Joel Whitburn's
TOP 10 HITS
POP

A 70-Year History of Every Top 10 Hit
1940-2010

ISBN 0-89820-187-X
ISBN 978-0-89820-187-1

Record Research Inc.
P.O. Box 200
Menomonee Falls, Wisconsin 53052-0200 U.S.A.

Phone: (262) 251-5408
Fax: (262) 251-9452
E-Mail: books@recordresearch.com
Website: www.recordresearch.com

AUTHOR'S NOTE

Put this book on your coffee table and it'll get a party started. Aunt Joyce will hum a few bars of every Billy Eckstine hit listed; brother Keith will easily recall all of Creedence Clearwater Revival's Top 10s; cousin Kaitlin will quote Blink 182's lyrics; and nephew Tyler just might do the 'Superman' dance at the mention of "Crank That (Soulja Boy)." It's a whole lotta fun making new memories as you take a trip down memory lane with this simple yet sweeping list of America's favorite songs.

Arranged by artist, this handy guide follows the proven format of other books I've published covering the pop charts; but it stands out in this respect: there is no split at 1955 dividing pre-rock hits from rock era hits! I love seeing the sequential hit listings of Les Paul & Mary Ford, Nat "King" Cole, Patti Page, Frankie Laine, Perry Como and other artists who have their chart discographies split between my *Pop Hits 1940-1954* and *Top Pop Singles 1955-2010* books. *Top 10 Pop Hits* looks at the pop era from the big band swing of 1940 and on through seven decades!

For the book's starting point, I chose Billboard magazine's first national Top 10 popular songs chart, "Best Selling Retail Records," which debuted on July 27, 1940. This was the first pop chart to show a specific recording's title and its artist. (Previously, Billboard combined all versions of a song into one listing on their popularity charts.) At #1 on that July 27th chart was "I'll Never Smile Again" by the Tommy Dorsey Orchestra, featuring vocals by Frank Sinatra & The Pied Pipers. At #2 was Tommy's brother, Jimmy, with "The Breeze And I."

My coverage of Top 10 hits follows the other pop song charts that Billboard introduced: "Most Played In Juke Boxes" in 1944, "Records Most Played By Disc Jockeys" in 1945 and the first to rank 100 songs, the "Top 100," in 1955. On August 4, 1958, Billboard debuted the chart that remains the standard ranking of song popularity today, the "Hot 100." (By fall of 1958, Billboard ceased publishing the "Best Sellers," "Juke Box," "Disc Jockey," and "Top 100" charts.)

In 1984 Billboard published its first "Hot 100 Airplay" chart which, beginning in 1987, would also include songs that could not make the "Hot 100" chart as they were not commercially released singles. Any song that made the Top 10 on this Airplay chart but not the "Hot 100" is included in this book. In 1998 Billboard revised their rules to allow airplay-only tracks to appear on the "Hot 100."

What information is included for each Top 10 hit? The columns on the left of each page show each title's peak date (date it reached its peak position on the chart), peak position, and the total weeks title was on the chart. ❶ indicates a #1 song. The superscript number to the right of the peak position is the number of weeks at peak for #1, #2, and #3 hits. The symbols in the GOLD column designate the following: for RIAA certifications of physical sales: ● = gold and ▲ = platinum; for RIAA certifications of digital downloads: ○ = digital gold and △ = digital platinum; non-certified million sellers = ⊙. The artist name and title are shown exactly as printed on the record label. For the first time in my pop books, I'm listing both the songwriter and the B-side. B-sides are listed only when a commercial record contained a different song; not shown are the B-sides that were alternate versions of the A-side (instrumental, remix, dub, etc.) or album snippets. Letters in brackets indicate if songs are Instrumental [I], Novelty [N], Comedy [C], Foreign [F], Live [L], Reissue [R], Spoken [S] and Christmas [X].

Finally, to top off this 'Cream of the Pop Crop,' I've included a photo display of the Top 50 "Chart Kings & Queens" listing the artists with the most Top 10 pop hits. Check it out -- you may be surprised!

Joel Whitburn

A

PEAK DATE	PEAK POS	WKS CHR	GOLD	ARTIST / Song Title	Songwriter...B-side	Label & Number
				AALIYAH		
7/2/94	5	24	●	1 Back & Forth	R. Kelly	Blackground 42174
10/15/94	6	20	●	2 At Your Best (You Are Love)	Ernie Isley/Marvin Isley/O'Kelly Isley/Ronald Isley/Rudolph Isley/Chris Jasper	Blackground 42239
11/15/97	9	20	●	3 The One I Gave My Heart To	Diane Warren...*Hot Like Fire*	Blackground 98002
10/10/98	4	30		4 Are You That Somebody?	Stephen Garrett/Tim Mosley	Blackground
6/17/00	❶^1	32		5 Try Again	Stephen Garrett/Tim Mosley	Blackground 38722
4/5/03	3^1	30		6 Miss You	Johnta Austin/Teddy Bishop	Blackground 000384
				ABBA		
8/24/74	6	17		1 Waterloo	Stig Anderson/Benny Andersson/Bjorn Ulvaeus...*Watch Out*	Atlantic 3035
4/9/77	❶^1	22	●	2 Dancing Queen	Stig Anderson/Benny Andersson/Bjorn Ulvaeus...*That's Me*	Atlantic 3372
7/8/78	3^2	18	●	3 Take A Chance On Me	Benny Andersson/Bjorn Ulvaeus...*I'm A Marionette*	Atlantic 3457
3/14/81	8	26		4 The Winner Takes It All	Benny Andersson/Bjorn Ulvaeus...*Elaine*	Atlantic 3776
				ABBOTT, Gregory		
1/17/87	❶^1	22	▲	1 Shake You Down	Gregory Abbott...*Wait Until Tomorrow*	Columbia 06191
				ABC		
11/9/85	9	22		1 Be Near Me	Martin Fry/Mark White...*A To Z*	Mercury 880626
9/19/87	5	19		2 When Smokey Sings	Martin Fry/Mark White...*Chicago (Part 1)*	Mercury 888604
				ABDUL, Paula		
2/11/89	❶^3	25	▲	1 Straight Up	Elliot Wolff...*Cold Hearted*	Virgin 99256
5/20/89	❶^2	22	●	2 Forever Your Girl	Oliver Leiber...*Next To You*	Virgin 99230
9/2/89	❶^1	21		3 Cold Hearted	Elliot Wolff...*One Or The Other*	Virgin 99196
12/2/89	3^1	20		4 (It's Just) The Way That You Love Me	Oliver Leiber	Virgin 92282
2/10/90	❶^3	23	●	5 Opposites Attract	Oliver Leiber...*One Or The Other*	Virgin 99158
				PAULA ABDUL (with The Wild Pair)		
6/15/91	❶^5	19	●	6 Rush, Rush	Peter Lord	Virgin 98828
9/14/91	❶^1	16		7 The Promise Of A New Day	Paula Abdul/Peter Lord/V. Jeffrey Smith/Sandra St. Victor	Captive/Virgin 98752
11/30/91	6	20		8 Blowing Kisses In The Wind	Paula Abdul/Peter Lord/V. Jeffrey Smith/Sandra St. Victor...*Spellbound*	Captive/Virgin 98683
				ACE		
5/31/75	3^2	16		1 How Long	Paul Carrack...*Sniffin' About*	Anchor 21000
				ACE OF BASE		
11/6/93	2^3	36	▲	1 All That She Wants	Jonas Berggren/Ulf Ekberg	Arista 12614
3/12/94	❶^6	41	▲	2 The Sign	Jonas Berggren...*Young And Proud*	Arista 12653
6/18/94	4	31	●	3 Don't Turn Around	Albert Hammond/Diane Warren...*Dancer In A Daydream*	Arista 12691
8/22/98	10	20	●	4 Cruel Summer	Sarah Dallin/Siobhan Fahey/Steve Jolley/Tony Swain/Keren Woodward	Arista 13505
				ADAMS, Bryan		
5/28/83	10	19		1 Straight From The Heart	Bryan Adams/Eric Kagna...*One Good Reason*	A&M 2536
1/19/85	6	19		2 Run To You	Bryan Adams/Jim Vallance...*I'm Ready*	A&M 2686
6/22/85	❶^2	19		3 Heaven	Bryan Adams/Jim Vallance...*Heaven "Live"*	A&M 2729
8/31/85	5	17		4 Summer Of '69	Bryan Adams/Jim Vallance...*The Best Was Yet To Come*	A&M 2739
5/16/87	6	16		5 Heat Of The Night	Bryan Adams/Jim Vallance...*Another Day*	A&M 2921
7/27/91	❶^7	22	▲^{3}	6 (Everything I Do) I Do It For You	Bryan Adams/Michael Kamen/Mutt Lange	A&M 1567
11/16/91	2^1	20	●	7 Can't Stop This Thing We Started	Bryan Adams/Mutt Lange...*(Everything I Do) I Do It For You*	A&M 1576
11/20/93	7	28		8 Please Forgive Me	Bryan Adams...*Can't Stop This Thing We Started (live)*	A&M 0422
1/22/94	❶^3	22	▲	9 All For Love	Bryan Adams/Michael Kamen/Mutt Lange	A&M 0476
				BRYAN ADAMS ROD STEWART STING		
6/3/95	❶^5	24		10 Have You Ever Really Loved A Woman?	Bryan Adams/Michael Kamen/Mutt Lange...*Low Life*	A&M 1028
12/7/96	8	20	●	11 I Finally Found Someone	Bryan Adams/Marvin Hamlisch/Mutt Lange/Barbra Streisand...*Evergreen (Spanish version* - Streisand)	Columbia 78480
				BARBRA STREISAND and BRYAN ADAMS		
				ADAMS, Oleta		
3/23/91	5	23		1 Get Here	Brenda Russell...*Watch What Happens*	Fontana 878476
				AD LIBS, The		
2/27/65	8	10		1 The Boy From New York City	John Taylor...*Kicked Around*	Blue Cat 102
				AEROSMITH		
4/10/76	6	20		1 Dream On	Steven Tyler...*Somebody*	Columbia 10278
1/29/77	10	17		2 Walk This Way	Joe Perry/Steven Tyler...*Uncle Salty*	Columbia 10449
4/30/88	3^2	25		3 Angel	Desmond Child/Steven Tyler...*Girl Keeps Coming Apart*	Geffen 28249
10/28/89	5	16	●	4 Love In An Elevator	Joe Perry/Steven Tyler...*Young Lust*	Geffen 22845
2/10/90	4	18		5 Janie's Got A Gun	Tom Hamilton/Steven Tyler...*Voodoo Medicine Man*	Geffen 22727
5/5/90	9	17		6 What It Takes	Desmond Child/Joe Perry/Steven Tyler...*Monkey On My Back*	Geffen 19944
9/5/98	❶^4	20	●	7 I Don't Want To Miss A Thing	Diane Warren...*Taste Of India / Animal Crackers*	Columbia 78952
4/7/01	7	20		8 Jaded	Marti Frederiksen/Steven Tyler...*Under My Skin / Angel's Eye*	Columbia 79555
				AFTER 7		
6/23/90	7	21	●	1 Ready Or Not	Babyface/L.A. Reid	Virgin 98995
10/27/90	6	25	●	2 Can't Stop	Babyface/L.A. Reid	Virgin 98961
				AFTER THE FIRE		
4/30/83	5	21		1 Der Kommissar	Andy Piercy/Robert Ponger...*Dancing In The Shadows*	Epic 03559
				AGUILERA, Christina		
7/31/99	❶^5	25	▲	1 Genie In A Bottle	David Frank/Steve Kipner/Pam Sheyne...*Blessed*	RCA 65692
1/15/00	❶^2	24	●	2 What A Girl Wants	Shelly Peiken/Guy Roche...*We're A Miracle*	RCA 65960
7/1/00	3^2	22		3 I Turn To You	Diane Warren...*Por Siempre Tu*	RCA 60251
10/14/00	❶^4	21		4 Come On Over Baby (all i want is you)	Johan Aberg/Christina Aguilera/Chaka Blackmon/Ray Cham/Eric Dawkins/Ron Fair/Shelly Peiken/Paul Rein/Guy Roche...*Ven Conmigo (solamente tu)*	RCA 60341

PEAK DATE	PEAK POS	WKS CHR	GOLD	ARTIST / Song Title	Songwriter...B-side	Label & Number
				AGUILERA, Christina (cont'd)		
6/2/01	❶⁵	20		5 Lady Marmalade	Bob Crewe/Kenny Nolan	Interscope 497066
				CHRISTINA AGUILERA, LIL' KIM, MYA and PINK		
2/1/03	2¹	27	○	6 Beautiful	Linda Perry	RCA 51195
7/15/06	6	20	○	7 Ain't No Other Man	Christina Aguilera/Harold Beatty/Kara DioGuardi/Chris Martin/Charles Roane	RCA 86851
10/18/08	7	18		8 Keeps Gettin' Better	Christina Aguilera/Linda Perry	RCA
				A-HA		
10/19/85	❶¹	27		1 Take On Me	Magne Furuholmen/Morten Harket/Pal Waaktaar...*Love Is Reason*	Warner 29011
				AIKEN, Clay		
6/28/03	❶²	16	▲	1 This Is The Night	Chris Braide/Gary Burr/Aldo Nova...*Bridge Over Troubled Water*	RCA 51785
4/3/04	4	8		2 Solitaire	Phil Cody/Neil Sedaka...*The Way*	RCA 60199
				AIR SUPPLY		
5/3/80	3⁴	23		1 Lost In Love	Graham Russell...*I Don't Want To Lose You*	Arista 0479
9/13/80	2⁴	27	●	2 All Out Of Love	Graham Russell...*Old Habits Die Hard*	Arista 0520
1/31/81	5	22		3 Every Woman In The World	Dominic Bugatti/Frank Musker...*Having You Near Me*	Arista 0564
7/25/81	❶¹	19	●	4 The One That You Love	Graham Russell...*I Want To Give It All*	Arista 0604
11/21/81	5	20		5 Here I Am (Just When I Thought I Was Over You)	Norman Sallitt...*Don't Turn Me Away*	Arista 0626
3/20/82	5	20		6 Sweet Dreams	Graham Russell...*Don't Turn Me Away*	Arista 0655
9/4/82	5	18		7 Even The Nights Are Better	Ken Bell/Terry Skinner/J.L. Wallace...*One Step Closer*	Arista 0692
10/8/83	2³	25	●	8 Making Love Out Of Nothing At All	Jim Steinman...*Late Again (live)*	Arista 9056
				AKENS, Jewel		
3/20/65	3²	14		1 The Birds And The Bees	Barry Stuart...*Tic Tac Toe*	Era 3141
				AKON		
10/9/04	8	27	○	1 Locked Up	Aliaune Thiam	SRC 002245
				AKON Feat. Styles P.		
4/23/05	4	20	△	2 Lonely	Gene Allan/Aliaune Thiam/Bobby Vinton	SRC 005049
11/12/05	4	24	△	3 Soul Survivor	Jay Jenkins/Aliaune Thiam	Def Jam 005290
				YOUNG JEEZY featuring Akon		
11/4/06	2⁵	30	△²	4 Smack That	Marshall Mathers/Luis Resto/Mike Strange/Aliaune Thiam	SRC 007877
				AKON Featuring Eminem		
12/2/06	❶²	29	△	5 I Wanna Love You	Calvin Broadus/Aliaune Thiam	SRC
				AKON Featuring Snoop Dogg		
4/7/07	❶²	23	△	6 Don't Matter	Anthony Lawson/Aliaune Thiam	SRC
4/14/07	2¹	40		7 The Sweet Escape	Gwen Stefani/Aliaune Thiam/Giorgio Tunifort	Interscope 008526
				GWEN STEFANI Featuring Akon		
5/26/07	6	18		8 I Tried	Anthony Henderson/Steven Howse/Bryon McCane/Charles Scruggs/Aliaune Thiam	Full Surface
				BONE THUGS-N-HARMONY Featuring Akon		
8/4/07	7	19	△	9 Sorry, Blame It On Me	Durrone Moore/Clinton Sparks/Aliaune Thiam	SRC
9/22/07	5	22	△	10 Bartender	Faheem Najm/Aliaune Thiam	Konvict 11814
				T-PAIN Featuring Akon		
9/6/08	5	27		11 Dangerous	Cristian Bahamonde/Jason Harrow/Don Sales/Aliaune Thiam	KonLive
				KARDINAL OFFISHALL Featuring Akon		
11/29/08	8	22	△²	12 Right Now (Na Na Na)	Aliaune Thiam/Giorgio Tuinfort	SRC 012518
2/13/10	5	40	△²	13 Sexy Chick	David Guetta/Jean Claude Sindres/Aliaune Thiam/Giorgio Tuinfort/Sandy Wilhelm	Astralwerks
				DAVID GUETTA Featuring Akon		
				ALBERT, Morris		
10/25/75	6	32	●	1 Feelings	Morris Albert...*This World Today Is A Mess*	RCA Victor 10279
				AL B. SURE!		
7/16/88	7	21		1 Nite And Day	Al Brown/Kyle West...*Nuit Et Jour*	Warner 28192
				ALI, Tatyana		
9/12/98	6	17	●	1 Daydreamin'	Walter Becker/LaShawn Daniels/Donald Fagen/Shawn Hamilton/Freddie Jerkins/Rodney Jerkins/Peter Pankey	MJJ Music 78855
				ALIAS		
11/24/90	2¹	23		1 More Than Words Can Say	Freddy Curci/Steve DeMarchi...*Say What I Wanna Say*	EMI 50324
				ALIVE AND KICKING		
8/8/70	7	14		1 Tighter, Tighter	Tommy James/Bob King...*Sunday Morning*	Roulette 7078
				ALL-AMERICAN REJECTS, The		
1/21/06	9	39	△	1 Dirty Little Secret	Tyson Ritter/Nick Wheeler	Doghouse
1/13/07	8	23		2 It Ends Tonight	Tyson Ritter/Nick Wheeler	Doghouse
3/7/09	4	36		3 Gives You Hell	Chris Gaylor/Mike Kennerty/Tyson Ritter/Nick Wheeler	Doghouse
				ALLEN, Rex		
10/10/53	8	15		1 Crying In The Chapel	Artie Glenn...*I Thank The Lord*	Decca 28758
				ALL-4-ONE		
3/12/94	5	22	●	1 So Much In Love	William Jackson/Roy Straigis/George Williams...*Something About You*	Blitzz/Atlantic 87271
5/21/94	❶¹¹	30	▲	2 I Swear	Gary Baker/Frank Meyers...*Here If You're Ready*	Blitzz/Atlantic 87243
8/26/95	5	29	●	3 I Can Love You Like That	Maribeth Derry/Steve Diamond/Jennifer Kimball...*All-4-1*	Blitzz/Atlantic 87134
				ALLMAN BROTHERS BAND, The		
10/13/73	2¹	16		1 Ramblin Man	Dickey Betts...*Pony Boy*	Capricorn 0027
				ALL SAINTS		
8/22/98	4	19		1 Never Ever	Robert Jazayeri/Shaznay Lewis/Sean Mather...*I Remember*	London 570178
				ALLURE		
11/22/97	4	25	●	1 All Cried Out	Curtis Bedeau/Gerard Charles/Hugh Clarke/Brian George/Lucien George/Paul George...*Head Over Heels* (w/Tone & AZ)	Crave 78678
				ALLURE featuring 112		

PEAK DATE	PEAK POS	WKS CHR	GOLD	ARTIST / Song Title	Songwriter...B-side	Label & Number
				ALPERT, Herb, & The Tijuana Brass		
12/8/62	6	14		1 The Lonely Bull	Sol Lake...*Acapulco 1922* [I]	A&M 703
11/27/65	7	16		2 Taste Of Honey	Ric Marlow/Bobby Scott...*3rd Man Theme* [I]	A&M 775
				HERB ALPERT:		
6/22/68	❶4	14	●	3 This Guy's In Love With You	Burt Bacharach/Hal David...*A Quiet Tear* (& Tijuana Brass)	A&M 929
10/20/79	❶2	25	●	4 Rise	Andy Armer/Randy Badazz...*Aranjuez (Mon Amour)* [I]	A&M 2151
6/20/87	5	19		5 Diamonds	Jimmy Jam Harris/Terry Lewis...*African Flame*	A&M 2929
				HERB ALPERT (with Janet Jackson)		
				AMBROSIA		
11/18/78	3³	21		1 How Much I Feel	David Pack...*Ready For Camarillo*	Warner 8640
6/7/80	3³	19		2 Biggest Part Of Me	David Pack...*Livin' On My Own*	Warner 49225
				AMERICA		
3/25/72	❶3	14	●	1 A Horse With No Name	Dewey Bunnell...*Everyone I Meet Is From California*	Warner 7555
7/1/72	9	10		2 I Need You	Gerry Beckley...*Riverside*	Warner 7580
12/9/72	8	12		3 Ventura Highway	Dewey Bunnell...*Saturn Nights*	Warner 7641
11/9/74	4	18		4 Tin Man	Dewey Bunnell...*In The Country*	Warner 8014
3/8/75	5	14		5 Lonely People	Catherine Peek/Dan Peek...*Mad Dog*	Warner 8048
6/14/75	❶1	16		6 Sister Golden Hair	Gerry Beckley...*Midnight*	Warner 8086
10/16/82	8	20		7 You Can Do Magic	Russ Ballard...*Even The Score*	Capitol 5142
				AMERICAN BREED, The		
1/27/68	5	14	●	1 Bend Me, Shape Me	Scott English/Laurence Weiss...*Mindrocker*	Acta 811
				AMERICAN IDOL		
5/3/03	4	8	●	1 God Bless The U.S.A.	Lee Greenwood	RCA 51780
				AMERIE		
4/23/05	8	20	○	1 1 Thing	Rich Harrison/Amerie Rogers/Stanley Walden	Rise/Columbia 71958
				AMES, Ed		
3/25/67	8	13		1 My Cup Runneth Over	Tom Jones/Harvey Schmidt...*It Seems A Long Long Time*	RCA Victor 9002
				AMES BROTHERS, The		
2/11/50	❶2	14	◉	1 Rag Mop	Deacon Anderson/Johnnie Lee Wills...*Sentimental Me*	Coral 60140
6/10/50	❶1	27	◉	2 Sentimental Me	Jimmy Cassin/Jim Morehead...*Blue Prelude*	Coral 60173
10/28/50	5	19		3 Can Anyone Explain? (No, No, No!)	Bennie Benjamin/George Weiss...*Sittin' 'N Starin' 'N Rockin'*	Coral 60253
12/15/51	2¹	21		4 Undecided	Sid Robin/Charles Shavers...*Sentimental Journey*	Coral 60566
				AMES BROTHERS And LES BROWN And His Band Of Renown		
9/26/53	❶8	31	◉	5 You You You	Robert Mellin/Lotar Olias...*Once Upon A Tune*	RCA Victor 5325
5/29/54	6	18		6 The Man With The Banjo	Robert Mellin/Fritz Reichel...*Man, Man, Is For The Woman Made*	RCA Victor 5644
12/25/54	3⁴	15	◉	7 The Naughty Lady Of Shady Lane	Roy Bennett/Sid Tepper...*Addio*	RCA Victor 5897
8/26/57	5	24		8 Tammy	Ray Evans/Jay Livingston...*Rockin' Shoes*	RCA Victor 6930
10/28/57	5	20		9 Melodie D'Amour (Melody Of Love)	Leo Johns/Henri Salvador...*So Little Time*	RCA Victor 7046
				ANDERSON, Bill		
6/8/63	8	15		1 Still	Bill Anderson...*You Made It Easy*	Decca 31458
				ANDERSON, Leroy, And His "Pops" Concert Orchestra		
5/17/52	❶5	38	◉	1 Blue Tango	Leroy Anderson...*Belle Of The Ball* [I]	Decca 27875
				ANDERSON, Lynn		
2/13/71	3²	17	●	1 Rose Garden	Joe South...*Nothing Between Us*	Columbia 45252
				ANDREWS SISTERS		
12/14/40	8	3		1 Ferryboat Serenade (La Piccinina)	Harold Adamson/Eldo DiLazzaro...*Hit The Road*	Decca 3328
5/3/41	5	11		2 I'll Be With You In Apple Blossom Time	Neville Fleeson/Albert Von Tilzer...*I, Yi, Yi, Yi, Yi (I Like You Very Much)*	Decca 3622
11/7/42	6	4		3 Strip Polka	Johnny Mercer...*Mister Five By Five*	Decca 18470
1/15/44	❶9	19		4 Shoo-Shoo Baby	Phil Moore...*Down In The Valley*	Decca 18572
8/5/44	8	13		5 Straighten Up And Fly Right	Nat "King" Cole/Irving Mills...*Tico-Tico*	Decca 18606
2/10/45	❶10	20	◉	6 Rum And Coca-Cola	Morey Amsterdam/Paul Baron/Jeri Sullavan...*One Meat Ball*	Decca 18636
10/20/45	8	8		7 The Blond Sailor	Bell Leib/Mitchell Parish/Jacob Pfeil...*Lily Belle*	Decca 18700
2/9/46	9	5		8 Money Is The Root Of All Evil (Take It Away, Take It Away, Take It Away)	Alex Kramer/Joan Whitney...*Johnny Fedora*	Decca 23474
12/14/46	4	13		9 Rumors Are Flying	Bennie Benjamin/George Weiss...*Them That Has—Gets* (Andrews Sisters & Eddie Heywood)	Decca 23656
				ANDREWS SISTERS with LES PAUL		
1/11/47	7	4		10 Christmas Island	Lyle Moraine...*Winter Wonderland* [X]	Decca 23722
				ANDREWS SISTERS and GUY LOMBARDO And His Royal Canadians		
10/25/47	2¹	17		11 Near You	Francis Craig/Kermit Goell...*How Lucky You Are*	Decca 24171
11/1/47	7	2		12 The Lady From 29 Palms	Allie Wrubel...*The Turntable Song ('Round, An' 'Round, An' 'Round)*	Decca 23976
1/3/48	3²	11		13 Civilization (Bongo, Bongo, Bongo)	Bob Hilliard/Carl Sigman...*Bread And Butter Woman* [N]	Decca 23940
				DANNY KAYE - ANDREWS SISTERS		
5/22/48	3³	17		14 Toolie Oolie Doolie (The Yodel Polka)	Arthur Beul/Vaughn Horton...*I Hate To Lose You*	Decca 24380
10/9/48	8	12		15 You Call Everybody Darling	Sam Martin/Ben Trace/Clem Watts...*Underneath The Arches*	Decca 24490
11/6/48	5	14		16 Underneath The Arches	Reg Connelly/Bud Flanagan/Joseph McCarthy...*You Call Everybody Darling*	Decca 24490
1/7/50	❶5	25	◉	17 I Can Dream, Can't I?	Sammy Fain/Irving Kahal...*The Wedding Of Lili Marlene*	Decca 24705
6/24/50	❶2	21		18 I Wanna Be Loved	John Green/Edward Heyman/Billy Rose...*I've Just Got To Get Out Of The Habit*	Decca 27007
				BING CROSBY and the ANDREWS SISTERS:		
12/4/43	2⁴	9	◉	19 Pistol Packin' Mama	Al Dexter...*Vict'ry Polka*	Decca 23277
1/8/44	6	5		20 Vict'ry Polka	Sammy Cahn/Jule Styne...*Pistol Packin' Mama*	Decca 23277
10/14/44	❶6	14		21 (There'll Be A) Hot Time In The Town Of Berlin (When The Yanks Go Marching In)	Joe Bushkin/John DeVries...*Is You Or Is You Ain't (Ma' Baby)*	Decca 23350
10/21/44	2¹	13		22 Is You Is Or Is You Ain't (Ma' Baby)	Billy Austin/Louis Jordan...*(There'll Be A) Hot Time In The Town Of Berlin (When The Yanks Go Marching In)*	Decca 23350
12/16/44	❶8	21	◉	23 Don't Fence Me In	Cole Porter...*The Three Caballeros*	Decca 23364
3/3/45	8	5		24 The Three Caballeros	Ernesto Cortazar/Manuel Esperon/Ray Gilbert...*Don't Fence Me In*	Decca 23364

PEAK DATE	PEAK POS	WKS CHR	GOLD		ARTIST / Song Title	Songwriter...B-side	Label & Number
					ANDREWS SISTERS (cont'd)		
3/10/45	2¹	12		25	Ac-Cent-Tchu-Ate The Positive	Harold Arlen/Johnny Mercer...*There's A Fellow Waiting In Poughkeepsie*	Decca 23379
10/27/45	2¹	11		26	Along The Navajo Trail	Dick Charles/Eddie DeLange/Larry Markes...*Good, Good, Good (That's You—That's You)*	Decca 23437
11/2/46	2¹	19	⊙	27	South America, Take It Away	Harold Rome...*Get Your Kicks On "Route 66!--"*	Decca 23569
7/19/47	10	10		28	Tallahassee	Frank Loesser...*Go West, Young Man!*	Decca 23885
3/18/50	6	17		29	Quicksilver	Eddie Pola/Irving Taylor/George Wyle...*Have I Told You Lately That I Love You?*	Decca 24827
4/28/51	8	15		30	Sparrow In The Tree Top	Bob Merrill...*Forsaking All Others*	Decca 27477
					ANGELS, The		
8/31/63	❶³	14	⊙	1	My Boyfriend's Back	Bob Feldman/Jerry Goldstein/Richard Gottehrer...*(Love Me) Now*	Smash 1834
					ANIMALS, The		
9/5/64	❶³	11	⊙	1	The House Of The Rising Sun	Alan Price...*Talkin' 'Bout You*	MGM 13264
10/22/66	10	10		2	See See Rider	Ma Rainey...*She'll Return It*	MGM 13582
9/16/67	9	10		3	San Franciscan Nights	Vic Briggs/Eric Burdon/Barry Jenkins/Danny McCulloch/John Weider...*Good Times*	MGM 13769
					ANIMOTION		
5/4/85	6	24		1	Obsession	Michael DesBarres/Holly Knight...*Turn Around*	Mercury 880266
5/6/89	9	18		2	Room To Move	Simon Climie/Rob Fisher/Dennis Morgan...*Send It Over*	Polydor 871418
					ANKA, Paul		
9/9/57	❶¹	29	⊙	1	Diana	Paul Anka...*Don't Gamble With Love*	ABC-Paramount 9831
2/24/58	7	17		2	You Are My Destiny	Paul Anka...*When I Stop Loving You (That'll Be The Day)*	ABC-Paramount 9880
7/13/59	❶⁴	15		3	Lonely Boy	Paul Anka...*Your Love*	ABC-Paramount 10022
10/5/59	2³	18		4	Put Your Head On My Shoulder	Paul Anka...*Don't Ever Leave Me*	ABC-Paramount 10040
12/28/59	4	15		5	It's Time To Cry	Paul Anka...*Something Has Changed Me*	ABC-Paramount 10064
4/4/60	2²	14	⊙	6	Puppy Love	Paul Anka...*Adam And Eve*	ABC-Paramount 10082
7/4/60	8	13		7	My Home Town	Paul Anka...*Something Happened*	ABC-Paramount 10106
7/10/61	10	10		8	Dance On Little Girl	Paul Anka...*I Talk To You (On The Telephone)*	ABC-Paramount 10220
8/24/74	❶³	15	●	9	(You're) Having My Baby	Paul Anka...*Papa*	United Artists 454
1/25/75	7	16		10	One Man Woman/One Woman Man	Paul Anka...*Let Me Get To Know You*	United Artists 569
5/24/75	8	15		11	I Don't Like To Sleep Alone	Paul Anka...*How Can Anything Be Beautiful-After You*	United Artists 615
					PAUL ANKA with Odia Coates (above 3)		
2/7/76	7	20		12	Times Of Your Life	William Lane/Roger Nichols...*Water Runs Deep*	United Artists 737
					ANNETTE		
2/23/59	7	15		1	Tall Paul	Bob Roberts/Richard Sherman/Robert Sherman...*Ma - He's Making Eyes At Me*	Disneyland 118
3/28/60	10	12		2	O Dio Mio	Al Hoffman/Dick Manning...*It Took Dreams*	Buena Vista 354
					ANOTHER BAD CREATION		
4/13/91	9	23	●	1	Iesha	Dallas Austin/Michael Bivins...*Motown 2070*	Motown 2070
6/29/91	10	17		2	Playground	Dallas Austin/Michael Bivins/Kevin Wales...*Motown 2088*	Motown 2088
					ANTHONY, Marc		
11/27/99	3²	40	●	1	I Need To Know	Marc Anthony/Mark Cory Rooney...*Dimelo (I Need To Know)*	Columbia 79250
6/3/00	2²	32		2	You Sang To Me	Marc Anthony/Mark Cory Rooney...*Muy Dentro De Mi (You Sang To Me)*	Columbia 79406
					ANTHONY, Ray		
6/24/50	7	15		1	Sentimental Me	Jimmy Cassin/Jim Morehead...*Spaghetti Rag*	Capitol 923
7/15/50	4	21		2	Count Every Star	Bruno Coquatrix/Sammy Gallop...*The Darktown Strutters' Ball*	Capitol 979
10/14/50	5	13		3	Can Anyone Explain	Bennie Benjamin/George Weiss...*Skycoach*	Capitol 1131
11/18/50	4	17		4	Harbor Lights	Will Grosz/Jimmy Kennedy...*Nevertheless (I'm In Love With You)*	Capitol 1190
12/9/50	9	14		5	Nevertheless (I'm In Love With You)	Bert Kalmar/Harry Ruby...*Harbor Lights*	Capitol 1190
11/24/51	10	11		6	Undecided	Sid Robin/Charles Shavers...*Just A Moment More*	Capitol 1824
4/26/52	2¹	15		7	At Last	Mack Gordon/Harry Warren...*I'll See You In My Dreams*	Capitol 1912
6/28/52	10	4		8	As Time Goes By	Herman Hupfeld...*Scatterbrain*	Capitol 2104
10/10/53	2¹	13		9	Dragnet	Walter Schumann...*Dancing In The Dark* [I]	Capitol 2562
3/2/59	8	17		10	Peter Gunn	Henry Mancini...*Tango For Two (mmm Shall We Dance?)* [I]	Capitol 4041
					APOLLO 100		
2/26/72	6	14		1	Joy	Johann Sebastian Bach...*Exercise In A Minor* [I]	Mega 0050
					AQUA		
9/6/97	7	16		1	Barbie Girl	Karsten Dahlgaard/Claus Norreen/Soren Rasted [N]	MCA 55392
					ARCADIA		
12/14/85	6	16		1	Election Day	Simon LeBon/Nick Rhodes/Roger Taylor...*She's Moody And Grey, She's Mean And She's Restless*	Capitol 5501
					ARCHIES, The		
9/20/69	❶⁴	22	●	1	Sugar, Sugar	Jeff Barry/Andy Kim...*Melody Hill*	Calendar 1008
2/7/70	10	13	●	2	Jingle Jangle	Jeff Barry/Andy Kim...*Justine*	Kirshner 5002
					ARCHULETA, David		
8/30/08	2¹	23		1	Crush	Jess Cates/Dave Hodges/Emanuel Kiriakou	19 Records
					ARDEN, Toni		
1/28/50	7	14		1	I Can Dream, Can't I?	Sammy Fain/Irving Kahal...*A Little Love, A Little Kiss*	Columbia 38612
					TONI ARDEN with HUGO WINTERHALTER and his ORCHESTRA and Choir		
					ARGENT		
8/26/72	5	15		1	Hold Your Head Up	Rod Argent/Chris White...*Keep On Rollin'*	Epic 10852
					ARMEN, Kay		
1/15/44	7	3		1	The Dreamer	Frank Loesser/Arthur Schwartz...*How Sweet You Are*	Decca 18566
1/22/44	10	9		2	How Sweet You Are	Frank Loesser/Arthur Schwartz...*The Dreamer*	Decca 18566

PEAK DATE	PEAK POS	WKS CHR	GOLD	ARTIST / Song Title	Songwriter...B-side	Label & Number
				ARMSTRONG, Louis		
4/6/46	10	2		1 You Won't Be Satisfied (Until You Break My Heart) .... *ELLA FITZGERALD and LOUIS ARMSTRONG*	Freddy James/Larry Stock...*The Frim Fram Sauce*	Decca 23496
11/10/51	10	16		2 (When We Are Dancing) I Get Ideas	Dorcas Cochran/Lenny Sanders...*A Kiss To Build A Dream On*	Decca 27720
5/9/64	❶¹	22	⊙	3 Hello, Dolly! *LOUIS ARMSTRONG And The All Stars*	Jerry Herman...*A Lot Of Livin' To Do*	Kapp 573
				ARNOLD, Eddy		
12/25/65	6	14		1 Make The World Go Away	Hank Cochran...*The Easy Way*	RCA Victor 8679
				ARRESTED DEVELOPMENT		
7/18/92	6	22	●	1 Tennessee	Aerle Jones/Todd Thomas...*Natural*	Chrysalis 23829
10/10/92	8	23	●	2 People Everyday	Sly Stone/Todd Thomas...*Children Play With Earth*	Chrysalis 50397
2/20/93	6	24	●	3 Mr. Wendal	Todd Thomas...*Revolution*	Chrysalis 24810
				ARTISTS FOR HAITI		
2/27/10	2¹	5		1 We Are The World 25: For Haiti	Michael Jackson/Lionel Richie	WATW Foundation
				ASHANTI		
2/23/02	❶²	27		1 Always On Time *JA RULE (feat. Ashanti)*	Jeffrey Atkins/Irv Gotti/Marcus Vest...*Worldwide Gangsta*	Murder Inc. 588795
4/6/02	2⁷	28		2 What's Luv? *FAT JOE Featuring Ashanti*	Jeffrey Atkins/Joe Cartagena/Irving Lorenzo/Andre Parker/Christopher Rios...*Definition Of A Don* (w/**Remy Ma**)	Terror Squad 85233
4/20/02	❶¹⁰	32		3 Foolish	Mark DeBarge/Ashanti Douglas/Irv Gotti/Etterlene Jordan	Murder Inc. 588986
9/7/02	8	23		4 Happy	Ray Calhoun/Ashanti Douglas/Irvving Lorenzo/Andre Parker...*Call*	Murder Inc. 582935
2/15/03	2¹	20		5 Mesmerize *JA RULE feat. Ashanti*	Jeffrey Atkins/Thom Bell/Linda Creed/Ashanti Douglas/Irving Lorenzo/Andre Parker...*Pop N****s*	Murder Inc. 063773
8/2/03	2¹	21		6 Rock Wit U (Awww Baby)	Ashanti Douglas/Irving Lorenzo/Andre Parker	Murder Inc. 000540
9/20/03	4	26		7 Into You *FABOLOUS Featuring Ashanti or Tamia*	Ken Ifill/John Jackson/Tim Kelly/Ronald LaPread/Lionel Richie/Bob Robinson/Tamia Washington	Desert Storm 67452
11/8/03	7	20		8 Rain On Me	Burt Bacharach/Hal David/Ashanti Douglas/Irving Lorenzo/Andre Parker...*Breakup 2 Makeup*	Murder Inc. 001107
11/27/04	5	20	○	9 Wonderful *JA RULE featuring R. Kelly & Ashanti*	Jeffrey Atkins/R. Kelly/Irving Lorenzo/Kendred Smith...*Caught Up*	The Inc. 003482
				ASIA		
6/26/82	4	18		1 Heat Of The Moment	Geoffrey Downes/John Wetton...*Ride Easy*	Geffen 50040
9/17/83	10	13		2 Don't Cry	Geoffrey Downes/John Wetton...*Daylight*	Geffen 29571
				ASSOCIATION, The		
7/16/66	7	11		1 Along Comes Mary	Tandyn Almer...*Your Own Love*	Valiant 741
9/24/66	❶³	14	●	2 Cherish	Terry Kirkman...*Don't Blame It On Me*	Valiant 747
7/1/67	❶⁴	14	●	3 Windy	Ruthann Friedman...*Sometime*	Warner 7041
10/7/67	2²	14	●	4 Never My Love	Dick Addrisi/Don Addrisi...*Requiem For The Masses*	Warner 7074
3/2/68	10	9		5 Everything That Touches You	Terry Kirkman...*We Love Us*	Warner 7163
				ASTLEY, Rick		
3/12/88	❶²	24	●	1 Never Gonna Give You Up	Matt Aitken/Mike Stock/Pete Waterman	RCA 5347
6/18/88	❶¹	18		2 Together Forever	Matt Aitken/Mike Stock/Pete Waterman...*I'll Never Set You Free*	RCA 8319
9/17/88	10	16		3 It Would Take A Strong Strong Man	Matt Aitken/Mike Stock/Pete Waterman...*You Move Me*	RCA 8663
2/25/89	6	18		4 She Wants To Dance With Me	Rick Astley	RCA 8838
4/27/91	7	20		5 Cry For Help	Rick Astley/Rob Fisher...*Behind The Smile*	RCA 2774
				ATLANTA RHYTHM SECTION		
4/30/77	7	19		1 So In To You	Buddy Buie/Dean Daughtry/Robert Nix...*Everybody Gotta Go*	Polydor 14373
6/3/78	7	17		2 Imaginary Lover	Buddy Buie/Dean Daughtry/Robert Nix...*Silent Treatment*	Polydor 14459
				ATLANTIC STARR		
3/22/86	3²	23		1 Secret Lovers	David Lewis/Wayne Lewis...*Thank You*	A&M 2788
6/13/87	❶¹	22		2 Always	David Lewis/Jonathan Lewis/Wayne Lewis	Warner 28455
4/11/92	3¹	20	●	3 Masterpiece	Kenny Nolan...*Bring It Back Home Again*	Reprise 19076
				AUGUST, Jan		
12/28/46	7	2		1 Misirlou	Nick Roubanis...*Babalu* [I]	Diamond 2009
7/15/50	8	12		2 Bewitched *JAN AUGUST & Jerry Murad's HARMONICATS*	Lorenz Hart/Richard Rodgers...*Blue Prelude* [I]	Mercury 5399
				AUSTIN, Patti		
2/19/83	❶²	28	●	1 Baby, Come To Me *PATTI AUSTIN and JAMES INGRAM*	Rod Temperton...*Solero*	Qwest 50036
				AUTRY, Gene		
12/27/47	9	2	⊙	1 Here Comes Santa Claus (Down Santa Claus Lane)	Gene Autry/Oakley Haldeman...*An Old-Fashioned Tree* [X]	Columbia 37942
1/1/49	8	5		2 Here Comes Santa Claus (Down Santa Claus Lane)	Gene Autry/Oakley Haldeman...*An Old-Fashioned Tree* [X-R]	Columbia 20377
1/7/50	❶¹	6	⊙	3 Rudolph, The Red-Nosed Reindeer	Johnny Marks...*If It Doesn't Snow On Christmas* [X]	Columbia 38610
4/15/50	5	5	⊙	4 Peter Cottontail	Steve Nelson/Jack Rollins...*The Funny Little Bunny (With The Powder Puff Tail)*	Columbia 38750
12/30/50	3¹	7		5 Rudolph, The Red-Nosed Reindeer	Johnny Marks...*If It Doesn't Snow On Christmas* [X-R]	Columbia 38610
1/6/51	7	6	⊙	6 Frosty The Snow Man	Steve Nelson/Jack Rollins...*When Santa Claus Gets Your Letter* [X]	Columbia 38907
12/27/52	9	2		7 The Night Before Christmas Song *ROSEMARY CLOONEY & GENE AUTRY*	Johnny Marks...*Look Out The Window (The Winter Song)* [X]	Columbia 39876
				AVALON, Frankie		
2/17/58	7	15	⊙	1 DeDe Dinah	Peter DeAngelis/Bob Marcucci...*Ooh La La*	Chancellor 1011
9/1/58	9	13		2 Ginger Bread	Clint Ballard/Hank Hunter...*Blue Betty*	Chancellor 1021
3/9/59	❶⁵	17	⊙	3 Venus	Ed Marshall...*I'm Broke*	Chancellor 1031
7/6/59	8	13		4 Bobby Sox To Stockings	Richard DiCicco/Russ Faith...*A Boy Without A Girl*	Chancellor 1036
7/13/59	10	14		5 A Boy Without A Girl	Sid Jacobson/Ruth Sexter...*Bobby Sox To Stockings*	Chancellor 1036
10/26/59	7	16		6 Just Ask Your Heart	Pete Damato/Diane DeNota/Joe Ricci...*Two Fools*	Chancellor 1040
12/28/59	❶¹	16	⊙	7 Why	Peter DeAngelis/Bob Marcucci...*Swingin' On A Rainbow*	Chancellor 1045

PEAK DATE	PEAK POS	WKS CHR	GOLD	ARTIST / Song Title ... Songwriter...B-side	Label & Number
				AVERAGE WHITE BAND (AWB)	
2/22/75	❶[1]	17	●	1 Pick Up The Pieces ....Roger Ball/Malcolm Duncan/Alan Garrie/Robbie McIntosh/Onnie McIntyre/Hamish Stuart...*Work To Do* [I]	Atlantic 3229
6/21/75	10	15		2 Cut The Cake.............Roger Ball/Malcolm Duncan/Alan Gorrie/Robbie McIntosh/Onnie McIntyre/Hamish Stuart...*Person To Person*	Atlantic 3261
				AYRES, Mitchell, and his Fashions In Music	
7/27/40	10	1		1 Make-Believe Island ....Will Grosz/Charles Kenny/Nick Kenny...*Poor Ballerina*	Bluebird 10687
				AZ YET	
10/19/96	9	29	●	1 Last Night ....Keith Andes/Babyface	LaFace 24181
5/3/97	8	34	▲	2 Hard To Say I'm Sorry ....Peter Cetera/David Foster	LaFace 24223
				AZ YET Featuring Peter Cetera	

B

PEAK DATE	PEAK POS	WKS CHR	GOLD	ARTIST / Song Title ... Songwriter...B-side	Label & Number
				BABY BASH	
12/6/03	7	33	○	1 Suga Suga ....Frankie Bautista/Ronald Bryant...*Feelin Me / Early In Da Morning*	Universal 001055
				BABY BASH Feat. Frankie J	
4/2/05	3[1]	21	○	2 Obsession [No Es Amor] ....Anthony Santos	Columbia 70386
				FRANKIE J featuring Baby Bash	
11/3/07	7	30	△[2]	3 Cyclone ....Ronald Bryant/Faheem Najm/Jonathan Smith	Arista
				BABY BASH Featuring T-Pain	
				BABYFACE	
10/28/89	7	18		1 It's No Crime ....Babyface/L.A. Reid/Daryl Simmons	Solar 68966
4/28/90	6	18		2 Whip Appeal ....Babyface/Perri McKissack	Solar 74007
9/10/94	4	36	●	3 When Can I See You ....Babyface	Epic 77550
8/5/95	10	30	●	4 Someone To Love ....Babyface	Yab Yum 77895
				JON B Featuring Babyface	
11/9/96	6	20	▲	5 This Is For The Lover In You ....Howard Hewett/Dana Meyers	Epic 78443
				BABYFACE Featuring LL Cool J, Howard Hewett, Jody Watley and Jeffrey Daniels	
3/22/97	6	26	●	6 Every Time I Close My Eyes ....Babyface...*Lady, Lady*	Epic 78485
				BACHELORS, The	
6/20/64	10	13		1 Diane ....Lee Pollack/Erno Rapee...*Happy Land*	London 9639
				BACHMAN-TURNER OVERDRIVE	
11/9/74	❶[1]	17	●	1 You Ain't Seen Nothing Yet ....Randy Bachman...*Free Wheelin'*	Mercury 73622
				BACKSTREET BOYS	
9/6/97	2[2]	43	▲	1 Quit Playing Games (With My Heart) ....Herbert Crichlow/Max Martin...*Lay Down Beside Me*	Jive 42453
3/7/98	4	56		2 As Long As You Love Me ....Max Martin...*Everybody (Backstreet's Back)*	Jive 42510
5/9/98	4	22	▲	3 Everybody (Backstreet's Back) ....Max Martin/Denniz Pop	Jive 42510
9/26/98	4	22		4 I'll Never Break Your Heart ....Albert Manno/Eugene Wilde...*Quit Playing Games With My Heart (live)*	Jive 42528
2/6/99	5	21	▲	5 All I Have To Give ....Curtis Bedeau/Gerard Charles/Hugh Clarke/Brian George/Lucien George/Paul George	Jive 42562
6/26/99	6	31		6 I Want It That Way ....Andreas Carlsson/Max Martin	Jive 42595
3/18/00	6	24		7 Show Me The Meaning Of Being Lonely ....Herbert Crichlow/Max Martin	Jive
12/2/00	9	20		8 Shape Of My Heart ....Max Martin/Lisa Miskovsky/Rami Yacoub	Jive 42758
				BAD COMPANY	
11/2/74	5	15		1 Can't Get Enough ....Mick Ralphs...*Little Miss Fortune*	Swan Song 70015
9/20/75	10	15		2 Feel Like Makin' Love ....Mick Ralphs/Paul Rodgers...*Wild Fire Woman*	Swan Song 70106
				BAD ENGLISH	
11/11/89	❶[2]	22	●	1 When I See You Smile ....Diane Warren...*Rockin' Horse*	Epic 69082
3/10/90	5	19		2 Price Of Love ....Jonathan Cain/John Waite...*The Restless Ones*	Epic 73094
				BADFINGER	
4/18/70	7	15		1 Come And Get It ....Paul McCartney...*Rock Of All Ages*	Apple 1815
12/5/70	8	12		2 No Matter What ....Pete Ham...*Carry On Till Tomorrow*	Apple 1822
2/5/72	4	14	●	3 Day After Day ....Pete Ham...*Money*	Apple 1841
				BADU, Erykah	
10/7/00	6	20		1 Bag Lady ....Erykah Badu/Isaac Hayes/Harold Martin	Motown 158326
1/4/03	9	27		2 Love Of My Life (An Ode To Hip Hop) ....Eryka Badu/Lonnie Lynn/Robert Ozuna/James Poyser/Raphael Saadiq/Glenn Standridge	Fox/MCA 113987
				ERYKAH BADU Featuring Common	
				BAEZ, Joan	
10/2/71	3[1]	15	●	1 The Night They Drove Old Dixie Down ....Robbie Robertson...*When Time Is Stolen*	Vanguard 35138
				BAILEY, Pearl	
12/6/52	7	17		1 Takes Two To Tango ....Al Hoffman/Dick Manning...*Let There Be Love*	Coral 60817
				BAILEY, Philip	
2/2/85	2[2]	23	●	1 Easy Lover ....Philip Bailey/Phil Collins/Nathan East...*Woman* (Bailey)	Columbia 04679
				PHILIP BAILEY (with Phil Collins)	
				BAINBRIDGE, Merril	
11/23/96	4	30	●	1 Mouth ....Merril Bainbridge...*Julie*	Universal 56018
				BAKER, Anita	
11/1/86	8	22		1 Sweet Love ....Anita Baker/Gary Bias/Louis Johnson...*Watch Your Step*	Elektra 69557
12/17/88	3[1]	22		2 Giving You The Best That I Got ....Anita Baker/Randy Holland/Skip Scarborough...*Good Enough*	Elektra 69371
				BAKER, LaVern	
2/23/59	6	21	⊙	1 I Cried A Tear ....Al Julia...*Dix-A-Billy*	Atlantic 2007
				BALIN, Marty	
8/8/81	8	21		1 Hearts ....Jesse Barish...*Freeway*	EMI America 8084

PEAK DATE	PEAK POS	WKS CHR	GOLD	ARTIST / Song Title	Songwriter...B-side	Label & Number
				BALL, Kenny, and His Jazzmen		
3/17/62	2[1]	14		1 Midnight In Moscow	Kenny Ball/Jan Burgens...*American Patrol* [I]	Kapp 442
				BALLARD, Hank, And The Midnighters		
8/15/60	7	26	⊙	1 Finger Poppin' Time	Hank Ballard...*I Love You, I Love You So-o-o*	King 5341
11/21/60	6	16		2 Let's Go, Let's Go, Let's Go	Hank Ballard...*If You'd Forgive Me*	King 5400
				BANANARAMA		
9/29/84	9	18		1 Cruel Summer	Sarah Dallin/Siobhan Fahey/Steve Jolley/Tony Swain/Keren Woodward	London 810127
9/6/86	❶[1]	19		2 Venus	Robbie Van Leeuwen...*White Train*	London 886056
9/26/87	4	19		3 I Heard A Rumour	Matt Aitken/Sarah Dallin/Siobhan Fahey/Pete Waterman/Keren Woodward...*Clean Cut Boy*	London 886165
				BANGLES		
4/19/86	2[1]	20		1 Manic Monday	Prince...*In A Different Light*	Columbia 05757
12/20/86	❶[4]	23	●	2 Walk Like An Egyptian	Liam Sternberg...*Angels Don't Fall In Love*	Columbia 06257
2/6/88	2[1]	21		3 Hazy Shade Of Winter	Paul Simon...*She Lost You* (Joan Jett & The Blackhearts)	Def Jam 07630
1/7/89	5	20		4 In Your Room	Susanna Hoffs/Tom Kelly/Billy Steinberg...*Bell Jar*	Columbia 08090
4/1/89	❶[1]	19	●	5 Eternal Flame	Susanna Hoffs/Tom Kelly/Billy Steinberg...*What I Meant To Say*	Columbia 68533
				BANKS, Lloyd		
7/24/04	8	20	○	1 On Fire	Peter Harmsworth/Kwame Holland/Curtis Jackson/Christopher Lloyd/Marshall Mathers/Luis Resto...*Warrior*	G-Unit 002753
				BANNER, David		
10/15/05	7	20	○	1 Play	Michael Crooms/Lavell Crump...*Westside*	SRC 005047
				BARBER('S), Chris, Jazz Band		
3/2/59	5	15	⊙	1 Petite Fleur (Little Flower)	Sidney Bechet...*Wild Cat Blues* [I]	Laurie 3022
				BARE, Bobby		
2/2/59	2[1]	16	△	1 The All American Boy	Orville Lunsford/Bill Parsons...*Rubber Dolly* [N]	Fraternity 835
				BILL PARSONS		
11/16/63	10	11		2 500 Miles Away From Home	Bobby Bare/Charlie Williams...*It All Depends On Linda*	RCA Victor 8238
				BAREILLES, Sara		
3/8/08	4	41	△[3]	1 Love Song	Sara Bareilles	Epic
				BARENAKED LADIES		
10/17/98	❶[1]	20		1 One Week	Ed Robertson...*Shoe Box* (live) / *When You Dream*	Reprise 17174
				BARKER, Blue Lu		
2/5/49	4	14		1 A Little Bird Told Me	Harvey Brooks...*What Did You Do To Me?*	Capitol 15308
				BARNET, Charlie, And His Orchestra		
7/27/40	6	1		1 Where Was I?	Al Dubin/W. Frank Harling...*'Deed I Do*	Bluebird 10669
12/14/40	3[1]	6		2 Pompton Turnpike	Will Osborne/Dick Rogers...*I Don't Want To Cry Any More* [I]	Bluebird 10825
1/25/41	2[6]	11		3 I Hear A Rhapsody	Jack Baker/George Fragos/Dick Gasparre...*The Moon Is Cryin' For Me*	Bluebird 10934
				BARRON, Blue, and his Orchestra		
11/6/48	9	17		1 You Were Only Fooling	William Faber/Larry Fotine/Fred Meadows...*It's Easy When You Know How*	MGM 10185
3/12/49	❶[7]	20	⊙	2 Cruising Down The River	Eily Beadell/Nell Tollerton...*Powder Your Face With Sunshine* (Smile! Smile! Smile!)	MGM 10346
				BARRY, Len		
11/20/65	2[1]	15		1 1-2-3	Len Barry/Lamont Dozier/Brian Holland/Eddie Holland/John Madara/David White...*Bullseye*	Decca 31827
				BARTON, Eileen		
3/25/50	❶[10]	16	⊙	1 If I Knew You Were Comin' (I'd've Baked A Cake)	Al Hoffman/Bob Merrill/Clem Watts...*Poco, Loco In The Coco*	National 9103
1/19/52	10	11		2 Cry	Churchill Kohlman...*Hold Me Just A Little Longer, Daddy*	Coral 60592
				BASIE, Count, and his Orchestra		
10/6/45	10	1		1 Jimmy's Blues	Jimmy Rushing...*Taps Miller*	Columbia 36831
6/8/46	10	10		2 The Mad Boogie	Count Basie/Buster Harding...*Patience And Fortitude* [I]	Columbia 36946
10/26/46	8	4		3 Blue Skies	Irving Berlin...*The King*	Columbia 37070
2/22/47	❶[1]	7		4 Open The Door, Richard!	Dusty Fletcher/Don Howell/John Mason/Jack McVea...*Me And The Blues* [N]	RCA Victor 2127
5/10/47	7	3		5 Free Eats	Count Basie/Harry Sweets...*Bill's Mill*	RCA Victor 2148
7/19/47	8	4		6 One O'Clock Boogie	Count Basie/Milton Ebbins/James Mundy...*Meet Me At No Special Place* (And I'll Be There At No Particular Time) [I]	RCA Victor 2262
8/30/47	7	4		7 I Ain't Mad At You (You Ain't Mad At Me)	Count Basie/Milton Ebbins/Freddy Green...*The Jungle King* (You Ain't a Doggone Thing)	RCA Victor 2314
				BASIL, Toni		
12/11/82	❶[1]	27	▲	1 Mickey	Mike Chapman/Nicky Chinn...*Thief On The Loose*	Chrysalis 2638
				BASS, Fontella		
11/20/65	4	13		1 Rescue Me	Raynard Miner/Carl Smith...*Soul Of The Man*	Checker 1120
				BASSEY, Shirley		
3/27/65	8	13		1 Goldfinger	John Barry/Leslie Bricusse/Anthony Newley...*Strange How Love Can Be*	United Artists 790
				BAXTER, Les, his Chorus and Orchestra		
10/6/51	4	21		1 Because Of You	Arthur Hammerstein/Dudley Wilkinson...*Somewhere, Somehow, Someday*	Capitol 1760
4/19/52	10	17		2 Blue Tango	Leroy Anderson...*Please, Mr. Sun* [I]	Capitol 1966
5/30/53	2[3]	22		3 April In Portugal	Paul Ferrao/Jimmy Kennedy...*Suddenly* [I]	Capitol 2374
6/20/53	7	12		4 Ruby	Mitchell Parish/Heinz Roemheld...*A Little Love* (Can Go A Long, Long Way) [I]	Capitol 2457
9/11/54	4	12		5 The High And The Mighty	Dimitri Tiomkin/Ned Washington...*More Love Than Your Love* [I]	Capitol 2845
5/14/55	❶[2]	21	⊙	6 Unchained Melody	Alex North/Hy Zaret...*Medic* (Blue Star)	Capitol 3055
9/24/55	5	12		7 Wake The Town And Tell The People	Sammy Gallop/Jerry Livingston...*I'll Never Stop Loving You*	Capitol 3120
3/17/56	❶[6]	24	⊙	8 The Poor People Of Paris	Marguerite Monnot...*Theme From "Helen Of Troy"* [I]	Capitol 3336

PEAK DATE	PEAK POS	WKS CHR	GOLD	#	ARTIST / Song Title	Songwriter...B-side	Label & Number
					BAY CITY ROLLERS		
1/3/76	❶¹	17	●	1	Saturday Night	Phil Coulter/Bill Martin...*Marlina*	Arista 0149
4/3/76	9	15		2	Money Honey	Eric Faulkner/Stuart Wood...*Maryanne*	Arista 0170
8/13/77	10	17		3	You Made Me Believe In Magic	Len Boone...*Dance Dance Dance*	Arista 0256
					BAZUKA		
8/2/75	10	20		1	Dynomite-Part I	Tony Camillo...*Part II* [I]	A&M 1666
					Tony Camillo's BAZUKA		
					BEACH BOYS, The		
5/25/63	3¹	17	☉	1	Surfin' U.S.A.	Chuck Berry...*Shut Down*	Capitol 4932
9/14/63	7	14		2	Surfer Girl	Brian Wilson...*Little Deuce Coupe*	Capitol 5009
12/21/63	6	12		3	Be True To Your School	Brian Wilson...*In My Room*	Capitol 5069
3/21/64	5	11	☉	4	Fun, Fun, Fun	Brian Wilson...*Why Do Fools Fall In Love*	Capitol 5118
7/4/64	❶²	15	●	5	I Get Around	Brian Wilson...*Don't Worry Baby*	Capitol 5174
10/17/64	9	10		6	When I Grow Up (To Be A Man)	Brian Wilson...*She Knows Me Too Well*	Capitol 5245
12/19/64	8	11		7	Dance, Dance, Dance	Brian Wilson...*The Warmth Of The Sun*	Capitol 5306
5/29/65	❶²	14	☉	8	Help Me, Rhonda	Brian Wilson...*Kiss Me, Baby*	Capitol 5395
8/28/65	3²	11	☉	9	California Girls	Brian Wilson...*Let Him Run Wild*	Capitol 5464
1/29/66	2²	11	☉	10	Barbara Ann	Fred Fassert...*Girl Don't Tell Me*	Capitol 5561
5/7/66	3¹	11	☉	11	Sloop John B	(traditional)...*You're So Good To Me*	Capitol 5602
9/17/66	8	11		12	Wouldn't It Be Nice	Tony Asher/Brian Wilson...*God Only Knows*	Capitol 5706
12/10/66	❶¹	14	●	13	Good Vibrations	Mike Love/Brian Wilson...*Let's Go Away For Awhile*	Capitol 5676
8/14/76	5	17		14	Rock And Roll Music	Chuck Berry...*The T M Song*	Brother/Reprise 1354
11/5/88	❶¹	28	▲	15	Kokomo	Mike Love/Scott MacKenzie/Terry Melcher/John Phillips...*Tutti Frutti* (Little Richard)	Elektra 69385
					BEASTIE BOYS		
3/7/87	7	18		1	(You Gotta) Fight For Your Right (To Party!)	Mike Diamond/Adam Horovitz/Rick Rubin/Adam Yauch...*Paul Revere*	Def Jam 06595
					BEATLES, The		
2/1/64	❶⁷	15	●	1	I Want To Hold Your Hand	John Lennon/Paul McCartney...*I Saw Her Standing There*	Capitol 5112
3/14/64	3²	13	☉	2	Please Please Me	John Lennon/Paul McCartney...*From Me To You*	Vee-Jay 581
3/21/64	❶²	15	●	3	She Loves You	John Lennon/Paul McCartney...*I'll Get You*	Swan 4152
4/4/64	❶⁵	10		4	Can't Buy Me Love	John Lennon/Paul McCartney...*You Can't Do That*	Capitol 5150
4/4/64	2⁴	11	☉	5	Twist And Shout	Phil Medley/Bert Russell...*There's A Place*	Tollie 9001
5/9/64	2¹	11	☉	6	Do You Want To Know A Secret	John Lennon/Paul McCartney...*Thank You Girl*	Vee-Jay 587
5/30/64	❶¹	14	●	7	Love Me Do	John Lennon/Paul McCartney...*P.S. I Love You*	Tollie 9008
6/6/64	10	8		8	P.S. I Love You	John Lennon/Paul McCartney...*Love Me Do*	Tollie 9008
8/1/64	❶²	13	●	9	A Hard Day's Night	John Lennon/Paul McCartney...*I Should Have Known Better*	Capitol 5222
12/26/64	❶³	11	●	10	I Feel Fine	John Lennon/Paul McCartney...*She's A Woman*	Capitol 5327
12/26/64	4	9		11	She's A Woman	John Lennon/Paul McCartney...*I Feel Fine*	Capitol 5327
3/13/65	❶²	10		12	Eight Days A Week	John Lennon/Paul McCartney...*I Don't Want To Spoil The Party*	Capitol 5371
5/22/65	❶¹	11		13	Ticket To Ride	John Lennon/Paul McCartney...*Yes It Is*	Capitol 5407
9/4/65	❶³	13	●	14	Help!	John Lennon/Paul McCartney...*I'm Down*	Capitol 5476
10/9/65	❶⁴	11		15	Yesterday	John Lennon/Paul McCartney...*Act Naturally*	Capitol 5498
1/8/66	❶³	12	●	16	We Can Work It Out	John Lennon/Paul McCartney...*Day Tripper*	Capitol 5555
1/22/66	5	10		17	Day Tripper	John Lennon/Paul McCartney...*We Can Work It Out*	Capitol 5555
3/26/66	3¹	9	●	18	Nowhere Man	John Lennon/Paul McCartney...*What Goes On*	Capitol 5587
6/25/66	❶²	10	●	19	Paperback Writer	John Lennon/Paul McCartney...*Rain*	Capitol 5651
9/17/66	2¹	9		20	Yellow Submarine	John Lennon/Paul McCartney...*Eleanor Rigby* [N]	Capitol 5715
3/18/67	❶¹	10		21	Penny Lane	John Lennon/Paul McCartney...*Strawberry Fields Forever*	Capitol 5810
4/1/67	8	9		22	Strawberry Fields Forever	John Lennon/Paul McCartney...*Penny Lane*	Capitol 5810
8/19/67	❶¹	11	●	23	All You Need Is Love	John Lennon/Paul McCartney...*Baby You're A Rich Man*	Capitol 5964
12/30/67	❶³	11		24	Hello Goodbye	John Lennon/Paul McCartney...*I Am The Walrus*	Capitol 2056
4/20/68	4	11	▲	25	Lady Madonna	John Lennon/Paul McCartney...*The Inner Light*	Capitol 2138
9/28/68	❶⁹	19	▲⁴	26	Hey Jude	John Lennon/Paul McCartney...*Revolution*	Apple 2276
5/24/69	❶⁵	12	▲²	27	Get Back	John Lennon/Paul McCartney...*Don't Let Me Down*	Apple 2490
7/12/69	8	9	●	28	The Ballad Of John And Yoko	John Lennon/Paul McCartney...*Old Brown Shoe*	Apple 2531
11/29/69	❶¹	16	▲²	29	Come Together /	John Lennon/Paul McCartney	Apple 2654
		16		30	Something	George Harrison	
4/11/70	❶²	14	▲²	31	Let It Be	John Lennon/Paul McCartney...*You Know My Name (Look Up My Number)*	Apple 2764
6/13/70	❶²	10	▲	32	The Long And Winding Road	John Lennon/Paul McCartney...*For You Blue*	Apple 2832
7/24/76	7	16	●	33	Got To Get You Into My Life	John Lennon/Paul McCartney...*Helter Skelter*	Capitol 4274
1/6/96	6	11	●	34	Free As A Bird	George Harrison/John Lennon/Paul McCartney/Ringo Starr...*Christmas Time (Is Here Again)*	Apple 58497
					BEAU BRUMMELS, The		
6/5/65	8	12		1	Just A Little	Robert Durand/Ron Elliott...*They'll Make You Cry*	Autumn 10
					BECK		
4/30/94	10	24	●	1	Loser	Beck Hansen/Karl Stephenson...*Alcohol*	DGC/Bong Load 19270
					BEDINGFIELD, Daniel		
9/28/02	10	21		1	Gotta Get Thru This	Daniel Bedingfield	Island 570976
					BEDINGFIELD, Natasha		
4/29/06	5	42	△²	1	Unwritten	Natasha Bedingfield/Danielle Brisebois/Wayne Rodrigues	Epic
7/5/08	5	35	△²	2	Pocketful Of Sunshine	Natasha Bedingfield/Danielle Brisebois/John Shanks	Phonogenic
					BEE GEES		
9/28/68	8	13		1	I've Gotta Get A Message To You	Barry Gibb/Maurice Gibb/Robin Gibb...*Kitty Can*	Atco 6603
2/8/69	6	11		2	I Started A Joke	Barry Gibb/Maurice Gibb/Robin Gibb...*Kilburn Towers*	Atco 6639
1/30/71	3¹	14		3	Lonely Days	Barry Gibb/Maurice Gibb/Robin Gibb...*Man For All Seasons*	Atco 6795
8/7/71	❶⁴	15		4	How Can You Mend A Broken Heart	Barry Gibb/Robin Gibb...*Country Woman*	Atco 6824
8/9/75	❶²	17		5	Jive Talkin'	Barry Gibb/Maurice Gibb/Robin Gibb...*Wind Of Change*	RSO 510
12/13/75	7	16		6	Nights On Broadway	Barry Gibb/Maurice Gibb/Robin Gibb...*Edge Of The Universe*	RSO 515
9/4/76	❶¹	20		7	You Should Be Dancing	Barry Gibb/Maurice Gibb/Robin Gibb...*Subway*	RSO 853

PEAK DATE	PEAK POS	WKS CHR	GOLD	ARTIST / Song Title	Songwriter...B-side	Label & Number
				BEE GEES (cont'd)		
11/20/76	3⁴	23	●	8 Love So Right	Barry Gibb/Maurice Gibb/Robin Gibb...*You Stepped Into My Life*	RSO 859
12/24/77	❶³	33	●	9 How Deep Is Your Love	Barry Gibb/Maurice Gibb/Robin Gibb...*Can't Keep A Good Man Down*	RSO 882
2/4/78	❶⁴	27	▲	10 Stayin' Alive	Barry Gibb/Maurice Gibb/Robin Gibb...*If I Can't Have You*	RSO 885
3/18/78	❶⁸	20	▲	11 Night Fever	Barry Gibb/Maurice Gibb/Robin Gibb...*Down The Road*	RSO 889
1/6/79	❶²	21	▲	12 Too Much Heaven	Barry Gibb/Maurice Gibb/Robin Gibb...*Rest Your Love On Me*	RSO 913
3/24/79	❶²	20	▲	13 Tragedy	Barry Gibb/Maurice Gibb/Robin Gibb...*Until*	RSO 918
6/9/79	❶¹	19	●	14 Love You Inside Out	Barry Gibb/Maurice Gibb/Robin Gibb...*I'm Satisfied*	RSO 925
9/30/89	7	14		15 One	Barry Gibb/Maurice Gibb/Robin Gibb...*Wing And A Prayer*	Warner 22899
				BEGA, Lou		
11/13/99	3²	22		1 Mambo No. 5 (A Little Bit Of...)	Lou Bega/Christian Pletschacher/Perez Prado	RCA 65842
				BELAFONTE, Harry		
2/2/57	5	20	⊙	1 Banana Boat (Day-O)	William Attaway/Irving Burgie...*Star-O*	RCA Victor 6771
				BELL, Archie, & The Drells		
5/18/68	❶²	15	●	1 Tighten Up	Archie Bell/Billy Butler...*Part II*	Atlantic 2478
8/24/68	9	10		2 I Can't Stop Dancing	Kenny Gamble/Leon Huff...*You're Such A Beautiful Child*	Atlantic 2534
				BELL, William		
4/30/77	10	15	●	1 Tryin' To Love Two	William Bell/Paul Mitchell...*If Sex Was All We Had*	Mercury 73839
				BELLAMY BROTHERS		
5/1/76	❶¹	19		1 Let Your Love Flow	Larry Williams...*Inside Of My Guitar*	Warner/Curb 8169
				BELL BIV DeVOE		
6/9/90	3⁴	22	▲	1 Poison	Elliott Straite	MCA 53772
9/8/90	3³	22		2 Do Me!	Ricky Bell/Michael Bivins/Carl Bourelly/Ronnie DeVoe	MCA 53848
6/13/92	10	20		3 The Best Things In Life Are Free	Michael Bivins/Ronnie DeVoe/Jimmy Jam Harris/Terry Lewis/Ralph Tresvant	Perspective 0010
				LUTHER VANDROSS and JANET JACKSON with BBD and Ralph Tresvant		
				BELLE, Regina		
3/6/93	❶¹	23	●	1 A Whole New World (Aladdin's Theme)	Alan Menken/Tim Rice...*After The Kiss (instrumental)*	Columbia 74751
				PEABO BRYSON and REGINA BELLE		
				BELL NOTES, The		
3/9/59	6	16		1 I've Had It	Carl Bonura/Raymond Ceroni...*Be Mine*	Time 1004
				BELLS, The		
5/1/71	7	14	●	1 Stay Awhile	Ken Tobias...*Sing A Song Of Freedom*	Polydor 15023
				BELL SISTERS, The		
2/16/52	7	16		1 Bermuda	Cynthia Strother...*June Night*	RCA Victor 4422
4/12/52	10	11		2 Wheel Of Fortune	Bennie Benjamin/George Weiss...*Poor Whip-Poor-Will (Move Over, Move Over)*	RCA Victor 4520
				BENATAR, Pat		
12/20/80	9	24	●	1 Hit Me With Your Best Shot	Eddie Schwartz...*Prisoner Of Love*	Chrysalis 2464
12/10/83	5	22	●	2 Love Is A Battlefield	Mike Chapman/Holly Knight...*Hell Is For Children (live)*	Chrysalis 42732
1/5/85	5	20		3 We Belong	David Lowen/Dan Navarro...*Suburban King*	Chrysalis 42826
9/14/85	10	17		4 Invincible	Simon Climie/Holly Knight	Chrysalis 42877
				BENEKE, Tex, with the Glenn Miller Orchestra		
6/15/46	4	9		1 Hey! Ba-Ba-Re-Bop	Curley Hamner/Lionel Hampton...*The Whiffenpoof Song (Baa! Baa! Baa!)*	RCA Victor 1859
8/3/46	9	3		2 I Know	Ted Brooks/John Jennings...*Ev'rybody Loves My Baby (My Baby)*	RCA Victor 1914
10/19/46	9	5		3 Passe	Eddie DeLange/Joseph Meyer/Carl Sigman...*The Woodchuck Song*	RCA Victor 1951
11/2/46	4	18		4 Give Me Five Minutes More	Sammy Cahn/Jule Styne...*Texas Tex*	RCA Victor 1922
1/18/47	6	8		5 A Gal In Calico	Leo Robin/Arthur Schwartz...*Oh, But I Do*	RCA Victor 1991
3/15/47	3²	11		6 Anniversary Song	Saul Chaplin/Al Jolson...*Hoodle Addle*	RCA Victor 2126
5/1/48	5	17		7 St. Louis Blues March	W.C. Handy...*Cherokee Canyon* [I]	RCA Victor 2722
				TEX BENEKE and his Orchestra		
				BENNETT, Boyd, And His Rockets		
9/3/55	5	17	⊙	1 Seventeen	Boyd Bennett/Chuck Gorman/John Young...*Little Ole You-All*	King 1470
				BENNETT, Tony		
9/8/51	❶¹⁰	32	⊙	1 Because Of You	Arthur Hammerstein/Dudley Wilkinson...*I Won't Cry Anymore*	Columbia 39362
11/3/51	❶⁶	27	⊙	2 Cold, Cold Heart	Hank Williams...*While We're Young*	Columbia 39449
11/21/53	❶⁸	25	⊙	3 Rags To Riches	Richard Adler/Jerry Ross...*Here Comes That Heartache Again*	Columbia 40048
2/6/54	2²	19	⊙	4 Stranger In Paradise	George Forrest/Robert Wright...*Why Does It Have To Be Me?*	Columbia 40121
4/24/54	7	12		5 There'll Be No Teardrops Tonight	Hank Williams...*My Heart Won't Say Good-Bye*	Columbia 40169
9/4/54	8	7		6 Cinnamon Sinner	Lincoln Chase...*Take Me Back Again*	Columbia 40272
9/23/57	9	21		7 In The Middle Of An Island	Nick Acquaviva/Ted Varnick...*I Am*	Columbia 40965
				BENSON, George		
8/28/76	10	19		1 This Masquerade	Leon Russell...*Lady*	Warner 8209
6/10/78	7	19		2 On Broadway	Jerry Leiber/Barry Mann/Mike Stoller/Cynthia Weil...*We As Love* [L]	Warner 8542
9/27/80	4	23		3 Give Me The Night	Rod Temperton...*Dinorah, Dinorah*	Warner 49505
2/6/82	5	22		4 Turn Your Love Around	Bill Champlin/Jay Graydon/Steve Lukather...*Nature Boy*	Warner 49846
				BENTON, Brook		
4/6/59	3¹	18	⊙	1 It's Just A Matter Of Time	Brook Benton/Belford Hendricks/Clyde Otis...*Hurtin' Inside*	Mercury 71394
11/23/59	6	16	⊙	2 So Many Ways	Bobby Stevenson...*I Want You Forever*	Mercury 71512
3/21/60	5	15	⊙	3 Baby (You've Got What It Takes)	Clyde Otis/Murray Stein...*I Do*	Mercury 71565
6/27/60	7	13		4 A Rockin' Good Way (To Mess Around And Fall In Love)	Brook Benton/Luchi DeJesus...*I Believe*	Mercury 71629
				DINAH WASHINGTON & BROOK BENTON (above 2)		
9/19/60	7	17		5 Kiddio	Brook Benton/Clyde Otis...*The Same One*	Mercury 71652
7/10/61	2³	16		6 The Boll Weevil Song	Brook Benton/Clyde Otis...*Your Eyes* [N]	Mercury 71820

13

PEAK DATE	PEAK POS	WKS CHR	G O L D	ARTIST / Song Title	Songwriter...B-side	Label & Number
				BENTON, Brook (cont'd)		
1/19/63	3¹	12		7 Hotel Happiness	Leon Carr/Earl Shuman...*Still Waters Run Deep*	Mercury 72055
3/7/70	4	15	●	8 Rainy Night In Georgia	Tony Joe White...*Where Do I Go From Here*	Cotillion 44057
				BERLIN		
9/13/86	❶¹	21	●	1 Take My Breath Away	Giorgio Moroder/Tom Whitlock...*Radar Radio* (Giorgio Moroder w/Joe Pizzulo)	Columbia 05903
				BERRY, Chuck		
9/10/55	5	11	⊙	1 Maybellene	Chuck Berry/Russ Frato/Alan Freed...*Wee Wee Hours*	Chess 1604
5/13/57	3³	26	⊙	2 School Day	Chuck Berry...*Deep Feeling*	Chess 1653
12/23/57	8	19		3 Rock & Roll Music	Chuck Berry...*Blue Feeling*	Chess 1671
3/17/58	2³	16		4 Sweet Little Sixteen	Chuck Berry...*Reelin' & Rockin'*	Chess 1683
6/9/58	8	15		5 Johnny B. Goode	Chuck Berry...*Around & Around*	Chess 1691
7/11/64	10	11		6 No Particular Place To Go	Chuck Berry...*You Two*	Chess 1898
10/21/72	❶²	17	●	7 My Ding-A-Ling	Chuck Berry...*Johnny B. Goode (live)* [L-N]	Chess 2131
				BEYONCE		
12/28/02	4	23		1 '03 Bonnie & Clyde JAY-Z Featuring Beyonce Knowles	Darrell Harper/Prince/Rick Rouse/Tupac Shakur/Tyrone Wrice	Roc-A-Fella 063843
7/12/03	❶⁸	27	○	2 Crazy In Love BEYONCE (Featuring Jay-Z)	Shawn Carter/Rich Harrison/Beyonce Knowles/Eugene Record	Columbia
10/4/03	❶⁹	29	○	3 Baby Boy BEYONCE Featuring Sean Paul	Shawn Carter/Beyonce Knowles/Sean Paul/Scott Storch/Robert Waller	Columbia 76867
2/21/04	4	24		4 Me, Myself And I	Beyonce Knowles/Scott Storch/Robert Waller...*Krazy In Luv*	Columbia 76911
6/5/04	3²	22	○	5 Naughty Girl	Pete Bellotte/Angela Beyince/Beyonce Knowles/Giorgio Moroder/Scott Storch/Donna Summer/Robert Waller...*Everything I Do*	Columbia 76853
2/4/06	❶⁵	28	○	6 Check On It BEYONCE Featuring Bun-B & Slim Thug	Angela Beyince/Kasseem Dean/Sean Garrett/Beyonce Knowles/Stayve Thomas	Columbia 80277
8/12/06	4	17	○	7 Deja Vu BEYONCE Featuring Jay-Z	Shawn Carter/Rodney Jerkins/Beyonce Knowles/Keli Nicole Price/Makeba Riddick/Delisha Thomas	Columbia 88435
12/16/06	❶¹⁰	30	△²	8 Irreplaceable	Amund Bjorklund/Mikkel Eriksen/Tor Erik Hermansen/Beyonce Knowles/Espen Lind/Shaffer Smith	Columbia 05024
4/7/07	3¹	18	△	9 Beautiful Liar BEYONCE & SHAKIRA	Ian Dench/Mikkel Eriksen/Amanda Ghost/Tor Erik Hermansen/Beyonce Knowles	Columbia 10320
11/8/08	3⁴	20	△²	10 If I Were A Boy	Brittany Carlson/Toby Gad	Music World
12/13/08	❶⁴	27	△⁴	11 Single Ladies (Put A Ring On It)	Thaddis Harrell/Beyonce Knowles/Terius Nash/Chris Stewart	Music World
5/23/09	5	31	△²	12 Halo	Evan Bogart/Beyonce Knowles/Ryan Tedder	Music World
11/7/09	10	29	△	13 Sweet Dreams	Richard Butler/Beyonce Knowles/James Scheffer/Wayne Wilkins	Music World
4/3/10	3¹	33		14 Telephone LADY GAGA Featuring Beyonce	LaShawn Daniels/Lazonates Franklin/Stefani Germanotta/Rodney Jerkins/Beyonce Knowles	Streamline 014166
				B-52's, The		
11/18/89	3²	27	●	1 Love Shack	Kate Pierson/Fred Schneider/Keith Strickland/Cindy Wilson...*Channel Z*	Reprise 22817
3/10/90	3²	20	●	2 Roam	Kate Pierson/Fred Schneider/Keith Strickland/Robert Waldrop/Cindy Wilson...*Bushfire*	Reprise 22667
				BICE, Bo		
7/9/05	2¹	7	●	1 Inside Your Heaven	Andreas Carlsson/Savan Kotecha/Pelle Nylen...*Vehicle*	RCA 69495
				BIEBER, Justin		
2/6/10	5	20	△²	1 Baby JUSTIN BIEBER Featuring Ludacris	Justin Bieber/Christopher Bridges/Christine Milian/Terius Nash/Christopher Stewart	SchoolBoy
				BIG BOPPER		
11/3/58	6	25		1 Chantilly Lace	J.P. Richardson...*Purple People Eater Meets Witch Doctor* [N]	Mercury 71343
				BIG MOUNTAIN		
5/14/94	6	28	●	1 Baby, I Love Your Way	Peter Frampton...*Baby, Te Quiero Ati*	RCA 62780
				BILK, Mr. Acker		
5/26/62	❶¹	21	●	1 Stranger On The Shore	Acker Bilk/Robert Mellin...*Cielito Lindo* [I]	Atco 6217
				BILLY & LILLIE		
1/27/58	9	13	⊙	1 La Dee Dah	Bob Crewe/Frank Slay...*The Monster* (Billy Ford & Thunderbirds)	Swan 4002
				BILLY JOE & THE CHECKMATES		
3/17/62	10	13		1 Percolator (Twist)	Lou Bideu/Ernie Freeman...*Round & Round & Round & Round* [I]	Dore 620
				BISHOP, Elvin		
5/22/76	3²	17	●	1 Fooled Around And Fell In Love	Elvin Bishop...*Have A Good Time*	Capricorn 0252
				BIZ MARKIE		
3/17/90	9	22	▲	1 Just A Friend	Marcel Hall	Cold Chillin' 22784
				BLACK('S), Bill, Combo		
4/25/60	9	14	⊙	1 White Silver Sands	Charles Matthews/Gladys Reinhardt...*The Wheel* [I]	Hi 2021
				BLACK, Jeanne		
5/30/60	4	11	⊙	1 He'll Have To Stay	Audrey Allison/Joe Allison/Charles Green...*Under Your Spell Again* (Jeanne & Janie)	Capitol 4368
				BLACK BOX		
10/20/90	8	19		1 Everybody Everybody	Daniele Davoli/Mirko Limoni/Valerio Semplici	RCA 2628
6/22/91	8	18		2 Strike It Up	Daniele Davoli/Mirko Limoni/Valerio Semplici	RCA 2794
				BLACKBYRDS, The		
5/10/75	6	17		1 Walking In Rhythm	Barney Perry...*The Baby*	Fantasy 736
				BLACK EYED PEAS		
8/9/03	8	25	○	1 Where Is The Love? BLACK EYED PEAS (Featuring Justin Timberlake)	William Adams/Printz Board/Michael Fratantuno/Jaime Gomez/George Pajon/Allan Pineda/Justin Timberlake	A&M 000714
6/25/05	3³	26	○	2 Don't Phunk With My Heart	William Adams/Kalyanji Anandji/Curtis Bedeau/Cleveland Bell/Printz Board/Gerry Charles/Hugh Clarke/Stacy Ferguson/Brian George/Lou George/Paul Anthony George/Shyamlal Indivar/Victor May/George Pajon	A&M 004799
11/5/05	3⁶	36		3 My Humps	William Adams/David Payton	A&M 005585
4/18/09	❶¹²	33	△⁴	4 Boom Boom Pow	William Adams/Stacy Ferguson/Jaime Gomez/Allen Pineda	Interscope

PEAK DATE	PEAK POS	WKS CHR	GOLD	ARTIST / Song Title	Songwriter...B-side	Label & Number
				BLACK EYED PEAS (cont'd)		
7/11/09	**❶**¹⁴	56	△⁶	5 I Gotta Feeling	William Adams/Stacy Ferguson/Jaime Gomez/David Guetta/Allen Pineda	Interscope
11/7/09	7	24	△²	6 Meet Me Halfway	William Adams/Jean Baptiste/Stacy Ferguson/Jaime Gomez/Sylvia Gordon/Keith Harris/Allan Pineda	Interscope
3/6/10	**❶**²	25	△²	7 Imma Be	William Adams/Stacy Ferguson/Jaime Gomez/Allan Pineda	Interscope
6/19/10	9	18		8 Rock That Body	William Adams/Jean Baptiste/Stacy Ferguson/Robert Ginyard/Jaime Gomez/David Guetta/Mark Knight/Jaime Munson/Allan Pineda/Adam Walder	Interscope
12/18/10	4	11↑		9 The Time (Dirty Bit)	William Adams/John DeNicola/Damien LeRoy/Donald Markowitz/Allen Pineda/Franke Previte	Interscope
				BLACKstreet		
1/7/95	7	27	▲	1 Before I Let You Go	Chauncey Hannibal/Dave Hollister/Markell Riley/Teddy Riley/Leon Sylvers...*Baby Be Mine*	Interscope 98211
11/9/96	**❶**⁴	31	▲	2 No Diggity	Chauncey Hannibal/Teddy Riley/William Stewart/Larry Walters/Andre Young...*Billie Jean*	Interscope 97007
				BLACKstreet (Featuring Dr. Dre)		
5/23/98	3¹	20	●	3 I Get Lonely	René Elizondo/James Harris III/Janet Jackson/Terry Lewis	Virgin 38631
				JANET (Featuring BLACKstreet)		
				BLANC, Mel		
7/17/48	2⁵	9		1 Woody Woodpecker	Ramez Idriss/George Tibbles...*I'd Love To Live In Loveland With A Girl Like You* (Sportsmen) [N]	Capitol 15145
				THE SPORTSMEN and MEL BLANC And His Original Woody Woodpecker Voice		
2/17/51	9	11		2 I Taut I Taw A Puddy Tat	Warren Foster/Alan Livingston/Billy May...*Yosemite Sam* [N]	Capitol 1360
				BLAND, Billy		
5/16/60	7	20		1 Let The Little Girl Dance	Henry Glover/Carl Spencer...*Sweet Thing*	Old Town 1076
				BLANE, Marcie		
12/1/62	3⁴	16	☉	1 Bobby's Girl	Henry Hoffman/Gary Klein...*A Time To Dream*	Seville 120
				BLAQUE		
6/12/99	8	20	●	1 808	R. Kelly/Natina Reed	Track Masters 78857
1/22/00	5	29		2 Bring It All To Me	Billy Lawrence/Leshan Lewis/Mark Cory Rooney/William Shelby/Violet Smith/Kevin Spencer/Nidra Sylvers/Linda Van Horssen	Track Masters
				BLAQUE (Feat. *NSYNC)		
				BLESSID UNION OF SOULS		
5/6/95	8	31		1 I Believe	Jeff Pence/Matt Senatore/Eliot Sloan...*Heaven*	EMI 58320
				BLEYER, Archie, Orchestra and Chorus		
7/17/54	2²	17		1 Hernando's Hideaway	Richard Adler/Jerry Ross...*S'il Vous Plait*	Cadence 1241
				BLIGE, Mary J.		
12/5/92	7	31	●	1 Real Love	Mark Morales/Mark Cory Rooney	Uptown/MCA 54455
6/3/95	3¹	20	▲	2 I'll Be There For You/You're All I Need To Get By	Nick Ashford/Robert Diggs/Valerie Simpson/Clifford Smith	Def Jam 851878
				METHOD MAN featuring Mary J. Blige		
2/24/96	2²	20	▲	3 Not Gon' Cry	Babyface...*My Funny Valentine* (Chaka Khan)	Arista 12957
11/3/01	**❶**⁶	41		4 Family Affair	Mary J. Blige/Melvin Bradford/Mike Elizondo/Camara Kambon/Luchana Lodge/Bruce Miller/Louis Pierre/Andre Young...*Checkin' For Me*	MCA 155894
2/11/06	3¹	33		5 Be Without You	Johnta Austin/Mary J. Blige/Bryan Michael Cox/Jason Perry	Geffen
3/3/07	2¹	20		6 Runaway Love	Christopher Bridges/Doug Davis/Keri Lyn Hilson/Jamal Jones/Ricky Walters	DTP
				LUDACRIS Featuring Mary J. Blige		
				BLINK-182		
2/19/00	6	23		1 All The Small Things	Tom DeLonge/Mark Hoppus...*M&M's*	MCA 155606
				BLONDIE		
4/28/79	**❶**¹	21	●	1 Heart Of Glass	Debbie Harry/Chris Stein...*11:59*	Chrysalis 2295
4/19/80	**❶**⁶	25	●	2 Call Me	Debbie Harry/Giorgio Moroder...*(instrumental - Giorgio Moroder)*	Chrysalis 2414
1/31/81	**❶**¹	26	●	3 The Tide Is High	John Holt...*Suzy And Jeffrey*	Chrysalis 2465
3/28/81	**❶**²	20	●	4 Rapture	Debbie Harry/Chris Stein...*Walk Like Me*	Chrysalis 2485
				BLOODSTONE		
7/21/73	10	19	▲	1 Natural High	Charles McCormick...*Peter's Jones*	London 1046
				BLOOD, SWEAT & TEARS		
4/12/69	2³	13	●	1 You've Made Me So Very Happy	Berry Gordy/Brenda Holloway/Patrice Holloway/Frank Wilson...*Blues - Part II*	Columbia 44776
7/5/69	2³	13	●	2 Spinning Wheel	David Clayton-Thomas...*More And More*	Columbia 44871
11/29/69	2¹	13	●	3 And When I Die	Laura Nyro/Jerry Sears...*Sometimes In Winter*	Columbia 45008
				BLOOM, Bobby		
11/28/70	8	16		1 Montego Bay	Jeff Barry/Bobby Bloom...*Try A Little Harder*	L&R/MGM 157
				BLUE MAGIC		
8/10/74	8	21	●	1 Sideshow	Vinnie Barrett/Bobby Eli...*Just Don't Want To Be Lonely*	Atco 6961
				BLUES IMAGE		
7/11/70	4	15	●	1 Ride Captain Ride	Frank Konte/Mike Pinera...*Pay My Dues*	Atco 6746
				BLUES MAGOOS		
2/11/67	5	14		1 (We Ain't Got) Nothin' Yet	Michael Esposito/Ronald Gilbert/Ralph Scala/Emil Thielhelm...*Gotta Get Away*	Mercury 72622
				BLUES TRAVELER		
8/5/95	8	49		1 Run-Around	John Popper...*Trust In Trust*	A&M 0982
				BLUE SWEDE		
4/6/74	**❶**¹	17	●	1 Hooked On A Feeling	Mark James...*Gotta Have Your Love*	EMI 3627
10/19/74	7	11		2 Never My Love	Dick Addrisi/Don Addrisi...*Pinewood Rally*	EMI 3938
				BLUNT, James		
3/11/06	**❶**¹	38	△²	1 You're Beautiful	James Blunt/Amanda Ghost/Sacha Skarbek	Custard/Atlantic

PEAK DATE	PEAK POS	WKS CHR	GOLD	ARTIST / Song Title	Songwriter...B-side	Label & Number
				B.O.B.		
5/1/10	❶²	28	⟁²	1 Nothin' On You	Peter Hernandez/Philip Lawrence/Ari Levine/Bobby Simmons...*Bet I*	RebelRock 524312
				B.O.B. Featuring Bruno Mars		
6/5/10	2¹	30	⟁³	2 Airplanes	Jeremy Dussolliet/Justin Franks/Alexander Grant/Bobby Simmons/Timothy Sommers	RebelRock
				B.O.B. Featuring Hayley Williams		
9/4/10	10	20	⟁	3 Magic	Rivers Cuomo/Lukasz Gottwald/Bobby Simmons	RebelRock
				B.O.B. Featuring Rivers Cuomo		
				BOBBETTES, The		
9/23/57	6	24		1 Mr. Lee	Heather Dixon/Helen Gathers/Emma Pought/Jannie Pought/Laura Webb...*Look At The Stars*	Atlantic 1144
				BOB B. SOXX And The Blue Jeans		
1/12/63	8	13		1 Zip-A-Dee Doo-Dah	Ray Gilbert/Allie Wrubel...*Flip And Nitty*	Philles 107
				BOLTON, Michael		
1/20/90	❶³	23		1 How Am I Supposed To Live Without You	Michael Bolton/Doug James...*Forever Eyes*	Columbia 73017
5/5/90	3¹	18		2 How Can We Be Lovers	Michael Bolton/Desmond Child/Diane Warren...*That's What Love Is All About*	Columbia 73257
8/4/90	7	19		3 When I'm Back On My Feet Again	Diane Warren...*Walk Away*	Columbia 73342
6/1/91	4	17		4 Love Is A Wonderful Thing	Michael Bolton/Andy Goldmark...*Soul Provider*	Columbia 73719
9/14/91	7	18		5 Time, Love And Tenderness	Diane Warren...*That's What Love Is All About*	Columbia 73889
11/23/91	❶¹	20		6 When A Man Loves A Woman	Calvin Lewis/Andrew Wright...*Save Me*	Columbia 74020
1/22/94	6	24	●	7 Said I Loved You...But I Lied	Michael Bolton/Mutt Lange...*Soul Provider*	Columbia 77260
				BONDS, Gary (U.S.)		
11/28/60	6	14		1 New Orleans	Frank Guida/Joseph Royster...*Please Forgive Me*	Legrand 1003
6/26/61	❶²	15	⊙	2 Quarter To Three	Gary Anderson/Gene Barge/Frank Guida/Joseph Royster...*Time Ole Story*	Legrand 1008
9/4/61	5	11		3 School Is Out	Gary Anderson/Gene Barge...*One Million Tears*	Legrand 1009
2/24/62	9	16		4 Dear Lady Twist	Frank Guida...*Havin' So Much Fun*	Legrand 1015
5/12/62	9	10		5 Twist, Twist Senora	Gary Anderson...*Food Of Love*	Legrand 1018
				BONE THUGS-N-HARMONY		
5/18/96	❶⁸	20	⟁²	1 Tha Crossroads	Anthony Henderson/Stanley Howse/Steven Howse/Byron McCane/Tim Middleton/Charles Scruggs	Ruthless 6335
6/21/97	4	20	▲	2 Look Into My Eyes	Tony Cowan/Anthony Henderson/Steven Howse/Byron McCane/Tim Middleton/Charles Scruggs	Ruthless 6343
5/26/07	6	18		3 I Tried	Anthony Henderson/Steven Howse/Bryon McCane/Charles Scruggs/Aliaune Thiam	Full Surface
				BONE THUGS-N-HARMONY Featuring Akon		
				BON JOVI		
11/29/86	❶¹	24		1 You Give Love A Bad Name	Jon Bon Jovi/Desmond Child/Richie Sambora...*Raise Your Hands*	Mercury 884953
2/14/87	❶⁴	21		2 Livin' On A Prayer	Jon Bon Jovi/Desmond Child/Richie Sambora...*Wild In The Streets*	Mercury 888184
6/6/87	7	17		3 Wanted Dead Or Alive	Jon Bon Jovi/Richie Sambora...*I'd Die For You*	Mercury 888467
11/19/88	❶²	20		4 Bad Medicine	Jon Bon Jovi/Desmond Child/Richie Sambora...*99 In The Shade*	Mercury 870657
2/18/89	3¹	20		5 Born To Be My Baby	Desmond Child/Richie Sambora...*Love For Sale*	Mercury 872156
5/13/89	❶¹	22		6 I'll Be There For You	Jon Bon Jovi/Richie Sambora...*Homebound Train*	Mercury 872564
7/29/89	7	16		7 Lay Your Hands On Me	Jon Bon Jovi/Richie Sambora...*Runaway (live)*	Mercury 874452
12/16/89	9	19		8 Living In Sin	Jon Bon Jovi...*Love Is War*	Mercury 876070
9/8/90	❶¹	21	▲	9 Blaze Of Glory	Jon Bon Jovi...*You Really Got Me Now* (w/Little Richard)	Mercury 875896
				JON BON JOVI		
3/6/93	10	20		10 Bed Of Roses	Jon Bon Jovi...*Lay Your Hands On Me (live)*	Jambco 864852
12/10/94	4	32	▲	11 Always	Jon Bon Jovi...*Never Say Goodbye / Edge Of A Broken Heart*	Mercury 856227
				BOOKER T. & THE MG'S		
9/29/62	3¹	16	●	1 Green Onions	Steve Cropper/Al Jackson/Booker T. Jones/Lewie Steinberg...*Behave Yourself* [I]	Stax 127
2/8/69	9	18		2 Hang 'Em High	Dominic Frontiere...*Over Easy* [I]	Stax 0013
5/3/69	6	13	●	3 Time Is Tight	Steve Cropper/Donald Dunn/Al Jackson/Booker T. Jones...*Johnny, I Love You* [I]	Stax 0028
				BOONE, Debby		
10/15/77	❶¹⁰	25	▲	1 You Light Up My Life	Joe Brooks...*Hasta Manana*	Warner/Curb 8455
				BOONE, Pat		
9/17/55	❶²	20	⊙	1 Ain't That A Shame	Dave Bartholomew/Fats Domino...*Tennessee Saturday Night*	Dot 15377
11/19/55	7	14		2 At My Front Door (Crazy Little Mama)	Ewart Abner/John Moore...*No Other Arms*	Dot 15422
4/7/56	4	22	⊙	3 I'll Be Home	Stan Lewis/Ferdinand Washington...*Tutti' Frutti*	Dot 15443
6/2/56	8	15		4 Long Tall Sally	Enotris Johnson...*Just As Long As I'm With You*	Dot 15457
7/28/56	❶⁴	23	⊙	5 I Almost Lost My Mind	Ivory Joe Hunter...*I'm In Love With You*	Dot 15472
10/20/56	5	24	⊙	6 Friendly Persuasion (Thee I Love)	Dimitri Tiomkin/Paul Francis Webster...*Chains Of Love*	Dot 15490
10/20/56	10	14		7 Chains Of Love	Ahmet Ertegun/Van Walls...*Friendly Persuasion (Thee I Love)*	Dot 15490
2/9/57	❶¹	22	⊙	8 Don't Forbid Me	Charles Singleton...*Anastasia*	Dot 15521
4/13/57	5	13		9 Why Baby Why	Luther Dixon/Larry Harrison...*I'm Waiting Just For You*	Dot 15545
6/3/57	❶⁷	34	⊙	10 Love Letters In The Sand	J. Fred Coots/Charles Kenny/Nick Kenny...*Bernardine*	Dot 15570
9/9/57	6	21	⊙	11 Remember You're Mine	Bernie Lowe/Kal Mann...*There's A Gold Mine In The Sky*	Dot 15602
12/16/57	❶⁶	26	⊙	12 April Love	Sammy Fain/Paul Francis Webster...*When The Swallows Come Back To Capistrano*	Dot 15660
3/10/58	4	19	⊙	13 A Wonderful Time Up There	Lee Roy Abernathy...*It's Too Soon To Know*	Dot 15690
3/24/58	4	16		14 It's Too Soon To Know	Deborah Chessler...*A Wonderful Time Up There*	Dot 15690
6/16/58	5	14		15 Sugar Moon	Danny Wolfe...*Cherie, I Love You*	Dot 15750
7/21/58	7	13		16 If Dreams Came True	Robert Allen/Al Stillman...*That's How Much I Love You*	Dot 15785
6/19/61	❶¹	15	⊙	17 Moody River	Gary Bruce...*A Thousand Years*	Dot 16209
7/28/62	6	13		18 Speedy Gonzales	David Hill/Buddy Kaye/Ethel Lee...*The Locket* [N]	Dot 16368
				BOSTON		
12/25/76	5	19	○	1 More Than A Feeling	Tom Scholz...*Smokin'*	Epic 50266
10/7/78	4	18		2 Don't Look Back	Tom Scholz...*The Journey*	Epic 50590
11/8/86	❶²	18		3 Amanda	Tom Scholz...*My Destination*	MCA 52756
2/14/87	9	15		4 We're Ready	Tom Scholz...*The Launch: Countdown/Ignition/Third Stage Separation*	MCA 52985
				BOSWELL, Connee		
2/9/46	9	5		1 Let It Snow! Let It Snow! Let It Snow!	Sammy Cahn/Jule Styne...*Walkin' With My Honey (Soon, Soon, Soon)* [X]	Decca 18741
				CONNEE BOSWELL and RUSS MORGAN and HIS ORCHESTRA		
10/23/54	10	11		2 If I Give My Heart To You	Jimmy Brewster/Jimmie Crane/Al Jacobs...*T-E-N-N-E-S-S-E-E*	Decca 29148

PEAK DATE	PEAK POS	WKS CHR	GOLD	ARTIST / Song Title	Songwriter...B-side	Label & Number
				BOUNTY KILLER		
3/2/02	5	20		1 Hey Baby..	Tom Dumont/Tony Kanal/Rodney Price/Gwen Stefani	Interscope
				NO DOUBT Featuring Bounty Killer		
				BOWIE, David		
9/20/75	❶²	21	●	1 Fame..*Right*	Carlos Alomar/David Bowie/John Lennon...*Right*	RCA Victor 10320
4/3/76	10	21		2 Golden Years............................*Can You Hear Me*	David Bowie...*Can You Hear Me*	RCA Victor 10441
5/21/83	❶¹	20	●	3 Let's Dance...............*Cat People (Putting Out Fire)*	David Bowie...*Cat People (Putting Out Fire)*	EMI America 8158
8/27/83	10	18		4 China Girl.....................................*Shake It*	David Bowie/Iggy Pop...*Shake It*	EMI America 8165
11/3/84	8	18		5 Blue Jean..........................*Dancing With The Big Boys*	David Bowie...*Dancing With The Big Boys*	EMI America 8231
10/12/85	7	14		6 Dancing In The Street.....................................	Marvin Gaye/Ivy Hunter/William Stevenson	EMI America 8288
				MICK JAGGER/DAVID BOWIE		
				BOW WOW		
8/13/05	4	24	○	1 Let Me Hold You..	Jermaine Dupri/Brenda Russell/Ernest Wilson	Columbia 74625
				BOW WOW Featuring Omarion		
10/1/05	3²	21	○	2 Like You..	Jaron Alson/Johnta Austin/Ricky Bell/Jermaine Dupri/Ralph Tresvant	Columbia 80449
				BOW WOW (feat. Ciara)		
12/16/06	9	21	○	3 Shortie Like Mine...	Johnta Austin/Bryan-Michael Cox/Jermaine Dupri/Shawntae Harris	Columbia
				BOW WOW Featuring Chris Brown & Johnta Austin		
				BOX TOPS, The		
9/23/67	❶⁴	16	●	1 The Letter.................................*Happy Times*	Wayne Carson Thompson...*Happy Times*	Mala 565
4/27/68	2²	15	●	2 Cry Like A Baby......................*The Door You Closed To Me*	Spooner Oldham/Dan Penn...*The Door You Closed To Me*	Mala 593
				BOYCE, Tommy, & Bobby Hart		
2/24/68	8	14		1 I Wonder What She's Doing Tonite...........*The Ambushers*	Tommy Boyce/Bobby Hart...*The Ambushers*	A&M 893
				BOYD, Jimmy		
12/27/52	❶²	5	⊙	1 I Saw Mommy Kissing Santa Claus............*Thumbelina* [X-N]	Tommy Connor...*Thumbelina* [X-N]	Columbia 39871
4/18/53	4	12		2 Tell Me A Story..........*The Little Boy And The Old Man* [N]	Terry Gilkyson...*The Little Boy And The Old Man* [N]	Columbia 39945
				JIMMY BOYD - FRANKIE LAINE		
				BOY MEETS GIRL		
12/17/88	5	25		1 Waiting For A Star To Fall..................*No Apologies*	George Merrill/Shannon Rubicam...*No Apologies*	RCA 8691
				BOYS CLUB		
1/14/89	8	21		1 I Remember Holding You......................*It's Alright*	Joe Pasquale...*It's Alright*	MCA 53430
				BOYZ II MEN		
9/7/91	3³	24	▲	1 Motownphilly..	Dallas Austin/Michael Bivins/Nathan Morris/Shawn Stockman	Motown 2090
12/14/91	2⁴	22	●	2 It's So Hard To Say Goodbye To Yesterday...................	Freddie Perren/Christine Yarian	Motown 2136
8/15/92	❶¹³	32	▲	3 End Of The Road..	Babyface/L.A. Reid/Daryl Simmons	Motown 2178
1/16/93	3³	20	●	4 In The Still Of The Nite (I'll Remember)..................	Fred Parris	Motown 2193
8/27/94	❶¹⁴	33	▲	5 I'll Make Love To You.....................................	Babyface	Motown 2257
12/3/94	❶⁶	27	▲	6 On Bended Knee..	Jimmy Jam Harris/Terry Lewis	Motown 0244
6/17/95	2¹	28	●	7 Water Runs Dry..	Babyface	Motown 0358
12/2/95	❶¹⁶	27	▲²	8 One Sweet Day.................................*(live version)*	Walter Afanasieff/Mariah Carey/Michael McCary/Nathan Morris/Wanya Morris/Shawn Stockman...*(live version)*	Columbia 78074
				MARIAH CAREY & BOYZ II MEN		
10/4/97	❶¹	20	▲	9 4 Seasons Of Loneliness...................................	Jimmy Jam Harris/Terry Lewis	Motown 0684
2/14/98	7	20	▲	10 A Song For Mama..	Babyface	Motown 0720
				BRADLEY, Will, And His Orchestra		
11/30/40	2¹	15		1 Beat Me Daddy (Eight To The Bar) Parts I & II.............	Hughie Prince/Don Raye/Eleanore Sheehy	Columbia 35530
				WILL BRADLEY and his ORCHESTRA featuring RAY McKINLEY and Freddie Slack		
12/21/40	10	1		2 Down The Road A Piece.................*Celery Stalks At Midnight*	Don Raye...*Celery Stalks At Midnight*	Columbia 35707
				WILL BRADLEY TRIO		
1/11/41	2¹	7		3 Scrub Me, Mama, With A Boogie Beat.............*There I Go*	Don Raye...*There I Go*	Columbia 35743
2/8/41	5	3		4 There I Go.................*Scrub Me, Mama, With A Boogie Beat*	Irving Weiser/Hy Zaret...*Scrub Me, Mama, With A Boogie Beat*	Columbia 35743
2/8/41	9	1		5 High On A Windy Hill.....................*Love Of My Life*	Alex Kramer/Joan Whitney...*Love Of My Life*	Columbia 35912
				WILL BRADLEY AND HIS ORCHESTRA FEATURING RAY McKINLEY (above 3)		
				BRANCH, Michelle		
5/25/02	6	28		1 All You Wanted...	Michelle Branch	Maverick
11/30/02	5	37		2 The Game Of Love...	Alex Ander/Rick Nowels	Arista 15203
				SANTANA featuring Michelle Branch		
				BRANDY		
12/31/94	6	28	●	1 I Wanna Be Down..	Keith Crouch/Kipper Jones	Atlantic 87225
3/11/95	4	20	▲	2 Baby.....................................*I Wanna Be Down*	Keith Crouch/Kipper Jones/Rahsaan Patterson...*I Wanna Be Down*	Atlantic 87173
10/14/95	9	20		3 Brokenhearted..	Keith Crouch/Kipper Jones	Atlantic 87150
3/9/96	2²	33	▲	4 Sittin' Up In My Room........*My Love, Sweet Love* (Patti LaBelle)	Babyface...*My Love, Sweet Love* (Patti LaBelle)	Arista 12929
6/6/98	❶¹³	27	▲²	5 The Boy Is Mine..	LaShawn Daniels/Freddie Jerkins/Rodney Jerkins/Brandy Norwood/Japhe Tejeda	Atlantic 84089
				BRANDY & MONICA		
1/16/99	❶²	22		6 Have You Ever?..................*Top Of The World* (Fat Joe & Big Pun)	Diane Warren...*Top Of The World* (Fat Joe & Big Pun)	Atlantic 84198
3/16/02	7	18		7 What About Us?...	LaShawn Daniels/Freddie Jerkins/Rodney Jerkins/Kenisha Pratt	Atlantic 85217
				BRANIGAN, Laura		
11/27/82	2³	36	▲	1 Gloria.......................................*Living A Lie*	Giancarlo Bigazzi/Umberto Tozzi/Trevor Veitch...*Living A Lie*	Atlantic 4048
5/21/83	7	17		2 Solitaire....................*I'm Not The Only One*	Martine Clemenceau/Diane Warren...*I'm Not The Only One*	Atlantic 89868
6/30/84	4	25		3 Self Control..............................*Silent Partners*	Giancarlo Bigazzi/Steve Piccolo/Raffaele Riefoli...*Silent Partners*	Atlantic 89676
				BRAXTON, Toni		
10/9/93	7	26	●	1 Another Sad Love Song....................................	Babyface/Daryl Simmons	LaFace 24047
1/22/94	3³	35	●	2 Breathe Again..	Babyface	LaFace 24054
5/28/94	7	31		3 You Mean The World To Me..........*Seven Whole Days (live)*	Babyface/L.A. Reid/Daryl Simmons...*Seven Whole Days (live)*	LaFace 24064
7/27/96	❶¹	41	▲	4 You're Makin' Me High........................*Let It Flow*	Babyface/Bryce Wilson...*Let It Flow*	LaFace 24160
12/7/96	❶¹¹	42	▲	5 Un-Break My Heart.....................*(Spanish version)*	Diane Warren...*(Spanish version)*	LaFace 24200
5/6/00	2²	37	●	6 He Wasn't Man Enough.....................................	LaShawn Daniels/Freddie Jerkins/Rodney Jerkins/Harvey Mason	LaFace 24463

PEAK DATE	PEAK POS	WKS CHR	GOLD	ARTIST / Song Title	Songwriter...B-side	Label & Number
				BREAD		
8/22/70	❶¹	17	●	1 Make It With You	David Gates...*Why Do You Keep Me Waiting*	Elektra 45686
11/14/70	10	11		2 It Don't Matter To Me	David Gates...*Call On Me*	Elektra 45701
5/15/71	4	12		3 If...	David Gates...*Take Comfort*	Elektra 45720
11/27/71	3²	12	●	4 Baby I'm - A Want You	David Gates...*Truckin'*	Elektra 45751
3/4/72	5	13		5 Everything I Own	David Gates...*I Don't Love You*	Elektra 45765
2/19/77	9	16		6 Lost Without Your Love	David Gates...*Change Of Heart*	Elektra 45365
				BREAKFAST CLUB		
5/30/87	7	19		1 Right On Track	Stephen Bray/Dan Gilroy	MCA 52954
				BREATHE		
8/6/88	2²	29		1 Hands To Heaven	David Glasper/Marcus Lillington...*Life And Times*	A&M 2991
12/3/88	3²	22		2 How Can I Fall?	David Glasper/Marcus Lillington...*Monday Morning Blues*	A&M 1224
3/18/89	10	16		3 Don't Tell Me Lies	David Glasper/Marcus Lillington...*Liberties Of Love*	A&M 1267
				BRENNAN, Walter		
5/26/62	5	11		1 Old Rivers	Cliff Crofford...*The Epic Ride Of John H. Glenn* [S]	Liberty 55436
				BREWER, Teresa		
3/18/50	❶⁴	17	⊙	1 Music! Music! Music!	Bernie Baum/Stephan Weiss...*Copenhagen*	London 30023
				TERESA BREWER with THE DIXIELAND ALL STARS		
2/14/53	❶⁷	24	⊙	2 Till I Waltz Again With You	Sidney Prosen...*Hello Bluebird*	Coral 60873
12/26/53	2²	20	⊙	3 Ricochet (Rick-O-Shay)	Larry Coleman/Joe Darion/Norman Gimbel...*Too Young To Tango*	Coral 61043
5/22/54	6	9		4 Jilted	Robert Colby/Dick Manning...*Le Grand Tour De L'Amour*	Coral 61152
1/8/55	6	12		5 Let Me Go, Lover!	*The Moon Is On Fire*	Coral 61315
				TERESA BREWER with The Lancers		
5/12/56	5	23		6 A Tear Fell	Dorian Burton/Eugene Randolph...*Bo Weevil*	Coral 61590
8/11/56	7	20		7 A Sweet Old Fashioned Girl	Bob Merrill...*Goodbye, John*	Coral 61636
11/25/57	8	12		8 You Send Me	Charles Cooke...*Would I Were*	Coral 61898
				BREWER & SHIPLEY		
4/10/71	10	14		1 One Toke Over The Line	Mike Brewer/Tom Shipley...*Oh Mommy*	Kama Sutra 516
				BRICK		
1/29/77	3²	21		1 Dazz	Reggie Hargis/Eddie Irons/Ray Ransom...*Southern Sunset*	Bang 727
				BRICKELL, Edie		
3/4/89	7	19		1 What I Am	Edie Brickell/Kenny Withrow...*I Do*	Geffen 27696
				BRIDGES, Alicia		
12/23/78	5	31	●	1 I Love The Nightlife (Disco 'Round)	Alicia Bridges/Susan Hutcheson...*Self Applause*	Polydor 14483
				BRISTOL, Johnny		
10/5/74	8	17		1 Hang On In There Baby	Johnny Bristol...*Take Care Of You For Me*	MGM 14715
				B-ROCK & THE BIZZ		
5/3/97	10	19	●	1 MyBabyDaddy	Baron Agee	Tony Mercedes 24221
				BROOKLYN BRIDGE Featuring Johnny Maestro		
2/1/69	3²	12	●	1 Worst That Could Happen	Jimmy Webb...*Your Kite, My Kite*	Buddah 75
				BROOKLYN DREAMS		
3/17/79	4	19	●	1 Heaven Knows	Pete Bellotte/Giorgio Moroder/Donna Summer...*Only One Man* (Summer)	Casablanca 959
				DONNA SUMMER with Brooklyn Dreams		
				BROOKS, Donnie		
9/5/60	7	20		1 Mission Bell	William Michael...*Do It For Me*	Era 3018
				BROOKS, Garth		
9/11/99	5	10	●	1 Lost In You	Gordon Kennedy/Wayne Kirkpatrick/Tommy Sims...*It Don't Matter To The Sun*	Capitol 58788
				GARTH BROOKS AS CHRIS GAINES		
				BROOKS, Meredith		
7/12/97	2⁴	30	●	1 Bitch	Meredith Brooks...*Down By The River*	Capitol 58634
				BROTHER BONES & HIS SHADOWS		
2/5/49	10	16		1 Sweet Georgia Brown	Ben Bernie/Kenneth Casey/Maceo Pinkard...*Margie* [I]	Tempo 652
				BROTHERS FOUR, The		
4/18/60	2⁴	20	⊙	1 Greenfields	Richard Dehr/Terry Gilkyson/Frank Miller...*Angelique-O*	Columbia 41571
				BROTHERS JOHNSON, The		
7/10/76	3³	17	●	1 I'll Be Good To You	George Johnson/Louis Johnson/Senora Sam...*The Devil*	A&M 1806
9/24/77	5	19		2 Strawberry Letter 23	Shuggie Otis...*Dancin' And Prancin'*	A&M 1949
5/24/80	7	19		3 Stomp!	George Johnson/Louis Johnson/Valerie Johnson/Rod Temperton...*Let's Swing*	A&M 2216
				BROWN, Arthur [The Crazy World Of]		
10/19/68	2¹	13	●	1 Fire	Arthur Brown/Vincent Crane/Michael Finesilver/Peter Kerr...*Rest Cure*	Atlantic 2556
				BROWN, Bobby		
10/15/88	8	26	●	1 Don't Be Cruel	Babyface/L.A. Reid/Daryl Simmons	MCA 53327
1/14/89	❶¹	24	●	2 My Prerogative	Bobby Brown/Gene Griffin	MCA 53383
3/18/89	3¹	17		3 Roni	Babyface/Darnell Bristol	MCA 53463
6/10/89	3²	21	●	4 Every Little Step	Babyface/L.A. Reid	MCA 53618
8/5/89	2³	20	▲	5 On Our Own	Babyface/L.A. Reid/Daryl Simmons	MCA 53662
11/4/89	7	21		6 Rock Wit'cha	Babyface/Daryl Simmons	MCA 53652
7/21/90	❶²	18	●	7 She Ain't Worth It	Antonina Armato/Bobby Brown/Ian Prince	MCA 53831
				GLENN MEDEIROS Featuring Bobby Brown		
9/12/92	3³	20	●	8 Humpin' Around	Babyface/Bobby Brown/L.A. Reid/Daryl Simmons	MCA 54342
12/26/92	7	23	●	9 Good Enough	Babyface/L.A. Reid/Daryl Simmons	MCA 54517

PEAK DATE	PEAK POS	WKS CHR	GOLD	ARTIST / Song Title	Songwriter...B-side	Label & Number
				BROWN, Chris		
11/26/05	❶⁵	38	△	1 Run It!	Chris Butler/Sean Garrett/Scott Storch	Jive 71831
2/18/06	7	21	○	2 Yo (Excuse Me Miss)	Johnta Austin/Vidal Davis/Andre Harris	Jive 80865
11/11/06	10	23	○	3 Say Goodbye	Brian-Michael Cox/Kendrick Dean/Adonis Shropshire	Jive
12/16/06	9	21	○	4 Shortie Like Mine	Johnta Austin/Bryan-Michael Cox/Jermaine Dupri/Shawntae Harris	Columbia
				BOW WOW Featuring Chris Brown & Johnta Austin		
11/10/07	❶³	26	△²	5 Kiss Kiss	Chris Brown/Faheem Najm	Jive 17392
				CHRIS BROWN Featuring T-Pain		
2/16/08	2⁶	29	△	6 With You	Johnta Austin/Amund Bjorklund/Mikkel Eriksen/Tor Erik Hermansen/Espen Lind	Jive
4/5/08	10	12		7 Shawty Get Loose	Niatia Kirkland/Faheem Najm	Jive 27082
				LIL MAMA Featuring Chris Brown & T-Pain		
4/26/08	3⁴	35	△	8 No Air	James Fauntleroy/Eric Griggs/Harvey Mason Jr./Steve Russell/Damon Thomas	19 Records
				JORDIN SPARKS & CHRIS BROWN		
8/16/08	2²	33		9 Forever	Rob Allen/Chris Brown/Jamal Jones/Andre Merritt/Brian Seals	Jive
				BROWN, Foxy		
4/12/97	7	20	●	1 I'll Be	Sam Barnes/Shawn Carter/Rene Moore/J.C. Olivier/Angela Winbush...*La Familia*	Violator 574028
				FOXY BROWN Featuring Jay-Z		
				BROWN, James		
9/4/65	8	13		1 Papa's Got A Brand New Bag (Part I)	James Brown...*Part II*	King 5999
12/18/65	3³	12		2 I Got You (I Feel Good)	James Brown...*I Can't Help It (I Just Do-Do-Do)*	King 6015
6/4/66	8	9		3 It's A Man's Man's Man's World	James Brown...*Is It Yes Or Is It No?*	King 6035
8/26/67	7	12		4 Cold Sweat (Part 1)	James Brown/Alfred Ellis...*(Part 2)*	King 6110
4/27/68	6	12		5 I Got The Feelin'	James Brown...*If I Ruled The World*	King 6155
10/19/68	10	11		6 Say It Loud - I'm Black And I'm Proud (Part 1)	James Brown...*(Part 2)*	King 6187
3/1/86	4	19		7 Living In America	Dan Hartman/Charlie Midnight...*Farewell* (Vince DiCola)	Scotti Brothers 05682
				BROWN, Les, And His Orchestra		
4/7/45	❶⁷	16		1 My Dreams Are Getting Better All The Time	Mann Curtis/Vic Mizzy...*He's Home For A Little While*	Columbia 36779
5/5/45	❶⁹	28	⊙	2 Sentimental Journey	Les Brown/Bud Green/Ben Homer...*Twilight Time*	Columbia 36769
6/30/45	10	1		3 'Tain't Me	Lemuel Davis/Jack Palmer...*I'll Always Be With You*	Columbia 36804
9/29/45	3²	13		4 Till The End Of Time	Buddy Kaye/Ted Mossman...*He'll Have To Cross The Atlantic (To Get To The Pacific)*	Columbia 36828
3/30/46	6	4		5 Doctor, Lawyer, Indian Chief	Hoagy Carmichael/Paul Francis Webster...*Day By Day*	Columbia 36945
4/13/46	2²	15		6 You Won't Be Satisfied (Until You Break My Heart)	Freddy James/Larry Stock...*Come To Baby, Do!*	Columbia 36884
7/6/46	10	5		7 I Got The Sun In The Morning	Irving Berlin...*It Couldn't Be True! (Or Could It?)*	Columbia 36977
11/30/46	6	11		8 The Whole World Is Singing My Song	Mann Curtis/Vic Mizzy...*I Guess I'll Get The Papers (And Go Home)*	Columbia 37066
2/15/47	8	1		9 Sooner Or Later	Ray Gilbert/Charles Wolcott...*Years And Years Ago*	Columbia 37153
				Doris Day (vocal; all of above, except #5)		
3/5/49	❶¹	17		10 I've Got My Love To Keep Me Warm	Irving Berlin...*I'm A-Tellin' You, Sam* [I]	Columbia 38324
12/15/51	2¹	21		11 Undecided	Sid Robin/Charles Shavers...*Sentimental Journey*	Coral 60566
				AMES BROTHERS And LES BROWN And His Band Of Renown		
				BROWN, Peter		
7/8/78	8	28		1 Dance With Me	Peter Brown/Robert Rans...*For Your Love*	Drive 6269
				PETER BROWN with Betty Wright		
				BROWN, Sleepy		
2/14/04	❶¹	39	○	1 The Way You Move	Patrick Brown/Carlton Mahone/Antwan Patton...*Hey Ya!*	Arista 54962
				OUTKAST Featuring Sleepy Brown		
				BROWNE, Jackson		
5/6/72	8	12		1 Doctor My Eyes	Jackson Browne...*Looking Into You*	Asylum 11004
10/16/82	7	19		2 Somebody's Baby	Jackson Browne/Danny Kortchmar...*The Crow On The Cradle* (w/Graham Nash & David Lindley)	Asylum 69982
				BROWNS, The		
8/24/59	❶⁴	17	⊙	1 The Three Bells	Bert Reisfeld/Jean Villard...*Heaven Fell Last Night*	RCA Victor 7555
5/2/60	5	15		2 The Old Lamplighter	Nat Simon/Charles Tobias...*Teen-Ex*	RCA Victor 7700
				BROWNSTONE		
2/25/95	8	27	●	1 If You Love Me	Gordon Chambers/Nichole Gilbert/Dave Hall	MJJ Music 77732
				BROWNSVILLE STATION		
1/19/74	3¹	19	●	1 Smokin' In The Boy's Room	Cub Coda/Michael Lutz...*Barefootin'*	Big Tree 16011
				BRYANT, Anita		
6/13/60	5	17		1 Paper Roses	Fred Spielman/Janice Torre...*Mixed Emotions*	Carlton 528
8/29/60	10	14		2 In My Little Corner Of The World	Bob Hilliard/Lee Pockriss...*Anyone Would Love You*	Carlton 530
				BRYSON, Peabo		
8/18/84	10	25		1 If Ever You're In My Arms Again	Michael Masser/Tom Snow/Cynthia Weil...*There's No Getting Over You*	Elektra 69728
4/18/92	9	20	▲	2 Beauty And The Beast	Howard Ashman/Alan Menken...*The Beast Lets Belle Go*	Epic 74090
				CELINE DION and PEABO BRYSON		
3/6/93	❶¹	23	●	3 A Whole New World (Aladdin's Theme)	Alan Menken/Tim Rice...*After The Kiss (instrumental)*	Columbia 74751
				PEABO BRYSON and REGINA BELLE		
				B.T. EXPRESS		
11/16/74	2²	18	●	1 Do It ('Til You're Satisfied)	Billy Nichols	Scepter 12395
3/29/75	4	15	●	2 Express	Barbara Lomas/Louis Risbrook/William Risbrook/Dennis Rowe/Richard Thompson/Carlos Ward/Orlando Woods [I]	Roadshow 7001
				B2K		
2/1/03	❶¹	22		1 Bump, Bump, Bump	R. Kelly/Varick Smith	Epic 79842
				B2K & P. DIDDY		
				BUCHANAN and GOODMAN — see GOODMAN, Dickie		
				BUCKCHERRY		
3/1/08	9	24	△	1 Sorry	Martin Frederiksen/Keith Nelson/Josh Todd	Eleven Seven
				BUCKINGHAM, Lindsey		
1/16/82	9	19		1 Trouble	Lindsey Buckingham...*Mary Lee Jones*	Asylum 47223

PEAK DATE	PEAK POS	WKS CHR	GOLD	ARTIST / Song Title	Songwriter...B-side	Label & Number
				BUCKINGHAMS, The		
2/18/67	❶²	13	⊙	1 Kind Of A Drag	James Holvay...*You Make Me Feel So Good*	U.S.A. 860
5/13/67	6	14		2 Don't You Care	Gary Beisber/James Guercio/James Holvay...*Why Don't You Love Me*	Columbia 44053
8/12/67	5	12		3 Mercy, Mercy, Mercy	Gail Levy/Vincent Levy/Joe Zawinul...*You Are Gone*	Columbia 44182
				BUCKNER & GARCIA		
3/27/82	9	19	●	1 Pac-Man Fever	Jerry Buckner/Gary Garcia [N]	Columbia 02673
				BUFFALO SPRINGFIELD, The		
3/25/67	7	15		1 For What It's Worth (Stop, Hey What's That Sound)	Stephen Stills...*Do I Have To Come Right Out And Say It*	Atco 6459
				BUFFETT, Jimmy		
7/23/77	8	22		1 Margaritaville	Jimmy Buffett...*Miss You So Badly*	ABC 12254
				BUN-B		
2/4/06	❶⁵	28	○	1 Check On It	Angela Beyince/Kasseem Dean/Sean Garrett/Beyonce Knowles/Stayve Thomas	Columbia 80277
				BEYONCE Featuring Bun-B & Slim Thug		
				BURDON, Eric, And War		
8/22/70	3¹	21	●	1 Spill The Wine	Thomas Allen/Harold Brown/Morris Dickerson/Leroy Jordan/Charles Miller/Lee Oskar/Howard Scott...*Magic Mountain*	MGM 14118
				BURNETTE, Johnny		
12/26/60	8	15		1 You're Sixteen	Richard Sherman/Robert Sherman...*I Beg Your Pardon*	Liberty 55285
				BURNETTE, Rocky		
7/26/80	8	19		1 Tired Of Toein' The Line	Rocky Burnette/Ron Coleman...*Boogie Down In Mobile, Alabama*	EMI America 8043
				BUSTA RHYMES		
4/20/96	8	20	▲	1 Woo-Hah!! Got You All In Check	Rashad Smith/Trevor Smith...*Everything Remains Raw*	Elektra 64335
2/7/98	9	19	●	2 Dangerous	Rashad Smith/Trevor Smith/Henry Stone/Fred Stonewall...*You Won't Tell, I Won't Tell*	Elektra 64131
5/9/98	10	20	●	3 Turn It Up [Remix]/Fire It Up	Glen Larson/Stu Phillips/Trevor Smith...*Rhymes Galore*	Elektra 64104
4/17/99	3¹	20	●	4 What's It Gonna Be?!	Darrell Allamby/Antoinette Roberson/Trevor Smith...*Tear Da Roof Off*	Elektra 64051
				BUSTA RHYMES Featuring Janet		
5/31/03	3³	24		5 I Know What You Want	Rashia Fisher/Leroy Jones/William Lewis/Roger McNair/Trevor Smith/Ricardo Thomas...*Call The Ambulance*	J Records 21258
				BUSTA RHYMES AND MARIAH CAREY (feat. The Flipmode Squad)		
8/20/05	2³	40	△	6 Don't Cha	Thomas Callaway/Trevor Smith	A&M 004685
				THE PUSSYCAT DOLLS Featuring Busta Rhymes		
				BUTLER, Jerry		
12/5/60	7	15		1 He Will Break Your Heart	Jerry Butler/Calvin Carter/Curtis Mayfield...*Thanks To You*	Vee-Jay 354
11/7/64	5	13		2 Let It Be Me	Gilbert Becaud/Mann Curtis...*Ain't That Loving You Baby*	Vee-Jay 613
				BETTY EVERETT & JERRY BUTLER		
4/19/69	4	13	●	3 Only The Strong Survive	Jerry Butler/Kenny Gamble/Leon Huff...*Just Because I Really Love You*	Mercury 72898
				BUTTERFIELD, Billy, And His Orchestra		
2/10/45	10	2		1 There Goes That Song Again	Sammy Cahn/Jule Styne...*Moonlight In Vermont*	Capitol 182
11/9/46	6	7		2 Rumors Are Flying	Bennie Benjamin/George Weiss...*The Sharp Scarf*	Capitol 282
				BUTTONS, Red		
6/13/53	9	9		1 The Ho Ho Song	Red Buttons/Joe Darion/Jack Wolf...*Strange Things Are Happening (Ho Ho, Hee Hee, Ha Ha)* [N]	Columbia 39981
				B*WITCHED		
4/17/99	9	15	●	1 C'est La Vie	Tracey Ackerman/Lindsay Armaou/Martin Brannigan/Ray Hedges/Edele Lynch/Keavy Lynch/Sinead O'Carroll...*B*Witched Quiz Show / Get Happy*	Epic 79084
				BYRDS, The		
6/26/65	❶¹	13	⊙	1 Mr. Tambourine Man	Bob Dylan...*I Knew I'd Want You*	Columbia 43271
12/4/65	❶³	14	⊙	2 Turn! Turn! Turn! (To Everything There Is A Season)	Pete Seeger...*She Don't Care About Time*	Columbia 43424
				BYRNES, Edward		
5/11/59	4	13	⊙	1 Kookie, Kookie (Lend Me Your Comb)	Irving Taylor...*You're The Top* (Brynes) [N]	Warner 5047
				EDWARD BYRNES and CONNIE STEVENS		

C

PEAK DATE	PEAK POS	WKS CHR	GOLD	ARTIST / Song Title	Songwriter...B-side	Label & Number
				CAFFERTY, John, And The Beaver Brown Band		
10/27/84	7	18		1 On The Dark Side	*Wild Summer Nights*	Scotti Brothers 04594
				CAILLAT, Colbie		
10/27/07	5	47	△	1 Bubbly	Colbie Caillat/Jason Reeves	Universal Republic
				CALDWELL, Bobby		
3/24/79	9	20		1 What You Won't Do For Love	Bobby Caldwell/Alfons Kettner...*Love Won't Wait*	Clouds 11
				CALLING, The		
3/16/02	5	45		1 Wherever You Will Go	Alex Band/Aaron Kamin	RCA 60518
				CALLOWAY		
5/5/90	2¹	23	●	1 I Wanna Be Rich	Reggie Calloway/Vincent Calloway/Melvin Gentry/Belinda Lipscomb	Solar 74005
				CALLOWAY, Cab		
3/14/42	8	1		1 Blues In The Night (My Mama Done Tol' Me)	Harold Arlen/Johnny Mercer...*Says Who? Says You, Says I!*	Okeh 6422
				CALVERT, Eddie		
1/16/54	6	14		1 Oh, Mein Papa	Paul Burkhard/Geoffrey Parsons/John Turner...*Mystery Street* [I]	Essex 336
				CAMEO		
11/22/86	6	21		1 Word Up	Larry Blackmon/Tomi Jenkins...*Urban Warrior*	Atlanta Artists 884933

PEAK DATE	PEAK POS	WKS CHR	GOLD	ARTIST / Song Title	Songwriter...B-side	Label & Number
				CAMPBELL, Glen		
1/11/69	3¹	15	●	1 Wichita Lineman	Jimmy Webb...*Fate Of Man*	Capitol 2302
4/12/69	4	12	●	2 Galveston	Jimmy Webb...*How Come Every Time I Itch I Wind Up Scratchin' You*	Capitol 2428
10/31/70	10	12		3 It's Only Make Believe	Jack Nance/Conway Twitty...*Pave Your Way Into Tomorrow*	Capitol 2905
9/6/75	❶²	23	●	4 Rhinestone Cowboy	Larry Weiss...*Lovelight*	Capitol 4095
4/30/77	❶¹	21	●	5 Southern Nights	Allen Toussaint...*William Tell Overture*	Capitol 4376
				CAMPBELL, Tevin		
2/29/92	6	25	●	1 Tell Me What You Want Me To Do	Tevin Campbell/Sally Jo Dakota/Narada Michael Walden	Qwest 19131
1/15/94	9	26	●	2 Can We Talk	Babyface/Daryl Simmons...*Look What We'd Have (If You Were Mine)*	Qwest 18346
5/21/94	9	22		3 I'm Ready	Babyface	Qwest 18264
				CAMP ROCK CAST		
7/12/08	9	7		1 This Is Me [Demi Lovato & Joe Jonas]	Andy Dodd/Adam Watts	Walt Disney
				CAM'RON		
7/6/02	4	21		1 Oh Boy	Cameron Giles/Laron James/Justin Smith/Norman Whitfield...*The Roc (Just Fire)*	Roc-A-Fella 582864
				CAM'RON feat. Juelz Santana		
11/2/02	3¹	21		2 Hey Ma	Cameron Giles/Laron James/Darryl Pittman/Lionel Richie...*Boy Boy*	Roc-A-Fella 063958
				CAM'RON (feat. Juelz Santana, Freekey Zekey and Toya)		
				C & C MUSIC FACTORY		
2/9/91	❶²	25	▲	1 Gonna Make You Sweat (Everybody Dance Now)	Robert Clivilles/Freedom Williams	Columbia 73604
5/18/91	3¹	20	●	2 Here We Go	Robert Clivilles/Freedom Williams	Columbia 73690
9/7/91	4	16	●	3 Things That Make You Go Hmmmm...	Robert Clivilles/Freedom Williams	Columbia 73687
				C + C MUSIC FACTORY Featuring Freedom Williams (above 3)		
				CANDYMAN		
11/10/90	9	23	▲	1 Knockin' Boots	Willie Clarke/John Shaffer/Norman Whitfield/Betty Wright...*Keep On Watcha Doin'*	Epic 73450
				CANNON, Freddy		
6/29/59	6	15	⊙	1 Tallahassee Lassie	Bob Crewe/Frank Picariello/Frank Slay...*You Know*	Swan 4031
1/11/60	3¹	15	⊙	2 Way Down Yonder In New Orleans	Henry Creamer/Turner Layton...*Fractured*	Swan 4043
6/23/62	3²	15	⊙	3 Palisades Park	Chuck Barris...*June, July, and August*	Swan 4106
				CANTRELL, Blu		
7/21/01	2²	34		1 Hit 'Em Up Style (Oops!)	Dallas Austin	Arista 13974
				CAPITOLS, The		
7/2/66	7	14		1 Cool Jerk	Donald Storball...*Hello Stranger*	Karen 1524
				CAPRIS, The		
2/27/61	3¹	14		1 There's A Moon Out Tonight	Alfonso Gentile/Joseph Luccisano/Alfred Striano...*Indian Girl*	Old Town 1094
				CAPTAIN & TENNILLE		
6/21/75	❶⁴	23	●	1 Love Will Keep Us Together	Howard Greenfield/Neil Sedaka...*Gentle Stranger*	A&M 1672
11/29/75	4	17	●	2 The Way I Want To Touch You	Toni Tennille...*Broddy Bounce*	A&M 1725
3/27/76	3³	19	●	3 Lonely Night (Angel Face)	Neil Sedaka...*Smile For Me One More Time*	A&M 1782
7/10/76	4	16	●	4 Shop Around	Berry Gordy/Smokey Robinson...*Butterscotch Castle*	A&M 1817
11/20/76	4	20	●	5 Muskrat Love	Willis Ramsey...*Honey Come Love Me*	A&M 1870
11/18/78	10	22		6 You Never Done It Like That	Howard Greenfield/Neil Sedaka..."D" Keyboard Blues*	A&M 2063
2/16/80	❶¹	27	●	7 Do That To Me One More Time	Toni Tennille...*Deep In The Dark*	Casablanca 2215
				CARA, Irene		
9/13/80	4	26		1 Fame	Michael Gore/Dean Pitchford...*Never Alone* (Contemporary Gospel Chorus)	RSO 1034
5/28/83	❶⁶	25	●	2 Flashdance...What A Feeling	Irene Cara/Keith Forsey/Giorgio Moroder...*Love Theme From "Flashdance"* (Helen St. John)	Casablanca 811440
6/9/84	8	19		3 Breakdance	Irene Cara/Giorgio Moroder...*Cue Me Up*	Geffen 29328
				CARAVELLES, The		
12/21/63	3¹	13		1 You Don't Have To Be A Baby To Cry	Bob Merrill/Terry Shand...*The Last One To Know*	Smash 1852
				CARDIGANS, The		
3/1/97	2⁸	49		1 Lovefool	Nina Persson/Peter Svensson	Mercury
				CAREY, Mariah		
8/4/90	❶⁴	22	●	1 Vision Of Love	Mariah Carey	Columbia 73348
11/10/90	❶³	26	●	2 Love Takes Time	Mariah Carey/Ben Margulies...*Sent From Up Above*	Columbia 73455
3/9/91	❶²	19	●	3 Someday	Mariah Carey/Ben Margulies...*Alone In Love*	Columbia 73561
5/25/91	❶²	19	●	4 I Don't Wanna Cry	Mariah Carey/Narada Michael Walden...*You Need Me*	Columbia 73743
10/12/91	❶³	20	●	5 Emotions	Mariah Carey/Robert Clivilles/David Cole...*Vanishing*	Columbia 73977
1/25/92	2¹	20		6 Can't Let Go	Walter Afanasieff/Mariah Carey...*To Be Around You*	Columbia 74088
4/11/92	5	20		7 Make It Happen	Mariah Carey/Robert Clivilles/David Cole...*Emotions (special edit)*	Columbia 74239
6/20/92	❶²	20		8 I'll Be There	Hal Davis/Berry Gordy/Willie Hutch/Bob West...*So Blessed* [L]	Columbia 74330
9/11/93	❶⁸	29	▲	9 Dreamlover	Mariah Carey/Dave Hall...*Do You Think Of Me*	Columbia 77080
12/25/93	❶⁴	30	▲	10 Hero	Walter Afanasieff/Mariah Carey...*Everything Fades Away*	Columbia 77224
3/19/94	3⁶	23		11 Without You	Tom Evans/Pete Ham...*Never Forget You*	Columbia 77358
10/1/94	2¹	20	●	12 Endless Love	Lionel Richie	Columbia 77629
				LUTHER VANDROSS & MARIAH CAREY		
9/30/95	❶⁸	25	▲²	13 Fantasy	Adrian Belew/Mariah Carey/Chris Frantz/Dave Hall/Steven Stanley/Tina Weymouth	Columbia 78043
12/2/95	❶¹⁶	27	▲²	14 One Sweet Day	Walter Afanasieff/Mariah Carey/Michael McCary/Nathan Morris/Wanya Morris/Shawn Stockman...*(live version)*	Columbia 78074
				MARIAH CAREY & BOYZ II MEN		
5/4/96	❶²	32	▲	15 Always Be My Baby	Mariah Carey/Jermaine Dupri/Manuel Seal...*Slipping Away*	Columbia 78276
8/17/96	9	20		16 Forever	Walter Afanasieff/Mariah Carey	Columbia
9/13/97	❶³	20	▲	17 Honey	Mariah Carey/Sean Combs/Kamaal Fareed/Stephen Hague/Steve Jordan/Ronald Larkins/Larry Price/Bob Robinson	Columbia 78648
5/23/98	❶¹	20	▲	18 My All	Walter Afanasieff/Mariah Carey...*Breakdown*	Columbia 78821
3/20/99	4	20		19 I Still Believe	Antonina Armato/Giuseppe Cantarelli...*I Still Believe/Pure Imagination* (w/Krayzie Bone & Da Brat)	Columbia 79093
10/9/99	❶²	20	●	20 Heartbreaker	Mariah Carey/Shawn Carter/Lincoln Chase/Jeffrey E. Cohen/Shirley Ellis/Narada Michael Walden	Columbia 79260
				MARIAH CAREY (Featuring Jay-Z)		

PEAK DATE	PEAK POS	WKS CHR	GOLD	ARTIST / Song Title ... Songwriter...B-side	Label & Number
				CAREY, Mariah (cont'd)	
2/19/00	❶[1]	20	●	21 Thank God I Found You .... Mariah Carey/James Harris III/Terry Lewis	Columbia 79338
				MARIAH with Joe & 98°	
8/4/01	2[2]	14	●	22 Loverboy .... Larry Blackmon/Mariah Carey/Thomas Jenkins	Virgin 38791
5/31/03	3[3]	24		23 I Know What You Want .... Rashia Fisher/Leroy Jones/William Lewis/Roger McNair/Trevor Smith/Ricardo Thomas...*Call The Ambulance*	J Records 21258
				BUSTA RHYMES AND MARIAH CAREY (feat. The Flipmode Squad)	
6/4/05	❶[14]	43	△	24 We Belong Together .... Johnta Austin/Babyface/Darnell Bristol/Mariah Carey/Jermaine Dupri/Sid Johnson/Patrick Moten/Manuel Seal/Sandra Sully/Bobby Womack	Island 005162
9/10/05	2[6]	26	○	25 Shake It Off .... Johnta Austin/Mariah Carey/Bryan Michael Cox/Jermaine Dupri	Island
12/31/05	❶[2]	21	○	26 Don't Forget About Us .... Johnta Austin/Mariah Carey/Bryan Michael Cox/Jermaine Dupri	Island 006059
4/12/08	❶[2]	20	△	27 Touch My Body .... Mariah Carey/Crystal Johnson/Terius Nash/Chris Stewart	Island 011159
9/19/09	7	21	△	Obsessed .... Mariah Carey/Terius Nash/Christopher Stewart	Island 013290
				CARLE, Frankie, and his Orchestra	
2/10/45	8	1		1 Saturday Night (Is The Loneliest Night In The Week) .... Sammy Cahn/Jule Styne...*Carle Boogie*	Columbia 36777
3/24/45	4	14		2 A Little On The Lonely Side .... James Cavanaugh/Dick Robertson/Frank Weldon...*I Had A Little Talk With The Lord*	Columbia 36760
3/16/46	❶[11]	20		3 Oh! What It Seemed To Be .... Bennie Benjamin/Frankie Carle/George Weiss...*As Long As I Live*	Columbia 36892
8/3/46	10	8		4 One More Tomorrow .... Eddie DeLange/Ernesto Lecuona/Josef Myrow...*I'm Gonna Make Believe*	Columbia 36978
10/19/46	❶[9]	18		5 Rumors Are Flying .... Bennie Benjamin/George Weiss...*Without You*	Columbia 37069
12/21/46	6	4		6 It's All Over Now .... Don Marcotte/Sunny Skylar...*Either It's Love Or It Isn't*	Columbia 37146
4/12/47	9	2		7 Roses In The Rain .... Frankie Carle/Al Frisch/Fred Wise...*You Are There*	Columbia 37252
3/20/48	5	16		8 Beg Your Pardon .... Francis Craig/Beasley Smith...*The Dream Peddler*	Columbia 38036
12/4/48	10	1		9 Twelfth Street Rag .... Euday Bowman/Andy Razaf...*Sweet Lorraine* [I]	Columbia 35572
				At The Piano...Horace Heidt Presents FRANKIE CARLE	
4/16/49	8	12		10 Cruising Down The River (On A Sunday Afternoon) .... Eily Beadell/Nell Tollerton...*Mississippi Flyer*	Columbia 38411
				CARLISLE, Belinda	
8/9/86	3[2]	21		1 Mad About You .... Paula Brown/Mitchell Young Evans/James Whelan...*I Never Wanted A Rich Man*	I.R.S. 52815
12/5/87	❶[1]	21		2 Heaven Is A Place On Earth .... Rick Nowels/Ellen Shipley...*We Can Change*	MCA 53181
3/19/88	2[1]	16		3 I Get Weak .... Diane Warren...*Should I Let You In?*	MCA 53242
6/18/88	7	17		4 Circle In The Sand .... Rick Nowels/Ellen Shipley...*We Can Change*	MCA 53308
				CARLISLE, Bob	
6/21/97	10	15		1 Butterfly Kisses .... Bob Carlisle/Keith Thomas...*You Must Have Been An Angel*	Diadem 1221
				CARLTON, Carl	
11/23/74	6	15		1 Everlasting Love .... Buzz Cason/Mac Gayden...*I Wanna Be Your Main Squeeze*	Back Beat 27001
				CARLTON, Larry	
11/14/81	10	22		1 The Theme From Hill Street Blues .... Mike Post...*Aaron's Tune* [I]	Elektra 47186
				MIKE POST featuring Larry Carlton	
				CARLTON, Vanessa	
5/18/02	5	41		1 A Thousand Miles .... Vanessa Carlton...*Twilight*	A&M 497676
				CARMEN, Eric	
3/6/76	2[3]	19	●	1 All By Myself .... Eric Carmen...*Everything*	Arista 0165
2/13/88	4	25		2 Hungry Eyes .... John DeNicola/Franke Previte...*Where Are You Tonight* (Tom Johnston)	RCA 5315
8/13/88	3[1]	20		3 Make Me Lose Control .... Eric Carmen/Dean Pitchford...*That's Rock 'N Roll*	Arista 9686
				CARMICHAEL, Hoagy	
10/13/45	6	3		1 Hong Kong Blues .... Hoagy Carmichael...*How Little We Know*	ARA 123
1/11/47	2[4]	19		2 Ole Buttermilk Sky .... Jack Brooks/Hoagy Carmichael...*Ginger And Spice*	ARA 155
2/8/47	❶[2]	15		3 Huggin' And Chalkin' .... Kermit Goell/Clancy Hayes...*I May Be Wrong, But, I Think You're Wonderful* [N]	Decca 23675
				CARNES, Kim	
5/24/80	4	19		1 Don't Fall In Love With A Dreamer .... Kim Carnes/Dave Ellingson...*Goin' Home To The Rock/Gideon Tanner* (Rogers)	United Artists 1345
				KENNY ROGERS with Kim Carnes	
8/16/80	10	19		2 More Love .... Smokey Robinson...*Changin'*	EMI America 8045
5/16/81	❶[9]	26	●	3 Bette Davis Eyes .... Jackie DeShannon/Donna Weiss...*Miss You Tonite*	EMI America 8077
				CARPENTERS	
7/25/70	❶[4]	17	●	1 (They Long To Be) Close To You .... Burt Bacharach/Hal David...*I Kept On Loving You*	A&M 1183
10/31/70	2[4]	17	●	2 We've Only Just Begun .... Roger Nichols/Paul Williams...*All Of My Life*	A&M 1217
3/13/71	3[2]	13	●	3 For All We Know .... James Griffin/Fred Karlin/Robb Wilson...*Don't Be Afraid*	A&M 1243
6/19/71	2[2]	12	●	4 Rainy Days And Mondays .... Roger Nichols/Paul Williams...*Saturday*	A&M 1260
10/16/71	2[2]	13	●	5 Superstar .... Bonnie Bramlett/Leon Russell...*Bless The Beasts And Children*	A&M 1289
2/26/72	2[2]	12	●	6 Hurting Each Other .... Gary Geld/Peter Udell...*Maybe It's You*	A&M 1322
8/26/72	7	10	●	7 Goodbye To Love .... John Bettis/Richard Carpenter...*Crystal Lullaby*	A&M 1367
4/21/73	3[2]	14	●	8 Sing .... Joe Raposo...*Druscilla Penny*	A&M 1413
7/28/73	2[1]	14	●	9 Yesterday Once More .... John Bettis/Richard Carpenter...*Road Ode*	A&M 1446
12/1/73	❶[2]	20	●	10 Top Of The World .... John Bettis/Richard Carpenter...*Heather*	A&M 1468
1/25/75	❶[1]	17	●	11 Please Mr. Postman .... Robert Bateman/Georgia Dobbins/William Garrett/Brian Holland...*This Masquerade*	A&M 1646
5/24/75	4	13		12 Only Yesterday .... John Bettis/Richard Carpenter...*Happy*	A&M 1677
				CARR, Cathy	
6/16/56	2[1]	24		1 Ivory Tower .... Jack Fulton/Lois Steele...*Please, Please Believe Me*	Fraternity 734
				CARR, Joe "Fingers"	
8/26/50	7	13		1 Sam's Song .... Jack Elliott/Lew Quadling...*Ivory Rag*	Capitol 962
				JOE "FINGERS" CARR And The Carr-Hops	
				CARR, Vikki	
11/4/67	3[2]	15		1 It Must Be Him .... Gilbert Becaud/Mack David...*That's All*	Liberty 55986
				CARRACK, Paul	
2/13/88	9	24		1 Don't Shed A Tear .... Rob Friedman/Eddie Schwartz...*Merilee*	Chrysalis 43164
				CARROLL, David, And His Orchestra	
3/5/55	8	17		1 Melody Of Love .... Hans Engelmann/Tom Glazer...*La Golondrina* [I]	Mercury 70516

PEAK DATE	PEAK POS	WKS CHR	GOLD	ARTIST / Song Title	Songwriter...B-side	Label & Number
				CARROLL, Helen		
11/23/46	7	6		1 Ole Buttermilk Sky	Jack Brooks/Hoagy Carmichael...*Let's Sail To Dreamland*	RCA Victor 1982
				HELEN CARROLL and THE SATISFIERS		
				CARS, The		
2/27/82	4	22		1 Shake It Up	Ric Ocasek...*Cruiser*	Elektra 47250
4/28/84	7	17		2 You Might Think	Ric Ocasek...*Heartbeat City*	Elektra 69744
9/29/84	3³	19		3 Drive	Ric Ocasek...*Stranger Eyes*	Elektra 69706
1/11/86	7	17		4 Tonight She Comes	Ric Ocasek...*Just What I Needed*	Elektra 69589
				CARSON, Mindy		
5/6/50	6	11		1 My Foolish Heart	Ned Washington/Victor Young...*Candy And Cake*	RCA Victor 3204
				CARTER, Clarence		
10/5/68	6	16	●	1 Slip Away	William Armstrong/Marcus Daniel/Wilbur Terrell...*Funky Fever*	Atlantic 2508
9/19/70	4	14	●	2 Patches	Ronald Dunbar/General Johnson...*Say It One More Time*	Atlantic 2748
				CARTER, Mel		
8/28/65	8	15		1 Hold Me, Thrill Me, Kiss Me	Harry Noble...*A Sweet Little Girl*	Imperial 66113
				CASCADA		
3/11/06	10	31	△	1 Everytime We Touch	Stuart Mackillop/Maggie Reilly/Peter Risavy	Robbins 72130
				CASCADES, The		
3/9/63	3¹	16		1 Rhythm Of The Rain	John Gummoe...*Let Me Be*	Valiant 6026
				CASE		
2/20/99	10	20		1 Faded Pictures	Joe L. Thomas/Josh Thompson	Def Jam 566494
				CASE & JOE		
4/28/01	4	22		2 Missing You	Tim Kelley/Bob Robinson/Joe L. Thomas/Joshua Thompson...*Not Your Friend*	Def Soul 572839
12/8/01	6	25		3 Livin' It Up	Jeffrey Atkins/Irv Gotti/Robert Mays/Stevie Wonder...*The Inc.* (w/Caddillac Tah & Black Child)	Murder Inc. 588741
				JA RULE (feat. Case)		
				CASH, Johnny		
8/23/69	2³	12	●	1 A Boy Named Sue	Shel Silverstein...*San Quentin* [L-N]	Columbia 44944
				CASINOS, The		
3/11/67	6	13		1 Then You Can Tell Me Goodbye	John D. Loudermilk...*I Still Love You*	Fraternity 977
				CASSIDY		
3/27/04	4	24		1 Hotel	Kasseem Dean/Bernard Edwards/R. Kelly/Barry Reese/Nile Rodgers	J Records 56053
				CASSIDY feat. R. Kelly		
				CASSIDY, David		
12/25/71	9	12	●	1 Cherish	Terry Kirkman...*All I Wanna Do Is Touch You*	Bell 45,150
				CASSIDY, Shaun		
7/16/77	❶¹	22	●	1 Da Doo Ron Ron	Jeff Barry/Ellie Greenwich/Phil Spector...*Holiday*	Warner/Curb 8365
10/22/77	3²	24	●	2 That's Rock 'N' Roll	Eric Carmen...*I Wanna Be With You*	Warner/Curb 8423
1/14/78	7	16	●	3 Hey Deanie	Eric Carmen...*Strange Sensation*	Warner/Curb 8488
				CASSIE		
7/22/06	3⁴	27	○	1 Me & U	Ryan Leslie	Bad Boy 94376
				CASTOR, Jimmy		
6/24/72	6	12	●	1 Troglodyte (Cave Man)	Jimmy Castor...*I Promise To Remember* [N]	RCA Victor 1029
				CATES, George, And His Orchestra		
6/2/56	4	22		1 Moonglow And Theme From "Picnic"	Eddie DeLange/Will Hudson/Irving Mills...*Rio Batucada* [I]	Coral 61618
				CAVALLARO, Carmen, And His Orchestra		
8/4/45	3¹⁰	19	⊙	1 Chopin's Polonaise	Frederic Chopin...*Enlloro (Voodoo Moon)* [I]	Decca 18677
12/22/45	❶⁶	20	⊙	2 I Can't Begin To Tell You	Mack Gordon/James Monaco...*I Can't Believe That You're In Love With Me*	Decca 23457
11/22/47	8	8		3 You Do	Mack Gordon/Josef Myrow...*How Soon (Will I Be Seeing You)*	Decca 24101
1/24/48	6	14		4 How Soon (Will I Be Seeing You)	Carroll Lucas/Jack Owens...*You Do*	Decca 24101
				BING CROSBY with CARMEN CAVALLARO (above 3)		
4/15/50	5	9		5 (Put Another Nickel In) Music! Music! Music!	Bernie Baum/Stephan Weiss...*O, Katharina*	Decca 24881
				CEE-LO		
12/4/10	9	22↑		1 F**k You!	Brody Brown/Thomas Callaway/Peter Hernandez/Philip Lawrence/Ari Levine...*Georgia*	Elektra 526196
				CEE LO GREEN		
				CETERA, Peter		
8/2/86	❶²	21		1 Glory Of Love	Peter Cetera/David Foster/Diane Nini...*On The Line*	Full Moon 28662
12/6/86	❶¹	21		2 The Next Time I Fall	Bobby Caldwell/Paul Gordon...*Holy Moly* (Cetera)	Full Moon 28597
				PETER CETERA w/ AMY GRANT		
10/1/88	4	18		3 One Good Woman	Peter Cetera/Patrick Leonard...*One More Story*	Full Moon 27824
5/13/89	6	20	●	4 After All	Dean Pitchford/Tom Snow...*Dangerous Times* (Cher)	Geffen 27529
				CHER and PETER CETERA		
5/3/97	8	34	▲	5 Hard To Say I'm Sorry	Peter Cetera/David Foster	LaFace 24223
				AZ YET Featuring Peter Cetera		
				CHACKSFIELD, Frank, And His Orchestra		
6/20/53	5	13		1 Terry's Theme From "Limelight"	Charlie Chaplin/Geoffrey Parsons...*Limelight* [I]	London 1342
11/7/53	2⁴	23	⊙	2 Ebb Tide	Robert Maxwell/Carl Sigman...*Waltzing Bugle Boy* [I]	London 1358
				CHAD & JEREMY		
10/17/64	7	14		1 A Summer Song	Clive Metcalfe/Keith Noble/Chad Stuart...*No Tears For Johnnie*	World Artists 1027
				CHAIRMEN OF THE BOARD		
3/21/70	3¹	15	●	1 Give Me Just A Little More Time	Lamont Dozier/Ronald Dunbar/Brian Holland/Eddie Holland...*Since The Days Of Pigtails (and Fairy Tales)*	Invictus 9074

PEAK DATE	PEAK POS	WKS CHR	GOLD	ARTIST / Song Title	Songwriter...B-side	Label & Number
				CHAKACHAS, The		
3/25/72	8	15	●	1 Jungle Fever	Bill Ador...*Cha Ka Cha* [I]	Polydor 15030
				CHAMBERLAIN, Richard		
8/4/62	10	14		1 Theme From Dr. Kildare (Three Stars Will Shine Tonight)	Jerry Goldsmith/Pete Rugolo/Hal Winn...*A Kiss To Build A Dream On*	MGM 13075
				CHAMILLIONAIRE		
6/3/06	❶²	31	○	1 Ridin'	Anthony Henderson/Juan Salinas/Oscar Salinas/Hakeem Seriki...*Southern Takeover* (w/Killer Mike & Pastor Troy)	Universal 006026
				CHAMILLIONAIRE Featuring Krayzie Bone		
9/2/06	7	20	○	2 Get Up	Phalon Alexander/Ciara Harris/Hakeem Seriki	LaFace 88451
				CIARA Featuring Chamillionaire		
				CHAMPS, The		
3/17/58	❶⁵	19	⊙	1 Tequila	Chuck Rio...*Train To Nowhere* [I]	Challenge 1016
				CHANDLER, Gene		
2/17/62	❶³	15	⊙	1 Duke Of Earl	Gene Chandler/Earl Edwards/Bernice Williams...*Kissin' In The Kitchen*	Vee-Jay 416
				CHANDLER, Karen		
3/7/53	5	18		1 Hold Me, Thrill Me, Kiss Me	Harry Noble...*One Dream (Tells Me)*	Coral 60831
				CHANGING FACES		
9/17/94	3¹	21	▲	1 Stroke You Up	R. Kelly	Big Beat 98279
6/7/97	8	25	▲	2 G.H.E.T.T.O.U.T.	R. Kelly...*Goin' Nowhere*	Big Beat 98026
				CHANNEL, Bruce		
3/10/62	❶³	15	⊙	1 Hey! Baby	Bruce Channel/Margaret Cobb...*Dream Girl*	Smash 1731
				CHANTAY'S		
5/4/63	4	16		1 Pipeline	Brian Carman/Bob Spickard...*Move It* [I]	Dot 16440
				CHAPIN, Harry		
12/21/74	❶¹	19	●	1 Cat's In The Cradle	Harry Chapin/Sandra Chapin...*Vacancy*	Elektra 45203
				CHAPMAN, Tracy		
8/27/88	6	21		1 Fast Car	Tracy Chapman...*For You*	Elektra 69412
6/15/96	3⁵	39	▲	2 Give Me One Reason	Tracy Chapman...*The Rape of the World*	Elektra 64346
				CHARIOTEERS, The		
12/1/45	9	4		1 Don't Forget Tonight Tomorrow	Jay Milton/Ukie Sherin...*Lily Belle*	Columbia 36854
				FRANK SINATRA and THE CHARIOTEERS		
3/8/47	6	3		2 Open The Door, Richard	Dusty Fletcher/Don Howell/John Mason/Jack McVea...*You Can't See The Sun When You're Cryin'* [N]	Columbia 37240
4/10/48	6	5		3 Now Is The Hour (Maori Farewell Song)	Maewa Kaihan/Clement Scott/Dorothy Stewart...*Peculiar* (Clark)	Columbia 38115
				BUDDY CLARK and THE CHARIOTEERS		
				CHARLENE		
5/22/82	3³	20		1 I've Never Been To Me	Ken Hirsch/Ron Miller...*Somewhere In My Life*	Motown 1611
				CHARLES, Jimmy		
9/26/60	5	15		1 A Million To One	Phil Medley...*Hop Scotch Hop*	Promo 1002
				CHARLES, Ray		
8/17/59	6	15	⊙	1 What'd I Say (Part I & II)	Ray Charles	Atlantic 2031
11/14/60	❶¹	13	⊙	2 Georgia On My Mind	Hoagy Carmichael/Stuart Gorrell...*Carry Me Back To Old Virginny*	ABC-Paramount 10135
5/1/61	8	13		3 One Mint Julep	Rudy Toombs...*Let's Go* [I]	Impulse! 200
10/9/61	❶²	13		4 Hit The Road Jack	Percy Mayfield...*The Danger Zone*	ABC-Paramount 10244
1/13/62	9	12		5 Unchain My Heart	Teddy Powell/Bobby Sharp...*But On The Other Hand Baby*	ABC-Paramount 10266
6/2/62	❶⁵	18	●	6 I Can't Stop Loving You	Don Gibson...*Born To Lose*	ABC-Paramount 10330
9/8/62	2¹	11		7 You Don't Know Me	Eddy Arnold/Cindy Walker...*Careless Love*	ABC-Paramount 10345
12/29/62	7	12		8 You Are My Sunshine	Jimmie Davis/Charles Mitchell...*Your Cheating Heart*	ABC-Paramount 10375
5/25/63	8	11		9 Take These Chains From My Heart	Hy Heath/Fred Rose...*No Letter Today*	ABC-Paramount 10435
10/19/63	4	12		10 Busted	Harlan Howard...*Making Believe*	ABC-Paramount 10481
2/19/66	6	15		11 Crying Time	Buck Owens...*When My Dreamboat Comes Home*	ABC-Paramount 10739
				CHARLES, Ray, Singers		
6/13/64	3¹	15		1 Love Me With All Your Heart	Carlos Rigual/Michael Vaughn...*Sweet Little Mountain Bird*	Command 4046
				CHEAP TRICK		
7/21/79	7	19	●	1 I Want You To Want Me	Rick Nielsen...*Clock Strikes Ten* [L]	Epic 50680
7/9/88	❶²	27		2 The Flame	Dick Graham/Robert Mitchell...*Through The Night*	Epic 07745
10/8/88	4	17		3 Don't Be Cruel	Otis Blackwell/Elvis Presley...*I Know What I Want (live)*	Epic 07965
				CHECKER, Chubby		
9/19/60	❶¹	18	⊙	1 The Twist	Hank Ballard...*Toot*	Parkway 811
2/27/61	❶³	16		2 Pony Time	John Berry/Don Covay...*Oh, Susannah*	Parkway 818
8/7/61	8	23		3 Let's Twist Again	Dave Appell/Kal Mann...*Everything's Gonna' Be All Right*	Parkway 824
11/13/61	7	13		4 The Fly	John Madara/David White...*That's The Way It Goes*	Parkway 830
1/13/62	❶²	21	⊙	5 The Twist	Hank Ballard...*Twistin' U.S.A.*	Parkway 811
4/14/62	3¹	14		6 Slow Twistin'	Kal Mann...*La Paloma Twist* (Checker)	Parkway 835
				CHUBBY CHECKER (with Dee Dee Sharp)		
11/10/62	10	13		7 Popeye The Hitchhiker	Dave Appell/Kal Mann...*Limbo Rock*	Parkway 849
12/22/62	2²	23	⊙	8 Limbo Rock	Dave Appell/Kal Mann...*Popeye (The Hitchhiker)*	Parkway 849
				CHEECH & CHONG		
10/12/74	9	13		1 Earache My Eye (Featuring Alice Bowie)	Tommy Chong/Gaye Delorme/Cheech Marin...*Turn That Thing Down (Featuring Alice Bowie)* [N]	Ode 66102
				CHEERS, The		
10/29/55	6	11		1 Black Denim Trousers	Jerry Leiber/Mike Stoller...*Some Night In Alaska*	Capitol 3219

PEAK DATE	PEAK POS	WKS CHR	GOLD	ARTIST / Song Title	Songwriter...B-side	Label & Number
				CHER		
4/23/66	2¹	11		1 Bang Bang (My Baby Shot Me Down)	Sonny Bono...*Needles And Pins*	Imperial 66160
12/23/67	9	13		2 You Better Sit Down Kids	Sonny Bono...*Mama (When My Dollies Have Babies)*	Imperial 66261
11/6/71	❶²	16	●	3 Gypsys, Tramps & Thieves	Bob Stone...*He'll Never Know*	Kapp 2146
3/25/72	7	13		4 The Way Of Love	Jack Dieval/Al Stillman...*Don't Put It On Me*	Kapp 2158
10/6/73	❶²	20	●	5 Half-Breed	Al Capps/Mary Dean...*Melody*	MCA 40102
3/23/74	❶¹	16	●	6 Dark Lady	John Durrill...*Two People Clinging To A Thread*	MCA 40161
5/12/79	8	19	●	7 Take Me Home	Michele Aller/Bob Esty...*My Song (Too Far Gone)*	Casablanca 965
3/5/88	10	26		8 I Found Someone	Michael Bolton/Mark Mangold...*Dangerous Times*	Geffen 28191
5/13/89	6	20	●	9 After All	Dean Pitchford/Tom Snow...*Dangerous Times* (Cher)	Geffen 27529
				CHER and PETER CETERA		
9/23/89	3²	23	●	10 If I Could Turn Back Time	Diane Warren...*Some Guys*	Geffen 22886
12/23/89	8	18		11 Just Like Jesse James	Desmond Child/Diane Warren...*Starting Over*	Geffen 22844
3/13/99	❶⁴	31	▲	12 Believe	Paul Barry/Brian Higgins/Stuart McLennen/Steve Torch	Warner 17119
				CHERRY, Don		
9/30/50	7	15		1 Mona Lisa	Ray Evans/Jay Livingston...*The 3rd Man Theme*	Decca 27048
				VICTOR YOUNG And His Orchestra And Chorus And DON CHERRY		
12/9/50	4	21		2 Thinking Of You	Bert Kalmar/Harry Ruby...*Here In My Arms*	Decca 27128
1/7/56	4	22		3 Band Of Gold	Bob Musel/Jack Taylor...*Rumble Boogie*	Columbia 40597
				CHERRY, Eagle-Eye		
1/23/99	5	28		1 Save Tonight	Eagle-Eye Cherry	Work
				CHERRY, Neneh		
6/24/89	3¹	24	●	1 Buffalo Stance	Neneh Cherry/Cameron McVey/Jamie Morgan/Phil Ramocon	Virgin 99231
9/30/89	8	14		2 Kisses On The Wind	Neneh Cherry/Cameron McVey...*Buffalo Blues*	Virgin 99183
				CHESTER, Bob, and his Orchestra		
10/12/40	6	6		1 Practice Makes Perfect	Ernest Gold/Don Roberts...*Don't Let It Get You Down*	Bluebird 10838
				CHIC		
2/25/78	6	28	●	1 Dance, Dance, Dance (Yowsah, Yowsah, Yowsah)	Bernard Edwards/Kenny Lehman/Nile Rodgers...*Sao Paulo*	Atlantic 3435
12/9/78	❶⁶	25	▲	2 Le Freak	Bernard Edwards/Nile Rodgers...*Savoir Faire*	Atlantic 3519
5/5/79	7	19	●	3 I Want Your Love	Bernard Edwards/Nile Rodgers...*(Funny) Bone*	Atlantic 3557
8/18/79	❶¹	19	●	4 Good Times	Bernard Edwards/Nile Rodgers...*A Warm Summer Night*	Atlantic 3584
				CHICAGO		
6/6/70	9	14		1 Make Me Smile	James Pankow...*Colour My World*	Columbia 45127
9/12/70	4	12		2 25 Or 6 To 4	Robert Lamm/James Pankow...*Where Do We Go From Here*	Columbia 45194
1/2/71	7	13		3 Does Anybody Really Know What Time It Is?	Robert Lamm...*Listen*	Columbia 45264
8/14/71	7	13		4 Beginnings	Robert Lamm...*Colour My World*	Columbia 45417
9/23/72	3²	12	●	5 Saturday In The Park	Robert Lamm...*Alma Mater*	Columbia 45657
8/18/73	10	16		6 Feelin' Stronger Every Day	Peter Cetera/James Pankow...*Jenny*	Columbia 45880
12/8/73	4	19	●	7 Just You 'N' Me	James Pankow...*Critic's Choice*	Columbia 45933
5/11/74	9	15		8 (I've Been) Searchin' So Long	James Pankow...*Byblos*	Columbia 46020
8/10/74	6	15		9 Call On Me	Lee Loughnane...*Prelude To Aire*	Columbia 46062
6/7/75	5	11		10 Old Days	James Pankow...*Hideaway*	Columbia 10131
10/23/76	❶²	21	▲	11 If You Leave Me Now	Peter Cetera...*Together Again*	Columbia 10390
12/3/77	4	17		12 Baby, What A Big Surprise	Peter Cetera...*Takin' It On Uptown*	Columbia 10620
9/11/82	❶²	24	●	13 Hard To Say I'm Sorry	Peter Cetera/David Foster...*Sonny Think Twice*	Full Moon 29979
10/20/84	3²	25		14 Hard Habit To Break	Steve Kipner/John Parker...*Remember The Feeling*	Warner 29214
1/19/85	3²	22		15 You're The Inspiration	Peter Cetera/David Foster...*Once In A Lifetime*	Warner 29126
2/21/87	3¹	23		16 Will You Still Love Me?	Richard Baskin/David Foster/Tom Keane...*25 Or 6 To 4*	Warner 28512
8/27/88	3¹	21		17 I Don't Wanna Live Without Your Love	Albert Hammond/Diane Warren...*I Stand Up*	Reprise 27855
12/10/88	❶²	24	●	18 Look Away	Diane Warren...*Come In From The Night*	Reprise 27766
3/25/89	10	17		19 You're Not Alone	Jim Scott...*It's Alright*	Reprise 27757
2/24/90	5	18		20 What Kind Of Man Would I Be?	Bobby Caldwell/Charles Sandford/Jason Scheff...*25 Or 6 To 4*	Reprise 22741
				CHIFFONS, The		
3/30/63	❶⁴	15	⊙	1 He's So Fine	Ronnie Mack...*Oh My Lover*	Laurie 3152
7/13/63	5	10		2 One Fine Day	Gerry Goffin/Carole King...*Why Am I So Shy*	Laurie 3179
6/25/66	10	10		3 Sweet Talkin' Guy	Elliot Greenberg/Doug Morris...*Did You Ever Go Steady*	Laurie 3340
				CHILD, Jane		
4/14/90	2³	21	●	1 Don't Wanna Fall In Love	Jane Child...*World Lullabye*	Warner 19933
				CHI-LITES, The		
12/11/71	3²	14		1 Have You Seen Her	Barbara Acklin/Eugene Record...*Yes I'm Ready (If I Don't Get To Go)*	Brunswick 55462
5/27/72	❶¹	15		2 Oh Girl	Eugene Record...*Being In Love*	Brunswick 55471
				CHINGY		
8/9/03	2⁵	33		1 Right Thurr	Howard Bailey/Shamar Daugherty/Alonzo Lee...*Mobb Wit Me*	Capitol 77995
11/8/03	3³	21	○	2 Holidae In	Howard Bailey/Christopher Bridges/Shamar Daugherty/Alonzo Lee...*Represent*	Capitol 52816
				CHINGY featuring Ludacris & Snoop Dogg		
3/13/04	2⁵	20	○	3 One Call Away	Howard Bailey/Shamar Daugherty/Alonzo Lee/Sedrick Martin...*Bagg Up*	Capitol 48595
				CHINGY featuring J. Weav		
10/7/06	9	20		4 Pullin' Me Back	Howard Bailey/Jermaine Dupri/Brian Morgan/Jaco Pastorius/Jim Phillips	Slot-A-Lot 69129
				CHINGY Featuring Tyrese		
				CHIPMUNKS, The		
12/22/58	❶⁴	13	⊙	1 The Chipmunk Song	David Seville...*Almost Good* (Seville) [X-N]	Liberty 55168
3/16/59	3²	12	⊙	2 Alvin's Harmonica	David Seville...*Mediocre* (Seville) [N]	Liberty 55179
				CHORDETTES, The		
11/27/54	❶⁷	20	⊙	1 Mr. Sandman	Pat Ballard...*I Don't Wanna See You Cryin'*	Cadence 1247
7/14/56	5	20		2 Born To Be With You	Don Robertson...*Love Never Changes*	Cadence 1291

PEAK DATE	PEAK POS	WKS CHR	GOLD	ARTIST / Song Title	Songwriter...B-side	Label & Number
				CHORDETTES, The (cont'd)		
9/30/57	8	15		3 Just Between You And Me	Jack Keller/Cathy Lynn...*Soft Sands*	Cadence 1330
3/31/58	2^2	15		4 Lollipop	Julius Dixon/Beverly Ross...*Baby Come-A Back-A*	Cadence 1345
				CHORDS, The		
7/31/54	5	16		1 Sh-Boom	James Edwards/Carl Feaster/Claude Feaster/James Keyes/Floyd McRae...*Cross Over The Bridge*	Cat 45-104
				CHRISTIE, Lou		
6/1/63	6	15		1 Two Faces Have I	Lou Christie/Twyla Herbert...*All That Glitters Isn't Gold*	Roulette 4481
2/19/66	❶^1	15	●	2 Lightnin' Strikes	Lou Christie/Twyla Herbert...*Cryin' In The Streets*	MGM 13412
10/25/69	10	12		3 I'm Gonna Make You Mine	Tony Romeo...*I'm Gonna Get Married*	Buddah 116
				CHUMBAWAMBA		
11/29/97	6	31		1 Tubthumping	Judith Abbott/Duncan Bruce/Paul Greco/Darren Hamer/Anne Holden/Nigel Hunter/Louise Watts/Allan Whalley ...*Farewell To The Crown / Football Song*	Republic 56146
				CHURCHILL, Savannah, And The Four Tunes		
11/17/51	5	17		1 (It's No) Sin	George Hoven/Chester Shull...*I Don't Believe In Tomorrow*	RCA Victor 4280
				CIARA		
9/11/04	❶^7	38	○	1 Goodies	Sean Garrett/Ciara Harris/La Marquis Jefferson/Craig Love/Jonathan Smith	LaFace 57550
				CIARA featuring Petey Pablo		
1/8/05	2^7	39	△	2 1,2 Step	Phalon Alexander/Missy Elliott/Ciara Harris	LaFace 66687
				CIARA featuring Missy Elliott		
5/21/05	2^1	23	○	3 Oh	Christopher Bridges/Vidal Davis/Andre Harris/Ciara Harris	LaFace 68177
				CIARA featuring Ludacris		
9/17/05	3^1	28	○	4 Lose Control	Juan Atkins/Richard Davis/Missy Elliott/Isaac Freeman/Ciara Harris/Curtis Hudson...*On & On*	Atlantic 93787
				MISSY ELLIOTT Featuring Ciara & Fat Man Scoop		
10/1/05	3^2	21	○	5 Like You (feat. Ciara)	Jaron Alson/Johnta Austin/Ricky Bell/Jermaine Dupri/Ralph Tresvant	Columbia 80449
				BOW WOW (feat. Ciara)		
7/15/06	10	21		6 So What	Phalon Alexander/Darion Crawford/Ciara Harris/Shawn Johnson/Zach Wallace/Cedric Williams	DTP 006546
				FIELD MOB featuring Ciara		
9/2/06	7	20	○	7 Get Up	Phalon Alexander/Ciara Harris/Hakeem Seriki	LaFace 88451
				CIARA Featuring Chamillionaire		
4/11/09	10	12		8 Love Sex Magic	Michael Elizondo/James Fauntleroy/Robin Tadross/Justin Timberlake	LaFace
				CIARA Featuring Justin Timberlake		
				CITY HIGH		
5/26/01	8	28		1 What Would You Do?	Robby Pardlo/Ryan Toby	Booga Base. 497489
				CLANTON, Jimmy		
8/25/58	4	18	◉	1 Just A Dream	Jimmy Clanton/Cosimo Matassa...*You Aim To Please*	Ace 546
2/1/60	5	16		2 Go, Jimmy, Go	Doc Pomus/Mort Shuman...*I Trusted You*	Ace 575
10/6/62	7	13		3 Venus In Blue Jeans	Howard Greenfield/Jack Keller...*Highway Bound*	Ace 8001
				CLAPTON, Eric		
8/5/72	10	15		1 Layla	...*I Am Yours*	Atco 6809
				DEREK AND THE DOMINOS		
9/14/74	❶^1	14	●	2 I Shot The Sheriff	Bob Marley...*Give Me Strength*	RSO 409
4/1/78	3^3	23	●	3 Lay Down Sally	Eric Clapton/Marcy Levy/George Terry...*Next Time You See Her*	RSO 886
1/20/79	9	18		4 Promises	Richard Feldman/Roger Linn...*Watch Out For Lucy*	RSO 910
5/2/81	10	17		5 I Can't Stand It	Eric Clapton...*Black Rose*	RSO 1060
3/28/92	2^4	26	▲	6 Tears In Heaven	Eric Clapton/Will Jennings...*Tracks And Lines*	Duck/Reprise 19038
8/17/96	5	43	●	7 Change The World	Gordon Kennedy/Wayne Kirkpatrick/Tommy Sims...*Danny Boy*	Reprise 17621
				CLARK, Buddy		
3/15/47	6	8		1 How Are Things In Gloca Mora	E.Y. Harburg/Burton Lane...*If This Isn't Love*	Columbia 37223
5/10/47	❶^2	23	◉	2 Linda	Jack Lawrence...*Love Is A Random Thing*	Columbia 37215
				RAY NOBLE and his ORCHESTRA with BUDDY CLARK		
7/5/47	❶^6	15	◉	3 Peg O' My Heart	Alfred Bryan/Fred Fisher...*Come To Me, Bend To Me*	Columbia 37392
1/17/48	3^1	15		4 I'll Dance At Your Wedding	Herb Magidson/Ben Oakland...*Those Things Money Can't Buy*	Columbia 37967
				RAY NOBLE and his ORCHESTRA with BUDDY CLARK		
1/17/48	5	7		5 Ballerina	Bob Russell/Carl Sigman...*It Had To Be You*	Columbia 38040
4/10/48	6	5		6 Now Is The Hour (Maori Farewell Song)	Maewa Kaihan/Clement Scott/Dorothy Stewart...*Peculiar* (Clark)	Columbia 38115
				BUDDY CLARK and THE CHARIOTEERS		
8/14/48	❶^5	24	◉	7 Love Somebody	Alex Kramer/Joan Whitney...*Confess*	Columbia 38174
12/18/48	7	13		8 My Darling My Darling	Frank Loesser...*That Certain Party*	Columbia 38353
				DORIS DAY and BUDDY CLARK (above 2)		
7/30/49	3^1	19		9 Baby, It's Cold Outside	Frank Loesser...*My One And Only Highland Fling*	Columbia 38463
				DINAH SHORE and BUDDY CLARK		
10/8/49	4	16		10 You're Breaking My Heart	Pat Genaro/Sunny Skylar...*Song Of Surrender*	Columbia 38546
				CLARK, Claudine		
9/1/62	5	15		1 Party Lights	Claudine Clark...*Disappointed*	Chancellor 1113
				CLARK, Dave, Five		
4/25/64	6	14	◉	1 Glad All Over	Dave Clark/Mike Smith...*I Know You*	Epic 9656
5/2/64	4	11		2 Bits And Pieces	Dave Clark/Mike Smith...*All Of The Time*	Epic 9671
7/18/64	4	11		3 Can't You See That She's Mine	Dave Clark/Mike Smith...*No Time To Lose*	Epic 9692
9/12/64	3^1	10		4 Because	Dave Clark...*Theme Without A Name*	Epic 9704
8/7/65	7	11		5 I Like It Like That	Chris Kenner/Allen Toussaint...*Hurting Inside*	Epic 9811
9/25/65	4	11		6 Catch Us If You Can	Dave Clark/Lenny Davidson...*On The Move*	Epic 9833
12/25/65	❶^1	12	◉	7 Over And Over	Bobby Day...*I'll Be Yours (My Love)*	Epic 9863
5/13/67	7	10		8 You Got What It Takes	Tyran Carlo/Berry Gordy/Gwen Gordy...*Doctor Rhythm*	Epic 10144
				CLARK, Dee		
6/26/61	2^1	16	◉	1 Raindrops	Dee Clark...*I Want To Love You*	Vee-Jay 383
				CLARK, Petula		
1/23/65	❶^2	15	●	1 Downtown	Tony Hatch...*You'd Better Love Me*	Warner 5494
5/1/65	3^1	12		2 I Know A Place	Tony Hatch...*Jack And John*	Warner 5612
2/5/66	❶^2	13	◉	3 My Love	Tony Hatch...*Where Am I Going*	Warner 5684

PEAK DATE	PEAK POS	WKS CHR	GOLD	ARTIST / Song Title	Songwriter...B-side	Label & Number
				CLARK, Petula (cont'd)		
8/20/66	9	9		4 I Couldn't Live Without Your Love	Tony Hatch/Jackie Trent...*Your Way Of Life*	Warner 5835
4/15/67	3¹	12		5 This Is My Song	Charlie Chaplin...*High*	Warner 7002
7/8/67	5	10		6 Don't Sleep In The Subway	Tony Hatch/Jackie Trent...*Here Comes The Morning*	Warner 7049
				CLARK, Sanford		
9/22/56	7	21		1 The Fool	Naomi Ford...*Lonesome For A Letter*	Dot 15481
				CLARKSON, Kelly		
10/5/02	❶²	20	●	1 A Moment Like This	Jorgen Elofsson/John Reid...*Before Your Love*	RCA 60622
7/19/03	9	20	○	2 Miss Independent	Christina Aguilera/Kelly Clarkson/Rhett Lawrence...*Low*	RCA 56533
11/20/04	6	46	●	3 Breakaway	Bridget Benenate/Matthew Gerrard/Avril Lavigne...*Since U Been Gone*	RCA 66958
4/9/05	2¹	46	△	4 Since U Been Gone	Lukasz Gottwald/Max Martin...*Breakaway*	RCA 66958
6/11/05	6	34	△	5 Behind These Hazel Eyes	Kelly Clarkson/Lukasz Gottwald/Max Martin...*Beautiful Disaster (live)*	RCA 69520
11/19/05	7	37	△	6 Because Of You	Kelly Clarkson/David Hodges/Ben Moody...*Behind These Hazel Eyes*	RCA 76273
5/12/07	8	16	○	7 Never Again	Kelly Clarkson/Jimmy Messer	RCA
2/7/09	❶²	24		8 My Life Would Suck Without You	Lukasz Gottwald/Claude Kelly/Max Martin	RCA
				CLASH, The		
1/22/83	8	24		1 Rock The Casbah	Nicky Headon/Mick Jones/Paul Simonon/Joe Strummer...*Long Time Jerk*	Epic 03245
				CLASSICS IV		
2/10/68	3³	15		1 Spooky	Buddy Buie/J.R. Cobb/Harry Middlebrooks/Mike Sharpiro...*Poor People*	Imperial 66259
12/28/68	5	15	●	2 Stormy	Buddy Buie/J.R. Cobb...*24 Hours Of Loneliness*	Imperial 66328
3/29/69	2¹	12		3 Traces	Buddy Buie/J.R. Cobb/Emory Gordy...*Mary, Mary Row Your Boat*	Imperial 66352
				CLAY, Tom		
8/14/71	8	9		1 What The World Needs Now Is Love/Abraham, Martin and John	Burt Bacharach/Hal David/Dick Holler...*The Victors* [S]	Mowest 5002
				CLAYTON, Adam, & Larry Mullen		
6/22/96	7	20	●	1 Theme From Mission: Impossible	Lalo Schifrin [I]	Mother/Island 576670
				CLIFFORD, Buzz		
3/13/61	6	14		1 Baby Sittin' Boogie	Johnny Parker...*Driftwood* [N]	Columbia 41876
				CLIMAX		
2/26/72	3²	15	●	1 Precious And Few	Walter Nims...*Park Preserve*	Carousel 30055
				CLIMAX BLUES BAND		
5/21/77	3¹	22		1 Couldn't Get It Right	Colin Cooper/John Cuffley/Peter Haycock/Derek Holt/Fred Jones...*Sav'ry Gravy*	Sire 736
				CLINE, Patsy		
11/27/61	9	11		1 Crazy	Willie Nelson...*Who Can I Count On*	Decca 31317
				CLOONEY, Rosemary		
7/28/51	❶⁸	20	☉	1 Come On-a My House	William Saroyan/David Seville...*Rose Of The Mountain*	Columbia 39467
7/26/52	❶³	27	☉	2 Half As Much	Curley Williams...*Poor Whip - Poor-Will*	Columbia 39710
8/2/52	2³	17		3 Botch-A-Me (Ba-Ba-Baciami Piccina)	Luigi Astore/Riccardo Morbelli/Eddie Stanley...*On The First Warm Day*	Columbia 39767
12/27/52	9	2		4 The Night Before Christmas Song	Johnny Marks...*Look Out The Window (The Winter Song)* [X]	Columbia 39876
				ROSEMARY CLOONEY & GENE AUTRY		
9/25/54	❶⁶	27	☉	5 Hey There	Richard Alder/Jerry Ross...*This Ole House*	Columbia 40266
11/6/54	❶³	27		6 This Ole House	Stuart Hamblen...*Hey There*	Columbia 40266
12/18/54	9	12		7 Mambo Italiano	Bob Merrill...*We'll Be Together Again*	Columbia 40361
5/20/57	10	16		8 Mangos	Dee Libbey/Sid Wayne...*Independent (On My Own)*	Columbia 40835
				CLUB NOUVEAU		
3/21/87	❶²	17	●	1 Lean On Me	Bill Withers...*Pump It Up (reprise)*	King Jay 28430
				COASTERS, The		
6/17/57	8	24		1 Young Blood	Jerry Leiber/Doc Pomus/Mike Stoller...*Searchin'*	Atco 6087
7/29/57	3¹	26	☉	2 Searchin'	Jerry Leiber/Mike Stoller...*Young Blood*	Atco 6087
7/21/58	❶¹	16	☉	3 Yakety Yak	Jerry Leiber/Mike Stoller...*Zing! Went The Strings Of My Heart*	Atco 6116
3/9/59	2³	15	☉	4 Charlie Brown	Jerry Leiber/Mike Stoller...*Three Cool Cats* [N]	Atco 6132
6/22/59	9	12		5 Along Came Jones	Jerry Leiber/Mike Stoller...*That Is Rock & Roll* [N]	Atco 6141
10/12/59	7	16	☉	6 Poison Ivy	Jerry Leiber/Mike Stoller...*I'm A Hog For You*	Atco 6146
				COBRA STARSHIP		
8/22/09	7	25	△	1 Good Girls Go Bad	Kara DioGuardi/Jacob Kasher/Kevin Rudolf/Gabe Saporta	Decaydance
				COBRA STARSHIP Featuring Leighton Meester		
				COCHRAN, Eddie		
9/29/58	8	16		1 Summertime Blues	Jerry Capehart/Eddie Cochran...*Love Again*	Liberty 55144
				COCHRANE, Tom		
8/22/92	6	26	●	1 Life Is A Highway	Tom Cochrane...*Emotional Truth*	Capitol 44815
				COCKER, Joe		
5/30/70	7	12		1 The Letter	Wayne Carson Thompson...*Space Captain* [L]	A&M 1174
				JOE COCKER with Leon Russell & The Shelter People		
3/29/75	5	17		2 You Are So Beautiful	Bruce Fisher/Billy Preston...*It's A Sin When You Love Somebody*	A&M 1641
11/6/82	❶³	23	▲	3 Up Where We Belong	Will Jennings/Jack Nitzsche/Buffy Sainte-Marie...*Sweet Li'l Woman* (Cocker)	Island 99996
				JOE COCKER and JENNIFER WARNES		
				COFFEY, Dennis, And The Detroit Guitar Band		
1/8/72	6	17	●	1 Scorpio	Dennis Coffey...*Sad Angel* [I]	Sussex 226
				COLDPLAY		
5/7/05	8	20	○	1 Speed Of Sound	Guy Berryman/Jon Buckland/Will Champion/Chris Martin	Capitol
6/28/08	❶¹	51	△³	2 Viva La Vida	Guy Berryman/Jon Buckland/Will Champion/Chris Martin	Capitol

PEAK DATE	PEAK POS	WKS CHR	GOLD	ARTIST / Song Title	Songwriter...B-side	Label & Number
				COLE, Cozy		
10/20/58	3³	21		1 Topsy II	Edgar Battle/Eddie Durham...*Topsy I* [I]	Love 5004
				COLE, Keyshia		
9/9/06	3¹	22		1 (When You Gonna) Give It Up To Me	Donovan Bennett/Jason Henriques/Sean Paul/Nigel Staff...*Never Gonna Be The Same*	VP/Atlantic 94413
				SEAN PAUL Featuring Keyshia Cole		
4/14/07	10	22		2 Last Night	Sean Combs/Jack Knight/Shannon Lawrence/Mario Winans	Bad Boy 89995
				DIDDY Featuring Keyshia Cole		
9/29/07	7	23		3 Let It Go	Keyshia Cole/Missy Elliott/Kim Jones/James Mtume	Imani 009976
				KEYSHIA COLE Featuring Missy Elliott & Lil' Kim		
				COLE, Nat "King"		
7/1/44	9	5		1 Straighten Up And Fly Right	Nat "King" Cole/Irving Mills...*I Can't See For Lookin'*	Capitol 154
9/7/46	10	1		2 You Call It Madness (But I Call It Love)	Russ Columbo/Con Conrad/Gladys DuBois...*Oh, But I Do*	Capitol 274
12/28/46	❶⁶	25		3 (I Love You) For Sentimental Reasons	William Best/Deek Watson...*The Best Man*	Capitol 304
12/28/46	3¹	7		4 The Christmas Song (Merry Christmas To You)	Mel Torme/Robert Wells...*In The Cool Of Evening* [X]	Capitol 311
				THE KING COLE TRIO (all of above)		
5/8/48	❶⁸	18	⊙	5 Nature Boy	Eden Ahbez...*Lost April*	Capitol 15054
				KING COLE		
7/8/50	❶⁸	27	⊙	6 Mona Lisa	Ray Evans/Jay Livingston...*The Greatest Inventor (Of Them All)*	Capitol 1010
11/4/50	5	14		7 Orange Colored Sky	Milton DeLugg/Willie Stein...*Jam-Bo*	Capitol 1184
				NAT "KING" COLE and STAN KENTON		
1/6/51	9	1		8 Frosty The Snow Man	Steve Nelson/Jack Rollins...*Little Christmas Tree* [X-N]	Capitol 1203
6/23/51	❶⁵	29	⊙	9 Too Young	Sylvia Dee/Sid Lippman...*That's My Girl*	Capitol 1449
7/12/52	8	12		10 Walkin' My Baby Back Home	Fred Ahlert/Roy Turk...*Funny (Not Much)*	Capitol 2130
				NAT KING COLE and BILLY MAY and His Orchestra		
8/30/52	8	25		11 Somewhere Along The Way	Kurt Adams/Sammy Gallop...*What Does It Take*	Capitol 2069
5/9/53	2¹	21		12 Pretend	Lew Douglas/Frank Lavere/Cliff Parman...*Don't Let Your Eyes Go Shopping (For Your Heart)*	Capitol 2346
5/1/54	6	19		13 Answer Me, My Love	Fred Rauch/Carl Sigman/Gerhard Winkler...*Why*	Capitol 2687
10/9/54	10	11		14 Smile	Charlie Chaplin/Geoffrey Parsons/John Turner...*It's Crazy*	Capitol 2897
4/16/55	7	16		15 Darling Je Vous Aime Beaucoup	Anna Sosenko...*The Sand And The Sea*	Capitol 3027
7/9/55	2¹	20	⊙	16 A Blossom Fell	Howard Barnes/Harold Cornelius/Dominic John...*If I May*	Capitol 3095
7/16/55	8	10		17 If I May	Rose Marie McCoy/Charles Singleton...*A Blossom Fell*	Capitol 3095
				NAT "KING" COLE and THE FOUR KNIGHTS		
7/29/57	6	27		18 Send For Me	Ollie Jones...*My Personal Possession*	Capitol 3737
5/26/58	5	19		19 Looking Back	Brook Benton/Belford Hendricks/Clyde Otis...*Do I Like It*	Capitol 3939
9/22/62	2²	16		20 Ramblin' Rose	Joe Sherman/Noel Sherman...*The Good Times*	Capitol 4804
6/29/63	6	12		21 Those Lazy-Hazy-Crazy Days Of Summer	Hans Carste/Charles Tobias...*In The Cool Of The Day*	Capitol 4965
				COLE, Natalie		
11/22/75	6	17		1 This Will Be	Chuck Jackson/Marvin Yancy...*Joey*	Capitol 4109
4/30/77	5	21	●	2 I've Got Love On My Mind	Chuck Jackson/Marvin Yancy...*Unpredictable You*	Capitol 4360
4/15/78	10	21	●	3 Our Love	Chuck Jackson/Marvin Yancy...*La Costa*	Capitol 4509
5/7/88	5	17		4 Pink Cadillac	Bruce Springsteen...*I Wanna Be That Woman*	EMI/Manhattan 50117
7/8/89	7	19		5 Miss You Like Crazy	Preston Glass/Gerry Goffin/Michael Masser...*Good To Be Back*	EMI 50185
				COLE, Paula		
5/10/97	8	21		1 Where Have All The Cowboys Gone?	Paula Cole...*hush, hush, hush.*	Warner 17373
				COLLINS, Judy		
12/21/68	8	11		1 Both Sides Now	Joni Mitchell...*Who Knows Where The Time Goes*	Elektra 45639
				COLLINS, Phil		
2/5/83	10	21		1 You Can't Hurry Love	Lamont Dozier/Brian Holland/Eddie Holland...*Do You Know, Do You Care?*	Atlantic 89933
4/21/84	❶³	24	●	2 Against All Odds (Take A Look At Me Now)	Phil Collins...*The Search* (Larry Carlton & Michel Colombier)	Atlantic 89700
2/2/85	2²	23	●	3 Easy Lover	Philip Bailey/Phil Collins/Nathan East...*Woman* (Bailey)	Columbia 04679
				PHILIP BAILEY (with Phil Collins)		
3/30/85	❶²	18		4 One More Night	Phil Collins...*The Man With The Horn*	Atlantic 89588
7/6/85	❶¹	17	●	5 Sussudio	Phil Collins...*I Like The Way*	Atlantic 89560
9/28/85	4	18		6 Don't Lose My Number	Phil Collins...*We Said Hello Goodbye*	Atlantic 89536
11/30/85	❶¹	21		7 Separate Lives	Stephen Bishop...*I Don't Wanna Know* (Collins)	Atlantic 89498
				PHIL COLLINS and MARILYN MARTIN		
5/10/86	7	16		8 Take Me Home	Phil Collins...*Only You Know And I Know*	Atlantic 89472
10/22/88	❶²	25	●	9 Groovy Kind Of Love	Carole Bayer Sager/Toni Wine...*Big Noise*	Atlantic 89017
1/21/89	❶²	18		10 Two Hearts	Phil Collins/Lamont Dozier...*The Robbery* (Anne Dudley)	Atlantic 88980
12/23/89	❶⁴	18	●	11 Another Day In Paradise	Phil Collins...*Heat On The Street*	Atlantic 88774
3/31/90	3¹	17		12 I Wish It Would Rain Down	Phil Collins...*You've Been In Love (That Little Bit Too Long)*	Atlantic 88738
6/30/90	4	19		13 Do You Remember?	Phil Collins...*I Wish It Would Rain Down*	Atlantic 87955
10/6/90	4	22		14 Something Happened On The Way To Heaven	Phil Collins/Daryl Stuermer...*Lionel (Do You Remember?)*	Atlantic 87885
				COLLINS, Tyler		
8/4/90	6	21		1 Girls Nite Out	Sheri Byers/Darryl Ross	RCA 2630
				COLONNA, Jerry		
7/28/45	7	4		1 Bell Bottom Trousers	Moe Jaffe...*I Cried For You* [N]	Capitol 204
				COLOR ME BADD		
6/8/91	2⁴	23	▲²	1 I Wanna Sex You Up	Elliott Straite	Giant 19382
9/21/91	❶²	20	●	2 I Adore Mi Amor	Bryan Abrams/Mark Calderon/Hamza Lee/Kevin Thornton/Sam Watters	Giant 19204
1/25/92	❶¹	28	●	3 All 4 Love	Bryan Abrams/Mark Calderon/Howard Thompson/Kevin Thornton/Sam Watters...*Color Me Badd*	Giant 19236
				COLTER, Jessi		
6/21/75	4	17		1 I'm Not Lisa	Jessi Colter...*For The First Time*	Capitol 4009
				COLVIN, Shawn		
7/26/97	7	32		1 Sunny Came Home	Shawn Colvin/John Leventhal...*What I Get Paid For*	Columbia 78528
				COMMANDER CODY And His Lost Planet Airmen		
6/3/72	9	14		1 Hot Rod Lincoln	Charlie Ryan/W.S. Stevenson...*My Home In My Hand* [N]	Paramount 0146

28

PEAK DATE	PEAK POS	WKS CHR	GOLD	ARTIST / Song Title	Songwriter...B-side	Label & Number
				COMMODORES		
4/24/76	5	23		1 Sweet Love	Lionel Richie...*Better Never Than Forever*	Motown 1381
11/27/76	7	16		2 Just To Be Close To You	Lionel Richie...*Thumpin' Music*	Motown 1402
8/27/77	4	22		3 Easy	Lionel Richie...*Can't Let You Tease Me*	Motown 1418
11/5/77	5	16	○	4 Brick House	William King/Ronald LaPread/Thomas McClary/Walter Orange/Lionel Richie/Milan Williams...*Captain Quick Draw*	Motown 1425
8/12/78	❶²	20		5 Three Times A Lady	Lionel Richie...*Look What You've Done To Me*	Motown 1443
10/13/79	4	17		6 Sail On	Lionel Richie...*Thumpin' Music*	Motown 1466
11/17/79	❶¹	20		7 Still	Lionel Richie...*Such A Woman*	Motown 1474
9/5/81	8	22		8 Lady (You Bring Me Up)	Howard Hudson/Shirley King/William King...*Gettin' It*	Motown 1514
12/5/81	4	20		9 Oh No	Lionel Richie...*Lovin' You*	Motown 1527
4/20/85	3¹	22		10 Nightshift	Franne Golde/Dennis Lambert/Walter Orange...*I Keep Running*	Motown 1773
				COMMON		
1/4/03	9	27		1 Love Of My Life (An Ode To Hip Hop)	Eryka Badu/Lonnie Lynn/Robert Ozuna/James Poyser/Raphael Saadiq/Glenn Standridge	Fox/MCA 113987
				ERYKAH BADU Featuring Common		
				COMO, Perry		
6/3/44	8	7		1 Long Ago (And Far Away)	Ira Gershwin/Jerome Kern...*I Love You*	Victor 1569
1/27/45	10	2		2 I Dream Of You (More Than You Dream I Do)	Marjorie Goetschius/Edna Osser...*I'm Confessin' (That I Love You)*	Victor 1629
8/11/45	3¹	13		3 If I Loved You	Oscar Hammerstein/Richard Rodgers...*I'm Gonna Love That Gal (Like She's Never Been Loved Before)*	Victor 1676
9/15/45	❶¹⁰	19	⊙	4 Till The End Of Time	Buddy Kaye/Ted Mossman...*(Did You Ever Get) That Feeling In The Moonlight*	Victor 1709
10/6/45	4	17		5 I'm Gonna Love That Gal (Like She's Never Been Loved Before)	Frances Ash...*If I Loved You*	Victor 1676
11/3/45	9	11		6 (Did You Ever Get) That Feeling In The Moonlight	James Cavanaugh/Ira Schuster/Larry Stock...*Till The End Of Time*	Victor 1709
1/5/46	3¹	14		7 Dig You Later (A Hubba-Hubba-Hubba)	Harold Adamson/Jimmy McHugh...*Here Comes Heaven Again* [N]	Victor 1750
2/16/46	5	8		8 I'm Always Chasing Rainbows	Harry Carroll/Joseph McCarthy...*You Won't Be Satisfied (Until You Break My Heart)*	Victor 1788
4/13/46	5	14		9 You Won't Be Satisfied (Until You Break My Heart)	Freddy James/Larry Stock...*I'm Always Chasing Rainbows*	Victor 1788
5/4/46	❶³	21	⊙	10 Prisoner Of Love	Russ Columbo/Clarence Gaskill/Leo Robin...*All Through The Day*	RCA Victor 1814
5/25/46	8	5		11 All Through The Day	Oscar Hammerstein/Jerome Kern...*Prisoner Of Love*	RCA Victor 1814
6/29/46	4	13		12 They Say It's Wonderful	Irving Berlin...*If You Were The Only Girl*	RCA Victor 1857
8/3/46	❶¹	17		13 Surrender	Bennie Benjamin/George Weiss...*More Than You Know*	RCA Victor 1877
12/28/46	10	1		14 Winter Wonderland	Felix Bernard/Richard Smith...*That Christmas Feeling* [X]	RCA Victor 1968
2/1/47	9	7		15 Sonata	Alex Alstone/Ervin Drake/Jimmy Shirl...*That's The Beginning Of The End*	RCA Victor 2033
6/28/47	❶³	13		16 Chi-Baba Chi-Baba (My Bambino Go To Sleep)	Mack David/Al Hoffman/Jerry Livingston...*When You Were Sweet Sixteen*	RCA Victor 2259
8/30/47	2⁵	17		17 I Wonder Who's Kissing Her Now	Frank Adams/Will Hough/Joseph Howard/Harold Orlob...*When Tonight Is Just A Memory*	RCA Victor 2315
10/11/47	2¹	19	⊙	18 When You Were Sweet Sixteen	James Thornton...*Chi-Baba Chi-Baba (My Bambino Go To Sleep)*	RCA Victor 2259
4/17/48	4	18	⊙	19 Because	Guy d'Hardelot/Edward Teschemacher...*If You Had All The World And Its Gold*	RCA Victor 2653
2/26/49	4	17		20 Far Away Places	Alex Kramer/Joan Whitney...*Missouri Waltz*	RCA Victor 3316
5/7/49	❶²	15		21 "A"-You're Adorable	Buddy Kaye/Sid Lippman/Fred Wise...*Where Is Sometime?*	RCA Victor 2899
6/11/49	2¹	25		22 Forever And Ever	Malia Rosa/Franz Winkler...*I Don't See Me In Your Eyes Anymore*	RCA Victor 2892
7/9/49	5	16		23 Bali Ha'i	Oscar Hammerstein/Richard Rodgers...*Some Enchanted Evening*	RCA Victor 2896
7/30/49	❶⁵	26		24 Some Enchanted Evening	Oscar Hammerstein/Richard Rodgers...*Bali Ha'i*	RCA Victor 2896
1/21/50	3¹	19		25 A Dreamer's Holiday	Kim Gannon/Mabel Wayne...*The Meadows Of Heaven*	RCA Victor 3036
6/3/50	❶²	17		26 Hoop-Dee-Doo	Milton DeLugg/Frank Loesser...*On The Outgoing Tide*	RCA Victor 3747
11/18/50	7	12		27 Patricia	Benny Davis...*Watchin' The Trains Go By*	RCA Victor 3905
12/9/50	3³	18		28 A Bushel And A Peck	Frank Loesser...*She's A Lady* [N]	RCA Victor 3930
				PERRY COMO and BETTY HUTTON		
2/10/51	5	17		29 You're Just In Love	Irving Berlin...*It's A Lovely Day Today*	RCA Victor 3945
3/3/51	❶⁸	24	⊙	30 If	Stanley Damerell/Tolchard Evans/Robert Hargreaves...*Zing Zing—Zoom Zoom*	RCA Victor 3997
8/9/52	3¹	18		31 Maybe	Allan Flynn/Frank Madden...*Watermelon Weather*	RCA Victor 4744
				PERRY COMO and EDDIE FISHER		
1/10/53	❶⁵	21	⊙	32 Don't Let The Stars Get In Your Eyes	Slim Willet...*Lies*	RCA Victor 5064
3/28/53	6	12		33 Wild Horses	Johnny Burke/Robert Schumann...*I Confess*	RCA Victor 5152
6/27/53	3²	16		34 Say You're Mine Again	Dave Heisler/Charles Nathan...*My One And Only Heart*	RCA Victor 5277
8/15/53	❶⁴	22		35 No Other Love	Oscar Hammerstein/Richard Rodgers...*Keep It Gay*	RCA Victor 5317
12/12/53	9	13		36 You Alone (Solo Tu)	Robert Allen/Al Stillman...*Pa-Paya Mama*	RCA Victor 5447
4/10/54	❶⁸	22	⊙	37 Wanted	Jack Fulton/Lois Steele...*Look Out The Window (And See How I'm Standing in the Rain)*	RCA Victor 5647
11/6/54	4	18	⊙	38 Papa Loves Mambo	Al Hoffman/Dick Manning/Bickley Reichner...*The Things I Didn't Do*	RCA Victor 5857
1/8/55	8	3		39 (There's No Place Like) Home For The Holidays	Robert Allen/Al Stillman...*Silk Stockings* [X]	RCA Victor 5950
3/5/55	2³	14		40 Ko Ko Mo (I Love You So)	Eunice Levy/Jake Porter/Forest Wilson...*You'll Always Be My Lifetime Sweetheart*	RCA Victor 5994
10/15/55	5	14		41 Tina Marie	Bob Merrill...*Fooled*	RCA Victor 6192
4/7/56	10	17		42 Juke Box Baby	Joe Sherman/Noel Sherman...*Hot Diggity (Dog Ziggity Boom)*	RCA Victor 6427
5/5/56	❶¹	23	⊙	43 Hot Diggity (Dog Ziggity Boom)	Al Hoffman/Dick Manning...*Juke Box Baby*	RCA Victor 6427
7/14/56	8	17		44 Glendora	Ray Stanley...*More*	RCA Victor 6554
7/21/56	4	18		45 More	Alex Alstone/Tom Glazer...*Glendora*	RCA Victor 6554
4/6/57	❶²	29	⊙	46 Round And Round	Joe Shapiro/Lou Stallman...*Mi Casa, Su Casa (My House Is Your House)*	RCA Victor 6815
2/24/58	4	17	⊙	47 Magic Moments	Burt Bacharach/Hal David...*Catch A Falling Star*	RCA Victor 7128
3/24/58	❶¹	23	●	48 Catch A Falling Star	Lee Pockriss/Paul Vance...*Magic Moments*	RCA Victor 7128
5/12/58	6	16		49 Kewpie Doll	Roy Bennett/Sid Tepper...*Dance Only With Me*	RCA Victor 7202
1/23/71	10	17		50 It's Impossible	Armando Manzanero/Sid Wayne...*Long Life, Lots Of Happiness*	RCA Victor 0387
				CONLEY, Arthur		
5/13/67	2¹	15	●	1 Sweet Soul Music	Arthur Conley/Sam Cooke/Otis Redding...*Let's Go Steady*	Atco 6463
				CONNIFF, Ray		
8/13/66	9	12		1 Somewhere, My Love	Maurice Jarre/Paul Francis Webster...*Midsummer In Sweden*	Columbia 43626
				CONTI, Bill		
7/2/77	❶¹	20	●	1 Gonna Fly Now	Carol Connors/Bill Conti/Ayn Robbins...*Reflections* [I]	United Artists 940
				CONTOURS, The		
10/20/62	3³	18	⊙	1 Do You Love Me	Berry Gordy...*Move, Mr. Man*	Gordy 7005
				COOK, David		
6/7/08	3¹	20	△	1 The Time Of My Life	Regie Hamm	Fremantle

29

PEAK DATE	PEAK POS	WKS CHR	GOLD	ARTIST / Song Title	Songwriter...B-side	Label & Number
				COOKE, Sam		
12/2/57	❶³	26	⊙	1 You Send Me	Charles Cooke...*Summertime*	Keen 3-4013
10/3/60	2²	16	⊙	2 Chain Gang	Sam Cooke...*I Fall In Love Every Day*	RCA Victor 7783
3/24/62	9	15		3 Twistin' The Night Away	Sam Cooke...*One More Time*	RCA Victor 7983
5/25/63	10	11		4 Another Saturday Night	Sam Cooke...*Love Will Find A Way*	RCA Victor 8164
2/27/65	7	11		5 Shake	Sam Cooke...*A Change Is Gonna Come*	RCA Victor 8486
				COOKIES, The		
4/27/63	7	13		1 Don't Say Nothin' Bad (About My Baby)	Gerry Goffin/Carole King...*Softly In The Night*	Dimension 1008
				COOLIDGE, Rita		
9/10/77	2¹	27	●	1 (Your Love Has Lifted Me) Higher And Higher	Gary Jackson/Raynard Miner/Carl Smith...*Who's To Bless And Who's To Blame*	A&M 1922
11/26/77	7	20	●	2 We're All Alone	Boz Scaggs...*Southern Lady*	A&M 1965
				COOLIO		
7/30/94	3⁵	25	▲	1 Fantastic Voyage	Fred Alexander/Norman Beavers/Marvin Craig/Bryan Dobbs/Artis Ivey/Fred Lewis/Tiemeyer McCain/Thomas Shelby/Stephen Shockley/Otis Stokes/Mark Wood	Tommy Boy 7617
9/9/95	❶³	38	▲³	2 Gangsta's Paradise COOLIO featuring L.V.	Artis Ivey/Doug Rasheed/Larry Sanders	MCA 55104
4/27/96	5	21	●	3 1,2,3,4 (Sumpin' New)	Artis Ivey/Anthony Sear	Tommy Boy 7721
				COOPER, Alice		
7/29/72	7	13		1 School's Out	Michael Bruce/Alice Cooper...*Gutter Cat*	Warner 7596
8/13/77	9	21		2 You And Me	Alice Cooper/Dick Wagner...*It's Hot Tonight*	Warner 8349
11/25/89	7	19	●	3 Poison	Desmond Child/Alice Cooper/John McCurry...*Trash*	Epic 68958
				CORINA		
8/10/91	6	21		1 Temptation	Corina Ayala/Carlos Berrios...*Loving You Like Crazy*	Cutting/Atco 98775
				CORNELIUS BROTHERS & SISTER ROSE		
7/3/71	3²	18	●	1 Treat Her Like A Lady	Eddie Cornelius...*Over At My Place*	United Artists 50721
7/15/72	2²	14	●	2 Too Late To Turn Back Now	Eddie Cornelius...*Lift Your Love Higher*	United Artists 50910
				CORNELL, Don		
5/24/52	5	19		1 I'll Walk Alone	Sammy Cahn/Jule Styne...*That's The Chance You Take*	Coral 60659
6/21/52	3¹	17		2 I'm Yours	Robert Mellin...*My Mother's Pearls*	Coral 60690
11/29/52	7	8		3 I	Buddy Arnold/Milton Berle/Robert Mellin...*Be Fair*	Coral 60860
1/2/54	10	10		4 The Gang That Sang "Heart Of My Heart" DON CORNELL, ALAN DALE AND JOHNNY DESMOND	Ben Ryan...*I Think I'll Fall In Love Today*	Coral 61076
11/20/54	2¹	18		5 Hold My Hand	Jack Lawrence/Richard Myers...*I'm Blessed*	Coral 61206
10/22/55	7	13		6 The Bible Tells Me So	Dale Evans...*Love Is A Many-Splendored Thing*	Coral 61467
				CORTEZ, Dave "Baby"		
5/11/59	❶¹	17		1 The Happy Organ	Dave "Baby" Cortez/Ken Wood...*Love Me As I Love You* [I]	Clock 1009
9/15/62	10	14		2 Rinky Dink	Dave "Baby" Cortez...*Getting Right* [I]	Julia/Chess 1829
				COSBY, Bill		
10/14/67	4	11		1 Little Ole Man (Uptight-Everything's Alright)	Henry Cosby/Sylvia Moy/Stevie Wonder...*Hush Hush* [N]	Warner 7072
				COUGAR, John — see MELLENCAMP		
				COUNT FIVE		
10/15/66	5	12		1 Psychotic Reaction	Craig Atkinson/Sean Byrne/Roy Chaney/Kenn Ellner/John Michalski...*They're Gonna Get You*	Double Shot 104
				COUNTING CROWS		
5/14/94	5	47		1 Mr. Jones	Steve Bowman/David Bryson/Adam Duritz/Charlie Gillingham/Matt Malley	DGC
2/8/97	6	28		2 A Long December	David Bryson/Adam Duritz/Charlie Gillingham/Matt Malley/Ben Mize/Dan Vickrey...*Hanginaround*	DGC 97216
				COVER GIRLS, The		
3/3/90	8	19		1 We Can't Go Wrong	David Cole/Tony Moran/Andy Tripoli...*Love Mission*	Capitol 44498
7/18/92	9	20		2 Wishing On A Star	Billie Rae Calvin...*Funk Boutique*	Epic 74343
				COWBOY CHURCH SUNDAY SCHOOL, The		
4/2/55	8	21		1 Open Up Your Heart (And Let The Sunshine In)	Stuart Hamblen...*The Lord Is Counting On You*	Decca 29367
				COWSILLS, The		
12/2/67	2²	16	●	1 The Rain, The Park & Other Things	Steve Duboff/Artie Kornfeld...*River Blue*	MGM 13810
7/13/68	10	13		2 Indian Lake	Tony Romeo...*Newspaper Blanket*	MGM 13944
5/10/69	2²	15	●	3 Hair	Galt MacDermot/James Rado/Gerome Ragni...*What Is Happy?*	MGM 14026
				COX, Deborah		
12/5/98	2⁸	29	▲	1 Nobody's Supposed To Be Here	Anthony Crawford/Montell Jordan	Arista 13550
10/23/99	8	20		2 We Can't Be Friends DEBORAH COX with R.L. from Next	Anthony Crawford/Jim Russell...*It's Over Now*	Arista 13724
				CRAIG, Francis, and His Orchestra		
8/30/47	❶¹⁷	25		1 Near You	Francis Craig/Kermit Goell...*Red Rose*	Bullet 1001
2/14/48	3³	20		2 Beg Your Pardon	Francis Craig/Beasley Smith...*I'm Looking For A Sweetheart*	Bullet 1012
				CRAMER, Floyd		
11/28/60	2⁴	20	⊙	1 Last Date	Floyd Cramer...*Sweetie Baby* [I]	RCA Victor 7775
4/17/61	4	13		2 On The Rebound	Floyd Cramer...*Mood Indigo* [I]	RCA Victor 7840
7/17/61	8	12		3 San Antonio Rose	Bob Wills...*I Can Just Imagine* [I]	RCA Victor 7893
				CRANBERRIES, The		
2/12/94	8	24	●	1 Linger	Noel Hogan/Dolores O'Riordan...*How*	Island 862800
				CRANE, Les		
12/4/71	8	12		1 Desiderata	Max Ehrmann/Fred Warner...*A Different Drummer* [S]	Warner 7520

PEAK DATE	PEAK POS	WKS CHR	GOLD		ARTIST / Song Title	Songwriter...B-side	Label & Number
					CRASH TEST DUMMIES		
4/16/94	4	24	●	1	Mmm Mmm Mmm Mmm	Brad Roberts...*Superman's Song*	Arista 12654
					CRAWFORD, Johnny		
6/23/62	8	13		1	Cindy's Birthday	Jeff Hooven/Hal Winn...*Something Special*	Del-Fi 4178
					CRAZY TOWN		
3/24/01	❶²	23		1	Butterfly	Michael Balzary/Seth Binzer/John Frusciante/Anthony Kiedis/Bret Mazur/Chad Smith	Columbia 79549
					CREAM		
8/31/68	5	26	●	1	Sunshine Of Your Love	Pete Brown/Jack Bruce/Eric Clapton...*SWLABR*	Atco 6544
11/9/68	6	11		2	White Room	Pete Brown/Jack Bruce...*Those Were The Days*	Atco 6617
					CREED		
7/22/00	7	57		1	Higher	Scott Stapp/Mark Tremonti	Wind-Up
11/11/00	❶¹	47		2	With Arms Wide Open	Scott Stapp/Mark Tremonti	Wind-Up 18004
2/9/02	4	29		3	My Sacrifice	Scott Stapp/Mark Tremonti	Wind-Up
9/28/02	6	34		4	One Last Breath	Scott Stapp/Mark Tremonti	Wind-Up
					CREEDENCE CLEARWATER REVIVAL		
3/8/69	2³	14	▲	1	Proud Mary	John Fogerty...*Born On The Bayou*	Fantasy 619
6/28/69	2¹	14	▲	2	Bad Moon Rising	John Fogerty...*Lodi*	Fantasy 622
9/27/69	2¹	13	●	3	Green River	John Fogerty...*Commotion*	Fantasy 625
12/20/69	3¹	15	▲	4	Down On The Corner /	John Fogerty	
		14		5	Fortunate Son	John Fogerty	Fantasy 634
3/7/70	2²	10	▲	6	Travelin' Band /	John Fogerty	
		10		7	Who'll Stop The Rain	John Fogerty	Fantasy 637
6/6/70	4	11	▲	8	Up Around The Bend	John Fogerty...*Run Through The Jungle*	Fantasy 641
10/3/70	2¹	13	▲	9	Lookin' Out My Back Door	John Fogerty...*Long As I Can See The Light*	Fantasy 645
3/13/71	8	10	●	10	Have You Ever Seen The Rain	John Fogerty...*Hey Tonight*	Fantasy 655
8/21/71	6	9	●	11	Sweet Hitch-Hiker	John Fogerty...*Door To Door*	Fantasy 665
					CRESCENDOS, The		
3/3/58	5	18	☉	1	Oh Julie	Noel Ball/Ken Moffitt...*My Little Girl*	Nasco 6005
					CRESTS, The		
2/9/59	2²	21	☉	1	16 Candles	Luther Dixon/Allyson Khent...*Beside You*	Coed 506
					CREW-CUTS, The		
7/3/54	8	18		1	Crazy 'Bout Ya Baby	Pat Barrett/Rudi Maugeri...*Angela Mia*	Mercury 70341
8/7/54	❶⁹	20	☉	2	Sh-Boom	James Edwards/Carl Feaster/Claude Feaster/James Keyes/Floyd McRae...*I Spoke Too Soon*	Mercury 70404
3/12/55	3¹	13		3	Earth Angel	Jesse Belvin...*Ko Ko Mo (I Love You So)*	Mercury 70529
4/9/55	6	14		4	Ko Ko Mo (I Love You So)	Eunice Levy/Jake Porter/Forest Wilson...*Earth Angel*	Mercury 70529
9/17/55	10	8		5	Gum Drop	Rudy Toombs...*Song Of The Fool*	Mercury 70668
					CRICKETS, The — see HOLLY, Buddy		
					CROCE, Jim		
9/2/72	8	13		1	You Don't Mess Around With Jim	Jim Croce...*Photographs And Memories*	ABC 11328
7/21/73	❶²	22	●	2	Bad, Bad Leroy Brown	Jim Croce...*A Good Time Man Like Me Ain't Got No Business (Singin' the Blues)*	ABC 11359
11/17/73	10	17		3	I Got A Name	Charles Fox/Norman Gimbel...*Alabama Rain*	ABC 11389
12/29/73	❶²	15	●	4	Time In A Bottle	Jim Croce...*Hard Time Losin' Man*	ABC 11405
4/27/74	9	14		5	I'll Have To Say I Love You In A Song	Jim Croce...*Salon And Saloon*	ABC 11424
					CROSBY, Bing		
8/31/40	3¹	10		1	Sierra Sue	Joseph Carey...*Marcheta*	Decca 3133
10/19/40	❶⁹	16		2	Only Forever	Johnny Burke/James Monaco...*When The Moon Comes Over Madison Square Or (The Love Lament Of A Western Gent)*	Decca 3300
12/7/40	2²	15		3	Trade Winds	Cliff Friend/Charles Tobias...*A Song Of Old Hawaii*	Decca 3299
4/12/41	7	3	☉	4	New San Antonio Rose	Bob Wills...*It Makes No Difference Now*	Decca 3590
5/10/41	2¹	9		5	Dolores	Louis Alter/Frank Loesser...*De Camptown Races*	Decca 3644
8/23/41	6	5		6	'Til Reveille	Stanley Cowan/Bobby Worth...*My Old Kentucky Home*	Decca 3886
9/13/41	6	4		7	You And I	Meredith Willson...*Brahms' Lullaby*	Decca 3840
12/20/41	5	6		8	Shepherd Serenade	Kermit Goell/Fred Spielman...*The Anniversary Waltz*	Decca 4065
3/7/42	3²	6		9	Deep In The Heart Of Texas	June Hershey/Don Swander...*Let's All Meet At My House*	Decca 4162
4/4/42	9	1		10	I Don't Want To Walk Without You	Frank Loesser/Jule Styne...*Moonlight Cocktail*	Decca 4184
6/6/42	9	1		11	Miss You	Charles Tobias/Harry Tobias...*Blues In The Night (My Mama Done Tol' Me)*	Decca 4183
10/31/42	❶¹¹	15	☉	12	White Christmas	Irving Berlin...*Let's Start The New Year Right* [X]	Decca 18429
2/6/43	3¹	11		13	Moonlight Becomes You	Johnny Burke/Jimmy Van Heusen...*Constantly*	Decca 18513
9/11/43	❶⁷	18	☉	14	Sunday, Monday Or Always	Johnny Burke/Jimmy Van Heusen...*If You Please*	Decca 18561
11/27/43	2¹	14		15	People Will Say We're In Love	Oscar Hammerstein/Richard Rodgers...*Oh! What A Beautiful Mornin'*	Decca 18564
12/25/43	5	9		16	Oh! What A Beautiful Mornin'	Oscar Hammerstein/Richard Rodgers...*People Will Say We're In Love*	Decca 18564
					BING CROSBY And TRUDY ERWIN (above 2)		
12/25/43	3²	5	☉	17	I'll Be Home For Christmas (If Only In My Dreams)	Kim Gannon/Walter Kent/Buck Ram...*Danny Boy* [X]	Decca 18570
1/8/44	7	1		18	White Christmas	Irving Berlin...*Let's Start The New Year Right* [X-R]	Decca 18429
3/25/44	3¹	15		19	Poinciana (Song Of The Tree)	Buddy Bernier/Nat Simon...*San Fernando Valley*	Decca 18586
4/29/44	❶⁵	22		20	San Fernando Valley	Gordon Jenkins...*Poinciana (Song Of The Tree)*	Decca 18586
5/6/44	❶⁵	18		21	I Love You	Cole Porter...*I'll Be Seeing You*	Decca 18595
7/1/44	❶⁴	25		22	I'll Be Seeing You	Sammy Fain/Irving Kahal...*I Love You*	Decca 18595
7/22/44	5	5		23	Long Ago (And Far Away)	Ira Gershwin/Jerome Kern...*Amor*	Decca 18608
8/5/44	❶⁹	27	☉	24	Swinging On A Star	Johnny Burke/Jimmy Van Heusen...*Going My Way*	Decca 18597
8/19/44	2³	16		25	Amor	Gabriel Ruiz/Sunny Skylar...*Long Ago (And Far Away)*	Decca 18608
10/28/44	4	12	☉	26	Too-Ra-Loo-Ra-Loo-Ral (That's An Irish Lullaby)	James Shannon...*I'll Remember April*	Decca 18621
12/30/44	5	3		27	White Christmas	Irving Berlin...*Let's Start The New Year Right* [X-R]	Decca 18429
2/10/45	5	5		28	Evelina	Harold Arlen/E.Y. Harburg...*The Eagle And Me*	Decca 18635
4/28/45	4	10		29	Just A Prayer Away	David Kapp/Charles Tobias...*My Mother's Waltz*	Decca 23392
6/2/45	5	7		30	Yah-Ta-Ta Yah-Ta-Ta (Talk, Talk, Talk)	Johnny Burke/Jimmy Van Heusen...*You've Got Me Where You Want Me* [N]	Decca 23410
					BING CROSBY and JUDY GARLAND		

PEAK DATE	PEAK POS	WKS CHR	GOLD	ARTIST / Song Title ... Songwriter...B-side	Label & Number
				CROSBY, Bing (cont'd)	
6/23/45	3²	14		31 You Belong To My Heart .... Ray Gilbert/Agustin Lara...*Baia*	Decca 23413
6/23/45	6	2		32 Baia .... Ary Barroso/Ray Gilbert... *You Belong To My Heart*	Decca 23413
				BING CROSBY and XAVIER CUGAT And His Orchestra (above 2)	
8/25/45	3¹	15		33 On The Atchison, Topeka And The Santa Fe .... Johnny Mercer/Harry Warren...*I'd Rather Be Me*	Decca 18690
9/1/45	8	6		34 If I Loved You .... Oscar Hammerstein/Richard Rodgers...*Close As Pages In A Book*	Decca 18686
12/1/45	❶²	16		35 It's Been A Long Long Time .... Sammy Cahn/Jule Styne...*Whose Dream Are You*	Decca 18708
				BING CROSBY with LES PAUL And His Trio	
12/22/45	❶⁶	20	⊙	36 I Can't Begin To Tell You .... Mack Gordon/James Monaco...*I Can't Believe That You're In Love With Me*	Decca 23457
				BING CROSBY with CARMEN CAVALLARO	
12/29/45	❶²	4		37 White Christmas .... Irving Berlin...*Let's Start The New Year Right* [X-R]	Decca 18429
1/26/46	8	9		38 Aren't You Glad You're You? .... Johnny Burke/Jimmy Van Heusen...*In The Land Of Beginning Again*	Decca 18720
2/9/46	3¹	12		39 Symphony .... Alex Alstone/Roger Bernstein/Jack Lawrence/Andre Tabet...*Beautiful Love*	Decca 18735
3/30/46	10	4	⊙	40 McNamara's Band .... Guy Bonham/Wamp Carlson/Dwight Latham/Shamus O'Connor/J.J. Stamford...*Dear Old Donegal*	Decca 23495
				BING CROSBY and THE JESTERS	
4/6/46	9	3		41 Personality .... Johnny Burke/Jimmy Van Heusen...*Would You?*	Decca 18790
4/27/46	3⁴	16		42 Sioux City Sue .... Ray Freedman/Dick Thomas...*You Sang My Love Song To Somebody Else*	Decca 23508
				BING CROSBY and THE JESTERS	
1/4/47	❶¹	6		43 White Christmas .... Irving Berlin...*God Rest Ye Merry Gentlemen* [X-R]	Decca 23778
2/15/47	8	6		44 A Gal In Calico .... Leo Robin/Arthur Schwartz...*Oh, But I Do*	Decca 23739
				BING CROSBY with The Calico Kids	
11/1/47	9	4		45 Feudin' And Fightin' .... Al Dubin/Burton Lane...*Goodbye, My Lover, Goodbye*	Decca 23975
				BING CROSBY and THE JESTERS	
11/22/47	8	8		46 You Do .... Mack Gordon/Josef Myrow...*How Soon (Will I Be Seeing You)*	Decca 24101
				BING CROSBY with CARMEN CAVALLARO	
12/6/47	7	7	⊙	47 Whiffenpoof Song .... Todd Galloway/Meade Minnigerode/George Pomeroy...*Kentucky Babe*	Decca 23990
				BING CROSBY with FRED WARING and the GLEE CLUB	
1/3/48	3¹	5		48 White Christmas .... Irving Berlin...*God Rest Ye Merry Gentlemen* [X-R]	Decca 23778
1/24/48	6	14		49 How Soon (Will I Be Seeing You) .... Carroll Lucas/Jack Owens...*You Do*	Decca 24101
				BING CROSBY with CARMEN CAVALLARO	
1/24/48	10	8		50 Ballerina .... Bob Russell/Carl Sigman...*Golden Earrings*	Decca 24278
4/24/48	❶³	23	⊙	51 Now Is The Hour (Maori Farewell Song) .... Maewa Kaihau/Clement Scott/Dorothy Stewart...*Silver Threads Among The Gold*	Decca 24279
1/8/49	6	6		52 White Christmas .... Irving Berlin...*God Rest Ye Merry Gentlemen* [X-R]	Decca 23778
2/12/49	2³	19		53 Far Away Places .... Alex Kramer/Joan Whitney...*Tarra Ta-Lara Ta-Lar*	Decca 24532
3/12/49	3⁵	17	⊙	54 Galway Bay .... Arthur Colahan...*My Girl's An Irish Girl*	Decca 24295
7/23/49	3²	20		55 Some Enchanted Evening .... Oscar Hammerstein/Richard Rodgers...*Bali Ha'i*	Decca 24609
12/3/49	4	12		56 Mule Train .... Fred Glickman/Hy Heath/Johnny Lange...*Dear Hearts And Gentle People*	Decca 24798
1/7/50	5	4		57 White Christmas .... Irving Berlin...*God Rest Ye Merry Gentlemen* [X-R]	Decca 23778
1/28/50	2⁴	17	⊙	58 Dear Hearts And Gentle People .... Sammy Fain/Bob Hilliard...*Mule Train*	Decca 24798
3/11/50	4	13		59 Chattanoogie Shoe Shine Boy .... Jack Stapp/Harry Stone...*Bibbidi - Bobbidi - Boo*	Decca 24863
8/12/50	3⁵	19		60 Sam's Song (The Happy Tune) .... Jack Elliott/Lew Quadling...*Play A Simple Melody* [N]	Decca 9-27112
9/23/50	2²	19	⊙	61 Play A Simple Melody .... Irving Berlin...*Sam's Song (The Happy Tune)* [N]	Decca 9-27112
				GARY CROSBY and FRIEND (above 2)	
12/16/50	8	13		62 Harbor Lights .... Will Grosz/Jimmy Kennedy...*Beyond The Reef*	Decca 9-27219
5/5/51	8	10		63 When You And I Were Young Maggie Blues .... Jack Frost/Jimmy McHugh...*Moonlight Bay* [N]	Decca 9-27577
				BING and GARY CROSBY	
1/7/56	7	3		64 White Christmas .... Irving Berlin...*God Rest Ye Merry Gentlemen* [X-R]	Decca 23778
11/10/56	3¹	31	⊙	65 True Love .... Cole Porter...*Well Did You Evah?* (w/Frank Sinatra)	Capitol 3507 / Decca 23778
				BING CROSBY and GRACE KELLY	
				BING CROSBY and the ANDREWS SISTERS:	
12/4/43	2⁴	9	⊙	66 Pistol Packin' Mama .... Al Dexter...*Vict'ry Polka*	Decca 23277
1/8/44	6	5		67 Vict'ry Polka .... Sammy Cahn/Jule Styne...*Pistol Packin' Mama*	Decca 23277
10/14/44	❶⁶	14		68 (There'll Be A) Hot Time In The Town Of Berlin (When The Yanks Go Marching In) .... Joe Bushkin/John DeVries...*Is You Or Is You Ain't (Ma' Baby)*	Decca 23350
10/21/44	2¹	13		69 Is You Is Or Is You Ain't (Ma' Baby) .... Billy Austin/Louis Jordan...*(There'll Be A) Hot Time In The Town Of Berlin (When The Yanks Go Marching In)*	Decca 23350
12/16/44	❶⁸	21	⊙	70 Don't Fence Me In .... Cole Porter...*The Three Caballeros*	Decca 23364
3/3/45	8	5		71 The Three Caballeros .... Ernesto Cortazar/Manuel Esperon...*Don't Fence Me In*	Decca 23364
3/10/45	2¹	12		72 Ac-Cent-Tchu-Ate The Positive .... Harold Arlen/Johnny Mercer...*There's A Fellow Waiting In Poughkeepsie*	Decca 23379
10/27/45	2¹	11		73 Along The Navajo Trail .... Dick Charles/Eddie DeLange/Larry Markes...*Good, Good, Good (That's You—That's You)*	Decca 23437
11/2/46	2¹	19	⊙	74 South America, Take It Away .... Harold Rome...*Get Your Kicks On "Route 66!--"*	Decca 23569
7/19/47	10	10		75 Tallahassee .... Frank Loesser...*Go West, Young Man!*	Decca 23885
3/18/50	6	17		76 Quicksilver .... Eddie Pola/Irving Taylor/George Wyle...*Have I Told You Lately That I Love You?*	Decca 24827
4/28/51	8	15		77 Sparrow In The Tree Top .... Bob Merrill...*Forsaking All Others*	Decca 27477
				CROSBY, Bob, And His Orchestra	
1/4/41	2¹	4		1 Down Argentina Way .... Mack Gordon/Harry Warren...*Two Dreams Met*	Decca 3404
				CROSBY, STILLS & NASH	
8/27/77	7	21		1 Just A Song Before I Go .... Graham Nash...*Dark Star*	Atlantic 3401
8/21/82	9	15		2 Wasted On The Way .... Graham Nash...*Delta*	Atlantic 4058
				CROSS, Christopher	
4/26/80	2⁴	21		1 Ride Like The Wind .... Christopher Cross...*Minstrel Gigolo*	Warner 49184
8/30/80	❶¹	21		2 Sailing .... Christopher Cross...*Poor Shirley*	Warner 49507
10/17/81	❶³	24	●	3 Arthur's Theme (Best That You Can Do) .... Peter Allen/Burt Bacharach/Christopher Cross/Carole Bayer Sager...*Minstrel Gigolo*	Warner 49787
2/4/84	9	17		4 Think Of Laura .... Christopher Cross...*Words Of Wisdom*	Warner 29658
				CROW, Sheryl	
10/8/94	2⁶	33	●	1 All I Wanna Do .... David Baerwald/Bill Bottrell/Wyn Cooper/Sheryl Crow/Kevin Gilbert...*Solidify*	A&M 0702
3/25/95	5	26		2 Strong Enough .... David Baerwald/Bill Bottrell/Sheryl Crow/Kevin Gilbert/Brian MacLeod/David Ricketts...*What I Can Do For You*	A&M 0798
1/25/97	10	27		3 If It Makes You Happy .... Sheryl Crow/Jeff Trott...*Keep On Growing*	A&M 1874
11/28/98	9	23		4 My Favorite Mistake .... Sheryl Crow/Jeff Trott...*There Goes The Neighborhood*	A&M 2776
4/5/03	4	34	●	5 Picture .... Robert Ritchie	Universal 172274
				KID ROCK Featuring Allison Moorer or Sheryl Crow	
				CROWDED HOUSE	
4/25/87	2¹	24		1 Don't Dream It's Over .... Neil Finn...*That's What I Call Love*	Capitol 5614
7/25/87	7	21		2 Something So Strong .... Neil Finn/Mitchell Froom...*I Walk Away*	Capitol 5695

PEAK DATE	PEAK POS	WKS CHR	GOLD	ARTIST / Song Title	Songwriter...B-side	Label & Number
				CRUZ, Taio		
3/20/10	**0**[1]	29	△[3]	1 Break Your Heart	Christopher Bridges/Taio Cruz/Fraser Smith	Mercury 014302
				TAIO CRUZ Featuring Ludacris		
8/21/10	**2**[3]	34↑	△[3]	2 Dynamite	Taio Cruz/Lukasz Gottwald/Benjamin Levin/Karl Martin/Bonnie McKee	Mercury
				CRYSTALS, The		
11/3/62	**0**[2]	18	⊙	1 He's A Rebel	Gene Pitney...*I Love You Eddie*	Philles 106
6/8/63	**3**[1]	13	⊙	2 Da Doo Ron Ron (When He Walked Me Home)	Jeff Barry/Ellie Greenwich/Phil Spector...*Git' It*	Philles 112
9/14/63	6	12		3 Then He Kissed Me	Jeff Barry/Ellie Greenwich/Phil Spector...*Brother Julius*	Philles 115
				CUFF LINKS, The		
10/25/69	9	12		1 Tracy	Lee Pockriss/Paul Vance...*Where Do You Go?*	Decca 32533
				CUGAT, Xavier, and his Waldorf-Astoria Orchestra		
3/22/41	**3**[4]	13		1 Perfidia	Alberto Dominguez/Milton Leeds...*Nana* [I]	Victor 26334
3/20/43	**2**[7]	19		2 Brazil (Aquarela Do Brasil)	Ary Barroso/S.K. Russell...*Chiu-Chiu* [I]	Columbia 36651
7/29/44	10	9		3 Amor	Gabriel Ruiz/Sunny Skylar...*Let Me Love You Tonight* [F]	Columbia 36718
6/23/45	**3**[2]	14		4 You Belong To My Heart	Ray Gilbert/Agustin Lara...*Baia*	Decca 23413
6/23/45	6	2		5 Baia	Ary Barroso/Ray Gilbert...*You Belong To My Heart*	Decca 23413
				BING CROSBY and XAVIER CUGAT And His Orchestra (above 2)		
6/23/45	6	7		6 Good, Good, Good (That's You - That's You)	Doris Fisher/Allan Roberts...*Toca-Tu Samba*	Columbia 36793
9/21/46	6	13		7 South America, Take It Away!	Harold Rome...*Chiquita Banana (The Banana Song)*	Columbia 37051
				CULTURE CLUB		
3/26/83	**2**[3]	25		1 Do You Really Want To Hurt Me	Michael Craig/Roy Hay/Jon Moss/George O'Dowd...*You Know I'm Not Crazy*	Epic/Virgin 03368
6/18/83	**2**[2]	18		2 Time (Clock Of The Heart)	Michael Craig/Roy Hay/Jon Moss/George O'Dowd...*Romance Beyond The Alphabet*	Epic/Virgin 03796
8/27/83	9	16		3 I'll Tumble 4 Ya	Michael Craig/Roy Hay/Jon Moss/George O'Dowd...*Mystery Boy*	Epic/Virgin 03912
12/3/83	10	17		4 Church Of The Poison Mind	Michael Craig/Roy Hay/Jon Moss/George O'Dowd...*Mystery Boy*	Epic/Virgin 04144
2/4/84	**0**[3]	22	●	5 Karma Chameleon	Michael Craig/Roy Hay/Jon Moss/George O'Dowd/Phil Pickett...*That's The Way (I'm Only Trying To Help You)*	Virgin/Epic 04221
4/21/84	5	16		6 Miss Me Blind	Michael Craig/Roy Hay/Jon Moss/George O'Dowd...*Colour By Numbers*	Virgin/Epic 04388
				CUMMINGS, Burton		
1/8/77	10	21	●	1 Stand Tall	Burton Cummings...*Burch Magic*	Portrait 70001
				CUOMO, Rivers		
9/4/10	10	20	△	1 Magic	Rivers Cuomo/Lukasz Gottwald/Bobby Simmons	RebelRock
				B.O.B. Featuring Rivers Cuomo		
				CURB, Mike, Congregation		
6/10/72	**0**[3]	21	●	1 The Candy Man	Leslie Bricusse/Anthony Newley...*I Want To Be Happy* (Davis)	MGM 14320
				SAMMY DAVIS, JR. with The Mike Curb Congregation		
				CURE, The		
10/21/89	**2**[1]	17		1 Love Song	Simon Gallup/Roger O'Donnell/Robert Smith/Porl Thompson/Laurence Tolhurst/Boris Williams...*2 Late*	Elektra 69280
				CUTTING CREW		
5/2/87	**0**[2]	19		1 (I Just) Died In Your Arms	Nick Van Eede...*For The Longest Time*	Virgin 99481
11/21/87	9	21		2 I've Been In Love Before	Nick Van Eede...*Life In A Dangerous Time*	Virgin 99425
				CYRKLE, The		
7/9/66	**2**[1]	13	⊙	1 Red Rubber Ball	Paul Simon/Bruce Woodley...*How Can I Leave Her*	Columbia 43589
				CYRUS, Billy Ray		
7/18/92	4	25	▲	1 Achy Breaky Heart	Don Von Tress	Mercury 866522
				CYRUS, Miley		
5/3/08	10	27		1 See You Again	Antonina Armato/Miley Cyrus/Tim James	Hollywood
7/26/08	9	15		2 7 Things	Antonina Armato/Miley Cyrus/Tim James	Hollywood
5/2/09	4	28	△[2]	3 The Climb	Jessi Alexander/Jon Mabe	Walt Disney
7/25/09	10	5		4 He Could Be The One	Mitch Allan/Kara DioGuardi	Walt Disney
				HANNAH MONTANA		
8/29/09	**2**[3]	28	△[3]	5 Party In The U.S.A.	Jessica Cornish/Lukasz Gottwald/Claude Kelly	Hollywood
6/5/10	8	10		6 Can't Be Tamed	Antonina Armato/Miley Cyrus/Tim James/Paul Neumann/Marek Pompetzki	Hollywood

D

PEAK DATE	PEAK POS	WKS CHR	GOLD	ARTIST / Song Title	Songwriter...B-side	Label & Number
				DA BRAT		
8/13/94	6	20	▲	1 Funkdafied	Jermaine Dupri/Shawntae Harris	So So Def 77532
8/9/97	6	21	▲	2 Not Tonight	Robert Bell/Ronald Bell/George Brown/Missy Elliott/Shawntae Harris/Kim Jones/Lisa Lopes/Angie Martinez/Meekaaeel Muhammed/Claydes Smith/James Taylor/Dennis Thomas/Earl Toon	Undeas 98019
				LIL' KIM Featuring Da Brat, Left Eye, Missy "Misdemeanor" Elliott and Angie Martinez		
				DADDY DEWDROP		
5/8/71	9	16		1 Chick-A-Boom (Don't Ya Jes' Love It)	Janis Lee Guinn/Linda Martin...*John Jacob Jingleheimer Smith* [N]	Sunflower 105
				DALE, Alan		
1/2/54	10	10		1 The Gang That Sang "Heart Of My Heart"	Ben Ryan...*I Think I'll Fall In Love Today*	Coral 61076
				DON CORNELL, ALAN DALE AND JOHNNY DESMOND		
7/9/55	10	7		2 Sweet And Gentle	Otilio Portal/George Thorn...*You Still Mean The Same To Me*	Coral 61435
				DALE & GRACE		
11/23/63	**0**[2]	15	⊙	1 I'm Leaving It Up To You	Don Harris/Dewey Terry...*That's What I Like About You*	Montel 921
3/7/64	8	9		2 Stop And Think It Over	Jack Graffagnino...*Bad Luck*	Montel 922
				DAMIAN, Michael		
6/3/89	**0**[1]	21	●	1 Rock On	David Essex...*Where Is She?* (Blue Future)	Cypress 1420
				DAMN YANKEES		
1/12/91	**3**[2]	29	●	1 High Enough	Jack Blades/Ted Nugent/Tommy Shaw...*Piledriver*	Warner 19595

PEAK DATE	PEAK POS	WKS CHR	G O L D	ARTIST / Song Title	Songwriter...B-side	Label & Number
				DAMONE, Vic		
10/25/47	7	7		1 I Have But One Heart "O Marinariello"	Johnny Farrow/Marty Symes...*Ivy*	Mercury 5053
12/6/47	7	9		2 You Do	Mack Gordon/Josef Myrow...*Angela Mia*	Mercury 5056
5/21/49	6	21	⊙	3 Again	Dorcas Cochran/Lionel Newman...*I Love You So Much It Hurts*	Mercury 5261
8/27/49	❶⁴	26	⊙	4 You're Breaking My Heart	Pat Genaro/Sunny Skylar...*Four Winds And Seven Seas*	Mercury 5271
9/10/49	10	6		5 My Bolero	Jimmy Kennedy/Nat Simon...*Through A Long And Sleepless Night*	Mercury 5313
8/5/50	7	11		6 Tzena, Tzena, Tzena	Gordon Jenkins/Spencer Ross...*I Love That Girl*	Mercury 5454
1/13/51	4	15		7 My Heart Cries For You	Percy Faith/Carl Sigman...*Music By The Angels*	Mercury 5563
6/23/51	4	17		8 My Truly, Truly Fair	Bob Merrill...*My Life's Desire*	Mercury 5646
6/28/52	8	9		9 Here In My Heart	Bill Borrelli/Pat Genaro/Lou Levinson...*Tomorrow Never Comes*	Mercury 5858
5/23/53	10	7		10 April In Portugal	Paul Ferrao/Jimmy Kennedy...*I'm Walking Behind You*	Mercury 70128
10/24/53	10	11		11 Ebb Tide	Robert Maxwell/Carl Sigman...*If I Could Make You Mine*	Mercury 70216
7/7/56	4	25	⊙	12 On The Street Where You Live	Alan Jay Lerner/Frederick Loewe...*We All Need Love*	Columbia 40654
				DANA, Vic		
4/3/65	10	12		1 Red Roses For A Blue Lady	Roy Brodsky/Sid Tepper...*Blue Ribbons (For Her Curls)*	Dolton 304
				D'ANGELO		
3/30/96	10	20	●	1 Lady	D'Angelo Archer/Raphael Saadiq	EMI 58543
				DANIELS, Charlie, Band		
8/11/73	9	12		1 Uneasy Rider	Charlie Daniels...*Funky Junky* [N]	Kama Sutra 576
9/15/79	3²	18	▲	2 The Devil Went Down To Georgia	Tom Crain/Charlie Daniels/Joe DiGregorio/Fred Edwards/Charles Hayward/Jim Marshall...*Rainbow Ride*	Epic 50700
				DANITY KANE		
9/9/06	8	20		1 Show Stopper	Angela Hunte/Kristal Oliver/Calvin Puckett/Frank Romano/Jim Scheffer	Bad Boy
5/24/08	10	22	△	2 Damaged	Sean Combs/Mario Winans...*Bad Girl*	Bad Boy 512402
				DANLEERS, The		
7/28/58	7	13		1 One Summer Night	Danny Webb...*Wheelin' And A-Dealin'*	Mercury 71322
				DANNY & THE JUNIORS		
1/6/58	❶⁷	21	⊙	1 At The Hop	John Madara/Artie Singer/David White...*Sometimes (When I'm All Alone)*	ABC-Paramount 9871
				D'ARBY, Terence Trent		
5/7/88	❶¹	25	●	1 Wishing Well	Terence Trent D'Arby/Sean Oliver...*Elevators & Hearts*	Columbia 07675
8/13/88	4	21		2 Sign Your Name	Terence Trent D'Arby...*Greasy Chicken*	Columbia 07911
				DARIN, Bobby		
8/4/58	3¹	15	⊙	1 Splish Splash	Bobby Darin/Jean Murray...*Judy, Don't Be Moody*	Atco 6117
11/17/58	9	19	⊙	2 Queen Of The Hop	Woody Harris...*Lost Love*	Atco 6127
6/8/59	2¹	17	⊙	3 Dream Lover	Bobby Darin...*Bullmoose*	Atco 6140
10/5/59	❶⁹	26	⊙	4 Mack The Knife	Marc Blitzstein/Kurt Weill...*Was There A Call For Me*	Atco 6147
2/29/60	6	14		5 Beyond The Sea	Jack Lawrence/Charles Trenet...*That's The Way Love Is*	Atco 6158
10/16/61	5	11		6 You Must Have Been A Beautiful Baby	Johnny Mercer/Harry Warren...*Sorrow Tomorrow*	Atco 6206
8/25/62	3¹	12		7 Things	Bobby Darin...*Jailer Bring Me Water*	Atco 6229
3/16/63	3²	14		8 You're The Reason I'm Living	Bobby Darin...*Now You're Gone*	Capitol 4897
6/15/63	10	10		9 18 Yellow Roses	Bobby Darin...*Not For Me*	Capitol 4970
11/5/66	8	11		10 If I Were A Carpenter	Tim Hardin...*Rainin'*	Atlantic 2350
				DARREN, James		
12/4/61	3²	17		1 Goodbye Cruel World	Gloria Shayne...*Valerie*	Colpix 609
3/17/62	6	11		2 Her Royal Majesty	Gerry Goffin/Carole King...*If I Could Only Tell You*	Colpix 622
				DAUGHTRY		
2/10/07	4	29	△	1 It's Not Over	Chris Daughtry/Gregg Wattenberg/Mark Wilkerson/Brett Young	RCA
6/2/07	5	37	△	2 Home	Chris Daughtry	RCA
				DAVID, Craig		
3/2/02	10	20		1 7 Days	Craig David/Darren Hill/Mark Hill	Wildstar 85232
				DAVIS, Mac		
9/23/72	❶³	18	●	1 Baby Don't Get Hooked On Me	Mac Davis...*Poem For My Little Lady*	Columbia 45618
10/26/74	9	14		2 Stop And Smell The Roses	Mac Davis/Doc Severinsen...*Poor Boy Boogie*	Columbia 10018
				DAVIS, Paul		
3/18/78	7	40		1 I Go Crazy	Paul Davis...*Reggae Kinda Way*	Bang 733
5/22/82	6	20		2 '65 Love Affair	Paul Davis...*We're Still Together*	Arista 0661
				DAVIS, Sammy Jr.		
7/16/55	9	11		1 Something's Gotta Give	Johnny Mercer...*Love Me Or Leave Me*	Decca 29484
6/10/72	❶³	21	●	2 The Candy Man	Leslie Bricusse/Anthony Newley...*I Want To Be Happy* (Davis)	MGM 14320
				SAMMY DAVIS, JR. with The Mike Curb Congregation		
				DAVIS, Skeeter		
3/23/63	2¹	17	⊙	1 The End Of The World	Sylvia Dee/Arthur Kent...*Somebody Loves You*	RCA Victor 8098
11/2/63	7	13		2 I Can't Stay Mad At You	Gerry Goffin/Carole King...*It Was Only A Heart*	RCA Victor 8219
				DAVIS, Spencer, Group		
2/25/67	7	13		1 Gimme Some Lovin'	Steve Winwood...*Blues In F*	United Artists 50108
5/6/67	10	9		2 I'm A Man	Jimmy Miller/Steve Winwood...*Can't Get Enough Of It*	United Artists 50144
				DAVIS, Tyrone		
2/22/69	5	13	●	1 Can I Change My Mind	Barry Dispenza/Carl Wolfolk...*A Woman Needs To Be Loved*	Dakar 602
5/23/70	3¹	13	●	2 Turn Back The Hands Of Time	Jack Daniels/Bonnie Thompson...*I Keep Coming Back*	Dakar 616
				DAWN — see ORLANDO, Tony		

PEAK DATE	PEAK POS	WKS CHR	GOLD	ARTIST / Song Title	Songwriter...B-side	Label & Number
				DAY, Bobby		
10/13/58	2²	21	⊙	1 Rock-in Robin	Leon Rene...*Over And Over*	Class 229
				DAY, Dennis		
5/17/47	8	5		1 Mam'selle	Mack Gordon/Edmund Goulding...*Stella By Starlight*	RCA Victor 2211
1/6/51	10	3		2 Christmas In Killarney	James Cavanaugh/John Redmond/Frank Weldon...*I'm Praying To St. Christopher* [X]	RCA Victor 3970
				DAY, Doris		
8/14/48	❶⁵	24	⊙	1 Love Somebody	Alex Kramer/Joan Whitney...*Confess*	Columbia 38174
				DORIS DAY and BUDDY CLARK		
9/11/48	2¹	21	⊙	2 It's Magic	Sammy Cahn/Jule Styne...*Put 'Em In A Box, Tie 'Em With A Ribbon (And Throw 'Em In The Deep Blue Sea)*	Columbia 38188
12/18/48	7	13		3 My Darling My Darling	Frank Loesser...*That Certain Party*	Columbia 38353
				DORIS DAY and BUDDY CLARK		
7/9/49	2²	19		4 Again	Dorcas Cochran/Lionel Newman...*Everywhere You Go*	Columbia 38467
7/1/50	9	15		5 Bewitched	Lorenz Hart/Richard Rodgers...*Imagination*	Columbia 38698
4/14/51	10	10		6 Would I Love You (Love You, Love You)	Bob Russell/Harold Spina...*Lullaby Of Broadway*	Columbia 39159
				HARRY JAMES & his ORCH. with DORIS DAY		
8/18/51	7	17		7 (Why Did I Tell You I Was Going To) Shanghai	Milton DeLugg/Bob Hilliard...*My Life's Desire*	Columbia 39423
5/24/52	❶¹	19		8 A Guy Is A Guy	Oscar Brand...*Who Who Who*	Columbia 39673
8/30/52	7	14		9 Sugarbush	Josef Marais...*How Lovely Cooks The Meat*	Columbia 39693
				DORIS DAY - FRANKIE LAINE		
1/31/53	10	7		10 Mister Tap Toe	Richard Dehr/Terry Gilkyson/Frank Miller...*Your Mother And Mine*	Columbia 39906
2/27/54	❶⁴	22	⊙	11 Secret Love	Sammy Fain/Paul Francis Webster...*The Deadwood Stage (Whip-crack - Away!)*	Columbia 40108
11/27/54	3²	17		12 If I Give My Heart To You	Jimmy Brewster/Jimmie Crane/Al Jacobs...*Anyone Can Fall In Love*	Columbia 40300
8/18/56	2³	27	⊙	13 Whatever Will Be, Will Be (Que Sera, Sera)	Ray Evans/Jay Livingston...*I've Gotta Sing Away These Blues*	Columbia 40704
7/28/58	6	14		14 Everybody Loves A Lover	Richard Adler/Robert Allen...*Instant Love*	Columbia 41195
				DAYNE, Taylor		
1/23/88	7	25	●	1 Tell It To My Heart	Ernie Gold/Seth Swirsky	Arista 9612
5/7/88	7	18		2 Prove Your Love	Arnie Roman/Seth Swirsky...*Upon The Journey's End* (w/Billy T. Scott)	Arista 9676
9/24/88	3²	30		3 I'll Always Love You	Jimmy George...*Where Does That Boy Hang Out*	Arista 9700
1/21/89	2¹	20		4 Don't Rush Me	Alexandra Forbes/Jeffrey Franzel...*In The Darkness*	Arista 9722
12/16/89	5	18		5 With Every Beat Of My Heart	Arthur Baker/Tommy Faragher/Lotti Golden...*All I Ever Wanted*	Arista 9895
4/7/90	❶¹	20	●	6 Love Will Lead You Back	Diane Warren...*You Meant The World To Me*	Arista 9938
7/14/90	4	18		7 I'll Be Your Shelter	Diane Warren...*Ain't No Good*	Arista 2005
				DAZZ BAND		
7/17/82	5	23		1 Let It Whip	Reggie Andrews/Leon Chancler...*Everyday Love*	Motown 1609
				DEAN, Jimmy		
11/6/61	❶⁵	16	●	1 Big Bad John	Jimmy Dean...*I Won't Go Huntin' With You Jake* [S]	Columbia 42175
5/26/62	8	11		2 P.T. 109	Fred Burch/Marijohn Wilkin...*Walk On, Boy*	Columbia 42338
				DeBARGE		
4/27/85	3²	22	1	Rhythm Of The Night	Diane Warren...*Queen Of My Heart*	Gordy 1770
8/10/85	6	19	2	Who's Holding Donna Now	David Foster/Randy Goodrum/Jay Graydon...*Be My Lady*	Gordy 1793
				DeBARGE, El		
7/5/86	3¹	19		1 Who's Johnny	Ina Wolf/Peter Wolf...*Love Me In A Special Way*	Gordy 1842
				DeBURGH, Chris		
5/23/87	3²	26		1 The Lady In Red	Chris DeBurgh...*The Vision*	A&M 2848
				DeCASTRO SISTERS, The		
1/1/55	2¹	20		1 Teach Me Tonight	Sammy Cahn/Gene DePaul...*It's Love*	Abbott 3001
				DEE, Joey, & the Starliters		
1/27/62	❶³	18	⊙	1 Peppermint Twist - Part I	Joey Dee/Henry Glover...*Part II*	Roulette 4401
5/5/62	6	12		2 Shout - Part I	O'Kelly Isley/Ronald Isley/Rudolph Isley...*Part II*	Roulette 4416
				DEE, Kiki		
8/7/76	❶⁴	20	●	1 Don't Go Breaking My Heart	Elton John/Bernie Taupin...*Snow Queen*	Rocket/MCA 40585
				ELTON JOHN and KIKI DEE		
				DEEE-LITE		
11/17/90	4	23	●	1 Groove Is In The Heart	Dmitry Brill/Herbie Hancock/Kier Kirby/Towa Tei...*What Is Love?*	Elektra 64934
				DEELE, The		
5/21/88	10	21		1 Two Occasions	Babyface/Darnell Bristol/Sid Johnson	Solar 70015
				DEEP BLUE SOMETHING		
1/20/96	5	36		1 Breakfast At Tiffany's	Todd Pipes...*A Water Prayer*	Interscope 98138
				DEEP PURPLE		
9/21/68	4	10		1 Hush	Joe South...*One More Rainy Day*	Tetragrammaton 1503
7/28/73	4	16	●	2 Smoke On The Water	Ritchie Blackmore/Ian Gillan/Roger Glover/Jon Lord/Ian Paice	Warner 7710
				DEES, Rick, And His Cast Of Idiots		
10/16/76	❶¹	25	▲	1 Disco Duck (Part I)	Rick Dees...*(Part II)* [N]	RSO 857
				DEF LEPPARD		
3/26/88	10	16		1 Hysteria	Steve Clark/Phil Collen/Joe Elliott/Mutt Lange/Rick Savage...*Ride Into The Sun*	Mercury 870004
7/23/88	2¹	24	○	2 Pour Some Sugar On Me	Steve Clark/Phil Collen/Joe Elliott/Mutt Lange/Rick Savage...*Ring Of Fire*	Mercury 870298
10/8/88	❶¹	23		3 Love Bites	Steve Clark/Phil Collen/Joe Elliott/Mutt Lange/Rick Savage...*Billy's Got A Gun (live)*	Mercury 870402
1/21/89	3²	18		4 Armageddon It	Steve Clark/Phil Collen/Joe Elliott/Mutt Lange/Rick Savage...*Release Me* (Stumpus Maximus & The Good Ol' Boys)	Mercury 870692
				DeFRANCO FAMILY Featuring Tony DeFranco		
11/17/73	3¹	17	●	1 Heartbeat - It's A Lovebeat	William Hudspeth/Michael Kennedy...*Sweet, Sweet Loretta*	20th Century 2030

PEAK DATE	PEAK POS	WKS CHR	GOLD	ARTIST / Song Title	Songwriter...B-side	Label & Number
				DEGRAW, Gavin		
1/1/05	10	28	○	1 I Don't Want To Be	Gavin DeGraw	J Records
				DeJOHN SISTERS		
2/12/55	6	13		1 (My Baby Don't Love Me) **No More**	Dux DeJohn/Julie DeJohn/Leo DeJohn...*Theresa (The Little Flower)*	Epic 9085
				DEKKER, Desmond, & The Aces		
6/28/69	9	10		1 Israelites	Desmond Dekker/Leslie Kong...*My Precious World (The Man)*	Uni 55129
				DEL AMITRI		
11/4/95	10	36		1 Roll To Me	Justin Currie...*Long Way Down*	A&M 1114
				DELEGATES, The		
11/18/72	8	8		1 Convention '72	Nick Cenci/Nick Kousaleous...*Funky Butt* [N]	Mainstream 5525
				DELFONICS, The		
4/6/68	4	15		1 La-La-Means I Love You	Thom Bell/William Hart...*Can't Get Over Losing You*	Philly Groove 150
3/21/70	10	14	●	2 Didn't I (Blow Your Mind This Time)	Thom Bell/William Hart...*Down Is Up, Up Is Down*	Philly Groove 161
				DELLS, The		
8/24/68	10	13		1 Stay In My Corner	Wade Flemons/Bobby Miller/Barrett Strong...*Love Is So Simple*	Cadet 5612
9/27/69	10	11		2 Oh, What A Night	John Funches/Marvin Junior...*Believe Me*	Cadet 5649
				DELL-VIKINGS, The		
5/6/57	4	31	⊙	1 Come Go With Me	Clarence Quick...*How Can I Find True Love*	Dot 15538
8/5/57	9	18		2 Whispering Bells	Clarence Quick...*Don't Be A Fool*	Dot 15592
				DELTA RHYTHM BOYS		
9/1/45	9	3		1 It's Only A Paper Moon	Harold Arlen/E.Y. Harburg/Billy Rose...*(I'm Gonna Hurry You Out Of My Mind And) Cry You Out Of My Heart*	Decca 23425
				ELLA FITZGERALD and DELTA RHYTHM BOYS		
11/24/45	10	3		2 The Honeydripper	Joe Liggins...*Baby, Are You Kiddin'?*	Decca 23451
				JIMMIE LUNCEFORD And His Orchestra and DELTA RHYTHM BOYS		
2/15/47	8	14		3 (I Love You) For Sentimental Reasons	William Best/Deek Watson...*It's A Pity To Say Goodnight*	Decca 23670
				ELLA FITZGERALD And DELTA RHYTHM BOYS		
				DEM FRANCHIZE BOYZ		
4/1/06	7	25		1 Lean Wit It, Rock Wit It	Maurice Gleaton/Charles Hammond/Robert Hill/D'Angelo Hunt/Bernard Leverette/Gerald Tiller/Jamal Willingham	So So Def 50656
				DEM FRANCHIZE BOYZ Feat. Lil Peanut & Charlay		
				DENNIS, Cathy		
3/17/90	10	21		1 C'mon And Get My Love	Danny Poku	FFRR 886798
				D MOB Introducing Cathy Dennis		
2/2/91	9	22		2 Just Another Dream	Cathy Dennis/Danny Poku	Polydor 877962
5/18/91	2²	20		3 Touch Me (All Night Long)	Patrick Adams/Cathy Dennis/C. Delyle Gregory	Polydor 879466
9/21/91	8	20		4 Too Many Walls	Cathy Dennis/Anne Dudley	Polydor 867134
				DENNIS, Clark		
7/5/47	8	10		1 Peg O' My Heart	Alfred Bryan/Fred Fisher...*Bless You (For Being An Angel)*	Capitol 346
				DENNY, Martin (The Exotic Sounds of)		
6/1/59	4	16	⊙	1 Quiet Village	Les Baxter...*Llama Serenade* [I]	Liberty 55162
				DENVER, John		
8/28/71	2¹	23	●	1 Take Me Home, Country Roads	Bill Danoff/John Denver/Taffy Nivert...*Poems, Prayers And Promises*	RCA Victor 0445
3/3/73	9	19		2 Rocky Mountain High	John Denver/Mike Taylor...*Spring*	RCA Victor 0829
3/30/74	❶¹	18	●	3 Sunshine On My Shoulders	John Denver/Richard Kniss/Mike Taylor...*Around And Around*	RCA Victor 0213
7/27/74	❶²	17	●	4 Annie's Song	John Denver...*Cool An' Green An' Shady*	RCA Victor 0295
11/9/74	5	16	●	5 Back Home Again	John Denver...*It's Up To You*	RCA Victor 10065
6/7/75	❶¹	19	●	6 Thank God I'm A Country Boy	John Martin Sommers...*My Sweet Lady* [L]	RCA Victor 10239
9/27/75	❶¹	18	●	7 I'm Sorry /	John Denver	
		10		8 Calypso	John Denver	RCA Victor 10353
				DEODATO		
3/31/73	2¹	12		1 Also Sprach Zarathustra (2001)	Richard Strauss...*Spirit Of Summer* [I]	CTI 12
				DEPECHE MODE		
7/14/90	8	24	●	1 Enjoy The Silence	Martin L. Gore...*Memphisto*	Sire/Reprise 19885
				DEREK AND THE DOMINOS — see CLAPTON, Eric		
				DERULO, Jason		
11/14/09	❶¹	32	△³	1 Whatcha Say	Kisean Anderson/Jason Derulo/Jonathan Rotem	Beluga Heights 522765
4/24/10	5	34	△²	2 In My Head	Jason Derulo/Claude Kelly/Jonathan Rotem	Beluga Heights
7/17/10	9	28	○	3 Ridin' Solo	Jason Derulo/Jonathan Rotem	Beluga Heights
				DERWIN, Hal		
12/7/46	5	10		1 The Old Lamplighter	Nat Simon/Charles Tobias...*I Guess I'll Get The Papers And Go Home*	Capitol 288
				DeSARIO, Teri		
3/1/80	2²	23	●	1 Yes, I'm Ready	Barbara Mason...*With Your Love* (DeSario)	Casablanca 2227
				TERI DeSARIO with K.C.		
				DeSHANNON, Jackie		
7/24/65	7	13		1 What The World Needs Now Is Love	Burt Bacharach/Hal David...*I Remember The Boy*	Imperial 66110
8/30/69	4	14	●	2 Put A Little Love In Your Heart	Jackie DeShannon/Jimmy Holiday/Randy Myers...*Always Together*	Imperial 66385
				DESMOND, Johnny		
1/2/54	10	10		1 The Gang That Sang "Heart Of My Heart"	Ben Ryan...*I Think I'll Fall In Love Today*	Coral 61076
				DON CORNELL, ALAN DALE AND JOHNNY DESMOND		
1/9/54	9	7		2 Woman	Dick Gleason...*The River Seine*	Coral 61069

PEAK DATE	PEAK POS	WKS CHR	GOLD	ARTIST / Song Title	Songwriter...B-side	Label & Number
				DESMOND, Johnny (cont'd)		
4/30/55	6	11		3 Play Me Hearts And Flowers (I Wanna Cry)	Mann Curtis/Sanford Green...*I'm So Ashamed*	Coral 61379
9/17/55	3[1]	16		4 The Yellow Rose Of Texas	Don George...*You're In Love With Someone*	Coral 61476
				DES'REE		
3/11/95	5	44		1 You Gotta Be	Ashley Ingram/Des'ree Weeks...*Competitive World*	550 Music/Epic 77551
				DESTINY'S CHILD		
3/28/98	3[1]	35	▲	1 No, No, No Part 2	Mary Brown/Robert Fusari/Calvin Gaines/Vincent Herbert...*(Part 1)*	Columbia 78618
				DESTINY'S CHILD (featuring Wyclef Jean)		
7/17/99	❶[1]	20	●	2 Bills, Bills, Bills	Kevin Briggs/Kandi Burruss/Beyonce Knowles/LeToya Luckett/Kelly Rowland	Columbia 79175
3/18/00	❶[3]	32	●	3 Say My Name	LaShawn Daniels/Freddie Jerkins/Rodney Jerkins/Beyonce Knowles/LeToya Luckett/LaTavia Roberson/Kelly Rowland	Columbia 79342
8/19/00	3[5]	32		4 Jumpin', Jumpin'	Chad Elliott/Beyonce Knowles/Rufus Moore...*Upside Down*	Columbia 79446
11/18/00	❶[11]	28		5 Independent Women Part I	Sam Barnes/Beyonce Knowles/J.C. Olivier/Mark Cory Rooney...*8 Days Of Christmas*	Columbia 79493
4/14/01	2[7]	20		6 Survivor	Anthony Dent/Beyonce Knowles/Mathew Knowles	Columbia 79566
8/4/01	❶[2]	19		7 Bootylicious	Robert Fusari/Beyonce Knowles/Falonte Moore/Stevie Nicks	Columbia 79622
12/1/01	10	20		8 Emotion	Robin Barry/Barry Gibb	Columbia 79672
10/30/04	3[4]	23	○	9 Lose My Breath	Shawn Carter/LaShawn Daniels/Sean Garrett/Freddie Jerkins/Rodney Jerkins/Beyonce Knowles/Kelly Rowland/Michelle Williams...*Game Over*	Columbia 70096
2/12/05	3[1]	21	○	10 Soldier	Dwayne Carter/Sean Garrett/Clifford Harris/Rich Harrison/Beyonce Knowles/Kelly Rowland/Michelle Williams	Columbia 70702
				DESTINY'S CHILD (feat. T.I. and Lil Wayne)		
				DeVAUGHN, William		
6/29/74	4	18	●	Be Thankful For What You Got	William DeVaughn...*Part 2*	Roxbury 0236
				DeVORZON, Barry, and Perry Botkin, Jr.		
12/11/76	8	22 ● 1		Nadia's Theme (The Young And The Restless)	Perry Botkin Jr./Barry DeVorzon...*Down The Line* [I]	A&M 1856
				DEXTER, Al, and his Troopers		
10/30/43	❶[1]	17	⊙	1 Pistol Packin' Mama	Al Dexter...*Rosalita*	Okeh 6708
				DEXYS MIDNIGHT RUNNERS		
4/23/83	❶[1]	23		1 Come On Eileen	Kevin Adams/Jimmy Patterson/Kevin Rowland...*Let's Make This Precious*	Mercury 76189
				DeYOUNG, Dennis		
11/10/84	10	22		1 Desert Moon	Dennis DeYoung...*Gravity*	A&M 2666
				D4L		
1/14/06	❶[1]	26	○	1 Laffy Taffy	Dennis Butler/Larry Johnson/Michael Johnson/Adrian Parks/Richard Sims/Lefabian Williams	DeeMoney 68009
				D.H.T.		
8/20/05	8	27	○	1 Listen To Your Heart	Per Gessle/Mats Persson	Robbins 72116
				DIAMOND, Neil		
10/15/66	6	12		1 Cherry, Cherry	Neil Diamond...*I'll Come Running*	Bang 528
5/27/67	10	11		2 Girl, You'll Be A Woman Soon	Neil Diamond...*You'll Forget*	Bang 542
8/16/69	4	14	▲	3 Sweet Caroline (Good Times Never Seemed So Good)	Neil Diamond...*Dig In*	Uni 55136
12/27/69	6	14	▲	4 Holly Holy	Neil Diamond...*Hurtin' You Don't Come Easy*	Uni 55175
10/10/70	❶[1]	15	▲	5 Cracklin' Rosie	Neil Diamond...*Lordy*	Uni 55250
5/8/71	4	10		6 I Am...I Said	Neil Diamond...*Done Too Soon*	Uni 55278
7/1/72	❶[1]	13	●	7 Song Sung Blue	Neil Diamond...*Gitchy Goomy*	Uni 55326
11/23/74	5	15		8 Longfellow Serenade	Neil Diamond...*Rosemary's Wine*	Columbia 10043
12/2/78	❶[2]	17	▲	9 You Don't Bring Me Flowers	Alan Bergman/Marilyn Bergman/Neil Diamond	Columbia 10840
				BARBRA & NEIL		
1/10/81	2[3]	20		10 Love On The Rocks	Neil Diamond...*Acapulco*	Capitol 4939
3/28/81	6	16		11 Hello Again	Neil Diamond/Alan Lindgren...*Amazed And Confused*	Capitol 4960
6/13/81	8	17		12 America	Neil Diamond...*Songs Of Life*	Capitol 4994
11/13/82	5	19		13 Heartlight	Burt Bacharach/Neil Diamond/Carole Bayer Sager...*You Don't Know Me*	Columbia 03219
				DIAMONDS, The		
4/6/57	2[8]	26	⊙	1 Little Darlin'	Maurice Williams...*Faithful And True*	Mercury 71060
11/11/57	10	11		2 Silhouettes	Bob Crewe/Frank Slay...*Daddy Cool*	Mercury 71197
2/3/58	4	21	⊙	3 The Stroll	Nancy Lee/Clyde Otis...*Land Of Beauty*	Mercury 71242
				DICK AND DEEDEE		
9/25/61	2[2]	15	⊙	1 The Mountain's High	Dick Gosting...*I Want Someone*	Liberty 55350
				DIDO		
4/28/01	3[3]	39	○	1 Thankyou	Dido Armstrong/Paul Herman	Arista 13996
				DINNING, Mark		
2/8/60	❶[2]	18	⊙	1 Teen Angel	Jean Surrey/Red Surrey...*Bye Now Baby*	MGM 12845
				DINNING SISTERS Featuring Jean Dinning		
5/31/47	9	4		1 My Adobe Hacienda	Louise Massey/Lee Penny...*If I Had My Life To Live Over*	Capitol 389
11/20/48	5	16		2 Buttons And Bows	Ray Evans/Jay Livingston...*San Antonio Rose*	Capitol 15184
				DINO		
8/12/89	7	25	●	1 I Like It	Dino Esposito	4th & B'way 7483
10/20/90	6	18		2 Romeo	Dino Esposito	Island 878012
				DION / Dion and The Belmonts		
5/18/59	5	15	⊙	1 A Teenager In Love	Doc Pomus/Mort Shuman...*I've Cried Before*	Laurie 3027
2/8/60	3[1]	16		2 Where Or When	Lorenz Hart/Richard Rodgers...*That's My Desire*	Laurie 3044
				DION and THE BELMONTS (above 2)		
10/23/61	❶[2]	14	⊙	3 Runaround Sue	Dion DiMucci/Ernie Maresca...*Runaway Girl*	Laurie 3110
2/24/62	2[1]	18	⊙	4 The Wanderer	Ernie Maresca...*The Majestic*	Laurie 3115
6/9/62	3[1]	12		5 Lovers Who Wander	Dion DiMucci/Ernie Maresca...*(I Was) Born To Cry*	Laurie 3123
8/18/62	8	11		6 Little Diane	Dion DiMucci...*Lost For Sure*	Laurie 3134
12/22/62	10	11		7 Love Came To Me	Dion DiMucci/John Falbo...*Little Girl*	Laurie 3145

PEAK DATE	PEAK POS	WKS CHR	GOLD	ARTIST / Song Title	Songwriter...B-side	Label & Number
				DION / Dion and The Belmonts — cont'd		
2/23/63	2³	13	⊙	8 Ruby Baby	Jerry Leiber/Mike Stoller...*He'll Only Hurt You*	Columbia 42662
10/26/63	6	11		9 Donna The Prima Donna	Dion DiMucci/Ernie Maresca...*You're Mine*	Columbia 42852
12/28/63	6	11		10 Drip Drop	Jerry Leiber/Mike Stoller...*No One's Waiting For Me*	Columbia 42917
				DION DI MUCI (above 2)		
12/14/68	4	14	●	11 Abraham, Martin And John	Dick Holler...*Daddy Rollin' (In Your Arms)*	Laurie 3464
				DION, Celine		
3/2/91	4	24		1 Where Does My Heart Beat Now	Robert Johnson/Taylor Rhodes...*I Feel Too Much*	Epic 73536
4/18/92	9	20	▲	2 Beauty And The Beast	Howard Ashman/Alan Menken...*The Beast Lets Belle Go*	Epic 74090
				CELINE DION and PEABO BRYSON		
7/11/92	4	22		3 If You Asked Me To	Diane Warren...*Love You Blind*	Epic 74277
2/12/94	❶⁴	33	▲	4 The Power Of Love	Mary Applegate/Candy Derouse/Gunther Mende/Jennifer Rush...*No Living Without Loving You*	550 Music/Epic 77230
3/23/96	❶⁶	33	▲	5 Because You Loved Me	Diane Warren...*I Don't Know*	550 Music/Epic 78237
10/26/96	2⁵	30	▲	6 It's All Coming Back To Me Now	Jim Steinman...*The Power Of The Dream*	550 Music/Epic 78345
4/5/97	4	20	●	7 All By Myself	Eric Carmen...*Because You Loved Me (live)*	550 Music/Epic 78529
2/28/98	❶²	20		8 My Heart Will Go On (Love Theme From 'Titanic')	James Horner/Will Jennings...*Rose* (James Horner)	550 Music/Epic 78825
12/5/98	❶⁶	18	▲	9 I'm Your Angel	R. Kelly	Jive 42557
				R. KELLY & CELINE DION		
3/4/00	6	28		10 That's The Way It Is	Andreas Carlsson/Kristian Lundin/Max Martin...*I Want You To Need Me*	550 Music/Epic 79473
				DIRE STRAITS		
4/7/79	4	15		1 Sultans Of Swing	Mark Knopfler...*Southbound Again*	Warner 8736
9/21/85	❶³	22		2 Money For Nothing	Mark Knopfler/Sting...*Love Over Gold (live)*	Warner 28950
1/25/86	7	21		3 Walk Of Life	Mark Knopfler...*One World*	Warner 28878
				DISCO TEX & THE SEX-O-LETTES		
2/8/75	10	15		1 Get Dancin'	Bob Crewe/Kenny Nolan...*Part II*	Chelsea 3004
				DIVINE		
11/28/98	❶¹	27	▲	1 Lately	Will Baker/Chris Kelly...*My Love*	Red Ant 15316
				DIVINYLS		
5/18/91	4	18		1 I Touch Myself	Christina Amphlett/Tom Kelly/Mark McEntee/Billy Steinberg...*Follow Through*	Virgin 98873
				DIXIEBELLES, The		
11/30/63	9	13		1 (Down At) Papa Joe's	Jerry Smith...*Rock, Rock, Rock*	Sound Stage 7 2507
				DIXIE CHICKS		
8/31/02	7	20		1 Long Time Gone	Darrell Scott...*Don't Waste Your Heart*	Monument 79790
3/8/03	7	29	○	2 Landslide	Stevie Nicks	Monument 79857
3/3/07	4	4	△	3 Not Ready To Make Nice	Martie Maguire/Natalie Maines/Emily Robison/Dan Wilson...*Everybody Knows*	Columbia 84335
				DIXIE CUPS, The		
6/6/64	❶³	13	⊙	1 Chapel Of Love	Jeff Barry/Ellie Greenwich/Phil Spector...*Ain't That Nice*	Red Bird 001
				D.J. JAZZY JEFF & THE FRESH PRINCE		
8/3/91	4	18	▲	1 Summertime	Robert Bell/Ronald Bell/George Brown/Lamar Mahone/Robert Mickens/Craig Simpkins/Claydes Smith/Will Smith/Alton Taylor/Dennis Thomas/Rich West	Jive 1465
				DJ SAMMY & YANOU Featuring Do		
8/10/02	8	27	○	1 Heaven	Bryan Adams/Jim Vallance	Robbins 72057
				D.N.A. — See VEGA, Suzanne		
				DOBKINS, Carl Jr.		
8/3/59	3³	24		1 My Heart Is An Open Book	Hal David/Lee Pockriss...*My Pledge To You*	Decca 30803
				DR. DRE		
3/20/93	2¹	27	▲	1 Nuthin' But A "G" Thang	Calvin Broadus/Leon Haywood	Death Row 53819
7/3/93	8	20	●	2 Dre Day	Calvin Broadus/Colin Wolfe/Andre Young	Death Row 53827
				DR. DRE (with Snoop Doggy Dogg) (above 2)		
4/22/95	10	20	●	3 Keep Their Heads Ringin'	Sam Sneed/Andre Young...*Take A Hit* (Mack 10)	Priority 53188
6/22/96	6	24		4 California Love	Joe Cocker/Tupac Shakur/Chris Stainton/Larry Troutman/Roger Troutman/Andre Young...*How Do U Want It* (2 PAC w/KC & JoJo)	Death Row 854652
				2 PAC (featuring Dr. Dre and Roger Troutman)		
11/9/96	❶⁴	31	▲	5 No Diggity	Chauncey Hannibal/Teddy Riley/William Stewart/Larry Walters/Andre Young...*Billie Jean*	Interscope 97007
				BLACKstreet (Featuring Dr. Dre)		
2/21/09	❶¹	17		6 Crack A Bottle	Curtis Jackson/Trevor Lawrence/Marshall Mathers/Dawaun Parker/Jean Renard/Andre Young	Web
				EMINEM, DR. DRE & 50 CENT		
				DR. HOOK		
6/3/72	5	15	●	1 Sylvia's Mother	Shel Silverstein...*Makin' It Natural*	Columbia 45562
3/17/73	6	20	●	2 The Cover Of "Rolling Stone"	Shel Silverstein...*Queen Of The Silver Dollar* [N]	Columbia 45732
				DR. HOOK AND THE MEDICINE SHOW (above 2)		
4/17/76	6	22	●	3 Only Sixteen	Sam Cooke...*Let Me Be Your Lover*	Capitol 4171
1/6/79	6	22	●	4 Sharing The Night Together	Ava Aldridge/Eddie Struzick...*You Make My Pants Want To Get Up And Dance*	Capitol 4621
8/11/79	6	25	●	5 When You're In Love With A Beautiful Woman	Even Stevens...*Knowing She's There*	Capitol 4705
5/24/80	5	21	●	6 Sexy Eyes	Chris Dunn/Robert Mather/Keith Stegall...*Help Me Mama*	Capitol 4831
				DR. JOHN		
6/30/73	9	20		1 Right Place Wrong Time	Malcolm Rebennack...*I Been Hoodood*	Atco 6914
				DOGGETT, Bill		
10/6/56	2³	29	⊙	1 Honky Tonk (Parts 1 & 2)	Billy Butler/Bill Doggett/Clifford Scott/Shep Shepherd [I]	King 4950
				DOLBY, Thomas		
5/14/83	5	22		1 She Blinded Me With Science	Thomas Dolby/Joe Kerr...*Flying North*	Capitol 5204
				DOMINO		
2/12/94	7	20	●	1 Getto Jam	Kevin Gilliam/Shawn Ivy	OutBurst 77298

PEAK DATE	PEAK POS	WKS CHR	GOLD	ARTIST Song Title	Songwriter...B-side	Label & Number
				DOMINO, Fats		
8/27/55	10	13	⊙	1 Ain't That A Shame	Dave Bartholomew/Fats Domino...*La-La*	Imperial 5348
7/14/56	3²	23	⊙	2 I'm In Love Again	Dave Bartholomew/Fats Domino...*My Blue Heaven*	Imperial 5386
1/19/57	2³	27	⊙	3 Blueberry Hill	Al Lewis/Vincent Rose/Larry Stock...*Honey Chile*	Imperial 5407
3/9/57	5	18	⊙	4 Blue Monday	Dave Bartholomew/Fats Domino...*What's The Reason I'm Not Pleasing You*	Imperial 5417
4/13/57	4	25	⊙	5 I'm Walkin'	Dave Bartholomew/Fats Domino...*I'm In The Mood For Love*	Imperial 5428
7/8/57	8	18		6 Valley Of Tears	Dave Bartholomew/Fats Domino...*It's You I Love*	Imperial 5442
7/22/57	6	12		7 It's You I Love	Dave Bartholomew/Fats Domino...*Valley Of Tears*	Imperial 5442
1/12/59	6	15	⊙	8 Whole Lotta Loving	Dave Bartholomew/Fats Domino...*Coquette*	Imperial 5553
9/14/59	8	13		9 I Want To Walk You Home	Fats Domino...*I'm Gonna Be A Wheel Some Day*	Imperial 5606
12/7/59	8	14		10 Be My Guest	Tommy Boyce/Fats Domino/John Marascalco...*I've Been Around*	Imperial 5629
8/15/60	6	14	⊙	11 Walking To New Orleans	Dave Bartholomew/Fats Domino/Robert Guidry...*Don't Come Knockin'*	Imperial 5675
				DONAHUE, Al, and his Orchestra		
4/19/41	7	2		1 The Wise Old Owl	Joe Ricardel...*You Should Be Set To Music*	Okeh 6037
				DONAHUE, Sam, And His Orchestra		
8/10/46	9	6		1 Dinah	Harry Akst/Sam Lewis/Joe Young...*Take Five* [I]	Capitol 260
8/17/46	8	7		2 Just The Other Day	Johnson Croom/Redd Evans...*I Left My Heart In Mississippi*	Capitol 275
11/16/46	8	2		3 Put That Kiss Back Where You Found It	Peter DeRose/Carl Sigman...*Scufflin'*	Capitol 293
4/12/47	7	7		4 A Rainy Night In Rio	Leo Robin/Arthur Schwartz...*It's Anybody's Love Song*	Capitol 325
5/3/47	5	7		5 My Melancholy Baby	Ernie Burnett/George Norton...*I Can't Believe It Was All Make Believe* [I]	Capitol 357
8/2/47	2¹	23		6 I Never Knew	Ted Fiorito/Gus Kahn...*Why Did It Have To End So Soon*	Capitol 405
11/1/47	9	2		7 Red Wing	Thurland Chattaway/F.A. Mills...*The Whistler*	Capitol 472
11/8/47	6	7		8 The Whistler	Hal Dickinson/Wilbur Hatch...*Red Wing*	Capitol 472
				DONALDSON, Bo, And The Heywoods		
6/15/74	❶²	19	●	1 Billy, Don't Be A Hero	Peter Callander/Mitch Murray...*Don't Ever Look Back*	ABC 11435
				DON & JUAN		
3/17/62	7	13		1 What's Your Name	Claude Johnson...*Chicken Necks*	Big Top 3079
				DONEGAN, Lonnie, And His Skiffle Group		
4/21/56	8	17		1 Rock Island Line	Lonnie Donegan...*John Henry*	London 1650
9/25/61	5	11		2 Does Your Chewing Gum Lose It's Flavor (On The Bedpost Over Night)	Marty Bloom/Ernest Breuer/Billy Rose...*Aunt Rhody* [L-N]	Dot 15911
				DONNER, Ral		
9/4/61	4	12		1 You Don't Know What You've Got (Until You Lose It)	George Burton/Paul Hampton...*So Close To Heaven*	Gone 5108
				DONOVAN		
9/3/66	❶¹	13	⊙	1 Sunshine Superman	Donovan Leitch...*The Trip*	Epic 10045
12/10/66	2³	12	●	2 Mellow Yellow	Donovan Leitch...*Sunny South Kensington*	Epic 10098
8/3/68	5	12		3 Hurdy Gurdy Man	Donovan Leitch...*Teen Angel*	Epic 10345
5/24/69	7	13		4 Atlantis	Donovan Leitch...*To Susan On The West Coast Waiting*	Epic 10434
				DOOBIE BROTHERS, The		
6/30/73	8	18		1 Long Train Runnin'	Tom Johnston...*Without You*	Warner 7698
3/15/75	❶¹	17		2 Black Water	Patrick Simmons...*Song To See You Through*	Warner 8062
4/14/79	❶¹	20		3 What A Fool Believes	Kenny Loggins/Michael McDonald...*Don't Stop To Watch The Wheels*	Warner 8725
10/25/80	5	16		4 Real Love	Patrick Henderson/Michael McDonald...*Thank You Love*	Warner 49503
7/15/89	9	14		5 The Doctor	Tom Johnston/Charlie Midnight/Eddie Schwartz...*Too High A Price*	Capitol 44376
				DOORS, The		
7/29/67	❶³	17	●	1 Light My Fire	John Densmore/Robby Krieger/Ray Manzarek/Jim Morrison...*The Crystal Ship*	Elektra 45615
8/3/68	❶²	12	●	2 Hello, I Love You	John Densmore/Robby Krieger/Ray Manzarek/Jim Morrison...*Love Street*	Elektra 45635
2/15/69	3¹	13	●	3 Touch Me	John Densmore/Robby Krieger/Ray Manzarek/Jim Morrison...*Wild Child*	Elektra 45646
				DOREY, Ray		
5/3/47	7	8		1 Mam'selle	Mack Gordon/Edmund Goulding...*The Man Who Paints The Rainbow*	Majestic 7217
				DORSEY, Jimmy, And His Orchestra		
7/27/40	2⁶	9		1 The Breeze And I	Ernesto Lecuona/Al Stillman...*Little Curly Hair In A High Chair*	Decca 3150
8/17/40	4	3		2 Six Lessons From Madame La Zonga	James Monaco/Charles Newman...*Boog-It*	Decca 3152
1/25/41	3⁴	10		3 I Hear A Rhapsody	Jack Baker/George Fragos/Dick Gasparre...*The Mem'ry Of A Rose*	Decca 3570
2/22/41	7	1		4 High On A Windy Hill	Alex Kramer/Joan Whitney...*I Understand*	Decca 3585
3/29/41	❶¹⁰	14	⊙	5 Amapola (Pretty Little Poppy)	Albert Gamse/Joseph Lacalle...*Donna Maria*	Decca 3629
6/7/41	❶²	10		6 My Sister And I	Alex Kramer/Joan Whitney/Hy Zaret...*In The Hush Of The Night*	Decca 3710
6/14/41	❶²	17		7 Maria Elena	Lorenza Barcelata...*Green Eyes (Aquellos Ojos Verdes)*	Decca 3698
7/12/41	7	3		8 The Things I Love	Harold Barlow/Lew Harris...*Once And For All*	Decca 3737
8/30/41	❶⁴	21	⊙	9 Green Eyes (Aquellos Ojos Verdes)	Nilo Menendez/Edil Rivera/Adolfo Utrera/Eddie Woods...*Maria Elena*	Decca 3698
9/6/41	2²	13		10 Yours (Quiereme Mucho)	Albert Gamse/Gonzalo Roig/Jack Sherr...*When The Sun Comes Out*	Decca 3657
9/27/41	❶¹	14		11 Blue Champagne	Frank Ryerson/Grady Watts...*All Alone And Lonely*	Decca 3775
10/11/41	5	9		12 Jim	Caesar Petrillo/Edward Ross/Nelson Shawn...*A New Shade Of Blue*	Decca 3963
10/25/41	10	1		13 Time Was (Duerme)	Miguel Prado/S.K. Russell...*Isle Of Pines*	Decca 3859
1/31/42	10	1		14 I Said No	Frank Loesser/Jule Styne...*This Is No Laughing Matter*	Decca 4102
4/25/42	9	1		15 I Remember You	Johnny Mercer/Victor Schertzinger...*If You Build A Better Mousetrap*	Decca 4132
5/9/42	❶⁶	15		16 Tangerine	Johnny Mercer/Victor Schertzinger...*Ev'rything I Love*	Decca 4123
6/13/42	9	1		17 Jersey Bounce	Tiny Bradshaw/Edward Johnson/Bobby Plater/Robert Wright...*My Little Cousin* [I]	Decca 4288
8/29/42	10	1		18 My Devotion	Roc Hillman/Johnny Napton...*Sorghum Switch*	Decca 18372
1/15/44	2¹	9		19 They're Either Too Young Or Too Old	Frank Loesser/Arthur Schwartz...*Star Eyes*	Decca 18571
1/22/44	3²	13		20 Star Eyes	Gene DePaul/Don Raye...*They're Either Too Young Or Too Old*	Decca 18571
2/26/44	5	11		21 My Ideal	Newell Chase/Leo Robin/Richard Whiting...*Besame Mucho (Kiss Me Much)*	Decca 18574
3/4/44	❶⁷	23	⊙	22 Besame Mucho (Kiss Me Much)	Sunny Skylar/Consuelo Velazquez...*My Ideal*	Decca 18574
4/15/44	4	16		23 When They Ask About You	Sam Stept...*My First Love*	Decca 18582
6/30/45	8	1		24 Can't You Read Between The Lines?	Sammy Cahn/Jule Styne...*Negra Consentida (My Pet Brunette)*	Decca 18676
7/14/45	8	6		25 There! I've Said It Again	Redd Evans/Dave Mann...*Dream*	Decca 18670
7/27/46	8	10		26 Doin' What Comes Natur'lly	Irving Berlin...*All That Glitters Is Not Gold*	Decca 18872

PEAK DATE	PEAK POS	WKS CHR	G O L D	ARTIST / Song Title	Songwriter...B-side	Label & Number
				DORSEY, Jimmy, And His Orchestra (cont'd)		
1/17/48	10	1		27 Ballerina	Bob Russell/Carl Sigman...*(Love's Got Me In A) Lazy Mood*	MGM 10035
6/17/57	2⁴	38	⊙	28 So Rare	Jerry Herst/Jack Sharpe...*Sophisticated Swing*	Fraternity 755
				JIMMY DORSEY and his Original "Dorseyland" Jazz Band		
				DORSEY, Lee		
10/30/61	7	13		1 Ya Ya	Lee Dorsey/Morgan Robinson...*Give Me You*	Fury 1053
9/3/66	8	12		2 Working In The Coal Mine	Allen Toussaint...*Mexico*	Amy 958
				DORSEY, Tommy, And His Orchestra		
7/27/40	❶¹²	15	⊙	1 I'll Never Smile Again	Ruth Lowe...*Marcheta*	Victor 26628
7/27/40	8	1		2 Imagination	Johnny Burke/Jimmy Van Heusen...*Charming Little Faker*	Victor 26581
9/21/40	10	4		3 Trade Winds	Cliff Friend/Charles Tobias...*Only Forever*	Victor 26666
10/26/40	7	3		4 Only Forever	Johnny Burke/James Monaco...*Trade Winds*	Victor 26666
11/16/40	5	3		5 Our Love Affair	Roger Edens/Arthur Freed...*That's For Me*	Victor 26736
12/28/40	3¹	5		6 We Three (My Echo, My Shadow and Me)	Nelson Cogane/Sammy Mysels/Dick Robertson...*Tell Me At Midnight*	Victor 26747
1/4/41	7	1		7 Star Dust	Hoagy Carmichael/Mitchell Parish...*Swanee River*	Victor 27233
3/15/41	2⁶	12		8 Oh! Look At Me Now	John DeVries...*You Might Have Belonged To Another*	Victor 27274
4/19/41	4	3		9 Do I Worry?	Stanley Cowan/Bobby Worth...*Little Man With A Candy Cigar*	Victor 27338
4/26/41	7	2		10 Dolores	Louis Alter/Frank Loesser...*I Tried*	Victor 27317
5/3/41	9	1		11 Everything Happens To Me	Tom Adair/Matt Dennis...*Whatcha Know Joe?*	Victor 27359
5/10/41	7	2		12 Let's Get Away From It All-Parts 1 & 2	Tom Adair/Matt Dennis	Victor 27377
8/9/41	4	14		13 Yes Indeed!	Sy Oliver...*Will You Still Be Mine?*	Victor 27421
11/22/41	3⁴	16		14 This Love Of Mine	Sol Parker/Henry Sanicola/Frank Sinatra...*Neiani*	Victor 27508
12/20/41	9	1		15 Two In Love	Meredith Willson...*A Sinner Kissed An Angel*	Victor 27611
9/26/42	5	3		16 Take Me	Rube Bloom/Mack David...*Be Careful, It's My Heart*	Victor 27923
10/3/42	3¹	9		17 Just As Though You Were Here	John Benson Brooks/Eddie DeLange...*Street Of Dreams*	Victor 27903
11/7/42	10	2		18 Daybreak	Harold Adamson/Ferde Grofe...*There Are Such Things*	Victor 27974
1/16/43	❶⁵	24	⊙	19 There Are Such Things	Stanley Adams/Abel Baer/George Meyer...*Daybreak*	Victor 27974
3/27/43	4	13		20 It Started All Over Again	Bill Carey/Carl Fischer...*Mandy, Make Up Your Mind*	Victor 1522
7/24/43	6	7		21 It's Always You	Johnny Burke/Jimmy Van Heusen...*In The Blue Of Evening*	Victor 1530
8/21/43	❶³	17		22 In The Blue Of Evening	Tom Adair/Al D'Artega...*It's Always You*	Victor 1530
1/22/44	5	6	⊙	23 Boogie Woogie	Clarence "Pine Top" Smith...*Weary Blues* [I]	Victor 26054
7/29/44	4	17		24 I'll Be Seeing You	Sammy Fain/Irving Kahal...*Let's Just Pretend*	Victor 1574
				Frank Sinatra (vocal; all of above, except #4, 13 & 23)		
1/27/45	4	9		25 I Dream Of You (More Than You Dream I Do)	Marjorie Goetschius/Edna Osser...*Opus No. 1*	Victor 1608
3/24/45	8	3		26 Opus No. I	Sy Oliver...*I Dream Of You (More Than You Dream I Do)* [I]	Victor 1608
4/7/45	10	4		27 More And More	E.Y. Harburg/Jerome Kern...*You're Drivin' Me Crazy*	Victor 1614
7/28/45	9	1		28 A Friend Of Yours	Johnny Burke/Jimmy Van Heusen...*There's No You*	Victor 1657
8/25/45	6	6		29 On The Atchison, Topeka & Santa Fe	Johnny Mercer/Harry Warren...*In The Valley*	Victor 1682
9/22/45	4	4		30 Boogie Woogie	Clarence "Pine Top" Smith...*There You Go* [I-R]	Victor 1715
10/6/45	8	3		31 Hong Kong Blues	Hoagy Carmichael...*You Came Along*	Victor 1722
4/5/47	9	5		32 How Are Things In Glocca Morra?	E.Y. Harburg/Burton Lane...*When I'm Not Near The Girl I Love*	RCA Victor 2121
11/13/48	4	21		33 Until	Bob Crosby/Jack Fulton/Hunter Kahler...*After Hour Stuff*	RCA Victor 3061
7/16/49	6	15		34 Again	Dorcas Cochran/Lionel Newman...*The Huckle-Buck*	RCA Victor 3028
8/27/49	5	21		35 The Huckle-Buck	Roy Alfred/Andy Gibson...*Again*	RCA Victor 3028
11/3/58	7	20		36 Tea For Two Cha Cha	Irving Caesar/Vincent Youmans...*My Baby Just Cares For Me* [I]	Decca 30704
				DOUGLAS, Carl		
12/7/74	❶²	18	●	1 Kung Fu Fighting	Carl Douglas...*Gamblin' Man*	20th Century 2140
				DOUGLAS, Mike		
2/5/66	6	9		1 The Men In My Little Girl's Life	Mary Candy/Eddie Deane/Gloria Shayne...*Stranger On The Shore* [S]	Epic 9876
				DOVELLS, The		
10/23/61	2²	16	⊙	1 Bristol Stomp	Dave Appell/Kal Mann...*Letters Of Love*	Parkway 827
6/15/63	3¹	14		2 You Can't Sit Down	Dee Clark/Kal Mann/Cornell Muldrow...*Wildwood Days*	Parkway 867
				DOWELL, Joe		
8/28/61	❶¹	16	⊙	1 Wooden Heart	Bert Kaempfert/Kay Twomey/Ben Weisman/Fred Wise...*Little Bo Peep*	Smash 1708
				DRAKE		
7/25/09	2⁴	24	△	1 Best I Ever Had	Aubrey Graham/Matthew Samuels	Cash Money
10/3/09	8	24		2 Forever	Dwayne Carter/Aubrey Graham/Marshall Mathers/Matthew Samuels/Kanye West	Harvey Mason
				DRAKE Featuring Kanye West, Lil Wayne & Eminem		
7/3/10	5	21		3 Find Your Love	Aubrey Graham/Kanye West	Young Money
9/4/10	6	23↑		4 Right Above It	Dwayne Carter/Aubrey Graham/Daniel Johnson	Cash Money
				LIL WAYNE Featuring Drake		
11/20/10	❶¹	14↑		5 What's My Name?	Esther Dean/Mikkel Eriksen/Tracy Hale/Tor Hermansen	SRP/Def Jam
				RIHANNA Featuring Drake		
				DRAMATICS, The		
9/25/71	9	15		1 Whatcha See Is Whatcha Get	Tony Hester...*Thankful For Your Love*	Volt 4058
4/22/72	5	13		2 In The Rain	Tony Hester...*(Gimme Some) Good Soul Music*	Volt 4075
				DRAPER, Rusty		
4/25/53	10	8		1 No Help Wanted	Bill Carlisle...*Texarkana Baby*	Mercury 70077
8/1/53	6	18	⊙	2 Gambler's Guitar	Jim Lowe...*Free Home Demonstration*	Mercury 70167
11/26/55	3²	16		3 The Shifting, Whispering Sands	V.C. Gilbert/Mary Hadler...*Time*	Mercury 70696
6/10/57	6	18		4 Freight Train	Paul James/Fred Williams...*Seven Come Eleven*	Mercury 71102
				DREAM		
12/30/00	2²	28	●	1 He Loves U Not	David Frank/Steve Kipner/Pam Sheyne	Bad Boy 79338
				DREAM ACADEMY, The		
2/22/86	7	21		1 Life In A Northern Town	Gilbert Gabriel/Nick Laird-Clowes...*Test Tape No. 3*	Warner 28841

PEAK DATE	PEAK POS	WKS CHR	GOLD	ARTIST / Song Title	Songwriter...B-side	Label & Number
				DREAMLOVERS, The		
9/18/61	10	12		1 When We Get Married	Donald Hogan...*Just Because*	Heritage 102
				DREAM WEAVERS, The		
1/21/56	7	23		1 It's Almost Tomorrow	Gene Adkinson/Wade Buff...*You've Got Me Wondering*	Decca 29683
				DRIFTERS, The		
8/17/59	2[1]	19	◉	1 There Goes My Baby	Benjamin Nelson/Lover Patterson/George Treadwell...*Oh My Love*	Atlantic 2025
10/17/60	❶[3]	18		2 Save The Last Dance For Me	Doc Pomus/Mort Shuman...*Nobody But Me*	Atlantic 2071
2/9/63	5	20		3 Up On The Roof	Gerry Goffin/Carole King...*Another Night With The Boys*	Atlantic 2162
4/27/63	9	10		4 On Broadway	Jerry Leiber/Barry Mann/Mike Stoller/Cynthia Weil...*Let The Music Play*	Atlantic 2182
8/22/64	4	14		5 Under The Boardwalk	Artie Resnick/Kenny Young...*I Don't Want To Go On Without You*	Atlantic 2237
				D.R.S.		
11/20/93	4	20	▲	1 Gangsta Lean	Tracy Carter/Chris Jackson/Milton Turner	Capitol 44958
				DRU HILL		
3/29/97	4	25	▲	1 In My Bed	Robert Brown/Daryl Simmons/Ronald Stacy...*Tell Me*	Island 854854
8/23/97	7	20	●	2 Never Make A Promise	Daryl Simmons...*In My Bed*	Island 572082
10/24/98	3[3]	20	●	3 How Deep Is Your Love	Mark Andrews/Warryn Campbell/Rick Cousin/Reggie Noble/Tamir Ruffin	Island 572424
				DRU HILL Featuring Redman		
7/24/99	❶[1]	17	●	4 Wild Wild West	Mohandas DeWese/Robert Fusari/Will Smith/Stevie Wonder...*Y'All Know* (Smith)	Overbrook 79157
				WILL SMITH featuring Dru Hill and Kool Moe Dee		
				D12		
5/15/04	6	18	○	1 My Band	Von Carlisle/DeShaun Holton/Rufus Johnson/Steven King/Marshall Mathers/Ondre Moore/Denaun Porter/Luis Resto	Shady
				DUCHIN, Eddy, and his Orchestra		
2/22/41	6	6		1 You Walk By	Ben Raleigh/Bernie Wayne...*Here's My Heart*	Columbia 35903
				DUKE, Patty		
8/14/65	8	11		1 Don't Just Stand There	Lor Crane/Bernice Ross...*Everything But Love*	United Artists 875
				DUPREE, Robbie		
7/12/80	6	23		1 Steal Away	Rick Chudacoff/Robbie Dupree...*I'm No Stranger*	Elektra 46621
				DUPREES, The		
9/22/62	7	13		1 You Belong To Me	Pee Wee King/Chilton Price/Redd Stewart...*Take Me As I Am*	Coed 569
				DURAN DURAN		
3/26/83	3[3]	23	●	1 Hungry Like The Wolf	Simon LeBon/Nick Rhodes/Andy Taylor/John Taylor/Roger Taylor	Harvest 5195
8/6/83	4	17		2 Is There Something I Should Know	Simon LeBon/Nick Rhodes/Andy Taylor/John Taylor/Roger Taylor...*Careless Memories*	Capitol 5233
12/24/83	3[3]	17		3 Union Of The Snake	Simon LeBon/Nick Rhodes/Andy Taylor/John Taylor/Roger Taylor...*Secret Oktober*	Capitol 5290
3/17/84	10	16		4 New Moon On Monday	Simon LeBon/Nick Rhodes/Andy Taylor/John Taylor/Roger Taylor...*Tiger Tiger*	Capitol 5309
6/23/84	❶[2]	21	●	5 The Reflex	Simon LeBon/Nick Rhodes/Andy Taylor/John Taylor/Roger Taylor...*New Religion*	Capitol 5345
12/15/84	2[4]	18	●	6 The Wild Boys	Simon LeBon/Nick Rhodes/Andy Taylor/John Taylor/Roger Taylor...*(I'm Looking For) Cracks In The Pavement*	Capitol 5417
7/13/85	❶[2]	17		7 A View To A Kill	John Barry/Simon LeBon/Nick Rhodes/John Taylor...*A View To A Kill* (John Barry)	Capitol 5475
1/10/87	2[1]	17		8 Notorious	Simon LeBon/Nick Rhodes/John Taylor...*Winter Marches On*	Capitol 5648
12/3/88	4	16		9 I Don't Want Your Love	Simon LeBon/Nick Rhodes/John Taylor	Capitol 44237
2/20/93	3[3]	22	●	10 Ordinary World	Warren Cuccurullo/Simon LeBon/Nick Rhodes/John Taylor...*Save A Prayer (live)*	Capitol 44908
6/19/93	7	25		11 Come Undone	Warren Cuccurullo/Simon LeBon/Nick Rhodes/John Taylor...*Time For Temptation*	Capitol 44918
				DYLAN, Bob		
9/4/65	2[2]	12		1 Like A Rolling Stone	Bob Dylan...*Gates Of Eden*	Columbia 43346
11/6/65	7	9		2 Positively 4th Street	Bob Dylan...*From A Buick 6*	Columbia 43389
5/21/66	2[1]	10		3 Rainy Day Women #12 & 35	Bob Dylan...*Pledging My Time*	Columbia 43592
9/6/69	7	14		4 Lay Lady Lay	Bob Dylan...*Peggy Day*	Columbia 44926
				DYSON, Ronnie		
8/29/70	8	14		1 (If You Let Me Make Love To You Then) Why Can't I Touch You?	Charles Courtney/Peter Link...*Girl Don't Come*	Columbia 45110

E

PEAK DATE	PEAK POS	WKS CHR	GOLD	ARTIST / Song Title	Songwriter...B-side	Label & Number
				EAGLES		
11/18/72	9	13		1 Witchy Woman	Don Henley/Bernie Leadon...*Earlybird*	Asylum 11008
3/1/75	❶[1]	19		2 Best Of My Love	Glenn Frey/Don Henley/J.D. Souther...*Ol' '55*	Asylum 45218
8/2/75	❶[1]	17		3 One Of These Nights	Glenn Frey/Don Henley...*Visions*	Asylum 45257
11/8/75	2[2]	14		4 Lyin' Eyes	Glenn Frey/Don Henley...*Too Many Hands*	Asylum 45279
3/13/76	4	23		5 Take It To The Limit	Don Henley/Randy Meisner...*After The Thrill Is Gone*	Asylum 45293
2/26/77	❶[1]	15	●	6 New Kid In Town	Glenn Frey/Don Henley/J.D. Souther...*Victim Of Love*	Asylum 45373
5/7/77	❶[1]	19	●	7 Hotel California	Don Felder/Glenn Frey/Don Henley...*Pretty Maids All In A Row*	Asylum 45386
11/10/79	❶[1]	15	●	8 Heartache Tonight	Glenn Frey/Don Henley/Bob Seger/J.D. Souther...*Teenage Jail*	Asylum 46545
2/2/80	8	15		9 The Long Run	Glenn Frey/Don Henley...*The Disco Strangler*	Asylum 46569
4/19/80	8	16		10 I Can't Tell You Why	Glenn Frey/Don Henley/Timothy B. Schmit...*The Greeks Don't Want No Freaks*	Asylum 46608
				EARTH, WIND & FIRE		
5/24/75	❶[1]	20	●	1 Shining Star	Philip Bailey/Maurice White...*Yearnin', Learnin'*	Columbia 10090
2/7/76	5	17	●	2 Sing A Song	Albert McKay/Maurice White	Columbia 10251
9/16/78	9	13	●	3 Got To Get You Into My Life	John Lennon/Paul McCartney...*I'll Write A Song For You*	Columbia 10796
2/10/79	8	17	●	4 September	Albert McKay/Maurice White/Allee Willis...*Love's Holiday*	ARC 10854
7/14/79	6	16	●	5 Boogie Wonderland	Jon Lind/Allee Willis	ARC 10956
				EARTH, WIND & FIRE with The Emotions		
9/15/79	2[2]	17	●	6 After The Love Has Gone	Bill Champlin/David Foster/Jay Graydon...*Rock That!*	ARC 11033
12/19/81	3[5]	24	●	7 Let's Groove	Wayne Vaughn/Maurice White	ARC 02536

PEAK DATE	PEAK POS	WKS CHR	GOLD	ARTIST / Song Title	Songwriter...B-side	Label & Number
				EASTON, Sheena		
5/2/81	❶²	21	●	1 Morning Train (Nine To Five)	Florrie Palmer...*Calm Before The Storm*	EMI America 8071
10/17/81	4	25		2 For Your Eyes Only	Bill Conti/Mike Leeson	Liberty 1418
3/26/83	6	18		3 We've Got Tonight	Bob Seger...*You Are So Beautiful* (Rogers)	Liberty 1492
				KENNY ROGERS and SHEENA EASTON		
10/29/83	9	22		4 Telefone (Long Distance Love Affair)	Greg Mathieson/Trevor Veitch...*Wish You Were Here Tonight*	EMI America 8172
11/24/84	7	25		5 Strut	Charlie Dore/Julian Littman...*Letters From The Road*	EMI America 8227
3/2/85	9	17		6 Sugar Walls	Prince...*Straight Talking*	EMI America 8253
3/4/89	2¹	25		7 The Lover In Me	Babyface/L.A. Reid/Daryl Simmons	MCA 53416
				ECKSTINE, Billy		
10/27/45	8	2		1 A Cottage For Sale	Larry Conley/Willard Robison...*(I Love The) Rhythm In A Riff*	National 9014
5/25/46	10	10		2 Prisoner Of Love	Russ Columbo/Clarence Gaskill/Leo Robin...*All I Sing Is Blues*	National 9017
6/3/50	6	19	⊙	3 My Foolish Heart	Ned Washington/Victor Young...*(We've Got A) Sure Thing*	MGM 10623
7/15/50	7	15		4 I Wanna Be Loved	John Green/Edward Heyman/Billy Rose...*Stardust*	MGM 10716
3/10/51	10	8		5 If	Stanley Damerell/Tolchard Evans/Robert Hargreaves...*When You Return*	MGM 10896
5/19/51	6	20	⊙	6 I Apologize	Al Goodhart/Al Hoffman/Ed Nelson...*Bring Back The Thrill*	MGM 10903
				EDDY, Duane		
7/28/58	6	14	⊙	1 Rebel-'Rouser	Duane Eddy/Lee Hazlewood...*Stalkin'* [I]	Jamie 1104
7/27/59	9	15	⊙	2 Forty Miles Of Bad Road	Al Casey/Duane Eddy...*The Quiet Three* [I]	Jamie 1126
7/4/60	4	15	⊙	3 Because They're Young	Don Costa/Wally Gold/Aaron Schroeder...*Rebel Walk* [I]	Jamie 1156
				EDEN'S CRUSH		
3/31/01	8	14	●	1 Get Over Yourself	Matthew Gerrard/John Keller/Michele Vice-Maslin	143/London 35063
				EDISON LIGHTHOUSE		
3/28/70	5	13	●	1 Love Grows (Where My Rosemary Goes)	Tony MacAulay/Barry Mason...*Every Lonely Day*	Bell 858
				EDMONDS, Kevon		
12/18/99	10	20	●	1 24/7	Angelo Ray/David Scott/Anthony Smith...*I Want You More*	RCA 65924
				EDMUNDS, Dave		
2/13/71	4	12		1 I Hear You Knocking	Dave Bartholomew/Pearl King...*Black Bill*	MAM 3601
				EDWARD BEAR		
3/3/73	3²	18	●	1 Last Song	Larry Evoy...*Best Friend*	Capitol 3452
				EDWARDS, Jonathan		
1/15/72	4	16	●	1 Sunshine	Jonathan Edwards...*Emma*	Capricorn 8021
				EDWARDS, Tommy		
9/29/58	❶⁶	22	⊙	1 It's All In The Game	Charles Dawes/Carl Sigman...*Please Love Me Forever*	MGM 12688
				E-40		
5/27/06	7	28		1 Snap Yo Fingers	Sean Joseph/Jonathan Smith/Earl Stevens	BME/TVT 2841
				LIL JON Feat. E-40 & Sean Paul of YoungBloodZ		
				EGAN, Walter		
8/26/78	8	22	●	1 Magnet And Steel	Walter Egan...*Tunnel O' Love*	Columbia 10719
				EIFFEL 65		
1/29/00	6	20		1 Blue (Da Ba Dee)	Massimo Gabutti/Maurizio Lobina/Gianfranco Randone	Republic 156638
				ELECTRIC LIGHT ORCHESTRA		
3/15/75	9	16		1 Can't Get It Out Of My Head	Jeff Lynne...*Illusions In G Major*	United Artists 573
2/14/76	10	17		2 Evil Woman	Jeff Lynne...*10538 Overture*	United Artists/Jet 729
9/24/77	7	23	●	3 Telephone Line	Jeff Lynne...*Poorboy (The Greenwood)*	United Artists/Jet 1000
7/21/79	8	15		4 Shine A Little Love	Jeff Lynne...*Jungle*	Jet 5057
9/8/79	4	15		5 Don't Bring Me Down	Jeff Lynne...*Dreaming Of 4000*	Jet 5060
10/11/80	8	17		6 Xanadu	Jeff Lynne...*Whenever You're Away From Me* (Newton-John & Gene Kelly)	MCA 41285
				OLIVIA NEWTON-JOHN/ELECTRIC LIGHT ORCHESTRA		
10/3/81	10	19		7 Hold On Tight	Jeff Lynne...*When Time Stood Still*	Jet 02408
				ELO		
				ELEGANTS, The		
8/25/58	❶¹	19	⊙	1 Little Star	Vito Picone/Arthur Venosa...*Getting Dizzy*	Apt 25005
				ELLIMAN, Yvonne		
5/13/78	❶¹	22	●	1 If I Can't Have You	Barry Gibb/Maurice Gibb/Robin Gibb...*Good Sign*	RSO 884
				ELLINGTON, Duke		
7/3/43	8	2		1 Don't Get Around Much Anymore (Never No Lament)	Duke Ellington/Bob Russell...*Cotton Tail* [I]	Victor 26610
2/19/44	6	7		2 Do Nothin' Till You Hear From Me	Duke Ellington/Bob Russell...*Chlo-E (Song of the Swamp)* [I]	Victor 1547
3/17/45	6	12		3 I'm Beginning To See The Light	Duke Ellington/Don George/Johnny Hodges/Harry James ...*Don't You Know I Care (Or Don't You Care to Know)*	Victor 1618
				ELLIOTT, Missy "Misdemeanor"		
8/9/97	6	21	▲	1 Not Tonight	Robert Bell/Ronald Bell/George Brown/Missy Elliott/Shawntae Harris/Kim Jones/Lisa Lopes/Angie Martinez/ Meekaaeel Muhammed/Claydes Smith/James Taylor/Dennis Thomas/Earl Toon	Undeas 98019
				LIL' KIM Featuring Da Brat, Left Eye, Missy "Misdemeanor" Elliott and Angie Martinez		
8/1/98	5	23	●	2 Make It Hot	Missy Elliott	Gold Mind 64110
				NICOLE Featuring Missy "Misdemeanor" Elliott and Mocha		
1/9/99	7	20	●	3 Trippin'	Missy Elliott/Tim Mosley/Darryl Pearson	Bad Boy 79185
				TOTAL (Feat. Missy Elliott)		
1/8/00	5	21	▲	4 Hot Boyz	Missy Elliott/Tim Mosley...*U Can't Resist* (w/Juvenile & B.G.)	Gold Mind 64029
				MISSY "MISDEMEANOR" ELLIOTT (Featuring Nas, Eve & Q-Tip)		
6/30/01	7	24		5 Get Ur Freak On	Missy Elliott/Tim Mosley	Gold Mind 67190
11/16/02	2¹⁰	25		6 Work It	Missy Elliott/Tim Mosley...*P***sycat*	Elektra 67340
3/8/03	8	20		7 Gossip Folks	Bill Bloom/Christopher Bridges/Missy Elliott/Tim Mosley/Frankie Smith	Elektra 67356
				MISSY ELLIOTT Featuring Ludacris		

PEAK DATE	PEAK POS	WKS CHR	GOLD	ARTIST / Song Title	Songwriter...B-side	Label & Number
				ELLIOTT, Missy (cont'd)		
1/8/05	2[7]	39	△	8 1,2 Step CIARA featuring Missy Elliott	Phalon Alexander/Missy Elliott/Ciara Harris	LaFace 66687
9/17/05	3[1]	28	○	9 Lose Control MISSY ELLIOTT Featuring Ciara & Fat Man Scoop	Juan Atkins/Richard Davis/Missy Elliott/Isaac Freeman/Ciara Harris/Curtis Hudson...*On & On*	Atlantic 93787
9/29/07	7	23		10 Let It Go KEYSHIA COLE Featuring Missy Elliott & Lil' Kim	Keyshia Cole/Missy Elliott/Kim Jones/James Mtume	Imani 009976
				ELLIS, Shirley		
1/11/64	8	14		1 The Nitty Gritty	Lincoln Chase...*Give Me A List*	Congress 202
1/30/65	3[2]	14		2 The Name Game	Lincoln Chase/Shirley Ellis...*Whisper To Me Wind* [N]	Congress 230
4/24/65	8	9		3 The Clapping Song (Clap Pat Clap Slap)	Lincoln Chase...*This Is Beautiful* [N]	Congress 234
				EMF		
7/20/91	❶[1]	23	●	1 Unbelievable	James Atkins/Derran Brownson/Mark Decloedt/Ian Dench/Zac Foley	EMI 50350
				EMINEM		
6/24/00	4	19		1 The Real Slim Shady	Thomas Coster/Mike Elizondo/Marshall Mathers/Andre Young	Aftermath 497334
6/29/02	2[5]	20	○	2 Without Me	Jeff Bass/Anne Dudley/Trevor Horn/Marshall Mathers	Aftermath
9/21/02	4	20		3 Cleanin' Out My Closet	Jeff Bass/Marshall Mathers	Aftermath
11/9/02	❶[12]	23	○	4 Lose Yourself	Jeff Bass/Marshall Mathers/Luis Resto	Shady 497815
10/30/04	6	19	○	5 Just Lose It	Mark Batson/Mike Elizondo/Marshall Mathers/Che Pope/Andre Young	Shady 003684
12/17/05	8	17		6 When I'm Gone	Marshall Mathers/Luis Resto	Shady 006085
2/25/06	6	21		7 Shake That EMINEM Featuring Nate Dogg	Nathan Hale/Steven King/Marshall Mathers/Luis Resto	Shady
11/4/06	2[5]	30	△[2]	8 Smack That AKON Featuring Eminem	Marshall Mathers/Luis Resto/Mike Strange/Aliaune Thiam	SRC 007877
2/21/09	❶[1]	17		9 Crack A Bottle EMINEM, DR. DRE & 50 CENT	Curtis Jackson/Trevor Lawrence/Marshall Mathers/Dawaun Parker/Jean Renard/Andre Young	Web
5/2/09	9	10		10 We Made You	Mark Batson/Walter Egan/Trevor Lawrence/Marshall Mathers/Dawaun Parker/Andre Young	Web
10/3/09	8	24		11 Forever DRAKE Featuring Kanye West, Lil Wayne & Eminem	Dwayne Carter/Aubrey Graham/Marshall Mathers/Matthew Samuels/Kanye West	Harvey Mason
5/22/10	❶[1]	25		12 Not Afraid	Matthew Burnett/Jordan Evans/Marshall Mathers/Luis Resto/Matthew Samuels	Web
7/31/10	❶[7]	29		13 Love The Way You Lie EMINEM Featuring Rihanna	Alexander Grant/Holly Hafermann/Marshall Mathers	Web
				EMOTIONS, The		
8/20/77	❶[5]	23	▲	1 Best Of My Love	Albert McKay/Maurice White...*A Feeling Is*	Columbia 10544
7/14/79	6	16	●	2 Boogie Wonderland EARTH, WIND & FIRE with The Emotions	Jon Lind/Allee Willis	ARC 10956
				ENGLAND DAN & JOHN FORD COLEY		
9/25/76	2[2]	24	●	1 I'd Really Love To See You Tonight	Parker McGee...*It's Not The Same*	Big Tree 16069
12/11/76	10	16		2 Nights Are Forever Without You	Parker McGee...*Showboat Gambler*	Big Tree 16079
4/15/78	9	14		3 We'll Never Have To Say Goodbye Again	Jeffrey Comanor...*Calling For You Again*	Big Tree 16110
5/26/79	10	18		4 Love Is The Answer	Todd Rundgren...*Running After You*	Big Tree 16131
				ENIGMA		
4/6/91	5	18	●	1 Sadeness Part 1	Michael Cretu [F]	Charisma 98864
5/7/94	4	26	●	2 Return To Innocence	Michael Cretu	Charisma 38423
				EN VOGUE		
7/21/90	2[1]	25	▲	1 Hold On	Terry Ellis/Denzil Foster/Cindy Herron/Maxine Jones/Thomas McElroy/Dawn Robinson...*Luv Lines*	Atlantic 87984
5/16/92	2[3]	30	●	2 My Lovin' (You're Never Gonna Get It)	Denzil Foster/Thomas McElroy...*Part Of Me*	EastWest 98586
9/12/92	6	24	●	3 Giving Him Something He Can Feel	Curtis Mayfield...*My Lovin' (You're Never Gonna Get It)*	EastWest 98560
10/31/92	8	20	●	4 Free Your Mind	Denzil Foster/Thomas McElroy...*Just Can't Stay Away*	EastWest 98487
2/26/94	3[3]	29	▲	5 Whatta Man SALT 'N' PEPA with En Vogue	Herby Azor/David Crawford	Next Plateau 857390
1/18/97	2[4]	35	▲	6 Don't Let Go (Love)	Patrick Brown/Marqueze Etheridge/Andrea Martin/Ivan Matias/Ray Murray/Rico Wade...*Hold On*	EastWest 64231
				ENYA		
11/10/01	10	31		1 Only Time	Enya/Nicky Ryan/Roma Ryan...*Oíche Chiun (Silent Night) / Willows On The Water*	Reprise 42420
4/24/04	2[8]	30	○	2 I Don't Wanna Know MARIO WINANS Featuring P. Diddy & Enya	Enya/Chauncey Hawkins/Michael Jones/Nicky Ryan/Roma Ryan/Erick Sermon/Parrish Smith/Mario Winans	Bad Boy
				ERIC B. & RAKIM		
8/26/89	9	18		1 Friends JODY WATLEY (With Eric B. & Rakim)	Eric Barrier/Andre Cymone/William Griffin/Jody Watley...*Private Life* (Watley)	MCA 53660
				ESCAPE CLUB, The		
11/12/88	❶[1]	27	●	1 Wild, Wild West	Johnnie Christo/John Holliday/Trevor Steel/Milan Zekavica...*We Can Run*	Atlantic 89048
8/10/91	8	25	●	2 I'll Be There	Johnnie Christo/John Holliday/Trevor Steel/Milan Zekavica...*Lately*	Atlantic 87683
				ESSEX, The		
7/6/63	❶[2]	13	☉	1 Easier Said Than Done	Larry Huff/William Linton...*Are You Going My Way*	Roulette 4494
				ESSEX, David		
3/9/74	5	25	●	1 Rock On	David Essex...*On And On*	Columbia 45940
				ESTEFAN, Gloria / Miami Sound Machine		
				MIAMI SOUND MACHINE:		
2/8/86	10	27	●	1 Conga	Enrique Garcia...*Mucho Money*	Epic 05457
5/10/86	8	19	●	2 Bad Boy	Larry Dermer/Joe Galdo/Rafael Vigil...*Surrender Paradise*	Epic 05805
9/20/86	5	24		3 Words Get In The Way	Gloria Estefan...*Movies*	Epic 06120
				GLORIA ESTEFAN and MIAMI SOUND MACHINE:		
8/1/87	5	17		4 Rhythm Is Gonna Get You	Gloria Estefan/Enrique Garcia...*Give It Up*	Epic 07059
3/5/88	6	23		5 Can't Stay Away From You	Gloria Estefan...*Let It Loose*	Epic 07641
5/14/88	❶[2]	23	●	6 Anything For You	Gloria Estefan...*(Spanish version)*	Epic 07759
8/20/88	3[1]	19		7 1-2-3	Gloria Estefan/Enrique Garcia	Epic 07921

PEAK DATE	PEAK POS	WKS CHR	GOLD	ARTIST / Song Title	Songwriter...B-side	Label & Number
				GLORIA ESTEFAN:		
9/16/89	❶¹	18	●	8 Don't Wanna Lose You	Gloria Estefan...*Si Voy A Perderte*	Epic 68959
3/3/90	6	21		9 Here We Are	Gloria Estefan...*1-2-3 (live)*	Epic 73084
3/30/91	❶²	19		10 Coming Out Of The Dark	Emilio Estefan/Gloria Estefan/Jon Secada...*(Spanish version)*	Epic 73666
10/16/99	2¹	20	●	11 Music Of My Heart	Diane Warren	Miramax/Epic 79245
				*NSYNC and GLORIA ESTEFAN		
				ESTELLE		
9/27/08	9	30	△²	1 American Boy	William Adams/Keith Harris/Josh Lopez/Caleb Spier/Estelle Swaray	Home School 422972
				ESTELLE Featuring Kanye West		
				ESTUS, Deon		
4/29/89	5	16		1 Heaven Help Me	Deon Estus/George Michael...*It's A Party*	Mika 871538
				DEON ESTUS (with George Michael)		
				ETHERIDGE, Melissa		
1/21/95	8	40		1 I'm The Only One	Melissa Etheridge...*Maggie May (live)*	Island 854068
				EUROPE		
3/28/87	8	18		1 The Final Countdown	Joey Tempest...*On Broken Wings*	Epic 06416
10/10/87	3²	19		2 Carrie	Mic Michaeli/Joey Tempest...*Love Chaser*	Epic 07282
				EURYTHMICS		
9/3/83	❶¹	26	●	1 Sweet Dreams (Are Made of This)	Annie Lennox/David A. Stewart...*I Could Give You (A Mirror)*	RCA 13533
3/31/84	4	20		2 Here Comes The Rain Again	Annie Lennox/David A. Stewart...*Paint A Rumour*	RCA 13725
7/13/85	5	19		3 Would I Lie To You?	Annie Lennox/David A. Stewart...*Here Comes That Sinking Feeling*	RCA 14078
				EVANESCENCE		
6/7/03	5	32	△	1 Bring Me To Life	David Hodges/Amy Lee/Ben Moody	Wind-Up
4/10/04	7	32	○	2 My Immortal	David Hodges/Amy Lee/Ben Moody	Wind-Up
9/9/06	10	22	△	3 Call Me When You're Sober	Terry Balsamo/Amy Lee	Wind-Up
				EVANS, Faith		
6/14/97	❶¹¹	33	▲³	1 I'll Be Missing You	Sean Combs/Faith Evans/Sting...*We'll Always Love Big Poppa* (The Lox) / *Cry On* (112)	Bad Boy 79097
				PUFF DADDY & FAITH EVANS (Featuring 112)		
12/12/98	7	20	●	2 Love Like This	Schon Crawford/Bernard Edwards/Clarence Emery/Faith Evans/Nile Rodgers	Bad Boy 79117
3/20/99	2³	28	▲	3 Heartbreak Hotel	Ken Karlin/Tamara Savage/Carsten Schack...*It's Not Right But It's Okay*	Arista 13619
				WHITNEY HOUSTON (Feat. Faith Evans & Kelly Price)		
4/3/99	9	19		4 All Night Long	Sean Combs/Schon Crawford/Faith Evans/Todd Gaither/Ron Lawrence/Bert Reed/Todd Russaw/Galen Underwood	Bad Boy 79203
				FAITH EVANS (feat. Puff Daddy)	...*Life Will Pass You By*	
				EVANS, Paul		
11/9/59	9	18		1 (Seven Little Girls) Sitting In The Back Seat	Bob Hilliard/Lee Pockriss...*Worshipping An Idol* [N]	Guaranteed 200
6/13/60	10	14		2 Happy-Go-Lucky-Me	Al Byron/Paul Evans...*Fish In The Ocean (Bubbly Bum Bum)* [N]	Guaranteed 208
				EVE		
1/8/00	5	21	▲	1 Hot Boyz	Missy Elliott/Tim Mosley...*U Can't Resist* (w/*Juvenile* & *B.G.*)	Gold Mind 64029
				MISSY "MISDEMEANOR" ELLIOTT (Featuring Nas, Eve & Q-Tip)		
8/18/01	2¹	33		2 Let Me Blow Ya Mind	Mike Elizondo/Eve Jeffers/Scott Storch/Andre Young...*That's What It Is* (w/*Styles* of The Lox)	Ruff Ryders 497562
				EVE Featuring Gwen Stefani		
9/14/02	2⁴	22		3 Gangsta Lovin'	Seven Aurelius/Eve Jeffers/Irving Lorenzo	Ruff Ryders 497817
				EVE Feat. Alicia Keys		
3/5/05	7	27	○	4 Rich Girl	Mark Batson/Jerry Bock/Kara DioGuardi/Mike Elizondo/Sheldon Harnick/Eve Jeffers/Chantal Keviazuk/Gwen Stefani/Andre Young	Interscope 003978
				GWEN STEFANI featuring Eve		
				EVERETT, Betty		
4/11/64	6	13		1 The Shoop Shoop Song (It's In His Kiss)	Rudy Clark...*Hands Off*	Vee-Jay 585
11/7/64	5	13		2 Let It Be Me	Gilbert Becaud/Mann Curtis...*Ain't That Loving You Baby*	Vee-Jay 613
				BETTY EVERETT & JERRY BUTLER		
				EVERLY BROTHERS, The		
6/17/57	2⁴	27	⊙	1 Bye Bye Love	Boudleaux Bryant/Felice Bryant...*I Wonder If I Care As Much*	Cadence 1315
10/14/57	❶⁴	26	⊙	2 Wake Up Little Susie	Boudleaux Bryant/Felice Bryant...*Maybe Tomorrow*	Cadence 1337
5/12/58	❶⁵	17	⊙	3 All I Have To Do Is Dream	Boudleaux Bryant...*Claudette*	Cadence 1348
8/25/58	❶¹	18	⊙	4 Bird Dog	Boudleaux Bryant...*Devoted To You*	Cadence 1350
9/22/58	10	14		5 Devoted To You	Boudleaux Bryant...*Bird Dog*	Cadence 1350
12/15/58	2¹	15		6 Problems	Boudleaux Bryant/Felice Bryant...*Love Of My Life*	Cadence 1355
9/21/59	4	16		7 ('Til) I Kissed You	Don Everly...*Oh, What A Feeling*	Cadence 1369
2/22/60	7	15		8 Let It Be Me	Gilbert Becaud/Mann Curtis/Pierre DeLanoe...*Since You Broke My Heart*	Cadence 1376
5/23/60	❶⁵	17	⊙	9 Cathy's Clown	Don Everly/Phil Everly...*Always It's You*	Warner 5151
7/18/60	8	13		10 When Will I Be Loved	Phil Everly...*Be Bop A-Lula*	Cadence 1380
10/10/60	7	12		11 So Sad (To Watch Good Love Go Bad)	Don Everly...*Lucille*	Warner 5163
3/20/61	8	12		12 Ebony Eyes	John D. Loudermilk...*Walk Right Back*	Warner 5199
3/27/61	7	13	⊙	13 Walk Right Back	Sonny Curtis...*Ebony Eyes*	Warner 5199
3/3/62	6	13		14 Crying In The Rain	Howard Greenfield/Carole King...*I'm Not Angry*	Warner 5250
6/23/62	9	11		15 That's Old Fashioned (That's The Way Love Should Be)	Bernie Baum/Bill Giant/Florence Kaye...*How Can I Meet Her?*	Warner 5273
				EVERY MOTHERS' SON		
7/8/67	6	15		1 Come On Down To My Boat	Wes Farrell/Jerry Goldstein...*I Believe In You*	MGM 13733
				EVERYTHING BUT THE GIRL		
2/17/96	2¹	55	●	1 Missing	Tracey Thorn/Ben Watt	Atlantic 87124
				EXCITERS, The		
1/19/63	4	13		1 Tell Him	Bert Russell...*Hard Way To Go*	United Artists 544
				EXILE		
9/30/78	❶⁴	23	●	1 Kiss You All Over	Mike Chapman/Nicky Chinn...*Don't Do It*	Warner/Curb 8589

PEAK DATE	PEAK POS	WKS CHR	GOLD	ARTIST / Song Title	Songwriter...B-side	Label & Number
				EXPOSE		
4/4/87	5	19		1 Come Go With Me	Lewis Martinee...*December*	Arista 9555
7/18/87	5	17		2 Point Of No Return	Lewis Martinee...*Extra Extra*	Arista 9579
10/31/87	7	22		3 Let Me Be The One	Lewis Martinee...*Love Is Our Destiny*	Arista 9617
2/20/88	❶[1]	20		4 Seasons Change	Lewis Martinee...*December*	Arista 9640
7/15/89	8	15	●	5 What You Don't Know	Lewis Martinee...*Walk Along With Me*	Arista 9836
10/21/89	10	20		6 When I Looked At Him	Lewis Martinee	Arista 9868
2/17/90	9	15		7 Tell Me Why	Lewis Martinee...*Let Me Down Easy*	Arista 9916
7/17/93	8	29	●	8 I'll Never Get Over You (Getting Over Me)	Diane Warren...*Give Me All Your Love*	Arista 12518
				EXTREME		
6/8/91	❶[1]	24	●	1 More Than Words	Nuno Bettencourt/Gary Cherone	A&M 1552
10/19/91	4	20		2 Hole Hearted	Nuno Bettencourt/Gary Cherone...*Suzi (Wants Her All Day What?)*	A&M 1564

F

PEAK DATE	PEAK POS	WKS CHR	GOLD	ARTIST / Song Title	Songwriter...B-side	Label & Number
				FABARES, Shelley		
4/7/62	❶[2]	15	☉	1 Johnny Angel	Lyn Duddy/Lee Pockriss...*Where's It Gonna Get Me?*	Colpix 621
				FABIAN		
5/11/59	9	13		1 Turn Me Loose	Doc Pomus/Mort Shuman...*Stop Thief!*	Chancellor 1033
7/20/59	3[2]	13		2 Tiger	Ollie Jones...*Mighty Cold (To A Warm Warm Heart)*	Chancellor 1037
12/28/59	9	15		3 Hound Dog Man	Doc Pomus/Mort Shuman...*This Friendly World*	Chancellor 1044
				FABOLOUS		
5/31/03	4	23		1 Can't Let You Go	John Jackson/Cynthia Loving/Justin Smith...*Damn*	Desert Storm 67428
				FABOLOUS featuring Mike Shorey & Lil' Mo		
9/20/03	4	26		2 Into You	Ken Ifill/John Jackson/Tim Kelly/Ronald LaPread/Lionel Richie/Bob Robinson/Tamia Washington	Desert Storm 67452
				FABOLOUS Featuring Ashanti or Tamia		
11/27/04	10	20		3 Breathe	Rick Davies/John Jackson/Justin Smith	Desert Storm 67616
8/25/07	8	21		4 Make Me Better	John Jackson/Tim Mosley/Shaffer Smith	Desert Storm 009027
				FABOLOUS Featuring Ne-Yo		
3/13/10	9	29	△	5 Say Aah	Ronald Ferebee/John Jackson/Tremaine Neverson/Tony Scales/Nathan Walker...*I Invented Sex*	Song Book 523577
				TREY SONGZ Featuring Fabolous		
				FABRIC, Bent, and His Piano		
9/29/62	7	18		1 Alley Cat	Frank Bjorn...*Markin' Time* [I]	Atco 6226
				FABULOUS THUNDERBIRDS, The		
7/12/86	10	19		1 Tuff Enuff	Kim Wilson...*Look At That, Look At That*	CBS Associated 05838
				FAITH, Percy, and his Orchestra		
10/21/50	7	11		1 All My Love ("Bolero")	Henri Contet/Paul Durand/Mitchell Parish...*This Is The Time*	Columbia 38918
5/26/51	10	9		2 On Top Of Old Smoky	Pete Seeger...*The Syncopated Clock*	Columbia 39328
				PERCY FAITH and his Orchestra and Chorus with BURL IVES		
7/5/52	❶[1]	22		3 Delicado	Waldyr Azevedo/Jack Lawrence...*Festival* [I]	Columbia 39708
5/16/53	❶[10]	24	☉	4 The Song From Moulin Rouge (Where Is Your Heart)	Georges Auric/William Engvick...*Midsummer Vigil (Swedish Rhapsody)*	Columbia 39944
2/22/60	❶[9]	21	●	5 The Theme From "A Summer Place"	Max Steiner...*Go-Go-Po-Go* [I]	Columbia 41490
				FAITH NO MORE		
9/8/90	9	21	●	1 Epic	Roddy Bottum/Mike Gordin/Billy Gould/Jim Martin/Michael Patton...*Edge Of The World*	Slash 19813
				FALCO		
3/29/86	❶[3]	17		1 Rock Me Amadeus	Ferdi Bolland/Rob Bolland/Johann Holzel	A&M 2821
				FALL OUT BOY		
9/17/05	8	42	△[2]	1 Sugar, We're Goin' Down	Andy Hurley/Patrick Stump/Joe Trohman/Pete Wentz	Island
1/14/06	9	31	△	2 Dance, Dance	Andy Hurley/Patrick Stump/Joe Trohman/Pete Wentz	Island
2/3/07	2[2]	20	△	3 This Ain't A Scene, It's An Arms Race	Andy Hurley/Patrick Stump/Joe Trohman/Pete Wentz	Fueled By Ramen
3/31/07	4	24	△	4 Cupid's Chokehold	Rick Davies/Roger Hodgson	Decaydance
				GYM CLASS HEROES Featuring Patrick Stump (of Fall Out Boy)		
				FALTERMEYER, Harold		
6/1/85	3[3]	19		1 Axel F	Harold Faltermeyer...*Shoot Out* [I]	MCA 52536
				FAME, Georgie		
4/13/68	7	14		1 The Ballad Of Bonnie And Clyde	Peter Callander/Mitch Murray...*Beware Of The Dog*	Epic 10283
				FANTASIA		
7/10/04	❶[1]	10		1 I Believe	Louis Biancaniello/Tamyra Gray/Sam Watters...*Chain Of Fools / Summertime*	J Records 63091
				FANTASTIC JOHNNY C, The		
12/23/67	7	18		1 Boogaloo Down Broadway	Jesse James...*Look What Love Can Make You Do*	Phil-L.A. of Soul 305
				FAR*EAST MOVEMENT		
10/30/10	❶[3]	24↑		1 Like A G6	Jae Won Choung/Dhar Holowell/Kevin Nishimura/James Roh/David Singer-Vine	CherryTree
				FAR*EAST MOVEMENT Featuring Cataracs & Dev		
				FARGO, Donna		
1/6/73	5	20	●	1 Funny Face	Donna Fargo...*How Close You Came (To Being Gone)*	Dot 17429
				FARRIS, Dionne		
5/6/95	4	38		1 I Know	Milton Davis/William Duvall...*Human*	Columbia 77750
				FASTBALL		
6/20/98	5	39		1 The Way	Tony Scalzo	Hollywood 5298

PEAK DATE	PEAK POS	WKS CHR	GOLD	ARTIST / Song Title	Songwriter...B-side	Label & Number
				FAT JOE		
4/6/02	2^7	28		1 What's Luv? .....Jeffrey Atkins/Joe Cartagena/Irving Lorenzo/Andre Parker/Christopher Rios...*Definition Of A Don* (w/Remy Ma)		Terror Squad 85233
				FAT JOE Featuring Ashanti		
7/30/05	9	20	○	2 Get It Poppin'	Joe Cartagena/Scott Storch	Terror Squad 93794
				FAT JOE (Feat. Nelly)		
				FEIST		
10/13/07	8	15		1 1234	Leslie Feist/Sally Seltmann	Cherrytree
				FELICIANO, Jose		
8/31/68	3^3	12		1 Light My Fire .....John Densmore/Robby Krieger/Ray Manzarek/Jim Morrison...*California Dreamin'*		RCA Victor 9550
				FENDER, Freddy		
5/31/75	❶^1	21	●	1 Before The Next Teardrop Falls	Vivian Keith/Ben Peters...*Waiting For Your Love*	ABC/Dot 17540
9/27/75	8	19	●	2 Wasted Days And Wasted Nights	Wayne Duncan/Freddy Fender...*I Love My Rancho Grande*	ABC/Dot 17558
				FENDERMEN, The		
7/11/60	5	18		1 Mule Skinner Blues	Jimmie Rodgers/George Vaughn...*Torture*	Soma 1137
				FERGIE		
8/19/06	❶^3	21	△	1 London Bridge	Stacy Ferguson/Sean Garrett/Mike Hartnett/Jamal Jones	will.i.am 007809
1/13/07	2^1	27	△^{2}	2 Fergalicious .....William Adams/Dania Birks/Juana Burns/Stacy Ferguson/Juanita Lee/Kim Nazel/Derrick Rahming/Fatimah Shaheed		will.i.am
				FERGIE Featuring will.i.am		
3/24/07	❶^2	29	△^{2}	3 Glamorous .....William Adams/Christopher Bridges/Stacy Ferguson/Jamal Jones/Elvis Williams		will.i.am
				FERGIE Featuring Ludacris		
9/8/07	❶^1	48	△^{2}	4 Big Girls Don't Cry	Stacy Ferguson/Tobias Gad	will.i.am
12/22/07	5	25	△	5 Clumsy	William Adams/Stacy Ferguson/Bobby Troup	will.i.am
				FERGUSON, Jay		
4/1/78	9	21		1 Thunder Island	Jay Ferguson...*Magic Moment*	Asylum 45444
				FERRANTE & TEICHER		
9/5/60	10	20		1 Theme From The Apartment	Charles Williams...*Lonely Room* [I]	United Artists 231
1/23/61	2^1	21		2 Exodus	Ernest Gold...*Twilight* [I]	United Artists 274
12/11/61	8	13		3 Tonight	Leonard Bernstein/Stephen Sondheim...*Dream Of Love* [I]	United Artists 373
1/17/70	10	15		4 Midnight Cowboy	John Barry...*Rock-A-Bye Baby* [I]	United Artists 50554
				FIASCO, Lupe		
3/22/08	10	20	△	1 Superstar	Wasalu Jaco/Rudy Lopez...*Dumb It Down*	Atlantic 350844
				LUPE FIASCO Featuring Matthew Santos		
				FIELD MOB		
7/15/06	10	21		1 So What .....Phalon Alexander/Darion Crawford/Ciara Harris/Shawn Johnson/Zach Wallace/Cedric Williams		DTP 006546
				FIELD MOB featuring Ciara		
				FIELDS, Ernie, Orch.		
12/14/59	4	19		1 In The Mood	Joe Garland/Andy Razaf...*Christopher Columbus* [I]	Rendezvous 110
				FIELDS, Gracie		
3/27/48	3^2	21		1 Now Is The Hour	Maewa Kaihan/Clement Scott/Dorothy Stewart...*Come Back To Sorrento*	London 110
				5TH DIMENSION, The		
7/8/67	7	12		1 Up -- Up And Away	Jimmy Webb...*Which Way To Nowhere*	Soul City 756
7/27/68	3^3	16	▲	2 Stoned Soul Picnic	Laura Nyro...*The Sailboat Song*	Soul City 766
4/12/69	❶^6	17	▲	3 Aquarius/Let The Sunshine In .....Galt MacDermot/James Rado/Gerome Ragni...*Don'tcha Hear Me Callin' To Ya*		Soul City 772
11/8/69	❶^3	15	▲	4 Wedding Bell Blues	Laura Nyro...*Lovin' Stew*	Soul City 779
12/26/70	2^2	14	▲	5 One Less Bell To Answer	Burt Bacharach/Hal David...*Feelin' Alright?*	Bell 940
6/17/72	8	16		6 (Last Night) I Didn't Get To Sleep At All	Tony Macaulay...*The River Witch*	Bell 45,195
11/25/72	10	15		7 If I Could Reach You	Randy McNeill...*Tomorrow Belongs To The Children*	Bell 45,261
				50 CENT		
3/8/03	❶^9	30	○	1 In Da Club	Mike Elizondo/Curtis Jackson/Andre Young...*Backdown*	Shady 497856
5/31/03	❶^4	23		2 21 Questions	Jimmie Cameron/Vella Cameron/Curtis Jackson/Kevin Risto...*Many Men*	Shady 080739
				50 CENT Feat. Nate Dogg		
7/12/03	2^3	24		3 Magic Stick	Michael Clervoix/Carlos Evans/Roy Hawkins/Curtis Jackson/Kim Jones/Rick Ravon	Queen Bee
				LIL' KIM (feat. 50 Cent)		
8/23/03	3^1	25	○	4 P.I.M.P.	Curtis Jackson/Brandon Parrott/Denaun Porter	Shady 000888
2/19/05	4	28	○	5 How We Do	Mike Elizondo/Curtis Jackson/Jayceon Taylor/Andre Young	Aftermath 003913
				THE GAME feat. 50 Cent		
3/5/05	❶^9	23	○	6 Candy Shop	Curtis Jackson/Scott Storch	Shady
				50 CENT Featuring Olivia		
3/26/05	3^1	29	○	7 Disco Inferno	Teraike Crawford/Curtis Jackson/Phillip Pitts	Shady 004142
4/16/05	2^5	23	○	8 Hate It Or Love It	Curtis Jackson/Andre Lyon/Jayceon Taylor/Marcello Valenzano	Aftermath
				THE GAME Featuring 50 Cent		
6/18/05	3^1	27		9 Just A Lil Bit	Curtis Jackson/Scott Storch	Shady 004726
10/1/05	6	19		10 Outta Control (Remix) .....Mark Batson/Mike Elizondo/Curtis Jackson/Albert Johnson/Kejuan Muchita/Che Pope/Andre Young		Shady 005439
				50 CENT Featuring Mobb Deep		
9/29/07	5	20		11 Ayo Technology	Nathan Hills/Curtis Jackson/Tim Mosley/Justin Timberlake	Shady 009807
				50 CENT Featuring Justin Timberlake & Timbaland		
2/21/09	❶^1	17		12 Crack A Bottle .....Curtis Jackson/Trevor Lawrence/Marshall Mathers/Dawaun Parker/Jean Renard/Andre Young		Web
				EMINEM, DR. DRE & 50 CENT		
				FINE YOUNG CANNIBALS		
4/15/89	❶^1	23	●	1 She Drives Me Crazy	Roland Gift/David Steele...*Pull The Sucker Off*	I.R.S./MCA 53483
7/8/89	❶^1	17		2 Good Thing	Roland Gift/David Steele...*Social Security*	I.R.S./MCA 53639
				FINGER ELEVEN		
1/5/08	6	50	△^{2}	1 Paralyzer	Scott Anderson/Sean Anderson/James Black/Rob Gommerman/Rick Jackett	Wind-Up
				FIREBALLS — see GILMER, Jimmy		

PEAK DATE	PEAK POS	WKS CHR	GOLD	ARTIST / Song Title	Songwriter...B-side	Label & Number
				FIREFALL		
12/11/76	9	22		1 You Are The Woman	Rick Roberts...*Sad Ol' Love Song*	Atlantic 3335
				FIREHOUSE		
9/28/91	5	22	●	1 Love Of A Lifetime	Bill Leverty/C.J. Snare...*Helpless*	Epic 73771
10/17/92	8	20		2 When I Look Into Your Eyes	Bill Leverty/C.J. Snare	Epic 74440
				FIRST CLASS		
10/5/74	4	17		1 Beach Baby	Gillian Shakespeare/John Shakespeare...*Both Sides Of The Story*	UK 49022
				FIRST EDITION — see ROGERS, Kenny		
				FISHER, Eddie		
12/16/50	5	18		1 Thinking Of You	Bert Kalmar/Harry Ruby...*If You Should Leave Me*	RCA Victor 3901
10/27/51	8	14		2 Turn Back The Hands Of Time	Jimmy Eaton/Con Hammond/Larry Wagner...*I Can't Go On Without You*	RCA Victor 4257
3/1/52	4	19		3 Tell Me Why	Al Alberts/Marty Gold...*Trust In Me*	RCA Victor 4444
4/12/52	2^2	30	☉	4 Any Time	Herbert Lawson...*Never Before*	RCA Victor 4359
4/12/52	7	17		5 Forgive Me	Milton Ager/Jack Yellen...*That's The Chance You Take*	RCA Victor 4574
5/3/52	10	10		6 That's The Chance You Take	Sylvia Dee/Sid Lippman...*Forgive Me*	RCA Victor 4574
6/28/52	3^3	19		7 I'm Yours	Robert Mellin...*Just A Little Lovin' (Will Go A Long Way)*	RCA Victor 4680
8/9/52	3^1	18		8 Maybe	Allan Flynn/Frank Madden...*Watermelon Weather*	RCA Victor 4744
				PERRY COMO and EDDIE FISHER		
9/6/52	❶^1	21		9 Wish You Were Here	Harold Rome...*The Hand Of Fate*	RCA Victor 4830
11/8/52	6	17		10 Lady Of Spain	Tolchard Evans/Erell Reaves...*Outside Of Heaven*	RCA Victor 4953
12/13/52	8	13		11 Outside Of Heaven	Chester Conn/Sammy Gallop...*Lady Of Spain*	RCA Victor 4953
1/31/53	7	8		12 Even Now	Richard Adler/Dan Howell/Jerry Ross...*If It Were Up To Me*	RCA Victor 5106
2/28/53	5	12		13 Downhearted	Bob Hilliard/Dave Mann...*How Do You Speak To An Angel?*	RCA Victor 5137
7/4/53	❶^7	25	☉	14 I'm Walking Behind You	Billy Reid...*Just Another Polka*	RCA Victor 5293
8/22/53	7	14		15 With These Hands	Benny Davis/Abner Silver...*When I Was Young*	RCA Victor 5365
11/14/53	4	16		16 Many Times	Jessie Barnes/Felix Stahl...*Just To Be With You*	RCA Victor 5453
1/2/54	❶^8	19	☉	17 Oh! My Pa-Pa (O Mein Papa)	Paul Burkhard/Geoffrey Parsons/John Turner...*I Never Missed Your Sweet "Hello" Until You Said "Goodbye"*	RCA Victor 5552
5/15/54	6	14		18 A Girl, A Girl (Zoom-Ba Di Alli Nella)	Al Bandini/Bennie Benjamin/George Weiss...*Anema E Core (With All My Heart and Soul)*	RCA Victor 5675
7/3/54	8	12		19 Green Years	Arthur Altman/Don Reid...*My Friend*	RCA Victor 5748
7/24/54	9	11		20 The Little Shoemaker	Geoffrey Parsons/Rudi Revil/John Turner...*The Magic Tango*	RCA Victor 5769
				HUGO WINTERHALTER'S ORCHESTRA and CHORUS and a Friend		
11/13/54	❶^3	24	☉	21 I Need You Now	Jimmie Crane/Al Jacobs...*Heaven Was Never Like This*	RCA Victor 5830
1/1/55	5	15		22 Count Your Blessings (Instead Of Sheep)	Irving Berlin...*Fanny*	RCA Victor 5871
6/25/55	6	13		23 Heart	Richard Adler/Jerry Ross...*Near To You*	RCA Victor 6097
2/4/56	7	19		24 Dungaree Doll	Sherman Edwards/Ben Raleigh...*Everybody's Got A Home But Me*	RCA Victor 6337
11/24/56	10	19		25 Cindy, Oh Cindy	Bob Barron/Burt Long...*Around The World*	RCA Victor 6677
				FISHER, Miss Toni		
12/28/59	3^2	17		1 The Big Hurt	Wayne Shanklin...*Memphis Belle*	Signet 275
				FITZGERALD, Ella		
1/4/41	9	1		1 Five O'Clock Whistle	Kim Gannon/Gene Irwin/Josef Myrow...*So Long*	Decca 3420
				ELLA FITZGERALD And Her Famous Orchestra		
4/1/44	10	8		2 Cow-Cow Boogie (Cuma-Ti-Yi-Yi-Ay)	Benny Carter/Gene DePaul/Don Raye...*When My Sugar Walks Down The Street*	Decca 18587
12/2/44	❶^2	18	☉	3 Into Each Life Some Rain Must Fall	Doris Fisher/Allan Roberts...*I'm Making Believe*	Decca 23356
12/9/44	❶^2	17		4 I'm Making Believe	Mack Gordon/James Monaco...*Into Each Life Some Rain Must Fall*	Decca 23356
				INK SPOTS and ELLA FITZGERALD (above 3)		
1/20/45	10	5		5 And Her Tears Flowed Like Wine	Joe Greene/Stan Kenton/Charles Lawrence...*Confessin' (That I Love You)*	Decca 18633
5/19/45	5	6		6 I'm Beginning To See The Light	Duke Ellington/Don George/Johnny Hodges/Harry James...*That's The Way It Is*	Decca 23399
				ELLA FITZGERALD and INK SPOTS		
9/1/45	9	3		7 It's Only A Paper Moon	Harold Arlen/E.Y. Harburg/Billy Rose...*(I'm Gonna Hurry You Out Of My Mind And) Cry You Out Of My Heart*	Decca 23425
				ELLA FITZGERALD and DELTA RHYTHM BOYS		
4/6/46	10	2		8 You Won't Be Satisfied (Until You Break My Heart)	Freddy James/Larry Stock...*The Frim Fram Sauce*	Decca 23496
				ELLA FITZGERALD and LOUIS ARMSTRONG		
8/31/46	7	6		9 Stone Cold Dead In The Market (He Had It Coming)	Wilmoth Houdini...*Petootie Pie*	Decca 23546
				ELLA FITZGERALD and LOUIS JORDAN And His Tympany Five		
2/15/47	8	14		10 (I Love You) For Sentimental Reasons	William Best/Deek Watson...*It's A Pity To Say Goodnight*	Decca 23670
				ELLA FITZGERALD And Delta RHYTHM BOYS		
10/2/48	6	21		11 My Happiness	Borney Bergantine/Betty Peterson...*Tea Leaves*	Decca 24446
7/23/49	9	13		12 Baby, It's Cold Outside	Frank Loesser...*Don't Cry, Cry Baby*	Decca 24644
				ELLA FITZGERALD And LOUIS JORDAN And His Tympany Five		
				FIVE		
8/1/98	10	26	●	1 When The Lights Go Out	Tim Lever/Mike Percy...*Straight Up Funk*	Arista 13495
				FIVE AMERICANS, The		
4/22/67	5	12		1 Western Union	John Durrill/Norman Ezell/Michael Rabon...*Now That It's Over*	Abnak 118
				FIVE MAN ELECTRICAL BAND		
8/28/71	3^1	18	●	1 Signs	Les Emmerson...*Hello Melinda Goodbye*	Lionel 3213
				FIVE STAIRSTEPS, The		
7/18/70	8	16	●	1 O-o-h Child	Stan Vincent...*Dear Prudence*	Buddah 165
				FIXX, The		
11/5/83	4	19		1 One Thing Leads To Another	Alfred Agies/Cy Curnin/Rupert Greenall/Jamie West-Oram/Adam Woods...*Opinions*	MCA 52264
				FLACK, Roberta		
4/15/72	❶^6	18	●	1 The First Time Ever I Saw Your Face	Ewan MacColl...*Trade Winds*	Atlantic 2864
8/12/72	5	13	●	2 Where Is The Love	Ralph MacDonald/William Salter...*Mood*	Atlantic 2879
				ROBERTA FLACK & DONNY HATHAWAY		
2/24/73	❶^5	16	●	3 Killing Me Softly With His Song	Charles Fox/Norman Gimbel...*Just Like A Woman*	Atlantic 2940
8/10/74	❶^1	16	●	4 Feel Like Makin' Love	Gene McDaniels...*When You Smile*	Atlantic 3025
5/13/78	2^2	20		5 The Closer I Get To You	Reggie Lucas/James Mtume...*Love Is The Healing* (Flack)	Atlantic 3463
				ROBERTA FLACK & DONNY HATHAWAY		
11/16/91	6	20		6 Set The Night To Music	Diane Warren...*Natural Thing* (Flack)	Atlantic 87607
				ROBERTA FLACK with Maxi Priest		

47

PEAK DATE	PEAK POS	WKS CHR	GOLD	ARTIST Song Title	Songwriter...B-side	Label & Number
				FLANAGAN, Ralph, and his Orchestra		
11/26/49	9	8		1 Don't Cry Joe (Let Her Go, Let Her Go, Let Her Go)	Joe Marsala...*Swing To 45*	RCA Victor 0002
3/4/50	3[1]	10		2 Rag Mop	Deacon Anderson/Johnnie Lee Wills...*You're Always There*	RCA Victor 3212
11/11/50	5	17		3 Harbor Lights	Will Grosz/Jimmy Kennedy...*Singing Winds* [I]	RCA Victor 3911
11/25/50	9	14		4 Nevertheless	Bert Kalmar/Harry Ruby...*The Red We Want Is The Red We've Got (In the Old Red, White and Blue)*	RCA Victor 3904
1/19/52	6	14		5 Slow Poke	Pee Wee King/Chilton Price/Redd Stewart...*Charmaine*	RCA Victor 4373
10/18/52	4	12		6 I Should Care	Sammy Cahn/Axel Stordahl/Paul Weston...*Tippin' In*	RCA Victor 4885
3/28/53	7	16		7 Hot Toddy	Ralph Flanagan...*Serenade* [I]	RCA Victor 5095
				FLEETWOOD MAC		
3/12/77	10	15		1 Go Your Own Way	Lindsey Buckingham...*Silver Springs*	Warner 8304
6/18/77	❶[1]	19	●	2 Dreams	Stevie Nicks...*Songbird*	Warner 8371
9/24/77	3[2]	18		3 Don't Stop	Christine McVie...*Never Going Back Again*	Warner 8413
12/17/77	9	14		4 You Make Loving Fun	Christine McVie...*Gold Dust Woman*	Warner 8483
11/3/79	8	15		5 Tusk	Lindsey Buckingham...*Never Make Me Cry*	Warner 49077
2/2/80	7	14		6 Sara	Stevie Nicks...*That's Enough For Me*	Warner 49150
7/24/82	4	17		7 Hold Me	Christine McVie/Robbie Patton...*Eyes Of The World*	Warner 29966
5/30/87	5	16		8 Big Love	Lindsey Buckingham...*You And I, Part I*	Warner 28398
11/7/87	4	21		9 Little Lies	Christine McVie/Eddy Quintela...*Ricky*	Warner 28291
				FLEETWOODS, The		
4/13/59	❶[4]	16	☉	1 Come Softly To Me	Gretchen Christopher/Barbara Ellis/Gary Troxel...*I Care So Much*	Dolphin 1
11/16/59	❶[1]	20	☉	2 Mr. Blue	Dewayne Blackwell...*You Mean Everything To Me*	Dolton 5
5/29/61	10	12		3 Tragedy	Fred Burch/Gerald Nelson...*Little Miss Sad One*	Dolton 40
				FLETCHER, "Dusty"		
2/22/47	3[1]	7		1 Open The Door, Richard! (Parts 1 & 2)	Dusty Fletcher/Don Howell/John Mason/Jack McVea [N]	National 4012
				FLOATERS, The		
9/17/77	2[2]	16	●	1 Float On	Arnold Ingram/James Mitchell/Marvin Willis...*Everything Happens For A Reason*	ABC 12284
				FLOCK OF SEAGULLS, A		
10/23/82	9	22		1 I Ran (So Far Away)	Frank Maudsley/Paul Reynolds/Ali Score/Mike Score...*Pick Me Up*	Jive 102
				FLO RIDA		
1/5/08	❶[10]	40	△[5]	1 Low	Tramar Dillard/Montay Humphrey/Faheem Najm...*Jealous*	Poe Boy 346620
				FLO RIDA Featuring T-Pain		
9/20/08	9	21	△	2 In The Ayer	William Adams/Tony Butler/Tramar Dilllard...*Elevator*	Poe Boy 506684
				FLO RIDA Featuring will.i.am		
2/28/09	❶[6]	26	△[4]	3 Right Round	Pete Burns/Steve Coy/Tramar Dillard/Justin Franks/Lukasz Gottwald/Allan Grigg/Philip Lawrence/Tim Lever/Mike Percy...*Shone*	Poe Boy 517992
5/16/09	5	18	△	4 Sugar	Jackie Boyz/Tramar Dillard...*Gotta Get It (Dancer)*	Poe Boy 519284
				FLO RIDA Featuring Wynter		
9/25/10	9	29	△	5 Club Can't Handle Me	Mike Caren/Tramar Dillard/David Guetta/Carmen Key/Kasia Livingston/Frederic Riesterer/Giorgio Tuinfort	Poe Boy
				FLO RIDA Featuring David Guetta		
				FLOYD, King		
1/30/71	6	20	●	1 Groove Me	King Floyd...*What Our Love Needs*	Chimneyville 435
				FLYING MACHINE, The		
11/22/69	5	14	●	1 Smile A Little Smile For Me	Tony MacAulay/Geoff Stephens...*Maybe We've Been Loving Too Long*	Congress 6000
				FOCUS		
6/2/73	9	19		1 Hocus Pocus	Jan Akkerman/Thijs Van Leer...*Hocus Pocus II* [I]	Sire 704
				FOGELBERG, Dan		
3/15/80	2[2]	22		1 Longer	Dan Fogelberg...*Along The Road*	Full Moon 50824
2/21/81	9	18		2 Same Old Lang Syne	Dan Fogelberg...*Hearts And Crafts*	Full Moon 50961
10/31/81	7	19		3 Hard To Say	Dan Fogelberg...*The Innocent Age*	Full Moon 02488
3/6/82	9	20		4 Leader Of The Band	Dan Fogelberg...*Times Like These*	Full Moon 02647
				FOGERTY, John		
3/2/85	10	18		1 The Old Man Down The Road	John Fogerty...*Big Train (From Memphis)*	Warner 29100
				FOLEY, Red		
11/4/44	7	11		1 Smoke On The Water	Zeke Clements/Earl Nunn...*There's A Blue Star Shining Bright (In A Window Tonight)*	Decca 6102
2/11/50	❶[8]	16	☉	2 Chattanoogie Shoe Shine Boy	Jack Stapp/Harry Stone...*Sugarfoot Rag*	Decca 46205
8/26/50	10	10		3 Goodnight Irene	Huddie Ledbetter/John Lomax...*Hillbilly Fever #2*	Decca 46255
				RED FOLEY-ERNEST TUBB		
9/30/50	7	9		4 Cincinnati Dancing Pig	Al Lewis/Guy Wood...*Somebody's Crying* [N]	Decca 46261
				FONTANA, Wayne — see MINDBENDERS, The		
				FONTANE SISTERS, The		
2/5/55	❶[3]	20	☉	1 Hearts Of Stone	Rudy Jackson/Eddy Ray...*Bless Your Heart*	Dot 15265
10/8/55	3[1]	15		2 Seventeen	Boyd Bennett/Chuck Gorman/John Young...*If I Could Be With You (One Hour Tonight)*	Dot 15386
				FORCE M.D.'S		
4/12/86	10	19		1 Tender Love	Jimmy Jam Harris/Terry Lewis	Warner 28818
				FORD, Lita		
6/17/89	8	25	●	1 Close My Eyes Forever	Lita Ford/Ozzy Osbourne...*Under The Gun* (Ford)	RCA 8899
				LITA FORD (with Ozzy Osbourne)		
				FORD, "Tennessee" Ernie		
12/17/49	9	9		1 Mule Train	Fred Glickman/Hy Heath/Johnny Lange...*Anticipation Blues*	Capitol 40258
11/18/50	3[1]	20		2 I'll Never Be Free	Bennie Benjamin/George Weiss...*Ain't Nobody's Business But My Own*	Capitol 1124
				KAY STARR and TENNESSEE ERNIE		
5/14/55	5	17		3 Ballad Of Davy Crockett	Tom Blackburn/George Bruns...*Farewell*	Capitol 3058
11/26/55	❶[8]	22	☉	4 Sixteen Tons	Merle Travis...*You Don't Have To Be A Baby To Cry*	Capitol 3262

PEAK DATE	PEAK POS	WKS CHR	GOLD	ARTIST / Song Title	Songwriter...B-side	Label & Number
				FOREIGNER		
6/18/77	4	22		1 Feels Like The First Time	Mick Jones...*Woman Oh Woman*	Atlantic 3394
10/22/77	6	21		2 Cold As Ice	Lou Gramm/Mick Jones...*I Need You*	Atlantic 3410
9/9/78	3^2	17	●	3 Hot Blooded	Lou Gramm/Mick Jones...*Tramontane*	Atlantic 3488
11/18/78	2^2	20	●	4 Double Vision	Lou Gramm/Mick Jones...*Lonely Children*	Atlantic 3514
9/5/81	4	23		5 Urgent	Mick Jones...*Girl On The Moon*	Atlantic 3831
11/28/81	2^{10}	23		6 Waiting For A Girl Like You	Lou Gramm/Mick Jones...*I'm Gonna Win*	Atlantic 3868
2/2/85	❶^2	21	●	7 I Want To Know What Love Is	Mick Jones...*Street Thunder*	Atlantic 89596
2/20/88	6	19		8 Say You Will	Lou Gramm/Mick Jones...*A Night To Remember*	Atlantic 89169
5/28/88	5	17		9 I Don't Want To Live Without You	Mick Jones...*Face To Face*	Atlantic 89101
				FORREST, Helen		
9/9/44	2^1	10		1 Time Waits For No One	Cliff Friend/Charles Tobias...*In A Moment Of Madness*	Decca 18600
				DICK HAYMES and HELEN FORREST:		
6/10/44	2^1	18		2 Long Ago (And Far Away)	Ira Gershwin/Jerome Kern...*Look For The Silver Lining*	Decca 23317
9/30/44	4	9		3 It Had To Be You	Isham Jones/Gus Kahn...*Together*	Decca 23349
11/4/44	3^2	12		4 Together	Lew Brown/B.G. DeSylva/Ray Henderson...*It Had To Be You*	Decca 23349
10/27/45	2^1	13		5 I'll Buy That Dream	Herb Magidson/Allie Wrubel...*Some Sunday Morning*	Decca 23434
10/27/45	9	5		6 Some Sunday Morning	Ray Heindorf/M.K. Jerome/Ted Koehler...*I'll Buy That Dream*	Decca 23434
3/16/46	7	5		7 I'm Always Chasing Rainbows	Harry Carroll/Joseph McCarthy...*Tomorrow Is Forever*	Decca 23472
4/6/46	4	11		8 Oh! What It Seemed To Be	Bennie Benjamin/Frankie Carle/George Weiss...*Give Me A Little Kiss, Will You Huh?*	Decca 23481
				FORT MINOR		
6/10/06	4	20	△	1 Where'd You Go	Mike Shinoda	Machine Shop
				FORT MINOR Featuring Holly Brook		
				FORTUNES, The		
10/9/65	7	11		1 You've Got Your Troubles	Roger Cook/Roger Greenaway...*I've Gotta Go*	Press 9773
				FOUNDATIONS, The		
2/22/69	3^3	15	●	1 Build Me Up Buttercup	Mike D'Abo/Tony MacAulay...*New Direction*	Uni 55101
				FOUR ACES		
11/17/51	4	22		1 Sin	George Hoven/Chester Shull...*Arizona Moon*	Victoria 101
1/26/52	2^6	24	☉	2 Tell Me Why	Al Alberts/Marty Gold...*A Garden In The Rain*	Decca 27860
4/19/52	7	16		3 Perfidia	Alberto Dominguez/Milton Leeds...*You Brought Me Love*	Decca 27987
9/20/52	9	10		4 Should I	Nacio Herb Brown/Arthur Freed...*There's Only Tonight*	Decca 28323
1/23/54	3^1	16	☉	5 Stranger In Paradise	George Forrest/Robert Wright...*The Gang That Sang "Heart Of My Heart"*	Decca 28927
1/30/54	7	18		6 The Gang That Sang "Heart Of My Heart"	Ben Ryan...*Stranger In Paradise*	Decca 28927
7/24/54	❶^1	18	☉	7 Three Coins In The Fountain	Sammy Cahn/Jule Styne...*Wedding Bells (Are Breaking Up That Old Gang Of Mine)*	Decca 29123
1/1/55	5	14		8 Mister Sandman	Pat Ballard...*(I'll Be With You) In Apple Blossom Time*	Decca 29344
3/12/55	3^1	21		9 Melody Of Love	Hans Engelmann/Tom Glazer...*There Is A Tavern In The Town*	Decca 29395
10/8/55	❶^6	21	☉	10 Love Is A Many-Splendored Thing	Sammy Fain/Paul Francis Webster...*Shine On Harvest Moon*	Decca 29625
				FOUR KING SISTERS		
8/9/41	7	2		1 The Hut-Sut Song (A Swedish Serenade)	Leo Killion/Ted McMichael/Jack Owens...*Music Makers*	Bluebird 11154
5/6/44	4	11		2 It's Love-Love-Love	Mack David/Alex Kramer/Joan Whitney...*Mairzy Doats And Dozy Doats (Mares Eat Oats and Does Eat Oats)*	Bluebird 0822
				FOUR KNIGHTS, The		
2/7/53	8	6		1 Oh, Happy Day	Don Howard/Nancy Reed...*A Million Tears*	Capitol 2315
4/17/54	2^1	24		2 I Get So Lonely (When I Dream About You)	Pat Ballard...*I Couldn't Stay Away From You*	Capitol 2654
				FOUR LADS, The		
12/5/53	10	13		1 Istanbul (Not Constantinople)	Jimmy Kennedy/Nat Simon...*I Should Have Told You Long Ago*	Columbia 40082
10/9/54	7	12		2 Skokiaan (South African Song)	Tom Glazer/August Msarurgwa...*Why Should I Love You?*	Columbia 40306
10/29/55	2^6	25	☉	3 Moments To Remember	Robert Allen/Al Stillman...*Dream On, My Love Dream On*	Columbia 40539
3/17/56	2^4	24	☉	4 No, Not Much!	Robert Allen/Al Stillman...*I'll Never Know*	Columbia 40629
6/16/56	3^3	20	☉	5 Standing On The Corner	Frank Loesser...*My Little Angel*	Columbia 40674
3/9/57	9	21		6 Who Needs You	Robert Allen/Al Stillman...*It's So Easy To Forget*	Columbia 40811
1/6/58	8	14		7 Put A Light In The Window	Kenny Jacobson/Rhoda Roberts...*The Things We Did Last Summer*	Columbia 41058
5/5/58	10	12		8 There's Only One Of You	Robert Allen/Al Stillman...*Blue Tattoo*	Columbia 41136
				4 P.M. (For Positive Music)		
2/4/95	8	32	●	1 Sukiyaki	Buzz Cason/Rohusuke Ei/Tom Leslie/Hachidai Nakamura...*For What More*	Next Plateau 857736
				FOUR PREPS, The		
3/10/58	2^3	20	☉	1 26 Miles (Santa Catalina)	Bruce Belland/Glenn Larson...*It's You*	Capitol 3845
6/9/58	3^2	14		2 Big Man	Bruce Belland/Glenn Larson...*Stop, Baby*	Capitol 3960
				4 SEASONS, The		
9/15/62	❶^5	14	☉	1 Sherry	Bob Gaudio...*I've Cried Before*	Vee-Jay 456
11/17/62	❶^5	16	☉	2 Big Girls Don't Cry	Bob Crewe/Bob Gaudio...*Connie-O*	Vee-Jay 465
3/2/63	❶^3	13	☉	3 Walk Like A Man	Bob Crewe/Bob Gaudio...*Lucky Ladybug*	Vee-Jay 485
8/24/63	3^1	13		4 Candy Girl	Larry Santos...*Marlena*	Vee-Jay 539
2/22/64	3^3	13		5 Dawn (Go Away)	Bob Gaudio/Sandy Linzer...*No Surfin' Today*	Philips 40166
5/16/64	6	10		6 Ronnie	Bob Crewe/Bob Gaudio...*Born To Wander*	Philips 40185
7/18/64	❶^2	12	●	7 Rag Doll	Bob Crewe/Bob Gaudio...*Silence Is Golden*	Philips 40211
9/26/64	10	8		8 Save It For Me	Bob Crewe/Bob Gaudio...*Funny Face*	Philips 40225
12/11/65	3^1	16		9 Let's Hang On!	Bob Crewe/Sandy Linzer/Denny Randell...*On Broadway Tonight*	Philips 40317
3/5/66	9	9		10 Working My Way Back To You	Sandy Linzer/Denny Randell...*Too Many Memories*	Philips 40350
10/15/66	9	10		11 I've Got You Under My Skin	Cole Porter...*Huggin' My Pillow*	Philips 40393
1/21/67	10	10		12 Tell It To The Rain	Chubby Cifelli/Mike Petrillo...*Show Girl*	Philips 40412
7/15/67	9	10		13 C'mon Marianne	Raymond Bloodworth/L. Russell Brown...*Let's Ride Again*	Philips 40460
11/15/75	3^2	20		14 Who Loves You	Bob Gaudio/Judy Parker	Warner/Curb 8122
3/13/76	❶^3	27	●	15 December, 1963 (Oh, What a Night)	Bob Gaudio/Judy Parker...*Slip Away*	Warner/Curb 8168

49

PEAK DATE	PEAK POS	WKS CHR	GOLD	ARTIST / Song Title	Songwriter...B-side	Label & Number
				FOUR TOPS		
6/19/65	❶²	14	⊙	1 I Can't Help Myself	Lamont Dozier/Brian Holland/Eddie Holland...*Sad Souvenirs*	Motown 1076
8/28/65	5	9		2 It's The Same Old Song	Lamont Dozier/Brian Holland/Eddie Holland...*Your Love Is Amazing*	Motown 1081
10/15/66	❶²	15	●	3 Reach Out I'll Be There	Lamont Dozier/Brian Holland/Eddie Holland...*Until You Love Someone*	Motown 1098
1/21/67	6	10		4 Standing In The Shadows Of Love	Lamont Dozier/Brian Holland/Eddie Holland...*Since You've Been Gone*	Motown 1102
4/8/67	4	10		5 Bernadette	Lamont Dozier/Brian Holland/Eddie Holland...*I Got A Feeling*	Motown 1104
1/13/73	10	12		6 Keeper Of The Castle	Dennis Lambert/Brian Potter...*Jubilee With Soul*	Dunhill/ABC 4330
4/7/73	4	15	●	7 Ain't No Woman (Like The One I've Got)	Dennis Lambert/Brian Potter...*The Good Lord Knows*	Dunhill/ABC 4339
				FOUR TUNES, The		
11/17/51	5	17		1 (It's No) Sin	George Hoven/Chester Shull...*I Don't Believe In Tomorrow*	RCA Victor 4280
				SAVANNAH CHURCHILL And The Four Tunes		
8/7/54	6	15	⊙	2 I Understand Just How You Feel	Pat Best...*Sugar Lump*	Jubilee 5132
				FOX, Samantha		
2/14/87	4	23		1 Touch Me (I Want Your Body)	Jon Astrop/Pete Harris/Mark Shreeve...*Drop Me A Line*	Jive 1006
6/4/88	3¹	27		2 Naughty Girls (Need Love Too)	Curtis Bedeau/Gerard Charles/Hugh Clarke/Brian George/Lucien George/Paul George	Jive 1089
2/11/89	8	23	●	3 I Wanna Have Some Fun	Curtis Bedeau/Gerard Charles/Hugh Clarke/Brian George/Lucien George/Paul George...*Don't Cheat On Me*	Jive 1154
				FOXX, Inez, with Charlie Foxx		
9/7/63	7	18		1 Mockingbird	Charlie Foxx/Inez Foxx...*Jaybirds*	Symbol 919
				FOXX, Jamie		
2/21/04	❶¹	22		1 Slow Jamz	Burt Bacharach/Hal David/Carl Mitchell/Kanye West...*Badunkadunk*	Atlantic 88288
				TWISTA Featuring Kanye West & Jamie Foxx		
9/17/05	❶¹⁰	39	△²	2 Gold Digger	Ray Charles/Renald Richard/Kanye West...*Diamonds From Sierra Leone*	Roc-A-Fella 005118
				KANYE WEST featuring Jamie Foxx		
2/11/06	8	22		3 Unpredictable	Derrick Baker/Christopher Bridges/Harold Lilly/James Scheffer	J Records 75974
				JAMIE FOXX (feat. Ludacris)		
5/16/09	2¹	27		4 Blame It	J.T. Brown/Jamie Foxx/Christopher Henderson/Brandon Melancon/Faheem Najm/Nate Walker...*Too Many Rules*	J Records 46266
				JAMIE FOXX Featuring T-Pain		
				FOXY		
11/11/78	9	21		1 Get Off	Carlos Driggs/Ish Ledesma...*You Make Me Hot*	Dash 5046
				FRAMPTON, Peter		
5/8/76	6	18		1 Show Me The Way	Peter Frampton...*Shine On* [L]	A&M 1795
11/13/76	10	18		2 Do You Feel Like We Do	Peter Frampton...*Penny For Your Thoughts* [L]	A&M 1867
7/30/77	2³	20		3 I'm In You	Peter Frampton...*St. Thomas (Know How I Feel)*	A&M 1941
				FRANCIS, Connie		
3/24/58	4	22	⊙	1 Who's Sorry Now	Bert Kalmar/Harry Ruby/Ted Snyder...*You Were Only Fooling (While I Was Falling In Love)*	MGM 12588
1/19/59	2²	18		2 My Happiness	Borney Bergantine/Betty Peterson...*Never Before*	MGM 12738
6/29/59	5	17	⊙	3 Lipstick On Your Collar	George Goehring/Edna Lewis...*Frankie*	MGM 12793
7/6/59	9	15		4 Frankie	Howard Greenfield/Neil Sedaka...*Lipstick On Your Collar*	MGM 12793
12/28/59	7	15		5 Among My Souvenirs	Edgar Leslie/Lawrence Wright...*God Bless America*	MGM 12841
4/11/60	8	13	⊙	6 Mama	Harold Barlow/Phil Brito...*Teddy*	MGM 12878
6/27/60	❶²	18	⊙	7 Everybody's Somebody's Fool	Howard Greenfield/Jack Keller...*Jealous Of You*	MGM 12899
9/26/60	❶²	17		8 My Heart Has A Mind Of Its Own	Howard Greenfield/Jack Keller...*Malaguena*	MGM 12923
12/26/60	7	13		9 Many Tears Ago	Winfield Scott...*Senza Mamma (With No One)*	MGM 12964
3/20/61	4	15		10 Where The Boys Are	Howard Greenfield/Neil Sedaka...*No One*	MGM 12971
5/29/61	7	10		11 Breakin' In A Brand New Broken Heart	Howard Greenfield/Jack Keller...*Someone Else's Boy*	MGM 12995
8/7/61	6	11		12 Together	Lew Brown/B.G. DeSylva/Ray Henderson...*Too Many Rules*	MGM 13019
1/13/62	10	12		13 When The Boy In Your Arms (Is The Boy In Your Heart)	Roy Bennett/Sid Tepper...*Baby's First Christmas*	MGM 13051
3/31/62	❶¹	13		14 Don't Break The Heart That Loves You	Benny Davis/Ted Murry...*Drop It Joe*	MGM 13059
6/9/62	7	9		15 Second Hand Love	Hank Hunter/Phil Spector...*Gonna Git That Man*	MGM 13074
9/1/62	9	9		16 Vacation	Connie Francis/Hank Hunter/Gary Weston...*The Biggest Sin Of All*	MGM 13087
				FRANKE & THE KNOCKOUTS		
6/6/81	10	19		1 Sweetheart	William Elworthy/Franke Previte...*Don't Stop*	Millennium 11801
				FRANKIE GOES TO HOLLYWOOD		
3/16/85	10	16	●	1 Relax	Peter Gill/Holly Johnson/Mark O'Toole...*One September Monday*	Island 99805
				FRANKIE J		
12/6/03	7	33	○	1 Suga Suga	Frankie Bautista/Ronald Bryant...*Feelin Me / Early In Da Morning*	Universal 001055
				BABY BASH Feat. Frankie J		
4/2/05	3¹	21	○	2 Obsession [No Es Amor]	Anthony Santos	Columbia 70386
				FRANKIE J featuring Baby Bash		
				FRANKLIN, Aretha		
4/15/67	9	11	●	1 I Never Loved A Man (The Way I Love You)	Ronnie Shannon...*Do Right Woman-Do Right Man*	Atlantic 2386
6/3/67	❶²	12	●	2 Respect	Otis Redding...*Dr. Feelgood*	Atlantic 2403
9/9/67	4	11	●	3 Baby I Love You	Ronnie Shannon...*Going Down Slow*	Atlantic 2427
11/4/67	8	9	●	4 (You Make Me Feel Like) A Natural Woman	Gerry Goffin/Carole King/Jerry Wexler...*Baby, Baby, Baby*	Atlantic 2441
1/20/68	2²	12	●	5 Chain Of Fools	Don Covay...*Prove It*	Atlantic 2464
3/30/68	5	12	●	6 (Sweet Sweet Baby) Since You've Been Gone	Aretha Franklin/Ted White...*Ain't No Way*	Atlantic 2486
6/15/68	7	10	●	7 Think	Aretha Franklin/Ted White...*You Send Me*	Atlantic 2518
9/7/68	6	9	●	8 The House That Jack Built	Bob Lance/Fran Robins...*I Say A Little Prayer*	Atlantic 2546
10/5/68	10	11	●	9 I Say A Little Prayer	Burt Bacharach/Hal David...*The House That Jack Built*	Atlantic 2546
6/5/71	6	12	●	10 Bridge Over Troubled Water	Paul Simon...*Brand New Me*	Atlantic 2796
9/11/71	2²	12	●	11 Spanish Harlem	Jerry Leiber/Phil Spector...*Lean On Me*	Atlantic 2817
11/27/71	9	9	●	12 Rock Steady	Aretha Franklin...*Oh Me Oh My (I'm A Fool For You Baby)*	Atlantic 2838
5/6/72	5	12	●	13 Day Dreaming	Aretha Franklin...*I've Been Loving You Too Long*	Atlantic 2866
2/23/74	3¹	21	●	14 Until You Come Back To Me (That's What I'm Gonna Do)	Morris Broadnax/Clarence Paul/Stevie Wonder...*If You Don't Think*	Atlantic 2995
8/31/85	3¹	19		15 Freeway Of Love	Jeffrey E. Cohen/Narada Michael Walden...*Until You Say You Love Me*	Arista 9354
11/30/85	7	19		16 Who's Zoomin' Who	Aretha Franklin/Preston Glass/Narada Michael Walden...*Sweet Bitter Love*	Arista 9410
4/18/87	❶²	17		17 I Knew You Were Waiting (For Me)	Simon Climie/Dennis Morgan	Arista 9559
				ARETHA FRANKLIN AND GEORGE MICHAEL		

PEAK DATE	PEAK POS	WKS CHR	GOLD	ARTIST / Song Title	Songwriter...B-side	Label & Number
				FRAY, The		
6/3/06	8	42	△²	1 Over My Head (Cable Car)	Joe King/Isaac Slade	Epic
10/7/06	3¹	58	△³	2 How To Save A Life	Joe King/Isaac Slade	Epic
2/14/09	7	39	△²	3 You Found Me	Joe King/Isaac Slade	Epic
				FREBERG, Stan		
10/10/53	❶⁴	10	☉	1 St. George And The Dragonet	Daws Butler/Stan Freberg/Walter Schumann...*Little Blue Riding Hood* [N]	Capitol 2596
10/10/53	9	4		2 Little Blue Riding Hood	Daws Butler/Stan Freberg/Miklos Rozsa/Walter Schumann...*St. George And The Dragonet* [N]	Capitol 2596
				FRED, John, & His Playboy Band		
1/20/68	❶²	16	●	1 Judy In Disguise (With Glasses)	Andrew Bernard/John Fred...*When The Lights Go Out*	Paula 282
				FREDDIE AND THE DREAMERS		
4/10/65	❶²	11	☉	1 I'm Telling You Now	Freddie Garrity/Mitch Murray...*What Have I Done To You*	Tower 125
				FREE		
10/17/70	4	16		1 All Right Now	Andy Fraser/Paul Rodgers...*Mouthful Of Grass*	A&M 1206
				FREEMAN, Bobby		
6/9/58	5	17		1 Do You Want To Dance	Bobby Freeman...*Big Fat Woman*	Josie 835
8/29/64	5	12		2 C'mon And Swim	Thomas Coman/Sly Stone...*Part 2*	Autumn 2
				FREEMAN, Ernie		
12/30/57	4	18		1 Raunchy	Bill Justis/Sid Manker...*Puddin'* [I]	Imperial 5474
				FREE MOVEMENT, The		
11/13/71	5	26		1 I've Found Someone Of My Own	Frank Robinson...*I Can't Convince My Heart*	Decca 32818
				FRENCH, Nicki		
6/24/95	2¹	27	●	1 Total Eclipse Of The Heart	Jim Steinman...*Pride And Passion*	Critique 15539
				FREY, Glenn		
3/16/85	2¹	24		1 The Heat Is On	Harold Faltermeyer/Keith Forsey...*Shoot Out* (Harold Faltermeyer)	MCA 52512
11/16/85	2²	21		2 You Belong To The City	Glenn Frey/Jack Tempchin...*Smuggler's Blues*	MCA 52651
				FRIEND AND LOVER		
6/22/68	10	14		1 Reach Out Of The Darkness	Jim Post...*Time On Your Side (You're Only 15 Years Old)*	Verve Forecast 5069
				FRIENDS OF DISTINCTION, The		
6/7/69	3¹	16	●	1 Grazing In The Grass	Harry Elston/Philemon Hou...*I Really Hope You Do*	RCA Victor 0107
5/2/70	6	13		2 Love Or Let Me Be Lonely	Jerry Peters/Anita Poree/Skip Scarborough...*This Generation*	RCA Victor 0319
				FRIJID PINK		
4/4/70	7	13	●	1 House Of The Rising Sun	Alan Price...*Drivin' Blues*	Parrot 341
				FUGEES		
6/22/96	2³	35		1 Killing Me Softly	Charles Fox/Norman Gimbel	Ruffhouse
				FUGEES (feat. Lauryn Hill)		
				FULLER, Bobby, Four		
3/12/66	9	11		1 I Fought The Law	Sonny Curtis...*Little Annie Lou*	Mustang 3014
				FURTADO, Nelly		
5/26/01	9	24		1 I'm Like A Bird	Nelly Furtado	DreamWorks
11/10/01	5	25		2 Turn Off The Light	Nelly Furtado...*I'm Like A Bird*	DreamWorks 459093
7/8/06	❶⁶	26	△	3 Promiscuous	Tim Clayton/Nelly Furtado/Nathan Hills/Tim Mosley	Mosley 006818
				NELLY FURTADO Featuring Timbaland		
2/24/07	❶¹	30		4 Say It Right	Nelly Furtado/Nathan Hills/Tim Mosley	Mosley
4/21/07	❶²	26		5 Give It To Me	Tim Clayton/Nelly Furtado/Nathan Hills/Timothy Mosley/Justin Timberlake	Mosley 008759
				TIMBALAND Featuring Nelly Furtado and Justin Timberlake		

G

PEAK DATE	PEAK POS	WKS CHR	GOLD	ARTIST / Song Title	Songwriter...B-side	Label & Number
				GABRIEL, Peter		
7/26/86	❶¹	21		1 Sledgehammer	Peter Gabriel...*Don't Break This Rhythm*	Geffen 28718
3/7/87	8	23		2 Big Time	Peter Gabriel...*We Do What We're Told*	Geffen 28503
				GALLERY		
6/24/72	4	22	●	1 Nice To Be With You	Jim Gold...*Ginger Haired Man*	Sussex 232
				GAME, The		
2/19/05	4	28	○	1 How We Do	Mike Elizondo/Curtis Jackson/Jayceon Taylor/Andre Young	Aftermath 003913
4/16/05	2⁵	23	○	2 Hate It Or Love It	Curtis Jackson/Andre Lyon/Jayceon Taylor/Marcello Valenzano	Aftermath
				THE GAME Featuring 50 Cent (above 2)		
				GARFUNKEL, Art		
11/10/73	9	14		1 All I Know	Jimmy Webb...*Mary Was An Only Child*	Columbia 45926
				GARLAND, Judy		
9/21/40	3²	10		1 I'm Nobody's Baby	Milton Ager/Benny Davis/Lester Santly...*Buds Won't Bud*	Decca 3174
4/3/43	3¹	10		2 For Me And My Gal	Ray Goetz/Edgar Leslie/George Meyer...*When You Wore A Tulip (And I Wore A Big, Red Rose)*	Decca 18480
				JUDY GARLAND and GENE KELLY		
12/30/44	4	10		3 The Trolley Song	Ralph Blane/Hugh Martin...*Boys And Girls Like You*	Decca 23361
6/2/45	5	7		4 Yah-Ta-Ta Yah-Ta-Ta (Talk, Talk, Talk)	Johnny Burke/Jimmy Van Heusen...*You've Got Me Where You Want Me* [N]	Decca 23410
				BING CROSBY and JUDY GARLAND		
10/6/45	9	1		5 On The Atchison, Topeka And The Santa Fe	Johnny Mercer/Harry Warren...*If I Had You*	Decca 23436
				JUDY GARLAND and THE MERRY MACS		

PEAK DATE	PEAK POS	WKS CHR	G O L D	ARTIST Song Title	Songwriter...B-side	Label & Number
				GARNETT, Gale		
10/17/64	4	17		1 We'll Sing In The Sunshine	Gale Garnett...*Prism Song*	RCA Victor 8388
				GARRETT, Betty		
11/13/48	8	11		1 Buttons And Bows	Ray Evans/Jay Livingston...*The Matador*	MGM 10244
				GARRETT, Leif		
2/17/79	10	21		1 I Was Made For Dancin'	Michael Lloyd...*Living Without Your Love*	Scotti Brothers 403
				GAYE, Marvin		
7/20/63	10	14		1 Pride And Joy	Marvin Gaye/William Stevenson/Norman Whitfield...*One Of These Days*	Tamla 54079
1/30/65	6	14		2 How Sweet It Is To Be Loved By You	Lamont Dozier/Brian Holland/Eddie Holland...*Forever*	Tamla 54107
5/15/65	8	12		3 I'll Be Doggone	Warren Moore/Smokey Robinson/Marvin Tarplin...*You've Been A Long Time Coming*	Tamla 54112
11/20/65	8	12		4 Ain't That Peculiar	Warren Moore/Smokey Robinson/Robert Rogers/Marvin Tarplin...*She's Got To Be Real*	Tamla 54122
12/14/68	❶⁷	15	⊙	5 I Heard It Through The Grapevine	Barrett Strong/Norman Whitfield...*You're What's Happening (In The World Today)*	Tamla 54176
6/28/69	4	15		6 Too Busy Thinking About My Baby	Janie Bradford/Barrett Strong/Norman Whitfield...*Wherever I Lay My Hat (That's My Home)*	Tamla 54181
10/18/69	7	12		7 That's The Way Love Is	Barrett Strong/Norman Whitfield...*Gonna Keep On Tryin' Till I Win Your Love*	Tamla 54185
4/10/71	2³	15		8 What's Going On	Renaldo Benson/Alfred Cleveland/Marvin Gaye...*God Is Love*	Tamla 54201
8/21/71	4	12		9 Mercy Mercy Me (The Ecology)	Marvin Gaye...*Sad Tomorrows*	Tamla 54207
11/6/71	9	9		10 Inner City Blues (Make Me Wanna Holler)	Marvin Gaye/James Myx...*Wholy Holy*	Tamla 54209
2/3/73	7	12		11 Trouble Man	Marvin Gaye...*Don't Mess With Mister "T"*	Tamla 54228
9/8/73	❶²	19	○	12 Let's Get It On	Marvin Gaye/Ed Townsend...*I Wish It Would Rain*	Tamla 54234
6/25/77	❶¹	18		13 Got To Give It Up (Pt. I)	Marvin Gaye...*(Pt. II)*	Tamla 54280
1/29/83	3³	21	▲	14 Sexual Healing	Marvin Gaye	Columbia 03302
				MARVIN GAYE & TAMMI TERRELL:		
11/4/67	5	13		15 Your Precious Love	Nick Ashford/Valerie Simpson...*Hold Me Oh My Darling*	Tamla 54156
1/20/68	10	11		16 If I Could Build My Whole World Around You	Johnny Bristol/Vernon Bullock/Harvey Fuqua...*If This World Were Mine*	Tamla 54161
5/25/68	8	13		17 Ain't Nothing Like The Real Thing	Nick Ashford/Valerie Simpson...*Little Ole Boy, Little Ole Girl*	Tamla 54163
9/14/68	7	12		18 You're All I Need To Get By	Nick Ashford/Valerie Simpson...*Two Can Have A Party*	Tamla 54169
				GAYLE, Crystal		
11/26/77	2³	26	●	1 Don't It Make My Brown Eyes Blue	Richard Leigh...*It's All Right With Me*	United Artists 1016
2/12/83	7	29		2 You And I	Frank Myers...*All My Life, All My Love* (Rabbitt)	Elektra 69936
				EDDIE RABBITT with Crystal Gayle		
				GAYLORDS, The		
3/28/53	2¹	22	⊙	1 Tell Me You're Mine	Dico Vasin/Ronnie Vincent...*Cuban Love Song*	Mercury 70067
2/27/54	7	12		2 From The Vine Came The Grape	Paul Cunningham/Leonard Whitcup...*Stolen Moments*	Mercury 70296
8/21/54	2¹	19		3 The Little Shoemaker	Geoffrey Parsons/Rudi Revil/John Turner...*Mecque, Mecque*	Mercury 70403
				THE GAYLORDS, Three Friends and a Stranger		
				GAYNOR, Gloria		
1/25/75	9	17		1 Never Can Say Goodbye	Clifton Davis...*We Just Can't Make It*	MGM 14748
3/10/79	❶³	27	▲	2 I Will Survive	Dino Fekaris/Freddie Perren...*Substitute*	Polydor 14508
				G-CLEFS, The		
12/4/61	9	16		1 I Understand (Just How You Feel)	Robert Burns...*Little Girl I Love You*	Terrace 7500
				GEDDES, David		
10/4/75	4	13		1 Run Joey Run	Jack Perricone/Paul Vance...*Honey Don't Blow It*	Big Tree 16044
				GEILS, J., Band		
2/6/82	❶⁶	25	●	1 Centerfold	Seth Justman...*Rage In The Cage*	EMI America 8102
4/10/82	4	16		2 Freeze-Frame	Seth Justman/Peter Wolf...*Flamethrower*	EMI America 8108
				GENESIS		
2/11/84	6	20		1 That's All!	Tony Banks/Phil Collins/Mike Rutherford...*Second Home By The Sea*	Atlantic 89724
7/19/86	❶¹	17		2 Invisible Touch	Tony Banks/Phil Collins/Mike Rutherford...*The Last Domino*	Atlantic 89407
10/11/86	4	16		3 Throwing It All Away	Tony Banks/Phil Collins/Mike Rutherford...*Do The Neurotic*	Atlantic 89372
1/31/87	4	21		4 Land Of Confusion	Tony Banks/Phil Collins/Mike Rutherford...*Feeding The Fire*	Atlantic 89336
4/4/87	3¹	15		5 Tonight, Tonight, Tonight	Tony Banks/Phil Collins/Mike Rutherford...*In The Glow Of The Night (Part One)*	Atlantic 89290
6/27/87	3¹	17		6 In Too Deep	Tony Banks/Phil Collins/Mike Rutherford...*I'd Rather Be You*	Atlantic 89316
4/11/92	7	20		7 I Can't Dance	Tony Banks/Phil Collins/Mike Rutherford...*On The Shoreline*	Atlantic 87532
				GENTRY, Bobbie		
8/26/67	❶⁴	14	●	1 Ode To Billie Joe	Bobbie Gentry...*Mississippi Delta*	Capitol 5950
				GENTRYS, The		
10/30/65	4	13		1 Keep On Dancing	Willie Young...*Make Up Your Mind*	MGM 13379
				GEORGE, Barbara		
1/27/62	3¹	19		1 I Know (You Don't Love Me No More)	Barbara George...*Love (Is Just A Chance You Take)*	A.F.O. 302
				GEORGIA SATELLITES		
2/21/87	2¹	20		1 Keep Your Hands To Yourself	Dan Baird...*Can't Stand The Pain*	Elektra 69502
				GERARDO		
4/13/91	7	18	●	1 Rico Suave	Gerardo Mejia/Christian Warren...*(Spanglish version)*	Interscope 98871
				GERRY AND THE PACEMAKERS		
7/4/64	4	12		1 Don't Let The Sun Catch You Crying	Gerry Marsden...*Away From You*	Laurie 3251
9/5/64	9	11		2 How Do You Do It?	Mitch Murray...*You'll Never Walk Alone*	Laurie 3261
3/20/65	6	11		3 Ferry Cross The Mersey	Gerry Marsden...*Pretend*	Laurie 3284
				GETZ, Stan		
7/18/64	5	12		1 The Girl From Ipanema	Norman Gimbel/Antonio Carlos Jobim...*Blowin' In The Wind* (Getz)	Verve 10323
				GETZ/GILBERTO		

PEAK DATE	PEAK POS	WKS CHR	GOLD	ARTIST / Song Title	Songwriter...B-side	Label & Number
				GIBB, Andy		
7/30/77	❶⁴	31	●	1 I Just Want To Be Your Everything	Barry Gibb...*In The End*	RSO 872
3/4/78	❶²	29	●	2 (Love Is) Thicker Than Water	Andy Gibb/Barry Gibb...*Words And Music*	RSO 883
6/17/78	❶⁷	25	▲	3 Shadow Dancing	Andy Gibb/Barry Gibb/Maurice Gibb/Robin Gibb...*Let It Be Me*	RSO 893
9/23/78	5	16	●	4 An Everlasting Love	Barry Gibb...*Flowing Rivers*	RSO 904
12/16/78	9	18	●	5 (Our Love) Don't Throw It All Away	Barry Gibb/Blue Weaver...*One More Look At The Night*	RSO 911
3/8/80	4	15		6 Desire	Barry Gibb/Maurice Gibb/Robin Gibb...*Waiting For You*	RSO 1019
				GIBB, Barry		
1/10/81	3²	22	●	1 Guilty	Barry Gibb/Maurice Gibb/Robin Gibb...*Life Story* (Streisand)	Columbia 11390
3/21/81	10	16		2 What Kind Of Fool	Albhy Galuten/Barry Gibb...*The Love Inside* (Streisand)	Columbia 11430
				BARBRA STREISAND & BARRY GIBB (above 2)		
				GIBBS, Georgia		
4/22/50	5	11		1 (If I Knew You Were Comin') I'd've Baked A Cake	Al Hoffman/Bob Merrill/Clem Watts...*Stay With The Happy People*	Coral 60169
9/8/51	6	9		2 While You Danced, Danced, Danced	Stephan Weiss...*While We're Young*	Mercury 5681
5/17/52	❶⁷	20	⊙	3 Kiss Of Fire	Lester Allen/Robert Hill...*A Lasting Thing*	Mercury 5823
5/2/53	5	24		4 Seven Lonely Days	Marshall Brown/Alden Schuman/Earl Schuman...*If You Take My Heart Away*	Mercury 70095
4/2/55	2¹	19	⊙	5 Tweedle Dee	Winfield Scott...*You're Wrong, All Wrong*	Mercury 70517
5/14/55	❶³	20	⊙	6 Dance With Me Henry (Wallflower)	Hank Ballard/Etta James/Johnny Otis...*Every Road Must Have A Turning*	Mercury 70572
				GIBSON, Debbie		
9/5/87	4	28	●	1 Only In My Dreams	Debbie Gibson	Atlantic 89322
12/19/87	4	22		2 Shake Your Love	Debbie Gibson	Atlantic 89187
4/9/88	3¹	17		3 Out Of The Blue	Debbie Gibson	Atlantic 89129
6/25/88	❶¹	20		4 Foolish Beat	Debbie Gibson	Atlantic 89109
3/4/89	❶³	19	●	5 Lost In Your Eyes	Debbie Gibson...*Silence Speaks (A Thousand Words)*	Atlantic 88970
				GIBSON, Don		
5/5/58	7	21	⊙	1 Oh Lonesome Me	Don Gibson...*I Can't Stop Lovin' You*	RCA Victor 7133
				GILBERTO, Astrud		
7/18/64	5	12		1 The Girl From Ipanema	Norman Gimbel/Antonio Carlos Jobim...*Blowin' In The Wind* (Getz)	Verve 10323
				GETZ/GILBERTO		
				GILDER, Nick		
10/28/78	❶¹	31	▲	1 Hot Child In The City	Nick Gilder/James McCulloch...*Backstreet Noise*	Chrysalis 2226
				GILKYSON, Terry, and The Easy Riders		
4/28/51	2⁸	23	⊙	1 On Top Of Old Smoky	Pete Seeger...*Across The Wide Missouri*	Decca 27515
				THE WEAVERS and TERRY GILKYSON		
4/6/57	4	19	⊙	2 Marianne	Richard Dehr/Terry Gilkyson/Frank Miller...*Goodbye Chiquita*	Columbia 40817
				GILL, Johnny		
8/4/90	3²	23	●	1 Rub You The Right Way	Jimmy Jam Harris/Terry Lewis	Motown 2045
9/29/90	10	16		2 My, My, My	Babyface/Daryl Simmons	Motown 2033
				GILMER, Jimmy, and The Fireballs		
10/12/63	❶⁵	15	●	1 Sugar Shack	Keith McCormack/Faye Voss...*My Heart Is Free*	Dot 16487
3/2/68	9	14		2 Bottle Of Wine	Tom Paxton...*Can't You See I'm Tryin'*	Atco 6491
				THE FIREBALLS		
				GIN BLOSSOMS		
3/9/96	9	46		1 Follow You Down	Scott Johnson/Bill Leen/Phillip Rhodes/Jesse Valenzuela/Robin Wilson...*Til I Hear It From You*	A&M 1380
				GINUWINE		
11/23/96	6	27	▲	1 Pony	Stephen Garrett/Elgin Lumpkin/Tim Mosley	550 Music/Epic 78373
10/27/01	4	30		2 Differences	Elgin Lumpkin/Troy Oliver	Epic 79711
8/3/02	4	26		3 I Need A Girl (Part Two)	Sean Combs/Chauncey Hawkins/Michael Jones/Frank Romano/Adonis Shropshire/Mario Winans...*So Complete*	Bad Boy 79441
				P. DIDDY AND GINUWINE Featuring Loon, Mario Winans & Tammy Ruggeri		
8/2/03	8	20		4 In Those Jeans	Harvey Hester/Elgin Lumpkin	Epic
				GLASS TIGER		
10/11/86	2¹	24		1 Don't Forget Me (When I'm Gone)	Al Connelly/Alan Frew/Michael Hanson/Wayne Parker/Sam Reid/Jim Vallance...*Ancient Evenings*	Manhattan 50037
1/24/87	7	21		2 Someday	Al Connelly/Alan Frew/Michael Hanson/Wayne Parker/Sam Reid/Jim Vallance...*Vanishing Tribe*	Manhattan 50048
				GLEE CAST		
6/6/09	4	6	○	1 Don't Stop Believin'	Jonathan Cain/Stephen Perry/Neal Schon	Fox
11/27/10	8	3		2 Teenage Dream	Lukasz Gottwald/Benjamin Levin/Bonnie McKee/Katy Perry/Martin Sandberg	Fox
				GLENN, Darrell		
9/19/53	6	13		1 Crying In The Chapel	Artie Glenn...*Hang Up That Telephone*	Valley 105
				GLITTER, Gary		
9/9/72	7	11		1 Rock And Roll Part 2	Gary Glitter/Mike Leander...*Part 1* [I]	Bell 45,237
				GNARLS BARKLEY		
7/22/06	2⁷	29	△²	1 Crazy	Brian Burton/Thomas Callaway/GianFranco Reverberi/GianPiero Reverberi	Downtown 70002
				GODFREY, Arthur		
12/13/47	2⁸	18	⊙	1 Too Fat Polka (I Don't Want Her) (You Can Have Her) (She's Too Fat For Me)	Ross MacLean/Arthur Richardson...*For Me And My Gal* [N]	Columbia 37921
3/20/48	7	9		2 Slap 'Er Down, Agin, Paw	Polly Arnold/Eddie Asherman/Alice Cornett...*I'd Give A Million Tomorrows (For Just One Yesterday)* [N]	Columbia 38066
4/1/50	8	7		3 Go To Sleep, Go To Sleep, Go To Sleep	Sammy Cahn/Fred Spielman...*But Me, I Love You* [N]	Columbia 38744
				MARY MARTIN and ARTHUR GODFREY		
2/23/52	6	14		4 Dance Me Loose	Lee Erwin/Mel Howard...*Slow Poke*	Columbia 39632
				GO-GO'S		
4/10/82	2³	19	●	1 We Got The Beat	Charlotte Caffey...*Can't Stop The World*	I.R.S. 9903
8/21/82	8	14		2 Vacation	Charlotte Caffey/Kathy Valentine/Jane Wiedlin...*Beatnik Beach*	I.R.S. 9907

PEAK DATE	PEAK POS	WKS CHR	GOLD	ARTIST Song Title	Songwriter...B-side	Label & Number
				GOLD, Andrew		
6/11/77	7	21		1 Lonely Boy	Andrew Gold...*Must Be Crazy*	Asylum 45384
				GOLDEN EARRING		
3/26/83	10	27		1 Twilight Zone	George Kooymans...*King Dark*	21 Records 103
				GOLDSBORO, Bobby		
3/14/64	9	13		1 See The Funny Little Clown	Bobby Goldsboro...*Hello Loser*	United Artists 672
4/13/68	❶⁵	15	●	2 Honey	Bobby Russell...*Danny*	United Artists 50283
				GOODMAN, Benny, and his Orchestra		
4/26/41	6	3		1 There'll Be Some Changes Made	Billy Higgins/W. Benton Overstreet...*Jumpin' At The Woodside*	Columbia 35210
4/11/42	5	9		2 Somebody Else Is Taking My Place	Bob Ellsworth/Dick Howard/Russ Morgan...*That Did It, Marie*	Okeh 6497
4/25/42	2⁶	20		3 Jersey Bounce	Tiny Bradshaw/Edward Johnson/Bobby Plater/Robert Wright...*A String Of Pearls* [I]	Okeh 6590
8/22/42	10	1		4 Take Me	Rube Bloom/Mack David...*Idaho*	Columbia 36613
9/5/42	4	3		5 Idaho	Jesse Stone...*Take Me*	Columbia 36613
1/23/43	4	12		6 Why Don't You Do Right	Joe McCoy...*Six Flats Unfurnished*	Columbia 36652
6/12/43	❶³	11		7 Taking A Chance On Love	Vernon Duke/Ted Fetter/John Latouche...*Cabin In The Sky*	Columbia 35869
7/28/45	2¹	17		8 Gotta Be This Or That (Part 1)	Sunny Skylar...*(Part 2)*	Columbia 36813
9/29/45	10	1		9 It's Only A Paper Moon	Harold Arlen/E.Y. Harburg/Billy Rose...*I'm Gonna Love That Guy*	Columbia 36843
10/13/45	9	1		10 I'm Gonna Love That Guy	Frances Ash...*It's Only A Paper Moon*	Columbia 36843
1/5/46	2¹	14		11 Symphony	Alex Alstone/Roger Bernstein/Jack Lawrence/Andre Tabet...*My Guy's Come Back*	Columbia 36874
8/17/46	9	1		12 Blue Skies	Irving Berlin...*I Don't Know Enough About You*	Columbia 37053
1/18/47	6	6		13 A Gal In Calico	Leo Robin/Arthur Schwartz...*Benjie's Bubble*	Columbia 37187
1/8/49	7	12		14 On A Slow Boat To China	Frank Loesser...*I Hate To Lose You (I'm So Used To You Now)*	Capitol 15208
				GOODMAN, Dickie		
8/25/56	3¹	13	⊙	1 The Flying Saucer (Parts 1 & 2)	Bill Buchanan/Dickie Goodman [N]	Luniverse 101
				BUCHANAN and GOODMAN		
10/11/75	4	10	●	2 Mr. Jaws	Dickie Goodman/Bill Ramal...*Irv's Theme* [N]	Cash 451
				GOO GOO DOLLS		
1/27/96	5	36		1 Name	John Rzeznik/Robby Takac...*Burnin' Up / Hit Or Miss*	Warner 17758
8/1/98	❶¹⁸	47	△	2 Iris	John Rzeznik	Warner Sunset
2/13/99	8	35	○	3 Slide	John Rzeznik	Warner
				GORDON, Barry		
1/7/56	6	4	⊙	1 Nuttin' For Christmas	Roy Bennett/Sid Tepper...*Santa Claus Looks Just Like Daddy* [X-N]	MGM 12092
				GORE, Lesley		
6/1/63	❶²	13	⊙	1 It's My Party	John Gluck/Wally Gold/Herb Wiener...*Danny*	Mercury 72119
8/17/63	5	11		2 Judy's Turn To Cry	Edna Lewis/Beverly Ross...*Just Let Me Cry*	Mercury 72143
12/7/63	5	15		3 She's A Fool	Mark Barkan/Ben Raleigh...*The Old Crowd*	Mercury 72180
2/1/64	2³	13		4 You Don't Own Me	John Madara/David White...*Run Bobby, Run*	Mercury 72206
				GORME, Eydie		
3/2/63	7	15		1 Blame It On The Bossa Nova	Barry Mann/Cynthia Weil...*Guess I Should Have Loved Him More*	Columbia 42661
				GO WEST		
8/11/90	8	24		1 King Of Wishful Thinking	Peter Cox/Richard Drummie/Martin Page	EMI 50307
				GRACIE, Charlie		
4/13/57	❶²	17	⊙	1 Butterfly	Bernie Lowe/Kal Mann...*Ninety-Nine Ways*	Cameo 105
				GRAHAM, Larry		
9/20/80	9	20	●	1 One In A Million You	Sam Dees...*The Entertainer*	Warner 49221
				GRAMM, Lou		
4/18/87	5	20		1 Midnight Blue	Lou Gramm/Bruce Turgon...*Chain Of Love*	Atlantic 89304
1/27/90	6	21		2 Just Between You And Me	Lou Gramm/Holly Knight...*Tin Soldier*	Atlantic 88781
				GRAMMER, Billy		
1/12/59	4	20	⊙	1 Gotta Travel On	Paul Clayton/Larry Ehrlich/Ronnie Gilbert/Lee Hays/Fred Hellerman/Dave Lazer/Pete Seeger...*Chasing A Dream*	Monument 400
				GRAND FUNK RAILROAD		
9/29/73	❶¹	17	●	1 We're An American Band	Don Brewer...*Creepin'*	Capitol 3660
5/4/74	❶²	20	●	2 The Loco-Motion	Gerry Goffin/Carole King...*Destitute & Losin'*	Capitol 3840
2/22/75	3¹	13		3 Some Kind Of Wonderful	Gerry Goffin/Carole King...*Wild*	Capitol 4002
6/7/75	4	15		4 Bad Time	Mark Farner...*Good & Evil*	Capitol 4046
				GRAND FUNK (all of above)		
				GRANT, Amy		
12/6/86	❶¹	21		1 The Next Time I Fall	Bobby Caldwell/Paul Gordon...*Holy Moly* (Cetera)	Full Moon 28597
				PETER CETERA w/ AMY GRANT		
4/27/91	❶²	21		2 Baby Baby	Amy Grant/Keith Thomas	A&M 1549
8/17/91	2¹	19		3 Every Heartbeat	Amy Grant/Wayne Kirkpatrick/Charlie Peacock	A&M 1557
11/23/91	7	20		4 That's What Love Is For	Amy Grant/Mark Muller/Michael Omartian	A&M 1566
3/21/92	8	20		5 Good For Me	Amy Grant/Jay Gruska/Wayne Kirkpatrick/Tom Snow	A&M 1573
				GRANT, Earl		
10/13/58	7	19		1 The End	Sid Jacobson...*Hunky Dunky Doo*	Decca 30719
				GRANT, Eddy		
7/2/83	2⁵	22	▲	1 Electric Avenue	Eddy Grant...*Time Warp*	Portrait 03793
				GRANT, Gogi		
10/29/55	9	11		1 Suddenly There's A Valley	Biff Jones/Chuck Meyer...*Love Is*	Era 1003
6/16/56	❶⁸	28	⊙	2 The Wayward Wind	Stan Lebowsky/Herb Newman...*No More Than Forever*	Era 1013

PEAK DATE	PEAK POS	WKS CHR	GOLD	ARTIST / Song Title	Songwriter...B-side	Label & Number
				GRASS ROOTS, The		
7/1/67	8	12		1 Let's Live For Today	Michael Julien...*Depressed Feeling*	Dunhill 4084
11/2/68	5	15	●	2 Midnight Confessions	Lou Josie...*Who Will You Be Tomorrow*	Dunhill/ABC 4144
7/31/71	9	11		3 Sooner Or Later	Mitch Bottler/Ted McNamara/Adeneyi Paris/Ekundayo Paris/Gary Zekley...*I Can Turn Off The Rain*	Dunhill/ABC 4279
				GRATEFUL DEAD		
9/26/87	9	15		1 Touch Of Grey	Jerry Garcia/Robert Hunter...*My Brother Esau*	Arista 9606
				GRAY, Dobie		
5/12/73	5	21	●	1 Drift Away	Mentor Williams...*City Stars*	Decca 33057
8/2/03	9	35		2 Drift Away	Mentor Williams	Lava
				UNCLE KRACKER Featuring Dobie Gray		
				GRAY, Glen, & The Casa Loma Orchestra		
6/13/42	8	3		1 One Dozen Roses	Walter Donovan/Dick Jurgens/Roger Lewis/Joe Washburne...*The Mem'ry Of This Dance*	Decca 4299
6/19/43	7	8		2 Don't Get Around Much Anymore	Duke Ellington/Bob Russell...*Don't Do It, Darling*	Decca 18479
1/22/44	4	6		3 My Shining Hour	Harold Arlen/Johnny Mercer...*My Heart Tells Me (Should I Believe My Heart?)*	Decca 18567
1/29/44	❶5	20		4 My Heart Tells Me (Should I Believe My Heart?)	Mack Gordon/Harry Warren...*My Shining Hour*	Decca 18567
9/22/45	9	2		5 Gotta Be This Or That	Sunny Skylar...*While You're Away*	Decca 18691
				GRAY, Macy		
5/20/00	5	27		1 I Try	Macy Gray/Jinsoo Lim/Jeremy Ruzumna/David Wilder	Epic 79421
				GREAT WHITE		
8/12/89	5	26	●	1 Once Bitten Twice Shy	Ian Hunter...*Slow Ride*	Capitol 44366
				GREAVES, R.B.		
11/22/69	2¹	15	●	1 Take A Letter Maria	R.B. Greaves...*Big Bad City*	Atco 6714
				GREEN, Al		
2/12/72	❶1	16	●	1 Let's Stay Together	Al Green/Al Jackson/Willie Mitchell...*Tomorrow's Dream*	Hi 2202
5/27/72	4	12	●	2 Look What You Done For Me	Al Green/Al Jackson/Willie Mitchell...*La-La For You*	Hi 2211
9/2/72	3²	12	●	3 I'm Still In Love With You	Al Green/Al Jackson/Willie Mitchell...*Old Time Lovin'*	Hi 2216
12/23/72	3²	15	●	4 You Ought To Be With Me	Al Green/Al Jackson/Willie Mitchell...*What Is This Feeling*	Hi 2227
4/14/73	10	11	●	5 Call Me (Come Back Home)	Al Green/Al Jackson/Willie Mitchell...*What A Wonderful Thing Love Is*	Hi 2235
9/8/73	10	15	●	6 Here I Am (Come And Take Me)	Al Green/Mabon Hodges...*I'm Glad You're Mine*	Hi 2247
12/21/74	7	19	●	7 Sha-La-La (Make Me Happy)	Al Green...*School Days*	Hi 2274
1/14/89	9	17		8 Put A Little Love In Your Heart	Jackie DeShannon/Jimmy Holiday/Randy Myers	A&M 1255
				ANNIE LENNOX & AL GREEN	...*A Great Big Piece Of Love* (The Spheres Of Celestial Influence)	
				GREEN, Larry, and his Orchestra		
10/25/47	3⁴	13		1 Near You	Francis Craig/Kermit Goell...*Pic-A-Nic-In*	RCA Victor 2421
4/3/48	8	7		2 Beg Your Pardon	Francis Craig/Beasley Smith...*Can It Ever Be The Same?*	RCA Victor 2647
				GREENBAUM, Norman		
4/18/70	3³	15	●	1 Spirit In The Sky	Norman Greenbaum...*Milk Cow*	Reprise 0885
				GREEN DAY		
3/18/95	6	40	○	1 When I Come Around	Billie Joe Armstrong/Mike Pritchard/Frank Wright	Reprise
3/5/05	2⁵	36	○	2 Boulevard Of Broken Dreams	Billie Joe Armstrong/Mike Pritchard/Frank Wright	Reprise
10/15/05	6	27	△	3 Wake Me Up When September Ends	Billie Joe Armstrong/Mike Pritchard/Frank Wright	Reprise
				GREENE, Lorne		
12/5/64	❶1	12		1 Ringo	Hal Blair/Don Robertson...*Bonanza* [S]	RCA Victor 8444
				GRIFFIN, Ken, at the Organ		
5/22/48	❶7	23	⊙	1 You Can't Be True, Dear	Hal Cotton/Gerhard Ebeler/Ken Griffin/Hans Otten...*Doodle Doo Do*	Rondo 228
				Jerry Wayne (vocal)		
7/10/48	2⁷	15		2 You Can't Be True, Dear	Hal Cotton/Gerhard Ebeler/Ken Griffin/Hans Otten...*Cuckoo Waltz* [I]	Rondo 128
				GRIFFITH, Andy		
1/23/54	9	6		1 What It Was, Was Football (Parts I & II)	Andy Griffith [C]	Capitol 2693
				DEACON ANDY GRIFFITH		
				GROCE, Larry		
3/20/76	9	15		1 Junk Food Junkie	Larry Groce...*Muddy Boggy Banjo Man* [L-N]	Warner/Curb 8165
				GROOVE THEORY		
11/4/95	5	33	●	1 Tell Me	Darryl Brown/Amel Larrieux/Bryce Wilson	Epic 77961
				GROSS, Henry		
6/5/76	6	20	●	1 Shannon	Henry Gross...*Pokey*	Lifesong 45002
				GUESS WHO, The		
5/31/69	6	14	●	1 These Eyes	Randy Bachman/Burton Cummings...*Lightfoot*	RCA Victor 0102
8/23/69	10	11	●	2 Laughing	Randy Bachman/Burton Cummings...*Undun*	RCA Victor 0195
2/28/70	5	14		3 No Time	Randy Bachman/Burton Cummings...*Proper Stranger*	RCA Victor 0300
5/9/70	❶3	15	●	4 American Woman /	Randy Bachman/Burton Cummings/Jim Kale/Garry Peterson	
		13		5 No Sugar Tonight	Randy Bachman/Burton Cummings/Jim Kale/Garry Peterson	RCA Victor 0325
12/5/70	10	10		6 Share The Land	Burton Cummings...*Bus Rider*	RCA Victor 0388
10/5/74	6	16		7 Clap For The Wolfman	Burton Cummings/Bill Wallace/Kurt Winter...*Road Food*	RCA Victor 0324
				GUETTA, David		
2/13/10	5	40	△²	1 Sexy Chick	David Guetta/Jean Claude Sindres/Aliaune Thiam/Giorgio Tuinfort/Sandy Wilhelm	Astralwerks
				DAVID GUETTA Featuring Akon		
9/25/10	9	29	△	2 Club Can't Handle Me	Mike Caren/Tramar Dillard/David Guetta/Carmen Key/Kasia Livingston/Frederic Riesterer/Giorgio Tuinfort	Poe Boy
				FLO RIDA Featuring David Guetta		
				GUITAR, Bonnie		
6/10/57	6	22		1 Dark Moon	Ned Miller...*Big Mike*	Dot 15550

PEAK DATE	PEAK POS	WKS CHR	GOLD	ARTIST / Song Title	Songwriter...B-side	Label & Number
				GUNS N' ROSES		
9/10/88	❶²	24	●	1 Sweet Child O' Mine	Steven Adler/Saul Hudson/Duff McKagan/Axl Rose/Izzy Stradlin...*It's So Easy*	Geffen 27963
12/24/88	7	17	○	2 Welcome To The Jungle	Steven Adler/Saul Hudson/Duff McKagan/Axl Rose/Izzy Stradlin...*Mr. Brownstone*	Geffen 27759
3/11/89	5	17		3 Paradise City	Steven Adler/Saul Hudson/Duff McKagan/Axl Rose/Izzy Stradlin...*Move To The City*	Geffen 27570
6/3/89	4	18	●	4 Patience	Steven Adler/Saul Hudson/Duff McKagan/Axl Rose/Izzy Stradlin...*Rocket Queen*	Geffen 22996
11/16/91	10	20	●	5 Don't Cry	Saul Hudson/Duff McKagan/Axl Rose/Izzy Stradlin...*Mr. Brownstone*	Geffen 19027
8/29/92	3²	20	●	6 November Rain	Saul Hudson/Duff McKagan/Axl Rose/Izzy Stradlin...*Sweet Child O' Mine*	Geffen 19067
				GYM CLASS HEROES		
3/31/07	4	24	△	1 Cupid's Chokehold	Rick Davies/Roger Hodgson	Decaydance
				GYM CLASS HEROES Featuring Patrick Stump (of Fall Out Boy)		

H

PEAK DATE	PEAK POS	WKS CHR	GOLD	ARTIST / Song Title	Songwriter...B-side	Label & Number
				HALEY, Bill, And His Comets		
11/6/54	7	27	⊙	1 Shake, Rattle And Roll	Jesse Stone...*A.B.C. Boogie*	Decca 29204
7/9/55	❶⁸	24	⊙	2 Rock Around The Clock	Jimmy DeKnight/Max Freedman...*Thirteen Women*	Decca 29124
1/14/56	9	17		3 Burn That Candle	Winfield Scott...*Rock-A-Beatin' Boogie*	Decca 29713
2/11/56	6	19	⊙	4 See You Later, Alligator	Robert Guidry...*The Paper Boy (On Main Street, U.S.A.)*	Decca 29791
				HALL, Daryl		
10/4/86	5	15		1 Dreamtime	John Beebe/Daryl Hall...*Let It Out*	RCA 14387
				HALL, Daryl, & John Oates		
6/26/76	4	28	●	1 Sara Smile	Daryl Hall/John Oates...*Soldering*	RCA Victor 10530
10/30/76	7	20		2 She's Gone	Daryl Hall/John Oates...*I'm Just A Kid (Don't Make Me Feel Like A Man)*	Atlantic 3332
3/26/77	❶²	20	●	3 Rich Girl	Daryl Hall...*London Luck, & Love*	RCA 10860
4/11/81	❶³	23	●	4 Kiss On My List	Janna Allen/Daryl Hall...*Africa*	RCA 12142
7/4/81	5	21		5 You Make My Dreams	Sara Allen/Daryl Hall/John Oates...*Gotta Lotta Nerve (Perfect Perfect)*	RCA 12217
11/7/81	❶²	23	●	6 Private Eyes	Janna Allen/Sara Allen/Daryl Hall/Warren Pash...*Tell Me What You Want*	RCA 12296
1/30/82	❶¹	21	●	7 I Can't Go For That (No Can Do)	Sara Allen/Daryl Hall/John Oates...*Unguarded Minute*	RCA 12357
5/22/82	9	16		8 Did It In A Minute	Janna Allen/Sara Allen/Daryl Hall...*Head Above Water*	RCA 13065
12/18/82	❶⁴	23	●	9 Maneater	Sara Allen/Daryl Hall/John Oates...*Delayed Reaction*	RCA 13354
4/9/83	7	18		10 One On One	Daryl Hall...*Art Of Heartbreak*	RCA 13421
6/25/83	6	16		11 Family Man	Tim Cross/Richard Fenn/Mike Oldfield/Morris Pert/Marge Reilly...*Open All Night*	RCA 13507
12/17/83	2⁴	18		12 Say It Isn't So	Daryl Hall...*Kiss On My List*	RCA 13654
4/7/84	8	17		13 Adult Education	Sara Allen/Daryl Hall/John Oates...*Maneater*	RCA 13714
12/8/84	❶²	23	●	14 Out Of Touch	Daryl Hall/John Oates...*Cold, Dark And Yesterday*	RCA 13916
2/16/85	5	19		15 Method Of Modern Love	Janna Allen/Daryl Hall...*Bank On Your Love*	RCA 13970
6/11/88	3¹	16		16 Everything Your Heart Desires	Daryl Hall...*Realove*	Arista 9684
				HAMILTON, George IV		
12/22/56	6	20	⊙	1 A Rose And A Baby Ruth	John D. Loudermilk...*If You Don't Know*	ABC-Paramount 9765
1/13/58	10	19		2 Why Don't They Understand	Jack Fishman/Joe Henderson...*Even Tho'*	ABC-Paramount 9862
				HAMILTON, Roy		
5/21/55	6	16		1 Unchained Melody	Alex North/Hy Zaret...*From Here To Eternity*	Epic 9102
				HAMILTON, Russ		
9/16/57	4	23	⊙	1 Rainbow	Russ Hamilton...*We Will Make Love*	Kapp 184
				HAMILTON, JOE FRANK & REYNOLDS		
7/17/71	4	14	●	1 Don't Pull Your Love	Dennis Lambert/Brian Potter...*Funk-In-Wagnal*	Dunhill/ABC 4276
8/23/75	❶¹	17	●	2 Fallin' In Love	Ann Hamilton/Dan Hamilton...*So Good At Lovin' You*	Playboy 6024
				HAMLISCH, Marvin		
5/18/74	3²	16	●	1 The Entertainer	Scott Joplin...*Solace* [I]	MCA 40174
				HAMMER, Jan		
11/9/85	❶¹	22		1 Miami Vice Theme	Jan Hammer...*Evan / The Original Miami Vice Theme* [I]	MCA 52666
				HAMMOND, Albert		
12/16/72	5	16	●	1 It Never Rains In Southern California	Albert Hammond/Mike Hazlewood...*Anyone Here In The Audience*	Mums 6011
				HAMPTON, Lionel, And His Orchestra		
4/27/46	9	8		1 Hey! Ba-Ba-Re-Bop	Curley Hamner/Lionel Hampton...*Slide, Hamp, Slide*	Decca 18754
3/4/50	7	10		2 Rag Mop	Deacon Anderson/Johnnie Lee Wills...*For You My Love*	Decca 24855
				HANSON		
5/24/97	❶³	22	▲	1 MMMBop	Isaac Hanson/Taylor Hanson/Zachary Hanson	Mercury 574261
12/13/97	9	20	●	2 I Will Come To You	Isaac Hanson/Taylor Hanson/Zachary Hanson/Barry Mann/Cynthia Weil...*Cried*	Mercury 568132
				HAPPENINGS, The		
8/27/66	3²	14		1 See You In September	Sherman Edwards/Sid Wayne...*He Thinks He's A Hero*	B.T. Puppy 520
5/27/67	3³	13		2 I Got Rhythm	George Gershwin/Ira Gershwin...*You're In A Bad Way*	B.T. Puppy 527
				HARMONICATS		
6/21/47	❶⁸	26	⊙	1 Peg O' My Heart	Alfred Bryan/Fred Fisher...*Fantasy Impromptu* [I]	Vitacoustic 1
7/15/50	8	12		2 Bewitched	Lorenz Hart/Richard Rodgers...*Blue Prelude* [I]	Mercury 5399
				JAN AUGUST & Jerry Murad's HARMONICATS		
				HARRIS, Major		
6/21/75	5	18	●	1 Love Won't Let Me Wait	Vinnie Barrett/Bobby Eli...*After Loving You*	Atlantic 3248

PEAK DATE	PEAK POS	WKS CHR	GOLD	ARTIST / Song Title ... Songwriter...B-side	Label & Number
				HARRIS, Phil	
4/6/46	2²	10		1 One-Zy Two-Zy .... Dave Franklin/Irving Taylor...*Some Little Bug* [N]	ARA 136
4/6/46	10	3		2 The Dark Town Poker Club .... Jean Havez/William Vodery/Bert Williams...*Jelly Bean* [N]	ARA 116
9/13/47	8	4		3 Smoke, Smoke, Smoke (That Cigarette) .... Merle Travis/Tex Williams...*Crawdad Song* [N]	RCA Victor 2370
1/21/50	10	8		4 The Old Master Painter .... Haven Gillespie/Beasley Smith...*St. James Infirmary*	RCA Victor 3114
3/11/50	8	6		5 Chattanoogie Shoe-Shine Boy .... Jack Stapp/Harry Stone...*That's A Plenty* [N]	RCA Victor 3216
12/2/50	❶⁵	15	⊙	6 The Thing .... Charles Grean...*Goofus* [N]	RCA Victor 3968
				HARRIS, Richard	
6/22/68	2¹	13		1 MacArthur Park .... Jimmy Webb...*Didn't We*	Dunhill 4134
				HARRIS, Rolf	
7/13/63	3¹	11		1 Tie Me Kangaroo Down, Sport .... Rolf Harris...*The Big Black Hat* [N]	Epic 9596
				HARRIS, Thurston	
11/11/57	6	17		1 Little Bitty Pretty One .... Bobby Day...*I Hope You Won't Hold It Against Me*	Aladdin 3398
				HARRISON, George	
12/26/70	❶⁴	14	●	1 My Sweet Lord .... George Harrison...*Isn't It A Pity*	Apple 2995
3/27/71	10	9		2 What Is Life .... George Harrison...*Apple Scruffs*	Apple 1828
6/30/73	❶¹	14		3 Give Me Love - (Give Me Peace On Earth) .... George Harrison...*Miss O'Dell*	Apple 1862
7/4/81	2³	16		4 All Those Years Ago .... George Harrison...*Writing's On The Wall*	Dark Horse 49725
1/16/88	❶¹	22		5 Got My Mind Set On You .... Rudy Clark...*Lay His Head*	Dark Horse 28178
				HARRISON, Wilbert	
5/18/59	❶²	16	⊙	1 Kansas City .... Jerry Leiber/Mike Stoller...*Listen, My Darling*	Fury 1023
				HART, Corey	
9/1/84	7	23		1 Sunglasses At Night .... Corey Hart...*At The Dance*	EMI America 8203
8/17/85	3²	20		2 Never Surrender .... Corey Hart...*Water From The Moon*	EMI America 8268
				HARTMAN, Dan	
8/18/84	6	25		1 I Can Dream About You .... Dan Hartman...*Blue Shadows* (The Blasters)	MCA 52378
				HATHAWAY, Donny	
8/12/72	5	13	●	1 Where Is The Love .... Ralph MacDonald/William Salter...*Mood*	Atlantic 2879
5/13/78	2²	20	●	2 The Closer I Get To You .... Reggie Lucas/James Mtume...*Love Is The Healing* (Flack)	Atlantic 3463
				ROBERTA FLACK & DONNY HATHAWAY (above 2)	
				HAWKES, Chesney	
11/2/91	10	20		1 The One And Only .... Nik Kershaw...*It's Gonna Be Tough*	Chrysalis 23730
				HAWKINS, Edwin, Singers	
5/31/69	4	10	●	1 Oh Happy Day .... Edwin Hawkins...*Jesus, Lover Of My Soul*	Pavilion 20,001
				THE EDWIN HAWKINS' SINGERS Featuring Dorothy Combs Morrison	
7/11/70	6	17		2 Lay Down (Candles In The Rain) .... Melanie Safka...*Candles In The Rain* (Melanie)	Buddah 167
				MELANIE with The Edwin Hawkins Singers	
				HAWKINS, Erskine, and his Orchestra	
9/14/40	10	1		1 Dolimite .... William Johnson...*Too Many Dreams* [I]	Bluebird 10812
5/26/45	9	8		2 Tippin' In .... Bobby Smith...*Remember* [I]	Victor 1639
				HAWKINS, Sophie B.	
6/27/92	5	21		1 Damn I Wish I Was Your Lover .... Sophie B. Hawkins...*Don't Stop Swaying*	Columbia 74164
10/28/95	6	44		2 As I Lay Me Down .... Sophie B. Hawkins...*I Need Nothing Else*	Columbia 77801
				HAYES, Bill	
3/26/55	❶⁵	20	⊙	1 The Ballad Of Davy Crockett .... Tom Blackburn/George Bruns...*Farewell*	Cadence 1256
				HAYES, Isaac	
11/20/71	❶²	13	●	1 Theme From Shaft .... Isaac Hayes...*Cafe Regio's*	Enterprise 9038
				HAYES, Richard	
1/28/50	2¹	12		1 The Old Master Painter .... Haven Gillespie/Beasley Smith...*Open Door — Open Arms*	Mercury 5342
9/23/50	10	12		2 Our Lady Of Fatima .... Gladys Gollahon...*Honestly I Love You*	Mercury 5466
3/31/51	9	10		3 The Aba Daba Honeymoon .... Walter Donovan/Arthur Fields...*I Don't Want To Love You*	Mercury 5586
				RICHARD HAYES & KITTY KALLEN (above 2)	
12/15/51	9	10		4 Out In The Cold Again .... Rube Bloom/Ted Koehler...*Once*	Mercury 5724
				HAYMAN, Richard	
5/30/53	3²	19		1 Ruby .... Mitchell Parish/Heinz Roemheld...*Love Mood* [I]	Mercury 70115
				HAYMES, Dick	
7/10/43	2⁴	11		1 It Can't Be Wrong .... Kim Gannon/Max Steiner...*In My Arms*	Decca 18557
7/24/43	❶⁴	16	⊙	2 You'll Never Know .... Mack Gordon/Harry Warren...*Wait For Me Mary*	Decca 18556
8/21/43	7	7		3 In My Arms .... Ted Grouya/Frank Loesser...*It Can't Be Wrong*	Decca 18557
11/27/43	5	6		4 Put Your Arms Around Me, Honey (I Never Knew Any Girl Like You) .... Junie McCree/Albert Von Tilzer...*For The First Time (I've Fallen In Love)*	Decca 18565
6/23/45	9	3		5 Laura .... Johnny Mercer/David Raksin...*The Night Is Young And You're So Beautiful*	Decca 18666
7/7/45	7	3		6 The More I See You .... Mack Gordon/Harry Warren...*I Wish I Knew*	Decca 18662
9/29/45	6	6		7 I Wish I Knew .... Mack Gordon/Harry Warren...*The More I See You*	Decca 18662
10/27/45	3¹	9		8 Till The End Of Time .... Buddy Kaye/Ted Mossman...*Love Letters*	Decca 18699
11/17/45	6	10		9 That's For Me .... Oscar Hammerstein/Richard Rodgers...*It Might As Well Be Spring*	Decca 18706
12/29/45	5	12		10 It Might As Well Be Spring .... Oscar Hammerstein/Richard Rodgers...*That's For Me*	Decca 18706
3/29/47	9	5		11 How Are Things In Glocca Morra .... E.Y. Harburg/Burton Lane...*'Twas Only An Irishman's Dream*	Decca 23830
5/31/47	3¹	11		12 Mam'selle .... Mack Gordon/Edmund Goulding...*Stella By Starlight*	Decca 23861
11/8/47	9	7		13 I Wish I Didn't Love You So .... Frank Loesser...*Naughty Angeline*	Decca 23977
5/29/48	2¹	23	⊙	14 Little White Lies .... Walter Donaldson...*The Treasure Of Sierra Madre*	Decca 24280
6/19/48	9	13		15 You Can't Be True, Dear .... Hal Cotton/Gerhard Ebeler/Ken Griffin/Hans Otten...*Nature Boy*	Decca 24439

57

PEAK DATE	PEAK POS	WKS CHR	GOLD	ARTIST / Song Title	Songwriter...B-side	Label & Number
				HAYMES, Dick (cont'd)		
9/18/48	9	18		16 It's Magic	Sammy Cahn/Jule Styne...*It's You Or No One*	Decca 23826
8/13/49	6	20		17 Room Full Of Roses	Tim Spencer...*A Chapter In My Life Called Mary*	Decca 24632
9/3/49	5	18		18 Maybe It's Because	Harry Ruby/Johnnie Scott...*It Happens Every Spring*	Decca 24650
1/28/50	4	13		19 The Old Master Painter	Haven Gillespie/Beasley Smith...*Why Was I Born?*	Decca 24801
8/5/50	10	11		20 Count Every Star	Bruno Coquatrix/Sammy Gallop...*If You Were Only Mine*	Decca 27042
				DICK HAYMES and ARTIE SHAW		
				DICK HAYMES and HELEN FORREST:		
6/10/44	2¹	18		21 Long Ago (And Far Away)	Ira Gershwin/Jerome Kern...*Look For The Silver Lining*	Decca 23317
9/30/44	4	9		22 It Had To Be You	Isham Jones/Gus Kahn...*Together*	Decca 23349
11/4/44	3²	12		23 Together	Lew Brown/B.G. DeSylva/Ray Henderson...*It Had To Be You*	Decca 23349
10/27/45	2¹	13		24 I'll Buy That Dream	Herb Magidson/Allie Wrubel...*Some Sunday Morning*	Decca 23434
10/27/45	9	5		25 Some Sunday Morning	Ray Heindorf/M.K. Jerome/Ted Koehler...*I'll Buy That Dream*	Decca 23434
3/16/46	7	5		26 I'm Always Chasing Rainbows	Harry Carroll/Joseph McCarthy...*Tomorrow Is Forever*	Decca 23472
4/6/46	4	11		27 Oh! What It Seemed To Be	Bennie Benjamin/Frankie Carle/George Weiss...*Give Me A Little Kiss, Will You Huh?*	Decca 23481
				HEAD, Murray		
5/18/85	3¹	20		1 One Night In Bangkok	Benny Andersson/Tim Rice/Björn Ulvaeus...*Merano*	RCA 13988
				HEAD, Roy		
10/16/65	2²	11		1 Treat Her Right	Roy Head...*So Long, My Love*	Back Beat 546
				HEALEY, Jeff, Band		
9/2/89	5	22		1 Angel Eyes	John Hiatt/Fred Koller...*Don't Let Your Chance Go By*	Arista 9808
				HEART		
11/6/76	9	23		1 Magic Man	Ann Wilson/Nancy Wilson...*How Deep It Goes*	Mushroom 7011
1/10/81	8	16		2 Tell It Like It Is	George Davis/Lee Diamond...*Strange Euphoria*	Epic 50950
8/24/85	10	21		3 What About Love?	Brian Allen/Sheron Alton/Jim Vallance...*Heart Of Darkness*	Capitol 5481
12/7/85	4	24		4 Never	Walter Bloch/Holly Knight/Ann Wilson...*Shell Shock*	Capitol 5512
3/22/86	❶¹	20		5 These Dreams	Martin Page/Bernie Taupin...*Shell Shock*	Capitol 5541
6/21/86	10	16		6 Nothin' At All	Mark Mueller...*The Wolf*	Capitol 5572
7/11/87	❶³	21		7 Alone	Tom Kelly/Billy Steinberg...*Barracuda (live)*	Capitol 44002
10/3/87	7	22		8 Who Will You Run To	Diane Warren...*Magic Man (live)*	Capitol 44040
5/26/90	2²	20	●	9 All I Wanna Do Is Make Love To You	Mutt Lange...*Call Of The Wild*	Capitol 44507
				HEATWAVE		
11/12/77	2²	27	▲	1 Boogie Nights	Rod Temperton...*All You Do Is Dial*	Epic 50370
7/15/78	7	17	▲	2 The Groove Line	Rod Temperton...*Happiness Togetherness*	Epic 50524
				HEBB, Bobby		
8/20/66	2²	15	●	1 Sunny	Bobby Hebb...*Bread*	Philips 40365
				HEIDT, Horace, and his Musical Knights		
5/24/41	2¹	6		1 G'bye Now	Ray Evans/Harold Johnson/Jay Levison/John Olsen...*Do You Believe In Fairy Tales?*	Columbia 36026
7/5/41	3²	6		2 The Hut-Sut Song (A Swedish Serenade)	Leo Killion/Ted McMichael/Jack Owens...*The Way You Look At Me*	Columbia 36138
7/26/41	8	2		3 Good Bye Dear, I'll Be Back In A Year	Mack Kay...*Walkin' Round In Circles*	Columbia 36148
10/4/41	2²	11		4 I Don't Want To Set The World On Fire	Bennie Benjamin/Eddie Durham/Sol Marcus/Eddie Seiler...*Mama*	Columbia 36295
12/13/41	7	5		5 Shepherd Serenade	Kermit Goell/Fred Spielman...*Delilah*	Columbia 36370
3/21/42	7	4	⊙	6 Deep In The Heart Of Texas	June Hershey/Don Swander...*Loretta*	Columbia 36525
2/3/45	10	2		7 Don't Fence Me In	Cole Porter...*I Promise You*	Columbia 36761
				HEIGHTS, The		
11/14/92	❶²	20	●	1 How Do You Talk To An Angel	Barry Coffing/Steve Tyrell...*Walkin' Nerve*	Capitol 44890
				HELMS, Bobby		
11/18/57	7	23	⊙	1 My Special Angel	Jimmy Duncan...*Standing At The End Of My World*	Decca 30423
1/13/58	6	6	⊙	2 Jingle Bell Rock	Joe Beal/Jim Boothe...*Captain Santa Claus (And His Reindeer Space Patrol)* [X]	Decca 30513
				HENDERSON, Joe		
7/7/62	8	12		1 Snap Your Fingers	Grady Martin/Alex Zinetis...*If You See Me Cry*	Todd 1072
				HENDERSON, Skitch		
11/2/46	9	9		1 Five Minutes More	Sammy Cahn/Jule Styne...*You'll See What A Kiss Can Do*	Capitol 287
				HENLEY, Don		
1/23/82	6	19		1 Leather And Lace	Stevie Nicks...*Bella Donna* (Nicks)	Modern 7341
				STEVIE NICKS (with Don Henley)		
1/8/83	3³	19	●	2 Dirty Laundry	Don Henley/Danny Kortchmar...*Lilah*	Asylum 69894
2/9/85	5	22		3 The Boys Of Summer	Mike Campbell/Don Henley...*A Month Of Sundays*	Geffen 29141
5/4/85	9	19		4 All She Wants To Do Is Dance	Danny Kortchmar...*Building The Perfect Beast*	Geffen 29065
8/26/89	8	18		5 The End Of The Innocence	Don Henley/Bruce Hornsby...*If Dirt Were Dollars*	Geffen 22925
9/26/92	2⁶	24	●	6 Sometimes Love Just Ain't Enough	Glen Burtnick/Patty Smyth...*Out There* (Smyth)	MCA 54403
				PATTY SMYTH with Don Henley		
				HENRY, Clarence "Frogman"		
4/24/61	4	16		1 But I Do	Paul Gayten/Robert Guidry...*Just My Baby And Me*	Argo 5378
				HERMAN, Woody, And His Orchestra		
4/26/41	5	4		1 Blue Flame	James Noble...*Fur Trappers' Ball* [I]	Decca 3643
6/28/41	10	1		2 G'bye Now	Ray Evans/Harold Johnson/Jay Levison/John Olsen...*Until Tomorrow*	Decca 3745
2/14/42	❶¹	11		3 Blues In The Night (My Mama Done Tol' Me)	Harold Arlen/Johnny Mercer...*This Time The Dream's On Me*	Decca 4030
9/12/42	5	4		4 Amen	Bill Hardy/Vic Schoen/Roger Segure...*Deliver Me To Tennessee*	Decca 18346
3/4/44	7	11		5 Do Nothin' Till You Hear From Me	Duke Ellington/Bob Russell...*By The River Of The Roses*	Decca 18578
4/8/44	10	8		6 The Music Stopped	Harold Adamson/Jimmy McHugh...*I Couldn't Sleep A Wink Last Night*	Decca 18577
7/15/44	10	5		7 Milkman, Keep Those Bottles Quiet	Gene DePaul/Don Raye...*Irresistible You*	Decca 18603
5/12/45	4	12	⊙	8 Laura	Johnny Mercer/David Raksin...*I Wonder*	Columbia 36785
5/26/45	2²	14		9 Caldonia	Fleecie Moore...*Happiness Is A Thing Called Joe*	Columbia 36789

PEAK DATE	PEAK POS	WKS CHR	GOLD	ARTIST / Song Title	Songwriter...B-side	Label & Number
				HERMAN, Woody, And His Orchestra (cont'd)		
8/11/45	9	6		10 A Kiss Goodnight	Reba Herman/Freddie Slack/Floyd Victor...*Goosey Gander*	Columbia 36815
2/16/46	7	4		11 Let It Snow! Let It Snow! Let It Snow!	Sammy Cahn/Jule Styne...*Everybody Knew But Me* [X]	Columbia 36909
7/27/46	8	10		12 Surrender	Bennie Benjamin/George Weiss...*The Good Earth*	Columbia 36985
5/8/48	3¹	12		13 Sabre Dance	Aram Khachaturian/Lester Lee/Allan Roberts...*Swing Low, Sweet Clarinet* [I]	Columbia 38102
				HERMAN'S HERMITS		
3/27/65	2²	15		1 Can't You Hear My Heartbeat	Ken Hawker/John Shakespeare...*I Know Why*	MGM 13310
5/1/65	❶³	11	●	2 Mrs. Brown You've Got A Lovely Daughter	Trevor Peacock...*I Gotta Dream On*	MGM 13341
5/15/65	5	13		3 Silhouettes	Bob Crewe/Frank Slay...*Walkin' With My Angel*	MGM 13332
7/10/65	4	10		4 Wonderful World	Lou Adler/Herb Alpert/Barbara Campbell...*Traveling Light*	MGM 13354
8/7/65	❶¹	10		5 I'm Henry VIII, I Am	Fred Murray/R.P. Weston...*The End Of The World*	MGM 13367
10/16/65	7	10		6 Just A Little Bit Better	Kenny Young...*Sea Cruise*	MGM 13398
1/22/66	8	9		7 A Must To Avoid	P.F. Sloan...*The Man With The Cigar*	MGM 13437
3/12/66	3¹	9		8 Listen People	Graham Gouldman...*Got A Feeling*	MGM 13462
5/7/66	9	8		9 Leaning On The Lamp Post	Noel Gay...*Hold On!*	MGM 13500
11/5/66	5	11		10 Dandy	Ray Davies...*My Reservation's Been Confirmed*	MGM 13603
3/25/67	4	12	●	11 There's A Kind Of Hush	Les Reed/Geoff Stephens...*No Milk Today*	MGM 13681
				HERTH, Milt		
3/20/48	6	13		1 I'm Looking Over A Four Leaf Clover	Mort Dixon/Harry Woods...*Bye Bye Blackbird*	Decca 24319
				RUSS MORGAN And HIS ORCHESTRA with MILT HERTH At The Organ and the Ames Brothers		
				HEYWOOD, Eddie		
10/13/56	2²	31	⊙	1 Canadian Sunset	Eddie Heywood...*This Is Real (We're In Love, We're In Love, We're In Love)* [I]	RCA Victor 6537
				HUGO WINTERHALTER with EDDIE HEYWOOD		
				HIBBLER, Al		
6/4/55	3¹	19		1 Unchained Melody	Alex North/Hy Zaret...*Daybreak*	Decca 29441
12/31/55	4	22		2 He	Richard Mullan/Jack Richards...*Breeze (Blow My Baby Back To Me)*	Decca 29660
9/22/56	10	20		3 After The Lights Go Down Low	Leroy Lovett/Alan White...*I Was Telling Her About You*	Decca 29982
				HICKS, Taylor		
7/1/06	❶¹	8		1 Do I Make You Proud	Tracie Ackerman/Andy Watkins/Paul Wilson...*Takin' It To The Streets*	J Records 85833
				HI-FIVE		
5/18/91	❶¹	23		1 I Like The Way (The Kissing Game)	Bernard Belle/Teddy Riley/Dave Way...*Sweetheart*	Jive 1424
8/31/91	8	21		2 I Can't Wait Another Minute	Eric White...*I Know Love*	Jive 1445
10/17/92	5	20		3 She's Playing Hard To Get	Timmy Allen/William Walton...*Whenever You Say*	Jive 42067
				HIGGINS, Bertie		
4/17/82	8	29	●	1 Key Largo	Bertie Higgins/Sonny Limbo...*White Line Fever*	Kat Family 02524
				HIGH SCHOOL MUSICAL CAST		
2/11/06	4	11	○	1 Breaking Free [Zac Efron & Vanessa Hudgens]	Jamie Houston	Walt Disney
8/4/07	6	8		2 What Time Is It	Matthew Gerrard/Robbie Nevil	Walt Disney 000507
				HIGHWAYMEN, The		
9/4/61	❶²	17	⊙	1 Michael	(traditional)...*Santiano*	United Artists 258
				HILDEGARDE		
8/18/45	6	2		1 June Is Bustin' Out All Over	Oscar Hammerstein/Richard Rodgers...*This Was A Real Nice Clambake*	Decca 23428
5/11/46	7	14		2 The Gypsy	Billy Reid...*One-Zy Two-Zy (I Love You-zy)*	Decca 23511
				HILDEGARDE with GUY LOMBARDO AND HIS ROYAL CANADIANS (above 2)		
				HILL, Dan		
3/4/78	3²	22	●	1 Sometimes When We Touch	Dan Hill/Barry Mann...*Still Not Used To*	20th Century 2355
9/12/87	6	24		2 Can't We Try	Beverly Hill/Dan Hill...*Pleasure Centre*	Columbia 07050
				DAN HILL (with Vonda Sheppard)		
				HILL, Faith		
10/10/98	7	48	▲	1 This Kiss	Beth Nielsen Chapman/Robin Lerner/Annie Roboff...*Better Days*	Warner 17247
4/22/00	2⁵	53	●	2 Breathe	Stephanie Bentley/Holly Lamar...*It All Comes Down To Love*	Warner 16884
1/13/01	6	56		3 The Way You Love Me	Michael Delaney/Keith Follese...*Never Gonna Be Your Lady*	Warner 16818
6/30/01	10	20		4 There You'll Be	Diane Warren...*Breathe*	Warner 16739
7/19/97	7	20	▲	5 It's Your Love	Stephony Smith...*She Never Lets It Go To Her Heart* (McGraw)	Curb 73019
				TIM McGRAW with Faith Hill		
				HILL, Lauryn		
6/22/96	2³	35		1 Killing Me Softly	Charles Fox/Norman Gimbel	Ruffhouse
				FUGEES (feat. Lauryn Hill)		
11/14/98	❶²	21	●	2 Doo Wop (That Thing)	Lauryn Hill...*Lost Ones*	Ruffhouse 78868
				HILLTOPPERS, The		
11/1/52	7	19		1 Trying	Billy Vaughn...*You Made Up My Mind*	Dot 15018
7/4/53	8	12		2 I'd Rather Die Young (Than Grow Old Without You)	Beasley Smith/Billy Vaughn/Randy Wood...*P.S. I Love You*	Dot 15085
8/8/53	4	21	⊙	3 P.S. I Love You	Gordon Jenkins/Johnny Mercer...*I'd Rather Die Young (Than Grow Old Without You)*	Dot 15085
11/21/53	8	11		4 To Be Alone	Billy Vaughn...*Love Walked In*	Dot 15105
11/28/53	8	10		5 Love Walked In	George Gershwin/Ira Gershwin...*To Be Alone*	Dot 15105
2/20/54	10	11		6 Till Then	Sol Marcus/Eddie Seiler/Guy Wood...*I Found Your Letter*	Dot 15132
3/20/54	8	11		7 From The Vine Came The Grape	Paul Cunningham/Leonard Whitcup...*Time Will Tell*	Dot 15127
12/31/55	8	19		8 Only You (And You Alone)	Buck Ram/Ande Rand...*Until The Real Thing Comes Along*	Dot 15423
4/6/57	3¹	16		9 Marianne	Richard Dehr/Terry Gilkyson/Frank Miller...*You're Wasting Your Time*	Dot 15537
				HILSON, Keri		
8/25/07	3⁴	38		1 The Way I Are	Floyd Hills/Keri Hilson/John Maultsby/Garland Mosley/Tim Mosley/Balewa Muhammad/Candice Nelson	Mosley
				TIMBALAND Featuring Keri Hilson		
6/20/09	3³	31		2 Knock You Down	Marcella Araica/Kevin Cossom/Floyd Nathaniel Hills/Keri Hilson/Shaffer Smith/Kanye West	Mosley
				KERI HILSON Featuring Kanye West & Ne-Yo		

PEAK DATE	PEAK POS	WKS CHR	GOLD	ARTIST / Song Title	Songwriter...B-side	Label & Number
				HINDER		
10/14/06	3⁴	33	△	1 Lips Of An Angel	Joe Garvey/Cody Hanson/Brian Howes/Mark King/Mike Rodden/Austin Winkler	Universal Republic
				HIRT, Al		
2/29/64	4	16		1 Java	Freddy Friday/Allen Toussaint/Alvin Tyler...*I Can't Get Started* [I]	RCA Victor 8280
				HOLDEN, Ron		
6/13/60	7	19		1 Love You So	Ron Holden...*My Babe*	Donna 1315
				RON HOLDEN with The Thunderbirds		
				HOLIDAY, J.		
10/6/07	5	23	○	1 Bed	Carlos McKinney/Terius Nash	Music Line 61202
				HOLLIES, The		
9/17/66	5	14		1 Bus Stop	Graham Gouldman...*Don't Run And Hide*	Imperial 66186
12/10/66	7	10		2 Stop Stop Stop	Allan Clarke/Tony Hicks/Graham Nash...*It's You*	Imperial 66214
8/12/67	9	13		3 Carrie-Anne	Allan Clarke/Tony Hicks/Graham Nash...*Signs That Will Never Change*	Epic 10180
3/21/70	7	18		4 He Ain't Heavy, He's My Brother	Bob Russell/Bobby Scott...*Cos You Like To Love Me*	Epic 10532
9/2/72	2²	15	▲	5 Long Cool Woman (In A Black Dress)	Harold Clarke/Roger Cook/Roger Greenaway...*Look What We've Got*	Epic 10871
8/3/74	6	21	●	6 The Air That I Breathe	Albert Hammond/Mike Hazlewood...*No More Riders*	Epic 11100
				HOLLY, Buddy / The Crickets		
9/23/57	❶¹	22	I	1 That'll Be The Day	Jerry Allison/Buddy Holly/Norman Petty...*I'm Lookin' For Someone To Love*	Brunswick 55009
				THE CRICKETS		
12/30/57	3³	22	⊙	2 Peggy Sue	Jerry Allison/Buddy Holly/Norman Petty...*Everyday*	Coral 61885
				BUDDY HOLLY		
1/20/58	10	20		3 Oh, Boy!	Norman Petty/Bill Tilghman/Sunny West...*Not Fade Away*	Brunswick 55035
				THE CRICKETS		
				HOLLYWOOD ARGYLES		
7/11/60	❶¹	15	⊙	1 Alley-Oop	Dallas Frazier...*Sho' Know A Lot About Love* [N]	Lute 5905
				HOLMAN, Eddie		
2/21/70	2¹	14	●	1 Hey There Lonely Girl	Leon Carr/Earl Shuman...*It's All In The Game*	ABC 11240
				HOLMES, Clint		
6/16/73	2²	23	●	1 Playground In My Mind	Lee Pockriss/Paul Vance...*There's No Future In My Future*	Epic 10891
				HOLMES, Leroy, And His Orchestra		
8/28/54	9	14	⊙	1 The High And The Mighty	Dimitri Tiomkin/Ned Washington...*Lisa* [I]	MGM 11761
				HOLMES, Rupert		
12/22/79	❶³	21	●	1 Escape (The Pina Colada Song)	Rupert Holmes...*Drop It*	Infinity 50,035
3/29/80	6	17		2 Him	Rupert Holmes...*Get Outta Yourself*	MCA 41173
				HONDELLS, The		
10/31/64	9	12		1 Little Honda	Brian Wilson...*Hot Rod High*	Mercury 72324
				HONEYCOMBS, The		
11/14/64	5	13		1 Have I The Right?	Alan Blaikley/Howard Blaikley...*Please Don't Pretend Again*	Interphon 7707
				HONEY CONE, The		
6/12/71	❶¹	16	●	1 Want Ads	General Johnson/Barney Perkins/Greg Perry...*We Belong Together*	Hot Wax 7011
				HONEYDRIPPERS, The		
1/5/85	3¹	20		1 Sea Of Love	Phil Battiste/George Khoury...*I Get A Thrill*	Es Paranza 99701
				HOOBASTANK		
6/19/04	2¹	38	○	1 The Reason	Dan Estrin/Doug Robb...*Running Away*	Island 0002875
				HOOTIE & THE BLOWFISH		
2/18/95	10	44		1 Hold My Hand	Mark Bryan/Dean Felber/Darius Rucker/Jim Sonefeld...*I Go Blind*	Atlantic 87230
7/8/95	9	35		2 Let Her Cry	Mark Bryan/Dean Felber/Darius Rucker/Jim Sonefeld	Atlantic 87231
10/21/95	6	32		3 Only Wanna Be With You	Mark Bryan/Dean Felber/Darius Rucker/Jim Sonefeld...*Where Were You*	Atlantic 87132
				HOPKIN, Mary		
11/2/68	2³	14	●	1 Those Were The Days	Gene Raskin...*Turn, Turn, Turn*	Apple 1801
				HORNSBY, Bruce, And The Range		
12/13/86	❶¹	22		1 The Way It Is	Bruce Hornsby...*The Wild Frontier*	RCA 5023
3/21/87	4	18		2 Mandolin Rain	Bruce Hornsby/John Hornsby...*The Red Plains (live)*	RCA 5087
7/2/88	5	16		3 The Valley Road	Bruce Hornsby/John Hornsby...*The Long Race*	RCA 7645
				HORTON, Johnny		
6/1/59	❶⁶	21	●	1 The Battle Of New Orleans	Jimmie Driftwood...*All For The Love Of A Girl*	Columbia 41339
4/25/60	3¹	18		2 Sink The Bismarck	Tillman Franks/Johnny Horton...*The Same Old Tale The Crow Told Me*	Columbia 41568
12/19/60	4	23		3 North To Alaska	Mike Phillips...*The Mansion You Stole*	Columbia 41782
				HOT		
7/16/77	6	27	●	1 Angel In Your Arms	Tom Brasfield/Herbert Ivey/Terry Woodford...*Just 'Cause I'm Guilty*	Big Tree 16085
				HOT BUTTER		
10/21/72	9	18		1 Popcorn	Gershon Kingsley...*At The Movies* [I]	Musicor 1458
				HOT CHOCOLATE		
4/26/75	8	14		1 Emma	Errol Brown/Tony Wilson...*A Love Like Yours*	Big Tree 16031
2/7/76	3³	21	●	2 You Sexy Thing	Errol Brown/Tony Wilson...*Amazing Skin Song*	Big Tree 16047
2/10/79	6	18	●	3 Every 1's A Winner	Errol Brown...*Power Of Love*	Infinity 50,002
				HOUSE OF PAIN		
10/10/92	3²	30	▲	1 Jump Around	Lawrence Muggerud/Erik Schrody	Tommy Boy 7526

PEAK DATE	PEAK POS	WKS CHR	GOLD	ARTIST / Song Title	Songwriter...B-side	Label & Number
				HOUSTON, Thelma		
4/23/77	❶¹	24		1 Don't Leave Me This Way	Kenny Gamble/Cary Gilbert/Leon Huff...*Today Will Soon Be Yesterday*	Tamla 54278
				HOUSTON, Whitney		
7/27/85	3¹	21	●	1 You Give Good Love	LaForrest Cope...*Greatest Love Of All*	Arista 9274
10/26/85	❶¹	22	●	2 Saving All My Love For You	Gerry Goffin/Michael Masser...*All At Once*	Arista 9381
2/15/86	❶²	23	●	3 How Will I Know	George Merrill/Shannon Rubicam/Narada Michael Walden...*Someone For Me*	Arista 9434
5/17/86	❶³	18	●	4 Greatest Love Of All	Linda Creed/Michael Masser...*Thinking About You*	Arista 9466
6/27/87	❶²	18	▲	5 I Wanna Dance With Somebody (Who Loves Me)	George Merrill/Shannon Rubicam...*Moment Of Truth*	Arista 9598
9/26/87	❶²	17		6 Didn't We Almost Have It All	Will Jennings/Michael Masser...*Shock Me* (w/Jermaine Jackson)	Arista 9616
1/9/88	❶¹	19	●	7 So Emotional	Tom Kelly/Billy Steinberg...*For The Love Of You*	Arista 9642
4/23/88	❶²	18		8 Where Do Broken Hearts Go	Chuck Jackson/Frank Wildhorn...*Where You Are*	Arista 9674
8/27/88	9	16		9 Love Will Save The Day	Toni Childs...*How Will I Know*	Arista 9720
11/12/88	5	17		10 One Moment In Time	John Bettis/Albert Hammond...*Love Is A Contact Sport*	Arista 9743
12/1/90	❶¹	19	●	11 I'm Your Baby Tonight	Babyface/L.A. Reid...*I'm Knockin'*	Arista 2108
2/23/91	❶²	23	●	12 All The Man That I Need	Michael Gore/Dean Pitchford...*Dancin' On The Smooth Edge*	Arista 2156
6/8/91	9	14		13 Miracle	Babyface/L.A. Reid...*After We Make Love*	Arista 2222
11/28/92	❶¹⁴	26	▲⁴	14 I Will Always Love You	Dolly Parton...*Jesus Loves Me*	Arista 12490
2/20/93	4	23	●	15 I'm Every Woman	Nick Ashford/Valerie Simpson...*Who Do You Love*	Arista 12519
4/3/93	4	20	●	16 I Have Nothing	David Foster/Linda Thompson...*Where You Are*	Arista 12527
11/25/95	❶¹	21	▲	17 Exhale (Shoop Shoop)	Babyface...*Dancin' On The Smooth Edge*	Arista 12885
5/4/96	8	20	●	18 Count On Me	Babyface/Michael Houston/Whitney Houston...*One Moment In Time* (Houston)	Arista 12976
				WHITNEY HOUSTON & CECE WINANS		
2/1/97	4	20	▲	19 I Believe In You And Me	Sandy Linzer/David Wolfert...*Somebody Bigger Than You And I*	Arista 13293
3/20/99	2³	28	▲	20 Heartbreak Hotel	Ken Karlin/Tamara Savage/Carsten Schack...*It's Not Right But It's Okay*	Arista 13619
				WHITNEY HOUSTON (Feat. Faith Evans & Kelly Price)		
7/3/99	4	20	●	21 It's Not Right But It's Okay	LaShawn Daniels/Toni Estes/Freddie Jerkins/Rodney Jerkins/Isaac Phillips	Arista 13681
1/1/00	4	28	▲	22 My Love Is Your Love	Jerry Duplessis/Wyclef Jean	Arista 13730
10/27/01	6	16	▲	23 The Star Spangled Banner	Francis Scott Key...*America The Beautiful* [L]	Arista 15054
				HOWARD, Adina		
5/6/95	2²	30	▲	1 Freak Like Me	George Clinton/William Collins/Gary Cooper	EastWest 64484
				HOWARD, Don		
1/24/53	4	15		1 Oh Happy Day	Don Howard/Nancy Reed...*You Went Away*	Essex 311
				HOWARD, Eddy, and His Orchestra		
8/3/46	❶⁸	25	⊙	1 To Each His Own	Ray Evans/Jay Livingston...*Cynthia's In Love*	Majestic 7188
12/7/46	6	14		2 The Rickety Rickshaw Man	Ervin Drake...*She's Funny That Way*	Majestic 7192
2/1/47	2¹	20		3 (I Love You) For Sentimental Reasons	William Best/Deek Watson...*Why Does It Get Late So Early*	Majestic 7204
4/26/47	2⁵	15		4 My Adobe Hacienda	Louise Massey/Lee Penny...*Midnight Masquerade*	Majestic 1117
6/21/47	2⁵	19		5 I Wonder, I Wonder, I Wonder	Daryl Hutchins...*Ask Anyone Who Knows*	Majestic 1124
11/1/47	7	3		6 Kate (Have I Come Too Early, Too Late)	Irving Berlin...*On The Avenue*	Majestic 1160
11/1/47	9	4		7 An Apple Blossom Wedding	Jimmy Kennedy/Nat Simon...*Blue Tail Fly*	Majestic 1156
2/28/48	8	16		8 Now Is The Hour (Maori Farewell Song)	Maewa Kaihan/Clement Scott/Dorothy Stewart...*True*	Majestic 1191
12/25/48	6	12		9 (I'd Love To Get You) On A Slow Boat To China	Frank Loesser...*I'd Love To Live In Loveland*	Mercury 5210
8/27/49	4	23		10 Room Full Of Roses	Tim Spencer...*Yes, Yes, In Your Eyes*	Mercury 5296
9/24/49	9	14		11 Maybe It's Because	Harry Ruby/Johnnie Scott...*Tell Me Why*	Mercury 5314
11/18/50	9	11		12 To Think You've Chosen Me	Bennie Benjamin/George Weiss...*The One Rose (That's Left In My Heart)*	Mercury 5517
11/17/51	❶⁸	24	⊙	13 Sin	George Haven/Chester Shull...*My Wife And I*	Mercury 5711
5/17/52	7	16		14 Be Anything (But Be Mine)	Irving Gordon...*She Took*	Mercury 5815
8/16/52	4	16		15 Auf Wiederseh'n, Sweetheart	John Sexton/Eberhard Storch/John Turner...*I Don't Want To Take A Chance*	Mercury 5871
				H-TOWN		
5/22/93	3⁷	25	▲	1 Knockin' Da Boots	Bishop Burrell/Dino Conner/Shazam Conner/Darryl Jackson	Luke 161
				HUES CORPORATION, The		
7/6/74	❶¹	18	●	1 Rock The Boat	Wally Holmes...*All Goin' Down Together*	RCA Victor 0232
				HUEY		
6/2/07	6	23	△	1 Pop, Lock And Drop It	Lawrence Franks/Dandre Smith	Jive 00352
				HUMAN BEINZ, The		
2/3/68	8	15		1 Nobody But Me	O'Kelly Isley/Rudolph Isley...*Sueno*	Capitol 5990
				HUMAN LEAGUE, The		
7/3/82	❶³	28	●	1 Don't You Want Me	John Callis/Philip Oakey/Philip Wright...*Seconds*	A&M/Virgin 2397
8/20/83	8	20		2 (Keep Feeling) Fascination	John Callis/Philip Oakey...*Total Panic*	A&M/Virgin 2547
11/22/86	❶¹	20		3 Human	Jimmy Jam Harris/Terry Lewis	A&M/Virgin 2861
				HUMPERDINCK, Engelbert		
5/27/67	4	14		1 Release Me (And Let Me Love Again)	Eddie Miller/William Stevenson...*Ten Guitars*	Parrot 40011
1/22/77	8	19	●	2 After The Lovin'	Ritchie Adams/Alan Bernstein...*Let's Remember The Good Times*	Epic/MAM 50270
				HUNT, Pee Wee, And His Orchestra		
8/28/48	❶⁸	32	⊙	1 Twelfth Street Rag	Euday Bowman/Andy Razaf...*Somebody Else, Not Me* [I]	Capitol 15105
9/12/53	3¹¹	25	⊙	2 Oh!	Byron Gay/Arnold Johnson...*San* [I]	Capitol 2442
				HUNTER, Tab		
2/16/57	❶⁶	21	⊙	1 Young Love	Ric Cartey/Carole Joyner...*Red Sails In The Sunset*	Dot 15533
				HURRICANE CHRIS		
7/28/07	7	20	△	1 A Bay Bay	Christopher Dooley/Earl Williams	Polo Grounds 11542
				HUSKY, Ferlin		
10/17/53	4	10		1 A Dear John Letter	Billy Barton/Charles Owen/Lewis Talley...*I'd Rather Die Young*	Capitol 2502
				JEAN SHEPARD with FERLIN HUSKEY		
4/29/57	4	27	⊙	2 Gone	Smokey Rogers...*Missing Persons*	Capitol 3628

PEAK DATE	PEAK POS	WKS CHR	GOLD	ARTIST / Song Title	Songwriter...B-side	Label & Number
				HUTTON, Betty		
7/29/44	7	7		1 His Rocking Horse Ran Away	Johnny Burke/Jimmy Van Heusen...*It Had To Be You* [N]	Capitol 155
9/30/44	5	12		2 It Had To Be You	Isham Jones/Gus Kahn...*His Rocking Horse Ran Away*	Capitol 155
4/14/45	4	10		3 Stuff Like That There	Ray Evans/Jay Livingston...*Blue Skies*	Capitol 188
2/9/46	❶²	20	⊙	4 Doctor, Lawyer, Indian Chief	Hoagy Carmichael/Paul Francis Webster...*A Square In The Social Circle*	Capitol 220
10/18/47	5	12		5 I Wish I Didn't Love You So	Frank Loesser...*The Sewing Machine*	Capitol 409
12/9/50	3³	18		6 A Bushel And A Peck	Frank Loesser...*She's A Lady* [N]	RCA Victor 3930
				PERRY COMO and BETTY HUTTON		
				HYLAND, Brian		
8/8/60	❶¹	15	⊙	1 Itsy Bitsy Teenie Weenie Yellow Polkadot Bikini	Lee Pockriss/Paul Vance...*Don't Dilly Dally, Sally* [N]	Leader 805/Kapp 342
7/28/62	3²	14		2 Sealed With A Kiss	Gary Geld/Peter Udell...*Summer Job*	ABC-Paramount 10336
12/5/70	3²	20	●	3 Gypsy Woman	Curtis Mayfield...*You And Me (#2)*	Uni 55240
				HYMAN, Dick		
3/3/56	8	20	⊙	1 Moritat (A Theme from "The Three Penny Opera")	Marc Blitzstein/Kurt Weill...*Baubles, Bangles And Beads* [I]	MGM 12149

I

PEAK DATE	PEAK POS	WKS CHR	GOLD	ARTIST / Song Title	Songwriter...B-side	Label & Number
				IAN, Janis		
9/13/75	3²	20		1 At Seventeen	Janis Ian...*Stars*	Columbia 10154
				ICEHOUSE		
5/21/88	7	21		1 Electric Blue	Iva Davies/John Oates...*Over My Head*	Chrysalis 43201
				IDES OF MARCH, The		
5/23/70	2¹	12		1 Vehicle	Jim Peterik...*Lead Me Home, Gently*	Warner 7378
				IDOL, Billy		
7/14/84	4	22		1 Eyes Without A Face	Billy Idol/Steve Stevens...*Blue Highway*	Chrysalis 42786
12/20/86	6	18		2 To Be A Lover	William Bell/Booker T. Jones...*All Summer Single*	Chrysalis 43024
11/21/87	❶¹	22		3 Mony Mony "Live"	Bobby Bloom/Ritchie Cordell/Bo Gentry/Tommy James...*Shakin' All Over "Live"* [L]	Chrysalis 43161
8/4/90	2¹	24	●	4 Cradle Of Love	Billy Idol/David Werner...*311 Man*	Chrysalis 23509
				IFIELD, Frank		
10/13/62	5	11		1 I Remember You	Johnny Mercer/Victor Schertzinger...*I Listen To My Heart*	Vee-Jay 457
				IGLESIAS, Enrique		
9/4/99	❶²	20		1 Bailamos	Paul Barry/Mark Taylor	Overbrook 97122
6/24/00	❶³	20		2 Be With You	Paul Barry/Enrique Iglesias/Mark Taylor...*Solo Me Importas Tu*	Interscope 490366
11/17/01	3³	34		3 Hero	Paul Barry/Enrique Iglesias/Mark Taylor	Interscope
8/28/10	4	37↑	△²	4 I Like It	Enrique Iglesias/Nadir Khayat/Armando Christian Perez/Lionel Richie	Universal Republic
				ENRIQUE IGLESIAS Featuring Pitbull		
2/5/11	4↑	9↑		5 Tonight (I'm Lovin' You)	Christopher Bridges/Lauren Christy/Justin Franks/Enrique Iglesias/Jacob Luttrell	Universal Republic
				ENRIQUE IGLESIAS Featuring Ludacris & DJ Frank E		
				IGLESIAS, Julio		
5/19/84	5	21	▲	1 To All The Girls I've Loved Before	Hal David/Albert Hammond...*I Don't Want To Wake You* (Iglesias)	Columbia 04217
				JULIO IGLESIAS & WILLIE NELSON		
				IMBRUGLIA, Natalie		
5/16/98	❶¹¹	44		1 Torn	Scott Cutler/Anne Preven/Phil Thornalley	RCA
				IMMATURE		
10/15/94	5	26	●	1 Never Lie	Claudio Cueni/Chris Stokes	MCA 54850
				IMPALAS, The		
5/11/59	2²	18	⊙	1 Sorry (I Ran All The Way Home)	Harry Giosasi/Artie Zwirn...*Fool, Fool, Fool*	Cub 9022
				IMPRESSIONS, The		
11/9/63	4	14		1 It's All Right	Curtis Mayfield...*You'll Want Me Back*	ABC-Paramount 10487
7/18/64	10	13		2 Keep On Pushing	Curtis Mayfield...*I Love You (Yeah)*	ABC-Paramount 10554
1/9/65	7	11		3 Amen	Jester Hairston...*Long, Long Winter*	ABC-Paramount 10602
				INC., The		
8/17/02	6	20		1 Down 4 U	Jeffrey Atkins/Seven Aurelius/Ashanti Douglas/Tiffany Lane/Irving Lorenzo/Andre Parker	Murder Inc.
				IRV GOTTI PRESENTS THE INC. Featuring Ja Rule, Ashanti, Charli Baltimore & Vita		
				INCUBUS		
7/28/01	9	39		1 Drive	Brandon Boyd/Mike Einziger/Alex Katunich/Chris Kilmore/Jose Pasillas	Immortal/Epic 79627
				INFORMATION SOCIETY		
10/22/88	3¹	25	●	1 What's On Your Mind (Pure Energy)	Paul Robb/Kurt Valaquen	Tommy Boy 27826
2/18/89	9	19		2 Walking Away	Paul Robb...*Make It Funkier*	Tommy Boy 27736
				INGLE, Red, And The Natural Seven		
6/28/47	❶¹	15	⊙	1 Temptation (Tim-Tayshun)	Nacio Herb Brown/Arthur Freed...*(I Love You) For Sentimental Reasons (I Love You) For Seventy Mental Reasons* [N]	Capitol 412
				RED INGLE AND THE NATURAL SEVEN with Cinderella G. Stump (Jo Stafford)		
				INGMANN, Jorgen, & His Guitar		
4/3/61	2²	17	⊙	1 Apache	Jerry Lordan...*Echo Boogie* [I]	Atco 6184
				INGRAM, James		
2/19/83	❶²	28	●	1 Baby, Come To Me	Rod Temperton...*Solero*	Qwest 50036
3/14/87	2¹	22	●	2 Somewhere Out There	James Horner/Barry Mann/Cynthia Weil	MCA 52973
				LINDA RONSTADT AND JAMES INGRAM		
10/20/90	❶¹	26		3 I Don't Have The Heart	Jud Friedman/Allan Rich...*Baby Be Mine*	Warner 19911

PEAK DATE	PEAK POS	WKS CHR	GOLD	ARTIST / Song Title	Songwriter...B-side	Label & Number
				INGRAM, Luther		
8/5/72	3²	16		1 (If Loving You Is Wrong) I Don't Want To Be Right	Homer Banks/Carl Hampton/Raymond Jackson...*Puttin' Game Down*	KoKo 2111
				INK SPOTS		
8/31/40	4	11		1 When The Swallows Come Back To Capistrano	Leon Rene...*What Can I Do*	Decca 3195
10/5/40	2⁶	14		2 Maybe	Allan Flynn/Frank Madden...*Whispering Grass (Don't Tell The Trees)*	Decca 3258
10/5/40	10	1		3 Whispering Grass (Don't Tell The Trees)	Doris Fisher/Fred Fisher...*Maybe*	Decca 3258
12/7/40	3¹	14		4 We Three (My Echo, My Shadow And Me)	Nelson Cogane/Sammy Mysels/Dick Robertson...*My Greatest Mistake*	Decca 3379
11/1/41	4	8		5 I Don't Want To Set The World On Fire	Bennie Benjamin/Eddie Durham/Sol Marcus/Eddie Seiler...*Hey Doc!*	Decca 3987
5/29/43	2¹	16		6 Don't Get Around Much Anymore	Duke Ellington/Bob Russell...*Street Of Dreams*	Decca 18503
4/1/44	10	8		7 Cow-Cow Boogie (Cuma-Ti-Yi-Yi-Ay)	Benny Carter/Gene DePaul/Don Raye...*When My Sugar Walks Down The Street*	Decca 18587
				INK SPOTS And ELLA FITZGERALD		
5/27/44	7	10		8 I'll Get By (As Long As I Have You)	Fred Ahlert/Roy Turk...*Someday I'll Meet You Again*	Decca 18579
12/2/44	❶²	18	⊙	9 Into Each Life Some Rain Must Fall	Doris Fisher/Allan Roberts...*I'm Making Believe*	Decca 23356
12/9/44	❶²	17		10 I'm Making Believe	Mack Gordon/James Monaco...*Into Each Life Some Rain Must Fall*	Decca 23356
5/19/45	5	6		11 I'm Beginning To See The Light	Duke Ellington/Don George/Johnny Hodges/Harry James...*That's The Way It Is*	Decca 23399
				INK SPOTS and ELLA FITZGERALD (above 3)		
5/25/46	❶¹³	23	⊙	12 The Gypsy	Billy Reid...*Everyone Is Saying Hello Again (Why Must We Say Goodbye?)*	Decca 18817
6/22/46	9	11		13 Prisoner Of Love	Russ Columbo/Clarence Gaskill/Leo Robin...*I Cover The Waterfront*	Decca 18864
9/21/46	❶¹	14	⊙	14 To Each His Own	Ray Evans/Jay Livingston...*I Never Had A Dream Come True*	Decca 23615
1/1/49	8	8		15 You Were Only Fooling (While I Was Falling In Love)	William Faber/Larry Fotine/Fred Meadows...*Say Something Sweet To Your Sweetheart*	Decca 24507
10/15/49	6	16		16 You're Breaking My Heart	Pat Genaro/Sunny Skylar...*Who Do You Know In Heaven (That Made You The Angel You Are?)*	Decca 24693
				INNER CIRCLE		
6/12/93	8	20	●	1 Bad Boys	Ian Lewis	Big Beat 98426
				INOJ		
9/26/98	6	16	●	1 Time After Time	Rob Hyman/Cyndi Lauper	So So Def 79016
				INTRUDERS, The		
5/18/68	6	14	●	1 Cowboys To Girls	Kenny Gamble/Leon Huff...*Turn The Hands Of Time*	Gamble 214
				INXS		
4/12/86	5	20		1 What You Need	Andy Farriss/Michael Hutchence...*Sweet As Sin*	Atlantic 89460
1/30/88	❶¹	25		2 Need You Tonight	Andy Farriss/Michael Hutchence...*I'm Coming (Home)*	Atlantic 89188
4/16/88	2²	17		3 Devil Inside	Andy Farriss/Michael Hutchence...*On The Rocks*	Atlantic 89144
7/23/88	3¹	17		4 New Sensation	Andy Farriss/Michael Hutchence...*Guns In The Sky*	Atlantic 89080
11/5/88	7	23		5 Never Tear Us Apart	Andy Farriss/Michael Hutchence...*Different World*	Atlantic 89038
10/27/90	9	13	●	6 Suicide Blonde	Andy Farriss/Michael Hutchence...*Everybody Wants U Tonight*	Atlantic 87860
2/16/91	8	20		7 Disappear	Jon Farriss/Michael Hutchence...*Middle Beast*	Atlantic 87784
				IRISH ROVERS, The		
5/25/68	7	12		1 The Unicorn	Shel Silverstein...*Black Velvet Band*	Decca 32254
				ISAAK, Chris		
3/2/91	6	24 ● 1		Wicked Game	Chris Isaak	Reprise 19704
				ISLEY BROTHERS, The		
5/3/69	2¹	14	●	1 It's Your Thing	O'Kelly Isley/Ronald Isley/Rudolph Isley...*Don't Give It Away*	T-Neck 901
10/6/73	6	20	●	2 That Lady (Part 1)	O'Kelly Isley/Ronald Isley/Rudolph Isley...*Part 2*	T-Neck 2251
9/27/75	4	18	●	3 Fight The Power (Part 1)	Ernie Isley/Marvin Isley/O'Kelly Isley/Ronald Isley/Rudolph Isley/Chris Jasper...*Part 2*	T-Neck 2256
5/26/90	10	16		4 This Old Heart Of Mine	Lamont Dozier/Brian Holland/Eddie Holland...*You're In My Heart*	Warner 19983
				ROD STEWART (with Ronald Isley)		
3/30/96	4	20	▲	5 Down Low (Nobody Has To Know)	R. Kelly	Jive 42373
				R. KELLY (featuring Ronald Isley and Ernie Isley)		
				IVES, Burl		
5/26/51	10	9		1 On Top Of Old Smoky	Pete Seeger...*The Syncopated Clock*	Columbia 39328
				PERCY FAITH and his Orchestra and Chorus with BURL IVES		
2/10/62	9	14		2 A Little Bitty Tear	Hank Cochran...*Shanghied*	Decca 31330
5/19/62	10	11		3 Funny Way Of Laughin'	Hank Cochran...*Mother Wouldn't Do That*	Decca 31371
				IVY THREE, The		
9/19/60	8	10		1 Yogi	Sid Jacobson/Charles Koppelman/Lou Stallman...*Was Judy There* [N]	Shell 720
				IYAZ		
1/9/10	2¹	34	△³	1 Replay	Kisean Anderson/Jason Derulo/Keidran Jones/Jonathan Rotem/Theron Thomas/Timothy Thomas	Beluga Heights

J

PEAK DATE	PEAK POS	WKS CHR	GOLD	ARTIST / Song Title	Songwriter...B-side	Label & Number
				JACKS, Terry		
3/2/74	❶³	21	●	1 Seasons In The Sun	Jacques Brel/Rod McKuen...*Put The Bone In*	Bell 45,432
				JACKSON, Janet		
5/17/86	4	21	●	1 What Have You Done For Me Lately	Jimmy Jam Harris/Janet Jackson/Terry Lewis...*He Doesn't Know I'm Alive*	A&M 2812
7/19/86	3¹	19	●	2 Nasty	Jimmy Jam Harris/Janet Jackson/Terry Lewis...*You'll Never Find (A Love Like Mine)*	A&M 2830
10/11/86	❶²	19	●	3 When I Think Of You	Jimmy Jam Harris/Janet Jackson/Terry Lewis...*Pretty Boy*	A&M 2855
1/24/87	5	18	●	4 Control	Jimmy Jam Harris/Janet Jackson/Terry Lewis...*Fast Girls*	A&M 2877
3/21/87	2¹	19	●	5 Let's Wait Awhile	Melanie Andrews/Jimmy Jam Harris/Janet Jackson/Terry Lewis...*Pretty Boy*	A&M 2906
6/20/87	5	19		6 Diamonds	Jimmy Jam Harris/Terry Lewis...*African Flame*	A&M 2929
				HERB ALPERT (with Janet Jackson)		
10/7/89	❶⁴	20	▲	7 Miss You Much	Jimmy Jam Harris/Terry Lewis...*You Need Me*	A&M 1445
1/6/90	2²	17		8 Rhythm Nation	Jimmy Jam Harris/Janet Jackson/Terry Lewis	A&M 1455
3/3/90	❶³	17	●	9 Escapade	Jimmy Jam Harris/Janet Jackson/Terry Lewis	A&M 1490
6/2/90	4	16	●	10 Alright	Jimmy Jam Harris/Janet Jackson/Terry Lewis	A&M 1479
8/18/90	2²	17		11 Come Back To Me	Jimmy Jam Harris/Janet Jackson/Terry Lewis...*Vuelve A Mi (Come Back To Me)*	A&M 1475

PEAK DATE	PEAK POS	WKS CHR	GOLD	#	ARTIST / Song Title	Songwriter...B-side	Label & Number
					JACKSON, Janet (cont'd)		
10/27/90	❶¹	16	●	12	Black Cat	Janet Jackson	A&M 1477
1/19/91	❶¹	22	●	13	Love Will Never Do (Without You)	Jimmy Jam Harris/Terry Lewis	A&M 1538
4/6/91	5	13		14	State Of The World	Jimmy Jam Harris/Terry Lewis...*Miss You Much*	A&M 8694
6/13/92	10	20		15	The Best Things In Life Are Free	Michael Bivins/Ronnie DeVoe/Jimmy Jam Harris/Terry Lewis/Ralph Tresvant	Perspective 0010
					LUTHER VANDROSS and JANET JACKSON with BBD and Ralph Tresvant		
5/15/93	❶⁸	23	▲	16	That's The Way Love Goes	Jimmy Jam Harris/Janet Jackson/Terry Lewis	Virgin 12650
9/11/93	4	27		17	If	Jimmy Jam Harris/Janet Jackson/Terry Lewis...*One More Chance*	Virgin 12676
12/11/93	❶²	23	▲	18	Again	Jimmy Jam Harris/Janet Jackson/Terry Lewis	Virgin 38404
3/19/94	10	20		19	Because Of Love	Jimmy Jam Harris/Janet Jackson/Terry Lewis...*Funky Big Band*	Virgin 38422
6/25/94	2¹	20	●	20	Any Time, Any Place	Jimmy Jam Harris/Janet Jackson/Terry Lewis...*And On And On*	Virgin 38435
12/24/94	8	22	●	21	You Want This	Jimmy Jam Harris/Janet Jackson/Terry Lewis...*70's Love Groove*	Virgin 38455
6/17/95	5	17	▲	22	Scream	Jimmy Jam Harris/Janet Jackson/Michael Jackson/Terry Lewis...*Childhood* (Michael Jackson)	Epic 78000
					MICHAEL JACKSON & JANET JACKSON		
10/21/95	3⁵	24	●	23	Runaway	Jimmy Jam Harris/Janet Jackson/Terry Lewis...*When I Think Of You*	A&M 1194
1/31/98	❶²	46	●	24	Together Again	René Elizondo/Jimmy Jam Harris/Janet Jackson/Terry Lewis...*Got 'Til It's Gone*	Virgin 38623
5/23/98	3¹	20		25	I Get Lonely	René Elizondo/James Harris III/Janet Jackson/Terry Lewis	Virgin 38631
					JANET (Featuring BLACKstreet)		
4/17/99	3¹	20	●	26	What's It Gonna Be?!	Darrell Allamby/Antoinette Roberson/Trevor Smith...*Tear Da Roof Off*	Elektra 64051
					BUSTA RHYMES Featuring Janet		
8/26/00	❶³	24	●	27	Doesn't Really Matter	Jimmy Jam Harris/Janet Jackson/Terry Lewis	Def Jam 562846
4/14/01	❶⁷	22		28	All For You	Wayne Garfield/Jimmy Jam Harris/Janet Jackson/Terry Lewis/Mauro Malavasi/David Romani	Virgin 97522
9/1/01	3²	20		29	Someone To Call My Lover	Dewey Bunnell/Jimmy Jam Harris/Janet Jackson/Terry Lewis	Virgin 38799
					JACKSON, Jermaine		
3/17/73	9	18		1	Daddy's Home	William Miller/James Shepard...*Take Me In Your Arms (Rock Me For A Little While)*	Motown 1216
7/12/80	9	23		2	Let's Get Serious	Lee Garrett/Stevie Wonder...*Je Vous Aime Beaucoup (I Love You)*	Motown 1469
					JACKSON, Joe		
12/11/82	6	27		1	Steppin' Out	Joe Jackson...*Chinatown*	A&M 2428
					JACKSON, Michael		
12/11/71	4	14		1	Got To Be There	Elliot Willensky...*Maria (You Were The Only One)*	Motown 1191
4/22/72	2²	13		2	Rockin' Robin	Leon Rene...*Love Is Here And Now You're Gone*	Motown 1197
10/14/72	❶¹	16		3	Ben	Don Black/Walter Scharf...*You Can Cry On My Shoulder*	Motown 1207
10/13/79	❶¹	21	▲	4	Don't Stop 'Til You Get Enough	Michael Jackson...*I Can't Help It*	Epic 50742
1/19/80	❶⁴	24	▲	5	Rock With You	Rod Temperton...*Working Day And Night*	Epic 50797
4/12/80	10	17	●	6	Off The Wall	Rod Temperton...*Get On The Floor*	Epic 50838
6/21/80	10	16	●	7	She's Out Of My Life	Tom Bahler...*Get On The Floor*	Epic 50871
1/8/83	2³	18	●	8	The Girl Is Mine	Michael Jackson...*Can't Get Outta The Rain* (Jackson)	Epic 03288
					MICHAEL JACKSON/PAUL McCARTNEY		
3/5/83	❶⁷	24	▲	9	Billie Jean	Michael Jackson...*Can't Get Outta The Rain*	Epic 03509
4/30/83	❶³	25	▲	10	Beat It	Michael Jackson...*Get On The Floor*	Epic 03759
7/16/83	5	15		11	Wanna Be Startin' Somethin'	Michael Jackson	Epic 03914
9/17/83	7	14		12	Human Nature	John Bettis/Steve Porcaro...*Baby Be Mine*	Epic 04026
11/26/83	10	16		13	P.Y.T. (Pretty Young Thing)	James Ingram/Quincy Jones...*Working Day And Night* (Jacksons)	Epic 04165
12/10/83	❶⁶	22	▲	14	Say Say Say	Michael Jackson/Paul McCartney...*Ode To A Koala Bear* (McCartney)	Columbia 04168
					PAUL McCARTNEY AND MICHAEL JACKSON		
3/3/84	4	14	▲	15	Thriller	Rod Temperton...*Can't Get Outta The Rain*	Epic 04364
9/19/87	❶¹	14	●	16	I Just Can't Stop Loving You	Michael Jackson...*Baby Be Mine*	Epic 07253
10/24/87	❶²	14		17	Bad	Michael Jackson...*I Can't Help It*	Epic 07418
1/23/88	❶¹	18		18	The Way You Make Me Feel	Michael Jackson	Epic 07645
3/26/88	❶²	17		19	Man In The Mirror	Glen Ballard/Siedah Garrett	Epic 07668
7/2/88	❶¹	14		20	Dirty Diana	Michael Jackson	Epic 07739
1/14/89	7	15		21	Smooth Criminal	Michael Jackson	Epic 08044
12/7/91	❶⁷	20	▲	22	Black Or White	Bill Bottrell/Michael Jackson	Epic 74100
3/7/92	3⁴	20	●	23	Remember The Time	Bernard Belle/Michael Jackson/Teddy Riley...*Black Or White*	Epic 74200
5/30/92	6	20		24	In The Closet	Michael Jackson/Teddy Riley	Epic 74266
9/11/93	7	20		25	Will You Be There	Michael Jackson	Epic 77060
6/17/95	5	17	▲	26	Scream	Jimmy Jam Harris/Janet Jackson/Michael Jackson/Terry Lewis...*Childhood* (Michael Jackson)	Epic 78000
					MICHAEL JACKSON & JANET JACKSON		
9/2/95	❶¹	20	▲	27	You Are Not Alone	R. Kelly...*Scream Louder*	Epic 78002
9/22/01	10	20		28	You Rock My World	LaShawn Daniels/Michael Jackson/Freddie Jerkins/Rodney Jerkins/Nora Payne	Epic 79656
					JACKSON, Stonewall		
7/13/59	4	16	⊙	1	Waterloo	John D. Loudermilk/Marijohn Wilkin...*Smoke Along The Track*	Columbia 41393
					JACKSON 5, The		
1/31/70	❶¹	19	▲	1	I Want You Back	Berry Gordy/Fonce Mizell/Freddie Perren/Deke Richards...*Who's Lovin You*	Motown 1157
4/25/70	❶²	13		2	ABC	Berry Gordy/Fonce Mizell/Freddie Perren/Deke Richards...*The Young Folks*	Motown 1163
6/27/70	❶²	13		3	The Love You Save	Berry Gordy/Fonce Mizell/Freddie Perren/Deke Richards...*I Found That Girl*	Motown 1166
10/17/70	❶⁵	16		4	I'll Be There	Hal Davis/Berry Gordy/Willie Hutch/Bob West...*One More Chance*	Motown 1171
2/27/71	2²	10		5	Mama's Pearl	Berry Gordy/Fonce Mizell/Freddie Perren/Deke Richards...*Darling Dear*	Motown 1177
5/8/71	2³	12		6	Never Can Say Goodbye	Clifton Davis...*She's Good*	Motown 1179
1/22/72	10	10		7	Sugar Daddy	Berry Gordy/Fonce Mizell/Freddie Perren/Deke Richards...*I'm So Happy*	Motown 1194
5/18/74	2²	22		8	Dancing Machine	Hal Davis/Donald Fletcher/Weldon Parks...*It's Too Late To Change The Time*	Motown 1286
					THE JACKSONS:		
2/19/77	6	21	▲	9	Enjoy Yourself	Kenny Gamble/Leon Huff...*Style Of Life*	Epic/Phil. Int. 50289
5/19/79	7	22	▲	10	Shake Your Body (Down To The Ground)	Michael Jackson/Randy Jackson...*That's What You Get (For Being Polite)*	Epic 50656
8/4/84	3³	15	●	11	State Of Shock	Randy Hansen/Michael Jackson...*Your Ways*	Epic 04503
					JADAKISS		
12/7/02	3⁴	20		1	Jenny From The Block	Miro Arbex/Sam Barnes/Andre Deyo/Jennifer Lopez/Michael Oliver/Troy Oliver/J.C. Olivier/ Lawrence Parker/Jayson Phillips/Scott Sterling/David Styles	Epic 79825
					JENNIFER LOPEZ Featuring Jadakiss & Styles		
					JADE		
3/27/93	4	35	●	1	Don't Walk Away	Vassal Benford/Ron Spearman	Giant 18686

PEAK DATE	PEAK POS	WKS CHR	GOLD	ARTIST / Song Title	Songwriter...B-side	Label & Number
				JAGGED EDGE		
3/10/01	9	21		1 Promise	Brandon Casey/Brian Casey/Bryan Michael Cox/Jermaine Dupri/Gary Smith/Lechas Young	So So Def 79545
9/15/01	3⁵	29		2 Where The Party At	Brandon Casey/Brian Casey/Bryan Michael Cox/Jermaine Dupri/Cornell Haynes...*Let's Get Married* (w/Run of Run-DMC)	So So Def 79626
				JAGGED EDGE featuring Nelly		
12/21/02	8	36		3 Don't Mess With My Man	Brandon Casey/Brian Casey/Bryan Michael Cox	Jive 40041
				NIVEA Featuring Brian & Brandon Casey of Jagged Edge		
12/20/03	6	27		4 Walked Outta Heaven	Brandon Casey/Brian Casey/Bryan Michael Cox...*Girls Gone Wild*	So So Def 76974
				JAGGER, Mick		
10/12/85	7	14		1 Dancing In The Street	Marvin Gaye/Ivy Hunter/William Stevenson	EMI America 8288
				MICK JAGGER/DAVID BOWIE		
				JAGGERZ, The		
3/21/70	2¹	13	●	1 The Rapper	Donnie Iris...*Born Poor*	Kama Sutra 502
				JAHEIM		
9/4/04	4	20	○	1 My Place	El DeBarge/Randy DeBarge/Randy Edelman/Kenny Gamble/Cornell Haynes/Leon Huff/Dorian Moore...*Flap Your Wings*	Derrty 003154
				NELLY Feat. Jaheim		
				JAMES, Harry, and His Orchestra		
4/12/41	9	1		1 Music Makers	Harry James...*Montevideo (Mon-te-vi-DAY-o)* [I]	Columbia 35932
8/30/41	10	1		2 Lament To Love	Mel Torme...*Dodgers' Fan Dance*	Columbia 36222
12/6/41	5	10	☉	3 You Made Me Love You (I Didn't Want To Do It)	Joseph McCarthy/James Monaco...*A Sinner Kissed An Angel* [I]	Columbia 36296
3/14/42	2⁵	13		4 I Don't Want To Walk Without You	Frank Loesser/Jule Styne...*B-19*	Columbia 36478
6/20/42	❶⁴	18		5 Sleepy Lagoon	Eric Coates/Jack Lawrence...*Trumpet Blues* [I]	Columbia 36549
8/1/42	4	10		6 One Dozen Roses	Walter Donovan/Dick Jurgens/Roger Lewis/Joe Washburne...*You're Too Good For Good-For-Nothing Me*	Columbia 36566
9/19/42	5	7		7 Strictly Instrumental	Edgar Battle/Bennie Benjamin/Sol Marcus/Eddie Seiler...*When You're A Long, Long Way From Home* [I]	Columbia 36579
10/3/42	9	1		8 He's My Guy	Gene DePaul/Don Raye...*You're In Love With Someone Else*	Columbia 36614
11/28/42	9	1		9 Manhattan Serenade	Harold Adamson/Louis Alter...*Daybreak*	Columbia 36644
12/19/42	2¹	9		10 Mister Five By Five	Gene DePaul/Don Raye...*That Soldier Of Mine*	Columbia 36650
2/13/43	❶²	18	☉	11 I Had The Craziest Dream	Mack Gordon/Harry Warren...*A Poem Set To Music*	Columbia 36659
3/6/43	❶¹³	20	☉	12 I've Heard That Song Before	Sammy Cahn/Jule Styne...*Moonlight Becomes You*	Columbia 36668
5/22/43	2²	13		13 Velvet Moon	Eddie DeLange/Josef Myrow...*Prince Charming* [I]	Columbia 36672
9/4/43	2¹	18		14 All Or Nothing At All	Arthur Altman/Jack Lawrence...*Flash*	Columbia 35587
				FRANK SINATRA with HARRY JAMES and his ORCHESTRA		
10/2/43	4	18		15 I Heard You Cried Last Night	Ted Grouya/Jerrie Kruger...*James Session*	Columbia 36677
2/12/44	4	10		16 Cherry	Don Redman...*Jump Town* [I]	Columbia 36683
6/10/44	❶⁶	28	☉	17 I'll Get By (As Long As I Have You)	Fred Ahlert/Roy Turk...*Flatbush Flanagan*	Columbia 36698
4/7/45	8	1		18 I Don't Care Who Knows It	Harold Adamson/Jimmy McHugh...*Guess I'll Hang My Tears Out To Dry*	Columbia 36778
4/14/45	❶²	19	☉	19 I'm Beginning To See The Light	Duke Ellington/Don George/Johnny Hodges/Harry James...*The Love I Long For*	Columbia 36758
7/28/45	8	3		20 If I Loved You	Oscar Hammerstein/Richard Rodgers...*Oh, Brother!*	Columbia 36806
9/22/45	8	4		21 11:60 P.M.	Seger Ellis/Don George...*Carnival*	Columbia 36827
11/3/45	2¹	14		22 I'll Buy That Dream	Herb Magidson/Allie Wrubel...*Memphis In June*	Columbia 36833
11/24/45	❶³	17	☉	23 It's Been A Long, Long Time	Sammy Cahn/Jule Styne...*Autumn Serenade*	Columbia 36838
12/22/45	6	10		24 Waitin' For The Train To Come In	Martin Block/Sunny Skylar...*I Can't Begin To Tell You*	Columbia 36867
2/9/46	5	12		25 I Can't Begin To Tell You	Mack Gordon/James Monaco...*Waitin' For The Train To Come In*	Columbia 36867
2/16/46	9	4		26 I'm Always Chasing Rainbows	Harry Carroll/Joseph McCarthy...*Baby, What You Do To Me*	Columbia 36899
11/16/46	10	2		27 This Is Always	Mack Gordon/Harry Warren...*I've Never Forgotten*	Columbia 37052
4/12/47	4	9		28 Heartaches	Al Hoffman/John Klenner...*I Tipped My Hat (And Slowly Rode Away)*	Columbia 37305
4/14/51	10	10		29 Would I Love You (Love You, Love You)	Bob Russell/Harold Spina...*Lullaby Of Broadway*	Columbia 39159
				HARRY JAMES & his ORCH. with DORIS DAY		
9/22/51	8	8		30 Castle Rock	Ervin Drake/Al Sears/Jimmy Shirl...*Deep Night*	Columbia 39527
				FRANK SINATRA & HARRY JAMES		
				JAMES, Joni		
11/29/52	❶⁶	23	☉	1 Why Don't You Believe Me	Lew Douglas/King Laney/Leroy Rodde...*Purple Shades*	MGM 11333
1/24/53	4	16	☉	2 Have You Heard	Lew Douglas/Frank Lavere/Leroy Rodde...*Wishing Ring*	MGM 11390
4/25/53	2³	17	☉	3 Your Cheatin' Heart	Hank Williams...*I'll Be Waiting For You*	MGM 11426
6/13/53	9	9		4 Almost Always	Lew Douglas/Frank Lavere/Kathleen Lichty...*Is It Any Wonder*	MGM 11470
10/3/53	8	12		5 My Love, My Love	Nick Acquaviva/Bob Haymes...*You're Fooling Someone*	MGM 11543
4/9/55	2¹	16	☉	6 How Important Can It Be?	Bennie Benjamin/George David Weiss...*This Is My Confession*	MGM 11919
11/5/55	6	15		7 You Are My Love	Jimmie Nabbie...*I Lay Me Down To Sleep*	MGM 12066
				JAMES, Sonny		
2/9/57	❶¹	21	☉	1 Young Love	Ric Cartey/Carole Joyner...*You're The Reason I'm In Love*	Capitol 3602
				JAMES, Tommy, And The Shondells		
7/16/66	❶²	12	●	1 Hanky Panky	Jeff Barry/Ellie Greenwich...*Thunderbolt*	Roulette 4686
4/22/67	4	17		2 I Think We're Alone Now	Ritchie Cordell...*Gone, Gone, Gone*	Roulette 4720
6/17/67	10	10		3 Mirage	Ritchie Cordell/Bo Gentry...*Run, Run, Baby, Run*	Roulette 4736
6/15/68	3¹	17		4 Mony Mony	Bobby Bloom/Ritchie Cordell/Bo Gentry/Tommy James...*One Two Three And I Fell*	Roulette 7008
2/1/69	❶²	16	☉	5 Crimson And Clover	Tommy James/Peter Lucia...*Some Kind Of Love*	Roulette 7028
5/3/69	7	10		6 Sweet Cherry Wine	Richie Grasso/Tommy James...*Breakaway*	Roulette 7039
7/26/69	2³	15		7 Crystal Blue Persuasion	Ed Gray/Tommy James/Mike Vale...*I'm Alive*	Roulette 7050
8/14/71	4	13		8 Draggin' The Line	Tommy James/Bob King...*Bits & Pieces*	Roulette 7103
				TOMMY JAMES		
				JAN & DEAN		
6/30/58	8	13		1 Jennie Lee	Jan Berry/Arnie Ginsburg...*Gotta Getta Date*	Arwin 108
				JAN & ARNIE		
9/14/59	10	12		2 Baby Talk	Melvin Schwartz...*Jeanette, Get Your Hair Done*	Dore 522
7/20/63	❶²	13	☉	3 Surf City	Jan Berry/Brian Wilson...*She's My Summer Girl*	Liberty 55580
1/18/64	10	11		4 Drag City	Jan Berry/Roger Christian/Brian Wilson...*Schlock Rod (Part 1)*	Liberty 55641
5/9/64	8	14		5 Dead Man's Curve	Jan Berry/Roger Christian/Artie Kornfeld/Brian Wilson...*The New Girl In School*	Liberty 55672
8/1/64	3¹	11		6 The Little Old Lady (From Pasadena)	Don Altfeld/Roger Christian...*My Mighty G.T.O.*	Liberty 55704

65

PEAK DATE	PEAK POS	WKS CHR	GOLD	ARTIST / Song Title	Songwriter...B-side	Label & Number
				JA RULE		
3/24/01	8	27		1 Put It On Me	Jeffrey Atkins/Tiheem Crocker/Irv Gotti/Paul Walcott...*Love Me, Hate Me*	Murder Inc. 572751
				JA RULE (feat. Lil' Mo and Vita)		
9/8/01	❶⁵	31		2 I'm Real	LeShaun Lewis/Jennifer Lopez/Troy Oliver/Mark Cory Rooney	Epic 79639
				JENNIFER LOPEZ featuring Ja Rule		
12/8/01	6	25		3 Livin' It Up	Jeffrey Atkins/Irv Gotti/Robert Mays/Stevie Wonder...*The Inc.* (w/Caddillac Tah & Black Child)	Murder Inc. 588741
				JA RULE (feat. Case)		
2/23/02	❶²	27		4 Always On Time	Jeffrey Atkins/Irv Gotti/Marcus Vest...*Worldwide Gangsta*	Murder Inc. 588795
				JA RULE (feat. Ashanti)		
3/9/02	❶⁶	27		5 Ain't It Funny	Jeffrey Atkins/Jennifer Lopez/Mark Cory Rooney	Epic
				JENNIFER LOPEZ featuring Ja Rule		
2/15/03	2¹	20		6 Mesmerize	Jeffrey Atkins/Thom Bell/Linda Creed/Ashanti Douglas/Irving Lorenzo/Andre Parker...*Pop N****s*	Murder Inc. 063773
				JA RULE feat. Ashanti		
11/27/04	5	20	○	7 Wonderful	Jeffrey Atkins/R. Kelly/Irving Lorenzo/Kendred Smith...*Caught Up*	The Inc. 003482
				JA RULE featuring R. Kelly & Ashanti		
				JAY & THE AMERICANS		
5/19/62	5	14		1 She Cried	Ted Daryll/Greg Richards...*Dawning*	United Artists 415
11/21/64	3²	15		2 Come A Little Bit Closer	Tommy Boyce/Wes Farrell/Bobby Hart...*Goodbye Boys Goodbye*	United Artists 759
7/31/65	4	13		3 Cara, Mia	Lee Lange/Tulio Trapani...*When It's All Over*	United Artists 881
3/8/69	6	14	●	4 This Magic Moment	Doc Pomus/Mort Shuman...*Since I Don't Have You*	United Artists 50475
				JAY AND THE TECHNIQUES		
9/23/67	6	17		1 Apples, Peaches, Pumpkin Pie	Maurice Irby...*Stronger Than Dirt*	Smash 2086
				JAYNETTS, The		
9/28/63	2²	12	⊙	1 Sally, Go 'Round The Roses	Zell Sanders/Lona Spector	Tuff 369
				JAY-Z		
4/12/97	7	20	●	1 I'll Be	Sam Barnes/Shawn Carter/Rene Moore/J.C. Olivier/Angela Winbush...*La Familia*	Violator 574028
				FOXY BROWN Featuring Jay-Z		
10/9/99	❶²	20	●	2 Heartbreaker	Mariah Carey/Shawn Carter/Lincoln Chase/Jeffrey E. Cohen/Shirley Ellis/Narada Michael Walden	Columbia 79260
				MARIAH CAREY (Featuring Jay-Z)		
6/23/01	6	21		3 Fiesta - Remix	R. Kelly...*Fiesta / True Baller*	Jive 42904
				R. KELLY (Featuring Jay-Z and Boo & Gotti)		
10/20/01	8	20		4 Izzo (H.O.V.A.)	Shawn Carter/Berry Gordy/Fonce Mizell/Freddie Perren/Deke Richards/Kanye West...*You Don't Know*	Roc-A-Fella 588701
12/28/02	4	23		5 '03 Bonnie & Clyde	Darrell Harper/Prince/Rick Rouse/Tupac Shakur/Tyrone Wrice	Roc-A-Fella 063843
				JAY-Z Featuring Beyonce Knowles		
4/12/03	8	19		6 Excuse Me Miss	Shawn Carter/Chad Hugo/Pharrell Williams...*The Bounce*	Roc-A-Fella 063717
7/12/03	❶⁸	27	○	7 Crazy In Love	Shawn Carter/Rich Harrison/Beyonce Knowles/Eugene Record	Columbia
				BEYONCE (Featuring Jay-Z)		
9/20/03	5	23		8 Frontin'	Shawn Carter/Chad Hugo/Pharrell Williams	Star Trak 58647
				PHARRELL Featuring Jay-Z		
12/27/03	10	18		9 Change Clothes	Shawn Carter/Chad Hugo/Pharrell Williams...*What More Can I Say*	Roc-A-Fella 001651
4/10/04	5	26	○	10 Dirt Off Your Shoulder	Shawn Carter/Tim Mosley...*Encore*	Roc-A-Fella 001936
8/12/06	4	17	○	11 Deja Vu	Shawn Carter/Rodney Jerkins/Beyonce Knowles/Keli Nicole Price/Makeba Riddick/Delisha Thomas	Columbia 88435
				BEYONCE (Featuring Jay-Z)		
11/25/06	8	15		12 Show Me What You Got	Jim Boxley/Shawn Carter/Mike McEwan/Johnny Pate/Carlton Ridenhour/Eric Sadler/Justin Smith	Roc-A-Fella
6/9/07	❶⁷	33	△³	13 Umbrella	Shawn Carter/Thaddis Harrell/Terius Nash/Christopher Stewart	SRP/Def Jam 008990
				RIHANNA feat. Jay-Z		
9/27/08	5	20		14 Swagga Like Us	Maya Arulpragasm/Dwayne Carter/Shawn Carter/Clifford Harris/Nicky Headon/Mick Jones/Wesley Pentz/Paul Simonon/Joe Strummer/Kanye West	Roc-A-Fella 012284
				JAY-Z & T.I. Featuring Kanye West & Lil Wayne		
10/3/09	2¹	23	△²	15 Run This Town	Alatas Athanasios/Jeff Bhasker/Shawn Carter/Robyn Fenty/Kanye West/Ernest Wilson...*D.O.A. (Death Of Auto-Tune)*	Roc Nation 521199
				JAY-Z, RIHANNA & KANYE WEST		
11/28/09	❶⁵	30	△³	16 Empire State Of Mind	Shawn Carter/Alicia Keys	Roc Nation 522671
				JAY-Z & ALICIA KEYS		
5/8/10	10	20		17 Young Forever	Shawn Carter/Marian Gold/Bernhard Lloyd/Frank Mertens/Kanye West...*On To The Next One*	Roc Nation 523738
				JAY-Z + MR. HUDSON		
				JEAN, Wyclef		
3/21/98	7	20	▲	1 Gone Till November	Wyclef Jean	Ruffhouse 78752
3/28/98	3¹	35	▲	2 No, No, No Part 2	Mary Brown/Robert Fusari/Calvin Gaines/Vincent Herbert...*(Part 1)*	Columbia 78618
				DESTINY'S CHILD (featuring Wyclef Jean)		
6/17/06	❶²	31	△²	3 Hips Don't Lie	Omar Alfanno/Luis Diaz/Jerry Duplessis/Wyclef Jean/Shakira Mebarak/Latavia Parker	Epic 84467
				SHAKIRA Featuring Wyclef Jean		
				JEFFERSON AIRPLANE / STARSHIP		
				JEFFERSON AIRPLANE:		
6/17/67	5	15		1 Somebody To Love	Dabney Slick...*She Has Funny Cars*	RCA Victor 9140
7/29/67	8	10		2 White Rabbit	Grace Slick...*Plastic Fantastic Lover*	RCA Victor 9248
				JEFFERSON STARSHIP:		
10/18/75	3³	17		3 Miracles	Marty Balin...*Ai Garimasu (There Is Love)*	Grunt 10367
5/13/78	8	14		4 Count On Me	Jesse Barish...*Show Yourself*	Grunt 11196
				STARSHIP:		
11/16/85	❶²	24	●	5 We Built This City	Dennis Lambert/Martin Page/Bernie Taupin/Peter Wolf...*Private Room*	Grunt 14170
3/15/86	❶¹	20		6 Sara	Ina Wolf/Peter Wolf...*Hearts Of The World (Will Understand)*	Grunt 14253
4/4/87	❶²	22	●	7 Nothing's Gonna Stop Us Now	Albert Hammond/Diane Warren...*Layin' It On The Line (live)*	Grunt 5109
8/29/87	9	16		8 It's Not Over ('Til It's Over)	Phil Galdston/Robbie Nevil/John Van Tongeren...*Babylon*	RCA/Grunt 5225
				JELLY BEANS, The		
8/8/64	9	12		1 I Wanna Love Him So Bad	Jeff Barry/Ellie Greenwich...*So Long*	Red Bird 10-003
				JENKINS, Gordon, And His Orchestra		
10/23/48	3¹	30	⊙	1 Maybe You'll Be There	Rube Bloom/Sammy Gallop...*Dark Eyes*	Decca 24403
5/28/49	2³	23		2 Again	Dorcas Cochran/Lionel Newman...*Skip To My Lou*	Decca 24602
11/12/49	3¹	19		3 Don't Cry Joe (Let Her Go, Let Her Go, Let Her Go)	Joe Marsala...*Perhaps, Perhaps, Perhaps (Quizas, Quizas, Quizas)*	Decca 24720
6/10/50	3¹	23		4 My Foolish Heart	Ned Washington/Victor Young...*Don't Do Something To Someone Else (That You Wouldn't Want Done To You)*	Decca 24830
7/15/50	4	18		5 Bewitched	Lorenz Hart/Richard Rodgers...*Where In The World*	Decca 24983
7/29/50	2¹	17	⊙	6 Tzena Tzena Tzena	Gordon Jenkins/Spencer Ross...*Goodnight Irene*	Decca 27077
8/19/50	❶¹³	25	⊙	7 Goodnight Irene	Huddie Ledbetter/John Lomax...*Tzena Tzena Tzena*	Decca 27077
				GORDON JENKINS and his Orchestra and THE WEAVERS (above 2)		

PEAK DATE	PEAK POS	WKS CHR	GOLD	ARTIST / Song Title	Songwriter...B-side	Label & Number
				JENKINS, Gordon (cont'd)		
10/7/50	10	10		8 I'm Forever Blowing Bubbles	John Kellette/Jean Kenbrovin...*You're Mine, You!*	Decca 27186
				GORDON JENKINS and ARTIE SHAW		
2/3/51	4	14		9 So Long (It's Been Good to Know Yuh)	Woody Guthrie...*Lonesome Traveler*	Decca 27376
				GORDON JENKINS and his Orchestra and THE WEAVERS		
				GORDON JENKINS And His Chorus And Orchestra:		
7/12/52	3[1]	13		10 Lover	Lorenz Hart/Richard Rodgers...*You Go To My Head*	Decca 28215
				JEREMIH		
6/13/09	4	20	△	1 Birthday Sex	Jeremy Felton/Keith James/Michael Schultz	Mick Schultz
				JESTERS, The		
1/5/46	10	5		1 Chickery Chick	Sylvia Dee/Sid Lippman...*Let Him Go—Let Him Tarry*	Decca 18725
				EVELYN KNIGHT and THE JESTERS		
3/30/46	10	4	⊙	2 McNamara's Band	Guy Bonham/Wamp Carlson/Dwight Latham/Shamus O'Connor/J.J. Stamford...*Dear Old Donegal*	Decca 23495
4/27/46	3[4]	16		3 Sioux City Sue	Ray Freedman/Dick Thomas...*You Sang My Love Song To Somebody Else*	Decca 23508
11/1/47	9	4		4 Feudin' And Fightin'	Al Dubin/Burton Lane...*Goodbye, My Lover, Goodbye*	Decca 23975
				BING CROSBY and THE JESTERS (above 3)		
				JESUS JONES		
7/27/91	2[1]	25		1 Right Here, Right Now	Mike Edwards...*Move Me*	SBK/Food 07345
11/9/91	4	20		2 Real, Real, Real	Mike Edwards...*Maryland*	SBK/Food 07364
				JETS, The		
6/21/86	3[2]	20		1 Crush On You	Jerry Knight/Aaron Zigman...*Right Before My Eyes*	MCA 52774
3/7/87	3[1]	26		2 You Got It All	Rupert Holmes...*Burn The Candle*	MCA 52968
8/1/87	7	16		3 Cross My Broken Heart	Stephen Bray/Tony Pierce...*Bad Guys* (The Heat)	MCA 53123
4/2/88	6	22		4 Rocket 2 U	Bobby Nunn...*Our Only Chance*	MCA 53254
6/25/88	4	20		5 Make It Real	Rick Kelly/Linda Mallah/Dan Powell...*Alla Tu/Make It Real*	MCA 53311
				JETT, Joan, & The Blackhearts		
3/20/82	❶[7]	20	▲	1 I Love Rock 'N Roll	Jake Hooker/Alan Merrill...*You Don't Know What You've Got*	Boardwalk 135
6/19/82	7	15		2 Crimson And Clover	Tommy James/Peter Lucia...*Oh Woe Is Me*	Boardwalk 144
10/1/88	8	26		3 I Hate Myself For Loving You	Desmond Child/Joan Jett...*Love Is Pain (live)*	Blackheart/CBS 07919
				JEWEL		
4/19/97	2[2]	65	▲	1 You Were Meant For Me	Jewel Kilcher/Steve Poltz...*Foolish Games*	Atlantic 87021
11/1/97	7	24	▲	2 Foolish Games	Jewel Kilcher...*You Were Meant For Me*	Atlantic 87021
1/23/99	6	16		3 Hands	Jewel Kilcher/Patrick Leonard	Atlantic
				JIBBS		
10/21/06	7	20	○	1 Chain Hang Low	Jovan Campbell/Derryl Howard/Maurice Wilson	Geffen 007034
				JIGSAW		
12/6/75	3[2]	21		1 Sky High	Des Dyer/Clive Scott...*Brand New Love Affair*	Chelsea 3022
				JIMMY EAT WORLD		
6/22/02	5	33		1 The Middle	Jim Adkins/Rick Burch/Zach Lind/Tom Linton	DreamWorks
				JIVE FIVE, The		
9/11/61	3[2]	19		1 My True Story	Eugene Pitt/Oscar Waltzer...*When I Was Single*	Beltone 1006
				J-KWON		
4/17/04	2[1]	30	○	1 Tipsy	Jerrell Jones/Joe Kent/Mark Williams	So So Def 58460
				JODECI		
8/28/93	4	24	●	1 Lately	Stevie Wonder [L]	Uptown/MCA 54652
				JOE		
2/20/99	10	20		1 Faded Pictures	Joe L. Thomas/Josh Thompson	Def Jam 566494
				CASE & JOE		
2/19/00	❶[1]	20	●	2 Thank God I Found You	Mariah Carey/James Harris III/Terry Lewis	Columbia 79338
				MARIAH with Joe & 98°		
7/1/00	4	44		3 I Wanna Know	Jolyon Skinner/Joe L. Thomas/Michele Williams	Jive
2/24/01	❶[4]	26	●	4 Stutter	Ernest Dixon/Roy Hamilton	Jive 42870
				JOE (Featuring Mystikal)		
				JOEL, Billy		
2/18/78	3[2]	27	●	1 Just The Way You Are	Billy Joel...*Get It Right The First Time*	Columbia 10646
1/6/79	3[3]	19	▲	2 My Life	Billy Joel...*52nd Street*	Columbia 10853
5/3/80	7	15		3 You May Be Right	Billy Joel...*Close To The Borderline*	Columbia 11231
7/19/80	❶[2]	21	▲	4 It's Still Rock And Roll To Me	Billy Joel...*Through The Long Night*	Columbia 11276
9/24/83	❶[1]	18	●	5 Tell Her About It	Billy Joel...*Easy Money*	Columbia 04012
11/12/83	3[5]	22		6 Uptown Girl	Billy Joel...*Careless Talk*	Columbia 04149
2/25/84	10	18		7 An Innocent Man	Billy Joel...*I'll Cry Instead*	Columbia 04259
8/31/85	9	16		8 You're Only Human (Second Wind)	Billy Joel...*Surprises*	Columbia 05417
7/26/86	10	15		9 Modern Woman	Billy Joel...*Sleeping With The Television On*	Epic 06118
10/18/86	10	18		10 A Matter Of Trust	Billy Joel...*Getting Closer*	Columbia 06108
12/9/89	❶[2]	19	●	11 We Didn't Start The Fire	Billy Joel...*House Of Blue Light*	Columbia 73021
3/17/90	6	16		12 I Go To Extremes	Billy Joel...*When In Rome*	Columbia 73091
10/16/93	3[1]	27		13 The River Of Dreams	Billy Joel...*No Man's Land*	Columbia 77086
				JOE PUBLIC		
5/23/92	4	21		1 Live And Learn	Joe Carter/Jake Sayles/Kevin Scott/Dwight Wyatt	Columbia 74012
				JOHN, Elton		
1/23/71	8	14		1 Your Song	Elton John/Bernie Taupin...*Take Me To The Pilot*	Uni 55265
7/15/72	6	15		2 Rocket Man	Elton John/Bernie Taupin...*Suzie (Dramas)*	Uni 55328
9/23/72	8	10		3 Honky Cat	Elton John/Bernie Taupin...*Slave*	Uni 55343
2/3/73	❶[3]	17	▲	4 Crocodile Rock	Elton John/Bernie Taupin...*Elderberry Wine*	MCA 40000

PEAK DATE	PEAK POS	WKS CHR	GOLD	ARTIST / Song Title	Songwriter...B-side	Label & Number
				JOHN, Elton (cont'd)		
6/2/73	2¹	15	●	5 Daniel	Elton John/Bernie Taupin...*Skyline Pigeon*	MCA 40046
12/8/73	2³	17	▲	6 Goodbye Yellow Brick Road	Elton John/Bernie Taupin...*Young Man's Blues*	MCA 40148
4/13/74	❶¹	18	▲	7 Bennie And The Jets	Elton John/Bernie Taupin...*Harmony* [L]	MCA 40198
7/27/74	2²	15	●	8 Don't Let The Sun Go Down On Me	Elton John/Bernie Taupin...*Sick City*	MCA 40259
11/2/74	4	14	●	9 The Bitch Is Back	Elton John/Bernie Taupin...*Cold Highway*	MCA 40297
1/4/75	❶²	14	●	10 Lucy In The Sky With Diamonds	John Lennon/Paul McCartney...*One Day At A Time*	MCA 40344
4/12/75	❶²	21	▲	11 Philadelphia Freedom	Elton John/Bernie Taupin...*I Saw Her Standing There* (w/John Lennon)	MCA 40364
8/16/75	4	13	●	12 Someone Saved My Life Tonight	Elton John/Bernie Taupin...*House Of Cards*	MCA 40421
11/1/75	❶³	15	▲	13 Island Girl	Elton John/Bernie Taupin...*Sugar On The Floor*	MCA 40461
8/7/76	❶⁴	20	●	14 Don't Go Breaking My Heart	Elton John/Bernie Taupin...*Snow Queen*	Rocket/MCA 40585
				ELTON JOHN and KIKI DEE		
12/25/76	6	14	●	15 Sorry Seems To Be The Hardest Word	Elton John/Bernie Taupin...*Shoulder Holster*	MCA/Rocket 40645
8/25/79	9	18	●	16 Mama Can't Buy You Love	Leroy Bell/Casey James...*Three Way Love Affair*	MCA 41042
7/19/80	3⁴	21	●	17 Little Jeannie	Elton John/Gary Osborne...*Conquer The Sun*	MCA 41236
1/28/84	4	23		18 I Guess That's Why They Call It The Blues	Elton John/Davey Johnstone/Bernie Taupin...*The Retreat*	Geffen 29460
8/11/84	5	19		19 Sad Songs (Say So Much)	Elton John/Bernie Taupin...*A Simple Man*	Geffen 29292
3/22/86	7	18		20 Nikita	Elton John/Bernie Taupin...*Restless*	Geffen 28800
1/23/88	6	21		21 Candle In The Wind	Elton John/Bernie Taupin...*Sorry Seems To Be The Hardest Word* (live) [L]	MCA 53196
8/27/88	2¹	18		22 I Don't Wanna Go On With You Like That	Elton John/Bernie Taupin...*Rope Around A Fool*	MCA 53345
2/1/92	❶¹	20	●	23 Don't Let The Sun Go Down On Me	Elton John/Bernie Taupin...*I Believe (When I Fall In Love It Will Be Forever)* (Michael) [L]	Columbia 74086
				GEORGE MICHAEL/ELTON JOHN		
9/19/92	9	22		24 The One	Elton John/Bernie Taupin...*Suit Of Wolves*	MCA 54423
8/6/94	4	26	●	25 Can You Feel The Love Tonight	Elton John/Tim Rice	Hollywood 64543
10/11/97	❶¹⁴	42	▲¹¹	26 Candle In The Wind 1997 /	Elton John/Bernie Taupin	
		42		27 Something About The Way You Look Tonight	Elton John/Bernie Taupin	Rocket 568108
				JOHN, Robert		
3/11/72	3³	17	●	1 The Lion Sleeps Tonight	Paul Campbell/Luigi Creatore/Roy Ilene/Hugo Peretti/Albert Stanton/George David Weiss...*Janet*	Atlantic 2846
10/6/79	❶¹	27	●	2 Sad Eyes	Robert John...*Am I Ever Gonna Hold You Again*	EMI America 8015
				JOHNNIE & JOE		
7/22/57	8	22	◉	1 Over The Mountain; Across The Sea	Rex Garvin...*My Baby's Gone, On, On*	Chess 1654
				JOHNNY AND THE HURRICANES		
9/7/59	5	17		1 Red River Rock	Tom King/Ira Mack/Fred Mendelsohn...*Buckeye* [I]	Warwick 509
				JOHNNY HATES JAZZ		
5/14/88	2³	19		1 Shattered Dreams	Clark Datchler...*My Secret Garden*	Virgin 99383
				JOHNS, Sammy		
5/3/75	5	17	●	1 Chevy Van	Sammy Johns...*Hang My Head And Moan*	GRC 2046
				JOHNSON, Betty		
2/9/57	9	22		1 I Dreamed	Charles Grean/Marvin Moore...*If It's Wrong To Love You*	Bally 1020
				JOHNSON, Don		
10/18/86	5	15		1 Heartbeat	Eric Kaz/Wendy Waldman...*Can't Take Your Memory*	Epic 06285
				JOHNSON, Marv		
2/8/60	10	22		1 You Got What It Takes	Tyran Carlo/Berry Gordy/Gwen Gordy/Marv Johnson...*Don't Leave Me*	United Artists 185
4/11/60	9	13		2 I Love The Way You Love	Berry Gordy...*Let Me Love You*	United Artists 208
				JOHNSON, Syleena		
5/22/04	7	20	○	1 All Falls Down	Lauryn Hill/Kanye West...*Get 'Em*	Roc-A-Fella 002018
				KANYE WEST featuring Syleena Johnson		
				JOHNSTON, Johnnie		
3/24/45	7	1		1 (All Of A Sudden) My Heart Sings	Jean Blanvillain/Henri Herpin/Harold Rome...*What A Sweet Surprise*	Capitol 186
6/16/45	5	5		2 Laura	Johnny Mercer/David Raksin...*There Must Be A Way*	Capitol 196
8/11/45	9	2		3 There Must Be A Way	Robert Cook/Sammy Gallop/David Saxon...*Laura*	Capitol 196
				JOJO		
9/30/06	3¹	22		1 Too Little Too Late	Josh Alexander/Ruth-Anne Cunningham/Billy Steinberg	Da Family
				JOLSON, Al		
3/8/47	2⁶	14	◉	1 Anniversary Song	Saul Chaplin/Al Jolson...*Avalon*	Decca 23714
				JONAS BROTHERS		
7/12/08	5	16		1 Burnin' Up	Joe Jonas/Kevin Jonas/Nick Jonas	Hollywood
8/16/08	8	2		2 Tonight	Greg Garbowsky/Joe Jonas/Kevin Jonas/Nick Jonas	Hollywood
				JON B		
8/5/95	10	30	●	1 Someone To Love	Babyface	Yab Yum 77895
				JON B Featuring Babyface		
6/20/98	7	15	▲	2 They Don't Know	Jon Buck/Tim Kelley/Bob Robinson...*Are U Still Down*	Yab Yum 78793
				JONES, Donell		
12/11/99	7	24	●	1 U Know What's Up	Delvis Damon/Ed Ferrell/Anthony Hamilton/Clifton Lighty/Darren Lighty/Bale'wa Muhammad	Untouchables 24420
				JONES, Howard		
6/15/85	5	23		1 Things Can Only Get Better	Howard Jones...*Why Look For The Key*	Elektra 69651
7/5/86	4	23		2 No One Is To Blame	Howard Jones...*The Chase*	Elektra 69549
				JONES, Jim		
2/3/07	5	27	r	1 We Fly High	Zukhan Bey/Jim Jones...*Reppin' Time*	Diplomats 5964
				JONES, Jimmy		
2/29/60	2¹	18	◉	1 Handy Man	Otis Blackwell/Jimmy Jones...*The Search Is Over*	Cub 9049
5/23/60	3³	15	◉	2 Good Timin'	Clint Ballard/Fred Tobias...*My Precious Angel*	Cub 9067

PEAK DATE	PEAK POS	WKS CHR	GOLD	ARTIST / Song Title	Songwriter...B-side	Label & Number
				JONES, Joe		
11/14/60	3¹	13	1	You Talk Too Much	Reggie Hall/Joe Jones...*I Love You Still*	Roulette 4304
				JONES, Mike		
2/18/06	5	20	○ 1	I'm N Luv (Wit A Stripper) T-PAIN Featuring Mike Jones	Mike Jones/Faheem Najm...*I'm Sprung 2*	Jive 77102
				JONES, Oran "Juice"		
11/15/86	9	19	● 1	The Rain	Vincent Bell...*Your Song*	Def Jam 06209
				JONES, Rickie Lee		
7/7/79	4	15	1	Chuck E.'s In Love	Rickie Lee Jones...*On Saturday Afternoons In 1963*	Warner 8825
				JONES, Spike, & His City Slickers		
11/14/42	3¹	10	1	Der Fuehrer's Face	Oliver Wallace...*I Wanna Go Back To West Virginia* [N]	Bluebird 11586
2/10/45	4	9	⊙ 2	Cocktails For Two	Sam Coslow/Arthur Johnston...*Leave The Dishes In The Sing, Ma* [N]	Victor 1628
5/5/45	5	6	3	Chloe	Carl Hoefle/Del Porter...*A Serenade To A Jerk* [N]	Victor 1654
11/24/45	10	1	4	Holiday For Strings	David Rose...*Drip, Drip, Drip-(Sloppy Lagoon)* [I-N]	Victor 1733
8/3/46	8	1	5	Hawaiian War Chant (Ta-Hu-Wa-Hu-Wai) SPIKE JONES and his WACKY WAKAKIANS	Ralph Freed/Johnny Noble...*The Glow-Worm* [N]	RCA Victor 1893
6/26/48	6	15	6	William Tell Overture	Gioacchino Rossini...*The Man On The Flying Trapeze* [N]	RCA Victor 2861
12/25/48	0³	8	⊙ 7	All I Want For Christmas (Is My Two Front Teeth)	Don Gardner...*Happy New Year* [X-N]	RCA Victor 3177
1/6/51	7	3	8	Rudolph The Red-Nosed Reindeer	Johnny Marks...*Mommy, Won't You Buy A Baby Brother (Or Sister For Me)* [X-N]	RCA Victor 3934
1/3/53	4	3	9	I Saw Mommy Kissing Santa Claus	Tommy Connor...*Winter* [X-N]	RCA Victor 5067
				JONES, Tom		
5/29/65	10	12	1	It's Not Unusual	Gordon Mills/Les Reed...*To Wait For Love (Is To Waste Your Life Away)*	Parrot 9737
7/31/65	3²	12	2	What's New Pussycat?	Burt Bacharach/Hal David...*Once Upon A Time*	Parrot 9765
9/13/69	6	16	3	I'll Never Fall In Love Again	Jimmy Currie/Lonnie Donegan...*Once Upon A Time*	Parrot 40018
1/31/70	5	11	● 4	Without Love (There Is Nothing)	Danny Small...*The Man Who Knows Too Much*	Parrot 40045
3/20/71	2¹	14	● 5	She's A Lady	Paul Anka...*My Way*	Parrot 40058
				JOPLIN, Janis		
3/20/71	0²	15	1	Me And Bobby McGee	Fred Foster/Kris Kristofferson...*Half Moon*	Columbia 45314
				JORDAN, Louis, And His Tympany Five		
8/5/44	0²	25	⊙ 1	G.I. Jive	Johnny Mercer...*Is You Is Or Is You Ain't (Ma' Baby)*	Decca 8659
9/9/44	2³	19	2	Is You Is Or Is You Ain't (Ma' Baby)	Billy Austin/Louis Jordan...*G.I. Jive*	Decca 8659
6/2/45	6	8	3	Caldonia	Fleecie Moore...*Somebody Done Changed The Lock On My Door*	Decca 8670
1/5/46	9	2	4	Buzz Me	Danny Baxter/Fleecie Moore...*Don't Worry 'Bout That Mule*	Decca 18734
8/31/46	7	16	⊙ 5	Choo Choo Ch'Boogie	Denver Darling/Milt Gabler/Vaughn Horton...*That Chick's Too Young To Fry*	Decca 23610
8/31/46	7	6	6	Stone Cold Dead In The Market (He Had It Coming) ELLA FITZGERALD and LOUIS JORDAN And His Tympany Five	Wilmoth Houdini...*Petootie Pie*	Decca 23546
2/15/47	6	6	7	Ain't Nobody Here But Us Chickens	Alex Kramer/Joan Whitney...*Let The Good Times Roll*	Decca 23741
3/15/47	6	4	8	Open The Door, Richard!	Dusty Fletcher/Don Howell/John Mason/Jack McVea...*It's So Easy* [N]	Decca 23841
7/23/49	9	13	9	Baby, It's Cold Outside ELLA FITZGERALD And LOUIS JORDAN And His Tympany Five	Frank Loesser...*Don't Cry, Cry Baby*	Decca 24644
				JORDAN, Montell		
4/15/95	0⁷	29	▲ 1	This Is How We Do It	Montell Jordan/Oji Pierce...*I Wanna*	PMP/RAL 851468
4/11/98	2²	21	▲ 2	Let's Ride MONTELL JORDAN Featuring Master P & Silkk "The Shocker"	Teddy Bishop/Montell Jordan/Percy Miller/Vyshonn Miller	Def Jam 568475
2/12/00	4	32	3	Get It On...Tonite	Darren Benbow/Joerg Evers/Montell Jordan/Juergen Korduletsch/Sergio Moore/Brian Palmer/Levar Wilson...*Once Upon A Time*	Def Soul 562622
				JOURNEY		
10/3/81	4	21	● 1	Who's Crying Now	Jonathan Cain/Steve Perry...*Mother, Father*	Columbia 02241
12/19/81	9	16	● 2	Don't Stop Believin'	Jonathan Cain/Steve Perry/Neal Schon...*Natural Thing*	Columbia 02567
2/27/82	2⁶	18	● 3	Open Arms	Jonathan Cain/Steve Perry/Neal Schon...*Little Girl*	Columbia 02687
3/19/83	8	17	4	Separate Ways (Worlds Apart)	Jonathan Cain/Steve Perry/Neal Schon...*Frontiers*	Columbia 03513
3/23/85	9	16	5	Only The Young	Jonathan Cain/Steve Perry/Neal Schon...*I'll Fall In Love Again* (Sammy Hagar)	Geffen 29090
5/31/86	9	15	6	Be Good To Yourself	Jonathan Cain/Steve Perry/Neal Schon...*Only The Young*	Columbia 05869
				JURGENS, Dick, and his Orchestra		
11/29/41	8	6	1	Elmer's Tune	Elmer Albrecht/Sammy Gallop/Dick Jurgens...*You're The Sunshine Of My Heart* [I]	Okeh 6209
				JUSTIS, Bill		
12/16/57	2¹	20	⊙ 1	Raunchy	Bill Justis/Sid Manker...*The Midnite Man* [I]	Phillips 3519
				JUVENILE		
8/7/04	0²	28	○ 1	Slow Motion JUVENILE Featuring Soulja Slim	Daniel Castillo/Terius Gray/James Tapp	Cash Money

K

PEAK DATE	PEAK POS	WKS CHR	GOLD	ARTIST / Song Title	Songwriter...B-side	Label & Number
				KAEMPFERT, Bert, And His Orchestra		
1/9/61	0³	17	▫ 1	Wonderland By Night	Lincoln Chase/Klauss-Gunter Neuman...*Dreaming The Blues* [I]	Decca 31141
				KAJAGOOGOO		
7/9/83	5	19	1	Too Shy	Nick Beggs/Christopher Hamill...*Take Another View*	EMI America 8161
				KALIN TWINS		
8/4/58	5	15	⊙ 1	When	Paul Evans/Jack Reardon...*Three O'Clock Thrill*	Decca 30642
				KALLEN, Kitty		
9/23/50	10	12	1	Our Lady Of Fatima	Gladys Gollahon...*Honestly I Love You*	Mercury 5466
3/31/51	9	10	2	The Aba Daba Honeymoon RICHARD HAYES & KITTY KALLEN (above 2)	Walter Donovan/Arthur Fields...*I Don't Want To Love You*	Mercury 5586

PEAK DATE	PEAK POS	WKS CHR	G O L D	ARTIST / Song Title	Songwriter...B-side	Label & Number
				KALLEN, Kitty (cont'd)		
6/5/54	**1**[9]	26	⊙	3 Little Things Mean A Lot	Edith Lindeman/Carl Stutz...*I Don't Think You Love Me Anymore*	Decca 29037
9/18/54	4	14		4 In The Chapel In The Moonlight	Billy Hill...*Take Everything But You*	Decca 29130
				KAMOZE, Ini		
12/17/94	**1**[2]	30	▲	1 Here Comes The Hotstepper	Fats Domino/Salaam Gibbs/Ini Kamoze/Chris Kenner/Kenton Nix	Columbia 77614
				KANSAS		
4/15/78	6	20		1 Dust In The Wind	Kerry Livgren...*Paradox*	Kirshner 4274
				KARAS, Anton		
4/29/50	**1**[11]	27	⊙	1 "The Third Man" Theme	Anton Karas...*The Cafe Mozart Waltz* [I]	London 45-30005
				KARDINAL OFFISHALL		
9/6/08	5	27		1 Dangerous	Cristian Bahamonde/Jason Harrow/Don Sales/Aliaune Thiam	KonLive
				KARDINAL OFFISHALL Featuring Akon		
				KATRINA AND THE WAVES		
6/22/85	9	21		1 Walking On Sunshine	Kimberley Rew...*Going Down To Liverpool*	Capitol 5466
				KAYE, Danny		
1/3/48	3[2]	11		1 Civilization (Bongo, Bongo, Bongo)	Bob Hilliard/Carl Sigman...*Bread And Butter Woman* [N]	Decca 23940
				DANNY KAYE - ANDREWS SISTERS		
				KAYE, Sammy, And His Orchestra		
5/24/41	10	1		1 Until Tomorrow (Goodnight My Love)	Sammy Kaye...*The Sidewalk Serenade*	Victor 27262
6/21/41	**1**[8]	15	⊙	2 Daddy	Bobby Troup...*Two Hearts That Pass In The Night*	Victor 27391
2/14/42	3[1]	5		3 Remember Pearl Harbor	Sammy Kaye/Don Reid...*Dear Mom*	Victor 27738
9/19/42	3[1]	7		4 I Left My Heart At The Stage Door Canteen	Irving Berlin...*South Wind*	Victor 27932
1/20/45	4	7		5 Don't Fence Me In	Cole Porter...*Always*	Victor 1610
1/20/45	7	8		6 There Goes That Song Again	Sammy Cahn/Jule Styne...*You Always Hurt The One You Love*	Victor 1606
1/27/45	10	4		7 Always	Irving Berlin...*Don't Fence Me In*	Victor 1610
1/27/45	10	3		8 You Always Hurt The One You Love	Doris Fisher/Allan Roberts...*There Goes That Song Again*	Victor 1606
3/24/45	6	7		9 Saturday Night (Is The Loneliest Night In The Week)	Sammy Cahn/Jule Styne...*I Don't Want To Love You (Like I Do)*	Victor 1635
4/14/45	10	5		10 Just A Prayer Away	David Kapp/Charles Tobias...*All Of My Life*	Victor 1642
4/14/45	10	1		11 All Of My Life	Irving Berlin...*Just A Prayer Away*	Victor 1642
8/11/45	10	1		12 Good, Good, Good (That's You–That's You)	Doris Fisher/Allan Roberts...*Gotta Be This Or That*	Victor 1684
9/15/45	6	7		13 Gotta Be This Or That	Sunny Skylar...*Good, Good, Good (That's You–That's You)*	Victor 1684
11/10/45	10	5		14 I'll Be Walkin' With My Honey (Soon, Soon, Soon)	Buddy Kaye/Sam Medoff...*Promises*	Victor 1713
11/17/45	**1**[4]	16		15 Chickery Chick	Sylvia Dee/Sid Lippman...*Let My Job Away*	Victor 1726
1/19/46	4	10		16 It Might As Well Be Spring	Oscar Hammerstein/Richard Rodgers...*Give Me The Simple Life*	Victor 1738
3/16/46	9	7		17 I Can't Begin To Tell You	Mack Gordon/James Monaco...*What Makes The Sunset?*	Victor 1720
3/30/46	6	8		18 Atlanta, GA	Arthur Shaftel/Sunny Skylar...*I Didn't Mean A Word I Said*	Victor 1795
4/27/46	**1**[1]	15		19 I'm A Big Girl Now	Milton Drake/Al Hoffman/Jerry Livingston...*Put Your Little Foot Right Out*	RCA Victor 1812
6/22/46	3[1]	17		20 The Gypsy	Billy Reid...*(Gee! I'm Glad To Be) The One That I Am*	RCA Victor 1844
6/29/46	3[1]	11		21 Laughing On The Outside, Crying On The Inside	Ben Raleigh/Bernie Wayne...*I've Never Forgotten*	RCA Victor 1856
12/14/46	8	8		22 Sooner Or Later (You're Gonna Be Comin' Around)	Ray Gilbert/Charles Wolcott...*Zip-A-Dee Doo-Dah*	RCA Victor 1976
12/21/46	**1**[7]	17	⊙	23 The Old Lamp-Lighter	Nat Simon/Charles Tobias...*Touch-Me-Not*	RCA Victor 1963
5/31/47	8	8		24 Red Silk Stockings And Green Perfume	Bob Hilliard/Sammy Mysels/Dick Sanford...*That's My Desire*	RCA Victor 2251
9/13/47	2[1]	22		25 That's My Desire	Helmy Kresa/Carroll Loveday...*Red Silk Stockings And Green Perfume*	RCA Victor 2251
11/1/47	5	5		26 An Apple Blossom Wedding	Jimmy Kennedy/Nat Simon...*The Echo Said "No"*	RCA Victor 2330
1/17/48	3[1]	16		27 Serenade Of The Bells	Al Goodhart/Kay Twomey/Al Urbano...*That's What Every Young Girl Should Know*	RCA Victor 2372
5/1/48	10	4		28 I Love You, Yes I Do	Henry Glover/Sally Nix...*The Last Polka*	RCA Victor 2674
7/3/48	8	10		29 Tell Me A Story	Terry Gilkyson...*I Wouldn't Be Surprised*	RCA Victor 2761
2/12/49	4	16		30 Lavender Blue (Dilly Dilly)	Eliot Daniel/Larry Morey...*Down Among The Sheltering Palms*	RCA Victor 3100
5/14/49	3[1]	22		31 Careless Hands	Bob Hilliard/Carl Sigman...*Powder Your Face With Sunshine*	RCA Victor 3321
8/27/49	2[1]	24		32 Room Full Of Roses	Tim Spencer...*It's Summertime Again*	RCA Victor 2908
9/3/49	3[1]	11		33 The Four Winds And The Seven Seas	Hal David/Don Rodney...*Out Of Love*	RCA Victor 2923
4/15/50	2[6]	24		34 It Isn't Fair	Richard Himber/Sylvester Sprigato/Frank Warshauer...*My Lily And My Rose*	RCA Victor 3115
				Don Cornell (vocal; #4, 24-29, 31, 32 & 34)		
5/27/50	5	12		35 Roses	Glenn Spencer/Tim Spencer...*Tiddley Winkie Woo*	RCA Victor 3754
11/18/50	**1**[4]	27	⊙	36 Harbor Lights	Will Grosz/Jimmy Kennedy...*Sugar Sweet*	Columbia 38963
				KC AND THE SUNSHINE BAND		
8/30/75	**1**[1]	15		1 Get Down Tonight	Harry Casey/Richard Finch...*You Don't Know*	T.K. 1009
11/22/75	**1**[2]	16		2 That's The Way (I Like It)	Harry Casey/Richard Finch...*What Makes You Happy*	T.K. 1015
9/11/76	**1**[1]	21		3 (Shake, Shake, Shake) Shake Your Booty	Harry Casey/Richard Finch...*Boogie Shoes*	T.K. 1019
6/11/77	**1**[1]	23		4 I'm Your Boogie Man	Harry Casey/Richard Finch...*Wrap Your Arms Around Me*	T.K. 1022
10/1/77	2[3]	20		5 Keep It Comin' Love	Harry Casey/Richard Finch...*Baby I Love You*	T.K. 1023
1/5/80	**1**[1]	26		6 Please Don't Go	Harry Casey/Richard Finch...*I Betcha Didn't Know That*	T.K. 1035
3/1/80	2[2]	23	●	7 Yes, I'm Ready	Barbara Mason...*With Your Love* (DeSario)	Casablanca 2227
				TERI DeSARIO with K.C.		
				K-CI & JOJO		
7/13/96	**1**[2]	24	▲[2]	1 How Do U Want It	James Jackson/Tupac Shakur...*California Love* (2 PAC w/Dr. Dre & Roger Troutman)	Death Row 854652
				2 PAC (featuring KC and JoJo)		
4/4/98	**1**[3]	36		2 All My Life	Rory Bennett/JoJo Hailey...*Don't Rush (Take Love Slowly)*	MCA 55420
8/14/99	2[1]	20		3 Tell Me It's Real	Rory Bennett/JoJo Hailey	MCA 55551
				K-DOE, Ernie		
5/22/61	**1**[1]	14	⊙	1 Mother-In-Law	Allen Toussaint...*Wanted, $10,000.00 Reward*	Minit 623
				KEITH		
2/11/67	7	14		1 98.6	George Fischoff/Tony Powers...*The Teeny Bopper Song*	Mercury 72639
				KELIS		
12/27/03	3[5]	22	○	1 Milkshake	Chad Hugo/Pharrell Williams	Star Trak 61026

PEAK DATE	PEAK POS	WKS CHR	GOLD	ARTIST / Song Title	Songwriter...B-side	Label & Number
				KELLY, R.		
4/9/94	❶⁴	25	▲	1 Bump N' Grind	R. Kelly...*Definition Of A Hotti*	Jive 42207
11/18/95	4	20	▲	2 You Remind Me Of Something	R. Kelly...*Homie, Lover, Friend*	Jive 42344
3/30/96	4	20	▲	3 Down Low (Nobody Has To Know)	R. Kelly	Jive 42373
				R. KELLY (featuring Ronald Isley and Ernie Isley)		
8/3/96	5	20	▲	4 I Can't Sleep Baby (If I)	R. Kelly...*Animation Soundtrack medley*	Jive 42377
12/21/96	2⁴	34	▲	5 I Believe I Can Fly	R. Kelly...*Religious Love*	Jive 42422
8/2/97	9	20	●	6 Gotham City	R. Kelly	Jive 42473
12/5/98	❶⁶	18	▲	7 I'm Your Angel	R. Kelly	Jive 42557
				R. KELLY & CELINE DION		
10/30/99	2³	20	●	8 Satisfy You	Sean Combs/Denzil Foster/Roger Greene/R. Kelly/Jay King/Thomas McElroy/Kelly Price/Jeffrey Walker	Bad Boy 79283
				PUFF DADDY (Featuring R. Kelly)		
6/23/01	6	21		9 Fiesta - Remix	R. Kelly...*Fiesta / True Baller*	Jive 42904
				R. KELLY (Featuring Jay-Z and Boo & Gotti)		
3/29/03	2⁵	42		10 Ignition	R. Kelly	Jive 40065
12/20/03	9	27		11 Step In The Name Of Love	R. Kelly	Jive 55572
3/27/04	4	24		12 Hotel	Kasseem Dean/Bernard Edwards/R. Kelly/Barry Reese/Nile Rodgers	J Records 56053
				CASSIDY feat. R. Kelly		
11/27/04	5	20	○	13 Wonderful	Jeffrey Atkins/R. Kelly/Irving Lorenzo/Kendred Smith...*Caught Up*	The Inc. 003482
				JA RULE featuring R. Kelly & Ashanti		
				KELLY, Willie, and his Orchestra		
6/19/43	6	4		1 You'll Never Know	Mack Gordon/Harry Warren...*Comin' In On A Wing And A Prayer*	Hit 7046
				KEMP, Hal, and his Orchestra		
3/15/41	5	2		1 It All Comes Back To Me Now	Alex Kramer/Joan Whitney/Hy Zaret...*Talkin' To My Heart*	Victor 27255
				KEMP, Johnny		
8/13/88	10	21	●	1 Just Got Paid	Gene Griffin/Johnny Kemp	Columbia 07744
				KEMP, Tara		
4/13/91	3¹	22	●	1 Hold You Tight	William Hammond/Tuhin Roy/Jake Smith	Giant 19458
7/20/91	7	18		2 Piece Of My Heart	Tara Kemp/Tuhin Roy/Jake Smith	Giant 19364
				KENDRICKS, Eddie		
11/10/73	❶²	19		1 Keep On Truckin' (Part 1)	Leonard Caston/Anita Poree/Frank Wilson...*(Part 2)*	Tamla 54238
3/9/74	2²	18		2 Boogie Down	Leonard Caston/Anita Poree/Frank Wilson...*Can't Help What I Am*	Tamla 54243
				KENNER, Chris		
7/31/61	2³	17	⊙	1 I Like It Like That, Part 1	Chris Kenner/Allen Toussaint...*Part 2*	Instant 3229
				KENNY G		
7/11/87	4	22		1 Songbird	Kenny G...*Midnight Motion* [I]	Arista 9588
1/8/00	7	5		2 Auld Lang Syne (The Millennium Mix)	(traditional) [I-S]	Arista 13769
				KENTON, Stan		
4/1/44	10	1		1 Do Nothin' 'Till You Hear From Me	Duke Ellington/Bob Russell...*Harlem Folk Dance*	Capitol 145
11/4/44	9	4		2 How Many Hearts Have You Broken	Al Kaufman/Marty Symes...*And Her Tears Flowed Like Wine*	Capitol 166
12/23/44	4	18		3 And Her Tears Flowed Like Wine	Joe Greene/Stan Kenton/Charles Lawrence...*How Many Hearts Have You Broken*	Capitol 166
9/1/45	2¹	15		4 Tampico	Doris Fisher/Allan Roberts...*Southern Scandal*	Capitol 202
11/17/45	6	9		5 It's Been A Long, Long Time	Sammy Cahn/Jule Styne...*Don't Let Me Dream*	Capitol 219
4/20/46	6	11		6 Shoo Fly Pie (And Apple Pan Dowdy)	Sammy Gallop/Guy Wood...*I Been Down In Texas*	Capitol 235
11/4/50	5	14		7 Orange Colored Sky	Milton DeLugg/Willie Stein...*Jam-Bo*	Capitol 1184
				NAT "KING" COLE and STAN KENTON		
				KE$HA		
1/2/10	❶⁹	38	△⁵	1 TiK ToK	Lukasz Gottwald/Benjamin Levin/Kesha Sebert	Kemosabe
1/23/10	7	20	△	2 Blah Blah Blah	Sean Foreman/Neon Hitch/Benjamin Levin/Kesha Sebert	Kemosabe
				Ke$ha Featuring 3OH!3		
5/22/10	9	18	○	3 My First Kiss	Sean Foreman/Lukasz Gottwald/Benjamin Levin/Nathaniel Motte	Photo Finish
				3OH!3 Featuring Ke$ha		
6/12/10	4	28	△²	4 Your Love Is My Drug	Joshua Coleman/Kesha Sebert/Pebe Sebert	Kemosabe
9/18/10	8	20	△	5 Take It Off	Lukasz Gottwald/Claude Kelly/Kesha Sebert	Kemosabe
11/13/10	❶¹	13↑		6 We R Who We R	Joshua Coleman/Lukasz Gottwald/Jacob Hindlin/Benjamin Levin/Kesha Sebert	Kemosabe
				KEYS, Alicia		
8/18/01	❶⁶	34	○	1 Fallin'	Alicia Keys...*Girlfriend*	J Records 21041
2/9/02	7	20		2 A Woman's Worth	Alicia Keys/Erika Rose...*(instrumental)*	J Records 21112
9/14/02	2⁴	22		3 Gangsta Lovin'	Seven Aurelius/Eve Jeffers/Irving Lorenzo...*(4 album snippets)*	Ruff Ryders 497817
				EVE Feat. Alicia Keys		
1/31/04	3¹	20		4 You Don't Know My Name	J.R. Bailey/Mel Kent/Alicia Keys/Harold Lilly/Kanye West/Ken Williams...*(3 versions)*	J Records 56599
7/3/04	4	40	○	5 If I Ain't Got You	Alicia Keys...*(2 versions)*	J Records 59351
10/2/04	8	28		6 Diary	Kerry Brothers/Alicia Keys...*If I Ain't Got You*	J Records 59965
				ALICIA KEYS Feat. Tony! Toni! Tone!		
10/30/04	❶⁶	26	○	7 My Boo	Jermaine Dupri/Alicia Keys/Usher Raymond/Manuel Seal/Adonis Shropshire...*(instrumental)*	LaFace 65246
				USHER & ALICIA KEYS		
12/1/07	❶⁵	39	△³	8 No One	Kerry Brothers/George Harry/Alicia Keys...*(3 versions)*	J Records 20102
11/28/09	❶⁵	30	△³	9 Empire State Of Mind	Shawn Carter/Alicia Keys...*(clean version)*	Roc Nation 522671
				JAY-Z & ALICIA KEYS		
				KHAN, Chaka		
11/24/84	3³	26	●	1 I Feel For You	Prince...*Chinatown*	Warner 29195
				KID CUDI		
5/9/09	3¹	27	△	1 Day 'N' Nite	Scott Mescudi/Oladipo Omishore...*Make Her Say*	Fool's Gold 013161
				KID ROCK		
4/5/03	4	34	●	1 Picture	Robert Ritchie...*(2 versions)*	Universal 172274
				KID ROCK Featuring Allison Moorer or Sheryl Crow		

PEAK DATE	PEAK POS	WKS CHR	GOLD	ARTIST / Song Title	Songwriter...B-side	Label & Number
				KIHN, Greg, Band		
5/7/83	2¹	22		1 Jeopardy	Greg Kihn/Steve Wright...*Fascination*	Beserkley 69847
				KILLERS, The		
6/11/05	10	38	△²	1 Mr. Brightside	Brandon Flowers/David Keuning...*(4 remixes)*	Island 004170
				KIM, Andy		
7/26/69	9	16	●	1 Baby, I Love You	Jeff Barry/Ellie Greenwich/Phil Spector...*Gee Girl*	Steed 716
9/28/74	❶¹	18	●	2 Rock Me Gently	Andy Kim...*Rock Me Gently Part II*	Capitol 3895
				KING, Ben E.		
3/13/61	10	16	⊙	1 Spanish Harlem	Jerry Leiber/Phil Spector...*First Taste Of Love*	Atco 6185
6/12/61	4	14	⊙	2 Stand By Me	Ben E. King/Jerry Leiber/Mike Stoller...*On The Horizon*	Atco 6194
4/26/75	5	14		3 Supernatural Thing - Part I	Patrick Grant/Gwen Guthrie...*Part II*	Atlantic 3241
12/20/86	9	21		4 Stand By Me	Ben E. King/Jerry Leiber/Mike Stoller...*Yakety Yak (The Coasters)*	Atlantic 89361
				KING, Carole		
6/19/71	❶⁵	17	●	1 It's Too Late	Carole King/Toni Stern...*I Feel The Earth Move*	Ode 66015
3/4/72	9	10		2 Sweet Seasons	Carole King/Toni Stern...*Pocket Money*	Ode 66022
11/9/74	2¹	16		3 Jazzman	Carole King/Dave Palmer...*You Go Your Way, I'll Go Mine*	Ode 66101
3/1/75	9	12	4	Nightingale	Carole King/Dave Palmer...*You're Something New*	Ode 66106
				KING, Claude		
7/21/62	6	16		1 Wolverton Mountain	Merle Kilgore/Claude King...*Little Bitty Heart*	Columbia 42352
				KING, Evelyn "Champagne"		
9/9/78	9	19	●	1 Shame	Reuben Cross/John Fitch...*Dancin', Dancin', Dancin'*	RCA 11122
				KING, Pee Wee, and his Golden West Cowboys		
1/5/52	❶³	24	⊙	1 Slow Poke	Pee Wee King/Chilton Price/Redd Stewart...*Whisper Waltz*	RCA Victor 0489
				KING, Wayne, and his Orchestra		
6/14/41	2¹	3		1 Maria Elena	Lorenza Barcelata...*You Are My Sunshine* [I]	Victor 26767
6/14/41	5	13		2 Souvenir De Vienne	Heinz Provost...*Because* [I]	Victor 26659
				KINGSMEN, The		
12/14/63	2⁶	16	⊙	1 Louie Louie	Richard Berry...*Haunted Castle*	Wand 143
3/6/65	4	12		2 The Jolly Green Giant	Lynn Easton...*Long Green* [N]	Wand 172
				KINGS OF LEON		
9/12/09	4	56	△	1 Use Somebody	Caleb Followill/Jared Followill/Matthew Followill/Nathan Followill	RCA
				KINGSTON, Sean		
8/11/07	❶⁴	22	△	1 Beautiful Girls	Kisean Anderson/Sly Jordan/Ben E. King/Jerry Lieber/Jonathan Rotem/Mike Stoller...*Me Love*	Beluga Heights 05578
2/9/08	7	25	△	2 Take You There	Kisean Anderson/Evan Bogart/John Rotem/Theron Thomas/Tim Thomas	Beluga Heights
7/25/09	5	21	△²	3 Fire Burning	Kisean Anderson/Bilal Hajii/Nadir Khayat	Beluga Heights
				KINGSTON TRIO, The		
11/17/58	❶¹	21	●	1 Tom Dooley	Dave Guard...*Ruby Red*	Capitol 4049
5/18/63	8	11		2 Reverend Mr. Black	Jed Peters/Billy Edd Wheeler...*One More Round*	Capitol 4951
				KINKS, The		
11/28/64	7	15	⊙	1 You Really Got Me	Ray Davies...*It's All Right*	Reprise 0306
2/6/65	7	12		2 All Day And All Of The Night	Ray Davies...*I Gotta Move*	Reprise 0334
4/24/65	6	11		3 Tired Of Waiting For You	Ray Davies...*Come On Now*	Reprise 0347
10/24/70	9	14		4 Lola	Ray Davies...*Mindless Child Of Motherhood*	Reprise 0930
7/16/83	6	17		5 Come Dancing	Ray Davies...*Noise*	Arista 1054
				KISS		
12/4/76	7	21	●	1 Beth	Peter Criss/Bob Ezrin/Stan Penridge...*Detroit Rock City*	Casablanca 863
4/21/90	8	17		2 Forever	Michael Bolton/Paul Stanley...*The Street Giveth And The Street Taketh Away*	Mercury 876716
				KITT, Eartha		
8/15/53	8	14		1 C'est Si Bon (It's So Good)	Henri Betti/Andre Hornez/Jerry Seelen...*African Lullaby* [F]	RCA Victor 5358
1/2/54	4	5		2 Santa Baby	Joan Javits/Phil Springer/Tony Springer...*Under The Bridges Of Paris* [X]	RCA Victor 5502
				KLF, The		
9/7/91	5	19	●	1 3 A.M. Eternal	James Cauty/William Drummond	Arista 2230
				KLYMAXX		
12/28/85	5	29		1 I Miss You	Lynn Malsby...*Video Kid*	Constellation 52606
				KNACK, The		
8/25/79	❶⁶	22	●	1 My Sharona	Berton Averre/Doug Fieger...*Let Me Out*	Capitol 4731
				KNIGHT, Evelyn		
10/21/44	6	17		1 Dance With A Dolly (With A Hole In Her Stocking)	Jimmy Eaton/Mickey Leader/Terry Shand...*Without A Sweetheart*	Decca 18614
1/5/46	10	5		2 Chickery Chick	Sylvia Dee/Sid Lippman...*Let Him Go—Let Him Tarry*	Decca 18725
				EVELYN KNIGHT and THE JESTERS		
1/8/49	9	15		3 Brush Those Tears From Your Eyes	Oakley Haldeman/Jimmy Lee/Al Trace...*A Little Bird Told Me*	Decca 24514
1/15/49	❶⁷	21	⊙	4 A Little Bird Told Me	Harvey Brooks...*Brush Those Tears From Your Eyes*	Decca 24514
3/5/49	❶¹	20		5 Powder Your Face With Sunshine (Smile! Smile! Smile!)	Carmen Lombardo/Stanley Rochinski...*One Sunday Afternoon*	Decca 24530
				KNIGHT, Gladys, & The Pips		
7/10/61	6	13		1 Every Beat Of My Heart	Johnny Otis...*Room In Your Heart*	Vee-Jay 386
				PIPS		
12/16/67	2³	17	⊙	2 I Heard It Through The Grapevine	Barrett Strong/Norman Whitfield...*It's Time To Go Now*	Soul 35039
2/13/71	9	15		3 If I Were Your Woman	Gloria Jones/Clay McMurray/Pam Sawyer...*The Tracks Of My Tears*	Soul 35078
4/7/73	2²	16		4 Neither One Of Us (Wants To Be The First To Say Goodbye)	Jim Weatherly...*Can't Give It Up No More*	Soul 35098

PEAK DATE	PEAK POS	WKS CHR	GOLD	ARTIST / Song Title	Songwriter...B-side	Label & Number
				KNIGHT, Gladys, & The Pips (cont'd)		
10/27/73	**❶**²	19	●	5 Midnight Train To Georgia	Jim Weatherly...*Window Raising Granny*	Buddah 383
1/19/74	4	16	●	6 I've Got To Use My Imagination	Gerry Goffin/Barry Goldberg...*I Can See Clearly Now*	Buddah 393
4/27/74	3¹	17	●	7 Best Thing That Ever Happened To Me	Jim Weatherly...*Once In A Lifetime Thing*	Buddah 403
7/13/74	5	17	●	8 On And On	Curtis Mayfield...*The Makings Of You*	Buddah 423
				KNIGHT, Jean		
8/14/71	2²	16	▲²	1 Mr. Big Stuff	Joe Broussard/Carol Washington/Ralph Williams...*Why I Keep Living These Memories*	Stax 0088
				KNIGHT, Jordan		
5/15/99	10	20	●	1 Give It To You	Jimmy Jam Harris/Jordan Knight/Terry Lewis/Robin Thicke	Interscope 97048
				KNOX, Buddy		
3/30/57	**❶**¹	23	⊙	1 Party Doll	Jimmy Bowen/Buddy Knox...*My Baby's Gone*	Roulette 4002
10/7/57	9	23		2 Hula Love	Buddy Knox...*Devil Woman*	Roulette 4018
				KOKOMO		
4/17/61	8	14		1 Asia Minor	Jimmy Wisner...*Roy's Tune* [I]	Felsted 8612
				KOOL & THE GANG		
3/9/74	4	22	●	1 Jungle Boogie	Kool & The Gang...*North, East, South, West*	De-Lite 559
7/6/74	6	19	●	2 Hollywood Swinging	Kool & The Gang...*Dujii*	De-Lite 561
1/12/80	8	24	●	3 Ladies Night	Kool & The Gang...*If You Feel Like Dancin'*	De-Lite 801
4/5/80	5	18	●	4 Too Hot	George Brown...*Tonight's The Night*	De-Lite 802
2/7/81	**❶**²	30	▲	5 Celebration	Kool & The Gang...*Morning Star*	De-Lite 807
5/22/82	10	17	●	6 Get Down On It	Kool & The Gang...*Steppin' Out*	De-Lite 818
2/11/84	2¹	24		7 Joanna	Kool & The Gang...*Place For Us*	De-Lite 829
3/9/85	10	24		8 Misled	Kool & The Gang...*Rollin'*	De-Lite 880431
6/8/85	9	19		9 Fresh	Kool & The Gang...*In The Heart*	De-Lite 880623
9/21/85	2³	25	●	10 Cherish	Kool & The Gang	De-Lite 880869
1/24/87	10	18		11 Victory	Kool & The Gang...*Bad Woman*	Mercury 888074
5/2/87	10	18		12 Stone Love	Kool & The Gang...*Dance Champion*	Mercury 888292
				K.P. & ENVYI		
3/14/98	6	20	●	1 Swing My Way	Javelin Hall/Michael Johnson...*Bass Is Lo* (Zae)	EastWest 64135
				KRAMER, Billy J., With The Dakotas		
6/13/64	7	15		1 Little Children	J. Leslie McFarland/Mort Shuman...*Bad To Me*	Imperial 66027
6/27/64	9	10		2 Bad To Me	John Lennon/Paul McCartney...*Little Children*	Imperial 66027
				KRAVITZ, Lenny		
8/24/91	2¹	19		1 It Ain't Over 'Til It's Over	Lenny Kravitz...*I'll Be Around*	Virgin 98795
2/17/01	4	32		2 Again	Lenny Kravitz...*Black Velveteen*	Virgin 38782
				KRAYZIE BONE		
6/3/06	**❶**²	31	○	1 Ridin'	Anthony Henderson/Juan Salinas/Oscar Salinas/Hakeem Seriki...*Southern Takeover* (w/Killer Mike & Pastor Troy)	Universal 006026
				CHAMILLIONAIRE Featuring Krayzie Bone		
				KRIS KROSS		
4/25/92	**❶**⁸	21	▲²	1 Jump	Jermaine Dupri...*Lil Boys In Da Hood*	Ruffhouse 74197
				KROEGER, Chad		
7/13/02	3²	22		1 Hero	Chad Kroeger	Roadrunner
				CHAD KROEGER Featuring Josey Scott		
10/25/03	8	35		2 Why Don't You & I	Chad Kroeger	Arista
				SANTANA Featuring Alex Band or Chad Kroeger		
				KRUPA, Gene, and his Orchestra		
3/8/41	2¹	6		1 High On A Windy Hill	Alex Kramer/Joan Whitney...*It All Comes Back To Me Now*	Okeh 5883
3/22/41	2¹	5		2 It All Comes Back To Me Now	Alex Kramer/Joan Whitney/Hy Zaret...*High On A Windy Hill*	Okeh 5883
8/2/41	9	1		3 Just A Little Bit South Of North Carolina	Bette Cannon/Arthur Shaftel/Sunny Skylar...*Let's Get Away From It All*	Okeh 6130
9/6/41	10	1		4 Let Me Off Uptown	Earl Bostic/Redd Evans...*Flamingo*	Okeh 6147
10/20/45	7	2		5 Along The Navajo Trail	Dick Charles/Eddie DeLange/Larry Markes...*A Tender Word Will Mend It All*	Columbia 36846
1/5/46	10	5		6 Chickery Chick	Sylvia Dee/Sid Lippman...*Just A Little Fond Affection*	Columbia 36877
8/3/46	9	6		7 Boogie Blues	Ray Biondi/Gene Krupa...*Lover*	Columbia 36986
9/2/50	9	15		8 Bonaparte's Retreat	Pee Wee King...*My Scandinavian Baby*	RCA Victor 3766
				GENE KRUPA and his CHICAGO JAZZ		
				KUHN, Dick, And His Orchestra		
10/23/43	8	3		1 Put Your Arms Around Me, Honey (I Never Knew Any Girl Like You)	Junie McCree/Albert Von Tilzer	
					...*I've Got Rings On My Fingers or, Mumbo Jumbo Jijjiboo J. O'Shea* [I]	Decca 4337
				K.W.S.		
10/17/92	6	26	●	1 Please Don't Go	Harry Casey/Richard Finch	Next Plateau 339
				KYSER, Kay, and his Orchestra		
7/27/40	4	1		1 Playmates	Saxie Dowell...*On The Isle Of May* [N]	Columbia 35375
1/4/41	6	5		2 Ferry-Boat Serenade	Harold Adamson/Eldo DiLazzaro...*The Call Of The Canyon*	Columbia 35627
4/26/41	3¹	3		3 Alexander The Swoose (Half Swan–Half Goose)	Glenn Burrs/Ben Forrest/Frank Furletti/Leonard Keller...*Why Cry Baby?* [N]	Columbia 36040
8/16/41	6	4		4 'Til Reveille	Stanley Cowan/Bobby Worth...*Say When*	Columbia 36137
1/24/42	7	3		5 (There'll Be Bluebirds Over) The White Cliffs Of Dover	Nat Burton/Walter Kent...*The Nadocky*	Columbia 36445
3/21/42	8	1		6 A Zoot Suit (For My Sunday Gal)	Ray Gilbert/Bob O'Brien...*When The Roses Bloom Again*	Columbia 36517
6/20/42	2⁸	22	⊙	7 Who Wouldn't Love You	Bill Carey/Carl Fischer...*How Do I Know It's Real*	Columbia 36526
6/20/42	8	3		8 Johnny Doughboy Found A Rose In Ireland	Al Goodhart/Kay Twomey...*Me And My Melinda*	Columbia 36558
7/18/42	**❶**⁸	13		9 Jingle Jangle Jingle	Joseph Lilley/Frank Loesser...*He Wears A Pair Of Silver Wings*	Columbia 36604
9/5/42	2⁴	11		10 He Wears A Pair Of Silver Wings	Michael Carr/Eric Maschwitz...*Jingle Jangle Jingle*	Columbia 36604
10/10/42	5	3	⊙	11 Strip Polka	Johnny Mercer...*Ev'ry Night About This Time*	Columbia 36635
10/31/42	2⁷	13	⊙	12 Praise The Lord And Pass The Ammunition!	Frank Loesser...*I Came Here To Talk For Joe*	Columbia 36640
7/3/43	4	5		13 Let's Get Lost	Frank Loesser/Jimmy McHugh...*The Fuddy Duddy Watchmaker*	Columbia 36673

PEAK DATE	PEAK POS	WKS CHR	GOLD	ARTIST / Song Title	Songwriter...B-side	Label & Number
				KYSER, Kay, and his Orchestra (cont'd)		
1/20/45	7	4		14 There Goes That Song Again	Sammy Cahn/Jule Styne...*I'm Gonna See My Baby*	Columbia 36757
6/30/45	3¹	10		15 Bell Bottom Trousers	Moe Jaffe...*Can't You Read Between The Lines* [N]	Columbia 36801
8/4/45	10	1		16 Can't You Read Between The Lines	Sammy Cahn/Jule Styne...*Bell Bottom Trousers*	Columbia 36801
9/1/45	10	4		17 Rosemary	Jimmie Dodd/John Jacob Loeb...*Horses Don't Bet On People*	Columbia 36824
4/27/46	5	2		18 One-Zy Two-Zy (I Love You-zy)	Dave Franklin/Irving Taylor...*There's No One But You*	Columbia 36960
12/14/46	❶²	19		19 Ole Buttermilk Sky	Jack Brooks/Hoagy Carmichael...*On The Wrong Side Of You*	Columbia 37073
12/21/46	3¹	13		20 The Old Lamp-Lighter	Nat Simon/Charles Tobias...*Huggin' And Chalkin'*	Columbia 37095
1/11/47	8	9		21 Huggin' And Chalkin'	Kermit Goell/Clancy Hayes...*The Old Lamp-Lighter* [N]	Columbia 37095
4/12/47	6	12		22 Managua, Nicaragua (Manag-wa, Nicarag-wa)	Irving Fields/Albert Gamse...*That's The Beginning Of The End*	Columbia 37214
7/3/48	❶⁶	15	⊙	23 Woody Wood-Pecker	Ramez Idriss/George Tibbles...*When Veronica Plays The Harmonica* [N]	Columbia 38197
11/27/48	2⁷	20	⊙	24 On A Slow Boat To China	Frank Loesser...*In The Market Place Of Old Monterey*	Columbia 38301

L

PEAK DATE	PEAK POS	WKS CHR	GOLD	ARTIST / Song Title	Songwriter...B-side	Label & Number
				LaBELLE, Patti / LaBELLE		
3/29/75	❶¹	18	●	1 Lady Marmalade LaBELLE	Bob Crewe/Kenny Nolan...*Space Children*	Epic 50048
6/14/86	❶³	23	●	2 On My Own PATTI LaBELLE AND MICHAEL McDONALD	Burt Bacharach/Carole Bayer Sager...*Stir It Up* (LaBelle)	MCA 52770
				LA BOUCHE		
2/24/96	6	38	●	1 Be My Lover	Anthony Brenner/Lane McCray/Gerald Saraf/Melanie Thornton	RCA 64446
				LACHEY, Nick		
5/13/06	6	25	○	1 What's Left Of Me	Jess Cates/Emmanuel Kiriakou/Nick Lachey/Lindy Robbins	Jive
				LADY ANTEBELLUM		
3/20/10	2²	60	△⁴	1 Need You Now	Dave Haywood/Josh Kear/Charles Kelley/Hillary Scott	Capitol
				LADY GAGA		
1/17/09	❶³	49	△⁴	1 Just Dance LADY GAGA Featuring Colby O'Donis	Stefani Germanotta/Nadir Khayat/Aliaune Thiam	Streamline 011524
4/11/09	❶¹	40	△⁴	2 Poker Face	Stefani Germanotta/Nadir Khayat	Streamline 012715
6/27/09	5	22	△	3 LoveGame	Stefani Germanotta/Nadir Khayat	Streamline 013062
10/17/09	6	27	△	4 Paparazzi	Robert Fusari/Stefani Germanotta	Streamline 013571
12/5/09	2⁷	34	△	5 Bad Romance	Stefani Germanotta/Nadir Khayat	Streamline 013969
4/3/10	3¹	33		6 Telephone LADY GAGA Featuring Beyonce	LaShawn Daniels/Lazonates Franklin/Stefani Germanotta/Rodney Jerkins/Beyonce Knowles	Streamline 014166
6/26/10	5	23		7 Alejandro	Stefani Germanotta/Nadir Khayat	Streamline 014501
				LAINE, Frankie		
10/4/47	4	25	⊙	1 That's My Desire FRANKIE LAINE And MANNIE KLEIN'S ALL STARS	Helmy Kresa/Carroll Loveday...*By The River Sainte Marie*	Mercury 5007
4/24/48	9	9		2 Shine	Lew Brown/Ford Dabney...*We'll Be Together Again*	Mercury 5091
10/1/49	❶⁸	22	⊙	3 That Lucky Old Sun	Haven Gillespie/Beasley Smith...*I Get Sentimental Over Nothing*	Mercury 5316
11/26/49	❶⁶	13	⊙	4 Mule Train FRANKIE LAINE and the Muleskinners	Fred Glickman/Hy Heath/Johnny Lange...*Carry Me Back To Old Virginny*	Mercury 5345
3/11/50	❶²	11	⊙	5 The Cry Of The Wild Goose	Terry Gilkyson...*Black Lace*	Mercury 5363
7/7/51	2²	21	⊙	6 Jezebel	Wayne Shanklin...*Rose, Rose, I Love You*	Columbia 39367
7/21/51	3¹	19		7 Rose, Rose, I Love You	Chris Langdon/Wilfrid Thomas...*Jezebel*	Columbia 39367
11/17/51	9	8		8 Hey, Good Lookin' FRANKIE LAINE - JO STAFFORD	Hank Williams...*Gambella (The Gamblin' Lady)*	Columbia 39570
12/15/51	3²	14		9 Jealousy (Jalousie)	Vera Bloom/Jacob Gade...*Flamenco*	Columbia 39585
4/5/52	6	10		10 Hambone FRANKIE LAINE & JO STAFFORD	Red Saunders/Leon Washington...*Let's Have A Party*	Columbia 39672
8/30/52	7	14		11 Sugarbush DORIS DAY - FRANKIE LAINE	Josef Marais...*How Lovely Cooks The Meat*	Columbia 39693
9/6/52	5	19	⊙	12 High Noon (Do Not Forsake Me)	Dimitri Tiomkin/Ned Washington...*Rock Of Gibraltar*	Columbia 39770
4/18/53	4	12		13 Tell Me A Story JIMMY BOYD - FRANKIE LAINE	Terry Gilkyson...*The Little Boy And The Old Man* [N]	Columbia 39945
4/25/53	2³	23	⊙	14 I Believe	Ervin Drake/Irvin Graham/Jimmy Shirl/Al Stillman...*Your Cheatin' Heart*	Columbia 39938
10/24/53	6	16		15 Hey Joe!	Boudleaux Bryant...*Sittin' In The Sun (Countin' My Money)*	Columbia 40036
1/19/57	3¹	22	⊙	16 Moonlight Gambler	Bob Hilliard/Phil Springer...*Lotus Land*	Columbia 40780
4/29/57	10	14		17 Love Is A Golden Ring FRANKIE LAINE with The Easy Riders	Richard Dehr/Terry Gilkyson/Frank Miller...*There's Not A Moment To Spare*	Columbia 40856
				LAMBERT, Adam		
5/1/10	10	30		1 Whataya Want From Me	Max Martin/Alecia Moore/Johan Schuster	19 Records
				LANCE, Major		
9/7/63	8	15		1 The Monkey Time	Curtis Mayfield...*Mama Didn't Know*	Okeh 7175
2/8/64	5	11		2 Um, Um, Um, Um, Um, Um	Curtis Mayfield...*Sweet Music*	Okeh 7187
				LANCERS, The		
1/8/55	6	12		1 Let Me Go, Lover! TERESA BREWER with The Lancers	*The Moon Is On Fire*	Coral 61315
				LANZA, Mario		
3/10/51	❶¹	34	⊙	1 Be My Love	Nicholas Brodszky/Sammy Cahn...*I'll Never Love You*	RCA Victor 1353
9/1/51	3²	34	⊙	2 The Loveliest Night Of The Year	Irving Aaronson/Paul Francis Webster...*La Donna È Mobile*	RCA Victor 3300
11/22/52	7	19		3 Because You're Mine	Nicholas Brodszky/Sammy Cahn...*The Song The Angels Sing*	RCA Victor 3914
				LARKS, The		
1/16/65	7	13		1 The Jerk	Don Julian...*Forget Me*	Money 106
				LaROSA, Julius		
2/21/53	4	9		1 Anywhere I Wander	Frank Loesser...*This Is Heaven*	Cadence 1230
11/14/53	2¹	20	⊙	2 Eh, Cumpari	Archie Bleyer/Julius LaRosa...*Till They've All Gone Home* [F]	Cadence 1232

PEAK DATE	PEAK POS	WKS CHR	GOLD	ARTIST / Song Title	Songwriter...B-side	Label & Number
				LA ROUX		
6/12/10	8	27		1 Bulletproof	Eleanor Jackson/Ben Langmaid	Big Life 013222
				LARSON, Nicolette		
2/17/79	8	19		1 Lotta Love	Neil Young...*Angels Rejoiced*	Warner 8664
				LAUPER, Cyndi		
3/10/84	2^2	25	▲	1 Girls Just Want To Have Fun	Robert Hazard...*Right Track Wrong Train*	Portrait 04120
6/9/84	❶^2	20	●	2 Time After Time	Rob Hyman/Cyndi Lauper...*I'll Kiss You*	Portrait 04432
9/8/84	3^3	18	●	3 She Bop	Rick Chertoff/Gary Corbett/Cyndi Lauper/Stephen Lunt...*Witness*	Portrait 04516
12/8/84	5	19		4 All Through The Night	Jules Shear...*Witness*	Portrait 04639
7/13/85	10	15		5 The Goonies 'R' Good Enough	Cyndi Lauper/Stephen Lunt/Arthur Stead...*What A Thrill*	Portrait 04918
10/25/86	❶^2	20		6 True Colors	Tom Kelly/Billy Steinberg...*Heading For The Moon*	Portrait 06247
2/14/87	3^1	17		7 Change Of Heart	Cyndi Lauper/Essra Mohawk...*Witness*	Portrait 06431
7/8/89	6	15		8 I Drove All Night	Tom Kelly/Billy Steinberg...*Maybe He'll Know*	Epic 68759
				LAVIGNE, Avril		
8/3/02	2^2	31		1 Complicated	Lauren Christy/Graham Edwards/Avril Lavigne/Scott Spock	Arista 15185
11/2/02	10	20	○	2 Sk8er Boi	Lauren Christy/Graham Edwards/Avril Lavigne/Scott Spock...*I'm With You*	Arista 50972
2/1/03	4	27	○	3 I'm With You	Lauren Christy/Graham Edwards/Avril Lavigne/Scott Spock...*Sk8er Boi*	Arista 50972
10/2/04	9	25	○	4 My Happy Ending	Avril Lavigne/Butch Walker...*Don't Tell Me*	RCA 62274
5/5/07	❶^1	24	△^{2}	5 Girlfriend	Lukasz Gottwald/Avril Lavigne	RCA
				LAWRENCE, Elliot, and his Orchestra		
7/27/46	9	2		1 Who Do You Love I Hope	Irving Berlin...*I Know*	Columbia 37047
11/1/47	4	13		2 Near You	Francis Craig/Kermit Goell...*How Lucky You Are*	Columbia 37838
				LAWRENCE, Steve		
4/13/57	5	20		1 Party Doll	Jimmy Bowen/Buddy Knox...*(The Bad Donkey) Pum-Pa-Lum*	Coral 61792
1/4/60	9	18		2 Pretty Blue Eyes	Teddy Randazzo/Bob Weinstein...*You're Nearer*	ABC-Paramount 10058
4/4/60	7	13		3 Footsteps	Hank Hunter/Barry Mann...*You Don't Know*	ABC-Paramount 10085
5/8/61	9	16		4 Portrait Of My Love	Cyril Ornadel/David West...*Oh How You Lied*	United Artists 291
1/12/63	❶^2	17	⊙	5 Go Away Little Girl	Gerry Goffin/Carole King...*If You Love Her Tell Her So*	Columbia 42601
				LAWRENCE, Vicki		
4/7/73	❶^2	20	●	1 The Night The Lights Went Out In Georgia	Bobby Russell...*Dime A Dance*	Bell 45,303
				LED ZEPPELIN		
1/31/70	4	15	●	1 Whole Lotta Love	John Bonham/John Paul Jones/Jimmy Page/Robert Plant...*Living Loving Maid (She's Just A Woman)*	Atlantic 2690
				LEE, Brenda		
4/18/60	4	24		1 Sweet Nothin's	Dub Allbritten/Ronnie Self...*Weep No More My Baby*	Decca 30967
7/4/60	6	14		2 That's All You Gotta Do	Jerry Reed...*I'm Sorry*	Decca 31093
7/18/60	❶^3	23	⊙	3 I'm Sorry	Dub Allbritten/Ronnie Self...*That's All You Gotta Do*	Decca 31093
10/24/60	❶^1	15		4 I Want To Be Wanted	Kim Gannon/Pino Spotti...*Just A Little*	Decca 31149
2/13/61	7	12		5 Emotions	Ramsey Kearney/Mel Tillis...*I'm Learning About Love*	Decca 31195
5/8/61	6	12		6 You Can Depend On Me	Charles Carpenter/Louis Dunlap/Earl Hines...*It's Never Too Late*	Decca 31231
7/31/61	4	12		7 Dum Dum	Jackie DeShannon/Sharon Sheeley...*Eventually*	Decca 31272
11/13/61	3^2	14		8 Fool #1	Kathryn Fulton...*Anybody But Me*	Decca 31309
3/3/62	4	13		9 Break It To Me Gently	Diane Lampert/Joe Seneca...*So Deep*	Decca 31348
5/26/62	6	11		10 Everybody Loves Me But You	Ronnie Self...*Here Comes That Feelin'*	Decca 31379
11/10/62	3^2	15		11 All Alone Am I	Arthur Altman/Manos Hadjidakis...*Save All Your Lovin' For Me*	Decca 31424
5/25/63	6	13		12 Losing You	Jean Renard/Carl Sigman...*He's So Heavenly*	Decca 31478
				LEE, Curtis		
8/7/61	7	11		1 Pretty Little Angel Eyes	Tommy Boyce/Curtis Lee...*Gee How I Wish You Were Here*	Dunes 2007
				LEE, Dickey		
10/6/62	6	14		1 Patches	Larry Kolber/Barry Mann...*More Or Less*	Smash 1758
				LEE, Johnny		
9/20/80	5	21	●	1 Lookin' For Love	Wanda Mallette/Bob Morrison/Patti Ryan...*Lyin' Eyes* (Eagles)	Full Moon 47004
				LEE, Murphy		
9/6/03	❶^4	30	○	1 Shake Ya Tailfeather NELLY/P. DIDDY/MURPHY LEE	Jayson Bridges/Tohri Harper/Cornell Haynes/Varick Smith	Bad Boy
				LEE, Peggy		
12/8/45	4	14		1 Waitin' For The Train To Come In	Martin Block/Sunny Skylar...*I'm Glad I Waited For You*	Capitol 218
7/20/46	7	6		2 I Don't Know Enough About You	Dave Barbour/Peggy Lee...*I Can See It Your Way*	Capitol 236
11/30/46	10	6		3 It's All Over Now	Don Marcotte/Sunny Skylar...*Aren't You Kind Of Glad We Did?*	Capitol 292
7/26/47	10	4		4 Chi-Baba Chi-Baba (My Bambino Go To Sleep)	Mack David/Al Hoffman/Jerry Livingston...*Ain'tcha Ever Comin' Back*	Capitol 419
1/31/48	2^1	18		5 Golden Earrings	Ray Evans/Jay Livingston/Victor Young...*I'll Dance At Your Wedding*	Capitol 15009
3/13/48	❶^9	21	⊙	6 Manana (Is Soon Enough For Me)	Dave Barbour/Peggy Lee...*All Dressed Up With A Broken Heart*	Capitol 15022
6/18/49	2^1	9		7 Riders In The Sky (A Cowboy Legend)	Stan Jones...*Please Love Me Tonight*	Capitol 608
1/14/50	9	7		8 The Old Master Painter PEGGY LEE and MEL TORME	Haven Gillespie/Beasley Smith...*Bless You (For The Good That's In You)*	Capitol 791
7/12/52	3^1	13	⊙	9 Lover PEGGY LEE and GORDON JENKINS And His Orchestra	Lorenz Hart/Richard Rodgers...*You Go To My Head*	Decca 28215
8/25/58	8	15		10 Fever	Eddie Cooley/John Davenport...*You Don't Know*	Capitol 3998
				LEFT BANKE, The		
10/29/66	5	13		1 Walk Away Renee	Mike Brown/Bob Calilli/Tony Sansone...*I Haven't Got The Nerve*	Smash 2041
				LEMON PIPERS, The		
2/3/68	❶^1	13	●	1 Green Tambourine	Paul Leka/Shelley Pinz...*No Help From Me*	Buddah 23

PEAK DATE	PEAK POS	WKS CHR	GOLD	ARTIST / Song Title	Songwriter...B-side	Label & Number
				LEN		
11/13/99	9	25		1 Steal My Sunshine	Marc Costanzo/Gregg Diamond	Work
				LENNON, John		
3/28/70	3³	13	●	1 Instant Karma (We All Shine On) .... JOHN ONO LENNON	John Lennon...*Who Has Seen The Wind?* (Yoko Ono Lennon)	Apple 1818
11/13/71	3²	9		2 Imagine .... JOHN LENNON PLASTIC ONO BAND	John Lennon...*It's So Hard*	Apple 1840
11/16/74	❶¹	15		3 Whatever Gets You Thru The Night ..... JOHN LENNON With The PLASTIC ONO NUCLEAR BAND	John Lennon...*Beef Jerky*	Apple 1874
2/22/75	9	12		4 #9 Dream	John Lennon...*What You Got*	Apple 1878
12/27/80	❶⁵	22	●	5 (Just Like) Starting Over	John Lennon...*Kiss Kiss Kiss* (Yoko Ono)	Geffen 49604
3/21/81	2³	20	●	6 Woman	John Lennon...*Beautiful Boys* (Yoko Ono)	Geffen 49644
5/23/81	10	17		7 Watching The Wheels	John Lennon...*Yes, I'm Your Angel* (Yoko Ono)	Geffen 49695
3/3/84	5	14		8 Nobody Told Me	John Lennon...*O' Sanity* (Yoko Ono)	Polydor 817254
				LENNON, Julian		
1/12/85	9	19		1 Valotte	Justin Clayton/Julian Lennon/Carlton Morales...*Well I Don't Know*	Atlantic 89609
3/23/85	5	17		2 Too Late For Goodbyes	Julian Lennon...*Let Me Be*	Atlantic 89589
				LENNOX, Annie		
1/14/89	9	17		1 Put A Little Love In Your Heart .... ANNIE LENNOX & AL GREEN	Jackie DeShannon/Jimmy Holiday/Randy Myers ...*A Great Big Piece Of Love* (The Spheres Of Celestial Influence)	A&M 1255
				LESTER, Ketty		
4/14/62	5	14		1 Love Letters	Edward Heyman/Victor Young...*I'm A Fool To Want You*	Era 3068
				LETTERMEN, The		
1/27/62	7	14		1 When I Fall In Love	Edward Heyman/Victor Young...*Smile*	Capitol 4658
2/10/68	7	15		2 Goin' Out Of My Head/Can't Take My Eyes Off You	Bob Crewe/Bob Gaudio/Teddy Randazzo/Bob Weinstein...*I Believe* [L]	Capitol 2054
				LEVEL 42		
5/31/86	7	27		1 Something About You	Wally Badarou/Boon Gould/Phil Gould/Mark King/Mike Lindup...*Coup D'etat*	Polydor 883362
				LEVERT		
10/31/87	5	18	●	1 Casanova	Reggie Calloway...*Throwdown*	Atlantic 89217
				LEWIS, Barbara		
6/22/63	3²	14		1 Hello Stranger	Barbara Lewis...*Think A Little Sugar*	Atlantic 2184
				LEWIS, Bobby		
7/10/61	❶⁷	23	⊙	1 Tossin' And Turnin'	Ritchie Adams/Malou Rene...*Oh Yes, I Love You*	Beltone 1002
9/18/61	9	10		2 One Track Mind	Bobby Lewis/Malou Rene...*Are You Ready*	Beltone 1012
				LEWIS, Donna		
8/24/96	2⁹	41	●	1 I Love You Always Forever	Donna Lewis...*Simone*	Atlantic 87072
				LEWIS, Gary, And The Playboys		
2/20/65	❶²	12	●	1 This Diamond Ring	Bob Brass/Al Kooper/Irwin Levine...*Tijuana Wedding*	Liberty 55756
5/8/65	2²	11		2 Count Me In	Glen Hardin...*Little Miss Go-Go*	Liberty 55778
8/21/65	2¹	11		3 Save Your Heart For Me	Gary Geld/Peter Udell...*Without A Word Of Warning*	Liberty 55809
11/6/65	4	11		4 Everybody Loves A Clown	Gary Lewis/Leon Russell/Leslie Thomas...*Time Stands Still*	Liberty 55818
1/8/66	3⁴	12		5 She's Just My Style	Al Capps/Snuff Garrett/Gary Lewis/Leon Russell...*I Won't Make That Mistake Again*	Liberty 55846
4/9/66	9	9		6 Sure Gonna Miss Her	Bobby Russell...*I Don't Wanna Say Goodnight*	Liberty 55865
6/18/66	8	8		7 Green Grass	Roger Cook/Roger Greenaway...*I Can Read Between The Lines*	Liberty 55880
				LEWIS, Huey, and The News		
4/17/82	7	17		1 Do You Believe In Love	Mutt Lange...*Is It Me*	Chrysalis 2589
11/26/83	8	21		2 Heart And Soul	Mike Chapman/Nicky Chinn...*You Crack Me Up*	Chrysalis 42726
3/24/84	6	19	●	3 I Want A New Drug	Chris Hayes/Huey Lewis...*Finally Found A Home*	Chrysalis 42766
6/9/84	6	20		4 The Heart Of Rock & Roll	Johnny Colla/Huey Lewis...*Workin' For A Livin'* (live)	Chrysalis 42782
9/15/84	6	17		5 If This Is It	Johnny Colla/Huey Lewis...*Change Of Heart*	Chrysalis 42803
8/24/85	❶²	19	●	6 The Power Of Love	Johnny Colla/Chris Hayes/Huey Lewis...*Bad Is Bad*	Chrysalis 42876
9/20/86	❶³	19		7 Stuck With You	Chris Hayes/Huey Lewis...*Don't Ever Tell Me That You Love Me*	Chrysalis 43019
12/6/86	3²	16		8 Hip To Be Square	Bill Gibson/Sean Hopper/Huey Lewis...*Some Of My Lies Are True*	Chrysalis 43065
3/14/87	❶¹	15		9 Jacob's Ladder	Bruce Hornsby/John Hornsby...*The Heart Of Rock & Roll* (live)	Chrysalis 43097
5/30/87	9	14		10 I Know What I Like	Chris Hayes/Huey Lewis...*Forest For The Trees*	Chrysalis 43108
9/19/87	6	16		11 Doing It All For My Baby	Phil Cody/Michael Duke...*Naturally*	Chrysalis 43143
9/10/88	3²	15		12 Perfect World	Alex Call...*Slammin'*	Chrysalis 43265
				LEWIS, Jerry		
12/29/56	10	19	⊙	1 Rock-A-Bye Your Baby With A Dixie Melody	Sam Lewis/Jean Schwartz/Joe Young...*Come Rain Or Come Shine*	Decca 30124
				LEWIS, Jerry Lee		
9/9/57	3²	29	⊙	1 Whole Lot Of Shakin' Going On	Sunny David/Dave Williams...*It'll Be Me*	Sun 267
1/6/58	2⁴	21	⊙	2 Great Balls Of Fire	Otis Blackwell/Jack Hammer...*You Win Again*	Sun 281
4/7/58	7	15		3 Breathless	Otis Blackwell...*Down The Line*	Sun 288
				LEWIS, Leona		
4/5/08	❶⁴	39	△	1 Bleeding Love	Jesse McCartney/Ryan Tedder	J Records/SyCo
				LEWIS, Ramsey, Trio		
10/9/65	5	16		1 The "In" Crowd	Billy Page...*Since I Fell For You* [I-L]	Argo 5506
				LFO		
8/28/99	3⁴	17	▲	1 Summer Girls	Rich Cronin...*Can't Have You*	Logic/Arista 13692
12/11/99	10	17	●	2 Girl On TV	Dow Brain/Rich Cronin/Brad Young...*All I Need To Know*	Logic/Arista 13756

PEAK DATE	PEAK POS	WKS CHR	GOLD	ARTIST / Song Title ... Songwriter...B-side	Label & Number
				LIFEHOUSE	
6/16/01	2⁴	54		1 Hanging By A Moment .... Jason Wade	DreamWorks
8/27/05	5	62	○	2 You And Me .... Jude Cole/Jason Wade	Geffen
				LIGHTFOOT, Gordon	
2/20/71	5	15		1 If You Could Read My Mind .... Gordon Lightfoot...*Poor Little Allison*	Reprise 0974
6/29/74	❶¹	18	●	2 Sundown .... Gordon Lightfoot...*Too Late For Prayin'*	Reprise 1194
11/9/74	10	14		3 Carefree Highway .... Gordon Lightfoot...*Seven Island Suite*	Reprise 1309
11/20/76	2²	21		4 The Wreck Of The Edmund Fitzgerald .... Gordon Lightfoot...*The House You Live In*	Reprise 1369
				LIL' BOOSIE	
3/8/08	9	25		1 Independent .... Jeremy Allen/Webster Gradney/Torence Hatch/Claude McKnight...*I Miss You* WEBBIE Feat. Lil' Phat & Lil' Boosie	Trill 511418
				LIL BOW WOW — see BOW WOW	
				LIL' FLIP	
8/28/04	2²	23	○	1 Sunshine .... Carlos Hassan/Sandy Lal/Lea Quezada/Wesley Weston...*The Ghetto* LIL' FLIP Featuring Lea	Sucka Free 77009
				LIL JON & THE EAST SIDE BOYZ	
10/25/03	2¹	45		1 Get Low .... D'Angelo Holmes/Eric Jackson/Sammie Norris/Jonathan Smith...*Throw It Up* LIL JON & THE EAST SIDE BOYZ Featuring Ying Yang Twins	BME/TVT 2377
11/1/03	4	32		2 Damn! .... Jeffrey Grigsby/Sean Paul Joseph/Cedric Leonard/Jonathan Smith YOUNGBLOODZ Featuring Lil' Jon	So So Def 52215
2/14/04	9	26		3 Salt Shaker .... D'Angelo Holmes/Eric Jackson/L. Jefferson/C. Love/Jonathan Smith YING YANG TWINS Feat. Lil Jon & The East Side Boyz	TVT 2485
2/28/04	❶¹²	45	△	4 Yeah! .... Christopher Bridges/Sean Garrett/Jonathan Smith/Patrick Smith USHER Featuring Lil Jon & Ludacris	Arista 59149
11/27/04	7	22	○	5 Let's Go .... Derrick Baker/Robert Daisley/Maurice Marshall/Carl Mitchell/Ozzy Osbourne/Randy Rhoads/James Scheffer/Jonathan Smith Charles Young/Maurice Young...*Down Wit Da South* TRICK DADDY Featuring Twista and Lil Jon	Slip N Slide 93348
1/22/05	3³	22		6 Lovers & Friends .... Christopher Bridges/Usher Raymond/Jonathan Smith/M. Sterling LIL JON & THE EAST SIDE BOYZ Featuring Usher & Ludacris	BME/TVT
5/27/06	7	28		7 Snap Yo Fingers .... Sean Joseph/Jonathan Smith/Earl Stevens LIL JON Feat. E-40 & Sean Paul of YoungBloodZ	BME/TVT 2841
1/9/10	10	20	△	8 Do You Remember .... Jared Cotter/Sean Henriques/Robert Larow/Jay Sean/Jeremy Skaller/Jonathan Smith/Frankie Storm JAY SEAN Featuring Sean Paul & Lil Jon	Cash Money
				LIL' KIM	
8/9/97	6	21	▲	1 Not Tonight .... Robert Bell/Ronald Bell/George Brown/Missy Elliott/Shawntae Harris/Kim Jones/Lisa Lopes/Angie Martinez/ Meekaaeel Muhammed/Claydes Smith/James Taylor/Dennis Thomas/Earl Toon LIL' KIM Featuring Da Brat, Left Eye, Missy "Misdemeanor" Elliott and Angie Martinez	Undeas 98019
1/3/98	2²	6	▲	2 It's All About The Benjamins .... Deric Angelettie/Sean Combs/Sean Jacobs/Kim Jones/Jayson Phillips/David Styles/Christopher Wallace ...*Been Around The World* (Puff Daddy) PUFF DADDY & THE FAMILY Feat. The Notorious B.I.G./Lil' Kim/The Lox/Dave Grohl/Perfect/FuzzBubble/Rob Zombie	Bad Boy 79130
6/2/01	❶⁵	20		3 Lady Marmalade .... Bob Crewe/Kenny Nolan CHRISTINA AGUILERA, LIL' KIM, MYA and PINK	Interscope 497066
7/12/03	2³	24		4 Magic Stick .... Michael Clervoix/Carlos Evans/Roy Hawkins/Curtis Jackson/Kim Jones/Rick Ravon LIL' KIM (feat. 50 Cent)	Queen Bee
9/29/07	7	23		5 Let It Go .... Keyshia Cole/Missy Elliott/Kim Jones/James Mtume KEYSHIA COLE Featuring Missy Elliott & Lil' Kim	Imani 009976
				LIL MAMA	
6/30/07	10	11	○	1 Lip Gloss .... James Chambers/Niatia Kirkland	Jive 07519
4/5/08	10	12		2 Shawty Get Loose .... Niatia Kirkland/Faheem Najm LIL MAMA Featuring Chris Brown & T-Pain	Jive 27082
				LIL' MO	
3/24/01	8	27		1 Put It On Me .... Jeffrey Atkins/Tiheem Crocker/Irv Gotti/Paul Walcott...*Love Me, Hate Me* JA RULE (feat. Lil' Mo and Vita)	Murder Inc. 572751
5/31/03	4	23		2 Can't Let You Go .... John Jackson/Cynthia Loving/Justin Smith...*Damn* FABOLOUS featuring Mike Shorey & Lil' Mo	Desert Storm 67428
				LIL' ROMEO	
6/30/01	3¹	14		1 My Baby .... Berry Gordy/Fonce Mizell/Freddie Perren/Deke Richards	Soulja 50202
				LIL WAYNE	
2/12/05	3¹	21	○	1 Soldier .... Dwayne Carter/Sean Garrett/Clifford Harris/Rich Harrison/Beyonce Knowles/Kelly Rowland/Michelle Williams DESTINY'S CHILD (feat. T.I. and Lil Wayne)	Columbia 70702
2/17/07	9	24		2 You .... Jasper Cameron/Dwayne Carter/Gary Kemp/Maurice Sinclair LLOYD Featuring Lil Wayne	The Inc.
5/3/08	❶⁵	28		3 Lollipop .... Dwayne Carter/Stephen Garrett/Darius Harrison/James Scheffer/Rex Zamor LIL WAYNE Featuring Static Major	Cash Money 011599
8/9/08	6	23	△	4 A Milli .... Dwayne Carter	Cash Money
9/27/08	5	20		5 Swagga Like Us .... Maya Arulpragasm/Dwayne Carter/Shawn Carter/Clifford Harris/Nicky Headon/Mick Jones/Wesley Pentz/Paul Simonon/ Joe Strummer/Kanye West JAY-Z & T.I. Featuring Kanye West & Lil Wayne	Roc-A-Fella 012284
9/27/08	10	27	△	6 Got Money .... Dwayne Carter/Faheem Najm/Juan Salinas/Oscar Salinas LIL WAYNE Featuring T-Pain	Cash Money
10/11/08	7	24		7 Can't Believe It .... Dwayne Carter/Faheem Najm T-PAIN Featuring Lil Wayne	Konvict 36568
10/18/08	5	35	△³	8 Let It Rock .... Dwayne Carter/Kevin Rudolf KEVIN RUDOLF Feat. Lil Wayne	Cash Money 012077
10/3/09	8	24		9 Forever .... Dwayne Carter/Aubrey Graham/Marshall Mathers/Matthew Samuels/Kanye West DRAKE Featuring Kanye West, Lil Wayne & Eminem	Harvey Mason
10/17/09	❶²	40	△³	10 Down .... Dewayne Carter/Jared Cotter/Robert Larow/J Perkins/Jay Sean/Jeremy Skaller JAY SEAN Featuring Lil Wayne	Cash Money 013306
9/4/10	6	23↑		11 Right Above It .... Dwayne Carter/Aubrey Graham/Daniel Johnson LIL WAYNE Featuring Drake	Cash Money
1/1/11	9	6↑		12 6 Foot 7 Foot .... Dwayne Carter LIL WAYNE Featuring Cory Gunz	Cash Money
				LIND, Bob	
3/12/66	5	13		1 Elusive Butterfly .... Bob Lind...*Cheryl's Goin Home*	World Pacific 77808

PEAK DATE	PEAK POS	WKS CHR	GOLD	ARTIST / Song Title	Songwriter...B-side	Label & Number
				LINDEN, Kathy		
4/14/58	7	17		1 Billy	Joe Goodwin/James Kendis/Herman Paley...*If I Could Hold You In My Arms*	Felsted 8510
				LINDSAY, Mark		
2/14/70	10	16	●	1 Arizona	Kenny Young...*Man From Houston*	Columbia 45037
				LINEAR		
5/19/90	5	27	●	1 Sending All My Love	Tolga Katas/Charlie Pennachio	Atlantic 87961
				LINKIN PARK		
3/30/02	2[1]	38	○	1 In The End	Chester Bennington/Rob Bourdon/Brad Delson/Joseph Hahn/Mike Shinoda	Warner
4/21/07	7	23	△[2]	2 What I've Done	Chester Bennington/Rob Bourdon/Brad Delson/David Farrell/Joseph Hahn/Mike Shinoda	Machine Shop
6/6/09	6	20	△	3 New Divide	Chester Bennington/Rob Bourdon/Brad Delson/David Farrell/Joseph Hahn/Mike Shinoda	Machine Shop
				LIPPS, INC.		
5/31/80	❶[4]	23	▲	1 Funkytown	Steve Greenberg...*All Night Dancing*	Casablanca 2233
				LISA LISA AND CULT JAM		
10/25/86	8	26	●	1 All Cried Out	Curtis Bedeau/Gerard Charles/Hugh Clarke/Brian George/Lucien George/Paul George...*Behind My Eyes*	Columbia 05844
				LISA LISA AND CULT JAM WITH FULL FORCE FEATURING PAUL ANTHONY & BOW LEGGED LOU		
6/20/87	❶[1]	20	●	Head To Toe	Curtis Bedeau/Gerard Charles/Hugh Clarke/Brian George/Lucien George/Paul George...*You'll Never Change*	Columbia 07008
10/17/87	❶[1]	20 ●	3	Lost In Emotion	Curtis Bedeau/Gerard Charles/Hugh Clarke/Brian George/Lucien George/Paul George...*Motion Is Lost*	Columbia 07267
				LITTLE ANTHONY AND THE IMPERIALS		
10/13/58	4	19	⊙	1 Tears On My Pillow	Sylvester Bradford/Al Lewis...*Two People In The World*	End 1027
12/26/64	6	14		2 Goin' Out Of My Head	Teddy Randazzo/Bob Weinstein...*Make It Easy On Yourself*	DCP 1119
3/13/65	10	9		3 Hurt So Bad	Bobby Hart/Teddy Randazzo/Bob Weinstein...*Reputation*	DCP 1128
				LITTLE CAESAR and The Romans		
6/26/61	9	13		1 Those Oldies But Goodies (Remind Me Of You)	Nick Curinga/Paul Politi...*She Don't Wanna Dance (No More)*	Del-Fi 4158
				LITTLE DIPPERS, The		
3/28/60	9	14		1 Forever	Buddy Killen...*Two By Four*	University 210
				LITTLE EVA		
8/25/62	❶[1]	16	⊙	1 The Loco-Motion	Gerry Goffin/Carole King...*He Is The Boy*	Dimension 1000
				LITTLE RICHARD		
5/12/56	6	19	⊙	1 Long Tall Sally	Robert Blackwell/Enotris Johnson/Richard Penniman...*Slippin' And Slidin' (Peepin' And Hidin')*	Specialty 572
7/8/57	10	20		2 Jenny, Jenny	Enotris Johnson/Richard Penniman...*Miss Ann*	Specialty 606
10/28/57	8	18		3 Keep A Knockin'	Richard Penniman...*Can't Believe You Wanna Leave*	Specialty 611
3/17/58	10	15		4 Good Golly, Miss Molly	Otis Blackwell/John Marascalco...*Hey-Hey-Hey-Hey (Goin' Back To Birmingham)*	Specialty 624
				LITTLE RIVER BAND		
10/28/78	3[2]	20		1 Reminiscing	Graham Goble...*So Many Paths*	Harvest 4605
4/7/79	10	20		2 Lady	Graham Goble...*Take Me Home*	Harvest 4667
9/29/79	6	18		3 Lonesome Loser	David Briggs...*Shut Down Turn Off*	Capitol 4748
1/19/80	10	18		4 Cool Change	Glenn Shorrock...*Middle Man*	Capitol 4789
11/7/81	6	21		5 The Night Owls	Graham Goble...*Suicide Boulevard*	Capitol 5033
3/6/82	10	19		6 Take It Easy On Me	Graham Goble...*Orbit Zero*	Capitol 5057
				LL COOL J		
3/2/91	9	23	●	1 Around The Way Girl	James Todd Smith/Marlon Williams	Def Jam 73609
12/2/95	3[8]	21	▲	2 Hey Lover	James Todd Smith/Rod Temperton	Def Jam 577494
4/13/96	9	20	▲	3 Doin It	Grace Jones/James Todd Smith/Robert Smith	Def Jam 576120
8/24/96	3[1]	29	▲	4 Loungin	James Todd Smith/Robert Smith/Lenny White/Bernard Wright...*Summer Luv*	Def Jam 575062
11/9/96	6	20	▲	5 This Is For The Lover In You	Howard Hewett/Dana Meyers	Epic 78443
				BABYFACE Featuring LL Cool J, Howard Hewett, Jody Watley and Jeffrey Daniels		
11/16/02	4	22		6 Luv U Better	Charles Hugo/James Smith/Pharrell Williams...*Fa Ha*	Def Jam 063956
2/8/03	❶[4]	21		7 All I Have	Ron Bowser/William Jeffrey/Jennifer Lopez/Lisa Peters/Curtis Richardson/Makeba Riddick	Epic
				JENNIFER LOPEZ Featuring LL Cool J		
4/29/06	4	11		8 Control Myself	Afrika Bambaataa/Jermaine Dupri/Jennifer Lopez/John Miller/James Phillips/James Robie/James Todd Smith/Ryan Toby	Def Jam 006285
				LL COOL J featuring Jennifer Lopez		
				LLOYD		
2/17/07	9	24		1 You	Jasper Cameron/Dwayne Carter/Gary Kemp/Maurice Sinclair	The Inc.
				LLOYD Featuring Lil Wayne		
3/13/10	2[1]	25		2 BedRock	Jasper Cameron/Dwayne Carter/Aubrey Graham/Daniel Johnson/Carl Lilly/Onika Maraj/Jarvis Mills/Lloyd Polite/Michael Stevenson	Universal Motown
				YOUNG MONEY Featuring Lloyd		
				LOBO		
5/15/71	5	13		1 Me And You And A Dog Named Boo	Lobo...*Walk Away From It All*	Big Tree 112
11/18/72	2[2]	14	●	2 I'd Love You To Want Me	Lobo...*Am I True To Myself*	Big Tree 147
2/17/73	8	13		3 Don't Expect Me To Be Your Friend	Lobo...*A Big Red Kite*	Big Tree 158
				LOCKLIN, Hank		
8/1/60	8	22	⊙	1 Please Help Me, I'm Falling	Hal Blair/Don Robertson...*My Old Home Town*	RCA Victor 7692
				LOEB, Lisa, & Nine Stories		
8/6/94	❶[3]	30	●	1 Stay (I Missed You)	Lisa Loeb	RCA 62870
				LOGGINS, Dave		
8/10/74	5	18		1 Please Come To Boston	Dave Loggins...*Let Me Go Now*	Epic 11115
				LOGGINS, Kenny		
10/28/78	5	20		1 Whenever I Call You "Friend"	Kenny Loggins/Melissa Manchester...*Angelique*	Columbia 10794
				KENNY LOGGINS (with Stevie Nicks)		
10/11/80	7	22		2 I'm Alright	Kenny Loggins...*Lead The Way*	Columbia 11317
3/31/84	❶[3]	23	▲	3 Footloose	Kenny Loggins/Dean Pitchford...*Swear Your Love*	Columbia 04310

PEAK DATE	PEAK POS	WKS CHR	GOLD	ARTIST / Song Title	Songwriter...B-side	Label & Number
				LOGGINS, Kenny (cont'd)		
7/26/86	2[1]	21		4 Danger Zone	Giorgio Moroder/Tom Whitlock...*I'm Gonna Do It Right*	Columbia 05893
9/17/88	8	18		5 Nobody's Fool	Kenny Loggins/Mike Towers...*I'm Gonna Do It Right*	Columbia 07971
				LOGGINS & MESSINA		
1/27/73	4	16	●	1 Your Mama Don't Dance	Kenny Loggins/Jim Messina...*Golden Ribbons*	Columbia 45719
				LOLITA		
12/19/60	5	18		1 Sailor (Your Home Is The Sea)	Fini Busch/Werner Scharfenberger...*La Luna (Quando La Luna)* [F]	Kapp 349
				LOMBARDO, Guy, And His Royal Canadians		
5/24/41	6	4		1 The Band Played On	John Palmer/Charles Ward...*You Stepped Out Of A Dream*	Decca 3675
6/27/42	9	1		2 Johnny Doughboy Found A Rose In Ireland	Al Goodhart/Kay Twomey...*Bless 'Em All*	Decca 4278
3/25/44	5	10		3 Speak Low	Ogden Nash/Kurt Weill...*Take It Easy*	Decca 18573
4/22/44	❶[2]	19		4 It's Love-Love-Love	Mack David/Alex Kramer/Joan Whitney...*Can't You Do A Friend A Favor*	Decca 18589
10/28/44	7	11		5 Together	Lew Brown/B.G. DeSylva/Ray Henderson...*Come With Me My Honey (The Song Of Calypso Joe)*	Decca 18617
2/3/45	10	5		6 Always	Irving Berlin...*The Trolley Song*	Decca 18634
3/24/45	5	13		7 A Little On The Lonely Side	James Cavanaugh/Dick Robertson/Frank Weldon...*(All Of A Sudden) My Heart Sings*	Decca 18642
7/21/45	2[1]	13		8 Bell Bottom Trousers	Moe Jaffe...*Oh! Brother*	Decca 18683
8/18/45	6	2		9 June Is Bustin' Out All Over	Oscar Hammerstein/Richard Rodgers...*This Was A Real Nice Clambake*	Decca 23428
				HILDEGARDE with GUY LOMBARDO AND HIS ROYAL CANADIANS		
11/24/45	8	6		10 No Can Do	Nat Simon/Charles Tobias...*José Gonzalez*	Decca 18712
2/9/46	9	5		11 Money Is The Root Of All Evil (Take It Away, Take It Away, Take It Away)	Alex Kramer/Joan Whitney...*Johnny Fedora*	Decca 23474
				ANDREWS SISTERS and GUY LOMBARDO And His Royal Canadians		
2/16/46	10	8		12 Symphony	Alex Alstone/Roger Bernstein/Jack Lawrence/Andre Tabet...*Seems Like Old Times* [I]	Decca 18737
3/30/46	7	7		13 Seems Like Old Times	John Jacob Loeb/Carmen Lombardo...*Symphony*	Decca 18737
5/11/46	6	7		14 Shoo Fly Pie And Apple Pan Dowdy	Sammy Gallop/Guy Wood...*Give Me The Moon Over Brooklyn*	Decca 18809
5/11/46	7	14		15 The Gypsy	Billy Reid...*One-Zy Two-Zy (I Love You-zy)*	Decca 23511
1/11/47	7	4		16 Christmas Island	Lyle Moraine...*Winter Wonderland* [X]	Decca 23722
				ANDREWS SISTERS and GUY LOMBARDO And His Royal Canadians		
3/8/47	2[3]	13		17 Anniversary Song	Saul Chaplin/Al Jolson...*Uncle Remus Said*	Decca 23799
3/15/47	❶[1]	15		18 Managua - Nicaragua	Irving Fields/Albert Gamse...*What More Can I Ask For?*	Decca 23782
5/24/47	9	4		19 April Showers	B.G. DeSylva/Louis Silvers...*If I Had My Way*	Decca 23845
6/28/47	3[2]	17		20 I Wonder, I Wonder, I Wonder	Daryl Hutchins...*It Takes Time*	Decca 23865
1/31/48	10	6		21 I'm My Own Grandpaw	Moe Jaffe/Dwight Latham...*Frankie And Johnny* [N]	Decca 24288
4/23/49	8	19		22 Red Roses For A Blue Lady	Roy Brodsky/Sid Tepper...*Everywhere You Go*	Decca 24549
3/25/50	10	19		23 Enjoy Yourself (It's Later Than You Think)	Herb Magidson/Carl Sigman...*Rain Or Shine*	Decca 24825
4/29/50	5	14		24 Dearie	Bob Hilliard/Dave Mann...*(She's My Lily Of Laguna) My Lily And My Rose*	Decca 24899
5/6/50	❶[11]	27	⊙	25 The 3rd Man Theme	Anton Karas...*The Cafe Mozart Waltz* [I]	Decca 24839
10/21/50	10	15		26 All My Love ("Bolero")	Henri Contet/Paul Durand/Mitchell Parish...*The Swiss Bellringer*	Decca 27118
11/25/50	2[1]	20		27 Harbor Lights	Will Grosz/Jimmy Kennedy...*The Petite Waltz (La Petite Valse)*	Decca 27208
1/20/51	6	17		28 Tennessee Waltz	Pee Wee King/Redd Stewart...*Get Out Those Old Records*	Decca 27336
4/12/52	9	19		29 Blue Tango	Leroy Anderson...*At Last, At Last* [I]	Decca 28031
				LONDON, Julie		
12/17/55	9	20		1 Cry Me A River	Arthur Hamilton...*S'Wonderful*	Liberty 55006
				LONDON, Laurie		
4/14/58	❶[4]	19	●	1 He's Got The Whole World (In His Hands)	(traditional)...*Handed Down*	Capitol 3891
				LONDONBEAT		
4/13/91	❶[1]	19	●	1 I've Been Thinking About You	Jimmy Chambers/George Chandler/Jimmy Helms/Bill Henshall	Radioactive 54005
				LONDON SYMPHONY ORCHESTRA — see WILLIAMS, John		
				LONESTAR		
3/4/00	❶[2]	55	●	1 Amazed	Marv Green/Chris Lindsey/Aimee Mayo	BNA 65957
				LONG, Johnny, And His Orchestra		
1/23/43	10	1		1 (As Long As You're Not In Love With Anyone Else) Why Don't You Fall In Love With Me?	Al Lewis/Mabel Wayne...*Then You'll Know You're In The Carolines*	Decca 4375
3/4/44	5	8		2 No Love, No Nothin'	Leo Robin/Harry Warren...*You Better Give Me Lots Of Lovin', Honey*	Decca 4427
9/2/44	8	8		3 Time Waits For No One	Cliff Friend/Charles Tobias...*Featherhead*	Decca 4439
4/28/45	3[3]	12		4 My Dreams Are Getting Better All The Time	Mann Curtis/Vic Mizzy...*Candy*	Decca 18661
6/2/45	8	8		5 Candy	Mack David/Alex Kramer/Joan Whitney...*My Dreams Are Getting Better All The Time*	Decca 18661
12/15/45	7	10		6 Waitin' For The Train To Come In	Martin Block/Sunny Skylar...*Fishin' For The Moon*	Decca 18718
				JOHNNY LONG And His Orchestra And DICK ROBERTSON (above 3)		
				LONG, Shorty		
7/6/68	8	11		1 Here Comes The Judge	Billie Jean Brown/Suzanne De Passe/Shorty Long...*Sing What You Wanna* [N]	Soul 35044
				LOOKING GLASS		
8/26/72	❶[1]	16	●	1 Brandy (You're A Fine Girl)	Elliot Lurie...*One By One*	Epic 10874
				LOON		
5/25/02	2[4]	23		1 I Need A Girl (Part One)	Sean Combs/Chauncey Hawkins/Michael Jones/Jack Knight/Sonny Lester/Eric Matlock/J. Karen Thomas	Bad Boy 79436
				P. DIDDY Featuring Usher & Loon		
8/3/02	4	26		2 I Need A Girl (Part Two)	Sean Combs/Chauncey Hawkins/Michael Jones/Frank Romano/Adonis Shropshire/Mario Winans...*So Complete*	Bad Boy 79441
				P. DIDDY AND GINUWINE Featuring Loon, Mario Winans & Tammy Ruggeri		
				LOPEZ, Jennifer		
6/12/99	❶[5]	25	▲	1 If You Had My Love	LaShawn Daniels/Rodney Jerkins/Mark Cory Rooney...*No Me Ames* (w/Marc Anthony)	Epic/WORK 79163
12/4/99	8	20		2 Waiting For Tonight	Maria Christiansen/Michael Garvin/Phil Temple	Epic/WORK 79292
2/24/01	3[2]	21		3 Love Don't Cost A Thing	Georgette Franklin/Amille Harris/Greg Lawson/Jeremy Monroe/Damon Sharpe...*Let's Get Loud*	Epic 79547
9/8/01	❶[5]	31		4 I'm Real	LeShaun Lewis/Jennifer Lopez/Troy Oliver/Mark Cory Rooney	Epic 79639
3/9/02	❶[6]	27		5 Ain't It Funny	Jeffrey Atkins/Jennifer Lopez/Mark Cory Rooney	Epic
				JENNIFER LOPEZ featuring Ja Rule (above 2)		
6/29/02	10	23		6 I'm Gonna Be Alright	Sam Barnes/Denzil Foster/Jay King/Jennifer Lopez/Thomas McElroy/Troy Oliver/J.C. Olivier/Mark Cory Rooney...*Alive* (Lopez)	Epic 79759
				JENNIFER LOPEZ Featuring Nas		

PEAK DATE	PEAK POS	WKS CHR	GOLD	ARTIST / Song Title	Songwriter...B-side	Label & Number
				LOPEZ, Jennifer (cont'd)		
12/7/02	3[4]	20		7 Jenny From The Block .... Miro Arbex/Sam Barnes/Andre Deyo/Jennifer Lopez/Michael Oliver/Troy Oliver/J.C. Olivier/Lawrence Parker/	Jayson Phillips/Scott Sterling/David Styles	Epic 79825
				JENNIFER LOPEZ Featuring Jadakiss & Styles		
2/8/03	❶[4]	21		8 All I Have .... Ron Bowser/William Jeffrey/Jennifer Lopez/Lisa Peters/Curtis Richardson/Makeba Riddick		Epic
				JENNIFER LOPEZ Featuring LL Cool J		
4/29/06	4	11		9 Control Myself .... Afrika Bambaataa/Jermaine Dupri/Jennifer Lopez/John Miller/James Phillips/John Robie/James Todd Smith/Ryan Toby		Def Jam 006285
				LL COOL J featuring Jennifer Lopez		
				LOPEZ, Trini		
9/7/63	3[3]	14		1 If I Had A Hammer	Lee Hays/Pete Seeger...*Unchain My Heart* [L]	Reprise 20,198
				LOR, Denise		
10/16/54	8	14		1 If I Give My Heart To You	Jimmy Brewster/Jimmie Crane/Al Jacobs...*Hello Darling*	Majar 27-X45
				LORAIN, A'Me		
4/28/90	9	20		1 Whole Wide World	Arnie Roman/Elliot Wolff...*Stop Twistin' My Arm* (Barrence Whitfield & The Savages)	RCA 9099
				LORD TARIQ & PETER GUNZ		
3/28/98	9	28	▲	1 Deja Vu (Uptown Baby)	Walter Becker/Donald Fagen...*Marmalade*	Columbia 78755
				LORING, Gloria		
9/27/86	2[2]	21		1 Friends And Lovers	Paul Gordon/Jay Gruska...*You Always Knew* (Loring)	USA Carrere 06122
				GLORIA LORING & CARL ANDERSON		
				LOS BRAVOS		
10/1/66	4	12		1 Black Is Black	Michelle Grainger/Tony Hayes/Steve Wadey...*I Want A Name*	Press 60002
				LOS DEL RIO		
8/3/96	❶[14]	40	▲[4]	1 Macarena	Antonio Romero/Rafael Ruiz...*Can You Feel It* (Matrix) [F]	RCA 64407
				LOS INDIOS TABAJARAS		
11/16/63	6	14		1 Maria Elena	Lorenzo Barcelata...*Jungle Dream* [I]	RCA Victor 8216
				LOS LOBOS		
8/29/87	❶[3]	21		1 La Bamba	Ritchie Valens...*Charlena* [F]	Slash 28336
				LOVE AND ROCKETS		
8/5/89	3[1]	20		1 So Alive	Daniel Ash/David Haskins/Kevin Haskins...*Dreamtime*	RCA 8956
				LOVERBOY		
11/2/85	9	21		1 Lovin' Every Minute Of It	Mutt Lange...*Bullet In The Chamber*	Columbia 05569
3/29/86	10	18		2 This Could Be The Night	Jonathan Cain/Paul Dean/Mike Reno/Bill Wray...*It's Your Life*	Columbia 05765
				LOVE UNLIMITED ORCHESTRA		
2/9/74	❶[1]	22	●	1 Love's Theme	Barry White...*Sweet Moments* [I]	20th Century 2069
				LOVIN' SPOONFUL, The		
10/16/65	9	13		1 Do You Believe In Magic	John Sebastian...*On The Road Again*	Kama Sutra 201
1/22/66	10	12		2 You Didn't Have To Be So Nice	Steve Boone/John Sebastian...*My Gal*	Kama Sutra 205
4/9/66	2[2]	12		3 Daydream	John Sebastian...*Night Owl Blues*	Kama Sutra 208
6/11/66	2[2]	11		4 Did You Ever Have To Make Up Your Mind?	John Sebastian...*Didn't Want To Have To Do It*	Kama Sutra 209
8/13/66	❶[3]	11	●	5 Summer In The City	Steve Boone/John Sebastian/Mark Sebastian...*Butchie's Tune*	Kama Sutra 211
11/19/66	10	10		6 Rain On The Roof	John Sebastian...*Pow (Theme From "What's Up, Tiger Lily?")*	Kama Sutra 216
1/28/67	8	10		7 Nashville Cats	John Sebastian...*Full Measure*	Kama Sutra 219
				LOWE, Jim		
11/3/56	❶[3]	26	☉	1 The Green Door	Bob Davie/Marvin Moore...*(The Story Of) The Little Man In Chinatown*	Dot 15486
				LOX, The		
1/3/98	2[2]	6	▲	1 It's All About The Benjamins .... Deric Angelettie/Sean Combs/Sean Jacobs/Kim Jones/Jayson Phillips/David Styles/Christopher Wallace	...*Been Around The World* (Puff Daddy)	Bad Boy 79130
				PUFF DADDY & THE FAMILY Feat. The Notorious B.I.G./Lil' Kim/The Lox/Dave Grohl/Perfect/FuzzBubble/Rob Zombie		
				LSG		
12/6/97	4	20▲		1 My Body	Darrell Allamby/Lincoln Browder...*The Check Is In The Mail*	EastWest 64132
				L.T.D.		
12/24/77	4	19	●	1 (Every Time I Turn Around) Back In Love Again	Zane Grey/Len Hanks...*Material Things*	A&M 1974
				LUDACRIS		
10/5/02	10	23		1 Move B***h	Christopher Bridges/Craig Lawson/Bobby Sandimanie/Michael Tyler...*Keep It On The Hush*	Def Jam South 063949
				LUDACRIS feat. Mystikal and Infamous 2.0		
3/8/03	8	20		2 Gossip Folks	Bill Bloom/Christopher Bridges/Missy Elliott/Tim Mosley/Frankie Smith	Elektra 67356
				MISSY ELLIOTT Featuring Ludacris		
11/8/03	3[3]	21	○	3 Holidae In	Howard Bailey/Christopher Bridges/Shamar Daugherty/Alonzo Lee...*Represent*	Capitol 52816
				CHINGY featuring Ludacris & Snoop Dogg		
12/6/03	❶[1]	28	○	4 Stand Up	Christopher Bridges/Kanye West...*P-Poppin'*	Def Jam South 001183
				LUDACRIS featuring Shawnna		
2/28/04	❶[12]	45	△	5 Yeah!	Christopher Bridges/Sean Garrett/Jonathan Smith/Patrick Smith	Arista 59149
				USHER Featuring Lil Jon & Ludacris		
3/20/04	6	21		6 Splash Waterfalls	Christopher Bridges/Lawrence Mizell...*Blow It Out*	Def Jam South 001757
1/22/05	3[3]	22		7 Lovers & Friends	Christopher Bridges/Usher Raymond/Jonathan Smith/M. Sterling	BME/TVT
				LIL JON & THE EAST SIDE BOYZ Featuring Usher & Ludacris		
5/21/05	2[1]	23	○	8 Oh	Christopher Bridges/Vidal Davis/Andre Harris/Ciara Harris	LaFace 68177
				CIARA featuring Ludacris		
8/6/05	9	20		9 Pimpin' All Over The World	Christopher Bridges/Jamal Jones/Darnley Scantlebury...*Spur Of The Moment*	DTP 004851
				LUDACRIS featuring Bobby Valentino		
2/11/06	8	22		10 Unpredictable	Derrick Baker/Christopher Bridges/Harold Lilly/James Scheffer	J Records 75974
				JAMIE FOXX (feat. Ludacris)		
10/28/06	❶[2]	25	○	11 Money Maker	Christopher Bridges/Pharrell Williams	DTP 007488
				LUDACRIS Featuring Pharrell		
3/3/07	2[1]	20		12 Runaway Love	Christopher Bridges/Doug Davis/Keri Lyn Hilson/Jamal Jones/Ricky Walters	DTP
				LUDACRIS Featuring Mary J. Blige		

PEAK DATE	PEAK POS	WKS CHR	GOLD	ARTIST / Song Title	Songwriter...B-side	Label & Number
				LUDACRIS (cont'd)		
3/24/07	❶²	29	△² 13	Glamorous	William Adams/Christopher Bridges/Stacy Ferguson/Jamal Jones/Elvis Williams	will.i.am
				FERGIE Featuring Ludacris		
2/6/10	5	20	△² 14	Baby	Justin Bieber/Christopher Bridges/Christine Milian/Terius Nash/Christopher Stewart	SchoolBoy
				JUSTIN BIEBER Featuring Ludacris		
2/13/10	6	21	△ 15	How Low	James Boxley/Christopher Bridges/Carlton Ridenhour/Eric Sadler/Tyler Williams [N]	DTP
3/20/10	❶¹	29	△² 16	Break Your Heart	Christopher Bridges/Taio Cruz/Fraser Smith	Mercury 014302
				TAIO CRUZ Featuring Ludacris		
2/5/11	4↑	9↑	17	Tonight (I'm Lovin' You)	Christopher Bridges/Lauren Christy/Justin Franks/Enrique Iglesias/Jacob Luttrell	Universal Republic
				ENRIQUE IGLESIAS Featuring Ludacris & DJ Frank E		
				LUKE, Robin		
10/13/58	5	17	1	Susie Darlin'	Robin Luke...*Living's Loving You*	Dot 15781
				LULU		
10/21/67	❶⁵	17	● 1	To Sir With Love	Don Black/Mark London...*The Boat That I Row*	Epic 10187
				LUMAN, Bob		
10/24/60	7	14	1	Let's Think About Living	Boudleaux Bryant...*You've Got Everything* [N]	Warner 5172
				LUMIDEE		
8/16/03	3¹	20	1	Never Leave You - Uh Oooh, Uh Oooh!	Lumidee Cedeno/Stephen Marsden/Ted Mendez	Universal 000652
				LUNCEFORD, Jimmie, And His Orchestra		
2/21/42	4	5	1	Blues In The Night (My Mama Done Tol' Me) — Parts 1 & 2	Harold Arlen/Johnny Mercer	Decca 4125
11/24/45	10	3	2	The Honeydripper	Joe Liggins...*Baby, Are You Kiddin'?*	Decca 23451
				JIMMIE LUNCEFORD And His Orchestra and DELTA RHYTHM BOYS		
				LUND, Art		
6/7/47	❶²	13	⊙ 1	Mam'selle	Mack Gordon/Edmund Goulding...*Sleepy Time Gal*	MGM 10011
7/19/47	4	13	2	Peg O' My Heart	Alfred Bryan/Fred Fisher...*On The Old Spanish Trail*	MGM 10037
				LUNDBERG, Victor		
12/2/67	10	6	1	An Open Letter To My Teenage Son	Robert Thompson...*My Buddy Carl* [S]	Liberty 55996
				LUNIZ		
9/23/95	8	25	▲ 1	I Got 5 On It	Robert Bell/Ronald Bell/Donald Boyce/George Brown/Jerold Ellis/Denzil Foster/Anthony Gillmour/Garrick Husbands/Jay King/Thomas McElroy/Robert Mickens/Claydes Smith/Dennis Thomas/Rick Westfield...*So Much Drama*	Noo Trybe 38474
				L.V.		
9/9/95	❶³	38	▲³ 1	Gangsta's Paradise	Artis Ivey/Doug Rasheed/Larry Sanders	MCA 55104
				COOLIO featuring L.V.		
				LYMAN, Abe, and his Californians		
10/10/42	4	3	1	Amen	Bill Hardy/Vic Schoen/Roger Segure...*He Wears A Pair Of Silver Wings*	Bluebird 11542
3/10/45	4	5	2	Rum And Coca-Cola	Morey Amsterdam/Paul Baron/Jeri Sullavan...*Since You*	Columbia 36775
				ABE LYMAN and his Orchestra		
				LYMAN, Arthur, Group		
7/24/61	4	12	1	Yellow Bird	Alan Bergman/Marilyn Keith/Norman Luboff...*Havah Nagilah* [I]	Hi Fi 5024
				LYMON, Frankie, and The Teenagers		
4/14/56	6	21	⊙ 1	Why Do Fools Fall In Love	Jimmy Merchant/Herman Santiago...*Please Be Mine*	Gee 1002
				THE TEENAGERS Featuring FRANKIE LYMON		
				LYNN, Barbara		
8/11/62	8	13	1	You'll Lose A Good Thing	Barbara Lynn...*Lonely Heartache*	Jamie 1220
				LYNN, Vera		
5/22/48	9	7	1	You Can't Be True Dear	Hal Cotton/Gerhard Ebeler/Ken Griffin/Hans Otten...*Once Upon A Wintertime*	London 202
7/12/52	❶⁹	21	⊙ 2	Auf Wiederseh'n Sweetheart	John Sexton/Eberhard Storch/John Turner...*From The Time You Say Goodbye (The Parting Song)*	London 1227
11/29/52	7	10	⊙ 3	Yours	Albert Gamse/Gonzalo Roig/Jack Sherr...*The Love Of My Life*	London 1261
				LYNYRD SKYNYRD		
10/26/74	8	17	○ 1	Sweet Home Alabama	Ed King/Gary Rossington/Ronnie Van Zant...*Take Your Time*	MCA 40258
				LYTTLE, Kevin		
8/14/04	4	25	○ 1	Turn Me On	Arnold Hennings/Daron Jones/Michael Keith/Kevin Lyttle/Quinnes Parker/Raeon Primus/Marvin Scandrick/Courtney Sills	VP/Atlantic 88374

M

PEAK DATE	PEAK POS	WKS CHR	GOLD	ARTIST / Song Title	Songwriter...B-side	Label & Number
				M		
11/3/79	❶¹	24	● 1	Pop Muzik	Robin Scott...*M Factor*	Sire 49033
				MacGREGOR, Byron		
2/9/74	4	12	● 1	Americans	Gordon Sinclair...*America The Beautiful* (The Westbound Strings) [S]	Westbound 222
				MacGREGOR, Mary		
2/5/77	❶²	22	● 1	Torn Between Two Lovers	Phil Jarrell/Peter Yarrow...*I Just Want To Love You*	Ariola America 7638
				MACK, Craig		
11/12/94	9	25	▲ 1	Flava In Ya Ear	Craig Mack...*Shinika*	Bad Boy 79001
				MACK, Lonnie		
7/20/63	5	13	1	Memphis	Chuck Berry...*Down In The Dumps* [I]	Fraternity 906
				MacKENZIE, Gisele		
8/13/55	4	19	1	Hard To Get	Jack Segal...*Boston Fancy*	"X" 0137

PEAK DATE	PEAK POS	WKS CHR	GOLD	ARTIST / Song Title	Songwriter...B-side	Label & Number
				MacRAE, Gordon		
9/4/48	9	17		1 It's Magic	Sammy Cahn/Jule Styne...*Spring In December*	Capitol 15072
10/16/48	7	14		2 Hair Of Gold, Eyes Of Blue	Sunny Skylar...*Rambling Rose*	Capitol 15178
				JO STAFFORD AND GORDON MacRAE:		
11/13/48	10	6		3 Say Something Sweet To Your Sweetheart	Roy Brodsky/Sid Tepper...*Bluebird Of Happiness*	Capitol 15207
1/15/49	❶¹	17		4 My Darling, My Darling	Frank Loesser...*Girls Were Made To Take Care Of Boys*	Capitol 15270
4/30/49	4	15		5 "A" You're Adorable	Buddy Kaye/Sid Lippman/Fred Wise...*Need You*	Capitol 15393
5/7/49	7	12		6 Need You	Johnny Blackburn/Teepee Mitchell/Lew Porter..."A" You're Adorable	Capitol 15393
10/1/49	4	23		7 Whispering Hope	Alice Hawthorne...*A Thought In My Heart*	Capitol 690
4/8/50	10	11		8 Dearie	Bob Hilliard/Dave Mann...*Monday, Tuesday, Wednesday*	Capitol 858
				MADDOX, Johnny		
3/12/55	2⁷	20	⊙	1 The Crazy Otto	Luigi Creatore/Hugo Peretti/Edward White/Mack Wolfson...*Humoresque* [I]	Dot 15325
				MADNESS		
7/23/83	7	19		1 Our House	Christopher Foreman/Carl Smyth...*Cardiac Arrest*	Geffen 29668
				MADONNA		
6/16/84	10	30	●	1 Borderline	Reggie Lucas...*Think Of Me*	Sire 29354
10/20/84	4	16		2 Lucky Star	Madonna...*I Know It*	Sire 29177
12/22/84	❶⁶	19	●	3 Like A Virgin	Tom Kelly/Billy Steinberg...*Stay*	Sire 29210
3/23/85	2²	17		4 Material Girl	Peter Brown/Robert Rans...*Pretender*	Sire 29083
5/11/85	❶¹	21	●	5 Crazy For You	John Bettis/Jon Lind...*No More Words* (Berlin)	Geffen 29051
6/29/85	5	17		6 Angel	Stephen Bray/Madonna	Sire 29008
10/5/85	5	16		7 Dress You Up	Andrea LaRusso/Peggy Stanziale...*Shoo-Bee-Doo*	Sire 28919
6/7/86	❶¹	18		8 Live To Tell	Patrick Leonard/Madonna	Sire 28717
8/16/86	❶²	18		9 Papa Don't Preach	Brian Elliot/Madonna...*Pretender*	Sire 28660
11/15/86	3³	16	●	10 True Blue	Stephen Bray/Madonna...*Ain't No Big Deal*	Sire 28591
2/7/87	❶¹	18		11 Open Your Heart	Gardner Cole/Madonna/Peter Rafelson...*White Heat*	Sire 28508
5/2/87	4	17		12 La Isla Bonita	Bruce Gaitsch/Patrick Leonard/Madonna	Sire 28425
8/22/87	❶¹	16		13 Who's That Girl	Patrick Leonard/Madonna...*White Heat*	Sire 28341
10/24/87	2³	18		14 Causing A Commotion	Stephen Bray/Madonna...*Jimmy, Jimmy*	Sire 28224
4/22/89	❶³	16	▲	15 Like A Prayer	Patrick Leonard/Madonna...*Act Of Contrition*	Sire 27539
7/15/89	2²	16	●	16 Express Yourself	Stephen Bray/Madonna...*The Look Of Love*	Sire 22948
10/7/89	2²	15		17 Cherish	Patrick Leonard/Madonna...*Supernatural*	Sire 22883
3/31/90	8	13		18 Keep It Together	Stephen Bray/Madonna	Sire 19986
5/19/90	❶³	24	▲²	19 Vogue	Madonna/Shep Pettibone	Sire 19863
7/28/90	10	11	●	20 Hanky Panky	Patrick Leonard/Madonna...*More*	Sire 19789
1/5/91	❶²	16	▲	21 Justify My Love	Lenny Kravitz/Madonna...*Express Yourself (1990 remix)*	Sire 19485
3/23/91	9	8		22 Rescue Me	Madonna/Shep Pettibone	Sire 19490
8/8/92	❶¹	20	●	23 This Used To Be My Playground	Madonna/Shep Pettibone	Sire 18822
10/24/92	3¹	18	●	24 Erotica	Madonna/Shep Pettibone	Maverick/Sire 18782
1/30/93	7	17		25 Deeper And Deeper	Madonna/Shep Pettibone/Tony Shimkin	Maverick/Sire 18639
5/28/94	2⁴	26	●	26 I'll Remember	Patrick Leonard/Madonna/Richard Page...*Secret Garden*	Maverick/Sire 18247
11/5/94	3¹	22	●	27 Secret	Dallas Austin/Madonna	Maverick/Sire 18035
2/25/95	❶⁷	30	●	28 Take A Bow	Babyface/Madonna	Maverick/Sire 18000
12/16/95	6	20	●	29 You'll See	David Foster/Madonna...*Live To Tell (live)*	Maverick/Sire 17719
3/1/97	8	16		30 Don't Cry For Me Argentina	Tim Rice/Andrew Lloyd Webber	Warner 43809
4/4/98	2¹	20	●	31 Frozen	Patrick Leonard/Madonna...*Shanti/Ashtangi*	Maverick 17244
7/11/98	5	20	●	32 Ray Of Light	Madonna/Clive Muldoon/William Orbit...*Has To Be*	Maverick 17206
9/16/00	❶⁴	24	▲	33 Music	Mirwais Ahmadzai/Madonna...*Cyberraga*	Maverick 16826
2/3/01	4	21	●	34 Don't Tell Me	Mirwais Ahmadzai/Joe Henry/Madonna	Maverick 16825
11/9/02	8	17		35 Die Another Day	Mirwais Ahmadzai/Madonna	Warner 42492
12/3/05	7	20	△	36 Hung Up	Benny Andersson/Madonna/Stuart Price/Björn Ulvaeus	Warner 42845
4/12/08	3²	20	△²	37 4 Minutes	Nathan Hills/Madonna/Tim Mosley/Justin Timberlake	Warner 463036
				MADONNA Featuring Justin Timberlake		
				MADRIGUERA, Enric, and his Orchestra		
4/8/44	7	3		1 I Love You	Cole Porter...*Someday I'll Meet You Again*	Hit 7077
				MAIN INGREDIENT, The		
10/14/72	3¹	18	●	1 Everybody Plays The Fool	J.R. Bailey/Rudy Clark/Ken Williams...*Who Can I Turn To (When Nobody Needs Me)*	RCA Victor 0731
5/4/74	10	20	●	2 Just Don't Want To Be Lonely	Vinnie Barrett/Bobby Eli/John Freeman...*Goodbye My Love*	RCA Victor 0205
				MAMAS & THE PAPAS, The		
3/12/66	4	17	●	1 California Dreamin'	John Phillips/Michelle Phillips...*Somebody Groovy*	Dunhill 4020
5/7/66	❶³	12	●	2 Monday, Monday	John Phillips...*Got A Feelin'*	Dunhill 4026
7/30/66	5	9		3 I Saw Her Again	Dennis Doherty/John Phillips...*Even If I Could*	Dunhill 4031
1/21/67	5	12		4 Words Of Love	John Phillips...*Dancing In The Street*	Dunhill 4057
3/25/67	2³	10		5 Dedicated To The One I Love	Ralph Bass/Lowman Pauling...*Free Advice*	Dunhill 4077
6/3/67	5	9		6 Creeque Alley	John Phillips/Michelle Phillips...*Did You Ever Want To Cry*	Dunhill 4083
				MANCHESTER, Melissa		
8/9/75	6	17		1 Midnight Blue	Melissa Manchester/Carole Bayer Sager...*I Got Eyes*	Arista 0116
3/31/79	10	23		2 Don't Cry Out Loud	Peter Allen/Carole Bayer Sager...*We Had This Time*	Arista 0373
9/18/82	5	25		3 You Should Hear How She Talks About You	Dean Pitchford/Tom Snow...*Long Goodbyes*	Arista 0676
				MANCINI, Henry, And His Orchestra		
6/28/69	❶²	14	●	1 Love Theme From Romeo & Juliet	Nino Rota...*The Windmills Of Your Mind* [I]	RCA Victor 0131
				MANFRED MANN		
10/17/64	❶²	13	⊙	1 Do Wah Diddy Diddy	Jeff Barry/Ellie Greenwich...*What You Gonna Do?*	Ascot 2157
4/13/68	10	11		2 Mighty Quinn (Quinn The Eskimo)	Bob Dylan...*By Request - Edwin Garvey*	Mercury 72770
2/19/77	❶¹	20	●	3 Blinded By The Light	Bruce Springsteen...*Starbird No. 2*	Warner 8252

PEAK DATE	PEAK POS	WKS CHR	GOLD	ARTIST / Song Title	Songwriter...B-side	Label & Number
				MANGANO, Silvana		
6/27/53	5	17	⊙	1 Anna (El N. Zumbon)	Francesco Giordano/Armando Vatro...*I Loved You (T'ho Voluto Bene)* [F]	MGM 11457
				MANGIONE, Chuck		
6/10/78	4	25		1 Feels So Good	Chuck Mangione...*Maui-Waui* [I]	A&M 2001
				MANHATTANS, The		
7/24/76	❶²	26	▲	1 Kiss And Say Goodbye	Winfred Lovett...*Wonderful World Of Love*	Columbia 10310
7/19/80	5	25	▲	2 Shining Star	Leo Graham/Paul Richmond...*I'll Never Run Away From Love Again*	Columbia 11222
				MANHATTAN TRANSFER, The		
8/8/81	7	21		1 Boy From New York City	George Davis/John Taylor...*(The Word Of) Confirmation*	Atlantic 3816
				MANILOW, Barry		
1/18/75	❶¹	16	●	1 Mandy	Scott English/Richard Kerr...*Something's Comin' Up*	Bell 45,613
9/20/75	6	18		2 Could It Be Magic	Adrienne Anderson/Barry Manilow...*I Am Your Child*	Arista 0126
1/17/76	❶¹	20	●	3 I Write The Songs	Bruce Johnston...*A Nice Boy Like Me*	Arista 0157
5/22/76	10	15		4 Tryin' To Get The Feeling Again	David Pomeranz...*Beautiful Music*	Arista 0172
2/26/77	10	19		5 Weekend In New England	Randy Edelman...*Say The Words*	Arista 0212
7/23/77	❶¹	19		6 Looks Like We Made It	Will Jennings/Richard Kerr...*New York City Rhythm*	Arista 0244
4/22/78	3³	19	●	7 Can't Smile Without You	Chris Arnold/David Martin/Geoff Morrow...*Sunrise*	Arista 0305
8/12/78	8	16	●	8 Copacabana (At The Copa)	Jack Feldman/Barry Manilow/Bruce Sussman	Arista 0339
2/17/79	9	15		9 Somewhere In The Night	Will Jennings/Richard Kerr...*Leavin' In The Morning*	Arista 0382
12/1/79	9	14		10 Ships	Ian Hunter...*They Gave In To The Blues*	Arista 0464
1/31/81	10	16		11 I Made It Through The Rain	Jack Feldman/Gerard Kenny/Barry Manilow/Drey Shepperd/Bruce Sussman...*Only In Chicago*	Arista 0566
				MANN, Barry		
9/25/61	7	12		1 Who Put The Bomp (In The Bomp, Bomp, Bomp)	Gerry Goffin/Barry Mann...*Love, True Love* [N]	ABC-Paramount 10237
				MANTOVANI And His Orchestra		
12/8/51	10	19	⊙	1 Charmaine	Lew Pollack/Erno Rapee...*Just For A While* [I]	London 1020
6/13/53	8	10		2 The Moulin Rouge Theme (Where Is Your Heart)	Georges Auric/William Engvick...*Vola Colomba* [I]	London 1328
10/30/54	10	18	⊙	3 Cara Mia	Lee Lange/Tulio Trapani...*How, When Or Where*	London 1486
				DAVID WHITFIELD with MANTOVANI His Orchestra and Chorus		
				MARCELS, The		
4/3/61	❶³	14	⊙	1 Blue Moon	Lorenz Hart/Richard Rodgers...*Goodbye To Love*	Colpix 186
11/27/61	7	12		2 Heartaches	Al Hoffman/John Klenner...*My Love For You*	Colpix 612
				MARCH, Little Peggy		
4/27/63	❶³	14	⊙	1 I Will Follow Him	Arthur Altman/Norman Gimbel/Del Roma/J.W. Stole...*Wind-Up Doll*	RCA Victor 8139
				MARCY PLAYGROUND		
4/18/98	8	28		1 Sex And Candy	John Wozniak...*The Angel Of The Forever Sleep / Memphis*	Capitol 58695
				MARESCA, Ernie		
5/19/62	6	14		1 Shout! Shout! (Knock Yourself Out)	Thomas Bogdany/Ernie Maresca...*Crying Like A Baby Over You*	Seville 117
				MARIE, Teena		
3/30/85	4	24		1 Lovergirl	Teena Marie	Epic 04619
				MARIO		
8/24/02	4	21		1 Just A Friend 2002	Warryn Campbell/Marcel Hall/Harold Lilly/John Smith...*Girl In The Picture*	J Records 21219
1/1/05	❶⁹	36	○	2 Let Me Love You	Kameron Houff/Shaffer Smith/Scott Storch	J Records 61888
				MARKETTS, The		
2/1/64	3²	14		1 Out Of Limits	Michael Gordon...*Bella Dalena* [I]	Warner 5391
				MAR-KEYS		
8/7/61	3²	14		1 Last Night	Charles Axton/Chips Moman/Floyd Newman/Jerry Lee Smith...*Night Before* [I]	Satellite 107
				MARKY MARK And The Funky Bunch		
10/5/91	❶¹	20	●	1 Good Vibrations	Dan Hartman/Amir Shakir/Donnie Wahlberg/Mark Wahlberg...*So What Chu Sayin*	Interscope 98764
				MARKY MARK And The Funky Bunch Featuring Loleatta Holloway		
12/14/91	10	20	●	2 Wildside	Lou Reed/Donnie Wahlberg/Mark Wahlberg...*On The House Tip*	Interscope 98673
				MARMALADE, The		
5/9/70	10	15		1 Reflections Of My Life	Junior Campbell/Thomas McAleese...*Rollin' My Thing*	London 20058
				MAROON 5		
4/24/04	5	43	○	1 This Love	Jesse Carmichael/Adam Levine	Octone 63388
9/25/04	5	41	○	2 She Will Be Loved	Adam Levine/James Valentine...*Sunday Morning*	Octone 65248
5/12/07	❶³	26		3 Makes Me Wonder	Jesse Carmichael/Adam Levine/Mickey Madden	A&M
				MARS, Bruno		
5/1/10	❶²	28	△²	1 Nothin' On You	Peter Hernandez/Philip Lawrence/Ari Levine/Bobby Simmons...*Bet I*	RebelRock 524312
				B.O.B. Featuring Bruno Mars		
6/26/10	4	27	△²	2 Billionaire	Peter Hernandez/Philip Lawrence/Ari Levine/Travis McCoy	Fueled By Ramen
				TRAVIE McCOY Featuring Bruno Mars		
10/2/10	❶⁴	27↑	△	3 Just The Way You Are	Khari Cain/Peter Hernandez/Philip Lawrence/Ari Levine/Khalil Walton	Elektra
1/8/11	❶³	17↑	○	4 Grenade	Brody Brown/Peter Hernandez/Claude Kelly/Philip Lawrence/Ari Levine/Andrew Wyatt	Elektra
				MARTERIE, Ralph, And His Orchestra		
2/7/53	6	10	⊙	1 Pretend	Lew Douglas/Frank Lavere/Cliff Parman...*After Midnight* [I]	Mercury 70045
4/25/53	6	11	⊙	2 Caravan	Duke Ellington/Irving Mills/Juan Tizol...*While We Dream* [I]	Mercury 70097
				RALPH MARTERIE and his "Down Beat" Orchestra		
9/25/54	3³	15		3 Skokiaan	Tom Glazer/August Msarugwa...*Crazy 'Bout Lollipop* [I]	Mercury 70432
6/10/57	10	16		4 Shish-Kebab	Buddy Kaye...*Bop A Doo - Bop A Doo* [I]	Mercury 71092

PEAK DATE	PEAK POS	WKS CHR	GOLD	ARTIST / Song Title	Songwriter...B-side	Label & Number
				MARTHA & THE VANDELLAS		
9/21/63	4	14		1 Heat Wave	Lamont Dozier/Brian Holland/Eddie Holland...*A Love Like Yours (Don't Come Knocking Everyday)*	Gordy 7022
1/4/64	8	12		2 Quicksand	Lamont Dozier/Brian Holland/Eddie Holland...*Darling, I Hum Our Song*	Gordy 7025
10/17/64	2²	14	●	3 Dancing In The Street	Marvin Gaye/William Stevenson...*There He Is (At My Door)*	Gordy 7033
4/10/65	8	11		4 Nowhere To Run	Lamont Dozier/Brian Holland/Eddie Holland...*Motoring*	Gordy 7039
12/10/66	9	10		5 I'm Ready For Love	Lamont Dozier/Brian Holland/Eddie Holland...*He Doesn't Love Her Anymore*	Gordy 7056
4/15/67	10	14		6 Jimmy Mack	Lamont Dozier/Brian Holland/Eddie Holland...*Third Finger, Left Hand*	Gordy 7058
				MARTIKA		
7/22/89	❶²	20	●	1 Toy Soldiers	Michael Jay/Martika...*Exchange Of Hearts*	Columbia 68747
10/19/91	10	15		2 Love...Thy Will Be Done	Martika/Prince...*Mi Tierra*	Columbia 73853
				MARTIN, Dean		
3/5/49	10	4		1 Powder Your Face With Sunshine (Smile! Smile! Smile!)	Carmen Lombardo/Stanley Rochinski ...*Absence Makes The Heart Grow Fonder (For Somebody Else)*	Capitol 15351
12/19/53	2⁶	22	⊙	2 That's Amore	Jack Brooks/Harry Warren...*You're The Right One*	Capitol 2589
1/7/56	❶⁶	24	⊙	3 Memories Are Made Of This	Richard Dehr/Terry Gilkyson/Frank Miller...*Change Of Heart*	Capitol 3295
6/2/58	4	21		4 Return To Me	Danny DiMinno/Carmen Lombardo...*Forgetting You*	Capitol 3894
8/15/64	❶¹	15	●	5 Everybody Loves Somebody	Ken Lane/Irving Taylor...*A Little Voice*	Reprise 0281
11/14/64	6	11		6 The Door Is Still Open To My Heart	Chuck Willis...*Every Minute Every Hour*	Reprise 0307
12/11/65	10	10		7 I Will	Dick Glasser...*You're The Reason I'm In Love*	Reprise 0415
				MARTIN, Freddy, and his Orchestra		
6/28/41	2¹	9		1 The Hut-Sut Song (A Swedish Serenade)	Leo Killion/Ted McMichael/Jack Owens...*The Karlstad Ball*	Bluebird 11147
7/5/41	7	2		2 Intermezzo	Robert Henning/Heinz Provost...*Nice Dreamin' Baby*	Bluebird 11123
10/4/41	❶⁸	24	⊙	3 Piano Concerto In B Flat	Pyotr Ilyich Tchaikovsky...*Why Don't We Do This More Often?* [I]	Bluebird 11211
1/17/42	8	1		4 Tonight We Love	Ray Austin/Freddy Martin/Bobby Worth...*Carmen Carmela*	Bluebird 11320
5/19/45	6	7		5 Laura	Johnny Mercer/David Raksin...*A Song To Remember* [I]	Victor 1655
7/21/45	8	8		6 Dream	Johnny Mercer...*Everytime*	Victor 1645
9/29/45	7	2		7 Lily Belle	Dave Franklin/Irving Taylor...*And There You Are*	Victor 1712
1/5/46	❶²	17		8 Symphony	Alex Alstone/Roger Bernstein/Jack Lawrence/Andre Tabet...*In The Middle Of May*	Victor 1747
4/13/46	4	9		9 One-Zy, Two-Zy (I Love You-zy)	Dave Franklin/Irving Taylor...*Sleepy Baby*	RCA Victor 1826
5/4/46	7	6		10 Bumble Boogie	Jack Fina...*Now And Forever* [I]	RCA Victor 1829
7/13/46	2¹	6		11 Doin' What Comes Natur'lly	Irving Berlin...*Blue Champagne*	RCA Victor 1878
8/31/46	❶²	17		12 To Each His Own	Ray Evans/Jay Livingston...*You Put A Song In My Heart*	RCA Victor 1921
2/22/47	❶³	13		13 Managua, Nicaragua	Irving Fields/Albert Gamse...*Heaven Knows When*	RCA Victor 2026
9/20/47	5	9		14 The Lady From 29 Palms	Allie Wrubel...*Cumana*	RCA Victor 2347
4/17/48	6	11		15 Sabre Dance Boogie	Aram Khachaturian/Lester Lee/Allan Roberts...*After You've Gone*	RCA Victor 2721
5/29/48	5	11		16 The Dickey-Bird Song	Howard Dietz/Sammy Fain...*If Winter Comes*	RCA Victor 2617
12/4/48	4	17		17 On A Slow Boat To China	Frank Loesser...*Czardas*	RCA Victor 3123
12/10/49	8	17		18 I've Got A Lovely Bunch Of Coconuts	Fred Heatherton...*(There's a) Bluebird On Your Windowsill* [N]	RCA Victor 3047
4/15/50	5	10		19 (Put Another Nickel in) Music! Music! Music!	Bernie Baum/Stephan Weiss...*Wilhelmina*	RCA Victor 3217
				MARTIN, Marilyn		
11/30/85	❶¹	21		1 Separate Lives **PHIL COLLINS and MARILYN MARTIN**	Stephen Bishop...*I Don't Wanna Know* (Collins)	Atlantic 89498
				MARTIN, Mary		
10/7/44	6	8		1 I'll Walk Alone	Sammy Cahn/Jule Styne...*Good Night, Wherever You Are*	Decca 23340
4/1/50	8	7		2 Go To Sleep, Go To Sleep, Go To Sleep **MARY MARTIN and ARTHUR GODFREY**	Sammy Cahn/Fred Spielman...*But Me, I Love You* [N]	Columbia 38744
				MARTIN, Ricky		
5/8/99	❶⁵	20	▲	1 Livin' La Vida Loca	Desmond Child/Robi Rosa...*(Spanish version)*	C2/Columbia 79124
9/25/99	2²	20	●	2 She's All I Ever Had	Luis Gómez Escolar/George Noriega/Robi Rosa/Jon Secada...*Bella (She's All I Ever Had)*	C2/Columbia 79259
				MARTIN, Tony		
11/29/41	5	8		1 Tonight We Love (Concerto No. 1, B Flat Minor)	Ray Austin/Freddy Martin/Bobby Worth...*I Guess I'll Have To Dream The Rest*	Decca 3988
8/31/46	4	16	⊙	2 To Each His Own	Ray Evans/Jay Livingston...*I'll See You In My Dreams*	Mercury 3022
11/2/46	9	7		3 Rumors Are Flying	Bennie Benjamin/George Weiss...*And Then It's Heaven*	Mercury 3032
2/4/50	2¹	27	⊙	4 There's No Tomorrow	Leon Carr/Leo Corday/Al Hoffman...*A Thousand Violins*	RCA Victor 3078
2/4/50	3¹	13		5 I Said My Pajamas (And Put on My Pray'rs) **TONY MARTIN and FRAN WARREN**	Eddie Pola/George Wyle...*Have I Told You Lately That I Love You*	RCA Victor 3119
8/26/50	9	17		6 La Vie En Rose	Mack David/Luis Guglielmi/Edith Piaf...*Tonight*	RCA Victor 3819
3/10/51	8	12		7 A Penny A Kiss **TONY MARTIN and DINAH SHORE**	Ralph Care/Buddy Kaye...*In Your Arms*	RCA Victor 4019
10/13/51	3³	30	⊙	8 I Get Ideas	Dorcas Cochran/Lenny Sanders...*Tahiti, My Island*	RCA Victor 4141
12/8/51	9	12		9 Domino	Louis Ferrari/Don Raye...*It's All Over But The Memories*	RCA Victor 4343
6/21/52	6	15		10 Kiss Of Fire	Lester Allen/Robert Hill...*For The Very First Time*	RCA Victor 4671
1/16/54	10	11		11 Stranger In Paradise	George Forrest/Robert Wright...*I Love Paris*	RCA Victor 5535
5/15/54	5	16		12 Here	Dorcas Cochran/Harold Grant...*Philosophy*	RCA Victor 5665
6/30/56	10	20		13 Walk Hand In Hand	Johnny Cowell...*Flamenco Love*	RCA Victor 6493
				MARTIN, Vince		
12/22/56	9	19		1 Cindy, Oh Cindy **VINCE MARTIN with The Tarriers**	Bob Barron/Burt Long...*Only If You Praise The Lord*	Glory 247
				MARTINDALE, Wink		
11/2/59	7	17		1 Deck Of Cards	"T" Texas Tyler...*Love's Old Sweet Song* [S]	Dot 15968
				MARTINEZ, Angie		
8/9/97	6	21	▲	1 Not Tonight	Robert Bell/Ronald Bell/George Brown/Missy Elliott/Shawntae Harris/Kim Jones/Lisa Lopes/Angie Martinez/ Meekaaeel Muhammed/Claydes Smith/James Taylor/Dennis Thomas/Earl Toon **LIL' KIM Featuring Da Brat, Left Eye, Missy "Misdemeanor" Elliott and Angie Martinez**		Undeas 98019
				MARTINO, Al		
6/7/52	❶³	19		1 Here In My Heart	Bill Borrelli/Pat Genaro/Lou Levinson...*I Cried Myself To Sleep*	BBS 101
6/1/63	3¹	16		2 I Love You Because	Leon Payne...*Merry-Go-Round*	Capitol 4930
3/21/64	9	11		3 I Love You More And More Every Day	Don Robertson...*I'm Living My Heaven With You*	Capitol 5108

PEAK DATE	PEAK POS	WKS CHR	GOLD	ARTIST / Song Title	Songwriter...B-side	Label & Number
				MARVELETTES, The		
12/11/61	❶¹	23	●	1 Please Mr. Postman	Robert Bateman/Georgia Dobbins/William Garrett/Brian Holland...*So Long Baby*	Tamla 54046
6/23/62	7	15		2 Playboy	Robert Bateman/Brian Holland/William Stevenson...*All The Love I've Got*	Tamla 54060
2/26/66	7	12	●	3 Don't Mess With Bill	Smokey Robinson...*Anything You Wanna Do*	Tamla 54126
				MARX, Richard		
8/29/87	3¹	21		1 Don't Mean Nothing	Bruce Gaitsch/Richard Marx...*The Flame Of Love*	Manhattan 50079
12/12/87	3¹	21		2 Should've Known Better	Richard Marx...*Rhythm Of Life*	Manhattan 50083
3/26/88	2²	21		3 Endless Summer Nights	Richard Marx...*Have Mercy (live)*	EMI/Manhattan 50113
7/23/88	❶¹	21		4 Hold On To The Nights	Richard Marx...*Lonely Heart*	EMI/Manhattan 50106
6/24/89	❶¹	15		5 Satisfied	Richard Marx...*Should've Known Better (live)*	EMI 50189
8/12/89	❶³	21	▲	6 Right Here Waiting	Richard Marx...*Wait For The Sunrise*	EMI 50219
12/2/89	4	17		7 Angelia	Richard Marx...*Endless Summer Nights (live)*	EMI 50218
4/25/92	9	20		8 Hazard	Richard Marx...*Big Boy Now*	Capitol 44796
3/19/94	7	27		9 Now And Forever	Richard Marx...*Hazard (live)*	Capitol 58005
				MARY JANE GIRLS		
6/8/85	7	22		1 In My House	Rick James	Gordy 1741
				MA$E		
3/22/97	❶⁶	28	▲²	1 Can't Nobody Hold Me Down	Mason Betha/Carlos Broady/Clifton Chase/Sean Combs/Edward Fletcher/Melvin Glover/Steve Jordan/Nashiem Myrick/Greg Prestopino/Sylvia Robinson/Matthew Wilder	Bad Boy 79083
				PUFF DADDY Featuring Ma$e		
8/30/97	❶²	30		2 Mo Money Mo Problems	Mason Betha/Sean Combs/Bernard Edwards/Steve Jordan/Nile Rodgers/Christopher Wallace	Bad Boy 79100
				THE NOTORIOUS B.I.G. Featuring Puff Daddy & Ma$e		
12/13/97	5	20	▲	3 Feel So Good	Robert Bell/Ronald Bell/George Brown/Larry Dermer/Joe Galdo/Robert Mickens/Claydes Smith/Dennis Thomas/Rafael Vigil/Rick Westfield	Bad Boy 79122
1/24/98	4	15		4 Been Around The World	Mason Betha/David Bowie/Sean Combs/Ian Devaney/Andy Morris/Lisa Stansfield/Christopher Wallace...*It's All About The Benjamins (Puff Daddy)*	Bad Boy 79130
				PUFF DADDY & THE FAMILY Featuring The Notorious B.I.G. & Ma$e		
3/21/98	6	24	●	5 What You Want	Mason Betha/Sean Combs/Nashiem Myrick/Keisha Spivey...*Will They Die 4 You? (w/Puff Daddy & Lil' Kim)*	Bad Boy 79141
				Ma$e (Featuring Total)		
9/19/98	8	19	●	6 Lookin' At Me	Mason Betha/Sean Combs/Chad Hugo/Pharrell Williams...*24 Hrs. To Live (w/The Lox, Black Rob & DMX)*	Bad Boy 79176
				Ma$e featuring Puff Daddy		
				MASEKELA, Hugh		
7/20/68	❶²	12	●	1 Grazing In The Grass	Harry Elston/Philemon Hou...*Bajabula Bonke (The Healing Song)* [I]	Uni 55066
				MASON, Barbara		
7/31/65	5	14		1 Yes, I'm Ready	Barbara Mason...*Keep Him*	Arctic 105
				MASTER P		
4/11/98	2²	21	▲	1 Let's Ride	Teddy Bishop/Montell Jordan/Percy Miller/Vyshonn Miller	Def Jam 568475
				MONTELL JORDAN Featuring Master P & Silkk "The Shocker"		
				MATCHBOX TWENTY		
10/4/97	5	52		1 Push	Matt Serletic/Rob Thomas...*Back 2 Good*	Lava/Atlantic 84410
2/14/98	3⁸	58		2 3 AM	John Goff/Jay Stanley/Rob Thomas/Brian Yale	Lava/Atlantic
8/1/98	9	36		3 Real World	Rob Thomas	Lava/Atlantic
7/22/00	❶¹	39	●	4 Bent	Rob Thomas...*Push (acoustic)*	Lava/Atlantic 84704
1/27/01	5	42		5 If You're Gone	Rob Thomas	Lava/Atlantic
7/19/03	5	54	○	6 Unwell	Rob Thomas	Melisma/Atlantic
				MATHIS, Johnny		
6/17/57	5	34□	1	It's Not For Me To Say	Robert Allen/Al Stillman...*Warm And Tender*	Columbia 40851
10/21/57	❶¹	28	⊙	2 Chances Are	Robert Allen/Al Stillman...*The Twelfth Of Never*	Columbia 40993
11/18/57	9	17		3 The Twelfth Of Never	Jerry Livingston/Paul Francis Webster...*Chances Are*	Columbia 40993
11/17/62	6	12		4 Gina	Leon Carr/Paul Vance...*I Love Her That's Why*	Columbia 42582
3/9/63	9	12		5 What Will My Mary Say	Eddie Snyder/Paul Vance...*Quiet Girl*	Columbia 42666
6/3/78	❶¹	18	●	6 Too Much, Too Little, Too Late	Nat Kipner/John Vallins...*Emotion*	Columbia 10693
				JOHNNY MATHIS & DENIECE WILLIAMS		
				MAURIAT, Paul, and His Orchestra		
2/10/68	❶⁵	18	●	1 Love Is Blue	Andre Popp...*Alone In The World* [I]	Philips 40495
				MAXWELL		
5/29/99	4	25	●	1 Fortunate	R. Kelly...*Submerge: Til We We Become The Sun*	Rock Land 79135
				MAY, Billy, and His Orchestra		
7/12/52	8	12		1 Walkin' My Baby Back Home	Fred Ahlert/Roy Turk...*Funny (Not Much)*	Capitol 2130
				NAT KING COLE and BILLY MAY and His Orchestra		
				MAYFIELD, Curtis		
11/4/72	4	16	●	1 Freddie's Dead (Theme From "Superfly")	Curtis Mayfield...*Underground*	Curtom 1975
1/13/73	8	15	●	2 Superfly	Curtis Mayfield...*Underground*	Curtom 1978
				MC HAMMER		
6/16/90	8	17	○	1 U Can't Touch This	Stanley Burrell/Rick James/Alonzo Miller...*Dancin' Machine*	Capitol 15571
9/15/90	4	20	●	2 Have You Seen Her	Barbara Acklin/Stanley Burrell/Eugene Record	Capitol 44573
11/10/90	2²	18	●	3 Pray	Stanley Burrell/Prince	Capitol 44609
1/11/92	5	20	▲	4 2 Legit 2 Quit	Louis Burrell/Stanley Burrell/James Earley/Michael Kelly/Felton Pilate	Capitol 44785
1/11/92	7	20	●	5 Addams Groove	Stanley Burrell/Felton Pilate	Capitol 44794
				MC LYTE		
6/1/96	10	20	●	1 Keep On, Keepin' On	Jermaine Dupri/Lana Moorer	Flavor Unit 64302
				MC LYTE Featuring Xscape		
				McCAIN, Edwin		
10/3/98	5	24		1 I'll Be	Edwin McCain...*Grind Me In The Gears*	Lava/Atlantic 84191
				McCALL, C.W.		
1/10/76	❶¹	16	●	1 Convoy	Chip Davis/Bill Fries...*Long Lonesome Road* [N]	MGM 14839

PEAK DATE	PEAK POS	WKS CHR	GOLD	ARTIST Song Title	Songwriter...B-side	Label & Number
				McCANN, Peter		
8/6/77	5	22	●	1 Do You Wanna Make Love	Peter McCann...*Right Time Of The Night*	20th Century 2335
				McCARTNEY, Jesse		
5/17/08	10	24	△	1 Leavin'	Terius Nash/Christopher Stewart	Hollywood
				McCARTNEY, Paul / Wings		
4/17/71	5	12		1 Another Day	Linda McCartney/Paul McCartney...*Oh Woman Oh Why*	Apple 1829
				PAUL McCARTNEY		
9/4/71	❶[1]	13	●	2 Uncle Albert/Admiral Halsey	Linda McCartney/Paul McCartney...*Too Many People*	Apple 1837
				PAUL & LINDA McCARTNEY		
2/3/73	10	11		3 Hi, Hi, Hi	Linda McCartney/Paul McCartney...*C Moon*	Apple 1857
				WINGS		
6/2/73	❶[4]	18	●	4 My Love	Paul McCartney...*The Mess*	Apple 1861
				PAUL McCARTNEY & WINGS		
8/11/73	2[3]	14	●	5 Live And Let Die	Paul McCartney...*I Lie Around*	Apple 1863
				WINGS		
1/12/74	10	13		6 Helen Wheels	Paul McCartney...*Country Dreamer*	Apple 1869
3/30/74	7	14		7 Jet	Paul McCartney...*Mamunia*	Apple 1871
6/8/74	❶[1]	18	●	8 Band On The Run	Paul McCartney...*Nineteen Hundred And Eighty Five*	Apple 1873
1/11/75	3[1]	12		9 Junior's Farm	Paul McCartney...*Sally G*	Apple 1875
				PAUL McCARTNEY & WINGS (above 4)		
7/19/75	❶[1]	14	●	10 Listen To What The Man Said	Paul McCartney...*Love In Song*	Capitol 4091
5/22/76	❶[5]	19	●	11 Silly Love Songs	Paul McCartney...*Cook Of The House*	Capitol 4256
8/14/76	3[4]	16	●	12 Let 'Em In	Paul McCartney...*Beware My Love*	Capitol 4293
4/2/77	10	13		13 Maybe I'm Amazed	Paul McCartney...*Soily* [L]	Capitol 4385
5/20/78	❶[2]	18		14 With A Little Luck	Paul McCartney...*Backwards Traveller/Cuff Link*	Capitol 4559
5/19/79	5	16	●	15 Goodnight Tonight	Paul McCartney...*Daytime Nightime Suffering*	Columbia 10939
				WINGS (above 6)		
6/28/80	❶[3]	21	●	16 Coming Up (Live At Glasgow)	Paul McCartney...*Coming Up / Lunch Box/Odd Sox* [L]	Columbia 11263
				PAUL McCARTNEY & WINGS		
5/15/82	❶[7]	19	●	17 Ebony And Ivory	Paul McCartney...*Rainclouds* (McCartney)	Columbia 02860
				PAUL McCARTNEY (with Stevie Wonder)		
8/21/82	10	16		18 Take It Away	Paul McCartney...*I'll Give You A Ring*	Columbia 03018
				PAUL McCARTNEY		
1/8/83	2[3]	18	●	19 The Girl Is Mine	Michael Jackson...*Can't Get Outta The Rain* (Jackson)	Epic 03288
				MICHAEL JACKSON/PAUL McCARTNEY		
12/10/83	❶[6]	22	▲	20 Say Say Say	Michael Jackson/Paul McCartney...*Ode To A Koala Bear* (McCartney)	Columbia 04168
				PAUL McCARTNEY AND MICHAEL JACKSON		
12/8/84	6	18		21 No More Lonely Nights	Paul McCartney	Columbia 04581
2/8/86	7	17		22 Spies Like Us	Paul McCartney...*My Carnival* (& Wings)	Capitol 5537
				PAUL McCARTNEY (above 2)		
				McCLINTON, Delbert		
2/21/81	8	19		1 Giving It Up For Your Love	Jerry Williams...*My Sweet Baby*	MSS/Capitol 4948
				McCOO, Marilyn, & Billy Davis, Jr.		
1/8/77	❶[1]	26	●	1 You Don't Have To Be A Star (To Be In My Show)	James Dean/John Glover...*We've Got To Get It On Again*	ABC 12208
				McCOY, Travie		
6/26/10	4	27	△[2]	1 Billionaire	Peter Hernandez/Philip Lawrence/Ari Levine/Travis McCoy	Fueled By Ramen
				TRAVIE McCOY Featuring Bruno Mars		
				McCOY, Van		
7/26/75	❶[1]	19	●	1 The Hustle	Van McCoy...*Hey Girl, Come And Get It* [I]	Avco 4653
				McCOYS, The		
10/2/65	❶[1]	14	⊙	1 Hang On Sloopy	Wes Farrell/Bert Russell...*I Can't Explain It*	Bang 506
12/25/65	7	11		2 Fever	John Davenport...*Sorrow*	Bang 511
				McCRACKLIN, Jimmy		
3/10/58	7	16		1 The Walk	Jimmy McCracklin...*I'm To Blame*	Checker 885
				McCRAE, George		
7/13/74	❶[2]	17		1 Rock Your Baby	Harry Casey/Richard Finch...*(Pt. 2)*	T.K. 1004
				McCRAE, Gwen		
8/2/75	9	14		1 Rockin' Chair	Willie Clarke/Clarence Reid...*It Keeps On Raining*	Cat 1996
				McDANIELS, Gene		
5/8/61	3[2]	15		1 A Hundred Pounds Of Clay	Luther Dixon/Bob Elgin/Eddie Snyder...*Take A Chance On Love*	Liberty 55308
11/13/61	5	13		2 Tower Of Strength	Burt Bacharach/Bob Hilliard...*The Secret*	Liberty 55371
3/3/62	10	11		3 Chip Chip	Jeff Barry/Cliff Crawford/Artie Resnick...*Another Tear Falls*	Liberty 55405
				McDONALD, Michael		
10/23/82	4	19		1 I Keep Forgettin' (Every Time You're Near)	Jerry Leiber/Mike Stoller...*Losin' End*	Warner 29933
6/14/86	❶[3]	23	●	2 On My Own	Burt Bacharach/Carole Bayer Sager...*Stir It Up* (LaBelle)	MCA 52770
				PATTI LaBELLE AND MICHAEL McDONALD		
8/30/86	7	20		3 Sweet Freedom	Rod Temperton...*The Freedom Eights*	MCA 52857
				McFERRIN, Bobby		
9/24/88	❶[2]	26	●	1 Don't Worry Be Happy	Bobby McFerrin...*Simple Pleasures*	EMI/Manhattan 50146
				McGOVERN, Maureen		
8/4/73	❶[2]	15	●	1 The Morning After	Joel Hirschhorn/Al Kasha...*Midnight Storm*	20th Century 2010
				McGRAW, Tim		
7/19/97	7	20	▲	1 It's Your Love	Stephony Smith...*She Never Lets It Go To Her Heart* (McGraw)	Curb 73019
				TIM McGRAW with Faith Hill		
5/1/99	10	20		2 Please Remember Me	Rodney Crowell/Will Jennings...*For A Little While*	Curb 73080
12/4/04	3[1]	24	△	3 Over And Over	Jayson Bridges/Cornell Haynes	Derrty/Curb
				NELLY Featuring Tim McGraw		

PEAK DATE	PEAK POS	WKS CHR	GOLD	ARTIST / Song Title	Songwriter...B-side	Label & Number
				McGUIRE, Barry		
9/25/65	❶¹	11	◉	1 Eve Of Destruction	Steve Barri/P.F. Sloan...*What Exactly's The Matter With Me*	Dunhill 4009
				McGUIRE SISTERS, The		
8/7/54	7	15		1 Goodnight, Sweetheart, Goodnight	Calvin Carter/James Hudson...*Heavenly Feeling*	Coral 61187
11/27/54	10	10		2 Muskrat Ramble	Ray Gilbert/Edward Ory...*Lonesome Polecat*	Coral 61278
2/12/55	❶¹⁰	21	◉	3 Sincerely	Alan Freed/Harvey Fuqua...*No More*	Coral 61323
7/23/55	5	14		4 Something's Gotta Give	Johnny Mercer...*Rhythm 'N' Blues (Mama's Got The Rhythm - Papa's Got The Blues)*	Coral 61423
11/19/55	10	19		5 He	Richard Mullan/Jack Richards...*If You Believe*	Coral 61501
2/17/58	❶⁴	23		6 Sugartime	Odis Echols/Charlie Phillips...*Banana Split*	Coral 61924
				McINTYRE, Hal, and his Orchestra		
6/30/45	3³	19		1 Sentimental Journey	Les Brown/Bud Green/Ben Homer...*I'm Gonna See My Baby* [I]	Victor 1643
10/27/45	8	5		2 I'll Buy That Dream	Herb Magidson/Allie Wrubel...*I'd Do It All Over Again*	Victor 1679
6/22/46	8	4		3 The Gypsy	Billy Reid...*Cement Mixer (Put-Ti — Put-Ti)*	Cosmo 475
				McINTYRE, Joey		
4/10/99	10	14	●	1 Stay The Same	Joe Carrier/Joey McIntyre	C2/Columbia 79103
				McKENZIE, Scott		
7/1/67	4	12		1 San Francisco (Be Sure To Wear Flowers In Your Hair)	John Phillips...*What's The Difference*	Ode 103
				McKINLEY, Ray, and his Orchestra		
5/31/47	10	3		1 Red Silk Stockings And Green Perfume	Bob Hilliard/Sammy Mysels/Dick Sanford...*Jiminy Crickets*	Majestic 7216
12/27/47	8	5		2 Civilization (Bongo, Bongo, Bongo)	Bob Hilliard/Carl Sigman...*Those Things Money Can't Buy*	Majestic 7274
				McKNIGHT, Brian		
5/15/93	3¹	28		1 Love Is VANESSA WILLIAMS and BRIAN McKNIGHT	John Keller/Steve Krikorian	Giant 18630
5/16/98	6	40		2 Anytime	Brandon Barnes/Brian McKnight...*The Only One For Me*	Motown 860768
11/20/99	2⁸	37	○	3 Back At One	Brian McKnight	Motown 156501
				McLACHLAN, Sarah		
8/22/98	3¹	27	●	1 Adia	Pierre Marchand/Sarah McLachlan...*Angel / I Will Remember You*	Arista 13497
3/6/99	4	31	○	2 Angel	Sarah McLachlan...*Ice Cream (Live) / I Will Not Forget You (Live)*	Arista 13621
				McLEAN, Don		
1/15/72	❶⁴	19	●	1 American Pie (Parts I & II)	Don McLean	United Artists 50856
3/21/81	5	18		2 Crying	Joe Melson/Roy Orbison...*Genesis (In The Beginning)*	Millennium 11799
				McPHATTER, Clyde		
1/19/59	6	24		1 A Lover's Question	Brook Benton/Jimmy Williams...*I Can't Stand Up Alone*	Atlantic 1199
4/21/62	7	14		2 Lover Please	Billy Swan...*Let's Forget About The Past*	Mercury 71941
				McVEA, Jack, And His All Stars		
2/15/47	3¹	9		1 Open The Door Richard!	Dusty Fletcher/Don Howell/John Mason/Jack McVea...*Lonesome Blues* [N]	Black & White 792
				McVIE, Christine		
3/24/84	10	16		1 Got A Hold On Me	Christine McVie/Todd Sharp...*Who's Dreaming This Dream*	Warner 29372
				MEAD, Sister Janet		
4/13/74	4	13	●	1 The Lord's Prayer	Arnold Strals...*Brother Sun And Sister Moon*	A&M 1491
				MEAT LOAF		
11/6/93	❶⁵	22	▲	1 I'd Do Anything For Love (But I Won't Do That)	Jim Steinman	MCA 54626
				MECO		
10/1/77	❶²	20	▲	1 Star Wars Theme/Cantina Band	John Williams...*Funk* [I]	Millennium 604
				MEDEIROS, Glenn		
7/21/90	❶²	18	●	1 She Ain't Worth It GLENN MEDEIROS Featuring Bobby Brown	Antonina Armato/Bobby Brown/Ian Prince	MCA 53831
				MEDLEY, Bill		
11/28/87	❶¹	21	●	1 (I've Had) The Time Of My Life BILL MEDLEY AND JENNIFER WARNES	John DeNicola/Donald Markowitz/Franke Previte...*Love Is Strange* (Mickey & Sylvia)	RCA 5224
				MEESTER, Leighton		
8/22/09	7	25	△	1 Good Girls Go Bad COBRA STARSHIP Featuring Leighton Meester	Kara DioGuardi/Jacob Kasher/Kevin Rudolf/Gabe Saporta	Decaydance
				MEL AND TIM		
12/13/69	10	14	●	1 Backfield In Motion	Mel Harden/Tim McPherson...*Do Right Baby*	Bamboo 107
				MELANIE		
7/11/70	6	17		1 Lay Down (Candles In The Rain) MELANIE with The Edwin Hawkins Singers	Melanie Safka...*Candles In The Rain* (Melanie)	Buddah 167
12/25/71	❶³	18	●	2 Brand New Key	Melanie Safka...*Some Say (I Got Devil)*	Neighborhood 4201
				MELLENCAMP, John Cougar		
8/7/82	2⁴	28	●	1 Hurts So Good	George Green/John Mellencamp...*Close Enough*	Riva 209
10/2/82	❶⁴	22	●	2 Jack & Diane JOHN COUGAR (above 2)	John Mellencamp...*Can You Take It*	Riva 210
11/26/83	9	16		3 Crumblin' Down	George Green/John Mellencamp...*Golden Gates*	Riva 214
2/11/84	8	16		4 Pink Houses	John Mellencamp...*Serious Business*	Riva 215
10/12/85	6	20		5 Lonely Ol' Night	John Mellencamp...*The Kind Of Fella I Am*	Riva 880984
12/28/85	6	18		6 Small Town	John Mellencamp	Riva 884202
4/5/86	2¹	17		7 R.O.C.K. In The U.S.A. (A Salute To 60's Rock)	John Mellencamp...*Under The Boardwalk*	Riva 884455
10/3/87	9	16		8 Paper In Fire	John Mellencamp...*Never Too Old*	Mercury 888763
1/9/88	8	21		9 Cherry Bomb	John Mellencamp...*Shama Lama Ding Dong*	Mercury 888934

PEAK DATE	PEAK POS	WKS CHR	GOLD	ARTIST / Song Title	Songwriter...B-side	Label & Number
9/3/94	3²	42		10 Wild Night	Van Morrison...*Brothers (live)* (Mellencamp)	Mercury 858738
				JOHN MELLENCAMP & ME'SHELL NDEGEOCELLO		
				MELVIN, Harold, And The Blue Notes		
12/9/72	3²	17	●	1 If You Don't Know Me By Now	Kenny Gamble/Leon Huff...*Let Me Into Your World*	Philadelphia I. 3520
12/8/73	7	18	●	2 The Love I Lost (Part 1)	Kenny Gamble/Leon Huff...*(Part 2)*	Philadelphia I. 3533
				MEN AT WORK		
10/30/82	❶¹	27		1 Who Can It Be Now?	Colin Hay...*Anyone For Tennis*	Columbia 02888
1/15/83	❶⁴	25	▲	2 Down Under	Colin Hay/Roy Strykert...*Crazy*	Columbia 03303
6/4/83	3¹	16		3 Overkill	Colin Hay...*Till The Money Runs Out*	Columbia 03795
8/20/83	6	15		4 It's A Mistake	Colin Hay...*Shintaro*	Columbia 03959
				MENDES, Sergio, & Brasil '66		
7/6/68	4	14		1 The Look Of Love	Burt Bacharach/Hal David...*Like A Lover*	A&M 924
9/28/68	6	12		2 The Fool On The Hill	John Lennon/Paul McCartney...*So Many Stars*	A&M 961
7/9/83	4	23		3 Never Gonna Let You Go	Barry Mann/Cynthia Weil...*Carnaval*	A&M 2540
				SERGIO MENDES		
				MEN WITHOUT HATS		
9/10/83	3⁴	24		1 The Safety Dance	Ivan Doroschuk...*Living In China*	Backstreet 52232
				MERCER, Johnny		
9/5/42	7	6		1 Strip Polka	Johnny Mercer...*The Air-Minded Executive*	Capitol 103
3/17/45	❶²	16		2 Ac-Cent-Tchu-Ate The Positive	Harold Arlen/Johnny Mercer...*There's A Fellow Waiting In Poughkeepsie*	Capitol 180
3/31/45	❶¹	19		3 Candy	Mack David/Alex Kramer/Joan Whitney...*I'm Gonna See My Baby*	Capitol 183
				JOHNNY MERCER, JO STAFFORD		
7/28/45	❶⁸	19	⊙	4 On The Atchison, Topeka And Santa Fe	Johnny Mercer/Harry Warren...*Conversation While Dancing*	Capitol 195
3/2/46	❶²	15		5 Personality	Johnny Burke/Jimmy Van Heusen...*If I Knew Then*	Capitol 230
1/4/47	4	1		6 Winter Wonderland	Felix Bernard/Richard Smith...*A Gal In Calico* [X]	Capitol 316
				JOHNNY MERCER And The PIED PIPERS		
1/4/47	5	10		7 A Gal In Calico	Leo Robin/Arthur Schwartz...*Winter Wonderland*	Capitol 316
2/1/47	8	8		8 Zip-A-Dee-Doo-Dah	Ray Gilbert/Allie Wrubel...*Ev'rybody Has A Laughing Place*	Capitol 323
2/15/47	8	7		9 Huggin' And A Chalkin'	Kermit Goell/Clancy Hayes...*Take Me Back To Little Rock (Arkansas)* [N]	Capitol 334
11/1/47	4	8		10 Sugar Blues	Lucy Fletcher/Clarence Williams...*Why Should I Cry Over You?*	Capitol 448
7/9/49	3¹	19		11 Baby, It's Cold Outside	Frank Loesser...*I Never Heard You Say*	Capitol 567
				MARGARET WHITING AND JOHNNY MERCER		
				MERCHANT, Natalie		
10/28/95	10	31		1 Carnival	Natalie Merchant...*I May Know The Word*	Elektra 64413
				MERCY		
5/31/69	2²	13	●	1 Love (Can Make You Happy)	Jack Sigler...*Fire Ball*	Sundi 6811
				MERRY MACS, The		
7/11/42	4	8		1 Jingle Jangle Jingle	Joseph Lilley/Frank Loesser...*Cheatin' On The Sandman*	Decca 18361
11/28/42	8	4		2 Praise The Lord And Pass The Ammunition!	Frank Loesser...*Tweedle O Twill*	Decca 18498
3/18/44	❶⁵	15		3 Mairzy Doats	Milton Drake/Al Hoffman/Jerry Livingston...*I Got Ten Bucks And Twenty-Four Hours' Leave* [N]	Decca 18588
9/23/44	7	14		4 Pretty Kitty Blue Eyes	Mann Curtis/Vic Mizzy...*Sing Me A Song Of Texas*	Decca 18610
8/4/45	4	12		5 Sentimental Journey	Les Brown/Bud Green/Ben Homer...*Choo Choo Polka*	Decca 18684
10/6/45	9	1		6 On The Atchison, Topeka And The Santa Fe	Johnny Mercer/Harry Warren...*If I Had You*	Decca 23436
				JUDY GARLAND and THE MERRY MACS		
6/1/46	9	6		7 Laughing On The Outside (Crying On The Inside)	Ben Raleigh/Bernie Wayne...*Ashby De La Zooch (Castle Abbey)*	Decca 18811
				METALLICA		
6/8/96	10	20	●	1 Until It Sleeps	James Hetfield/Lars Ulrich...*Overkill*	Elektra 64276
				METHOD MAN		
6/3/95	3¹	20	▲	1 I'll Be There For You/You're All I Need To Get By	Nick Ashford/Robert Diggs/Valerie Simpson/Clifford Smith	Def Jam 851878
				METHOD MAN featuring Mary J. Blige		
				METRO STATION		
6/28/08	10	30	△²	1 Shake It	Trace Cyrus/Blake Healy/Mason Musso	Red Ink
				MFSB featuring The Three Degrees		
4/20/74	❶²	18	●	1 TSOP (The Sound Of Philadelphia)	Kenny Gamble/Leon Huff...*Something For Nothing* [I]	Philadelphia I. 3540
				M.I.A.		
9/27/08	4	20	△³	1 Paper Planes	Maya Arulpragasm/Nicky Headon/Mick Jones/Wesley Pentz/Paul Simonon/Joe Strummer	XL 010912
				MIAMI SOUND MACHINE — see ESTEFAN, Gloria		
				MICHAEL, George / Wham!		
11/17/84	❶³	24	▲	1 Wake Me Up Before You Go-Go	George Michael	Columbia 04552
				WHAM!		
2/16/85	❶³	21	▲	2 Careless Whisper	George Michael/Andrew Ridgeley	Columbia 04691
				WHAM! Featuring George Michael		
5/25/85	❶²	20	●	3 Everything She Wants	George Michael...*Like A Baby*	Columbia 04840
9/28/85	3¹	18		4 Freedom	George Michael...*Heartbeat*	Columbia 05409
2/1/86	3²	18		5 I'm Your Man	George Michael...*Do It Right*	Columbia 05721
				WHAM! (above 3)		
6/14/86	7	16		6 A Different Corner	George Michael	Columbia 05888
				GEORGE MICHAEL		
8/16/86	10	13		7 The Edge Of Heaven	George Michael...*Blue (live in China)*	Columbia 06182
				WHAM!		
4/18/87	❶²	17		8 I Knew You Were Waiting (For Me)	Simon Climie/Dennis Morgan	Arista 9559
				ARETHA FRANKLIN AND GEORGE MICHAEL		
				GEORGE MICHAEL:		
8/8/87	2¹	20	▲	9 I Want Your Sex	George Michael	Columbia 07164
12/12/87	❶⁴	20	●	10 Faith	George Michael...*Hand To Mouth*	Columbia 07623
2/27/88	❶²	17		11 Father Figure	George Michael	Columbia 07682

PEAK DATE	PEAK POS	WKS CHR	GOLD		ARTIST / Song Title	Songwriter...B-side	Label & Number
					MICHAEL, George (cont'd)		
5/28/88	❶³	18	●	12	One More Try	George Michael...*Look At Your Hands*	Columbia 07773
8/27/88	❶²	16		13	Monkey	George Michael	Columbia 07941
11/26/88	5	15		14	Kissing A Fool	George Michael	Columbia 08050
4/29/89	5	16		15	Heaven Help Me	Deon Estus/George Michael...*It's A Party*	Mika 871538
					DEON ESTUS (with George Michael)		
10/13/90	❶¹	14		16	Praying For Time	George Michael...*If You Were My Woman*	Columbia 73512
12/22/90	8	16		17	Freedom	George Michael...*Fantasy*	Columbia 73559
2/1/92	❶¹	20	●	18	Don't Let The Sun Go Down On Me	Elton John/Bernie Taupin...*I Believe (When I Fall In Love It Will Be Forever)* (Michael) [L]	Columbia 74086
					GEORGE MICHAEL/ELTON JOHN		
8/8/92	10	20	●	19	Too Funky	George Michael...*Crazyman Dance*	Columbia 74353
2/24/96	7	14	●	20	Jesus To A Child	George Michael...*One More Try (live gospel version)*	DreamWorks 59000
6/1/96	8	19	●	21	Fastlove	George Michael...*I'm Your Man '96*	DreamWorks 59001
					MICHAELS, Lee		
10/9/71	6	17	1		Do You Know What I Mean	Lee Michaels...*Keep The Circle Turning*	A&M 1262
					MICHEL'LE		
3/10/90	7	29	●	1	No More Lies	Larry Goodman/Michel'le Toussant/Andre Young...*Never Been In Love*	Ruthless 99149
					MIDLER, Bette		
7/21/73	8	16		1	Boogie Woogie Bugle Boy	Hughie Prince/Don Raye...*Delta Dawn*	Atlantic 2964
6/28/80	3³	25	●	2	The Rose	Amanda McBroom...*Stay With Me*	Atlantic 3656
6/10/89	❶¹	29	▲	3	Wind Beneath My Wings	Larry Henley/Jeff Silbar...*Oh Industry*	Atlantic 88972
12/15/90	2¹	26	▲	4	From A Distance	Julie Gold...*One More Round*	Atlantic 87820
					MIKE + THE MECHANICS		
3/8/86	6	24		1	Silent Running (On Dangerous Ground)	Brian Robertson/Mike Rutherford...*Par Avion*	Atlantic 89488
6/7/86	5	19		2	All I Need Is A Miracle	Christopher Neil/Mike Rutherford...*You Are The One*	Atlantic 89450
3/25/89	❶¹	20		3	The Living Years	Brian Robertson/Mike Rutherford...*Too Many Friends*	Atlantic 88964
					MILIAN, Christina		
8/21/04	5	30	○	1	Dip It Low	J. Jackson/Christina Milian/Tedra Moses/Paul Poli	Island 002034
					MILLER, Chuck		
8/27/55	9	14		1	The House Of Blue Lights	Don Raye/Freddie Slack...*Can't Help Wonderin'*	Mercury 70627
					MILLER, Glenn, and his Orchestra		
7/27/40	3¹	3		1	Imagination	Johnny Burke/Jimmy Van Heusen...*Say "Si Si" (Para Vigo Me Voy)*	Bluebird 10622
8/3/40	3⁴	7		2	Fools Rush In (Where Angels Fear to Tread)	Rube Bloom/Johnny Mercer...*Yours Is My Heart Alone*	Bluebird 10728
8/10/40	5	8		3	The Nearness Of You	Hoagy Carmichael/Ned Washington...*Mister Meadowlark*	Bluebird 10745
8/31/40	5	6	◉	4	Pennsylvania Six-Five Thousand	Jerry Gray/Carl Sigman...*Rug Cutter's Swing* [I]	Bluebird 10754
8/31/40	10	1		5	When The Swallows Come Back To Capistrano	Leon Rene...*A Cabana In Havana*	Bluebird 10776
9/7/40	2⁴	14		6	Blueberry Hill	Al Lewis/Vincent Rose/Larry Stock...*A Million Dreams Ago*	Bluebird 10768
10/5/40	9	1		7	Crosstown	James Cavanaugh/John Redmond/Nat Simon...*What's Your Story, Morning Glory*	Bluebird 10832
11/9/40	10	1		8	The Call Of The Canyon	Billy Hill...*Our Love Affair*	Bluebird 10845
11/23/40	8	2		9	Our Love Affair	Roger Edens/Arthur Freed...*The Call Of The Canyon*	Bluebird 10845
11/30/40	10	2		10	A Handful Of Stars	Jack Lawrence/Ted Shapiro...*Yesterthoughts*	Bluebird 10893
12/28/40	2²	6		11	A Nightingale Sang In Berkeley Square	Eric Maschwitz/Manning Sherwin...*Goodbye, Little Darlin', Goodbye*	Bluebird 10931
1/11/41	6	2		12	Five O'Clock Whistle	Kim Gannon/Gene Irwin/Josef Myrow...*Shadows On The Sand*	Bluebird 10900
1/18/41	7	4		13	Along The Santa Fe Trail	Edwina Coolidge/Al Dubin/Will Grosz...*Yes, My Darling Daughter*	Bluebird 10970
2/8/41	3¹	10		14	Anvil Chorus—Parts 1 & 2	Glenn Miller/Giuseppe Verdi [I]	Bluebird 10982
3/15/41	❶¹	8		15	Song Of The Volga Boatmen	(traditional)...*Chapel In The Valley* [I]	Bluebird 11029
4/5/41	3¹	4		16	I Dreamt I Dwelt In Harlem	Jerry Gray/Ben Smith/Leonard Ware/Robert Wright...*A Stone's Throw From Heaven* [I]	Bluebird 11063
8/16/41	7	5		17	The Booglie Wooglie Piggy	Roy Jacobs...*Boulder Buff*	Bluebird 11163
9/6/41	4	6		18	You And I	Meredith Willson...*The Angels Came Thru*	Bluebird 11215
11/29/41	❶⁹	23	◉	19	Chattanooga Choo Choo	Mack Gordon/Harry Warren...*I Know Why*	Bluebird 11230
12/20/41	❶¹	15		20	Elmer's Tune	Elmer Albrecht/Sammy Gallop/Dick Jurgens...*Delilah*	Bluebird 11274
12/27/41	5	2		21	Jingle Bells	James Pierpont...*Santa Claus Is Comin' To Town* (Alvino Rey Orchestra) [X]	Bluebird 11353
1/24/42	6	7		22	(There'll Be Blue Birds Over) The White Cliffs Of Dover	Nat Burton/Walter Kent...*We're The Couple In The Castle*	Bluebird 11397
2/7/42	❶²	18	◉	23	A String Of Pearls	Jerry Gray...*Day Dreaming* [I]	Bluebird 11382
2/14/42	7	4		24	Ev'rything I Love	Cole Porter...*Baby Mine*	Bluebird 11365
2/28/42	❶¹⁰	15	◉	25	Moonlight Cocktail	Kim Gannon/Lucky Roberts...*Happy In Love*	Bluebird 11401
5/9/42	7	11		26	Skylark	Hoagy Carmichael/Johnny Mercer...*The Story Of A Starry Night*	Bluebird 11462
5/23/42	10	1		27	Always In My Heart	Kim Gannon/Ernesto Lecuona...*When The Roses Bloom Again*	Bluebird 11438
6/6/42	2²	13		28	Don't Sit Under The Apple Tree (With Anyone Else But Me)	Lew Brown/Sam Stept/Charles Tobias...*The Lamplighter's Serenade*	Bluebird 11474
8/15/42	8	3		29	Sweet Eloise	Mack David/Russ Morgan...*Sleep Song*	Victor 27879
9/12/42	❶⁷	18	◉	30	(I've Got A Gal in) Kalamazoo	Mack Gordon/Harry Warren...*At Last*	Victor 27934
10/10/42	2¹	15		31	Serenade In Blue	Mack Gordon/Harry Warren...*That's Sabotage*	Victor 27935
12/26/42	7	8		32	Juke Box Saturday Night	Paul McGrane/Al Stillman...*Sleepy Town Train* [N]	Victor 1509
1/2/43	5	4		33	Dearly Beloved	Jerome Kern/Johnny Mercer...*I'm Old Fashioned*	Victor 27953
1/30/43	5	8		34	Moonlight Becomes You	Johnny Burke/Jimmy Van Heusen...*Moonlight Mood*	Victor 1520
5/29/43	❶¹	14		35	That Old Black Magic	Harold Arlen/Johnny Mercer...*A Pink Cocktail For A Blue Lady*	Victor 1523
1/22/44	9	3		36	Blue Rain	Johnny Mercer/Jimmy Van Heusen...*Caribbean Clipper*	Victor 1536
					TEX BENEKE with the Glenn Miller Orchestra:		
6/15/46	4	9		37	Hey! Ba-Ba-Re-Bop	Curley Hamner/Lionel Hampton...*The Whiffenpoof Song (Baa! Baa! Baa!)*	RCA Victor 1859
8/3/46	9	3		38	I Know	Ted Brooks/John Jennings...*Ev'rybody Loves My Baby (My Baby)*	RCA Victor 1914
10/19/46	9	5		39	Passe	Eddie DeLange/Joseph Meyer/Carl Sigman...*The Woodchuck Song*	RCA Victor 1951
11/2/46	4	18		40	Give Me Five Minutes More	Sammy Cahn/Jule Styne...*Texas Tex*	RCA Victor 1922
1/18/47	6	8		41	A Gal In Calico	Leo Robin/Arthur Schwartz...*Oh, But I Do*	RCA Victor 1991
3/15/47	3²	11		42	Anniversary Song	Saul Chaplin/Al Jolson...*Hoodle Addle*	RCA Victor 2126
					MILLER, Mitch, & his Orch. and Chorus		
7/22/50	3¹	12		1	Tzena Tzena Tzena	Gordon Jenkins/Spencer Ross...*The Sleigh*	Columbia 38885
9/3/55	❶⁶	19	◉	2	The Yellow Rose Of Texas	Don George...*Blackberry Winter*	Columbia 40540
9/22/56	8	17		3	Theme Song From "Song For A Summer Night"	Robert Allen...*(vocal version)* [I]	Columbia 40730

PEAK DATE	PEAK POS	WKS CHR	GOLD	ARTIST / Song Title	Songwriter...B-side	Label & Number
				MILLER, Ned		
2/16/63	6	13		1 From A Jack To A King	Ned Miller...*Parade Of Broken Hearts*	Fabor 114
				MILLER, Roger		
8/1/64	7	11		1 Dang Me	Roger Miller...*Got 2 Again* [N]	Smash 1881
11/7/64	9	13		2 Chug-A-Lug	Roger Miller...*Reincarnation* [N]	Smash 1926
3/20/65	4	13	●	3 King Of The Road	Roger Miller...*Atta Boy Girl*	Smash 1965
6/12/65	7	9		4 Engine Engine #9	Roger Miller...*The Last Word In Lonesome Is Me*	Smash 1983
12/18/65	8	11		5 England Swings	Roger Miller...*Good Old Days*	Smash 2010
				MILLER, Steve, Band		
1/12/74	❶1	20	●	1 The Joker	Eddie Curtis/Steve Miller...*Something To Believe In*	Capitol 3732
11/6/76	❶1	18		2 Rock'n Me	Steve Miller...*Shu Ba Da Du Ma Ma Ma Ma*	Capitol 4323
3/12/77	2²	20	●	3 Fly Like An Eagle	Steve Miller...*Lovin' Cup*	Capitol 4372
				STEVE MILLER (above 2)		
7/9/77	8	18		4 Jet Airliner	Paul Pena...*Babes In The Wood*	Capitol 4424
9/4/82	❶2	25	●	5 Abracadabra	Steve Miller...*Give It Up*	Capitol 5126
				MILLINDER, Lucky, And His Orchestra		
9/1/45	7	10		1 Who Threw The Whiskey In The Well	Johnny Brooks/Eddie DeLange...*Shipyard Social Function*	Decca 18674
				MILLI VANILLI		
4/1/89	2¹	26	▲	1 Girl You Know It's True	Kayode Adeyemo/Rodney Hollaman/Kevin Lyles/William Pettaway/Sean Spencer...*Magic Touch*	Arista 9781
7/1/89	❶1	21	●	2 Baby Don't Forget My Number	Roger Dalton/Frank Farian/Brad Howell/Franz Reuter...*Too Much Monkey Business*	Arista 9832
9/23/89	❶2	22		3 Girl I'm Gonna Miss You	Peter Bischof-Fallenstein/Frank Farian/Dietmar Kawohl...*All Or Nothing*	Arista 9870
11/25/89	❶2	23	▲	4 Blame It On The Rain	Diane Warren...*Dance With A Devil*	Arista 9904
2/24/90	4	14		5 All Or Nothing	David Clayton-Thomas/Frank Farian/Brad Howell/P.G. Wilder...*Dreams To Remember*	Arista 9923
				MILLS, Frank		
5/5/79	3¹	20	●	1 Music Box Dancer	Frank Mills...*The Poet And I* [I]	Polydor 14517
				MILLS, Hayley		
10/23/61	8	14		1 Let's Get Together	Richard Sherman/Robert Sherman...*Cobbler Cobbler*	Buena Vista 385
				MILLS, Stephanie		
11/15/80	6	25	●	1 Never Knew Love Like This Before	Reggie Lucas/James Mtume...*Still Mine*	20th Century 2460
				MILLS BROTHERS, The		
11/6/43	❶12	30	☉	1 Paper Doll	Johnny Black...*I'll Be Around*	Decca 18318
9/30/44	8	5		2 Till Then	Sol Marcus/Eddie Seiler/Guy Wood...*You Always Hurt The One You Love*	Decca 18599
10/7/44	❶5	33	☉	3 You Always Hurt The One You Love	Doris Fisher/Allan Roberts...*Till Then*	Decca 18599
6/23/45	6	11		4 I Wish	Doris Fisher/Allan Roberts...*Put Another Chair At The Table*	Decca 18663
8/10/46	7	15		5 I Don't Know Enough About You	Dave Barbour/Peggy Lee...*There's No One But You*	Decca 18834
6/28/47	2²	15		6 Across The Alley From The Alamo	Joe Greene...*Dream, Dream, Dream*	Decca 23863
2/26/49	8	9		7 I Love You So Much It Hurts	Floyd Tillman...*I've Got My Love To Keep Me Warm*	Decca 24550
4/2/49	9	11		8 I've Got My Love To Keep Me Warm	Irving Berlin...*I Love You So Much It Hurts*	Decca 24550
10/8/49	5	15		9 Someday (You'll Want Me To Want You)	Jimmie Hodges...*On A Chinese Honeymoon*	Decca 24694
5/6/50	5	15		10 Daddy's Little Girl	Bobby Burke/Horace Gerlach...*If I Live To Be A Hundred*	Decca 24872
12/16/50	4	17		11 Nevertheless (I'm In Love With You)	Bert Kalmar/Harry Ruby...*Thirsty For Your Kisses*	Decca 27253
2/9/52	7	12		12 Be My Life's Companion	Milton DeLugg/Bob Hilliard...*Love Lies*	Decca 27889
12/6/52	❶3	21	☉	13 The Glow-Worm	Paul Lincke/Johnny Mercer/Lilla Robinson...*After All*	Decca 28384
				MILSAP, Ronnie		
9/5/81	5	20		1 (There's) No Gettin' Over Me	Walt Aldridge/Tom Brasfield...*I Live My Whole Life At Night*	RCA 12264
				MIMMS, Garnet, & The Enchanters		
10/12/63	4	14		1 Cry Baby	Norman Meade/Bert Russell...*Don't Change Your Heart*	United Artists 629
				MIMS		
3/10/07	❶2	23	△	1 This Is Why I'm Hot	Leon Haywood/Albert Johnson/Curtis Lundy/Darryl McDaniels/Shawn Mims/Kejuan Muchita/Danny Schofield/ Joseph Simmons/Russell Simmons/Thomas Simons/Jonathan Smith/Earl Stevens/Winston Thomas/Charles Williams	Capitol 84997
				MINAJ, Nicki		
11/6/10	6	24↑	○	1 Bottoms Up	Miles Edrick/Milton James/Daniel Johnson/Onika Maraj/Tremaine Neverson/Tony Scales	Song Book
				TREY SONGZ Featuring Nicki Minaj		
				MINDBENDERS, The		
4/24/65	❶1	11	☉	1 Game Of Love	Clint Ballard...*One More Time*	Fontana 1509
				WAYNE FONTANA & THE MINDBENDERS		
5/28/66	2²	13	☉	2 A Groovy Kind Of Love	Carole Bayer Sager/Toni Wine...*Love Is Good*	Fontana 1541
				MINEO, Sal		
6/3/57	9	19		1 Start Movin' (In My Direction)	David Hill/Bobby Stevenson...*Love Affair*	Epic 9216
				MINOGUE, Kylie		
11/12/88	3²	27	●	1 The Loco-Motion	Gerry Goffin/Carole King...*I'll Still Be Loving You*	Geffen 27752
3/23/02	7	20	○	2 Can't Get You Out Of My Head	Rob Davis/Cathy Dennis	Capitol 77685
				MINT CONDITION		
4/11/92	6	24	●	1 Breakin' My Heart (Pretty Brown Eyes)	Jeffrey Allen/Lawrence Waddell/Stokley Williams	Perspective 0004
				MIRACLES, The		
2/20/61	2¹	16	☉	1 Shop Around	Berry Gordy/Smokey Robinson...*Who's Lovin You*	Tamla 54034
2/9/63	8	16		2 You've Really Got A Hold On Me	Smokey Robinson...*Happy Landing*	Tamla 54073
9/21/63	8	12		3 Mickey's Monkey	Lamont Dozier/Brian Holland...*Whatever Makes You Happy*	Tamla 54083
				SMOKEY ROBINSON & THE MIRACLES:		
12/16/67	4	15		4 I Second That Emotion	Alfred Cleveland/Smokey Robinson...*You Must Be Love*	Tamla 54159
3/1/69	8	14		5 Baby, Baby Don't Cry	Alfred Cleveland/Terry Johnson/Smokey Robinson...*Your Mother's Only Daughter*	Tamla 54178
12/12/70	❶2	16		6 The Tears Of A Clown	Henry Cosby/Smokey Robinson/Stevie Wonder...*Promise Me*	Tamla 54199

PEAK DATE	PEAK POS	WKS CHR	GOLD	ARTIST / Song Title	Songwriter...B-side	Label & Number
3/6/76	❶[1]	28		7 Love Machine (Part 1) — THE MIRACLES	William Griffin/Warren Moore...**(Part 2)**	Tamla 54262
				MR. BIG		
2/29/92	❶[3]	24	●	1 To Be With You	David Grahame/Eric Martin...**Green-Tinted Sixties Mind**	Atlantic 87580
				MR. HUDSON		
5/8/10	10	20		1 Young Forever — JAY-Z + MR. HUDSON	Shawn Carter/Marian Gold/Bernhard Lloyd/Frank Mertens/Kanye West...**On To The Next One**	Roc Nation 523738
				MR. MISTER		
12/7/85	❶[2]	22		1 Broken Wings	Steve George/John Lang/Richard Page...**Uniform Of Youth**	RCA 14136
3/1/86	❶[2]	20		2 Kyrie	Steve George/John Lang/Richard Page...**Run To Her**	RCA 14258
5/31/86	8	17		3 Is It Love	Steve George/John Lang/Pat Mastelotto/Richard Page...**32**	RCA 14313
				MITCHELL, Guy		
1/27/51	2[7]	21	☉	1 My Heart Cries For You	Percy Faith/Carl Sigman...**The Roving Kind**	Columbia 39067
2/24/51	4	17		2 The Roving Kind	Jessie Cavanaugh/Arnold Stanton...**My Heart Cries For You**	Columbia 39067
4/7/51	8	15		3 Sparrow In The Tree Top	Bob Merrill...**Christopher Columbus**	Columbia 39190
7/21/51	2[1]	19	☉	4 My Truly, Truly Fair	Bob Merrill...**Who Knows Love**	Columbia 39415
9/8/51	9	9		5 Belle, Belle, My Liberty Belle	Bob Merrill...**Sweetheart Of Yesterday**	Columbia 39512
5/24/52	4	21	☉	6 Pittsburgh, Pennsylvania	Bob Merrill...**The Doll With A Sawdust Heart**	Columbia 39663
12/8/56	❶[10]	26		7 Singing The Blues	Melvin Endsley...**Crazy With Love**	Columbia 40769
5/6/57	10	17		8 Rock-A-Billy	Eddie Deane/Woody Harris...**Hoot Owl**	Columbia 40877
12/14/59	❶[2]	20	☉	9 Heartaches By The Number	Harlan Howard...**Two**	Columbia 41476
				MITCHELL, Joni		
6/8/74	7	19		1 Help Me	Joni Mitchell...**Just Like This Train**	Asylum 11034
				MOBB DEEP		
10/1/05	6	19		1 Outta Control (Remix) — 50 CENT Featuring Mobb Deep	Mark Batson/Mike Elizondo/Curtis Jackson/Albert Johnson/Kejuan Muchita/Che Pope/Andre Young	Shady 005439
				MOCEDADES		
3/23/74	9	17		1 Eres Tu (Touch The Wind)	Juan Carlos Calderon...**Touch The Wind (Eres Tu)** [F]	Tara 100
				MODERNAIRES with PAULA KELLY		
9/21/46	3[1]	14		1 To Each His Own	Ray Evans/Jay Livingston...**Holiday For Strings**	Columbia 37063
				MODUGNO, Domenico		
8/18/58	❶[5]	16		1 Nel Blu Dipinto Di Blu (Volare)	Franco Migliacci/Domenico Modugno...**Mariti In Citta** [F]	Decca 30677
				MOKENSTEF		
8/26/95	7	23	●	1 He's Mine	Monifa Bethune/Kenya Hadley/Marquis Hair/Prince/Stephanie Sinclair/Roger Troutman	OutBurst 851704
				MOMENTS, The		
5/30/70	3[2]	15	●	1 Love On A Two-Way Street	Bert Keyes/Sylvia Robinson...**I Won't Do Anything**	Stang 5012
4/19/80	5	18	●	2 Special Lady	Al Goodman/Harry Ray/Lee Walter...**Deja Vu**	Polydor 2033
				MONEY, Eddie		
11/15/86	4	23		1 Take Me Home Tonight	Jeff Barry/Ellie Greenwich/Mike Leeson/Phil Spector/Peter Vale...**Calm Before The Storm**	Columbia 06231
12/24/88	9	21		2 Walk On Water	Jesse Harms...**Dancing With Mr. Jitters**	Columbia 08060
				MONEY, JT		
5/22/99	5	20	●	1 Who Dat — JT MONEY Featuring Sole	DiAndre Davis/Tonya Johnston/Tony Mercedes/Tab Nkhereanye/Christopher Stewart/Jeff Tompkins	Tony Mercedes 53469
				MONICA		
7/1/95	2[3]	29	▲	1 Don't Take It Personal (Just One Of Dem Days)	Dallas Austin/Derrick Simmons	Rowdy 35040
12/30/95	7	28	▲	2 Before You Walk Out Of My Life	Ken Karlin/Andrea Martin/Carsten Schack...**Like This And Like That**	Rowdy 35052
7/6/96	9	20		3 Why I Love You So Much	Daryl Simmons...**Ain't Nobody**	Rowdy 35072
4/19/97	4	32	▲	4 For You I Will	Diane Warren	Warner Sunset 87003
6/6/98	❶[13]	27	▲[2]	5 The Boy Is Mine — BRANDY & MONICA	LaShawn Daniels/Freddie Jerkins/Rodney Jerkins/Brandy Norwood/Japhe Tejeda	Atlantic 84089
10/3/98	❶[5]	23	▲	6 The First Night	Jermaine Dupri/Marilyn McLeod/Tamara Savage/Pam Sawyer...**Cross The Room**	Arista 13522
2/13/99	❶[4]	30	▲	7 Angel Of Mine	Ron Lawrence/Travon Potts...**The First Night**	Arista 13590
7/12/03	10	22		8 So Gone	Zyah Ahmonuel/Missy Elliott	J Records 21260
				MONIFAH		
10/17/98	9	26		1 Touch It	Albert Charles/Tijuan Frampton/John Guldberg/Jack Knight/Tim Stahl	Uptown 56207
				MONKEES, The		
11/5/66	❶[1]	15	●	1 Last Train To Clarksville	Tommy Boyce/Bobby Hart...**Take A Giant Step**	Colgems 1001
12/31/66	❶[7]	15	●	2 I'm A Believer	Neil Diamond...**(I'm Not Your) Steppin' Stone**	Colgems 1002
4/29/67	2[1]	10	●	3 A Little Bit Me, A Little Bit You	Neil Diamond...**The Girl I Knew Somewhere**	Colgems 1004
8/19/67	3[2]	10	●	4 Pleasant Valley Sunday	Gerry Goffin/Carole King...**Words**	Colgems 1007
12/2/67	❶[4]	12	●	5 Daydream Believer	John Stewart...**Goin' Down**	Colgems 1012
3/30/68	3[2]	10	●	6 Valleri	Tommy Boyce/Bobby Hart...**Tapioca Tundra**	Colgems 1019
				MONOTONES, The		
4/21/58	5	18	☉	1 Book Of Love	Warren Davis/George Malone/Charles Patrick...**You Never Loved Me**	Argo 5290
				MONROE, Vaughn, and his Orchestra		
12/28/40	5	4		1 There I Go	Irving Weiser/Hy Zaret...**Whatever Happened To You**	Bluebird 10848
10/24/42	5	4		2 My Devotion	Roc Hillman/Johnny Napton...**When I Grow Up**	Victor 27925
12/26/42	2[1]	16		3 When The Lights Go On Again (All Over the World)	Bennie Benjamin/Sol Marcus/Eddie Seiler...**Hip Hip Hooray**	Victor 27945
6/12/43	8	2		4 Let's Get Lost	Frank Loesser/Jimmy McHugh...**Happy-Go-Lucky**	Victor 1524
1/6/45	4	7		5 The Trolley Song	Ralph Blane/Hugh Martin...**The Very Thought Of You**	Victor 1605
3/3/45	8	1		6 Rum And Coca-Cola	Morey Amsterdam/Paul Baron/Jeri Sullavan...**There! I've Said It Again**	Victor 1637
5/12/45	❶[6]	29	☉	7 There! I've Said It Again	Redd Evans/Dave Mann...**Rum And Coca-Cola**	Victor 1637

PEAK DATE	PEAK POS	WKS CHR	GOLD	ARTIST / Song Title	Songwriter...B-side	Label & Number
				MONROE, Vaughn (cont'd)		
1/19/46	❶⁵	14	⊙	8 Let It Snow! Let It Snow! Let It Snow!	Sammy Cahn/Jule Styne...*When The Sandman Rides The Trail* [X]	Victor 1759
4/6/46	7	5		9 Seems Like Old Times	John Jacob Loeb/Carmen Lombardo...*Gee! I Wish (The 'G.I. Wish' Song)*	RCA Victor 1811
10/18/47	2⁵	15		10 I Wish I Didn't Love You So	Frank Loesser...*Tallahassee*	RCA Victor 2294
10/25/47	10	1		11 Kokomo, Indiana	Mack Gordon/Josef Myrow...*You Do*	RCA Victor 2361
11/22/47	5	8		12 You Do	Mack Gordon/Josef Myrow...*Kokomo, Indiana*	RCA Victor 2361
12/13/47	❶¹⁰	22	⊙	13 Ballerina	Bob Russell/Carl Sigman...*The Stars Will Remember*	RCA Victor 2433
1/24/48	3²	13		14 How Soon? (Will I Be Seeing You)	Carroll Lucas/Jack Owens...*True*	RCA Victor 2523
10/9/48	9	14		15 Cool Water	Bob Nolan...*The Legend Of Tiabi*	RCA Victor 2923
				VAUGHN MONROE and Sons of the Pioneers		
4/16/49	3²	22		16 Red Roses For A Blue Lady	Roy Brodsky/Sid Tepper...*Melancholy Minstrel*	RCA Victor-2889
5/14/49	❶¹²	22	⊙	17 Riders In The Sky (A Cowboy Legend)	Stan Jones...*Single Saddle*	RCA Victor 2902
9/10/49	❶²	18		18 Someday	Jimmie Hodges...*And It Still Goes*	RCA Victor 2986
10/22/49	6	17		19 That Lucky Old Sun (Just Rolls Around Heaven All Day)	Haven Gillespie/Beasley Smith...*Make Believe (You Are Glad When You're Sorry)*	RCA Victor 3018
12/3/49	10	9		20 Mule Train	Fred Glickman/Hy Heath/Johnny Lange...*Singing My Way Back Home*	RCA Victor 3106
2/4/50	4	7		21 Bamboo	Buddy Bernier/Nat Simon...*A Little Golden Cross*	RCA Victor 3143
5/26/51	7	8		22 Old Soldiers Never Die	Tom Glazer...*Love And Devotion*	RCA Victor 4146
6/2/51	3¹	17		23 Sound Off (The Duckworth Chant)	Willie Lee Duckworth...*Oh, Marry, Marry Me*	RCA Victor 4113
6/9/51	8	16		24 On Top Of Old Smoky	Pete Seeger...*Shall We Dance*	RCA Victor 4114
10/2/54	7	16		25 They Were Doin' The Mambo	Don Raye...*Mister Sandman*	RCA Victor 5767
				MONTANA, Hannah — see CYRUS, Miley		
				MONTE, Lou		
4/17/54	7	11		1 Darktown Strutters Ball (Italian Style)	Shelton Brooks...*I Know How You Feel*	RCA Victor 5611
1/12/63	5	10		2 Pepino The Italian Mouse	Ray Allen/Wanda Merrell...*What Did Washington Say (When He Crossed the Delaware)* [N]	Reprise 20,106
				MONTENEGRO, Hugo, His Orchestra And Chorus		
6/1/68	2¹	22		1 The Good, The Bad And The Ugly	Ennio Morricone...*March With Hope* [I]	RCA Victor 9423
				MONTEZ, Chris		
10/6/62	4	14		1 Let's Dance	Jim Lee...*You're The One*	Monogram 505
				MOODY BLUES, The		
4/17/65	10	14		1 Go Now!	Larry Banks/Milton Bennett...*Lose Your Money*	London 9726
11/4/72	2²	18	●	2 Nights In White Satin	Justin Hayward...*Cities*	Deram 85023
7/12/86	9	21		3 Your Wildest Dreams	Justin Hayward...*Talkin' Talkin'*	Polydor 883906
				MOONEY, Art, And His Orchestra		
2/21/48	❶⁵	18	⊙	1 I'm Looking Over A Four Leaf Clover	Mort Dixon/Harry Woods...*The Big Brass Band From Brazil*	MGM 10119
5/8/48	3²	15	⊙	2 Baby Face	Harry Akst/Benny Davis...*Encore, Cherie*	MGM 10156
10/23/48	5	22		3 Blue Bird Of Happiness	Harry Davies/Sandor Harmati/Edward Heyman...*Sunset To Sunrise*	MGM 10207
7/16/49	7	17		4 Again	Dorcas Cochran/Lionel Newman...*Five Foot Two, Eyes Of Blue (Has Anybody Seen My Girl)*	MGM 10398
6/25/55	6	17	⊙	5 Honey-Babe	Max Steiner/Paul Francis Webster...*No Regrets*	MGM 11900
				MOORE, Bob, and His Orch.		
10/2/61	7	15		1 Mexico	Boudleaux Bryant...*Hot Spot* [I]	Monument 446
				MOORE, Chante		
6/12/99	10	18	●	1 Chante's Got A Man	Jimmy Jam Harris/Terry Lewis/Chante Moore...*Your Home Is In My Heart* (w/Boyz II Men)	Silas/MCA 55544
				MOORE, Dorothy		
6/12/76	3⁴	22		1 Misty Blue	Bob Montgomery...*Here It Is*	Malaco 1029
				MOORE, Phil, Four		
3/24/45	3¹	10		1 My Dreams Are Getting Better All The Time	Mann Curtis/Vic Mizzy...*A Little On The Lonely Side*	Victor 1641
				MORGAN, Al		
9/24/49	4	26		1 Jealous Heart	Jenny Lou Carson...*Turnabout Is Fair Play*	London 30001
				MORGAN, Debelah		
1/6/01	8	29	●	1 Dance With Me	Richard Adler/Debelah Morgan/Giloh Morgan/Jerry Ross	Atlantic 84783
				MORGAN, Jane		
10/14/57	7	29	⊙	1 Fascination	Dante Marchetti	Kapp 191
				JANE MORGAN and The Troubadors		
				MORGAN, Jaye P.		
2/26/55	3¹	21		1 That's All I Want From You	Fritz Rotter...*Dawn*	RCA Victor 5896
9/17/55	6	14		2 The Longest Walk	Edward Pola/Fred Spielman...*Swanee*	RCA Victor 6182
				MORGAN, Russ, And His Orchestra		
4/18/42	5	11		1 Somebody Else Is Taking My Place	Bob Ellsworth/Dick Howard/Russ Morgan...*Prisionero Del Mar ('Neath A Tropical Moon)*	Decca 4098
7/15/44	6	16		2 Good Night, Wherever You Are	Al Hoffman/Dick Robertson/Frank Weldon...*Louise*	Decca 18598
12/9/44	3¹	12		3 Dance With A Dolly (With A Hole In Her Stockin')	Jimmy Eaton/Mickey Leader/Terry Shand...*There Goes That Song Again*	Decca 18625
1/13/45	3¹	14		4 There Goes That Song Again	Sammy Cahn/Jule Styne...*Dance With A Dolly (With A Hole In Her Stockin')*	Decca 18625
2/9/46	9	5		5 Let It Snow! Let It Snow! Let It Snow!	Sammy Cahn/Jule Styne...*Walkin' With My Honey (Soon, Soon, Soon)* [X]	Decca 18741
				CONNEE BOSWELL and RUSS MORGAN and HIS ORCHESTRA		
3/20/48	6	13		6 I'm Looking Over A Four Leaf Clover	Mort Dixon/Harry Woods...*Bye Bye Blackbird*	Decca 24319
				RUSS MORGAN And HIS ORCHESTRA with MILT HERTH At The Organ and the Ames Brothers		
3/26/49	❶⁷	22	⊙	7 Cruising Down The River	Eily Beadell/Nell Tollerton...*Sunflower*	Decca 24568
4/2/49	3¹	25		8 So Tired	Russ Morgan/Jack Stuart...*I Hear Music*	Decca 24521
4/16/49	5	15		9 Sunflower	Mack David...*Cruising Down The River*	Decca 24568
5/14/49	❶³	26		10 Forever And Ever	Malia Rosa/Franz Winkler...*You, You, You Are The One*	Decca 24569
2/18/50	7	10		11 Johnson Rag	Guy Hall/Henry Kleinkauf/Jack Lawrence...*Where Are You Blue Eyes?*	Decca 24819
6/10/50	7	17		12 Sentimental Me	Jimmy Cassin/Jim Morehead...*Copper Canyon*	Decca 24904
				MORISSETTE, Alanis		
4/13/96	4	32	●	1 Ironic	Glen Ballard/Alanis Morissette...*Not The Doctor (live) / Forgiven (live)*	Maverick 17698
7/27/96	6	30		2 You Learn	Glen Ballard/Alanis Morissette...*You Oughta Know (live)*	Maverick 17644

PEAK DATE	PEAK POS	WKS CHR	GOLD	ARTIST / Song Title	Songwriter...B-side	Label & Number
				MORISSETTE, Alanis (cont'd)		
10/26/96	3[6]	47		3 Head Over Feet	Glen Ballard/Alanis Morissette	Maverick
6/27/98	4	29		4 Uninvited	Alanis Morissette	Warner Sunset
11/28/98	2[1]	18		5 Thank U	Glen Ballard/Alanis Morissette	Maverick
				MORRISON, Mark		
6/7/97	2[1]	40	▲	1 Return Of The Mack	Mark Morrison	Atlantic 84868
				MORRISON, Van		
9/30/67	10	16	○	1 Brown Eyed Girl	Van Morrison...*Goodbye Baby (Baby Goodbye)*	Bang 545
1/2/71	9	12		2 Domino	Van Morrison...*Sweet Jannie*	Warner 7434
				MORROW, Buddy, and His Orchestra		
6/9/51	8	10		1 Rose, Rose, I Love You	Chris Langdon/Wilfrid Thomas...*(What Can I Say) After I Say I'm Sorry?*	RCA Victor 4135
				MORSE, Ella Mae		
1/15/44	4	15		1 Shoo-Shoo Baby	Phil Moore...*No Love, No Nothin'*	Capitol 143
2/19/44	4	12		2 No Love, No Nothin'	Leo Robin/Harry Warren...*Shoo-Shoo Baby*	Capitol 143
6/3/44	7	16		3 Milkman, Keep Those Bottles Quiet	Gene DePaul/Don Raye...*Tess's Torch Song (I Had A Man)*	Capitol 151
10/21/44	10	5		4 The Patty Cake Man	Roy Jordan...*Invitation To The Blues*	Capitol 163
4/5/52	3[6]	22	⊙	5 The Blacksmith Blues	Jack Holmes...*Love Me Or Leave Me*	Capitol 1922
				MOTELS, The		
7/17/82	9	23		1 Only The Lonely	Martha Davis...*Change My Mind*	Capitol 5114
11/19/83	9	20		2 Suddenly Last Summer	Martha Davis...*Some Things Never Change*	Capitol 5271
				MOTLEY CRUE		
10/28/89	6	16	●	1 Dr. Feelgood	Mick Mars/Nikki Sixx...*Sticky Sweet*	Elektra 69271
4/28/90	8	17		2 Without You	Mick Mars/Nikki Sixx...*Slice Of Your Pie*	Elektra 64985
				MOUTH & MACNEAL		
7/22/72	8	19	●	1 How Do You Do?	Hans Van Hemert/Harm Van Hoof...*Land Of Milk And Honey*	Philips 40715
				MRAZ, Jason		
9/20/08	6	76	△5	1 I'm Yours	Jason Mraz	Atlantic
				MULDAUR, Maria		
6/1/74	6	24		1 Midnight At The Oasis	David Nichtern...*Any Old Time*	Reprise 1183
				MULLINS, Shawn		
1/16/99	7	18		1 Lullaby	Shawn Mullins...*The Gulf Of Mexico*	Columbia 79080
				MUMBA, Samantha		
12/9/00	4	22		1 Gotta Tell You	Anders Bagge/Arnthor Birgisson/Samantha Mumba	Wild Card 497408
				MUNGO JERRY		
9/12/70	3[1]	13	●	1 In The Summertime	Ray Dorset...*Mighty Man*	Janus 125
				MURMAIDS, The		
1/11/64	3[2]	14		1 Popsicles And Icicles	David Gates...*Huntington Flats*	Chattahoochee 628
				MURPHEY, Michael		
6/21/75	3[2]	19	▲	1 Wildfire	Larry Cansler/Michael Murphey...*Night Thunder*	Epic 50084
				MURPHY, Eddie		
12/28/85	2[3]	22	▲	1 Party All The Time	Rick James	Columbia 05609
				MURPHY, Walter		
10/9/76	❶[1]	28	●	1 A Fifth Of Beethoven WALTER MURPHY & THE BIG APPLE BAND	Walter Murphy...*California Strut* [I]	Private Stock 45,073
				MURRAY, Anne		
9/26/70	8	16	●	1 Snowbird	Gene MacLellan...*Just Bidin' My Time*	Capitol 2738
4/14/73	7	18		2 Danny's Song	Kenny Loggins...*Drown Me*	Capitol 3481
7/13/74	8	20		3 You Won't See Me	John Lennon/Paul McCartney...*He Thinks I Still Care*	Capitol 3867
11/4/78	❶[1]	26	●	4 You Needed Me	Randy Goodrum...*I Still Wish The Very Best For You*	Capitol 4574
				MUSICAL YOUTH		
2/26/83	10	18		1 Pass The Dutchie	Lloyd Fergusson/Jackie Mittoo/Fitzroy Simpson...*Give Love A Chance*	MCA 52149
				MUSIC EXPLOSION, The		
7/8/67	2[2]	16	●	1 Little Bit O' Soul	Ken Hawker/John Shakespeare...*I See The Light*	Laurie 3380
				MYA		
5/16/98	6	20	●	1 It's All About Me MYA with Sisqo	Mark Andrews/Darryl Pearson	University 97024
12/2/00	2[3]	30		2 Case Of The Ex (Whatcha Gonna Do)	Traci Hale/Tab Nkhereanye/Christopher Stewart	University 97457
6/2/01	❶[5]	20		3 Lady Marmalade CHRISTINA AGUILERA, LIL' KIM, MYA and PINK	Bob Crewe/Kenny Nolan	Interscope 497066
				MY CHEMICAL ROMANCE		
1/20/07	9	26	△	1 Welcome To The Black Parade	Bob Bryar/Frank Iero/Ray Toro/Gerard Way/Mikey Way	Reprise
				MYLES, Alannah		
3/24/90	❶[2]	24	●	1 Black Velvet	David Tyson/Christopher Ward...*If You Want To*	Atlantic 88742
				MYSTIKAL		
2/24/01	❶[4]	26	●	1 Stutter JOE (Featuring Mystikal)	Ernest Dixon/Roy Hamilton	Jive 42870
10/5/02	10	23		2 Move B***h LUDACRIS feat. Mystikal and Infamous 2.0	Christopher Bridges/Craig Lawson/Bobby Sandimanie/Michael Tyler...*Keep It On The Hush*	Def Jam South 063949

PEAK DATE	PEAK POS	WKS CHR	GOLD	ARTIST / Song Title	Songwriter...B-side	Label & Number
				N		
				NAIM, Yael		
2/23/08	7	19	○	1 New Soul	Yael Naim	Tot Ou Tard
				NAKED EYES		
6/11/83	8	22		1 Always Something There To Remind Me	Burt Bacharach/Hal David...*The Time Is Now*	EMI America 8155
				NAPOLEON XIV		
8/13/66	3¹	6		1 They're Coming To Take Me Away, Ha-Haaa!	Jerry Samuels...*Yawa Em Ekat Ot Gnimoc Er'yeht! Aaah-Ah* [N]	Warner 5831
				NAS		
1/8/00	5	21	▲	1 Hot Boyz	Missy Elliott/Tim Mosley...*U Can't Resist* (w/**Juvenile** & **B.G.**)	Gold Mind 64029
				MISSY "MISDEMEANOR" ELLIOTT (Featuring Nas, Eve & Q-Tip)		
6/29/02	10	23		2 I'm Gonna Be Alright	Sam Barnes/Denzil Foster/Jay King/Jennifer Lopez/Thomas McElroy/Troy Oliver/J.C. Olivier/Mark Cory Rooney...*Alive* (Lopez)	Epic 79759
				JENNIFER LOPEZ Featuring Nas		
				NASH, Johnny		
11/9/68	5	15		1 Hold Me Tight	Johnny Nash...*Cupid*	JAD 207
11/4/72	❶⁴	20	●	2 I Can See Clearly Now	Johnny Nash...*How Good It Is*	Epic 10902
				NATE DOGG		
7/2/94	2³	20	▲	1 Regulate	Warren Griffin/Nathan Hale	Death Row 98280
				WARREN G. & NATE DOGG		
5/31/03	❶⁴	23		2 21 Questions	Jimmie Cameron/Vella Cameron/Curtis Jackson/Kevin Risto...*Many Men*	Shady 080739
				50 CENT Feat. Nate Dogg		
2/25/06	6	21		3 Shake That	Nathan Hale/Steven King/Marshall Mathers/Luis Resto	Shady
				EMINEM Featuring Nate Dogg		
				NATURAL SELECTION		
10/19/91	2²	21		1 Do Anything	Elliot Erickson/Frederick Thomas	EastWest 98724
				NATURAL SELECTION Featuring Niki Haris		
				NAUGHTON, David		
7/21/79	5	24	●	1 Makin' It	Dino Fekaris/Freddie Perren...*Still Makin' It*	RSO 916
				NAUGHTY BY NATURE		
11/9/91	6	21	▲²	1 O.P.P.	Vincent Brown/Anthony Criss/Kier Gist/Berry Gordy...*Wickedest Man Alive*	Tommy Boy 988
3/6/93	8	22	▲	2 Hip Hop Hooray	Vincent Brown/Anthony Criss/Kier Gist...*The Hood Comes First*	Tommy Boy 554
8/21/99	10	17	●	3 Jamboree	Vincent Brown/Anthony Criss/Kier Gist/Benny Golson...*On The Run*	Arista 13712
				NAUGHTY BY NATURE (Featuring Zhane)		
				NAZARETH		
3/13/76	8	23	●	1 Love Hurts	Boudleaux Bryant...*Hair Of The Dog*	A&M 1671
				NDEGEOCELLO, Me'Shell		
9/3/94	3²	42		1 Wild Night	Van Morrison...*Brothers (live)* (Mellencamp)	Mercury 858738
				JOHN MELLENCAMP & ME'SHELL NDEGEOCELLO		
				NELLY		
9/16/00	7	34	○	1 (Hot S**t) Country Grammar	Jason Epperson/Cornell Haynes	Fo' Reel 156800
6/23/01	3¹	29	○	2 Ride Wit Me	Jason Epperson/Cornell Haynes	Fo' Reel
				NELLY (Featuring City Spud)		
9/15/01	3⁵	29		3 Where The Party At	Brandon Casey/Brian Casey/Bryan Michael Cox/Jermaine Dupri/Cornell Haynes...*Let's Get Married* (w/Run of **Run-DMC**)	So So Def 79626
				JAGGED EDGE featuring Nelly		
4/6/02	5	20		4 Girlfriend	Wade J. Robson/Justin Timberlake...*Gone*	Jive 40013
				*NSYNC featuring Nelly		
6/29/02	❶⁷	26	○	5 Hot In Herre	Charles Brown/Cornell Haynes/Chad Hugo/Pharrell Williams	Fo' Reel 019279
8/17/02	❶¹⁰	29		6 Dilemma	Ryan Bowser/Kenny Gamble/Cornell Haynes/Antoine Macon/Bunny Sigler...*Air Force Ones* (w/Kyjuan, **Ali** & Murphy Lee)	Fo' Reel 019509
				NELLY Featuring Kelly Rowland		
1/4/03	3⁴	20		7 Air Force Ones	Robert Cleveland/Tohri Harper/Cornell Haynes/Ali Jones...*Dilemma*	Fo' Reel 019509
				NELLY Featuring Kyjuan, Ali and Murphy Lee		
9/6/03	❶⁴	30	○	8 Shake Ya Tailfeather	Jayson Bridges/Tohri Harper/Cornell Haynes/Varick Smith	Bad Boy
				NELLY/P. DIDDY/MURPHY LEE		
9/4/04	4	20	○	9 My Place	El DeBarge/Randy DeBarge/Randy Edelman/Kenny Gamble/Cornell Haynes/Leon Huff/Dorian Moore...*Flap Your Wings*	Derrty 003154
				NELLY Feat. Jaheim		
12/4/04	3¹	24	△	10 Over And Over	Jayson Bridges/Cornell Haynes	Derrty/Curb
				NELLY Featuring Tim McGraw		
7/30/05	9	20	○	11 Get It Poppin'	Joe Cartagena/Scott Storch	Terror Squad 93794
				FAT JOE (Feat. Nelly)		
1/21/06	❶²	28	△	12 Grillz	Jermaine Dupri/Cameron Gipp/Cornell Haynes/Ali Jones/James Phillips/Paul Slayton	Derrty 005897
				NELLY F/Paul Wall, Ali & Gipp		
10/23/10	3²	23↑	△	13 Just A Dream	David Harris/Damon Reinagle/James Scheffer	Derrty
				NELSON		
9/29/90	❶¹	26	●	1 (Can't Live Without Your) Love And Affection	Gunnar Nelson/Matthew Nelson/Marc Tanner...*Will You Love Me?*	DGC 19689
2/2/91	6	22		2 After The Rain	Gunnar Nelson/Matthew Nelson/Marc Tanner/Richard Wilson...*Fill You Up*	DGC 19667
				NELSON, Ricky		
6/3/57	4	17	⊙	1 I'm Walking	Dave Bartholomew/Fats Domino...*A Teenager's Romance*	Verve 10047
6/10/57	2¹	19	⊙	2 A Teenager's Romance	David Gillam...*I'm Walking*	Verve 10047
10/28/57	3¹	20	⊙	3 Be-Bop Baby	Pearl Lendhurst...*Have I Told You Lately That I Love You?*	Imperial 5463
1/13/58	2³	18	⊙	4 Stood Up	Willis Dickerson/Erma Herrold...*Waitin' In School*	Imperial 5483
4/21/58	4	12	⊙	5 Believe What You Say	Dorsey Burnette/Johnny Burnette...*My Bucket's Got A Hole In It*	Imperial 5503
8/4/58	❶²	15		6 Poor Little Fool	Sharon Sheeley...*Don't Leave Me This Way*	Imperial 5528
11/10/58	10	17		7 I Got A Feeling	Baker Knight...*Lonesome Town*	Imperial 5545
12/1/58	7	18	⊙	8 Lonesome Town	Baker Knight...*I Got A Feeling*	Imperial 5545
4/6/59	6	16		9 Never Be Anyone Else But You	Baker Knight...*It's Late*	Imperial 5565
4/6/59	9	13		10 It's Late	Dorsey Burnette...*Never Be Anyone Else But You*	Imperial 5565
8/3/59	9	12		11 Sweeter Than You	Baker Knight...*Just A Little Too Much*	Imperial 5595
8/17/59	9	13		12 Just A Little Too Much	Johnny Burnette...*Sweeter Than You*	Imperial 5595
5/22/61	9	15		13 Hello Mary Lou	Gene Pitney...*Travelin' Man*	Imperial 5741

PEAK DATE	PEAK POS	WKS CHR	GOLD	ARTIST / Song Title	Songwriter...B-side	Label & Number
				NELSON, Ricky (cont'd)		
5/29/61	❶²	16	●	14 Travelin' Man	Jerry Fuller...*Hello Mary Lou*	Imperial 5741
				RICK NELSON:		
4/21/62	5	13		15 Young World	Jerry Fuller...*Summertime*	Imperial 5805
9/22/62	5	11		16 Teen Age Idol	Jack Lewis...*I've Got My Eyes On You (And I Like What I See)*	Imperial 5864
2/2/63	6	12		17 It's Up To You	Jerry Fuller...*I Need You*	Imperial 5901
2/15/64	6	11		18 For You	Joe Burke/Al Dubin...*That's All She Wrote*	Decca 31574
11/4/72	6	19	●	19 Garden Party	Rick Nelson...*So Long Mama*	Decca 32980
				RICK NELSON & THE STONE CANYON BAND		
				NELSON, Sandy		
10/19/59	4	16		1 Teen Beat	Arthur Egnoian/Sandy Nelson...*Big Jump* [I]	Original Sound 5
12/18/61	7	16		2 Let There Be Drums	Sandy Nelson/Richie Podolor...*Quite A Beat!* [I]	Imperial 5775
				NELSON, Willie		
6/12/82	5	23	▲	1 Always On My Mind	Wayne Carson/Johnny Christopher/Mark James...*The Party's Over*	Columbia 02741
5/19/84	5	21	▲	2 To All The Girls I've Loved Before	Hal David/Albert Hammond...*I Don't Want To Wake You* (Iglesias)	Columbia 04217
				JULIO IGLESIAS & WILLIE NELSON		
				NENA		
3/3/84	2¹	23	●	1 99 Luftballons	Carlo Karges/Joern Fahrenkrog Peterson...*99 Red Ballons* [F]	Epic 04108
				NERVOUS NORVUS		
6/23/56	8	14		1 Transfusion	Jimmy Drake...*Dig* [N]	Dot 15470
				NEVIL, Robbie		
1/17/87	2²	23		1 C'est La Vie	Mark Holding/Robbie Nevil/Duncan Pain...*Time Waits For No One*	Manhattan 50047
8/1/87	10	16		2 Wot's It To Ya	Robbie Nevil/Brock Walsh	Manhattan 50075
				NEVILLE, Aaron		
1/28/67	2¹	14		1 Tell It Like It Is	George Davis/Lee Diamond...*Why Worry*	Par-Lo 101
12/23/89	2²	26	●	2 Don't Know Much	Barry Mann/Tom Snow/Cynthia Weil...*Cry Like A Rainstorm* (Ronstadt)	Elektra 69261
				LINDA RONSTADT (featuring Aaron Neville)		
10/19/91	8	20		3 Everybody Plays The Fool	J.R. Bailey/Rudy Clark/Ken Williams...*House On A Hill*	A&M 1563
				NEWBEATS, The		
9/19/64	2²	12	◉	1 Bread And Butter	Larry Parks/Jay Turnbow...*Tough Little Buggy*	Hickory 1269
				NEW EDITION		
1/5/85	4	25	●	1 Cool It Now	Vincent Brantley/Rick Timas	MCA 52455
9/17/88	7	21		2 If It Isn't Love	Jimmy Jam Harris/Terry Lewis	MCA 53264
8/31/96	3¹	20	●	3 Hit Me Off	Dinky Bingham/Ronnie DeVoe/Jeff Dyson	MCA 55210
1/11/97	7	20	●	4 I'm Still In Love With You	Jimmy Jam Harris/Terry Lewis...*You Don't Have To Worry*	MCA 55264
				NEW KIDS ON THE BLOCK		
10/8/88	10	28		1 Please Don't Go Girl	Maurice Starr...*Whatcha Gonna Do About It*	Columbia 07700
3/11/89	3¹	26	●	2 You Got It (The Right Stuff)	Maurice Starr	Columbia 08092
6/17/89	❶¹	21	●	3 I'll Be Loving You (Forever)	Maurice Starr	Columbia 68671
9/9/89	❶¹	17	▲	4 Hangin' Tough	Maurice Starr...*Didn't I (Blow Your Mind)*	Columbia 68960
11/4/89	2¹	18	●	5 Cover Girl	Maurice Starr...*Merry, Merry Christmas*	Columbia 69088
11/18/89	8	19		6 Didn't I (Blow Your Mind)	Thom Bell/William Hart...*Hangin' Tough*	Columbia 68960
1/6/90	7	16		7 This One's For The Children	Maurice Starr...*Funky, Funky Xmas* [X]	Columbia 73064
6/30/90	❶³	15	▲	8 Step By Step	Maurice Starr...*Valentine Girl*	Columbia 73343
9/8/90	7	12		9 Tonight	Al Lancellotti/Maurice Starr...*Hold On*	Columbia 73461
				NEWMAN, Randy		
1/28/78	2³	20	●	1 Short People	Randy Newman...*Old Man On The Farm* [N]	Warner 8492
				NEW SEEKERS, The		
1/15/72	7	11	●	1 I'd Like To Teach The World To Sing (In Perfect Harmony)	Bill Backer/Roger Cook/Roquel Davis/Roger Greenaway...*Boom-Town*	Elektra 45762
				NEWTON, Juice		
5/2/81	4	22	●	1 Angel Of The Morning	Chip Taylor...*Headin' For A Heartache*	Capitol 4976
9/19/81	2²	27	●	2 Queen Of Hearts	Hank DeVito...*River Of Love*	Capitol 4997
2/13/82	7	24		3 The Sweetest Thing (I've Ever Known)	Otha Young...*Ride 'Em Cowboy*	Capitol 5046
7/10/82	7	17		4 Love's Been A Little Bit Hard On Me	Gary Burr...*Ever True*	Capitol 5120
				NEWTON, Wayne		
8/5/72	4	20	●	1 Daddy Don't You Walk So Fast	Peter Callander/Geoff Stephens...*Echo Valley 2-6809*	Chelsea 0100
				NEWTON-JOHN, Olivia		
2/9/74	6	19	●	1 Let Me Be There	John Rostill...*Maybe Then I'll Think Of You*	MCA 40101
6/29/74	5	20	●	2 If You Love Me (Let Me Know)	John Rostill...*Brotherly Love*	MCA 40209
10/5/74	❶²	15	●	3 I Honestly Love You	Peter Allen/Jeff Barry...*Home Ain't Home Anymore*	MCA 40280
3/8/75	❶¹	16	●	4 Have You Never Been Mellow	John Farrar...*Water Under The Bridge*	MCA 40349
8/9/75	3²	15	●	5 Please Mr. Please	John Rostill/Bruce Welch...*And In The Morning*	MCA 40418
6/10/78	❶¹	24	▲	6 You're The One That I Want	John Farrar...*Alone At A Drive-In Movie*	RSO 891
				JOHN TRAVOLTA AND OLIVIA NEWTON-JOHN		
9/23/78	3²	19	●	7 Hopelessly Devoted To You	John Farrar...*Love Is A Many Splendored Thing*	RSO 903
9/30/78	5	16	●	8 Summer Nights	Warren Casey/Jim Jacobs...*Rock 'N' Roll Party Queen* (Louis St. Louis)	RSO 906
				JOHN TRAVOLTA, OLIVIA NEWTON-JOHN & CAST		
2/17/79	3²	20	●	9 A Little More Love	John Farrar...*Borrowed Time*	MCA 40975
8/2/80	❶⁴	23	●	10 Magic	John Farrar...*Fool Country*	MCA 41247
10/11/80	8	17		11 Xanadu	Jeff Lynne...*Whenever You're Away From Me* (Newton-John & Gene Kelly)	MCA 41285
				OLIVIA NEWTON-JOHN/ELECTRIC LIGHT ORCHESTRA		
11/21/81	❶¹⁰	26	▲	12 Physical	Steve Kipner/Terry Shaddick...*The Promise (The Dolphin Song)*	MCA 51182
4/3/82	5	14		13 Make A Move On Me	John Farrar/Tom Snow...*Falling*	MCA 52000
11/6/82	3⁴	21		14 Heart Attack	Paul Bliss/Steve Kipner...*Stranger's Touch*	MCA 52100
1/7/84	5	18		15 Twist Of Fate	Peter Beckett/Steve Kipner...*Take A Chance* (w/John Travolta)	MCA 52284

PEAK DATE	PEAK POS	WKS CHR	GOLD	ARTIST / Song Title	Songwriter...B-side	Label & Number
				NEW VAUDEVILLE BAND, The		
12/3/66	❶³	15	●	1 Winchester Cathedral	Geoff Stephens...*Wait For Me Baby*	Fontana 1562
				NEXT		
4/25/98	❶⁵	53	▲	1 Too Close	Raphael Brown/Robert Ford/Kier Gist/Robert Huggar/Darren Lighty/Denzil Miller/James Moore/Lawrence Smith/Kurt Walker...*Butta Love*	Arista 13456
9/9/00	7	21		2 Wifey	Ed Berkeley/Kier Gist/Robert Huggar	Arista 13881
				NE-YO		
3/18/06	❶²	25	○	1 So Sick	Mikkel Eriksen/Tor Erik Hermansen/Shaffer Smith...*Stay*	Def Jam 006190
9/23/06	7	22	○	2 Sexy Love	Mikkel Eriksen/Tor Erik Hermansen/Shaffer Smith	Def Jam 007342
5/19/07	2¹	20	○	3 Because Of You	Mikkel Eriksen/Tor Erik Hermansen/Shaffer Smith	Def Jam 008678
8/25/07	8	21		4 Make Me Better FABOLOUS Featuring Ne-Yo	John Jackson/Tim Mosley/Shaffer Smith	Desert Storm 009027
12/22/07	7	26	△	5 Hate That I Love You RIHANNA Featuring Ne-Yo	Mikkel Eriksen/Tor Erik Hermansen/Shaffer Smith	SRP/Def Jam
7/12/08	7	22	○	6 Bust It Baby Part 2 PLIES (Feat. Ne-Yo)	Shaffer Smith/Algernod Washington...*Who Hotter Than Me*	Slip n Slide 506620
9/27/08	7	39	△	7 Closer	Shaffer Smith	Def Jam 011222
12/13/08	7	28	△	8 Miss Independent	Mikkel Eriksen/Tor Erik Hermansen/Shaffer Smith	Def Jam 012111
6/20/09	3³	31		9 Knock You Down KERI HILSON Featuring Kanye West & Ne-Yo	Marcella Araica/Kevin Cossom/Floyd Nathaniel Hills/Keri Hilson/Shaffer Smith/Kanye West	Mosley
				NICHOLAS, Paul		
11/26/77	6	23	●	1 Heaven On The 7th Floor	Dominic Bugatti/Frank Musker...*Do You Want My Love*	RSO 878
				NICKELBACK		
12/22/01	❶⁴	49	○	1 How You Remind Me	Chad Kroeger/Mike Kroeger/Ryan Peake/Ryan Vikedal...*Leader Of Men*	Roadrunner 612053
2/14/04	7	50	○	2 Someday	Chad Kroeger/Mike Kroeger/Ryan Peake/Ryan Vikedal	Roadrunner
10/22/05	2¹	33	○	3 Photograph	Daniel Adair/Chad Kroeger/Mike Kroeger/Ryan Peake	Roadrunner
9/23/06	8	30		4 Far Away	Dan Adair/Chad Kroeger/Mike Kroeger/Ryan Peake	Roadrunner
9/22/07	6	49		5 Rockstar	Daniel Adair/Chad Kroeger/Mike Kroeger/Ryan Peake	Roadrunner
10/18/08	10	27		6 Gotta Be Somebody	Daniel Adair/Chad Kroeger/Mike Kroeger/Ryan Peake	Roadrunner
				NICKS, Stevie		
10/28/78	5	20		1 Whenever I Call You "Friend" KENNY LOGGINS (with Stevie Nicks)	Kenny Loggins/Melissa Manchester...*Angelique*	Columbia 10794
9/5/81	3⁶	21		2 Stop Draggin' My Heart Around STEVIE NICKS (with Tom Petty and The Heartbreakers)	Mike Campbell/Tom Petty...*Kind Of Woman* (Nicks)	Modern 7336
1/23/82	6	19		3 Leather And Lace STEVIE NICKS (with Don Henley)	Stevie Nicks...*Bella Donna* (Nicks)	Modern 7341
8/20/83	5	19		4 Stand Back	Stevie Nicks...*Garbo*	Modern 99863
1/25/86	4	18		5 Talk To Me	Charles Sandford...*One More Big Time Rock And Roll Star*	Modern 99582
				NICOLE		
8/1/98	5	23	●	1 Make It Hot NICOLE Featuring Missy "Misdemeanor" Elliott and Mocha	Missy Elliott	Gold Mind 64110
				NIESEN, Gertrude		
3/10/45	10	1		1 I Wanna Get Married	Phil Charig/Milton Pascal/Dan Shapiro...*Twelve O'Clock And All Is Well*	Decca 23382
				NIGHTINGALE, Maxine		
5/1/76	2²	20	●	1 Right Back Where We Started From	Vincent Edwards/Pierre Tubbs...*Believe In What You Do*	United Artists 752
9/15/79	5	23	●	2 Lead Me On	David Lasley/Allee Willis...*Love Me Like You Mean It*	Windsong 11530
				NIGHT RANGER		
6/9/84	5	24		1 Sister Christian	Kelly Keagy...*Chippin' Away*	MCA/Camel 52350
7/27/85	8	17		2 Sentimental Street	Jack Blades...*Night Machine*	MCA/Camel 52591
				NILSSON		
10/11/69	6	12		1 Everybody's Talkin'	Fred Neil...*Rainmaker*	RCA Victor 0161
2/19/72	❶⁴	19	●	2 Without You	Tom Evans/Pete Ham...*Gotta Get Up*	RCA Victor 0604
8/26/72	8	14		3 Coconut	Harry Nilsson...*Down* [N]	RCA Victor 0718
				NINA SKY		
8/7/04	4	26	○	1 Move Ya Body NINA SKY feat. Jabba	Natalie Albino/Nicole Albino/Lionel Bermingham/Cordell Burrell/Luis Diaz/Elijah Wells...*In A Dream*	J-Time 002570
				NINEDAYS		
7/22/00	6	27		1 Absolutely (Story Of A Girl)	John Hampson...*If I Am*	550 Music 79532
				1910 FRUITGUM CO.		
3/9/68	4	14	●	1 Simon Says	Elliot Chiprut...*Reflections From The Looking Glass*	Buddah 24
9/14/68	5	13	●	2 1, 2, 3, Red Light	Bobbi Trimachi/Sal Trimachi...*Sticky, Sticky*	Buddah 54
3/22/69	5	13	●	3 Indian Giver	Bobby Bloom/Ritchie Cordell/Bo Gentry...*Pow Wow*	Buddah 91
				98°		
11/21/98	3¹	20	▲	1 Because Of You	Anders Bagge/Arnthor Birgisson/Christian Karlsson/Patrick Tucker...*True To Your Heart* (w/Stevie Wonder)	Motown 860830
7/3/99	5	24	●	2 The Hardest Thing	David Frank/Steve Kipner...*Because Of You / Invisible Man*	Universal 156246
2/19/00	❶¹	20	●	3 Thank God I Found You MARIAH with Joe & 98°	Mariah Carey/James Harris III/Terry Lewis	Columbia 79338
9/30/00	2²	20	●	4 Give Me Just One Night (Una Noche)	Anders Bagge/Arnthor Birgisson/Claudia Ogalde...*(Spanish version)*	Universal 153296
				NIRVANA		
1/11/92	6	20	▲	1 Smells Like Teen Spirit	Kurt Cobain/Dave Grohl/Chris Novoselic...*Even In His Youth*	DGC 19050
				NITTY GRITTY DIRT BAND		
2/20/71	9	19		1 Mr. Bojangles	Jerry Jeff Walker...*Uncle Charlie Interview #2/Spanish Fandango*	Liberty 56197
				NIVEA		
12/21/02	8	36		1 Don't Mess With My Man NIVEA Featuring Brian & Brandon Casey of Jagged Edge	Brandon Casey/Brian Casey/Bryan Michael Cox	Jive 40041

PEAK DATE	PEAK POS	WKS CHR	GOLD	ARTIST / Song Title ... Songwriter...B-side	Label & Number
				NOBLE, Ray, and his Orchestra	
5/10/47	❶²	23	☉	1 Linda .... Jack Lawrence...*Love Is A Random Thing*	Columbia 37215
1/17/48	3¹	15		2 I'll Dance At Your Wedding .... Herb Magidson/Ben Oakland...*Those Things Money Can't Buy*	Columbia 37967
				RAY NOBLE and his ORCHESTRA with BUDDY CLARK (above 2)	
				NOBLES, Cliff, & Co.	
6/29/68	2³	14	●	1 The Horse .... Jesse James...*Love Is All Right* [I]	Phil-L.A. of Soul 313
				NO DOUBT	
12/7/96	❶¹⁶	63		1 Don't Speak .... Eric Stefani/Gwen Stefani	Trauma
3/2/02	5	20		2 Hey Baby .... Tom Dumont/Tony Kanal/Rodney Price/Gwen Stefani	Interscope
				NO DOUBT Featuring Bounty Killer	
11/23/02	3²	30		3 Underneath It All .... Gwen Stefani/David A. Stewart...*Hella Good / Hey Baby*	Interscope 497768
				NO DOUBT featuring Lady Saw	
1/31/04	10	28	○	4 It's My Life .... Tim Friese-Greene/Mark Hollis	Interscope
				NOLAN, Kenny	
3/12/77	3¹	27	●	1 I Like Dreamin' .... Kenny Nolan...*Time Ain't Time Enough*	20th Century 2287
				NO MERCY	
10/12/96	5	39	●	1 Where Do You Go .... Peter Bischof-Fallenstein/Franz Reuter	Arista 13225
				N.O.R.E.	
8/10/02	10	24		1 Nothin' .... Chad Hugo/Victor Santiago/Pharrell Williams...*Nahmeanuheard*	Def Jam 582914
				NOTORIOUS B.I.G., The	
3/18/95	6	24	▲	1 Big Poppa .... Christopher Wallace...*Warning*	Bad Boy 79015
7/15/95	2³	20		2 One More Chance/Stay With Me .... Christopher Wallace...*The What*	Bad Boy 79031
5/3/97	❶³	20		3 Hypnotize .... Deric Angelettie/Andy Armer/Randy Badazz/Sean Combs/Ron Lawrence/Christopher Wallace...*I Got A Story To Tell*	Bad Boy 79092
8/30/97	❶²	30		4 Mo Money Mo Problems .... Mason Betha/Sean Combs/Bernard Edwards/Steve Jordan/Nile Rodgers/Christopher Wallace	Bad Boy 79100
				THE NOTORIOUS B.I.G. Featuring Puff Daddy & Ma$e	
1/3/98	2²	6	▲	5 It's All About The Benjamins .... Deric Angelettie/Sean Combs/Sean Jacobs/Kim Jones/Jayson Phillips/David Styles/Christopher Wallace...*Been Around The World* (Puff Daddy)	Bad Boy 79130
				PUFF DADDY & THE FAMILY Feat. The Notorious B.I.G./Lil' Kim/The Lox/Dave Grohl/Perfect/FuzzBubble/Rob Zombie	
1/24/98	4	15		6 Been Around The World .... Mason Betha/David Bowie/Sean Combs/Ian Devaney/Andy Morris/Lisa Stansfield/Christopher Wallace...*It's All About The Benjamins*	Bad Boy 79130
				PUFF DADDY & THE FAMILY Featuring The Notorious B.I.G. & Ma$e	
				***NSYNC**	
2/27/99	8	22		1 (God Must Have Spent) A Little More Time On You .... Evan Rogers/Carl Sturken...*Sailing (live)*	RCA 65685
10/16/99	2¹	20	●	2 Music Of My Heart .... Diane Warren	Miramax/Epic 79245
				*NSYNC and GLORIA ESTEFAN	
1/22/00	5	29		3 Bring It All To Me .... Billy Lawrence/Leshan Lewis/Mark Cory Rooney/William Shelby/Violet Smith/Kevin Spencer/Nidra Sylvers/Linda Van Horssen	Track Masters
				BLAQUE (Feat. *NSYNC)	
4/15/00	4	23		4 Bye Bye Bye .... Andreas Carlsson/Kristian Lundin/Jake Schulze	Jive 42681
7/29/00	❶²	25	●	5 It's Gonna Be Me .... Andreas Carlsson/Rami Carlsson/Max Martin	Jive 42664
12/2/00	5	26		6 This I Promise You .... Richard Marx	Jive 42746
4/6/02	5	20		7 Girlfriend .... Wade J. Robson/Justin Timberlake...*Gone*	Jive 40013
				*NSYNC featuring Nelly	
				NUMAN, Gary	
6/7/80	9	25		1 Cars .... Gary Numan...*Metal*	Atco 7211
				NU SHOOZ	
6/14/86	3¹	23	●	1 I Can't Wait .... John Smith...*Make Your Mind Up*	Atlantic 89446

O

PEAK DATE	PEAK POS	WKS CHR	GOLD	ARTIST / Song Title ... Songwriter...B-side	Label & Number
				OAK RIDGE BOYS	
7/25/81	5	22	▲	1 Elvira .... Dallas Frazier...*A Woman Like You*	MCA 51084
				OASIS	
3/9/96	8	20	○	1 Wonderwall .... Noel Gallagher...*Talk Tonight / Round Are Way*	Epic 78216
				OCEAN	
5/1/71	2¹	14	●	1 Put Your Hand In The Hand .... Gene MacLellan...*Tear Down The Fences*	Kama Sutra 519
				OCEAN, Billy	
11/3/84	❶²	26	●	1 Caribbean Queen (No More Love On The Run) .... Keith Diamond/Billy Ocean	Jive 9199
2/23/85	2¹	21		2 Loverboy .... Keith Diamond/Mutt Lange/Billy Ocean	Jive 9284
6/8/85	4	22		3 Suddenly .... Keith Diamond/Billy Ocean...*Lucky Man*	Jive 9323
2/15/86	2¹	23		4 When The Going Gets Tough, The Tough Get Going .... Wayne Brathwaite/Barry Eastmond/Mutt Lange/Billy Ocean	Jive 9432
7/5/86	❶¹	21		5 There'll Be Sad Songs (To Make You Cry) .... Wayne Brathwaite/Barry Eastmond/Billy Ocean...*If I Should Lose You*	Jive 9465
9/27/86	10	16		6 Love Zone .... Wayne Brathwaite/Barry Eastmond/Billy Ocean	Jive 9510
4/9/88	❶²	20		7 Get Outta My Dreams, Get Into My Car .... Mutt Lange/Billy Ocean...*Showdown*	Jive 9678
				O'CONNELL, Helen	
1/26/52	8	13		1 Slow Poke .... Pee Wee King/Chilton Price/Redd Stewart...*I Wanna Play House With You*	Capitol 1837
				O'CONNOR, Sinead	
4/21/90	❶⁴	21	▲	1 Nothing Compares 2 U .... Prince...*Jump In The River*	Ensign/Chrysalis 23488
				O'DAY, Alan	
7/9/77	❶¹	25	●	1 Undercover Angel .... Alan O'Day...*Just You*	Pacific 001
				O'DONIS, Colby	
1/17/09	❶³	49	△⁴	1 Just Dance .... Stefani Germanotta/Nadir Khayat/Aliaune Thiam	Streamline 011524
				LADY GAGA Featuring Colby O'Donis	

PEAK DATE	PEAK POS	WKS CHR	GOLD	ARTIST / Song Title	Songwriter...B-side	Label & Number
				OHIO EXPRESS		
6/15/68	4	14	●	1 Yummy Yummy Yummy	Joey Levine/Artie Resnick...*Zig Zag*	Buddah 38
				OHIO PLAYERS		
2/8/75	❶[1]	17	●	1 Fire	William Beck/Leroy Bonner/Marshall Jones/Ralph Middlebrook/Marvin Pierce/Clarence Satchell/Jimmy Williams...*Together*	Mercury 73643
1/31/76	❶[1]	16	●	2 Love Rollercoaster	William Beck/Leroy Bonner/Marshall Jones/Ralph Middlebrook/Marvin Pierce/Clarence Satchell/Jimmy Williams...*It's All Over*	Mercury 73734
				O'JAYS, The		
10/7/72	3[1]	15	●	1 Back Stabbers	Leon Huff/Gene McFadden/John Whitehead...*Sunshine*	Philadelphia I. 3517
3/24/73	❶[1]	14	●	2 Love Train	Kenny Gamble/Leon Huff...*Who Am I*	Philadelphia I. 3524
3/2/74	10	16	●	3 Put Your Hands Together	Kenny Gamble/Leon Huff...*You Got Your Hooks In Me*	Philadelphia I. 3535
6/15/74	9	16	●	4 For The Love Of Money	Kenny Gamble/Leon Huff/Anthony Jackson...*People Keep Tellin' Me*	Philadelphia I. 3544
1/24/76	5	17	●	5 I Love Music (Part 1)	Kenny Gamble/Leon Huff...*(Part II)*	Philadelphia I. 3577
7/8/78	4	19	●	6 Use Ta Be My Girl	Kenny Gamble/Leon Huff...*This Time Baby*	Philadelphia I. 3642
				O'KAYSIONS, The		
10/5/68	5	14	●	1 Girl Watcher	Buck Trail...*Deal Me In*	ABC 11094
				O'KEEFE, Danny		
11/4/72	9	13		1 Good Time Charlie's Got The Blues	Danny O'Keefe...*The Valentine Pieces*	Signpost 70006
				OKLAHOMA! Original Cast Album		
12/18/43	9	2	⊙	1 Oklahoma!	Oscar Hammerstein/Richard Rodgers	Decca 359
				OLDFIELD, Mike		
5/11/74	7	16		1 Tubular Bells	Mike Oldfield [I]	Virgin 55100
				OLIVER		
7/12/69	3[2]	13	⊙	1 Good Morning Starshine	Galt MacDermot/James Rado/Gerome Ragni...*Can't You See*	Jubilee 5659
10/4/69	2[2]	14	●	2 Jean	Rod McKuen...*The Arrangement*	Crewe 334
				OLIVIA		
3/5/05	❶[9]	23	○	1 Candy Shop	Curtis Jackson/Scott Storch	Shady
				50 CENT Featuring Olivia		
				OLLIE & JERRY		
8/4/84	9	18		1 Breakin'...There's No Stopping Us	Ollie Brown/Jerry Knight...*Showdown*	Polydor 821708
				OLYMPICS, The		
9/15/58	8	14		1 Western Movies	Cliff Goldsmith/Fred Smith...*Well!* [N]	Demon 1508
				OMARION		
8/13/05	4	24	○	1 Let Me Hold You	Jermaine Dupri/Brenda Russell/Ernest Wilson	Columbia 74625
				BOW WOW Featuring Omarion		
				OMC		
7/26/97	4	51		1 How Bizarre	Pauly Fuemana/Alan Jansson	Mercury
				100 PROOF AGED IN SOUL		
11/14/70	8	14	●	1 Somebody's Been Sleeping	Angelo Bond/General Johnson/Greg Perry...*I've Come To Save You*	Hot Wax 7004
				ONEREPUBLIC		
11/10/07	2[4]	47	△[3]	1 Apologize	Ryan Tedder	Mosley
				TIMBALAND Featuring OneRepublic		
				112		
6/14/97	❶[11]	33	▲[3]	1 I'll Be Missing You	Sean Combs/Faith Evans/Sting...*We'll Always Love Big Poppa* (The Lox) / *Cry On* (112)	Bad Boy 79097
				PUFF DADDY & FAITH EVANS (Featuring 112)		
11/22/97	4	25	●	2 All Cried Out	Curtis Bedeau/Gerard Charles/Hugh Clarke/Brian George/Lucien George/Paul George...*Head Over Heels* (w/Tone & AZ)	Crave 78678
				ALLURE Featuring 112		
3/17/01	6	20		3 It's Over Now	Melvin Glover/Daron Jones/Michael Keith/Quinnes Parker/Sylvia Robinson/Marvin Scandrick	Bad Boy 79366
7/7/01	4	29		4 Peaches & Cream	Jason Boyd/Sean Combs/Daron Jones/Michael Keith/Quinnes Parker/Courtney Sills/Mario Winans...*Dance With Me*	Bad Boy 79387
				ONYX		
8/21/93	4	20	▲	1 Slam	Kirk Jones/Chylow Parker/Fred Scruggs/Tyrone Taylor	JMJ/RAL 77053
				ORBISON, Roy		
7/25/60	2[1]	21	⊙	1 Only The Lonely (Know The Way I Feel)	Joe Melson/Roy Orbison...*Here Comes That Song Again*	Monument 421
11/7/60	9	14		2 Blue Angel	Joe Melson/Roy Orbison...*Today's Teardrops*	Monument 425
6/5/61	❶[1]	17	⊙	3 Running Scared	Joe Melson/Roy Orbison...*Love Hurts*	Monument 438
10/9/61	2[1]	16	⊙	4 Crying	Joe Melson/Roy Orbison...*Candy Man*	Monument 447
3/31/62	4	12		5 Dream Baby (How Long Must I Dream)	Cindy Walker...*The Actress*	Monument 456
3/30/63	7	13		6 In Dreams	Roy Orbison...*Shahdaroba*	Monument 806
11/2/63	5	13		7 Mean Woman Blues	Claude DeMetrius...*Blue Bayou*	Monument 824
5/23/64	9	11		8 It's Over	Bill Dees/Roy Orbison...*Indian Wedding*	Monument 837
9/26/64	❶[3]	15		9 Oh, Pretty Woman	Bill Dees/Roy Orbison...*Yo Te Amo Maria*	Monument 851
				ROY ORBISON And The Candy Men		
4/15/89	9	18		10 You Got It	Jeff Lynne/Roy Orbison/Tom Petty...*The Only One*	Virgin 99245
				ORCHESTRAL MANOEUVRES IN THE DARK		
5/31/86	4	20		1 If You Leave	Martin H. Cooper/Malcolm Holmes/Paul Humphreys/Andrew McCluskey...*La Femme Accident*	A&M 2811
				ORLANDO, Tony (& DAWN)		
				DAWN:		
10/3/70	3[2]	18	●	1 Candida	Irwin Levine/Toni Wine...*Look At...*	Bell 903
1/23/71	❶[3]	18	●	2 Knock Three Times	L. Russell Brown/Irwin Levine...*Home*	Bell 938
				DAWN Featuring Tony Orlando:		
4/21/73	❶[4]	23	●	3 Tie A Yellow Ribbon Round The Ole Oak Tree	L. Russell Brown/Irwin Levine...*I Can't Believe How Much I Love You*	Bell 45,318
9/15/73	3[1]	16	●	4 Say, Has Anybody Seen My Sweet Gypsy Rose	L. Russell Brown/Irwin Levine...*The Spark Of Love Is Kindlin'*	Bell 45,374

PEAK DATE	PEAK POS	WKS CHR	GOLD	ARTIST / Song Title	Songwriter...B-side	Label & Number
				TONY ORLANDO & DAWN:		
10/26/74	7	13		5 Steppin' Out (Gonna Boogie Tonight)..	L. Russell Brown/Irwin Levine...*She Can't Hold A Candle To You*	Bell 45,601
5/3/75	❶³	14	●	6 He Don't Love You (Like I Love You)..	Jerry Butler/Calvin Carter/Curtis Mayfield...*Pick It Up*	Elektra 45240
				ORLEANS		
10/18/75	6	18	●	1 Dance With Me..	Johanna Hall/John Hall...*Ending Of A Song*	Asylum 45261
10/23/76	5	18	●	2 Still The One..	Johanna Hall/John Hall...*Siam Sam*	Asylum 45336
				ORLONS, The		
7/21/62	2²	14	◉	1 The Wah Watusi..	Dave Appell/Kal Mann...*Holiday Hill*	Cameo 218
12/8/62	4	15		2 Don't Hang Up..	Dave Appell/Kal Mann...*The Conservative*	Cameo 231
4/13/63	3¹	13		3 South Street..	Dave Appell/Kal Mann...*Them Terrible Boots*	Cameo 243
				OSBORNE, Joan		
2/3/96	4	22	●	1 One Of Us..	Eric Bazilian...*Dracula Moon*	Blue Gorilla 852368
				OSBOURNE, Ozzy		
6/17/89	8	25	●	1 Close My Eyes Forever..	Lita Ford/Ozzy Osbourne...*Under The Gun* (Ford)	RCA 8899
				LITA FORD (with Ozzy Osbourne)		
				OSMOND, Donny		
6/5/71	7	16	●	1 Sweet And Innocent..	Rick Hall/Billy Sherrill...*Flirtin'*	MGM 14227
9/11/71	❶³	15	●	2 Go Away Little Girl..	Gerry Goffin/Carole King...*The Wild Rover (Time To Ride)*	MGM 14285
1/15/72	9	10		3 Hey Girl..	Gerry Goffin/Carole King...*I Knew You When*	MGM 14322
4/1/72	3¹	12		4 Puppy Love..	Paul Anka...*Let My People Go*	MGM 14367
4/28/73	8	13		5 The Twelfth Of Never..	Jerry Livingston/Paul Francis Webster...*Life Is Just What You Make It*	MGM/Kolob 14503
6/3/89	2¹	18		6 Soldier Of Love..	Evan Rogers/Carl Sturken...*My Secret Touch*	Capitol 44369
				OSMOND, Donny And Marie		
9/14/74	4	15	●	1 I'm Leaving It (All) Up To You..	Don Harris/Dewey Terry...*The Umbrella Song*	MGM/Kolob 14735
1/25/75	8	16		2 Morning Side Of The Mountain..	Dick Manning/Larry Stock...*One Of These Days*	MGM/Kolob 14765
				OSMOND, Marie		
11/3/73	5	16	●	1 Paper Roses..	Fred Spielman/Janice Torre...*Least Of All You*	MGM/Kolob 14609
				OSMONDS, The		
2/13/71	❶⁵	15	●	1 One Bad Apple..	George Jackson...*He Ain't Heavy...He's My Brother*	MGM 14193
10/16/71	3³	13		2 Yo-Yo..	Joe South...*Keep On My Side*	MGM 14295
3/4/72	4	14		3 Down By The Lazy River..	Alan Osmond/Merrill Osmond...*He's The Light Of The World*	MGM 14324
10/19/74	10	13		4 Love Me For A Reason..	Johnny Bristol/Wade Brown/Dave Jones...*Fever*	MGM/Kolob 14746
				O'SULLIVAN, Gilbert		
7/29/72	❶⁶	18	●	1 Alone Again (Naturally)..	Gilbert O'Sullivan...*Save It*	MAM 3619
12/30/72	2²	16	●	2 Clair..	Gilbert O'Sullivan...*Ooh-Wakka-Doo-Wakka-Day*	MAM 3626
8/18/73	7	15	●	3 Get Down..	Gilbert O'Sullivan...*A Very Extraordinary Sort Of Girl*	MAM 3629
				OTIS, Johnny, Show		
8/4/58	9	16		1 Willie And The Hand Jive..	Johnny Otis...*Ring-A-Ling*	Capitol 3966
				O-TOWN		
1/6/01	10	12		1 Liquid Dreams..	Michael Norfleet/Quincy Patrick/Bradley Spalter/Joshua Thompson...*All For Love*	J Records 21001
7/28/01	3¹	20		2 All Or Nothing..	Wayne Hector/Steve Mac...*Liquid Dreams / Take Me Under (live) / We Fit Together*	J Records 21056
				OUTFIELD, The		
5/10/86	6	22		1 Your Love..	John Spinks...*61 Seconds*	Columbia 05796
				OUTKAST		
2/17/01	❶¹	23	○	1 Ms. Jackson..	Andre Benjamin/Antwan Patton/David Sheats...*Sole Sunday* (w/Goodie Mob)	LaFace 24525
12/13/03	❶⁹	32	△	2 Hey Ya!..	Andre Benjamin...*The Way You Move*	Arista 54962
2/14/04	❶¹	39	○	3 The Way You Move..	Patrick Brown/Carlton Mahone/Antwan Patton...*Hey Ya!*	Arista 54962
				OUTKAST Featuring Sleepy Brown		
6/19/04	9	21	○	4 Roses..	Andre Benjamin/Matt Boykin/Antwan Patton	Arista 57551
				OUTSIDERS, The		
4/16/66	5	15		1 Time Won't Let Me..	Chet Kelley/Tom King...*Was It Really Real*	Capitol 5573
				OWEN, Reg, And His Orchestra		
2/9/59	10	16		1 Manhattan Spiritual..	Billy Maxted...*Ritual Blues* [I]	Palette 5005
				OWENS, Jack		
12/6/47	2¹	20		1 How Soon (Will I Be Seeing You)..	Carroll Lucas/Jack Owens...*Begin The Beguine*	Tower 1258
				OWL CITY		
11/7/09	❶²	31	△³	1 Fireflies..	Adam Young	Universal Republic
				OZARK MOUNTAIN DAREDEVILS		
5/17/75	3²	21		1 Jackie Blue..	Steve Cash/Larry Lee...*Better Days*	A&M 1654

P

PEAK DATE	PEAK POS	WKS CHR	GOLD	ARTIST / Song Title	Songwriter...B-side	Label & Number
				PABLO, Petey		
7/3/04	7	39	○	1 Freek-A-Leek..	Moses Barrett/Corey Evans/Jonathan Smith	Jive 58745
9/11/04	❶⁷	38	○	2 Goodies..	Sean Garrett/Ciara Harris/La Marquis Jefferson/Craig Love/Jonathan Smith	LaFace 57550
				CIARA featuring Petey Pablo		
				PABLO CRUISE		
8/20/77	6	26		1 Whatcha Gonna Do?..	Dave Jenkins/Cory Lerios...*Atlanta June*	A&M 1920
8/26/78	6	18		2 Love Will Find A Way..	Dave Jenkins/Cory Lerios...*Always Be Together*	A&M 2048

PEAK DATE	PEAK POS	WKS CHR	GOLD	ARTIST / Song Title	Songwriter...B-side	Label & Number
				PAGE, Patti		
7/22/50	8	9		1 I Don't Care If The Sun Don't Shine	Mack David...*I'm Gonna Paper All My Walls With Love Letters*	Mercury 5396
10/28/50	❶⁵	23	⊙	2 All My Love (Bolero)	Henri Contet/Paul Durand/Mitchell Parish...*Roses Remind Me Of You*	Mercury 5455
12/16/50	❶¹³	26	⊙	3 The Tennessee Waltz	Pee Wee King/Redd Stewart...*Long Long Ago*	Mercury 5534
3/24/51	4	19		4 Would I Love You (Love You, Love You)	Bob Russell/Harold Spina...*Sentimental Music*	Mercury 5571
5/12/51	2¹	22		5 Mockin' Bird Hill	Vaughn Horton...*I Love You Because*	Mercury 5595
6/30/51	8	14		6 Mister And Mississippi	Irving Gordon...*These Things I Offer You*	Mercury 5645
9/29/51	5	16		7 Detour	Paul Westmoreland...*Who's Gonna Shoe My Pretty Little Feet*	Mercury 5682
11/10/51	4	14		8 And So To Sleep Again	Joe Marsala/Sunny Skylar...*One Sweet Letter*	Mercury 5706
3/1/52	9	11		9 Come What May	Vaughn Horton...*Retreat (Cries My Heart)*	Mercury 5772
8/23/52	9	11		10 Once In Awhile	Michael Edwards/Bud Green...*I'm Glad You're Happy With Someone Else (But I'm Sorry It Couldn't Be Me)*	Mercury 5867
9/27/52	❶¹⁰	22	⊙	11 I Went To Your Wedding	Jessie Mae Robinson...*You Belong To Me*	Mercury 5899
9/27/52	4	17		12 You Belong To Me	Pee Wee King/Chilton Price/Redd Stewart...*I Went To Your Wedding*	Mercury 5899
1/10/53	4	13		13 Why Don't You Believe Me	Lew Douglas/King Laney/Leroy Rodde...*Conquest*	Mercury 70025
3/21/53	❶⁸	21	⊙	14 The Doggie In The Window	Bob Merrill...*My Jealous Eyes* [N]	Mercury 70070
8/29/53	10	11		15 Butterflies	Bob Merrill...*This Is My Song*	Mercury 70183
12/19/53	3⁶	19		16 Changing Partners	Larry Coleman/Joe Darion...*Where Did My Snowman Go*	Mercury 70260
5/22/54	2⁴	21	⊙	17 Cross Over The Bridge	Bennie Benjamin/George Weiss...*Johnny Guitar*	Mercury 70302
7/3/54	8	8		18 Steam Heat	Richard Adler/Jerry Ross...*Lonely Days*	Mercury 70380
9/11/54	10	11		19 What A Dream	Chuck Willis...*I Cried*	Mercury 70416
12/25/54	8	7		20 Let Me Go, Lover!	Jenny Lou Carson/Al Hill...*Hocus-Pocus*	Mercury 70511
8/11/56	2²	27	⊙	21 Allegheny Moon	Al Hoffman/Dick Manning...*The Strangest Romance*	Mercury 70878
7/29/57	3¹	23		22 Old Cape Cod	Alan Jeffreys/Claire Rothrock/Milt Yakus...*Wondering*	Mercury 71101
7/21/58	9	12		23 Left Right Out Of Your Heart (Hi Lee Hi Lo Hi Lup Up Up)	Mort Garson/Earl Shuman...*Longing To Hold You Again*	Mercury 71331
6/26/65	8	14		24 Hush, Hush, Sweet Charlotte	Mack David/Frank DeVol...*Longing To Hold You Again*	Columbia 43251
				PAGE, Tommy		
4/14/90	❶¹	18	●	1 I'll Be Your Everything	Jordan Knight/Tommy Page/Danny Wood...*I'm Falling In Love*	Sire 19959
				PAIGE, Jennifer		
9/5/98	3⁴	25	●	1 Crush	Kevin Clark/Berny Cosgrove/Andy Goldmark/Mark Mueller	Edel America 64024
				PALMER, Robert		
5/3/86	❶¹	22	●	1 Addicted To Love	Robert Palmer...*Let's Fall In Love Tonight*	Island 99570
11/8/86	2¹	22		2 I Didn't Mean To Turn You On	Jimmy Jam Harris/Terry Lewis...*Get It Through Your Heart*	Island 99537
9/10/88	2²	20		3 Simply Irresistible	Robert Palmer...*Nova*	EMI/Manhattan 50133
				PANIC AT THE DISCO		
8/26/06	7	37	△	1 I Write Sins Not Tragedies	Ryan Ross/Spencer Smith/Brendon Urie/Brent Wilson	Decaydance
				PAPERBOY		
4/24/93	10	30	▲	1 Ditty	Aaron Clarke/David Ferguson/John Ferguson/Mitchell Johnson	Next Plateau 357012
				PAPER LACE		
8/17/74	❶¹	17	●	1 The Night Chicago Died	Peter Callander/Mitch Murray...*Can You Get It When You Want It*	Mercury 73492
				PARAMORE		
6/5/10	2¹	30	△³	1 Airplanes	Jeremy Dussolliet/Justin Franks/Alexander Grant/Bobby Simmons/Timothy Sommers	RebelRock
				B.o.B. Featuring Hayley Williams Of Paramore		
				PARIS SISTERS, The		
10/30/61	5	15		1 I Love How You Love Me	Larry Kolber/Barry Mann...*All Through The Night*	Gregmark 6
				PARKER, Fess		
5/21/55	5	17	⊙	1 Ballad Of Davy Crockett	Tom Blackburn/George Bruns...*I Gave My Love (Riddle Song)*	Columbia 40449
				PARKER, Ray Jr. / Raydio		
				RAYDIO:		
4/15/78	8	21	●	1 Jack And Jill	Ray Parker Jr....*Get Down*	Arista 0283
8/18/79	9	22		2 You Can't Change That	Ray Parker Jr....*Rock On*	Arista 0399
				RAY PARKER JR. & RAYDIO:		
6/20/81	4	27		3 A Woman Needs Love (Just Like You Do)	Ray Parker Jr....*So Into You*	Arista 0592
				RAY PARKER JR.:		
6/12/82	4	21		4 The Other Woman	Ray Parker Jr....*Stay The Night*	Arista 0669
8/11/84	❶³	21	●	5 Ghostbusters	Ray Parker Jr.	Arista 9212
				PARKER, Robert		
6/18/66	7	14		1 Barefootin'	Robert Parker...*Let's Go Baby (Where The Action Is)*	Nola 721
				PARR, John		
9/7/85	❶²	22		1 St. Elmo's Fire (Man In Motion)	David Foster/John Parr...*One Love* (David Foster)	Atlantic 89541
				PARSONS, Alan, Project		
10/16/82	3³	25		1 Eye In The Sky	Alan Parsons/Eric Woolfson...*Gemini*	Arista 0696
				PARSONS, Bill — see BARE, Bobby		
				PARTON, Dolly		
1/14/78	3²	19	●	1 Here You Come Again	Barry Mann/Cynthia Weil...*Me And Little Andy*	RCA 11123
2/21/81	❶²	26	●	2 9 To 5	Dolly Parton...*Sing For The Common Man*	RCA 12133
10/29/83	❶²	25	▲	3 Islands In The Stream	Barry Gibb/Maurice Gibb/Robin Gibb...*I Will Always Love You* (Rogers)	RCA 13615
				KENNY ROGERS with Dolly Parton		
				PARTRIDGE FAMILY, The		
11/21/70	❶³	19	●	1 I Think I Love You	Tony Romeo...*Somebody Wants To Love You*	Bell 910
3/27/71	6	12	●	2 Doesn't Somebody Want To Be Wanted	Mike Appel/Jim Cretecos/Wes Farrell...*You Are Always On My Mind*	Bell 963
6/12/71	9	9	●	3 I'll Meet You Halfway	Wes Farrell/Gerry Goffin...*Morning Rider On The Road*	Bell 996

PEAK DATE	PEAK POS	WKS CHR	GOLD	ARTIST / Song Title ... Songwriter ... B-side	Label & Number
				PASTOR, Tony, and his Orchestra	
6/28/41	9	1		1 Maria Elena .... Lorenza Barcelata...*Made Up My Mind*	Bluebird 11127
12/9/44	9	10		2 Dance With A Dolly (With a Hole In Her Stocking) .... Jimmy Eaton/Mickey Leader/Terry Shand...*Don't Blame Me*	Bluebird 0827
5/26/45	2²	15		3 Bell Bottom Trousers .... Moe Jaffe...*Five Salted Peanuts*	Victor 1661
5/25/46	10	2		4 Sioux City Sue .... Ray Freedman/Dick Thomas...*Loop-De-Loo*	Cosmo 471
6/7/47	8	2		5 Red Silk Stockings And Green Perfume .... Bob Hilliard/Sammy Mysels/Dick Sanford...*Get Up Those Stairs, Mademoiselle*	Columbia 37330
8/23/47	10	7		6 The Lady From Twenty-Nine Palms .... Allie Wrubel...*I'm Sorry I Didn't Say I'm Sorry (When I Made You Cry Last Night)*	Columbia 37562
				PATIENCE & PRUDENCE	
10/6/56	4	25		1 Tonight You Belong To Me .... Lee David/Billy Rose...*A Smile And A Ribbon* (Prudence)	Liberty 55022
				PAUL, Billy	
12/16/72	❶³	16	●	1 Me And Mrs. Jones .... Kenny Gamble/Cary Gilbert/Leon Huff...*Your Song*	Philadelphia I. 3521
				PAUL, Les, and Mary Ford	
12/1/45	❶²	16		1 It's Been A Long Long Time .... Sammy Cahn/Jule Styne...*Whose Dream Are You*	Decca 18708
				BING CROSBY with LES PAUL And His Trio	
12/14/46	4	13		2 Rumors Are Flying .... Bennie Benjamin/George Weiss...*Them That Has—Gets* (Andrews Sisters & Eddie Heywood)	Decca 23656
				ANDREWS SISTERS with LES PAUL	
8/5/50	9	17		3 Nola .... Felix Arndt...*Jealous* (w/Mary Ford) [I]	Capitol 1014
				LES PAUL	
1/13/51	6	14		4 Tennessee Waltz .... Pee Wee King/Redd Stewart...*Little Rock Getaway* (Paul)	Capitol 1316
3/24/51	2⁵	24	⊙	5 Mockin' Bird Hill .... Vaughn Horton...*Chicken Reel* (Paul)	Capitol 1373
4/21/51	❶⁹	25	⊙	6 How High The Moon .... Nancy Hamilton/Morgan Lewis...*Walkin' And Whistlin' Blues* (Paul)	Capitol 1451
9/15/51	7	16		7 Whispering .... Richard Coburn/Vincent Rose/John Schonberger...*The World Is Waiting For The Sunrise* (w/Mary Ford) [I]	Capitol 1748
				LES PAUL	
10/6/51	2²	16	⊙	8 The World Is Waiting For The Sunrise .... Eugene Lockhart/Ernest Seitz...*Whispering* (Paul)	Capitol 1748
11/24/51	5	13		9 Just One More Chance .... Sam Coslow/Arthur Johnston...*Jazz Me Blues* (Paul)	Capitol 1825
1/5/52	10	4		10 Jingle Bells .... James Pierpont...*Silent Night* (w/Mary Ford) [X-I]	Capitol 1881
				LES PAUL	
3/1/52	2¹	12		11 Tiger Rag .... Harry DeCosta/Edwin Edwards/James LaRocca/W.H. Ragas/Anthony Sbarbaro/Larry Shields...*It's A Lonesome Old Town*	Capitol 1920
10/11/52	5	14		12 Meet Mister Callaghan .... Eric Spear...*Take Me In Your Arms And Hold Me* (w/Mary Ford) [I]	Capitol 2193
11/29/52	8	8		13 Lady Of Spain .... Tolchard Evans/Erell Reaves...*My Baby's Coming Home* (w/Mary Ford) [I]	Capitol 2265
				LES PAUL (above 2)	
1/10/53	7	10		14 My Baby's Coming Home .... Sherman Feller/John Grady/William Leavitt...*Lady Of Spain* (Paul)	Capitol 2265
1/17/53	5	7		15 Bye Bye Blues .... David Bennett/Chauncey Gray/Fred Hamm/Bert Lown...*Mammy's Boogie* (Paul)	Capitol 2316
4/18/53	10	6		16 I'm Sitting On Top Of The World .... Ray Henderson/Sam Lewis/Joe Young...*Sleep* (Paul)	Capitol 2400
8/8/53	❶¹¹	31	⊙	17 Vaya Con Dios (May God Be With You) .... Inez James/Buddy Pepper/Larry Russell...*Johnny (Is The Boy For Me)* (Paul)	Capitol 2486
9/11/54	6	14		18 I'm A Fool To Care .... Ted Daffan...*Auctioneer*	Capitol 2839
10/30/54	10	9		19 Whither Thou Goest .... Guy Singer...*Mandolino* (Paul)	Capitol 2928
8/27/55	7	13		20 Hummingbird .... Don Robertson...*Goodbye, My Love*	Capitol 3165
				PAUL, Sean	
12/7/02	7	39		1 Gimme The Light .... Sean Paul/Troy Rami...*Can You Do The Work*	VP 6400
5/10/03	❶³	32		2 Get Busy .... Steven Marsden/Sean Paul...*I'm Still In Love With You*	VP/Atlantic 88020
10/4/03	❶⁹	29	○	3 Baby Boy .... Shawn Carter/Beyonce Knowles/Sean Paul/Scott Storch/Robert Waller	Columbia 76867
				BEYONCE Featuring Sean Paul	
11/12/05	6	28	○	4 We Be Burnin' .... Cezar Cunningham/Michael Jarrett/Stephen Marsden/Craig Marsh/Sean Paul/Delano Thomas	VP/Atlantic 93770
4/1/06	❶¹	31	△²	5 Temperature .... Rohan Fuller/Adrian Marshall/Sean Paul...*Breakout*	VP/Atlantic 94133
9/9/06	3¹	22		6 (When You Gonna) Give It Up To Me .... Donovan Bennett/Jason Henriques/Sean Paul/Nigel Staff...*Never Gonna Be The Same*	VP/Atlantic 94413
				SEAN PAUL Featuring Keyshia Cole	
3/17/07	9	20		7 Break It Off .... Donovan Bennett/Robyn Fenty/Kirk Ford/Sean Paul	Def Jam
				RIHANNA & SEAN PAUL	
1/9/10	10	20	△	8 Do You Remember .... Jared Cotter/Sean Henriques/Robert Larow/Jay Sean/Jeremy Skaller/Jonathan Smith/Frankie Storm	Cash Money
				JAY SEAN Featuring Sean Paul & Lil Jon	
				PAUL & PAULA	
2/9/63	❶³	15	●	1 Hey Paula .... Ray Hildebrand...*Bobby Is The One*	Philips 40084
4/20/63	6	10		2 Young Lovers .... Ray Hildebrand/Jill Jackson...*Ba-Hey-Be*	Philips 40096
				PAYNE, Freda	
7/25/70	3¹	20	●	1 Band Of Gold .... Lamont Dozier/Ronald Dunbar/Brian Holland/Eddie Holland...*The Easiest Way To Fall*	Invictus 9075
				PEACHES & HERB	
5/6/67	8	12		1 Close Your Eyes .... Chuck Willis...*I Will Watch Over You*	Date 1549
3/17/79	5	22	●	2 Shake Your Groove Thing .... Dino Fekaris/Freddie Perren...*All Your Love (Give It Here)*	Polydor/MVP 14514
5/5/79	❶⁴	23	▲	3 Reunited .... Dino Fekaris/Freddie Perren...*Easy As Pie*	Polydor/MVP 14547
				PEARL JAM	
12/23/95	7	20	●	1 I Got Id .... Eddie Vedder...*Long Road*	Epic 78199
6/26/99	2¹	21	●	2 Last Kiss .... Wayne Cochran...*Soldier Of Love*	Epic 79197
				PEBBLES	
4/23/88	5	20		1 Girlfriend .... Babyface/L.A. Reid	MCA 53185
7/9/88	2²	18		2 Mercedes Boy .... Perri McKissack	MCA 53279
10/27/90	4	22		3 Giving You The Benefit .... Babyface/L.A. Reid	MCA 53891
				PENGUINS, The	
2/5/55	8	15	⊙	1 Earth Angel (Will You Be Mine) .... Curtis Williams...*Hey Senorita*	DooTone 348
				PENISTON, Ce Ce	
1/18/92	5	33	●	1 Finally .... Felipe Delgado/Elbert Linnear/Ce Ce Peniston	A&M 1586
				PERFECT GENTLEMEN	
6/2/90	10	16		1 Ooh La La (I Can't Get Over You) .... Maurice Starr...*Rated PG*	Columbia 73211
				PERICOLI, Emilio	
7/7/62	6	14		1 Al Di La' .... Carlo Donida/Giulio Rapetti...*Sassi* (Gino Paoli) [F]	Warner 5259

PEAK DATE	PEAK POS	WKS CHR	GOLD	ARTIST / Song Title	Songwriter...B-side	Label & Number
				PERKINS, Carl		
5/19/56	2⁴	21	⊙	1 Blue Suede Shoes	Carl Perkins...*Honey, Don't!*	Sun 234
				PERRY, Katy		
7/5/08	❶⁷	23	△³	1 I Kissed A Girl	Cathy Dennis/Lukasz Gottwald/Max Martin/Katy Perry	Capitol
11/22/08	3¹	39	△⁴	2 Hot N Cold	Lukasz Gottwald/Max Martin/Katy Perry	Capitol
8/8/09	9	23		3 Waking Up In Vegas	Andreas Carlsson/Desmond Child/Katy Perry	Capitol
6/19/10	❶⁶	27	△³	4 California Gurls	Lukasz Gottwald/Benjamin Levin/Bonnie McKee/Katy Perry/Martin Sandberg...*Hot N Cold (remix)*	Capitol 41011
				KATY PERRY Featuring Snoop Dogg		
9/18/10	❶²	27↑	△²	5 Teenage Dream	Lukasz Gottwald/Benjamin Levin/Bonnie McKee/Katy Perry/Martin Sandberg	Captiol
12/18/10	❶⁴	14↑		6 Firework	Esther Dean/Mikkel Eriksen/Tor Hermansen/Katy Perry/Sandy Wilhelm	Capitol
				PERRY, Steve		
6/9/84	3¹	20		1 Oh Sherrie	Bill Cuomo/Randy Goodrum/Craig Krampf/Steve Perry...*Don't Tell Me Why You're Leaving*	Columbia 04391
				PETER AND GORDON		
6/27/64	❶¹	12	⊙	1 A World Without Love	John Lennon/Paul McCartney...*If I Were You*	Capitol 5175
2/20/65	9	11		2 I Go To Pieces	Del Shannon...*Love Me, Baby*	Capitol 5335
12/10/66	6	14		3 Lady Godiva	Mike Leander/Charles Mills...*The Town I Live In*	Capitol 5740
				PETER, PAUL & MARY		
10/13/62	10	12		1 If I Had A Hammer (The Hammer Song)	Lee Hays/Pete Seeger...*Gone The Rainbow*	Warner 5296
5/11/63	2¹	14		2 Puff The Magic Dragon	Leonard Lipton/Peter Yarrow...*Pretty Mary*	Warner 5348
8/17/63	2¹	15		3 Blowin' In The Wind	Bob Dylan...*Flora*	Warner 5368
10/26/63	9	10		4 Don't Think Twice, It's All Right	Bob Dylan...*Autumn To May*	Warner 5385
9/23/67	9	11		5 I Dig Rock And Roll Music	Dave Dixon/James Mason/Paul Stookey...*The Great Mandella (The Wheel Of Life)*	Warner 7067
12/20/69	❶¹	17	●	6 Leaving On A Jet Plane	John Denver...*The House Song*	Warner 7340
				PETERSEN, Paul		
1/26/63	6	16		1 My Dad	Barry Mann/Cynthia Weil...*Little Boy Sad*	Colpix 663
				PETERSON, Ray		
8/1/60	7	14		1 Tell Laura I Love Her	Jeff Barry/Ben Raleigh...*Wedding Day*	RCA Victor 7745
1/9/61	9	15		2 Corinna, Corinna	Bo Chapman/Mitchell Parish/J. Mayo Williams...*Be My Girl*	Dunes 2002
				PET SHOP BOYS		
5/10/86	❶¹	20		1 West End Girls	Chris Lowe/Neil Tennant...*A Man Could Get Arrested*	EMI America 8307
8/2/86	10	16		2 Opportunities (Let's Make Lots Of Money)	Chris Lowe/Neil Tennant...*Was That What It Was*	EMI America 8330
11/14/87	9	19		3 It's A Sin	Chris Lowe/Neil Tennant...*You Know Where You Went Wrong*	EMI America 43027
2/20/88	2²	18		4 What Have I Done To Deserve This?	Chris Lowe/Neil Tennant/Allee Willis...*A New Life (Pet Shop Boys)*	EMI/Manhattan 50107
				PET SHOP BOYS (and Dusty Springfield)		
5/21/88	4	15		5 Always On My Mind	Johnny Christopher/Mark James/Wayne Carson Thompson...*Do I Have To?*	EMI/Manhattan 50123
				PETTY, Tom, And The Heartbreakers		
2/2/80	10	18		1 Don't Do Me Like That	Tom Petty...*Casa Dega*	Backstreet 41138
9/5/81	3⁶	21		2 Stop Draggin' My Heart Around	Mike Campbell/Tom Petty...*Kind Of Woman* (Nicks)	Modern 7336
				STEVIE NICKS (with Tom Petty and The Heartbreakers)		
1/27/90	7	21		3 Free Fallin'	Jeff Lynne/Tom Petty...*Down The Line*	MCA 53748
				TOM PETTY		
				PHARRELL		
4/26/03	6	20		1 Beautiful	Calvin Broadus/Chad Hugo/Pharrell Williams...*Ballin'*	Doggystyle 77887
				SNOOP DOGG featuring Pharrell & Uncle Charlie Wilson		
9/20/03	5	23		2 Frontin'	Shawn Carter/Chad Hugo/Pharrell Williams	Star Trak 58647
				PHARRELL Featuring Jay-Z		
12/11/04	❶³	30	○	3 Drop It Like It's Hot	Calvin Broadus/Chad Hugo/Pharrell Williams	Doggystyle 003574
				SNOOP DOGG featuring Pharrell		
10/28/06	❶²	25	○	4 Money Maker	Christopher Bridges/Pharrell Williams	DTP 007488
				LUDACRIS Featuring Pharrell		
				PHILLIPS, "Little Esther"		
12/22/62	8	14		1 Release Me	Eddie Miller/William Stevenson...*Don't Feel Rained On*	Lenox 5555
				PHILLIPS, Phil		
8/24/59	2²	18	⊙	1 Sea Of Love	Phil Baptiste/George Khoury...*Juella*	Mercury 71465
				PHIL PHILLIPS with The Twilights		
				PICKETT, Bobby "Boris", And The Crypt-Kickers		
10/20/62	❶²	14	●	1 Monster Mash	Leonard Capizzi/Bobby Pickett...*Monsters' Mash Party* [N]	Garpax 44167
8/11/73	10	20		2 Monster Mash	Leonard Capizzi/Bobby Pickett...*Monsters' Mash Party* [N-R]	Parrot 348
				PICKETT, Wilson		
9/10/66	6	11		1 Land Of 1000 Dances	Chris Kenner...*You're So Fine*	Atlantic 2348
9/30/67	8	12		2 Funky Broadway	Arlester Christian...*I'm Sorry About That*	Atlantic 2430
				PIED PIPERS, The		
4/8/44	8	1		1 Mairzy Doats	Milton Drake/Al Hoffman/Jerry Livingston...*A Journey To A Star*	Capitol 148
12/2/44	2²	14		2 The Trolley Song	Ralph Blane/Hugh Martin...*Cuddle Up A Little Closer*	Capitol 168
5/5/45	❶¹	18		3 Dream	Johnny Mercer...*Tabby The Cat*	Capitol 185
6/15/46	8	4		4 In The Moon Mist	Jack Lawrence...*Madame Butterball*	Capitol 243
3/1/47	8	3		5 Open The Door Richard	Dusty Fletcher/Don Howell/John Mason/Jack McVea...*When Am I Gonna Kiss You Good Morning* [N]	Capitol 369
6/7/47	3¹	11		6 Mam'selle	Mack Gordon/Edmund Goulding...*It's The Same Old Dream*	Capitol 396
7/17/48	3²	27		7 My Happiness	Borney Bergantine/Betty Peterson...*Highway To Love*	Capitol 15094
				PILOT		
7/12/75	5	20	●	1 Magic	Bill Lyall/David Paton...*Just Let Me Be*	EMI 3992
				PINETOPPERS, The		
4/7/51	10	17		1 Mockin' Bird Hill	Vaughn Horton...*Big Parade Polka*	Coral 64061

PEAK DATE	PEAK POS	WKS CHR	GOLD	ARTIST / Song Title	Songwriter...B-side	Label & Number
				PINK		
4/8/00	7	32	●	1 There You Go	Kevin Briggs/Kandi Burruss/Alecia Moore	LaFace 24456
11/25/00	4	27		2 Most Girls	Babyface/Damon Thomas...*There You Go (remix)*	LaFace 24490
6/2/01	❶⁵	20		3 Lady Marmalade	Bob Crewe/Kenny Nolan	Interscope 497066
				CHRISTINA AGUILERA, LIL' KIM, MYA and PINK		
12/29/01	4	24	○	4 Get The Party Started	Linda Perry	Arista 15074
5/11/02	8	21		5 Don't Let Me Get Me	Dallas Austin/Alecia Moore...*Family Portrait*	Arista 50977
8/17/02	8	20		6 Just Like A Pill	Dallas Austin/Alecia Moore...*Don't Let Me Get Me (remix)*	Arista 15186
5/5/07	9	33	△	7 U + Ur Hand	Lukasz Gottwald/Max Martin/Alecia Moore/Rami	LaFace
9/29/07	9	36	△	8 Who Knew	Lukasz Gottwald/Max Martin/Alecia Moore	LaFace
9/27/08	❶¹	31		9 So What	Max Martin/Alecia Moore/Johan Schuster	LaFace
12/11/10	❶¹	16↑		10 Raise Your Glass	Max Martin/Alecia Moore/Johan Schuster	LaFace
				PINK FLOYD		
3/22/80	❶⁴	25	▲	1 Another Brick In The Wall Part II	Roger Waters...*One Of My Turns*	Columbia 11187
				PINZA, Ezio		
9/24/49	7	9		1 Some Enchanted Evening	Oscar Hammerstein/Richard Rodgers...*This Nearly Was Mine*	Columbia 4578
				PIPKINS, The		
7/18/70	9	12		1 Gimme Dat Ding	Albert Hammond/Mike Hazlewood...*To Love You* [N]	Capitol 2819
				PITBULL		
6/20/09	2¹	35	△²	1 I Know You Want Me (Calle Ocho)	Stefano Bosco/Patrick Gonella/Armando Christian Perez/Daniel Seraphine/David Wolinsky	J Records
9/19/09	8	23	△	2 Hotel Room Service	Hugh Brankin/Luther Campbell/Ross Campbell/Bernard Edwards/David Hobbs/Armando Christian Perez/John Reid/ Nile Rodgers/Mark Ross/James Scheffer/Graham Wilson/Christopher Wongwon	J Records
8/28/10	4	37↑	△²	3 I Like It	Enrique Iglesias/Nadir Khayat/Armando Christian Perez/Lionel Richie	Universal Republic
				ENRIQUE IGLESIAS Featuring Pitbull		
10/9/10	4	28↑		4 DJ Got Us Fallin' In Love	Savan Kotecha/Armando Christian Perez/Martin Sandberg/Johan Schuster...*OMG (club mix)*	LaFace 76763
				USHER Featuring Pitbull		
				PITNEY, Gene		
6/16/62	4	13		1 (The Man Who Shot) Liberty Valance	Burt Bacharach/Hal David...*Take It Like A Man*	Musicor 1020
11/3/62	2¹	14	⊙	2 Only Love Can Break A Heart	Burt Bacharach/Hal David...*If I Didn't Have A Dime*	Musicor 1022
10/3/64	7	16		3 It Hurts To Be In Love	Howard Greenfield/Helen Miller...*Hawaii*	Musicor 1040
12/12/64	9	12		4 I'm Gonna Be Strong	Barry Mann/Cynthia Weil...*E Se Domani (If Tomorrow)*	Musicor 1045
				PLAIN WHITE T'S		
7/28/07	❶²	35	△	1 Hey There Delilah	Tom Higgenson	Hollywood
				PLATTERS, The		
11/5/55	5	22	⊙	1 Only You (And You Alone)	Buck Ram/Ande Rand...*Bark, Battle And Ball*	Mercury 70633
2/18/56	❶²	24	⊙	2 The Great Pretender	Buck Ram...*I'm Just A Dancing Partner*	Mercury 70753
5/19/56	4	20		3 (You've Got) The Magic Touch	Buck Ram...*Winner Take All*	Mercury 70819
8/4/56	❶⁵	23		4 My Prayer	Georges Boulanger/Jimmy Kennedy...*Heaven On Earth*	Mercury 70893
4/21/58	❶¹	17	⊙	5 Twilight Time	Artie Dunn/Al Nevins/Morty Nevins/Buck Ram...*Out Of My Mind*	Mercury 71289
1/19/59	❶³	19	⊙	6 Smoke Gets In Your Eyes	Otto Harbach/Jerome Kern...*No Matter What You Are*	Mercury 71383
3/28/60	8	16		7 Harbor Lights	Jimmy Kennedy/Hugh Williams...*Sleepy Lagoon*	Mercury 71563
				PLAYER		
1/14/78	❶³	32	●	1 Baby Come Back	Peter Beckett/John Crowley...*Love Is Where You Find It*	RSO 879
6/3/78	10	17		2 This Time I'm In It For Love	Larry Keith/Steve Pippin...*Every Which Way*	RSO 890
				PLAYMATES, The		
12/1/58	4	15	⊙	1 Beep Beep	Carl Cicchetti/Donald Claps...*Your Love* [N]	Roulette 4115
				PLIES		
9/8/07	9	22	○	1 Shawty	Christopher Gholson/Ferrell Miles/Faheem Najm/Algernod Washington	Slip n Slide 230716
				PLIES (Feat. T-Pain)		
7/12/08	7	22	○	2 Bust It Baby Part 2	Shaffer Smith/Algernod Washington...*Who Hotter Than Me*	Slip n Slide 506620
				PLIES (Feat. Ne-Yo)		
				PM DAWN		
11/30/91	❶¹	20	●	1 Set Adrift On Memory Bliss	Attrell Cordes/Gary Kemp...*A Watcher's Point Of View (Don't 'Cha Think)*	Gee Street 866094
10/31/92	3⁴	28		2 I'd Die Without You	Attrell Cordes...*On A Clear Day*	Gee Street 24034
5/29/93	6	21		3 Looking Through Patient Eyes	Attrell Cordes/George Michael	Gee Street 862024
				POINTER SISTERS		
2/24/79	2²	23	●	1 Fire	Bruce Springsteen...*Love Is Like A Rolling Stone*	Planet 45901
10/25/80	3³	26	●	2 He's So Shy	Tom Snow/Cynthia Weil...*Movin' On*	Planet 47916
8/29/81	2³	24	●	3 Slow Hand	John Bettis/Michael Clark...*Holdin' Out For Love*	Planet 47929
4/14/84	5	20		4 Automatic	Mark Goldenberg/Brock Walsh...*Nightline*	Planet 13730
7/7/84	3²	24		5 Jump (For My Love)	Steve Mitchell/Marti Sharron/Gary Skardina...*Heart Beat*	Planet 13780
10/27/84	9	24		6 I'm So Excited	Trevor Lawrence/Anita Pointer/June Pointer/Ruth Pointer...*Dance Electric*	Planet 13857
2/16/85	6	23		7 Neutron Dance	Danny Sembello/Allee Willis...*Telegraph Your Love*	Planet 13951
				POISON		
5/16/87	9	16		1 Talk Dirty To Me	Bobby Dall/C.C. DeVille/Bret Michaels/Rikki Rockett...*Want Some, Need Some*	Enigma/Capitol 5686
7/9/88	6	19		2 Nothin' But A Good Time	Bobby Dall/C.C. DeVille/Bret Michaels/Rikki Rockett...*Look But You Can't Touch*	Enigma/Capitol 44145
12/24/88	❶³	21	●	3 Every Rose Has Its Thorn	Bobby Dall/C.C. DeVille/Bret Michaels/Rikki Rockett...*Livin' For The Minute*	Enigma/Capitol 44203
4/15/89	10	14		4 Your Mama Don't Dance	Kenny Loggins/Jim Messina...*Look What The Cat Dragged In*	Enigma/Capitol 44293
9/1/90	3¹	19	●	5 Unskinny Bop	Bobby Dall/C.C. DeVille/Bret Michaels/Rikki Rockett...*Swampjuice (Soul-O) / Valley Of Lost Souls*	Enigma/Capitol 44584
12/8/90	4	21	●	6 Something To Believe In	Bobby Dall/C.C. DeVille/Bret Michaels/Rikki Rockett...*Ball And Chain*	Enigma/Capitol 44617
				POLICE, The		
1/17/81	10	21		1 De Do Do Do, De Da Da Da	Sting...*Friends*	A&M 2275
4/11/81	10	18		2 Don't Stand So Close To Me	Sting...*A Sermon*	A&M 2301
12/5/81	3²	19		3 Every Little Thing She Does Is Magic	Sting...*Shambelle*	A&M 2371
7/9/83	❶⁸	22	●	4 Every Breath You Take	Sting...*Murder By Numbers*	A&M 2542

103

PEAK DATE	PEAK POS	WKS CHR	GOLD	ARTIST / Song Title	Songwriter...B-side	Label & Number
				POLICE, The (cont'd)		
10/8/83	3²	16		5 King Of Pain	Sting...*Someone To Talk To*	A&M 2569
3/3/84	8	16		6 Wrapped Around Your Finger	Sting...*Tea In The Sahara (live)*	A&M 2614
				PONI-TAILS		
9/15/58	7	16		1 Born Too Late	Charles Strouse/Fred Tobias...*Come On Joey Dance With Me*	ABC-Paramount 9934
				POPPY FAMILY, The		
6/6/70	2²	17	●	1 Which Way You Goin' Billy?	Terry Jacks...*Endless Sleep*	London 129
				POSNER, Mike		
7/17/10	6	29		1 Cooler Than Me	Eric Holljes/Mike Posner	J Records
				POST, Mike		
8/9/75	10	16		1 The Rockford Files	Pete Carpenter/Mike Post...*Dixie Lullabye* [I]	MGM 14772
11/14/81	10	22		2 The Theme From Hill Street Blues	Mike Post...*Aaron's Tune* [I]	Elektra 47186
				MIKE POST Featuring Larry Carlton		
				POURCEL('S), Franck, French Fiddles		
6/1/59	9	16		1 Only You	Buck Ram/Ande Rand...*Rainy Night In Paris* [I]	Capitol 4165
				POWELL, Jesse		
3/6/99	10	20		1 You	Jesse Powell/Carl Roland	Silas/MCA 55500
				POWERS, Joey		
1/4/64	10	13		1 Midnight Mary	Ben Raleigh/Artie Wayne...*Where Do You Want The World Delivered*	Amy 892
				POWER STATION, The		
5/11/85	6	18		1 Some Like It Hot	Robert Palmer/Andy Taylor/John Taylor...*The Heat Is On*	Capitol 5444
8/3/85	9	15		2 Get It On	Marc Bolan...*Go To Zero*	Capitol 5479
				POWTER, Daniel		
4/8/06	❶⁵	32	△³	1 Bad Day	Daniel Powter	Warner
				PRADO, Perez, And His Orchestra		
4/30/55	❶¹⁰	26	⊙	1 Cherry Pink And Apple Blossom White	Luis Guglielmi...*Rhythm Sticks* [I]	RCA Victor 5965
7/28/58	❶¹	21	●	2 Patricia	Bob Marcus/Perez Prado...*Why Wait* [I]	RCA Victor 7245
				PRATT & McCLAIN		
6/5/76	5	14		1 Happy Days	Charles Fox/Norman Gimbel...*Cruisin' With The Fonz*	Reprise 1351
				PRESLEY, Elvis		
4/21/56	❶⁸	27	▲²	1 Heartbreak Hotel	Mae Boren Axton/Thomas Durden/Elvis Presley...*I Was The One*	RCA Victor 6420
7/28/56	❶¹	24	▲	2 I Want You, I Need You, I Love You	Ira Kosloff/Maurice Mysels...*My Baby Left Me*	RCA Victor 6540
8/18/56	❶¹¹	28	▲⁴	3 Don't Be Cruel /	Otis Blackwell/Elvis Presley...	
	❶¹¹	28		4 Hound Dog	Jerry Leiber/Mike Stoller	RCA Victor 6604
11/3/56	❶⁵	23	▲³	5 Love Me Tender	Vera Matson/Elvis Presley...*Anyway You Want Me (That's How I Will Be)*	RCA Victor 6643
1/5/57	2²	19		6 Love Me	Jerry Leiber/Mike Stoller...*When My Blue Moon Turns To Gold Again*	RCA Victor EPA-992
2/9/57	❶³	17	▲	7 Too Much	Lee Rosenberg/Bernard Weinman...*Playing For Keeps*	RCA Victor 6800
4/13/57	❶⁹	30	▲²	8 All Shook Up	Otis Blackwell/Elvis Presley...*That's When Your Heartaches Begin*	RCA Victor 6870
7/8/57	❶⁷	25	▲²	9 (Let Me Be Your) Teddy Bear	Bernie Lowe/Kal Mann...*Loving You*	RCA Victor 7000
10/21/57	❶⁷	27	▲²	10 Jailhouse Rock	Jerry Leiber/Mike Stoller...*Treat Me Nice*	RCA Victor 7035
2/10/58	❶⁵	20	▲	11 Don't	Jerry Leiber/Mike Stoller...*I Beg Of You*	RCA Victor 7150
2/10/58	8	12		12 I Beg Of You	Rose Marie McCoy/Kelly Owens...*Don't*	RCA Victor 7150
4/28/58	2¹	15	▲	13 Wear My Ring Around Your Neck	Bert Carroll/Russell Moody...*Doncha' Think It's Time*	RCA Victor 7240
7/21/58	❶²	16	▲	14 Hard Headed Woman	Claude DeMetrius...*Don't Ask Me Why*	RCA Victor 7280
11/24/58	8	16		15 I Got Stung	David Hill/Aaron Schroeder...*One Night*	RCA Victor 7410
12/15/58	4	17	▲	16 One Night	Dave Bartholomew/Pearl King...*I Got Stung*	RCA Victor 7410
4/20/59	4	13		17 I Need Your Love Tonight	Bix Reichner/Sid Wayne...*(Now and Then There's) A Fool Such As I*	RCA Victor 7506
4/27/59	2¹	15	▲	18 (Now and Then There's) A Fool Such As I	Bill Trader...*I Need Your Love Tonight*	RCA Victor 7506
8/10/59	❶²	14	●	19 A Big Hunk O' Love	Aaron Schroeder/Sid Wyche...*My Wish Came True*	RCA Victor-7600
4/25/60	❶⁴	16	▲	20 Stuck On You	J. Leslie McFarland/Aaron Schroeder...*Fame And Fortune*	RCA Victor 7740
8/15/60	❶⁵	20	▲	21 It's Now Or Never	Wally Gold/Aaron Schroeder...*A Mess Of Blues*	RCA Victor 7777
11/28/60	❶⁶	16	▲²	22 Are You Lonesome To-night?	Lou Handman/Roy Turk...*I Gotta Know*	RCA Victor 7810
3/20/61	❶²	12	▲	23 Surrender	Doc Pomus/Mort Shuman...*Lonely Man*	RCA Victor 7850
6/5/61	5	9	●	24 I Feel So Bad	Chuck Willis...*Wild In The Country*	RCA Victor 7880
9/18/61	4	11	●	25 (Marie's The Name) His Latest Flame	Doc Pomus/Mort Shuman...*Little Sister*	RCA Victor 7908
10/2/61	5	13		26 Little Sister	Doc Pomus/Mort Shuman...*(Marie's The Name) His Latest Flame*	RCA Victor 7908
2/3/62	2¹	14	▲	27 Can't Help Falling In Love	Luigi Creatore/Hugo Peretti/George David Weiss...*Rock-A-Hula Baby*	RCA Victor 7968
4/21/62	❶²	13	▲	28 Good Luck Charm	Wally Gold/Aaron Schroeder...*Anything That's Part Of You*	RCA Victor 7992
9/8/62	5	10	●	29 She's Not You	Jerry Leiber/Doc Pomus/Mike Stoller...*Just Tell Her Jim Said Hello*	RCA Victor 8041
11/17/62	2⁵	16	▲	30 Return To Sender	Otis Blackwell/Winfield Scott...*Where Do You Come From*	RCA Victor 8100
8/10/63	3²	11	●	31 (You're The) Devil In Disguise	Bernie Baum/Bill Giant/Florence Kaye...*Please Don't Drag That String Around*	RCA Victor 8188
11/16/63	8	10		32 Bossa Nova Baby	Jerry Leiber/Mike Stoller...*Witchcraft*	RCA Victor 8243
6/12/65	3¹	14	▲	33 Crying In The Chapel	Artie Glenn...*I Believe In The Man In The Sky*	RCA Victor 0643
6/14/69	3¹	13	●	34 In The Ghetto	Mac Davis...*Any Day Now*	RCA Victor 9741
11/1/69	❶¹	15	●	35 Suspicious Minds	Mark James...*You'll Think Of Me*	RCA Victor 9764
1/31/70	6	13	●	36 Don't Cry Daddy	Mac Davis...*Rubberneckin'*	RCA Victor 9768
6/27/70	9	12	●	37 The Wonder Of You	Baker Knight...*Mama Liked The Roses* [L]	RCA Victor 9835
10/28/72	2¹	15	▲	38 Burning Love	Dennis Linde...*It's A Matter Of Time*	RCA Victor 0769
				PRESTON, Billy		
7/8/72	2¹	17	●	1 Outa-Space	Joe Greene/Billy Preston...*I Wrote A Simple Song* [I]	A&M 1320
7/7/73	❶²	22	●	2 Will It Go Round In Circles	Bruce Fisher/Billy Preston...*Blackbird*	A&M 1411
11/24/73	4	18	●	3 Space Race	Billy Preston...*We're Gonna Make It* [I]	A&M 1463
10/19/74	❶¹	18	●	4 Nothing From Nothing	Bruce Fisher/Billy Preston...*My Soul Is A Witness*	A&M 1544
4/19/80	4	29		5 With You I'm Born Again	Carol Connors/David Shire...*All I Wanted Was You* (Preston)	Motown 1477
				BILLY PRESTON & SYREETA		

PEAK DATE	PEAK POS	WKS CHR	GOLD	ARTIST / Song Title	Songwriter...B-side	Label & Number
				PRESTON, Johnny		
1/18/60	❶³	27	☉	1 Running Bear	J.P. Richardson...*My Heart Knows*	Mercury 71474
5/2/60	7	15		2 Cradle Of Love	Jack Fautheree/Wayne Gray...*City Of Tears*	Mercury 71598
				PRETENDERS, The		
3/19/83	5	24		1 Back On The Chain Gang	Chrissie Hynde...*My City Was Gone*	Sire 29840
12/27/86	10	18		2 Don't Get Me Wrong	Chrissie Hynde...*Dance!*	Sire 28630
				PRETTY POISON		
12/19/87	8	23	●	1 Catch Me (I'm Falling)	Whey Cooler/Jade Starling	Virgin 99416
				PRETTY RICKY		
6/25/05	7	22	○	1 Grind With Me	Derrick Baker/Marcus Cooper/Corey Mathis/James Scheffer/Diamond Smith/Joseph Smith/Spectacular Smith	Atlantic 93711
				PRICE, Kelly		
3/20/99	2³	28	▲	1 Heartbreak Hotel	Ken Karlin/Tamara Savage/Carsten Schack...*It's Not Right But It's Okay*	Arista 13619
				WHITNEY HOUSTON (Feat. Faith Evans & Kelly Price)		
				PRICE, Lloyd		
2/9/59	❶⁴	21		1 Stagger Lee	Harold Logan/Lloyd Price...*You Need Love*	ABC-Paramount 9972
6/15/59	2³	19		2 Personality	Harold Logan/Lloyd Price...*Have You Ever Had The Blues*	ABC-Paramount 10018
9/14/59	3²	14		3 I'm Gonna Get Married	Harold Logan/Lloyd Price...*Three Little Pigs*	ABC-Paramount 10032
				PRIEST, Maxi		
10/6/90	❶¹	30	●	1 Close To You	Gary Benson/Max Elliott/Winston Sela...*I Know Love*	Charisma 98951
11/16/91	6	20		2 Set The Night To Music	Diane Warren...*Natural Thing* (Flack)	Atlantic 87607
				ROBERTA FLACK with Maxi Priest		
				PRIMA, Louis, & Keely Smith		
6/16/45	6	6		1 Bell Bottom Trousers	Moe Jaffe...*Caldonia*	Majestic 7134
12/27/47	8	8		2 Civilization (Bongo, Bongo, Bongo)	Bob Hilliard/Carl Sigman...*Forsaking All Others* [N]	RCA Victor 2400
				PRIMITIVE RADIO GODS		
9/14/96	10	23		1 Standing Outside A Broken Phone Booth With Money In My Hand	Chris O'Connor	Ergo
				PRINCE		
5/21/83	6	22		1 Little Red Corvette	Prince...*All The Critics Love U In New York*	Warner 29746
10/22/83	8	18		2 Delirious	Prince...*Horny Toad*	Warner 29503
7/7/84	❶⁵	21	▲	3 When Doves Cry	Prince...*17 Days*	Warner 29286
				PRINCE and The Revolution:		
9/29/84	❶²	19	●	4 Let's Go Crazy	Prince...*Erotic City*	Warner 29216
11/17/84	2²	16	●	5 Purple Rain	Prince...*God*	Warner 29174
2/2/85	8	15		6 I Would Die 4 U	Prince...*Another Lonely Christmas*	Warner 29121
7/20/85	2¹	17		7 Raspberry Beret	Prince...*She's Always In My Hair*	Paisley Park 28972
9/21/85	7	14		8 Pop Life	Prince...*Hello*	Paisley Park 28998
4/19/86	❶²	18	●	9 Kiss	Prince...*Love Or $*	Paisley Park 28751
				PRINCE:		
4/25/87	3¹	14		10 Sign 'O' The Times	Prince...*La, La, La, He, He, Hee*	Paisley Park 28399
10/17/87	2¹	25		11 U Got The Look	Prince...*Housequake*	Paisley Park 28289
2/6/88	10	17		12 I Could Never Take The Place Of Your Man	Prince...*Hot Thing*	Paisley Park 28288
6/25/88	8	13		13 Alphabet St.	Prince...*Alphabet St. (cont.)*	Paisley Park 27900
8/5/89	❶¹	18	▲	14 Batdance	Prince...*200 Balloons*	Warner 22924
9/22/90	6	13	●	15 Thieves In The Temple	Prince...*Part II*	Paisley Park 19751
				PRINCE AND THE NEW POWER GENERATION:		
11/9/91	❶²	20	●	16 Cream	Prince...*Horny Pony*	Paisley Park 19175
2/15/92	3¹	21		17 Diamonds And Pearls	Prince	Paisley Park 19083
2/27/93	7	23	●	18 7	Prince	Paisley Park 18824
4/30/94	3³	26	●	19 The Most Beautiful Girl In The World	Prince...*Beautiful*	NPG 72514
				PRINCE		
				PROCLAIMERS, The		
8/21/93	3¹	20	●	1 I'm Gonna Be (500 Miles)	Charlie Reid/Craig Reid...*Better Days*	Chrysalis 24846
				PROCOL HARUM		
7/29/67	5	12		1 A Whiter Shade Of Pale	Gary Brooker/Keith Reid...*Lime Street Blues*	Deram 7507
				PRODUCT G&B, The		
4/8/00	❶¹⁰	26	▲	1 Maria Maria	Jerry Duplessis/Wyclef Jean/Karl Perazzo/Raul Rekow/Carlos Santana...*Migra*	Arista 13773
				SANTANA Featuring The Product G&B		
				PSEUDO ECHO		
7/18/87	6	15		1 Funky Town	Steve Greenberg...*Lies Are Nothing*	RCA 5217
				PUBLIC ANNOUNCEMENT		
5/16/98	5	22	▲	1 Body Bumpin' Yippie-Yi-Yo	Feloney Davis/Euclid Gray/Monica Gray	A&M 582444
				PUCKETT, Gary, And The Union Gap		
1/13/68	4	17	●	1 Woman, Woman	Jim Glaser/Jim Payne...*Don't Make Promises*	Columbia 44297
4/6/68	2³	15	●	2 Young Girl	Jerry Fuller...*I'm Losing You*	Columbia 44450
7/20/68	2²	13	●	3 Lady Willpower	Jerry Fuller...*Daylight Stranger*	Columbia 44547
10/26/68	7	11	●	4 Over You	Jerry Fuller...*If The Day Would Come*	Columbia 44644
10/11/69	9	11		5 This Girl Is A Woman Now	Abe Bernstein/Vic Millrose...*His Other Woman*	Columbia 44967
				PUDDLE OF MUDD		
5/11/02	5	38		1 Blurry	James Allen/Doug Ardito/Paul Phillips/Wes Scantlin	Flawless

PEAK DATE	PEAK POS	WKS CHR	GOLD	ARTIST / Song Title	Songwriter...B-side	Label & Number
				PUFF DADDY / P. DIDDY / DIDDY		
3/22/97	❶6	28	▲2	1 Can't Nobody Hold Me Down ...... Mason Betha/Carlos Broady/Clifton Chase/Sean Combs/Edward Fletcher/Melvin Glover/Steve Jordan/ PUFF DADDY Featuring Ma$e	Nashiem Myrick/Greg Prestopino/Sylvia Robinson/Matthew Wilder	Bad Boy 79083
6/14/97	❶11	33	▲3	2 I'll Be Missing You ...... Sean Combs/Faith Evans/Sting... **We'll Always Love Big Poppa** (The Lox) / **Cry On** (112) PUFF DADDY & FAITH EVANS (Featuring 112)		Bad Boy 79097
8/30/97	❶2	30		3 Mo Money Mo Problems ...... Mason Betha/Sean Combs/Bernard Edwards/Steve Jordan/Nile Rodgers/Christopher Wallace THE NOTORIOUS B.I.G. Featuring Puff Daddy & Ma$e		Bad Boy 79100
1/3/98	22	6	▲	4 It's All About The Benjamins ...... Deric Angelettie/Sean Combs/Sean Jacobs/Kim Jones/Jayson Phillips/David Styles/Christopher Wallace PUFF DADDY & THE FAMILY Feat. The Notorious B.I.G./Lil' Kim/The Lox/Dave Grohl/Perfect/FuzzBubble/Rob Zombie	...**Been Around The World**	Bad Boy 79130
1/24/98	4	15		5 Been Around The World ...... Mason Betha/David Bowie/Sean Combs/Ian Devaney/Andy Morris/Lisa Stansfield/Christopher Wallace PUFF DADDY & THE FAMILY Featuring The Notorious B.I.G. & Ma$e	...**It's All About The Benjamins**	Bad Boy 79130
7/25/98	4	20	▲	6 Come With Me ...... John Bonham/Sean Combs/Mark Curry/Jimmy Page/Robert Plant PUFF DADDY featuring Jimmy Page		Epic 78954
9/19/98	8	19	●	7 Lookin' At Me ...... Mason Betha/Sean Combs/Chad Hugo/Pharrell Williams...**24 Hrs. To Live** (w/The Lox, Black Rob & DMX) Ma$e featuring Puff Daddy		Bad Boy 79176
4/3/99	9	19		8 All Night Long ...... Sean Combs/Schon Crawford/Faith Evans/Todd Gaither/Ron Lawrence/Bert Reed/Todd Russaw/Galen Underwood FAITH EVANS (feat. Puff Daddy)	...**Life Will Pass You By**	Bad Boy 79203
10/30/99	23	20	●	9 Satisfy You ...... Sean Combs/Denzil Foster/Roger Greene/R. Kelly/Jay King/Thomas McElroy/Kelly Price/Jeffrey Walker PUFF DADDY (Featuring R. Kelly)		Bad Boy 79283
5/25/02	24	23		10 I Need A Girl (Part One) ...... Sean Combs/Chauncey Hawkins/Michael Jones/Jack Knight/Sonny Lester/Eric Matlock/J. Karen Thomas P. DIDDY Featuring Usher & Loon		Bad Boy 79436
8/3/02	4	26		11 I Need A Girl (Part Two) ...... Sean Combs/Chauncey Hawkins/Michael Jones/Frank Romano/Adonis Shropshire/Mario Winans...**So Complete** P. DIDDY AND GINUWINE Featuring Loon, Mario Winans & Tammy Ruggeri		Bad Boy 79441
2/1/03	❶1	22		12 Bump, Bump, Bump ...... R. Kelly/Varick Smith B2K & P. DIDDY		Epic 79842
9/6/03	❶4	30	○	13 Shake Ya Tailfeather ...... Jayson Bridges/Tohri Harper/Cornell Haynes/Varick Smith NELLY/P. DIDDY/MURPHY LEE		Bad Boy
4/24/04	28	30	○	14 I Don't Wanna Know ...... Enya/Chauncey Hawkins/Michael Jones/Nicky Ryan/Roma Ryan/Erick Sermon/Parrish Smith/Mario Winans MARIO WINANS Featuring P. Diddy & Enya		Bad Boy
11/4/06	9	20		15 Come To Me ...Sean Combs/Richard Frierson/Yakubu Izuagb/Shannon Lawrence/Nicole Scherzinger/Jacoby White/Mike Winans/Shay Winans...**Get Off** DIDDY Featuring Nicole Scherzinger		Bad Boy 94423
4/14/07	10	22		16 Last Night ...... Sean Combs/Jack Knight/Shannon Lawrence/Mario Winans DIDDY Featuring Keyshia Cole		Bad Boy 89995
				PURE PRAIRIE LEAGUE		
7/12/80	10	17		1 Let Me Love You Tonight ...... Dan Greer/Jeff Wilson/Steve Woodard...**Janny Lou**		Casablanca 2266
				PURIFY, James & Bobby		
11/26/66	6	14		1 I'm Your Puppet ...... Linda Oldham/Dan Penn...**So Many Reasons**		Bell 648
				PURSELL, Bill		
3/30/63	9	14		1 Our Winter Love ...... Johnny Cowell...**A Wound Time Can't Erase** [I]		Columbia 42619
				PUSSYCAT DOLLS, The		
8/20/05	23	40	△	1 Don't Cha ...... Thomas Callaway/Trevor Smith THE PUSSYCAT DOLLS Featuring Busta Rhymes		A&M 004685
12/31/05	5	26		2 Stickwitu ...... Frannie Golde/Kasia Livingston/Robert D. Palmer		A&M
9/23/06	31	30		3 Buttons ...... Calvin Broadus/Sean Garrett/Jamal Jones/Jason Perry/Nicole Scherzinger THE PUSSYCAT DOLLS featuring Big Snoop Dogg		A&M 006800
7/5/08	9	20		4 When I Grow Up ...... Rodney Jerkins/Jim McCarty/Paul Samwell-Smith/Theron Thomas/Timothy Thomas		Interscope 011750

Q

PEAK DATE	PEAK POS	WKS CHR	GOLD	ARTIST / Song Title	Songwriter...B-side	Label & Number
				Q-TIP		
1/8/00	5	21	▲	1 Hot Boyz ...... Missy Elliott/Tim Mosley...**U Can't Resist** (w/Juvenile & B.G.) MISSY "MISDEMEANOR" ELLIOTT (Featuring Nas, Eve & Q-Tip)		Gold Mind 64029
				QUAD CITY DJ'S		
8/17/96	31	42	▲	1 C'Mon N' Ride It (The Train) ...... Johnny McGowan/Nathaniel Orange/Michael Phillips/Barry White		Big Beat 98083
				QUARTERFLASH		
2/13/82	32	24	●	1 Harden My Heart ...... Marv Ross...**Don't Be Lonely**		Geffen 49824
				QUATRO, Suzi		
5/12/79	4	22	●	1 Stumblin' In ...... Mike Chapman/Nicky Chinn...**A Stranger To Paradise** SUZI QUATRO AND CHRIS NORMAN		RSO 917
				QUEEN		
4/24/76	9	24	●	1 Bohemian Rhapsody ...... Freddie Mercury...**I'm In Love With My Car**		Elektra 45297
2/4/78	4	27	▲	2 We Will Rock You/We Are The Champions ...... Brian May/Freddie Mercury		Elektra 45441
2/23/80	❶4	22	●	Crazy Little Thing Called Love ...... 3 ...... Freddie Mercury...**Spread Your Wings**		Elektra 46579
10/4/80	❶3	31 ▲ 4		Another One Bites The Dust ...... John Deacon...**Don't Try Suicide**		Elektra 47031
5/9/92	21	17	○	5 Bohemian Rhapsody ...... Freddie Mercury...**The Show Must Go On** [R]		Hollywood 64794
				QUEENSRYCHE		
6/1/91	9	17		1 Silent Lucidity ...... Chris DeGarmo...**The Mission (live)**		EMI 50345
				? (QUESTION MARK) & THE MYSTERIANS		
10/29/66	❶1	15	●	1 96 Tears ...... Rudy Martinez...**Midnight Hour**		Cameo 428
				QUIET RIOT		
11/19/83	5	21	●	1 Cum On Feel The Noize ...... Noddy Holder/Jim Lea...**Run For Cover**		Pasha 04005

R

PEAK DATE	PEAK POS	WKS CHR	GOLD	ARTIST / Song Title	Songwriter...B-side	Label & Number
				RABBITT, Eddie		
10/4/80	5	25	●	1 Drivin' My Life Away ...... David Malloy/Eddie Rabbitt/Even Stevens...**Pretty Lady**		Elektra 46656
2/28/81	❶2	28	●	2 I Love A Rainy Night ...... David Malloy/Eddie Rabbitt/Even Stevens...**Short Road To Love**		Elektra 47066

PEAK DATE	PEAK POS	WKS CHR	GOLD	ARTIST / Song Title	Songwriter...B-side	Label & Number
				RABBITT, Eddie (cont'd)		
10/17/81	5	22		3 Step By Step	David Malloy/Eddie Rabbitt/Even Stevens...*My Only Wish*	Elektra 47174
2/12/83	7	29		4 You And I	Frank Myers...*All My Life, All My Love* (Rabbitt)	Elektra 69936
				EDDIE RABBITT with Crystal Gayle		
				RAFFERTY, Gerry		
6/24/78	2[6]	20	●	1 Baker Street	Gerry Rafferty...*Big Change In The Weather*	United Artists 1192
				RAIDERS — see REVERE, Paul		
				RAITT, Bonnie		
10/19/91	5	20		1 Something To Talk About	Shirley Eikhard...*One Part Be My Lover*	Capitol 44724
				RAKIM		
6/8/02	9	20		1 Addictive	David Blake/Stephen Garrett/William Griffin	Aftermath 497710
				TRUTH HURTS featuring Rakim		
				RANDY & THE RAINBOWS		
8/24/63	10	17		1 Denise	Neil Levenson...*Come Back*	Rust 5059
				RARE EARTH		
6/13/70	4	20	●	1 Get Ready	Smokey Robinson...*Magic Key* [L]	Rare Earth 5012
10/3/70	7	14		2 (I Know) I'm Losing You	Cornelius Grant/Eddie Holland/Norman Whitfield...*When Joanie Smiles*	Rare Earth 5017
9/11/71	7	13		3 I Just Want To Celebrate	Dino Fekaris/Nick Zesses...*The Seed*	Rare Earth 5031
				RASCAL FLATTS		
4/29/06	6	51	△	1 What Hurts The Most	Steve Robson/Jeffrey Steele	Lyric Street
7/1/06	7	20	△	2 Life Is A Highway	Tom Cochrane	Walt Disney
				RASCALS, The		
4/30/66	❶[1]	14	⊙	1 Good Lovin'	Rudy Clark/Artie Resnick...*Mustang Sally*	Atlantic 2321
5/20/67	❶[4]	13	●	2 Groovin'	Eddie Brigati/Felix Cavaliere...*Sueno*	Atlantic 2401
8/12/67	10	9		3 A Girl Like You	Eddie Brigati/Felix Cavaliere...*It's Love*	Atlantic 2424
10/21/67	4	11		4 How Can I Be Sure	Eddie Brigati/Felix Cavaliere...*I'm So Happy Now*	Atlantic 2438
				THE YOUNG RASCALS (above 4)		
5/25/68	3[2]	13	●	5 A Beautiful Morning	Eddie Brigati/Felix Cavaliere...*Rainy Day*	Atlantic 2493
8/17/68	❶[5]	14	●	6 People Got To Be Free	Eddie Brigati/Felix Cavaliere...*My World*	Atlantic 2537
				RASPBERRIES		
10/7/72	5	18	●	1 Go All The Way	Eric Carmen...*With You In My Life*	Capitol 3348
				RAWLS, Lou		
9/4/76	2[2]	21	●	1 You'll Never Find Another Love Like Mine	Kenny Gamble/Leon Huff...*Let's Fall In Love All Over Again*	Philadelphia I. 3592
				RAY, Johnnie		
12/29/51	❶[11]	27	⊙	1 Cry	Churchill Kohlman...*The Little White Cloud That Cried*	Okeh 6840
1/12/52	2[2]	22		2 The Little White Cloud That Cried	Johnnie Ray...*Cry*	Okeh 6840
2/16/52	8	15		3 Here Am I - Broken Hearted	Lew Brown/B.G. DeSylva/Ray Henderson...*Please, Mr. Sun*	Columbia 39636
3/1/52	6	18		4 Please, Mr. Sun	Sid Frank/Ray Getzov...*Here Am I - Broken Hearted*	Columbia 39636
7/12/52	4	20		5 Walkin' My Baby Back Home	Fred Ahlert/Roy Turk...*Give Me Time*	Columbia 39750
5/2/53	8	6		6 Somebody Stole My Gal	Leo Wood...*Glad Rag Doll*	Columbia 39961
10/27/56	2[1]	28	⊙	7 Just Walking In The Rain	Johnny Bragg/Robert Riley...*In The Candlelight*	Columbia 40729
2/16/57	10	12		8 You Don't Owe Me A Thing	Marty Robbins...*Look Homeward, Angel*	Columbia 40803
				RAYBURN, Margie		
12/16/57	9	19		1 I'm Available	Dave Burgess...*If You Were*	Liberty 55102
				RAYDIO — see PARKER, Ray Jr.		
				RAY J		
4/5/08	3[1]	26	△	1 Sexy Can I	Victor Carraway/Noel Fisher/Willie Norwood/Christian Ward	Koch/Epic
				RAY J & YUNG BERG		
				RAYS, The		
11/4/57	3[2]	20	⊙	1 Silhouettes	Bob Crewe/Frank Slay...*Daddy Cool*	Cameo 117
				READY FOR THE WORLD		
10/12/85	❶[1]	21		1 Oh Sheila	Melvin Riley/Gordon Strozier/Gerald Valentine...*I'm The One Who Loves You*	MCA 52636
2/21/87	9	19		2 Love You Down	Melvin Riley...*Human Toy*	MCA 52947
				REAL McCOY		
11/12/94	3[11]	45	▲	1 Another Night	Frank Hassas/Olaf Jeglitza/Juergen Wind	Arista 12724
4/8/95	3[1]	20	●	2 Run Away	Frank Hassas/Olaf Jeglitza/Juergen Wind...*I Want You*	Arista 12808
				REBELS, The		
3/9/63	8	17		1 Wild Weekend	Tom Shannon/Phil Todaro...*Wild Weekend Cha-Cha* [I]	Swan 4125
				REDBONE		
4/13/74	5	23	●	1 Come And Get Your Love	Lolly Vegas...*Day To Day Life*	Epic 11035
				REDDING, Otis		
3/16/68	❶[4]	16	●	1 (Sittin' On) The Dock Of The Bay	Steve Cropper/Otis Redding...*Sweet Lorene*	Volt 157
				REDDY, Helen		
12/9/72	❶[1]	22	●	1 I Am Woman	Ray Burton/Helen Reddy...*More Than You Could Take*	Capitol 3350
9/15/73	❶[1]	20	●	2 Delta Dawn	Larry Collins/Alex Harvey...*If We Could Still Be Friends*	Capitol 3645
12/29/73	3[2]	16		3 Leave Me Alone (Ruby Red Dress)	Linda Laurie...*The Old Fashioned Way*	Capitol 3768
9/7/74	9	20		4 You And Me Against The World	Kenny Ascher/Paul Williams...*Love Song For Jeffrey*	Capitol 3897
12/28/74	❶[1]	17	●	5 Angie Baby	Alan O'Day...*I Think I'll Write A Song*	Capitol 3972
10/11/75	8	16		6 Ain't No Way To Treat A Lady	Harriet Schock...*Long Time Looking*	Capitol 4128

PEAK DATE	PEAK POS	WKS CHR	GOLD	ARTIST / Song Title	Songwriter...B-side	Label & Number
				RED HOT CHILI PEPPERS		
6/6/92	2[1]	26	●	1 Under The Bridge	Michael Balzary/John Frusciante/Anthony Kiedis/Chad Smith...*The Righteous & The Wicked*	Warner 18978
10/2/99	9	29	○	2 Scar Tissue	Michael Balzary/John Frusciante/Anthony Kiedis/Chad Smith...*Instrumental #1 / Gong Li*	Warner 16913
5/27/06	6	26	△2	3 Dani California	Michael Balzary/John Frusciante/Anthony Kiedis/Chad Smith	Warner
				REDMAN		
10/24/98	3[3]	20	●	1 How Deep Is Your Love	Mark Andrews/Warryn Campbell/Rick Cousin/Reggie Noble/Tamir Ruffin	Island 572424
				DRU HILL Featuring Redman		
				REED, Jerry		
2/27/71	8	24	●	1 Amos Moses	Jerry Reed...*The Preacher And The Bear* [N]	RCA Victor 9904
6/26/71	9	12		2 When You're Hot, You're Hot	Jerry Reed...*You've Been Cryin' Again* [N]	RCA Victor 9976
				REESE, Della		
11/30/59	2[1]	18	⊙	1 Don't You Know	Bobby Worth...*Soldier, Won't You Marry Me?*	RCA Victor 7591
				REEVES, Jim		
3/7/60	2[3]	23	⊙	1 He'll Have To Go	Audrey Allison/Joe Allison...*In A Mansion Stands My Love*	RCA Victor 7643
				REFLECTIONS, The		
5/30/64	6	12		1 (Just Like) Romeo & Juliet	Fred Gorman/Bob Hamilton...*Can't You Tell By The Look In My Eyes*	Golden World 9
				REGINA		
9/13/86	10	20		1 Baby Love	Stephen Bray/Mary Kessler/Regina Richards	Atlantic 89417
				REISMAN, Leo, and his Orchestra		
12/21/40	7	2		1 Down Argentina Way	Mack Gordon/Harry Warren...*You're Nearer*	Victor 26765
				R.E.M.		
12/5/87	9	20		1 The One I Love	Bill Berry/Peter Buck/Mike Mills/Michael Stipe...*Maps And Legends (live)*	I.R.S. 53171
4/8/89	6	19		2 Stand	Bill Berry/Peter Buck/Mike Mills/Michael Stipe...*Memphis Train Blues*	Warner 27688
6/22/91	4	21	●	3 Losing My Religion	Bill Berry/Peter Buck/Mike Mills/Michael Stipe...*Rotary Eleven*	Warner 19392
9/28/91	10	15		4 Shiny Happy People	Bill Berry/Peter Buck/Mike Mills/Michael Stipe...*Forty Second Song*	Warner 19242
				RENARD, Jacques, And His Orchestra		
4/10/43	3[2]	16		1 As Time Goes By	Herman Hupfeld...*I'm Sorry, Dear*	Brunswick 6205
				RENAY, Diane		
3/14/64	6	12		1 Navy Blue	Bob Crewe/Eddie Rambeau/Bud Rehak...*Unbelievable Guy*	20th Century 456
				RENE, Henri, and his Orchestra		
7/21/51	6	15		1 I'm In Love Again	Cole Porter...*Roller Coaster*	RCA Victor 4148
				HENRI RENE and his Orchestra featuring April Stevens		
8/18/51	10	5		2 Gimme A Little Kiss, Will Ya Huh?	Maceo Pinkard/Jack Smith/Roy Turk...*Dreamy Melody*	RCA Victor 4208
				APRIL STEVENS with HENRI RENE and his Orchestra		
11/21/53	8	5		3 The Velvet Glove	Harold Spina...*Elaine* [I]	RCA Victor 5405
				HENRI RENE and HUGO WINTERHALTER		
6/26/54	8	15		4 The Happy Wanderer (Val-De Ri, Val-De Ra)	Friedrich Moeller/Antonia Ridge/Florenz Siegesmund...*My Impossible Love*	RCA Victor 5715
				HENRI RENE'S MUSETTE and CHORUS		
				RENO, Mike		
7/14/84	7	20		1 Almost Paradise...Love Theme From **Footloose**	Eric Carmen/Dean Pitchford...*Strike Zone* (Loverboy)	Columbia 04418
				MIKE RENO and ANN WILSON		
				REO SPEEDWAGON		
3/21/81	❶[1]	28	▲	1 Keep On Loving You	Kevin Cronin...*Follow My Heart*	Epic 50953
5/30/81	5	20	●	2 Take It On The Run	Gary Richrath...*Someone Tonight*	Epic 01054
8/14/82	7	16		3 Keep The Fire Burnin'	Kevin Cronin...*I'll Follow You*	Epic 02967
3/9/85	❶[3]	18	●	4 Can't Fight This Feeling	Kevin Cronin...*Break His Spell*	Epic 04713
				REUNION		
11/16/74	8	15		1 Life Is A Rock (But The Radio Rolled Me)	Paul DiFranco/Norman Dolph/Joey Levine...*Are You Ready To Believe* [N]	RCA Victor 10056
				REVERE, Paul, And The Raiders		
5/14/66	4	14		1 Kicks	Barry Mann/Cynthia Weil...*Shake It Up*	Columbia 43556
7/30/66	6	11		2 Hungry	Barry Mann/Cynthia Weil...*There She Goes*	Columbia 43678
1/14/67	4	12		3 Good Thing	Mark Lindsay/Terry Melcher...*Undecided Man*	Columbia 43907
6/10/67	5	9		4 Him Or Me - What's It Gonna Be?	Mark Lindsay/Terry Melcher...*Legend Of Paul Revere*	Columbia 44094
7/24/71	❶[1]	22	▲	5 Indian Reservation (The Lament Of The Cherokee Reservation Indian)	John D. Loudermilk...*Terry's Tune*	Columbia 45332
				RAIDERS		
				REY, Alvino, and his Orchestra		
2/21/42	2[1]	10		1 I Said No!	Frank Loesser/Jule Styne...*Deep In The Heart Of Texas* [N]	Bluebird 11391
2/28/42	3[1]	9		2 Deep In The Heart Of Texas	June Hershey/Don Swander...*I Said No!*	Bluebird 11391
10/3/42	8	2		3 Strip Polka	Johnny Mercer...*The Major And The Minor* [N]	Bluebird 11573
6/8/46	5	9		4 Cement Mixer (Put-ti Put-ti)	Slim Gaillard/Lee Ricks...*We'll Gather Lilacs*	Capitol 248
10/11/47	3[3]	14		5 Near You	Francis Craig/Kermit Goell...*Oh Peter (You're So Nice)*	Capitol 452
3/6/48	6	8		6 I'm Looking Over A Four Leaf Clover	Mort Dixon/Harry Woods...*Spanish Cavalier*	Capitol 491
				REYNOLDS, Debbie		
3/31/51	3[1]	17	⊙	1 Aba Daba Honeymoon	Walter Donovan/Arthur Fields...*Row, Row, Row*	MGM 30282
				DEBBIE REYNOLDS and CARLETON CARPENTER		
8/19/57	❶[5]	31	⊙	2 Tammy	Ray Evans/Jay Livingston...*French Heels*	Coral 61851
				REYNOLDS, Jody		
6/30/58	5	17		1 Endless Sleep	Dolores Nance/Jody Reynolds...*Tight Capris* (w/The Storms)	Demon 1507
				RHODES, Betty		
11/23/46	5	11		1 Rumors Are Flying	Bennie Benjamin/George Weiss...*How Could I?*	RCA Victor 1944
12/4/48	9	9		2 Buttons And Bows	Ray Evans/Jay Livingston...*I Still Get A Thrill*	RCA Victor 3078

PEAK DATE	PEAK POS	WKS CHR	GOLD	ARTIST / Song Title	Songwriter...B-side	Label & Number
				RHYTHM HERITAGE		
2/28/76	❶¹	24	●	1 Theme From S.W.A.T.	Barry DeVorzon...*I Wouldn't Treat A Dog (The Way You Treated Me)* [I]	ABC 12135
				RHYTHM SYNDICATE		
8/3/91	2²	17		1 P.A.S.S.I.O.N.	Evan Rogers/Carl Sturken	Impact 54046
				RICH, Charlie		
12/15/73	❶²	22	●	1 The Most Beautiful Girl	Rory Bourke/Billy Sherrill/Norro Wilson...*I Feel Like Going Home*	Epic 11040
				RICH, Tony, Project		
3/23/96	2²	47	▲	1 Nobody Knows	David DuBose/Joe Rich	LaFace 24115
				RICHARD, Cliff		
9/25/76	6	22	●	1 Devil Woman	Terry Britten/Christine Hodgson...*Love On (Shine On)*	Rocket 40574
1/19/80	7	20		2 We Don't Talk Anymore	Alan Tarney...*Count Me Out*	EMI America 8025
11/22/80	10	22		3 Dreaming	Leo Sayer/Alan Tarney...*Dynamite*	EMI America 8057
				RICH BOY		
3/31/07	6	21		1 Throw Some D's	Robert Crawford/Bobby DeBarge/Jamal Jones/Marece Richards/Greg Williams...*D-Dude*	Zone 4 008391
				RICH BOY feat. Polow Da Don		
				RICHIE, Lionel		
8/15/81	❶⁹	27	▲	1 Endless Love	Lionel Richie	Motown 1519
				DIANA ROSS & LIONEL RICHIE		
11/27/82	❶²	18	●	2 Truly	Lionel Richie...*Just Put Some Love In Your Heart*	Motown 1644
3/26/83	4	18		3 You Are	Brenda Richie/Lionel Richie...*You Mean More To Me*	Motown 1657
6/11/83	5	16		4 My Love	Lionel Richie...*Round And Round*	Motown 1677
11/12/83	❶⁴	24		5 All Night Long (All Night)	Lionel Richie...*Wandering Stranger*	Motown 1698
2/4/84	7	19		6 Running With The Night	Lionel Richie/Cynthia Weil...*Serves You Right*	Motown 1710
5/12/84	❶²	24		7 Hello	Lionel Richie...*You Mean More To Me*	Motown 1722
8/25/84	3²	19		8 Stuck On You	Lionel Richie...*Round And Round*	Motown 1746
12/1/84	8	18		9 Penny Lover	Brenda Richie/Lionel Richie...*Tell Me*	Motown 1762
12/21/85	❶⁴	20		10 Say You, Say Me	Lionel Richie...*Can't Slow Down*	Motown 1819
9/13/86	2²	17		11 Dancing On The Ceiling	Lionel Richie/Carlos Rios...*Love Will Find A Way*	Motown 1843
11/29/86	9	18		12 Love Will Conquer All	Greg Phillinganes/Lionel Richie/Cynthia Weil...*The Only One*	Motown 1866
2/21/87	7	18		13 Ballerina Girl	Lionel Richie...*Deep River Woman*	Motown 1873
				RIDDLE, Nelson, and His Orchestra		
2/25/56	❶⁴	29	☉	1 Lisbon Antigua	Raul Portela...*Robin Hood* [I]	Capitol 3287
				RIGHTEOUS BROTHERS, The		
2/6/65	❶²	16	☉	1 You've Lost That Lovin' Feelin'	Barry Mann/Phil Spector/Cynthia Weil...*There's A Woman*	Philles 124
5/15/65	9	11		2 Just Once In My Life	Gerry Goffin/Carole King/Phil Spector...*The Blues*	Philles 127
8/28/65	4	13	☉	3 Unchained Melody	Alex North/Hy Zaret...*Hung On You*	Philles 129
1/8/66	5	9		4 Ebb Tide	Robert Maxwell/Carl Sigman...*(I Love You) For Sentimental Reasons*	Philles 130
4/9/66	❶³	13	●	5 (You're My) Soul And Inspiration	Barry Mann/Cynthia Weil...*B Side Blues*	Verve 10383
7/20/74	3²	17		6 Rock And Roll Heaven	Alan O'Day/John Stevenson...*I Just Wanna Be Me*	Haven 7002
				RIGHT SAID FRED		
2/8/92	❶³	21	▲	1 I'm Too Sexy	Fred Fairbrass/Richard Fairbrass/Rob Manzoli...*(Spanish version)* [N]	Charisma 98671
				RIHANNA		
7/30/05	2³	27	△	1 Pon De Replay	Alisha Brooks/Vada Nobles/Evan Rogers/Carl Sturken	Def Jam 004809
5/13/06	❶³	28	△	2 SOS	Evan Bogart/Ed Cobb/Jonathan Rotem	Def Jam 006315
7/22/06	6	20	△	3 Unfaithful	Mikkel Eriksen/Tor Erik Hermansen/Shaffer Smith	Def Jam
3/17/07	9	20		4 Break It Off	Donovan Bennett/Robyn Fenty/Kirk Ford/Sean Paul	Def Jam
				RIHANNA & SEAN PAUL		
6/9/07	❶⁷	33	△³	5 Umbrella	Shawn Carter/Thaddis Harrell/Terius Nash/Christopher Stewart	SRP/Def Jam 008990
				RIHANNA feat. Jay-Z		
12/22/07	7	26	△	6 Hate That I Love You	Mikkel Eriksen/Tor Erik Hermansen/Shaffer Smith	SRP/Def Jam
				RIHANNA Featuring Ne-Yo		
2/16/08	3⁴	30	△³	7 Don't Stop The Music	Tawanna Dabney/Mikkel Eriksen/Tor Erik Hermansen/Michael Jackson	SRP/Def Jam
5/24/08	❶¹	27	△²	8 Take A Bow	Mikkel Eriksen/Tor Erik Hermansen/Shaffer Smith	SRP/Def Jam
8/23/08	❶²	37	△³	9 Disturbia	Robert Allen/Chris Brown/Andre Merritt/Brian Seals	SRP/Def Jam 011653
10/18/08	❶⁶	28	△³	10 Live Your Life	Dan Balan/Clifford Harris/Makeba Riddick/Justin Smith	Grand Hustle 516201
				T.I. (Featuring Rihanna)		
10/3/09	2¹	23	△²	11 Run This Town	Alatas Athanasios/Jeff Bhasker/Shawn Carter/Robyn Fenty/Kanye West/Ernest Wilson...*D.O.A. (Death Of Auto-Tune)*	Roc Nation 521199
				JAY-Z, RIHANNA & KANYE WEST		
11/21/09	9	14		12 Russian Roulette	Charles Harmon/Shaffer Smith	SRP/Def Jam
1/30/10	8	20	△	13 Hard	Robyn Fenty/Jay Jenkins/Terius Nash/Christopher Stewart	SRP/Def Jam
				RIHANNA Featuring Jeezy		
3/27/10	❶⁵	22	△²	14 Rude Boy	Esther Dean/Mikkel Eriksen/Robyn Fenty/Tor Hermansen/Makeba Riddick/Thompson Swire	SRP/Def Jam
7/31/10	❶⁷	29		15 Love The Way You Lie	Alexander Grant/Holly Hafermann/Marshall Mathers	Web
				EMINEM Featuring Rihanna		
11/20/10	❶¹	14↑		16 What's My Name?	Esther Dean/Mikkel Eriksen/Tracy Hale/Tor Hermansen	SRP/Def Jam
				RIHANNA Featuring Drake		
12/4/10	❶¹	20↑		17 Only Girl (In The World)	Mikkel Eriksen/Tor Hermansen/Crystal Johnson/Sandy Wilhelm	SRP/Def Jam
				RILEY, Jeannie C.		
9/21/68	❶¹	13		1 Harper Valley P.T.A.	Tom T. Hall...*Yesterday All Day Long Today*	Plantation 3
				RIMES, LeAnn		
12/13/97	2⁴	69	▲³	1 How Do I Live	Diane Warren	Curb 73022
				RIP CHORDS, The		
2/8/64	4	14	☉	1 Hey Little Cobra	Carol Connors/Marshall Connors...*The Queen*	Columbia 42921
				RIPERTON, Minnie		
4/5/75	❶¹	18	●	1 Lovin' You	Minnie Riperton/Richard Rudolph...*The Edge Of A Dream*	Epic 50057

PEAK DATE	PEAK POS	WKS CHR	GOLD	ARTIST / Song Title	Songwriter...B-side	Label & Number
				RIVERS, Johnny		
7/11/64	2²	12	⊙	1 Memphis	Chuck Berry...*It Wouldn't Happen With Me* [L]	Imperial 66032
12/5/64	9	11		2 Mountain Of Love	Harold Dorman...*Moody River*	Imperial 66075
7/3/65	7	11		3 Seventh Son	Willie Dixon...*Un-Square Dance* [L]	Imperial 66112
4/23/66	3¹	11		4 Secret Agent Man	Steve Barri/P.F. Sloan...*You Dig*	Imperial 66159
11/12/66	❶¹	15	⊙	5 Poor Side Of Town	Lou Adler/Johnny Rivers...*A Man Can Cry*	Imperial 66205
3/11/67	3²	11		6 Baby I Need Your Lovin'	Lamont Dozier/Brian Holland/Eddie Holland...*Gettin' Ready For Tomorrow*	Imperial 66227
7/8/67	10	9		7 The Tracks Of My Tears	Warren Moore/Smokey Robinson/Marvin Tarplin...*Rewind Medley*	Imperial 66244
1/20/73	6	19	●	8 Rockin' Pneumonia - Boogie Woogie Flu	Huey Smith/John Vincent...*Come Home America*	United Artists 50960
10/22/77	10	24	●	9 Swayin' To The Music (Slow Dancin')	Jack Tempchin...*Outside Help*	Big Tree 16094
				RIVIERAS, The		
2/29/64	5	10		1 California Sun	Henry Glover...*H B Goose Step*	Riviera 1401
				R.L.		
10/23/99	8	20		1 We Can't Be Friends DEBORAH COX with R.L. from Next	Anthony Crawford/Jim Russell...*It's Over Now*	Arista 13724
				ROBBINS, Marty		
6/3/57	2¹	26	⊙	1 A White Sport Coat (And A Pink Carnation)	Marty Robbins...*Grown-Up Tears*	Columbia 40864
1/4/60	❶²	22	⊙	2 El Paso	Marty Robbins...*Running Gun*	Columbia 41511
3/20/61	3¹	15		3 Don't Worry	Marty Robbins...*Like All The Other Times*	Columbia 41922
				ROBERTS, Austin		
10/11/75	9	17		1 Rocky	Jay Stevens...*You Got The Power*	Private Stock 45,020
				ROBERTS, Kenny		
10/29/49	9	13		1 I Never See Maggie Alone	Everett Lynton/Harry Tilsley...*Wedding Bells*	Coral 64012
				ROBERTSON, Don		
6/2/56	6	20		1 The Happy Whistler	Don Robertson...*You're Free To Go* (w/Lou Dinning) [I]	Capitol 3391
				ROBIN S		
6/12/93	5	28	●	1 Show Me Love	Allan George/Fred McFarlane	Big Beat 10118
				ROBINSON, Smokey		
2/2/80	4	25		1 Cruisin'	Smokey Robinson/Marvin Tarplin...*Ever Had A Dream*	Tamla 54306
5/23/81	2³	25	●	2 Being With You	Smokey Robinson...*What's In Your Life For Me*	Tamla 54321
7/4/87	8	21		3 Just To See Her	Jimmy George/Louis Pardini...*I'm Gonna Love You Like There's No Tomorrow*	Motown 1877
10/3/87	10	19		4 One Heartbeat	Steve LeGassick/Brian Ray...*Love Will Set You Free*	Motown 1897
				ROBINSON, Vicki Sue		
8/14/76	10	25	●	1 Turn The Beat Around	Gerald Jackson/Pete Jackson...*Lack Of Respect*	RCA Victor 10562
				ROBYN		
8/2/97	7	28	●	1 Do You Know (What It Takes)	Robyn Carlsson/Herbert Crichlow/Max Martin/Denniz Pop	RCA 64865
11/29/97	7	24	●	2 Show Me Love	Robyn Carlsson/Max Martin	RCA 64970
				ROCKWELL		
3/24/84	2³	19	●	1 Somebody's Watching Me	Kennedy Gordy	Motown 1702
				RODGERS, Jimmie		
9/23/57	❶⁴	28	⊙	1 Honeycomb	Bob Merrill...*Their Hearts Were Full Of Spring*	Roulette 4015
12/16/57	3³	21	⊙	2 Kisses Sweeter Than Wine	Ronnie Gilbert/Lee Hays/Fred Hellerman/Huddie Ledbetter/Pete Seeger...*Better Loved You'll Never Be*	Roulette 4031
3/3/58	7	15		3 Oh-Oh, I'm Falling In Love Again	Al Hoffman/Dick Manning/Mark Markwell...*The Long Hot Summer*	Roulette 4045
6/16/58	3³	17		4 Secretly	Al Hoffman/Dick Manning/Mark Markwell...*Make Me A Wish*	Roulette 4070
9/1/58	10	13		5 Are You Really Mine	Al Hoffman/Dick Manning/Mark Markwell...*The Wizard*	Roulette 4090
				ROE, Tommy		
9/1/62	❶²	14	●	1 Sheila	Tommy Roe...*Save Your Kisses*	ABC-Paramount 10329
12/7/63	3²	14		2 Everybody	Tommy Roe...*Sorry I'm Late, Lisa*	ABC-Paramount 10478
7/30/66	8	14	●	3 Sweet Pea	Tommy Roe...*Much More Love*	ABC-Paramount 10762
11/5/66	6	13		4 Hooray For Hazel	Tommy Roe...*Need Your Love*	ABC 10852
3/15/69	❶⁴	15		5 Dizzy	Tommy Roe/Freddy Weller...*The You I Need*	ABC 11164
1/17/70	8	14	●	6 Jam Up Jelly Tight	Tommy Roe/Freddy Weller...*Moontalk*	ABC 11247
				ROGER		
6/22/96	6	24		1 California Love	Joe Cocker/Tupac Shakur/Chris Stainton/Larry Troutman/Roger Troutman/Andre Young...*How Do U Want It* (2 PAC w/KC & JoJo)	Death Row 854652
				2 PAC (featuring Dr. Dre and Roger Troutman)		
2/13/88	3¹	21		2 I Want To Be Your Man	Larry Troutman...*I Really Want To Be Your Man*	Reprise 28229
				ROGERS, Julie		
1/2/65	10	11		1 The Wedding	Fred Jay/Joaquin Prieto...*Without Your Love*	Mercury 72332
				ROGERS, Kenny / The First Edition		
3/16/68	5	10		1 Just Dropped In (To See What Condition My Condition Was In) THE FIRST EDITION	Mickey Newbury...*Shadow In The Corner Of Your Mind*	Reprise 0655
8/2/69	6	13		2 Ruby, Don't Take Your Love To Town KENNY ROGERS AND THE FIRST EDITION	Mel Tillis...*Girl Get Ahold Of Yourself*	Reprise 0829
6/18/77	5	19	●	3 Lucille	Roger Bowling/Hal Bynum...*Till I Get It Right*	United Artists 929
7/7/79	5	16		4 She Believes In Me	Steve Gibb...*Morgana Jones*	United Artists 1273
11/17/79	7	18		5 You Decorated My Life	Debbie Hupp/Bob Morrison...*One Man's Woman*	United Artists 1315
1/26/80	3⁴	19	●	6 Coward Of The County	Roger Bowling/Billy Edd Wheeler...*I Want To Make You Smile*	United Artists 1327
5/24/80	4	19		7 Don't Fall In Love With A Dreamer KENNY ROGERS with Kim Carnes	Kim Carnes/Dave Ellingson...*Goin' Home To The Rock/Gideon Tanner* (Rogers)	United Artists 1345
11/15/80	❶⁶	25	●	8 Lady	Lionel Richie...*Sweet Music Man*	Liberty 1380
8/15/81	3²	18		9 I Don't Need You	Rick Christian...*Without You In My Life*	Liberty 1415
3/26/83	6	18		10 We've Got Tonight KENNY ROGERS and SHEENA EASTON	Bob Seger...*You Are So Beautiful* (Rogers)	Liberty 1492

PEAK DATE	PEAK POS	WKS CHR	GOLD	ARTIST / Song Title	Songwriter...B-side	Label & Number
				ROGERS, Kenny (cont'd)		
10/29/83	❶²	25	▲ 11	Islands In The Stream KENNY ROGERS with Dolly Parton	Barry Gibb/Maurice Gibb/Robin Gibb...*I Will Always Love You* (Rogers)	RCA 13615
				ROLLING STONES, The		
12/5/64	6	13	1	Time Is On My Side	Norman Meade...*Congratulations*	London 9708
5/1/65	9	10	2	The Last Time	Mick Jagger/Keith Richards...*Play With Fire*	London 9741
7/10/65	❶⁴	14	● 3	(I Can't Get No) Satisfaction	Mick Jagger/Keith Richards...*The Under Assistant West Coast Promotion Man*	London 9766
11/6/65	❶²	12	⊙ 4	Get Off Of My Cloud	Mick Jagger/Keith Richards...*I'm Free*	London 9792
1/29/66	6	9	5	As Tears Go By	Mick Jagger/Andrew Loog Oldham/Keith Richards...*Gotta Get Away*	London 9808
3/19/66	2³	10	⊙ 6	19th Nervous Breakdown	Mick Jagger/Keith Richards...*Sad Day*	London 9823
6/11/66	❶²	11	⊙ 7	Paint It, Black	Mick Jagger/Keith Richards...*Stupid Girl*	London 901
8/13/66	8	9	8	Mothers Little Helper	Mick Jagger/Keith Richards...*Lady Jane*	London 902
10/29/66	9	7	9	Have You Seen Your Mother, Baby, Standing In The Shadow?	Mick Jagger/Keith Richards...*Who's Driving My Plane*	London 903
3/4/67	❶¹	12	● 10	Ruby Tuesday	Mick Jagger/Keith Richards...*Let's Spend The Night Together*	London 904
7/6/68	3³	12	⊙ 11	Jumpin' Jack Flash	Mick Jagger/Keith Richards...*Child Of The Moon*	London 908
8/23/69	❶⁴	15	● 12	Honky Tonk Women	Mick Jagger/Keith Richards...*You Can't Always Get What You Want*	London 910
5/29/71	❶²	12	13	Brown Sugar	Mick Jagger/Keith Richards...*Bitch*	Rolling Stones 19100
5/27/72	7	10	14	Tumbling Dice	Mick Jagger/Keith Richards...*Sweet Black Angel*	Rolling Stones 19103
10/20/73	❶¹	16	15	Angie	Mick Jagger/Keith Richards...*Silver Train*	Rolling Stones 19105
6/5/76	10	15	16	Fool To Cry	Mick Jagger/Keith Richards...*Hot Stuff*	Rolling Stones 19304
8/5/78	❶¹	20	● 17	Miss You	Mick Jagger/Keith Richards...*Far Away Eyes*	Rolling Stones 19307
11/11/78	8	13	18	Beast Of Burden	Mick Jagger/Keith Richards...*When The Whip Comes Down*	Rolling Stones 19309
9/6/80	3²	19	19	Emotional Rescue	Mick Jagger/Keith Richards...*Down In The Hole*	Rolling Stones 20001
10/31/81	2³	24	20	Start Me Up	Mick Jagger/Keith Richards...*No Use In Crying*	Rolling Stones 21003
12/24/83	9	14	21	Undercover Of The Night	Mick Jagger/Keith Richards...*All The Way Down*	Rolling Stones 99813
5/3/86	5	13	22	Harlem Shuffle	Earl Nelson/Bob Relf...*Had It With You*	Rolling Stones 05802
10/14/89	5	12	23	Mixed Emotions	Mick Jagger/Keith Richards...*Fancy Man Blues*	Rolling Stones 69008
				ROMANTICS, The		
1/28/84	3³	26	1	Talking In Your Sleep	Coz Canler/Jimmy Marinos/Wally Palmar/Mike Skill/Pete Solley...*I'm Hip*	Nemperor 04135
				ROME		
6/7/97	6	26	▲ 1	I Belong To You (Every Time I See Your Face)	Jerome Woods...*Crazy Love / Do You Like This*	RCA 64759
				RONDO, Don		
8/12/57	7	19	1	White Silver Sands	Charles Matthews...*Stars Fell On Alabama*	Jubilee 5288
				RONETTES, The		
10/12/63	2³	13	⊙ 1	Be My Baby	Jeff Barry/Ellie Greenwich/Phil Spector...*Tedesco And Pitman*	Philles 116
				RONNY & THE DAYTONAS		
9/26/64	4	13	⊙ 1	G.T.O.	John Wilkin...*Hot Rod Baby*	Mala 481
				RONSTADT, Linda		
2/15/75	❶¹	16	1	You're No Good	Clint Ballard...*I Can't Help It (If I'm Still In Love With You)*	Capitol 3990
6/21/75	2²	19	2	When Will I Be Loved	Phil Everly...*It Doesn't Matter Anymore*	Capitol 4050
11/15/75	5	13	3	Heat Wave	Lamont Dozier/Brian Holland/Eddie Holland...*Love Is A Rose*	Asylum 45282
12/10/77	5	18	4	It's So Easy	Buddy Holly/Norman Petty...*Lo Siento Mi Vida*	Asylum 45438
12/17/77	3⁴	23	▲ 5	Blue Bayou	Joe Melson/Roy Orbison...*Old Paint*	Asylum 45431
1/20/79	7	16	6	Ooh Baby Baby	Warren Moore/Smokey Robinson...*Blowing Away*	Asylum 45546
3/22/80	10	16	7	How Do I Make You	Billy Steinberg...*Rambler Gambler*	Asylum 46602
5/24/80	8	14	8	Hurt So Bad	Bobby Hart/Teddy Randazzo/Bob Weinstein...*Justine*	Asylum 46624
3/14/87	2¹	22	● 9	Somewhere Out There LINDA RONSTADT AND JAMES INGRAM	James Horner/Barry Mann/Cynthia Weil	MCA 52973
12/23/89	2²	26	● 10	Don't Know Much LINDA RONSTADT (featuring Aaron Neville)	Barry Mann/Tom Snow/Cynthia Weil...*Cry Like A Rainstorm* (Ronstadt)	Elektra 69261
				ROOFTOP SINGERS, The		
1/26/63	❶²	13	⊙ 1	Walk Right In	Gus Cannon/Hosie Woods...*Cool Water*	Vanguard 35017
				ROSE, David, and His Orchestra		
4/8/44	2³	19	⊙ 1	Holiday For Strings	David Rose...*Our Waltz* [I]	Victor 27853
7/7/62	❶¹	17	⊙ 2	The Stripper	David Rose...*Ebb Tide* [I]	MGM 13064
				ROSE ROYCE		
1/29/77	❶¹	23	▲ 1	Car Wash	Norman Whitfield...*Water*	MCA 40615
5/7/77	10	17	2	I Wanna Get Next To You	Norman Whitfield...*Sunrise*	MCA 40662
				ROSIE And The Originals		
1/23/61	5	13	1	Angel Baby	Rosie Hamlin...*Give Me Love*	Highland 1011
				ROSS, Diana		
9/19/70	❶³	14	1	Ain't No Mountain High Enough	Nick Ashford/Valerie Simpson...*Can't It Wait Until Tomorrow*	Motown 1169
8/18/73	❶¹	21	2	Touch Me In The Morning	Ron Miller...*I Won't Last A Day Without You*	Motown 1239
1/24/76	❶¹	17	3	Theme From Mahogany (Do You Know Where You're Going To)	Gerry Goffin/Michael Masser...*No One's Gonna Be A Fool Forever*	Motown 1377
5/29/76	❶²	18	4	Love Hangover	Marilyn McLeod/Pam Sawyer...*Kiss Me Now*	Motown 1392
9/6/80	❶⁴	29	● 5	Upside Down	Bernard Edwards/Nile Rodgers...*Friend To Friend*	Motown 1494
11/15/80	5	23	6	I'm Coming Out	Bernard Edwards/Nile Rodgers...*Friend To Friend*	Motown 1491
1/24/81	9	21	7	It's My Turn	Michael Masser/Carole Bayer Sager...*Together*	Motown 1496
8/15/81	❶⁹	27	▲ 8	Endless Love DIANA ROSS & LIONEL RICHIE	Lionel Richie	Motown 1519
12/19/81	7	20	9	Why Do Fools Fall In Love	Jimmy Merchant/Herman Santiago...*Think I'm In Love*	RCA 12349
3/6/82	8	14	10	Mirror, Mirror	Dennis Matkosky/Michael Sembello...*Sweet Nothings*	RCA 13021
11/13/82	10	17	11	Muscles	Michael Jackson...*I Am Me*	RCA 13348
4/13/85	10	27	12	Missing You	Lionel Richie...*We Are The Children Of The World*	RCA 13966

PEAK DATE	PEAK POS	WKS CHR	GOLD	ARTIST / Song Title	Songwriter...B-side	Label & Number
				ROTH, David Lee		
3/2/85	3¹	16		1 California Girls	Brian Wilson	Warner 29102
3/12/88	6	16		2 Just Like Paradise	David Lee Roth/Brett Tuggle...*The Bottom Line*	Warner 28119
				ROWLAND, Kelly		
8/17/02	❶¹⁰	29		1 Dilemma......Ryan Bowser/Kenny Gamble/Cornell Haynes/Antoine Macon/Bunny Sigler...*Air Force Ones* (w/Kyjuan, Ali & Murphy Lee)		Fo' Reel 019509
				NELLY Featuring Kelly Rowland		
				ROXETTE		
4/8/89	❶¹	19	●	1 The Look	Per Gessle...*Silver Blue*	EMI 50190
11/4/89	❶¹	22		2 Listen To Your Heart	Per Gessle/Mats Persson...*Half A Woman, Half A Shadow*	EMI 50223
3/3/90	2²	21		3 Dangerous	Per Gessle	EMI 50233
6/16/90	❶²	25	●	4 It Must Have Been Love	Per Gessle...*Chances*	EMI 50283
5/11/91	❶¹	19		5 Joyride	Per Gessle...*Come Back (Before You Leave)*	EMI 50342
8/31/91	2¹	18		6 Fading Like A Flower (Every Time You Leave)	Per Gessle...*I Remember You*	EMI 50355
				ROYAL, Billy Joe		
8/28/65	9	13		1 Down In The Boondocks	Joe South...*Oh, What A Night*	Columbia 43305
				ROYAL GUARDSMEN, The		
12/31/66	2⁴	12	●	1 Snoopy Vs. The Red Baron	Phil Gernhard/Dick Holler...*I Needed You* [N]	Laurie 3366
				ROYAL PHILHARMONIC ORCHESTRA		
1/30/82	10	20		1 Hooked On Classics.......Georges Bizet/George Gershwin/Edvard Grieg/George Frideric Handel/Wolfgang Amadeus Mozart/ Nikolai Rimsky-Korsakov/Jean Sibelius/Pyotr Ilyich Tchaikovsky [I]		RCA 12304
				ROYAL TEENS		
2/10/58	3²	16		1 Short Shorts	Tom Austin/Bill Crandall/Bill Dalton/Bob Gaudio...*Planet Rock*	ABC-Paramount 9882
				RUBY AND THE ROMANTICS		
3/23/63	❶¹	13		1 Our Day Will Come	Mort Garson/Bob Hilliard...*Moonlight And Music*	Kapp 501
				RUDOLF, Kevin		
10/18/08	5	35	△³	1 Let It Rock	Dwayne Carter/Kevin Rudolf	Cash Money 012077
				KEVIN RUDOLF Feat. Lil Wayne		
				RUFF ENDZ		
9/2/00	5	26		1 No More	Ed Ferrell/Clifton Lighty/Darren Lighty/Bale'wa Muhammad...*Are U Messing Around*	Epic 79400
				RUFFIN, David		
3/29/69	9	10		1 My Whole World Ended (The Moment You Left Me)......Johnny Bristol/Harvey Fuqua/Jimmy Roach/Pam Sawyer ...*I've Got To Find Myself A Brand New Baby*		Motown 1140
1/24/76	9	15		2 Walk Away From Love	Charles Kipps...*Love Can Be Hazardous To Your Health*	Motown 1376
				RUFFIN, Jimmy		
10/29/66	7	17		1 What Becomes Of The Brokenhearted	James Dean/Paul Riser/William Weatherspoon...*Baby I've Got It*	Soul 35022
5/3/80	10	14		2 Hold On To My Love	Robin Gibb/Blue Weaver	RSO 1021
				RUFUS Featuring Chaka Khan		
8/24/74	3³	17	●	1 Tell Me Something Good	Stevie Wonder...*Smokin' Room*	ABC 11427
				RUFUS		
4/12/75	10	13		2 Once You Get Started	Gavin Christopher...*Rufusized*	ABC 12066
4/3/76	5	21	●	3 Sweet Thing	Chaka Khan/Tony Maiden...*Circles*	ABC 12149
				RUNDGREN, Todd		
12/22/73	5	20		1 Hello It's Me	Todd Rundgren...*Cold Morning Light*	Bearsville 0009
				RUN-D.M.C.		
9/27/86	4	16	●	1 Walk This Way	Joe Perry/Steven Tyler...*King Of Rock*	Profile 5112
				RUSH, Merrilee, & THE Turnabouts		
6/29/68	7	16		1 Angel Of The Morning	Chip Taylor...*Reap What You Sow*	Bell 705
				RUSSELL, Andy		
4/22/44	10	2		1 Besame Mucho (Kiss Me Much)	Sunny Skylar/Consuelo Velazquez...*You're The Dream, I'm The Dreamer*	Capitol 149
6/24/44	5	9		2 Amor	Gabriel Ruiz/Sunny Skylar...*The Day After Forever*	Capitol 156
12/30/44	5	5		3 I Dream Of You	Marjorie Goetschius/Edna Osser...*Magic Is The Moonlight*	Capitol 175
2/16/46	7	9		4 I Can't Begin To Tell You	Mack Gordon/James Monaco...*Love Me*	Capitol 221
5/18/46	4	12		5 Laughing On The Outside (Crying On The Inside)	Ben Raleigh/Bernie Wayne...*They Say It's Wonderful*	Capitol 252
6/1/46	10	5		6 They Say It's Wonderful	Irving Berlin...*Laughing On The Outside (Crying On The Inside)*	Capitol 252
9/28/46	10	8		7 Pretending	Al Sherman/Marty Symes...*Who Do You Love I Hope*	Capitol 271
3/22/47	4	10		8 Anniversary Song	Saul Chaplin/Al Jolson...*My Best To You*	Capitol 368
				RUSSELL, Brenda		
6/4/88	6	25		1 Piano In The Dark	Scott Cutler/Jeff Hull/Brenda Russell...*This Time I Need You*	A&M 3003
				RYDELL, Bobby		
12/7/59	6	17		1 We Got Love	Bernie Lowe/Kal Mann...*I Dig Girls*	Cameo 169
3/28/60	2¹	16	⊙	2 Wild One	Dave Appell/Bernie Lowe/Kal Mann...*Little Bitty Girl*	Cameo 171
6/20/60	5	12	⊙	3 Swingin' School	Dave Appell/Bernie Lowe/Kal Mann...*Ding-A-Ling*	Cameo 175
9/5/60	4	15	⊙	4 Volare	Domenico Modugno/Mitchell Parish...*I'd Do It Again*	Cameo 179
11/17/62	10	11		5 The Cha-Cha-Cha	Dave Appell/Kal Mann...*The Best Man Cried*	Cameo 228
1/18/64	4	16		6 Forget Him	Mark Anthony...*Love, Love Go Away*	Cameo 280
				RYDER, Mitch, And THE Detroit Wheels		
1/29/66	10	12		1 Jenny Take A Ride!	Enotris Johnson/Richard Penniman...*Baby Jane (Mo-Mo Jane)*	New Voice 806
11/26/66	4	16		2 Devil With A Blue Dress On & Good Golly Miss Molly	Robert Blackwell/Shorty Long/John Marascalco/William Stevenson...*I Had It Made*	New Voice 817
3/25/67	6	11		3 Sock It To Me-Baby!	L. Russell Brown/Bob Crewe...*I Never Had It Better*	New Voice 820

PEAK DATE	PEAK POS	WKS CHR	GOLD	ARTIST Song Title	Songwriter...B-side	Label & Number

S

SADE
PEAK DATE	PEAK POS	WKS CHR		ARTIST / Song Title	Songwriter...B-side	Label & Number
5/18/85	5	20		1 Smooth Operator	Helen Adu/Ray St. John...*Spirit*	Portrait 04807
3/1/86	5	22		2 The Sweetest Taboo	Helen Adu/Martin Ditcham...*You're Not The Man*	Portrait 05713

SADLER, SSgt Barry
| 3/5/66 | ❶⁵ | 13 | ● | 1 The Ballad Of The Green Berets | Robin Moore/Barry Sadler...*Letter From Vietnam* | RCA Victor 8739 |

SAFARIS
| 8/1/60 | 6 | 18 | | 1 Image Of A Girl | Richard Clasky/Marvin Rosenberg...*4 Steps To Love* | Eldo 101 |

ST. PETERS, Crispian
| 7/23/66 | 4 | 12 | | 1 The Pied Piper | Steve Duboff/Artie Kornfeld...*Sweet Dawn My True Love* | Jamie 1320 |

SAKAMOTO, Kyu
| 6/15/63 | ❶³ | 14 | ⊙ | 1 Sukiyaki | Rohusuke Ei/Hachidai Nakamura...*Anoko No Namaewa Nantenkana* [F] | Capitol 4945 |

SALT-N-PEPA
| 12/4/93 | 4 | 25 | ● | 1 Shoop | Sandra Denton/Cheryl James/Otwane Roberts/Mark Sparks...*Emphatically No* | Next Plateau 857314 |
| 2/26/94 | 3³ | 29 | ▲ | 2 Whatta Man — SALT 'N' PEPA with En Vogue | Herby Azor/David Crawford | Next Plateau 857390 |

SAM & DAVE
| 11/4/67 | 2³ | 15 | ● | 1 Soul Man | Isaac Hayes/David Porter...*May I Baby* | Stax 231 |
| 3/23/68 | 9 | 13 | | 2 I Thank You | Isaac Hayes/David Porter...*Wrap It Up* | Stax 242 |

SAMMIE
| 4/4/09 | 3² | 27 | | 1 Kiss Me Thru The Phone — SOULJA BOY TELL'EM Featuring Sammie | Jim Scheffer/David Siegel/DeAndre Way | ColliPark |

SAM THE SHAM AND THE PHARAOHS
| 6/5/65 | 2² | 18 | ● | 1 Wooly Bully | Domingo Samudio...*Ain't Gonna Move* | MGM 13322 |
| 8/6/66 | 2² | 14 | ● | 2 Lil' Red Riding Hood | Ronald Blackwell...*Love Me Like Before* | MGM 13506 |

SANDLER, Adam
| 1/6/96 | 10 | 2 | ○ | 1 The Chanukah Song | Ian Maxstone-Graham/Lewis Morton/Adam Sandler [X-C-L] | Warner |

SANDPIPERS, The
| 9/17/66 | 9 | 11 | | 1 Guantanamera | Hector Angulo/Jose Marti/Pete Seeger...*What Makes You Dream, Pretty Girl* [F] | A&M 806 |

SANDS, Tommy
| 3/16/57 | 2² | 17 | ⊙ | 1 Teen-Age Crush | Audrey Allison/Joe Allison...*Hep Dee Hootie (Cutie Wootie)* | Capitol 3639 |

SANFORD/TOWNSEND BAND, The
| 9/17/77 | 9 | 18 | | 1 Smoke From A Distant Fire | Ed Sanford/Steve Stewart/John Townsend...*Lou* | Warner 8370 |

SANG, Samantha
| 3/18/78 | 3² | 27 | ▲ | 1 Emotion | Barry Gibb/Robin Gibb...*When Love Is Gone* | Private Stock 45,178 |

SANTAMARIA, Mongo
| 4/27/63 | 10 | 11 | | 1 Watermelon Man | Herbie Hancock...*Don't Bother Me No More* [I] | Battle 45909 |

SANTANA
3/21/70	9	13		1 Evil Ways	Clarence Henry...*Waiting*	Columbia 45069
1/9/71	4	13		2 Black Magic Woman	Peter Green...*Hope You're Feeling Better*	Columbia 45270
10/23/99	❶¹²	58	▲	3 Smooth — SANTANA Feat. Rob Thomas	Itaal Shur/Rob Thomas...*El Farol*	Arista 13718
4/8/00	❶¹⁰	26	▲	4 Maria Maria — SANTANA Featuring The Product G&B	Jerry Duplessis/Wyclef Jean/Karl Perazzo/Raul Rekow/Carlos Santana...*Migra*	Arista 13773
11/30/02	5	37		5 The Game Of Love — SANTANA featuring Michelle Branch	Alex Ander/Rick Nowels	Arista 15203
10/25/03	8	35		6 Why Don't You & I — SANTANA Featuring Alex Band or Chad Kroeger	Chad Kroeger	Arista

SANTANA, Juelz
7/6/02	4	21		1 Oh Boy — CAM'RON feat. Juelz Santana	Cameron Giles/Laron James/Justin Smith/Norman Whitfield...*The Roc (Just Fire)*	Roc-A-Fella 582864
11/2/02	3¹	21		2 Hey Ma — CAM'RON (feat. Juelz Santana, Freekey Zekey and Toya)	Cameron Giles/Laron James/Darryl Pittman/Lionel Richie...*Boy Boy*	Roc-A-Fella 063958
1/28/06	6	24	○	3 There It Go! (The Whistle Song)	Terrence Anderson/Laron James/Darron Joseph/Carlisle Young	Diplomats 005462

SANTO & JOHNNY
| 9/21/59 | ❶² | 18 | ⊙ | 1 Sleep Walk | Ann Farina/Johnny Farina/Santo Farina...*All Night Diner* [I] | Canadian American 103 |

SAVAGE GARDEN
5/10/97	4	33	●	1 I Want You	Darren Hayes/Daniel Jones...*Tears Of Pearls*	Columbia 78503
1/17/98	❶²	52		2 Truly Madly Deeply	Darren Hayes/Daniel Jones...*I'll Bet He Was Cool*	Columbia 78723
1/29/00	❶⁴	33	●	3 I Knew I Loved You	Darren Hayes/Daniel Jones	Columbia 79236

SAVITT, Jan, And His Orchestra
| 8/3/40 | 8 | 1 | | 1 Make-Believe Island | Will Grosz/Charles Kenny/Nick Kenny...*Ask Your Heart* | Decca 3188 |

SAYER, Leo
5/3/75	9	15		1 Long Tall Glasses (I Can Dance)	David Courtney/Leo Sayer...*In My Life*	Warner 8043
1/15/77	❶¹	21	●	2 You Make Me Feel Like Dancing	Vini Poncia/Leo Sayer...*Magdalena*	Warner 8283
5/14/77	❶¹	20	●	3 When I Need You	Albert Hammond/Carole Bayer Sager...*I Think We Fell In Love Too Fast*	Warner 8332
12/6/80	2⁵	23		4 More Than I Can Say	Jerry Allison/Sonny Curtis...*Millionaire*	Warner 49565

SCAGGS, Boz
| 10/9/76 | 3² | 22 | ● | 1 Lowdown | David Paich/Boz Scaggs...*Harbor Lights* | Columbia 10367 |

PEAK DATE	PEAK POS	WKS CHR	G O L D	ARTIST / Song Title	Songwriter...B-side	Label & Number
				SCALA, Primo		
10/2/48	6	16	1	Underneath The Arches ....Reg Connelly/Bud Flanagan/Joseph McCarthy...*Side By Side*		London 238
				PRIMO SCALA'S BANJO AND ACCORDION ORCHESTRA with THE KEYNOTES		
				SCANDAL — see SMYTH, Patty		
				SCARBURY, Joey		
8/15/81	2²	26	● 1	Theme From "Greatest American Hero" (Believe It Or Not)...............................Stephen Geyer/Mike Post...*That Little Bit Of Us*		Elektra 47147
				SCHERZINGER, Nicole		
11/4/06	9	20	1	Come To Me ...Sean Combs/Richard Frierson/Yakubu Izuagb/Shannon Lawrence/Nicole Scherzinger/Jacoby White/Mike Winans/Shay Winans...*Get Off*		Bad Boy 94423
				DIDDY Featuring Nicole Scherzinger		
				S CLUB 7		
5/12/01	10	20	1	Never Had A Dream Come True ....Cathy Dennis/Simon Ellis...*Spiritual Love*		A&M 7074
				SCORPIONS		
8/31/91	4	25	● 1	Wind Of Change ....Klaus Meine...*Money And Fame*		Mercury 868180
				SCOTT, Freddie		
9/7/63	10	12	1	Hey, Girl ....Gerry Goffin/Carole King...*The Slide*		Colpix 692
				SCOTT, Jack		
8/18/58	3¹	19	☉ 1	My True Love ....Jack Scott...*Leroy*		Carlton 462
2/16/59	8	16	2	Goodbye Baby ....Jack Scott...*Save My Soul*		Carlton 493
2/22/60	5	16	☉ 3	What In The World's Come Over You ....Jack Scott...*Baby, Baby*		Top Rank 2028
6/13/60	3²	17	☉ 4	Burning Bridges ....Melvin Miller...*Oh, Little One*		Top Rank 2041
				SCOTT, Linda		
5/1/61	3¹	14	1	I've Told Every Little Star ....Oscar Hammerstein/Jerome Kern...*Three Guesses*		Canadian American 123
8/28/61	9	14	2	Don't Bet Money Honey ....Linda Scott...*Starlight, Starbright*		Canadian American 127
				SEAL		
9/7/91	7	19	1	Crazy ....Seal...*Sparkle*		ZTT/Sire 19298
8/26/95	❶¹	36	● 2	Kiss From A Rose ....Seal...*I'm Alive*		ZTT/Sire 17896
1/18/97	10	20	3	Fly Like An Eagle ....Steve Miller		Warner Sunset 87046
				SEALS & CROFTS		
11/25/72	6	18	1	Summer Breeze ....Dash Crofts/Jim Seals...*East Of Ginger Trees*		Warner 7606
7/28/73	6	18	2	Diamond Girl ....Dash Crofts/Jim Seals...*Wisdom*		Warner 7708
7/24/76	6	26	3	Get Closer ....Dash Crofts/Jim Seals...*Don't Fail*		Warner 8190
				SEALS & CROFTS (Featuring Carolyn Willis)		
				SEAN, Jay		
10/17/09	❶²	40	△³ 1	Down ....Dewayne Carter/Jared Cotter/Robert Larow/J Perkins/Jay Sean/Jeremy Skaller		Cash Money 013306
				JAY SEAN Featuring Lil Wayne		
1/9/10	10	20	△ 2	Do You Remember ....Jared Cotter/Sean Henriques/Robert Larow/Jay Sean/Jeremy Skaller/Jonathan Smith/Frankie Storm		Cash Money
				JAY SEAN Featuring Sean Paul & Lil Jon		
				SEARCHERS, The		
1/16/65	3²	14	1	Love Potion Number Nine ....Jerry Leiber/Mike Stoller...*Hi-Heel Sneakers*		Kapp 27
				SEBASTIAN, John		
5/8/76	❶¹	14	● 1	Welcome Back ....John Sebastian...*Warm Baby*		Reprise 1349
				SECADA, Jon		
8/1/92	5	37	● 1	Just Another Day ....Miguel Morejon/Jon Secada...*(Spanish version)*		SBK/EMI 07383
7/2/94	10	31	2	If You Go ....Miguel Morejon/Jon Secada...*(Si Te Vas - Spanish version)*		SBK/EMI 58156
				SEDAKA, Neil		
12/7/59	9	18	1	Oh! Carol ....Howard Greenfield/Neil Sedaka...*One Way Ticket (To the Blues)*		RCA Victor 7595
5/9/60	9	15	2	Stairway To Heaven ....Howard Greenfield/Neil Sedaka...*Forty Winks Away*		RCA Victor 7709
2/13/61	4	15	3	Calendar Girl ....Howard Greenfield/Neil Sedaka...*The Same Old Fool*		RCA Victor 7829
1/6/62	6	14	4	Happy Birthday, Sweet Sixteen ....Howard Greenfield/Neil Sedaka...*Don't Lead Me On*		RCA Victor 7957
8/11/62	❶²	14	☉ 5	Breaking Up Is Hard To Do ....Howard Greenfield/Neil Sedaka...*As Long As I Live*		RCA Victor 8046
11/17/62	5	11	6	Next Door To An Angel ....Howard Greenfield/Neil Sedaka...*I Belong To You*		RCA Victor 8086
2/1/75	❶¹	20	7	Laughter In The Rain ....Phil Cody/Neil Sedaka...*Endlessly*		Rocket 40313
10/11/75	❶³	14	● 8	Bad Blood ....Phil Cody/Neil Sedaka...*Your Favorite Entertainer*		Rocket 40460
2/21/76	8	14	9	Breaking Up Is Hard To Do *[new version]* ....Howard Greenfield/Neil Sedaka...*Nana's Song* [R]		Rocket 40500
				SEDUCTION		
2/10/90	2²	23	● 1	Two To Make It Right ....David Cole		Vendetta 1464
				SEEKERS, The		
5/15/65	4	13	1	I'll Never Find Another You ....Tom Springfield...*Open Up Them Pearly Gates*		Capitol 5383
2/4/67	2²	16	● 2	Georgy Girl ....Jim Dale/Tom Springfield...*When The Stars Begin To Fall*		Capitol 5756
				SEGER, Bob		
3/12/77	4	21	1	Night Moves ....Bob Seger...*Ship Of Fools*		Capitol 4369
7/22/78	4	18	2	Still The Same ....Bob Seger...*Feel Like A Number*		Capitol 4581
				BOB SEGER & The Silver Bullet Band		
5/3/80	6	16	3	Fire Lake ....Bob Seger...*Long Twin Silver Line*		Capitol 4836
6/14/80	5	17	4	Against The Wind ....Bob Seger...*No Man's Land*		Capitol 4863
11/7/81	5	19	5	Tryin' To Live My Life Without You ....Eugene Williams...*Brave Strangers (live)* [L]		Capitol 5042
2/26/83	2⁴	21	6	Shame On The Moon ....Rodney Crowell...*House Behind A House*		Capitol 5187
				BOB SEGER & The Silver Bullet Band		
8/1/87	❶¹	18	7	Shakedown ....Harold Faltermeyer/Keith Forsey/Bob Seger...*The Aftermath*		MCA 53094
				SELENA		
9/2/95	8	23	1	I Could Fall In Love ....Keith Thomas...*Tu Solo Tu*		EMI Latin 18742

PEAK DATE	PEAK POS	WKS CHR	GOLD	ARTIST / Song Title	Songwriter...B-side	Label & Number
				SEMBELLO, Michael		
9/10/83	❶²	22		1 Maniac	Dennis Matkosky/Michael Sembello	Casablanca 812516
				SENSATIONS, The		
3/17/62	4	18		1 Let Me In	Yvonne Baker...*Oh Yes, I'll Be True*	Argo 5405
				SERENDIPITY SINGERS, The		
5/2/64	6	14		1 Don't Let the Rain Come Down (Crooked Little Man)	(traditional)...*Freedom's Star*	Philips 40175
				702		
3/22/97	10	20	●	1 Get It Together	Donell Jones...*Steelo*	Biv 10 0612
6/19/99	4	42	●	2 Where My Girls At?	Missy Elliott/Eric Seats/Rapture Stewart	Motown 860891
				SEVILLE, David		
4/28/58	❶³	19		1 Witch Doctor	David Seville...*Don't Whistle At Me Baby* [N]	Liberty 55132
				SHADOWS OF KNIGHT, The		
5/7/66	10	12		1 Gloria	Van Morrison...*Dark Side*	Dunwich 116
				SHAGGY		
8/19/95	3²	29	▲	1 Boombastic	Orville Burrell/King Floyd/Robert Livingston...*Summer Time* (w/Rayvon)	Virgin 38482
2/3/01	❶²	25		2 It Wasn't Me	Orville Burrell/Ricardo Ducent/Shaun Pizzonia/Brian Thompson	MCA 155782
				SHAGGY (Featuring Ricardo "RikRok" Ducent)		
3/31/01	❶¹	28		3 Angel	Eddie Curtis/Ahmet Ertegun/Steve Miller/Chip Taylor	MCA 155811
				SHAGGY Featuring Rayvon		
				SHAI		
11/21/92	2⁸	27	▲	1 If I Ever Fall In Love	Carl Martin	Gasoline Alley 54518
4/17/93	10	24	●	2 Comforter	Marc Gay/Carl Martin/Darnell Van Rensalier	Gasoline Alley 54596
9/18/93	10	25		3 Baby I'm Yours	Marc Gay/Carl Martin	Gasoline Alley 54574
				SHAKESPEAR'S SISTER		
9/19/92	4	20	●	1 Stay	Marcella Detroit/Siobhan Fahey/David A. Stewart...*The Trouble With Andre*	London 869730
				SHAKIRA		
12/29/01	6	24		1 Whenever, Wherever	Gloria Estefan/Tim Mitchell/Shakira Ripoll...*Suerte (Whenever, Wherever)*	Epic 79642
5/18/02	9	20		2 Underneath Your Clothes	Lester Mendez/Shakira Ripoll	Epic 79741
6/17/06	❶²	31	△²	3 Hips Don't Lie	Omar Alfanno/Luis Diaz/Jerry Duplessis/Wyclef Jean/Shakira Mebarak/Latavia Parker	Epic 84467
				SHAKIRA Featuring Wyclef Jean		
4/7/07	3¹	18	△	4 Beautiful Liar	Ian Dench/Mikkel Eriksen/Amanda Ghost/Tor Erik Hermansen/Beyonce Knowles	Columbia 10320
				BEYONCE & SHAKIRA		
				SHALAMAR		
3/22/80	8	23	●	1 The Second Time Around	William Shelby/Leon Sylvers...*Leave It All Up To Love*	Solar 11709
				SHANGRI-LAS, The		
9/26/64	5	11		1 Remember (Walkin' In The Sand)	George Morton...*It's Easier To Cry*	Red Bird 10-008
11/28/64	❶¹	12	⊙	2 Leader Of The Pack	Jeff Barry/Ellie Greenwich/George Morton...*What Is Love*	Red Bird 10-014
12/11/65	6	11		3 I Can Never Go Home Anymore	George Morton...*Bull Dog*	Red Bird 10-043
				SHANICE		
2/1/92	2³	26		1 I Love Your Smile	Jarvis Baker/Sylvester Jackson/Narada Michael Walden/Shanice Wilson	Motown 2093
1/30/93	4	24		2 Saving Forever For You	Diane Warren	Giant 18719
				SHANNON		
2/25/84	8	24	●	1 Let The Music Play	Chris Barbosa/Ed Chisholm	Mirage 99810
				SHANNON, Del		
4/24/61	❶⁴	17	⊙	1 Runaway	Max Crook/Del Shannon...*Jody*	Big Top 3067
7/31/61	5	13		2 Hats Off To Larry	Del Shannon...*Don't Gild The Lily, Lily*	Big Top 3075
1/30/65	9	14		3 Keep Searchin' (We'll Follow The Sun)	Del Shannon...*Broken Promises*	Amy 915
				SHARP, Dee Dee		
4/14/62	3¹	14		1 Slow Twistin'	Kal Mann...*La Paloma Twist* (Checker)	Parkway 835
				CHUBBY CHECKER (with Dee Dee Sharp)		
5/5/62	2²	18	⊙	2 Mashed Potato Time	Robert Bateman/Georgia Dobbins/William Garrett/Freddie Gorman/Brian Holland/Kal Mann...*Set My Heart At Ease*	Cameo 212
7/14/62	9	10		3 Gravy (For My Mashed Potatoes)	Dave Appell/Kal Mann...*Baby Cakes*	Cameo 219
12/8/62	5	13		4 Ride!	Dave Leon/Jon Sheldon...*The Night*	Cameo 230
4/13/63	10	11		5 Do The Bird	Dave Appell/Kal Mann...*Lover Boy*	Cameo 244
				SHAW, Artie, & his Orchestra		
12/21/40	❶¹³	23	⊙	1 Frenesi	Ray Charles/Alberto Dominguez/S.K. Russell...*Adios, Marquita Linda* [I]	Victor 26542
1/18/41	6	3	⊙	2 Star Dust	Hoagy Carmichael/Mitchell Parish...*Temptation* [I]	Victor 27230
2/8/41	10	1	⊙	3 Summit Ridge Drive	Artie Shaw...*Cross Your Heart* [I]	Victor 26763
				ARTIE SHAW and his GRAMERCY 5		
2/15/41	10	2		4 Concerto For Clarinet (Parts 1 & 2)	Artie Shaw [I]	Victor 36383
4/5/41	9	2		5 Dancing In The Dark	Howard Dietz/Arthur Schwartz...*(When Your Heart's On Fire) Smoke Gets In Your Eyes* [I]	Victor 27335
11/29/41	10	1		6 Blues In The Night	Harold Arlen/Johnny Mercer...*This Time The Dream's On Me* [I]	Victor 27609
11/4/44	10	2		7 It Had To Be You	Isham Jones/Gus Kahn...*Don't Take Your Love From Me* [I]	Victor 1593
2/10/45	5	7		8 Ac-cent-tchu-ate The Positive	Harold Arlen/Johnny Mercer...*Jumpin' On The Merry-Go-Round*	Victor 1612
8/5/50	10	11		9 Count Every Star	Bruno Coquatrix/Sammy Gallop...*If You Were Only Mine*	Decca 27042
				DICK HAYMES and ARTIE SHAW		
10/7/50	10	10		10 I'm Forever Blowing Bubbles	John Kellette/Jean Kenbrovin...*You're Mine, You!*	Decca 27186
				GORDON JENKINS and ARTIE SHAW		
				SHAW, Georgie		
2/27/54	7	14		1 Till We Two Are One	Tom Glazer/Billy Martin/Larry Martin...*Honeycomb*	Decca 28937
				SHAWNNA		
12/6/03	❶¹	28	○	1 Stand Up	Christopher Bridges/Kanye West...*P-Poppin'*	Def Jam South 001183
				LUDACRIS featuring Shawnna		

PEAK DATE	PEAK POS	WKS CHR	GOLD	ARTIST / Song Title	Songwriter...B-side	Label & Number
				SHAY, Dorothy		
9/13/47	4	12		1 Feudin' And Fightin'	Al Dubin/Burton Lane...*Say That We're Sweethearts Again*	Columbia 37189
				SHEILA E.		
10/6/84	7	26		1 The Glamorous Life	Sheila E....*Part II*	Warner 29285
				SHEP AND THE LIMELITES		
5/29/61	2¹	14	☉	1 Daddy's Home	William Miller/James Sheppard...*This I Know*	Hull 740
				SHEPARD, Jean		
10/17/53	4	10		1 A Dear John Letter JEAN SHEPARD with FERLIN HUSKEY	Billy Barton/Charles Owen/Lewis Talley...*I'd Rather Die Young*	Capitol 2502
				SHEPARD, Vonda		
9/12/87	6	24		1 Can't We Try DAN HILL (with Vonda Sheppard)	Beverly Hill/Dan Hill...*Pleasure Centre*	Columbia 07050
				SHERIFF		
2/4/89	❶¹	21	●	1 When I'm With You	Arnold Lanni...*Give Me Rock 'N' Roll*	Capitol 44302
				SHERMAN, Allan		
8/24/63	2³	10	☉	1 Hello Mudduh, Hello Fadduh! (A Letter From Camp)	Lou Busch/Allan Sherman...*Here's To The Crabgrass* [C-L]	Warner 5378
				SHERMAN, Bobby		
10/4/69	3²	13	●	1 Little Woman	Danny Janssen...*One Too Many Mornings*	Metromedia 121
1/10/70	9	11	●	2 La La La (If I Had You)	Danny Janssen...*Time*	Metromedia 150
4/11/70	9	14	●	3 Easy Come, Easy Go	Diane Hilderbrand/Jack Keller...*Sounds Along The Way*	Metromedia 177
9/19/70	5	15	●	4 Julie, Do Ya Love Me	Tom Bahler...*Spend Some Time Lovin' Me*	Metromedia 194
				SHINEDOWN		
6/20/09	7	41	△²	1 Second Chance	Dave Bassett/Brent Smith	Atlantic
				SHINER, Mervin		
4/8/50	8	6		1 Peter Cottontail	Steve Nelson/Jack Rollins...*Floppy* [N]	Decca 46221
				SHIRELLES, The		
1/30/61	❶²	19	☉	1 Will You Love Me Tomorrow	Gerry Goffin/Carole King...*Boys*	Scepter 1211
3/27/61	3²	16	☉	2 Dedicated To The One I Love	Ralph Bass/Lowman Pauling...*Look A Here Baby*	Scepter 1203
5/29/61	4	11		3 Mama Said	Willie Denson/Luther Dixon...*Blue Holiday*	Scepter 1217
2/3/62	8	14		4 Baby It's You	Burt Bacharach/Mack David/Barney Williams...*The Things I Want To Hear (Pretty Words)*	Scepter 1227
5/5/62	❶³	14	☉	5 Soldier Boy	Luther Dixon/Florence Green...*Love Is A Swingin' Thing*	Scepter 1228
5/25/63	4	14		6 Foolish Little Girl	Howard Greenfield...*Not For All The Money In The World*	Scepter 1248
				SHOCKING BLUE, The		
2/7/70	❶¹	14	●	1 Venus	Robbie Van Leeuwen...*Hot Sand*	Colossus 108
				SHONDELL, Troy		
10/23/61	6	13		1 This Time	Chips Moman...*Girl After Girl*	Liberty 55353
				SHOP BOYZ		
6/9/07	2⁶	22	△	1 Party Like A Rock Star	Demetrius Hardin/Rasheed Hightower/Jason Pittman/Richard Stephens/Brian Ward/William Whedbee	Universal Rep. 009015
				SHORE, Dinah		
1/25/41	10	1		1 Yes, My Darling Daughter	Jack Lawrence...*Down Argentina Way*	Bluebird 10920
3/15/41	9	1		2 I Hear A Rhapsody	Jack Baker/George Fragos/Dick Gasparre...*I Do, Do You? (Do You Believe In Love)*	Bluebird 11003
10/25/41	5	3		3 "Jim"	Caesar Petrillo/Edward Ross/Nelson Shawn...*I'm Through With Love*	Bluebird 11204
3/21/42	4	7		4 Blues In The Night	Harold Arlen/Johnny Mercer...*Sometimes*	Bluebird 11436
3/28/42	8	3		5 Miss You	Charles Tobias/Harry Tobias...*Is It Taboo? (To Fall in Love With You)*	Bluebird 11322
7/11/42	8	5		6 One Dozen Roses	Walter Donovan/Dick Jurgens/Roger Lewis/Joe Washburne...*All I Need Is You*	Victor 27881
12/26/42	10	1		7 Dearly Beloved...Jerome Kern/Johnny Mercer...*(As Long As You're Not in Love With Anyone Else) Why Don't You Fall In Love With Me?*		Victor 27970
1/23/43	3²	8		8 (As Long As You're Not in Love With Anyone Else) Why Don't You Fall In Love With Me?	Al Lewis/Mabel Wayne...*Dearly Beloved*	Victor 27970
3/20/43	4	12		9 You'd Be So Nice To Come Home To	Cole Porter...*Manhattan Serenade*	Victor 1519
5/8/43	5	2		10 "Murder," He Says	Frank Loesser/Jimmy McHugh...*Something To Remember You By*	Victor 1525
10/14/44	❶⁴	24	☉	11 I'll Walk Alone	Sammy Cahn/Jule Styne...*It Could Happen To You*	Victor 1586
2/24/45	8	1		12 Sleigh Ride In July	Johnny Burke/Jimmy Van Heusen...*Like Someone In Love*	Victor 1617
5/5/45	5	11		13 Candy	Mack David/Alex Kramer/Joan Whitney...*He's Home For A Little While*	Victor 1632
9/15/45	7	2		14 Along The Navajo Trail	Dick Charles/Eddie DeLange/Larry Markes...*Counting The Days*	Victor 1666
3/16/46	10	4		15 Personality	Johnny Burke/Jimmy Van Heusen...*Welcome To My Dream*	Victor 1781
4/13/46	6	9		16 Shoo-Fly Pie And Apple Pan Dowdy	Sammy Gallop/Guy Wood...*Here I Go Again*	Columbia 36943
5/4/46	3³	8		17 Laughing On The Outside (Crying On The Inside)	Ben Raleigh/Bernie Wayne...*The Gypsy*	Columbia 36964
5/18/46	❶⁸	21		18 The Gypsy	Billy Reid...*Laughing On The Outside (Crying On The Inside)*	Columbia 36964
6/1/46	9	4		19 All That Glitters Is Not Gold	Eddie Asherman/Alice Cornett/Lee Kuhn...*Come Rain Or Come Shine*	Columbia 36971
7/27/46	3²	17		20 Doin' What Comes Natur'lly DINAH SHORE with Spade Cooley and his Orchestra	Irving Berlin...*I Got Lost In His Arms*	Columbia 36976
11/16/46	5	3		21 You Keep Coming Back Like A Song	Irving Berlin...*(It's Gonna Depend On) The Way That The Wind Blows*	Columbia 37072
2/8/47	2²	16		22 (I Love You) For Sentimental Reasons	William Best/Deek Watson...*You'll Always Be The One I Love*	Columbia 37188
3/8/47	❶²	12		23 Anniversary Song	Saul Chaplin/Al Jolson...*Heartaches, Sadness And Tears*	Columbia 37234
11/8/47	2³	12		24 I Wish I Didn't Love You So	Frank Loesser...*(I've Been So Wrong, For So Long—But) I'm So Right Tonight*	Columbia 37506
11/22/47	4	11		25 You Do	Mack Gordon/Josef Myrow...*Kokomo, Indiana*	Columbia 37587
1/24/48	8	9		26 How Soon (Will I Be Seeing You)	Carroll Lucas/Jack Owens...*Fool That I Am*	Columbia 37952
11/6/48	❶¹⁰	25	☉	27 Buttons And Bows DINAH SHORE and her HAPPY VALLEY BOYS	Ray Evans/Jay Livingston...*Daddy-O*	Columbia 38284
2/5/49	9	12		28 Lavender Blue (Dilly Dilly)	Eliot Daniel/Larry Morey...*So Dear To My Heart*	Columbia 38299
7/30/49	3¹	19		29 Baby, It's Cold Outside DINAH SHORE and BUDDY CLARK	Frank Loesser...*My One And Only Highland Fling*	Columbia 38463
1/28/50	2¹	18		30 Dear Hearts And Gentle People	Sammy Fain/Bob Hilliard...*Speak A Word Of Love (I Wish, I Wish)*	Columbia 38605
1/6/51	3¹	19		31 My Heart Cries For You	Percy Faith/Carl Sigman...*Nobody's Chasing Me*	RCA Victor 3978

PEAK DATE	PEAK POS	WKS CHR	GOLD	ARTIST / Song Title	Songwriter...B-side	Label & Number
				SHORE, Dinah (cont'd)		
3/10/51	8	12		32 A Penny A Kiss	Ralph Care/Buddy Kaye...*In Your Arms*	RCA Victor 4019
				TONY MARTIN and DINAH SHORE		
8/11/51	3³	17		33 Sweet Violets	Cy Coben/Charles Grean...*If You Turn Me Down (Dee-Own-Down-Down)*	RCA Victor 4174
				SILHOUETTES, The		
2/24/58	❶²	15		1 Get A Job	Earl Beal/Ray Edwards/William Horton/Richard Lewis...*I Am Lonely*	Ember 1029
				SILK		
5/1/93	❶²	24	▲	1 Freak Me	Roy Murray/Keith Sweat	Keia/Elektra 64654
				SILKIE, The		
11/27/65	10	10		1 You've Got To Hide Your Love Away	John Lennon/Paul McCartney...*City Winds*	Fontana 1525
				SILKK THE SHOCKER		
4/11/98	2²	21	▲	1 Let's Ride	Teddy Bishop/Montell Jordan/Percy Miller/Vyshonn Miller	Def Jam 568475
				MONTELL JORDAN Featuring Master P & Silkk "The Shocker"		
				SILVER CONVENTION		
11/29/75	❶³	17	●	1 Fly, Robin, Fly	Silvester Levay/Stephen Prager...*Tiger Baby* [I]	Midland Int'l. 10339
6/12/76	2³	21	●	2 Get Up And Boogie (That's Right)	Silvester Levay/Stephen Prager...*Son Of A Gun*	Midland Int'l. 10571
				SIMON, Carly		
7/10/71	10	17		1 That's The Way I've Always Heard It Should Be	Jacob Brackman/Carly Simon...*Alone*	Elektra 45724
1/6/73	❶³	17	●	2 You're So Vain	Carly Simon...*His Friends Are More Than Fond Of Robin*	Elektra 45824
3/23/74	5	16	●	3 Mockingbird	Charlie Foxx/Inez Foxx...*Grownup* (Simon)	Elektra 45880
				CARLY SIMON & JAMES TAYLOR		
10/22/77	2³	25	●	4 Nobody Does It Better	Marvin Hamlisch/Carole Bayer Sager...*After The Storm*	Elektra 45413
6/24/78	6	18		5 You Belong To Me	Michael McDonald/Carly Simon...*In A Small Moment*	Elektra 45477
				SIMON, Joe		
6/21/75	8	17		1 Get Down, Get Down (Get On The Floor)	Raeford Gerald/Joe Simon...*In My Baby's Arms*	Spring 156
				SIMON, Paul		
4/1/72	4	13		1 Mother And Child Reunion	Paul Simon...*Paranoia Blues*	Columbia 45547
7/7/73	2²	14		2 Kodachrome	Paul Simon...*Tenderness*	Columbia 45859
10/6/73	2¹	16	●	3 Loves Me Like A Rock	Paul Simon...*Learn How To Fall*	Columbia 45907
				PAUL SIMON (with The Dixie Hummingbirds)		
2/7/76	❶³	17	●	4 50 Ways To Leave Your Lover	Paul Simon...*Some Folks Lives Roll Easy*	Columbia 10270
1/28/78	5	20	●	5 Slip Slidin' Away	Paul Simon...*Something So Right*	Columbia 10630
9/27/80	6	16		6 Late In The Evening	Paul Simon...*How The Heart Approaches What It Yearns*	Warner 49511
				SIMON & GARFUNKEL		
1/1/66	❶²	14	●	1 The Sound Of Silence	Paul Simon...*We've Got A Groovey Thing Goin'*	Columbia 43396
3/26/66	5	12		2 Homeward Bound	Paul Simon...*Leaves That Are Green*	Columbia 43511
6/11/66	3²	11		3 I Am A Rock	Paul Simon...*Flowers Never Bend With The Rainfall*	Columbia 43617
6/1/68	❶³	13	●	4 Mrs. Robinson	Paul Simon...*Old Friends/Bookends*	Columbia 44511
5/17/69	7	10		5 The Boxer	Paul Simon...*Baby Driver*	Columbia 44785
2/28/70	❶⁶	14	●	6 Bridge Over Troubled Water	Paul Simon...*Keep The Customer Satisfied*	Columbia 45079
5/30/70	4	13	●	7 Cecilia	Paul Simon...*The Only Living Boy In New York*	Columbia 45133
12/13/75	9	14		8 My Little Town	Paul Simon...*Rag Doll* (Garfunkel) / *You're Kind* (Simon)	Columbia 10230
				SIMPLE MINDS		
5/18/85	❶¹	22		1 Don't You (Forget About Me)	Keith Forsey/Steve Schiff...*A Brass Band If Africa*	A&M 2703
12/28/85	3²	20		2 Alive & Kicking	Charles Burchill/Mel Gaynor/John Gibbin/Jim Kerr/Michael McNeil...*Up On The Catwalk (live)*	A&M 2783
				SIMPLY RED		
7/12/86	❶¹	23		1 Holding Back The Years	Mick Hucknall/Neil Moss...*I Won't Feel Bad*	Elektra 69564
7/15/89	❶¹	22	●	2 If You Don't Know Me By Now	Kenny Gamble/Leon Huff...*Move On Out*	Elektra 69297
				SIMPSON, Ashlee		
9/18/04	5	21	○	1 Pieces Of Me	Kara DioGuardi/John Shanks/Ashlee Simpson	Geffen 003019
				SIMPSON, Jessica		
12/11/99	3⁵	20	▲	1 I Wanna Love You Forever	Louis Biancaniello/Sam Watters	Columbia 79262
				SINATRA, Frank		
8/28/43	2²	13		1 You'll Never Know	Mack Gordon/Harry Warren...*Close To You*	Columbia 36678
9/4/43	2¹	18	⊙	2 All Or Nothing At All	Arthur Altman/Jack Lawrence...*Flash* (James)	Columbia 35587
				FRANK SINATRA with HARRY JAMES and his ORCHESTRA		
9/18/43	9	4		3 Sunday, Monday Or Always	Johnny Burke/Jimmy Van Heusen...*If You Please*	Columbia 36679
10/2/43	10	1		4 Close To You	Al Hoffman/Carl Lampl/Jerry Livingston...*You'll Never Know*	Columbia 36678
10/30/43	6	9		5 People Will Say We're In Love	Oscar Hammerstein/Richard Rodgers...*Oh, What A Beautiful Mornin'*	Columbia 36682
3/25/44	4	14		6 I Couldn't Sleep A Wink Last Night	Harold Adamson/Jimmy McHugh...*A Lovely Way To Spend An Evening*	Columbia 36687
12/30/44	7	2		7 White Christmas	Irving Berlin...*If You Are But A Dream* [X]	Columbia 36756
1/27/45	7	5		8 I Dream Of You (More Than You Dream I Do)	Marjorie Goetschius/Edna Osser...*Saturday Night (Is The Loneliest Night In The Week)*	Columbia 36762
3/31/45	2¹	12		9 Saturday Night (Is The Loneliest Night In The Week)	Sammy Cahn/Jule Styne...*I Dream Of You (More Than You Dream I Do)*	Columbia 36762
6/30/45	5	7		10 Dream	Johnny Mercer...*There's No You*	Columbia 36797
6/30/45	8	2		11 I Should Care	Sammy Cahn/Axel Stordahl/Paul Weston...*When Your Lover Has Gone*	Columbia 36791
9/15/45	9	1		12 You'll Never Walk Alone	Oscar Hammerstein/Richard Rodgers...*If I Loved You*	Columbia 36825
10/6/45	7	2		13 If I Loved You	Oscar Hammerstein/Richard Rodgers...*You'll Never Walk Alone*	Columbia 36825
12/1/45	9	4		14 Don't Forget Tonight Tomorrow	Jay Milton/Ukie Sherin...*Lily Belle*	Columbia 36854
				FRANK SINATRA and THE CHARIOTEERS		
12/8/45	10	2		15 Nancy (With The Laughing Face)	Phil Silvers/Jimmy Van Heusen...*Cradle Song*	Columbia 36868
1/5/46	5	4		16 White Christmas	Irving Berlin...*Mighty Lak' A Rose* [X-R]	Columbia 36860
3/16/46	5	10		17 Day By Day	Sammy Cahn/Axel Stordahl/Paul Weston...*Oh! What It Seemed To Be*	Columbia 36905
3/23/46	❶⁸	17	⊙	18 Oh! What It Seemed To Be	Bennie Benjamin/Frankie Carle/George Weiss...*Day By Day*	Columbia 36905
6/1/46	7	3		19 All Through The Day	Oscar Hammerstein/Jerome Kern...*Two Hearts Are Better Than One*	Columbia 36962
7/20/46	2¹	14		20 They Say It's Wonderful	Irving Berlin...*The Girl That I Marry*	Columbia 36975

PEAK DATE	PEAK POS	WKS CHR	GOLD	ARTIST / Song Title	Songwriter...B-side	Label & Number
				SINATRA, Frank (cont'd)		
9/14/46	❶⁴	22	⊙	21 Five Minutes More	Sammy Cahn/Jule Styne...*How Cute Can You Be?*	Columbia 37048
10/19/46	6	12		22 The Coffee Song (They've Got An Awful Lot Of Coffee In Brazil)	Bob Hilliard/Dick Miles...*The Things We Did Last Summer*	Columbia 37089
12/14/46	8	6		23 The Things We Did Last Summer	Sammy Cahn/Jule Styne...*The Coffee Song (They've Got An Awful Lot Of Coffee In Brazil)*	Columbia 37089
12/28/46	6	3		24 White Christmas	Irving Berlin...*Jingle Bells* [X-R]	Columbia 37152
1/4/47	8	3		25 September Song	Maxwell Anderson/Kurt Weill...*Among My Souvenirs*	Columbia 37161
4/19/47	10	5		26 That's How Much I Love You	Eddy Arnold/Wally Fowler/J. Graydon Hall...*I Got A Gal I Love (In North And South Dakota)*	Columbia 37231
5/31/47	❶¹	10		27 Mam'selle	Mack Gordon/Edmund Goulding...*Stella By Starlight*	Columbia 37343
6/7/47	5	6		28 I Believe	Sammy Cahn/Jule Styne...*Time After Time*	Columbia 37300
11/8/47	8	1		29 So Far	Oscar Hammerstein/Richard Rodgers...*A Fellow Needs A Girl*	Columbia 37883
6/5/48	7	4		30 Nature Boy	Eden Ahbez...*S'posin'*	Columbia 38210
7/30/49	6	13		31 Some Enchanted Evening	Oscar Hammerstein/Richard Rodgers...*Bali Ha'i*	Columbia 38446
9/3/49	10	14		32 The Huckle Buck	Roy Alfred/Andy Gibson...*It Happens Every Spring*	Columbia 38486
11/5/49	9	12		33 Don't Cry Joe (Let Her Go, Let Her Go, Let Her Go)	Joe Marsala...*The Wedding Of Lilli Marlene*	Columbia 38555
2/25/50	10	7		34 Chattanoogie Shoe Shine Boy	Jack Stapp/Harry Stone...*God's Country*	Columbia 38708
9/2/50	5	12		35 Goodnight Irene	Huddie Ledbetter/John Lomax...*My Blue Heaven*	Columbia 38892
12/23/50	9	16		36 One Finger Melody	Kermit Goell/Al Hoffman/Fred Spielman...*Accidents Will Happen*	Columbia 39014
9/22/51	8	8		37 Castle Rock	Ervin Drake/Al Sears/Jimmy Shirl...*Deep Night*	Columbia 39527
				FRANK SINATRA & HARRY JAMES		
6/13/53	7	10		38 I'm Walking Behind You	Billy Reid...*Lean Baby*	Capitol 2450
5/15/54	2¹	22	⊙	39 Young-At-Heart	Carolyn Leigh/Johnny Richards...*Take A Chance*	Capitol 2703
7/10/54	4	13		40 Three Coins In The Fountain	Sammy Cahn/Jule Styne...*Rain (Falling From The Skies)*	Capitol 2816
7/9/55	❶²	21		41 Learnin' The Blues	Dolores Vicki Silvers...*If I Had Three Wishes*	Capitol 3102
11/26/55	5	17		42 Love And Marriage	Sammy Cahn/James Van Heusen...*The Impatient Years*	Capitol 3260
1/28/56	7	15		43 (Love Is) The Tender Trap	Sammy Cahn/James Van Heusen...*Weep They Will*	Capitol 3290
1/12/57	3¹	19		44 Hey! Jealous Lover	Sammy Cahn/Kay Twomey/Bee Walker...*You Forgot All The Words*	Capitol 3552
1/6/58	2¹	30		45 All The Way	Sammy Cahn/James Van Heusen...*Chicago*	Capitol 3793
2/17/58	6	16		46 Witchcraft	Cy Coleman/Carolyn Leigh...*Tell Her You Love Her*	Capitol 3859
7/2/66	❶¹	15	●	47 Strangers In The Night	Bert Kaempfert/Charles Singleton/Eddie Snyder...*Oh, You Crazy Moon*	Reprise 0470
12/24/66	4	11		48 That's Life	Kelly Gordon/Dean Kay...*The September Of My Years*	Reprise 0531
4/15/67	❶⁴	13	●	49 Somethin' Stupid	C. Carson Parks...*I Will Wait For You* (Frank)	Reprise 0561
				NANCY SINATRA & FRANK SINATRA		
				SINATRA, Nancy		
2/26/66	❶¹	14	●	1 These Boots Are Made For Walkin'	Lee Hazlewood...*The City Never Sleeps At Night*	Reprise 0432
5/14/66	7	8		2 How Does That Grab You, Darlin'?	Lee Hazlewood...*The Last Of The Secret Agents?*	Reprise 0461
12/31/66	5	13	●	3 Sugar Town	Lee Hazlewood...*Summer Wine* (w/Lee Hazlewood)	Reprise 0527
4/15/67	❶⁴	13	●	4 Somethin' Stupid	C. Carson Parks...*I Will Wait For You* (Frank)	Reprise 0561
				NANCY SINATRA & FRANK SINATRA		
				SINGING NUN, The		
12/7/63	❶⁴	13	⊙	1 Dominique	Jeanine Deckers...*Entre Les Etoiles (Among The Stars)* [F]	Philips 40152
				SIR MIX-A-LOT		
7/4/92	❶⁵	28	▲²	1 Baby Got Back	Anthony Ray...*Cake Boy*	Def American 18947
				SISQO		
5/16/98	6	20	●	1 It's All About Me	Mark Andrews/Darryl Pearson	University 97024
				MYA with Sisqo		
5/20/00	3³	28		2 Thong Song	Mark Andrews/Desmond Child/Tim Kelley/Bob Robinson/Robi Rosa...*Got To Get It*	Def Soul 562599
8/12/00	❶²	26	▲	3 Incomplete	Anthony Crawford/Montell Jordan...*Thong Song*	Def Soul 562854
				SISTER SLEDGE		
5/12/79	9	19		1 He's The Greatest Dancer	Bernard Edwards/Nile Rodgers...*Somebody Loves Me*	Cotillion 44245
6/16/79	2²	19	●	2 We Are Family	Bernard Edwards/Nile Rodgers...*Easier To Love*	Cotillion 44251
				SIXPENCE NONE THE RICHER		
5/1/99	2¹	33	●	1 Kiss Me	Matt Slocum...*Love*	Squint 79101
				69 BOYZ		
1/7/95	8	38	▲	1 Tootsee Roll	Albert Bryant	Down Low 6911
				SKID ROW		
9/23/89	4	20	●	1 18 And Life	Rachel Bolan/Dave Sabo...*Midnight/Tornado*	Atlantic 88883
2/3/90	6	20		2 I Remember You	Rachel Bolan/Dave Sabo...*Makin' A Mess*	Atlantic 88886
				SKYLARK		
5/26/73	9	21		1 Wildflower	Doug Edwards/David Richardson...*The Writing's On The Wall*	Capitol 3511
				SLACK, Freddie		
8/22/42	9	2		1 Cow-Cow Boogie	Benny Carter/Gene DePaul/Don Raye...*Here You Are*	Capitol 102
12/12/42	10	2		2 Mr. Five By Five	Gene DePaul/Don Raye...*The Thrill Is Gone*	Capitol 115
3/20/43	10	1		3 That Old Black Magic	Harold Arlen/Johnny Mercer...*Hit The Road To Dreamland*	Capitol 126
7/6/46	8	13		4 The House Of Blue Lights	Don Raye/Freddie Slack...*Hey Mr. Postman*	Capitol 251
				SLEDGE, Percy		
5/28/66	❶²	13	●	1 When A Man Loves A Woman	Calvin Lewis/Andrew Wright...*Love Me Like You Mean It*	Atlantic 2326
				SLIM THUG		
2/4/06	❶⁵	28	○	1 Check On It	Angela Beyince/Kasseem Dean/Sean Garrett/Beyonce Knowles/Stayve Thomas	Columbia 80277
				BEYONCE Featuring Bun B & Slim Thug		
				SLY & THE FAMILY STONE		
4/20/68	8	15		1 Dance To The Music	Sly Stone...*Let Me Hear It From You*	Epic 10256
2/15/69	❶⁴	19	●	2 Everyday People	Sly Stone...*Sing A Simple Song*	Epic 10407
10/18/69	2²	16		3 Hot Fun In The Summertime	Sly Stone...*Fun*	Epic 10497
2/14/70	❶²	13	●	4 Thank You Falettinme Be Mice Elf Agin	Sly Stone...*Everybody Is A Star*	Epic 10555
12/4/71	❶³	14	●	5 Family Affair	Sly Stone...*Luv N' Haight*	Epic 10805

PEAK DATE	PEAK POS	WKS CHR	GOLD	ARTIST / Song Title	Songwriter...B-side	Label & Number
				SLY FOX		
4/12/86	7	25		1 Let's Go All The Way	Gary Cooper...*Como Tu Te Llama? (What Is Your Name)*	Capitol 5552
				SMALL, Millie		
7/4/64	2^1	12	⊙	1 My Boy Lollipop	Morris Levy/Johnny Roberts/Robert Spencer...*Something's Gotta Be Done*	Smash 1893
				SMASH MOUTH		
1/24/98	2^1	60		1 Walkin' On The Sun	Greg Camp/Kevin Coleman/Paul DeLisle/Steve Harwell	Interscope
8/14/99	4	30		2 All Star	Greg Camp...*Then The Morning Comes*	Interscope 71007
				SMITH		
11/1/69	5	15		1 Baby It's You	Burt Bacharach/Mack David/Barney Williams...*I Don't Believe (I Believe)*	Dunhill/ABC 4206
				SMITH, Huey (Piano), And The Clowns		
4/14/58	9	13	⊙	1 Don't You Just Know It	Huey Smith/John Vincent...*High Blood Pressure*	Ace 545
				SMITH, Hurricane		
2/17/73	3^1	15		1 Oh, Babe, What Would You Say?	Hurricane Smith...*Getting To Know You*	Capitol 3383
				SMITH, Jack, And The Clark Sisters		
11/8/47	9	7		1 Civilization (Bongo, Bongo, Bongo)	Bob Hilliard/Carl Sigman...*Don't You Love Me Anymore*	Capitol 465
4/2/49	3^2	14		2 Cruising Down The River	Eily Beadell/Nell Tollerton...*Coca Roca*	Capitol 15372
				SMITH, Kate		
8/24/40	5	3		1 God Bless America	Irving Berlin...*The Star Spangled Banner*	Victor 26198
2/21/42	9	1		2 (There'll Be Bluebirds Over) The White Cliffs Of Dover	Nat Burton/Walter Kent...*Rose O'Day (The Filla-ga-dusha Song)*	Columbia 36448
2/28/42	8	3		3 Rose O'Day (The Filla-ga-dusha Song)	Al Lewis/Charles Tobias...*(There'll Be Bluebirds Over) The White Cliffs Of Dover*	Columbia 36448
1/20/45	8	2		4 Don't Fence Me In	Cole Porter...*There Goes That Song Again*	Columbia 36759
				SMITH, Michael W.		
7/13/91	6	21		1 Place In This World	Amy Grant/Wayne Kirkpatrick/Michael W. Smith...*Seed To Sow*	Reunion 19019
				SMITH, O.C.		
10/26/68	2^1	17	●	1 Little Green Apples	Bobby Russell...*Long Black Limousine*	Columbia 44616
				SMITH, Rex		
6/23/79	10	16	●	1 You Take My Breath Away	Bruce Hart/Stephen Lawrence...*You're Never Too Old To Rock & Roll*	Columbia 10908
				SMITH, Sammi		
3/27/71	8	16	●	1 Help Me Make It Through The Night	Kris Kristofferson...*When Michael Calls*	Mega 0015
				SMITH, Somethin', & The Redheads		
8/13/55	7	23		1 It's A Sin To Tell A Lie	Billy Mayhew...*My Baby Just Cares For Me*	Epic 9093
				SMITH, Will		
8/9/97	❶^4	25		1 Men In Black	Theresa McFaddin/Patrice Rushen/Will Smith	Columbia
3/14/98	❶^3	32	●	2 Gettin' Jiggy Wit It	Sam Barnes/Bernard Edwards/Joe Robinson/Nile Rodgers/Will Smith...*Men In Black*	Columbia 78804
7/24/99	❶^1	17	●	3 Wild Wild West	Mohandas DeWese/Robert Fusari/Will Smith/Stevie Wonder...*Y'All Know* (Smith)	Overbrook 79157
				WILL SMITH featuring Dru Hill and Kool Moe Dee		
6/18/05	7	28	○	4 Switch	Lennie Bennett/Kwame Holland/Will Smith...*Party Starter*	Overbrook 005272
				SMYTH, Patty / SCANDAL		
9/22/84	7	21		1 The Warrior	Nick Gilder/Holly Knight...*Less Than Half*	Columbia 04424
				SCANDAL Featuring Patty Smyth		
9/26/92	2^6	24	●	2 Sometimes Love Just Ain't Enough	Glen Burtnick/Patty Smyth...*Out There* (Smyth)	MCA 54403
				PATTY SMYTH with Don Henley		
				SNAP!		
8/11/90	2^1	22	▲	1 The Power	Benito Benites/Durron Butler/John Garrett	Arista 2013
1/2/93	5	39	●	2 Rhythm Is A Dancer	Thea Austin/Benito Benites/Durron Butler/John Garrett...*Who Stole It?*	Arista 12437
				SNOOP DOGG		
3/20/93	2^1	27	▲	1 Nuthin' But A "G" Thang	Calvin Broadus/Leon Haywood	Death Row 53819
7/3/93	8	20	●	2 Dre Day	Calvin Broadus/Colin Wolfe/Andre Young	Death Row 53827
				DR. DRE (with Snoop Doggy Dogg) (above 2)		
1/1/94	8	17	●	3 What's My Name?	Calvin Broadus	Death Row 98340
3/26/94	8	20	●	4 Gin & Juice	Calvin Broadus	Death Row 98318
				SNOOP DOGGY DOGG (above 2)		
4/26/03	6	20		5 Beautiful	Calvin Broadus/Chad Hugo/Pharrell Williams...*Ballin'*	Doggystyle 77887
				SNOOP DOGG featuring Pharrell & Uncle Charlie Wilson		
11/8/03	3^3	21	○	6 Holidae In	Howard Bailey/Christopher Bridges/Shamar Daugherty/Alonzo Lee...*Represent*	Capitol 52816
				CHINGY featuring Ludacris & Snoop Dogg		
12/11/04	❶^3	30	○	7 Drop It Like It's Hot	Calvin Broadus/Chad Hugo/Pharrell Williams	Doggystyle 003574
				SNOOP DOGG featuring Pharrell		
9/23/06	3^1	30		8 Buttons	Calvin Broadus/Sean Garrett/Jamal Jones/Jason Perry/Nicole Scherzinger	A&M 006800
				THE PUSSYCAT DOLLS featuring Big Snoop Dogg		
12/2/06	❶^2	29	△	9 I Wanna Love You	Calvin Broadus/Aliaune Thiam	SRC
				AKON Featuring Snoop Dogg		
3/1/08	7	20		10 Sensual Seduction	Calvin Broadus/Seneca Lovejoy/Demetrius Stewart	Doggystyle 010576
6/19/10	❶^6	27	△^{3}	11 California Gurls	Lukasz Gottwald/Benjamin Levin/Bonnie McKee/Katy Perry/Martin Sandberg...*Hot N Cold (remix)*	Capitol 41011
				KATY PERRY Featuring Snoop Dogg		
				SNOW		
3/13/93	❶^7	25	▲	1 Informer	Edmond Leary/Shawn Moltke/Darrin O'Brien...*Lonely Monday Morning*	EastWest 98471
				SNOW, Phoebe		
4/12/75	5	18		1 Poetry Man	Phoebe Snow...*Either Or Both*	Shelter 40353
				SNOW PATROL		
10/14/06	5	45		1 Chasing Cars	Nathan Connolly/Gary Lightbody/John Quinn/Tom Simpson/Paul Wilson	Polydor

PEAK DATE	PEAK POS	WKS CHR	GOLD	ARTIST / Song Title	Songwriter...B-side	Label & Number
				SNYDER, Bill, And His Orchestra		
6/17/50	3¹	19		1 Bewitched	Lorenz Hart/Richard Rodgers...*Drifting Sands* [I]	Tower 1473
				SOFT CELL		
7/17/82	8	43		1 Tainted Love	Ed Cobb...*Memorabilia*	Sire 49855
				SOLE		
5/22/99	5	20	●	1 Who Dat	DiAndre Davis/Tonya Johnston/Tony Mercedes/Tab Nkhereanye/Christopher Stewart/Jeff Tompkins	Tony Mercedes 53469
				JT MONEY Featuring Sole		
				SOMETHIN' FOR THE PEOPLE		
11/29/97	4	26	●	1 My Love Is The Shhh!	James Baker/Rochad Holiday/Tamara Powell/Curtis Wilson/Melvin Lee Wilson/Jeff Young	Warner 17327
				SOMETHIN' FOR THE PEOPLE featuring Trina & Tamara		
				SOMMERS, Joanie		
7/21/62	7	14		1 Johnny Get Angry	Hal David/Sherman Edwards...*(Theme From) A Summer Place*	Warner 5275
				SONG SPINNERS, The		
7/3/43	❶³	11		1 Comin' In On A Wing And A Prayer	Harold Adamson/Jimmy McHugh...*Johnny Zero*	Decca 18553
7/10/43	7	4		2 Johnny Zero	Mack David/Vee Lawnhurst...*Comin' In On A Wing And A Prayer*	Decca 18553
				SONGZ, Trey		
3/13/10	9	29	△	1 Say Aah	Ronald Ferebee/John Jackson/Tremaine Neverson/Tony Scales/Nathan Walker...*I Invented Sex*	Song Book 523577
				TREY SONGZ Featuring Fabolous		
11/6/10	6	24↑	○	2 Bottoms Up	Miles Edrick/Milton James/Daniel Johnson/Onika Maraj/Tremaine Neverson/Tony Scales	Song Book
				TREY SONGZ Featuring Nicki Minaj		
				SONIQUE		
4/22/00	8	24		1 It Feels So Good	Linus Burdick/Sonia Clarke	Caffeine 156247
				SONNY & CHER		
8/14/65	❶³	14	●	1 I Got You Babe	Sonny Bono...*It's Gonna Rain*	Atco 6359
9/25/65	10	10		2 Laugh At Me	Sonny Bono...*Tony* (Sonny's Group)	Atco 6369
				SONNY		
10/9/65	8	12		3 Baby Don't Go	Sonny Bono...*Walkin' The Quetzal*	Reprise 0392
2/25/67	6	11		4 The Beat Goes On	Sonny Bono...*Love Don't Come*	Atco 6461
12/25/71	7	15		5 All I Ever Need Is You	Jimmy Holiday/Eddie Reeves...*I Got You Babe (live)*	Kapp 2151
4/29/72	8	13		6 A Cowboys Work Is Never Done	Sonny Bono...*Somebody*	Kapp 2163
				SONS OF THE PIONEERS		
10/9/48	9	14		1 Cool Water	Bob Nolan...*The Legend Of Tiabi*	RCA Victor 2923
				VAUGHN MONROE and Sons of the Pioneers		
				S.O.S. BAND, The		
8/16/80	3²	21	▲	1 Take Your Time (Do It Right) Part 1	Harold Clayton/Umunto Sigidi...*Part 2*	Tabu 5522
				SOUL, David		
4/16/77	❶¹	19	●	1 Don't Give Up On Us	Tony MacAulay...*Black Bean Soup*	Private Stock 45,129
				SOUL, Jimmy		
5/18/63	❶²	14	⊙	1 If You Wanna Be Happy	Carmela Guida/Frank Guida/Joseph Royster...*Don't Release Me*	S.P.Q.R. 3305
				SOUL ASYLUM		
8/28/93	5	26	●	1 Runaway Train	Dave Pirner...*Never Really Been (live)*	Columbia 74966
				SOUL FOR REAL		
3/18/95	2⁴	25	●	1 Candy Rain	Sam Barnes/Dwight Meyers/J.C. Olivier/Terri Robinson	Uptown/MCA 54906
				SOULJA BOY TELL'EM		
9/15/07	❶⁷	32		1 Crank That (Soulja Boy)	DeAndre Way	ColliPark
4/4/09	3²	27		2 Kiss Me Thru The Phone	Jim Scheffer/David Siegel/DeAndre Way	ColliPark
				SOULJA BOY TELL'EM Featuring Sammie		
				SOUL SURVIVORS		
11/4/67	4	15		1 Expressway To Your Heart	Kenny Gamble/Leon Huff...*Hey Gyp*	Crimson 1010
				SOUL II SOUL		
12/16/89	4	28	▲	1 Back To Life	Beresford Romeo	Virgin 99171
				SOUNDS ORCHESTRAL		
5/8/65	10	14		1 Cast Your Fate To The Wind	Vince Guaraldi/Carel Werber...*To Wendy With Love* [I]	Parkway 942
				SOUTHER, J.D.		
12/15/79	7	21		1 You're Only Lonely	J.D. Souther...*Songs Of Love*	Columbia 11079
				SPANDAU BALLET		
10/8/83	4	18		1 True	Gary Kemp...*Gently*	Chrysalis 42720
				SPANKY AND OUR GANG		
6/24/67	9	8		1 Sunday Will Never Be The Same	Terry Cashman/Eugene Pistilli...*Distance*	Mercury 72679
				SPARKS, Jordin		
12/29/07	8	31	△	1 Tattoo	Ian Dench/Mikkel Eriksen/Amanda Ghost/Tor Erik Hermansen	19 Records
4/26/08	3⁴	35	△	2 No Air	James Fauntleroy/Eric Griggs/Harvey Mason Jr./Steve Russell/Damon Thomas	19 Records
				JORDIN SPARKS & CHRIS BROWN		
8/8/09	10	22		3 Battlefield	Louis Biancaniello/Ryan Tedder/Samuel Watters/Wayne Wilkins	19 Records
				SPARXXX, Bubba		
5/13/06	7	24		1 Ms. New Booty	Michael Crooms/Deongelo Holmes/Eric Jackson/Warren Mathis	New South 50658
				BUBBA SPARXXX Feat. Ying Yang Twins and Mr. ColliPark		

PEAK DATE	PEAK POS	WKS CHR	GOLD	ARTIST / Song Title	Songwriter...B-side	Label & Number
				SPEARS, Britney		
1/30/99	❶²	32	▲	1 ...Baby One More Time	Max Martin...*Autumn Goodbye*	Jive 42545
11/13/99	10	20		2 (You Drive Me) Crazy	Jorgen Elofsson/David Kreuger/Per Magnusson/Max Martin	Jive 42606
6/10/00	9	20		3 Oops!...I Did It Again	Max Martin/Rami Yacoub	Jive 42700
3/27/04	9	20	○	4 Toxic	Cathy Dennis/Henrik Jonback/Christian Karlsson/Pontus Winnberg	Jive 59214
10/13/07	3²	20	△	5 Gimme More	Tenesha Blacks/Mikkel Eriksen/Tor Erik Hermansen/Shanell Irving	Jive 18815
10/25/08	❶¹	23		6 Womanizer	Rapheal Akinyemi/Nikesha Briscoe	Jive
12/20/08	3¹	22		7 Circus	Lukasz Gottwald/Claude Kelly/Benjamin Levin	Jive
10/24/09	❶¹	20		8 3	Tiffany Amber/Max Martin/Johan Schuster	Jive
1/29/11	❶¹	2↑		9 Hold It Against Me	Lukasz Gottwald/Mathieu Jomphe/Max Martin/Bonnie McKee	Jive
				SPENCER, Tracie		
3/30/91	3¹	23		1 This House	Matt Sherrod/Paul Sherrod/Marty Spencer...*I Have A Song To Sing*	Capitol 44652
				SPICE GIRLS		
2/22/97	❶⁴	23	▲	1 Wannabe	Victoria Adams/Melanie Brown/Emma Bunton/Melanie Chisholm/Geri Halliwell/Matt Rowe/Richard Stannard...*Bumper To Bumper*	Virgin 38579
5/31/97	3³	21	●	2 Say You'll Be There	Victoria Adams/Melanie Brown/Emma Bunton/Melanie Chisholm/Geri Halliwell/Eliot Kennedy...*Take Me Home*	Virgin 38592
9/6/97	4	24	●	3 2 Become 1	Victoria Adams/Melanie Brown/Emma Bunton/Melanie Chisholm/Geri Halliwell/Matt Rowe/Richard Stannard...*One Of These Girls*	Virgin 38604
2/21/98	9	20		4 Too Much	Victoria Adams/Melanie Brown/Emma Bunton/Melanie Chisholm/Geri Halliwell/Andrew Watkins/Paul Wilson...*Outer Space Girls*	Virgin 38630
				SPIN DOCTORS		
4/10/93	7	29		1 Two Princes	Christopher Barron/Aaron Comess/Eric Schenkman/Mark White...*Off My Line (live)*	Epic Associated 74804
				SPINNERS		
11/18/72	3²	15	●	1 I'll Be Around	Thom Bell/Phil Hurt...*How Could I Let You Get Away*	Atlantic 2904
3/3/73	4	15	●	2 Could It Be I'm Falling In Love	Melvin Steals/Mervin Steals...*Just You And Me Baby*	Atlantic 2927
10/26/74	❶¹	19	●	3 Then Came You — DIONNE WARWICKE AND SPINNERS	Sherman Marshall/Phil Pugh...*Just As Long As We Have Love*	Atlantic 3202
10/25/75	5	18		4 "They Just Can't Stop It" The (Games People Play)	Bruce Hawes/Joe Jefferson/Charles Simmons...*I Don't Want To Lose You*	Atlantic 3284
12/4/76	2³	21		5 The Rubberband Man	Thom Bell/Linda Creed...*Now That We're Together*	Atlantic 3355
3/29/80	2²	25		6 Working My Way Back To You/Forgive Me, Girl	Sandy Linzer/Denny Randell/Michael Zager...*Disco Ride*	Atlantic 3637
7/19/80	4	19		7 Cupid/I've Loved You For A Long Time	Sam Cooke/Michael Zager...*Pipedream*	Atlantic 3664
				SPIVAK, Charlie, and his Orchestra		
8/2/41	10	1		1 Intermezzo (A Love Story)	Robert Henning/Heinz Provost...*Simpatica* [I]	Okeh 6120
1/10/42	8	2		2 This Is No Laughing Matter	Al Frisch/Buddy Kaye...*When I See An Elephant Fly*	Okeh 6458
10/3/42	2²	11		3 My Devotion	Roc Hillman/Johnny Napton...*I Left My Heart At The Stage Door Canteen*	Columbia 36620
10/17/42	8	2		4 I Left My Heart At The Stage Door Canteen	Irving Berlin...*My Devotion*	Columbia 36620
6/30/45	6	6		5 You Belong To My Heart	Ray Gilbert/Agustin Lara...*There Must Be A Way*	Victor 1663
7/21/45	9	6		6 There Must Be A Way	Robert Cook/Sammy Gallop/David Saxon...*You Belong To My Heart*	Victor 1663
11/17/45	4	12		7 It's Been A Long, Long Time	Sammy Cahn/Jule Styne...*If I Had A Dozen Hearts*	Victor 1721
4/13/46	5	7		8 Oh! What It Seemed To Be	Bennie Benjamin/Frankie Carle/George Weiss...*Take Care (When You Say "Te Quiero")*	RCA Victor 1806
1/11/47	5	14		9 (I Love You) For Sentimental Reasons	William Best/Deek Watson...*It's All Over Now*	RCA Victor 1981
4/26/47	5	11		10 Linda	Jack Lawrence...*So They Tell Me*	RCA Victor 2047
				SPORTSMEN, The		
6/26/48	6	14		1 You Can't Be True, Dear	Hal Cotton/Gerhard Ebeler/Ken Griffin/Hans Otten...*Toolie Oolie Doolie (The Yodel Polka)*	Capitol 15077
7/17/48	2⁵	9		2 Woody Woodpecker — THE SPORTSMEN and MEL BLANC And His Original Woody Woodpecker Voice	Ramez Idriss/George Tibbles...*I'd Love To Live In Loveland With A Girl Like You* (Sportsmen) [N]	Capitol 15145
				SPRINGFIELD, Dusty		
8/1/64	6	13		1 Wishin' And Hopin'	Burt Bacharach/Hal David...*Do Re Mi (Forget About The Do And Think About Me)*	Philips 40207
7/16/66	4	13	⊙	2 You Don't Have To Say You Love Me	Pino Donaggio/Simon Napier-Bell/Vicki Wickham...*Little By Little*	Philips 40371
1/18/69	10	12		3 Son-Of-A Preacher Man	John Hurley/Ronnie Wilkins...*Just A Little Lovin' (Early In The Mornin')*	Atlantic 2580
2/20/88	2²	18		4 What Have I Done To Deserve This? — PET SHOP BOYS (and Dusty Springfield)	Chris Lowe/Neil Tennant/Allee Willis...*A New Life* (Pet Shop Boys)	EMI/Manhattan 50107
				SPRINGFIELD, Rick		
8/1/81	❶²	32	●	1 Jessie's Girl	Rick Springfield...*Carry Me Away*	RCA 12201
11/7/81	8	22		2 I've Done Everything For You	Sammy Hagar...*Red Hot And Blue Love*	RCA 12166
5/22/82	2⁴	21		3 Don't Talk To Strangers	Rick Springfield...*Tonight*	RCA 13070
6/18/83	9	18		4 Affair Of The Heart	Rick Springfield/Danny Tate/Blaise Tosti...*Like Father, Like Son*	RCA 13497
5/5/84	5	16		5 Love Somebody	Bill Drescher/Rick Springfield...*The Great Lost Art Of Conversation*	RCA 13738
				SPRINGSTEEN, Bruce		
12/27/80	5	18		1 Hungry Heart	Bruce Springsteen...*Held Up Without A Gun*	Columbia 11391
6/30/84	2⁴	21	▲	2 Dancing In The Dark	Bruce Springsteen...*Pink Cadillac*	Columbia 04463
10/20/84	7	18	●	3 Cover Me	Bruce Springsteen...*Jersey Girl (live)*	Columbia 04561
1/19/85	9	17	●	4 Born In The U.S.A.	Bruce Springsteen...*Shut Out The Light*	Columbia 04680
4/13/85	6	20		5 I'm On Fire	Bruce Springsteen...*Johnny Bye Bye*	Columbia 04772
8/3/85	5	18		6 Glory Days	Bruce Springsteen...*Stand On It*	Columbia 04924
10/26/85	9	13		7 I'm Goin' Down	Bruce Springsteen...*Janey, Don't You Lose Heart*	Columbia 05603
1/25/86	6	15	●	8 My Hometown	Bruce Springsteen...*Santa Claus Is Comin' To Town*	Columbia 05728
12/27/86	8	12		9 War	Barrett Strong/Norman Whitfield...*Merry Christmas Baby* [L]	Columbia 06432
11/21/87	5	16		10 Brilliant Disguise	Bruce Springsteen...*Lucky Man*	Columbia 07595
2/6/88	9	16		11 Tunnel Of Love	Bruce Springsteen...*Two For The Road*	Columbia 07663
4/23/94	9	20	●	12 Streets Of Philadelphia	Bruce Springsteen...*If I Should Fall Behind*	Columbia 77384
				STACEY Q		
10/11/86	3¹	22		1 Two Of Hearts	Sue Gatlin/Tim Greene/John Mitchell...*Dancing Nowhere*	Atlantic 89381
				STAFFORD, Jim		
3/2/74	3¹	23	●	1 Spiders & Snakes	David Bellamy/Jim Stafford...*Undecided*	MGM 14648
8/24/74	7	14		2 Wildwood Weed	Don Bowman...*The Last Chant* [N-S]	MGM 14737
				STAFFORD, Jo		
4/29/44	8	4		1 I Love You	Cole Porter...*Long Ago (And Far Away)*	Capitol 153
5/20/44	6	12		2 Long Ago (And Far Away)	Ira Gershwin/Jerome Kern...*I Love You*	Capitol 153

PEAK DATE	PEAK POS	WKS CHR	GOLD	ARTIST / Song Title	Songwriter...B-side	Label & Number
				STAFFORD, Jo (cont'd)		
9/30/44	10	1		3 It Could Happen To You	Johnny Burke/Jimmy Van Heusen...*Someone To Love*	Capitol 158
3/31/45	❶¹	19		4 Candy	Mack David/Alex Kramer/Joan Whitney...*I'm Gonna See My Baby*	Capitol 183
				JOHNNY MERCER, JO STAFFORD		
6/30/45	7	6		5 There's No You	Tom Adair/Hal Hopper...*Out Of This World*	Capitol 191
7/28/45	9	1		6 Out Of This World	Harold Arlen/Johnny Mercer...*There's No You*	Capitol 191
10/27/45	4	4		7 That's For Me	Oscar Hammerstein/Richard Rodgers...*Gee, It's Good To Hold You*	Capitol 213
1/19/46	4	12		8 Symphony	Alex Alstone/Roger Bernstein/Jack Lawrence/Andre Tabet...*Day By Day*	Capitol 227
3/16/46	8	2		9 Day By Day	Sammy Cahn/Axel Stordahl/Paul Weston...*Symphony*	Capitol 227
11/16/46	10	2		10 The Things We Did Last Summer	Sammy Cahn/Jule Styne...*You Keep Coming Back Like A Song*	Capitol 297
12/28/46	9	1		11 White Christmas	Irving Berlin...*Silent Night* [X]	Capitol 319
1/25/47	10	5		12 Sonata	Leo Robin/Arthur Schwartz...*Through A Thousand Dreams*	Capitol 337
9/6/47	6	11		13 Feudin' And Fightin'	Al Dubin/Burton Lane...*Love And The Weather* [N]	Capitol 443
12/20/47	6	11		14 Serenade Of The Bells	Al Goodhart/Kay Twomey/Al Urbano...*The Gentleman Is A Dope*	Capitol 15007
7/16/49	4	17		15 Some Enchanted Evening	Oscar Hammerstein/Richard Rodgers...*I'm Gonna Wash That Man Right Outta My Hair*	Capitol 544
10/8/49	10	7		16 Ragtime Cowboy Joe	Maurice Abrahams/Grant Clarke/Lewis Muir...*The Last Mile Home*	Capitol 710
11/19/49	9	5		17 The Last Mile Home	Walton Farrar/Walter Kent...*Ragtime Cowboy Joe*	Capitol 710
9/9/50	8	11		18 No Other Love	Chopin/Bob Russell/Paul Weston...*Sometime*	Capitol 1053
9/23/50	9	7		19 Goodnight, Irene	Huddie Ledbetter/John Lomax...*Our Very Own*	Capitol 1142
1/20/51	7	13		20 Tennessee Waltz	Pee Wee King/Redd Stewart...*If You've Got The Money, I've Got The Time*	Columbia 39065
2/17/51	8	18		21 If	Stanley Damerell/Tolchard Evans/Robert Hargreaves...*It Is No Secret*	Columbia 39082
11/17/51	9	8		22 Hey, Good Lookin'	Hank Williams...*Gambella (The Gamblin' Lady)*	Columbia 39570
				FRANKIE LAINE - JO STAFFORD		
12/22/51	2²	17		23 Shrimp Boats	Paul Howard/Paul Weston...*Love, Mystery And Adventure*	Columbia 39581
4/5/52	6	10		24 Hambone	Red Saunders/Leon Washington...*Let's Have A Party*	Columbia 39672
				FRANKIE LAINE & JO STAFFORD		
5/10/52	9	12		25 Ay-Round The Corner (Bee-hind The Bush)	Josef Marais...*Heaven Drops Her Curtain Down (Twilight Theme Of An Autumn Fantasy)*	Columbia 39653
9/13/52	❶¹²	25	⊙	26 You Belong To Me	Pee Wee King/Chilton Price/Redd Stewart...*Pretty Boy (Pretty Girl)*	Columbia 39811
9/27/52	3³	20		27 Jambalaya	Hank Williams...*Early Autumn*	Columbia 39838
1/3/53	4	18		28 Keep It A Secret	Jessie Mae Robinson...*Once To Every Heart*	Columbia 39891
3/13/54	❶⁷	24	⊙	29 Make Love To Me!	George Brunies/Allan Copeland/Paul Mares/Walter Melrose/Bill Norvas/Benny Pollack/Leon Roppolo/Mel Stitzel...*Adi - Adios Amigo (Il Passerotto)*	Columbia 40143
				JO STAFFORD AND GORDON MacRAE:		
11/13/48	10	6		30 Say Something Sweet To Your Sweetheart	Roy Brodsky/Sid Tepper...*Bluebird Of Happiness*	Capitol 15207
1/15/49	❶¹	17		31 My Darling, My Darling	Frank Loesser...*Girls Were Made To Take Care Of Boys*	Capitol 15270
4/30/49	4	15		32 "A" You're Adorable	Buddy Kaye/Sid Lippman/Fred Wise...*Need You*	Capitol 15393
5/7/49	7	12		33 Need You	Johnny Blackburn/Teepee Mitchell/Lew Porter...*"A" You're Adorable*	Capitol 15393
10/1/49	4	23		34 Whispering Hope	Alice Hawthorne...*A Thought In My Heart*	Capitol 690
4/8/50	10	11		35 Dearie	Bob Hilliard/Dave Mann...*Monday, Tuesday, Wednesday*	Capitol 858
				STAFFORD, Terry		
4/11/64	3²	15	⊙	1 Suspicion	Doc Pomus/Mort Shuman...*Judy*	Crusader 101
				STAIND		
10/20/01	5	46	○	1 It's Been Awhile	Johnny April/Aaron Lewis/Mike Mushok/Jon Wysocki	Flip/Elektra
				STALLONE, Frank		
10/1/83	10	16		1 Far From Over	Vince DiCola/Frank Stallone...*Waking Up*	RSO 815023
				STAMPEDERS		
10/23/71	8	14		1 Sweet City Woman	Rich Dodson...*Gator Road*	Bell 45,120
				STANDLEY, Johnny		
11/22/52	❶²	19	⊙	1 It's In The Book (Parts 1 & 2)	Johnny Standley/Art Thorsen [C]	Capitol 2249
				STANSFIELD, Lisa		
4/7/90	3³	22	▲	1 All Around The World	Ian Devaney/Andy Morris/Lisa Stansfield...*Affection*	Arista 9928
				STAPLE SINGERS, The		
6/3/72	❶¹	15		1 I'll Take You There	Alvertis Isbell...*I'm Just Another Soldier*	Stax 0125
12/22/73	9	16	●	2 If You're Ready (Come Go With Me)	Homer Banks/Carl Hampton/Raymond Jackson...*Love Comes In All Colors*	Stax 0179
12/27/75	❶¹	15	●	3 Let's Do It Again	Curtis Mayfield...*After Sex*	Curtom 0109
				STARBUCK		
7/31/76	3²	22		1 Moonlight Feels Right	Bruce Blackman...*Lash LaRue*	Private Stock 45,039
				STARDUSTERS, The		
7/23/49	5	21		1 I Don't See Me In Your Eyes Anymore	Bennie Benjamin/George Weiss...*Because You Love Me*	Decca 24576
				STARLAND VOCAL BAND		
7/10/76	❶²	20	●	1 Afternoon Delight	Bill Danoff...*Starland*	Windsong 10588
				STARR, Edwin		
4/26/69	6	14		1 Twenty-Five Miles	Johnny Bristol/Harvey Fuqua/Edwin Starr...*Love Is My Destination*	Gordy 7083
8/29/70	❶³	15		2 War	Barrett Strong/Norman Whitfield...*He Who Picks A Rose*	Gordy 7101
				STARR, Kay		
4/9/49	7	16		1 So Tired	Russ Morgan/Jack Stuart...*Steady Daddy*	Capitol 15314
6/17/50	2¹	16		2 Hoop-Dee-Doo	Milton DeLugg/Frank Loesser...*A Woman Likes To Be Told*	Capitol 980
9/23/50	4	27		3 Bonaparte's Retreat	Pee Wee King...*Someday Sweetheart*	Capitol 936
11/18/50	3¹	20		4 I'll Never Be Free	Bennie Benjamin/George Weiss...*Ain't Nobody's Business But My Own*	Capitol 1124
				KAY STARR and TENNESSEE ERNIE		
12/2/50	7	8		5 Oh, Babe	Milton Kabak/Louis Prima...*Everybody's Somebody's Fool*	Capitol 1278
8/25/51	8	9		6 Come On-A My House	William Saroyan/David Seville...*Hold Me, Hold Me, Hold Me*	Capitol 1710
3/15/52	❶¹⁰	25	⊙	7 Wheel Of Fortune	Bennie Benjamin/George Weiss...*I Wanna Love You*	Capitol 1964
11/8/52	9	9		8 Comes A-Long A-Love	Al Sherman...*Three Letters*	Capitol 2213
3/7/53	3³	13		9 Side By Side	Harry Woods...*Noah!*	Capitol 2334
7/18/53	7	15		10 Half A Photograph	Bob Russell/Hal Stanley...*Allez-Vous-En*	Capitol 2464
1/23/54	7	13		11 Changing Partners	Larry Coleman/Joe Darion...*I'll Always Be In Love With You*	Capitol 2657

PEAK DATE	PEAK POS	WKS CHR	GOLD	ARTIST / Song Title	Songwriter...B-side	Label & Number
				STARR, Kay (cont'd)		
5/29/54	7	17		12 The Man Upstairs	Bob Russell/Hal Stanley...*If You Love Me (Really Love Me)*	Capitol 2769
6/5/54	4	18		13 If You Love Me (Really Love Me)	Marguerite Monnot/Geoffrey Parsons...*The Man Upstairs*	Capitol 2769
2/18/56	❶⁶	25	⊙	14 Rock And Roll Waltz	Roy Alfred/Shorty Allen...*I've Changed My Mind A Thousand Times*	RCA Victor 6359
10/14/57	9	12		15 My Heart Reminds Me	Camillo Bargoni/Al Stillman...*Flim Flam Floo*	RCA Victor 6981
				STARR, Ringo		
6/5/71	4	12	●	1 It Don't Come Easy	Ringo Starr...*Early 1970*	Apple 1831
5/13/72	9	10		2 Back Off Boogaloo	Ringo Starr...*Blindman*	Apple 1849
11/24/73	❶¹	16	●	3 Photograph	George Harrison/Ringo Starr...*Down And Out*	Apple 1865
1/26/74	❶¹	15	●	4 You're Sixteen	Richard Sherman/Robert Sherman...*Devil Woman*	Apple 1870
4/27/74	5	14		5 Oh My My	Vini Poncia/Ringo Starr...*Step Lightly*	Apple 1872
1/11/75	6	13		6 Only You	Buck Ram/Ande Rand...*Call Me*	Apple 1876
4/5/75	3²	14		7 No No Song	Hoyt Axton...*Snookeroo*	Apple 1880
				STARSHIP — see JEFFERSON AIRPLANE		
				STARS on 45		
6/20/81	❶¹	21	●	1 Medley	Jeff Barry/Andy Kim/John Lennon/Paul McCartney/Robbie Van Leeuwen...*Stars on 45*	Radio 3810
				STATLER BROTHERS, The		
1/8/66	4	13		1 Flowers On The Wall	Lew DeWitt...*Billy Christian*	Columbia 43315
				STEALERS WHEEL		
5/12/73	6	18		1 Stuck In The Middle With You	Joe Egan/Gerry Rafferty...*Jose*	A&M 1416
				STEAM		
12/6/69	❶²	16	●	1 Na Na Hey Hey Kiss Him Goodbye	Gary DeCarlo/Dale Frashuer/Paul Leka...*It's The Magic In You Girl*	Fontana 1667
				STEELE, Jon and Sondra		
6/12/48	2²	30	⊙	1 My Happiness	Borney Bergantine/Betty Peterson...*They All Recorded To Beat The Ban*	Damon 11133
				STEELY DAN		
2/10/73	6	17		1 Do It Again	Walter Becker/Donald Fagen...*Fire In The Hole*	ABC 11338
8/3/74	4	19		2 Rikki Don't Lose That Number	Walter Becker/Donald Fagen...*Any Major Dude Will Tell You*	ABC 11439
2/14/81	10	19		3 Hey Nineteen	Walter Becker/Donald Fagen...*Bodhisattva (live)*	MCA 51036
				STEFANI, Gwen		
8/18/01	2¹	33		1 Let Me Blow Ya Mind	Mike Elizondo/Eve Jeffers/Scott Storch/Andre Young...*That's What It Is* (w/Styles of The Lox)	Ruff Ryders 497562
				EVE Featuring Gwen Stefani		
3/5/05	7	27	○	2 Rich Girl	Mark Batson/Jerry Bock/Kara DioGuardi/Mike Elizondo/Sheldon Harnick/Eve Jeffers/Chantal Keviazuk/Gwen Stefani/Andre Young	Interscope 003978
				GWEN STEFANI featuring Eve		
5/7/05	❶⁴	31	△	3 Hollaback Girl	Charles Hugo/Gwen Stefani/Pharrell Williams	Interscope 004435
12/16/06	6	18		4 Wind It Up	Gwen Stefani/Pharrell Williams	Interscope
4/14/07	2¹	40		5 The Sweet Escape	Gwen Stefani/Aliaune Thiam/Giorgio Tunifort	Interscope 008526
				GWEN STEFANI Featuring Akon		
				STEPPENWOLF		
8/24/68	2³	13	●	1 Born To Be Wild	Mars Bonfire...*Everybody's Next One*	Dunhill/ABC 4138
11/30/68	3¹	16	●	2 Magic Carpet Ride	John Kay/Rushton Moreve...*Sookie Sookie*	Dunhill/ABC 4161
4/19/69	10	10		3 Rock Me	John Kay...*Jupiter's Child*	Dunhill/ABC 4182
				STEVENS, April		
7/21/51	6	15		1 I'm In Love Again	Cole Porter...*Roller Coaster*	RCA Victor 4148
				HENRI RENE and his Orchestra featuring April Stevens		
8/18/51	10	5		2 Gimme A Little Kiss, Will Ya Huh?	Maceo Pinkard/Jack Smith/Roy Turk...*Dreamy Melody*	RCA Victor 4208
				APRIL STEVENS with HENRI RENE and his Orchestra		
11/16/63	❶¹	15		3 Deep Purple	Peter DeRose/Mitchell Parish...*I've Been Carrying A Torch For You So Long*	Atco 6273
				NINO TEMPO & APRIL STEVENS		
				STEVENS, Cat		
11/6/71	7	12		1 Peace Train	Cat Stevens...*Where Do The Children Play*	A&M 1291
5/27/72	6	14		2 Morning Has Broken	Eleanor Farjeon...*I Want To Live In A Wigwam*	A&M 1335
6/1/74	10	17		3 Oh Very Young	Cat Stevens...*100 I Dream*	A&M 1503
10/12/74	6	14		4 Another Saturday Night	Sam Cooke...*Home In The Sky*	A&M 1602
				STEVENS, Connie		
5/11/59	4	13	⊙	1 Kookie, Kookie (Lend Me Your Comb)	Irving Taylor...*You're The Top* (Brynes) [N]	Warner 5047
				EDWARD BYRNES And CONNIE STEVENS		
5/2/60	3¹	24	⊙	2 Sixteen Reasons	Bill Post/Doree Post...*Little Sister*	Warner 5137
				STEVENS, Dodie		
4/13/59	3²	19	⊙	1 Pink Shoe Laces	Mickie Grant...*Coming Of Age*	Crystalette 724
				STEVENS, Ray		
8/4/62	5	11		1 Ahab, The Arab	Ray Stevens...*It's Been So Long* [N]	Mercury 71966
5/31/69	8	13	●	2 Gitarzan	Bill Everette/Ray Stevens...*Bagpipes-That's My Bag* [N]	Monument 1131
5/30/70	❶²	15	●	3 Everything Is Beautiful	Ray Stevens...*A Brighter Day*	Barnaby 2011
5/18/74	❶³	17	●	4 The Streak	Ray Stevens...*You've Got The Music Inside* [N]	Barnaby 600
				STEVENSON, B.W.		
9/29/73	9	16		1 My Maria	Daniel Moore/B.W. Stevenson...*August Evening Lady*	RCA Victor 0030
				STEVIE B		
12/8/90	❶⁴	23	●	1 Because I Love You (The Postman Song)	Warren Brooks	LMR/RCA 2724
				STEWART, Al		
3/5/77	8	17		1 Year Of The Cat	Al Stewart/Peter Wood...*Broadway Hotel*	Janus 266
12/9/78	7	18		2 Time Passages	Al Stewart/Peter White...*Almost Lucy*	Arista 0362

PEAK DATE	PEAK POS	WKS CHR	GOLD	ARTIST / Song Title	Songwriter...B-side	Label & Number
				STEWART, Amii		
4/21/79	❶¹	20	▲	1 Knock On Wood	Steve Cropper/Eddie Floyd...*When You Are Beautiful*	Ariola America 7736
				STEWART, Billy		
8/27/66	10	10		1 Summertime	George Gershwin/DuBose Heyward...*To Love To Love*	Chess 1966
				STEWART, Jermaine		
8/9/86	5	22	1	We Don't Have To Take Our Clothes Off	Preston Glass/Narada Michael Walden...*Give Your Love To Me*	Arista 9424
				STEWART, John		
8/4/79	5	18		1 Gold	John Stewart...*Comin' Out Of Nowhere*	RSO 931
				STEWART, Rod		
10/2/71	❶⁵	17	●	1 Maggie May	Martin Quittenton/Rod Stewart...*Reason To Believe*	Mercury 73224
11/13/76	❶⁸	23	●	2 Tonight's The Night (Gonna Be Alright)	Rod Stewart...*Fool For You*	Warner 8262
1/14/78	4	22	●	3 You're In My Heart (The Final Acclaim)	Rod Stewart...*You Got A Nerve*	Warner 8475
2/10/79	❶⁴	21	▲	4 Da Ya Think I'm Sexy?	Carmine Appice/Rod Stewart...*Scarred And Scared*	Warner 8724
2/7/81	5	20		5 Passion	Phil Chen/Jim Cregan/Gary Grainger/Kevin Savigar/Rod Stewart...*Better Off Dead*	Warner 49617
12/19/81	5	19		6 Young Turks	Carmine Appice/Duane Hitchings/Kevin Savigar/Rod Stewart...*Sonny*	Warner 49843
7/28/84	6	18		7 Infatuation	Duane Hitchings/Rowland Robinson/Rod Stewart...*She Won't Dance With Me*	Warner 29256
10/27/84	10	17		8 Some Guys Have All The Luck	Jeff Fortgang...*I Was Only Joking*	Warner 29215
8/9/86	6	18		9 Love Touch	Gene Black/Mike Chapman/Holly Knight...*Heart Is On The Line*	Warner 28668
4/1/89	4	25		10 My Heart Can't Tell You No	Simon Climie/Dennis Morgan...*The Wild Horse*	Warner 27729
1/27/90	3³	18		11 Downtown Train	Tom Waits...*The Killing Of Georgie (Part I And II)*	Warner 22685
5/26/90	10	16		12 This Old Heart Of Mine ROD STEWART (with Ronald Isley)	Lamont Dozier/Brian Holland/Eddie Holland...*You're In My Heart*	Warner 19983
5/18/91	5	18		13 Rhythm Of My Heart	John Capek/Marc Jordan...*Moment Of Glory*	Warner 19366
9/21/91	10	17		14 The Motown Song ROD STEWART (with The Temptations)	Larry John McNally...*Sweet Soul Music (live)*	Warner 19322
6/19/93	5	22	●	15 Have I Told You Lately	Van Morrison...*Gasoline Alley* [L]	Warner 18511
1/22/94	❶³	22	▲	16 All For Love BRYAN ADAMS ROD STEWART STING	Bryan Adams/Michael Kamen/Mutt Lange	A&M 0476
				STIGERS, Curtis		
11/23/91	9	20		1 I Wonder Why	Glen Ballard/Curtis Stigers...*Nobody Loves You Like I Do*	Arista 12331
				STING		
8/3/85	3²	18		1 If You Love Somebody Set Them Free	Sting...*Another Day*	A&M 2738
10/26/85	8	20		2 Fortress Around Your Heart	Sting...*Consider Me Gone (live)*	A&M 2767
12/5/87	7	18		3 We'll Be Together	Sting...*Conversation With A Dog*	A&M 2983
3/16/91	5	15		4 All This Time	Sting...*I Miss You Kate*	A&M 1541
1/22/94	❶³	22	▲	5 All For Love BRYAN ADAMS ROD STEWART STING	Bryan Adams/Michael Kamen/Mutt Lange	A&M 0476
				STOLOFF, Morris		
6/2/56	❶³	27	⊙	1 Moonglow and Theme From "Picnic" MORRIS STOLOFF Conducting The Columbia Pictures Orchestra	Eddie DeLange/Will Hudson/Irving Mills...*Theme From "Picnic"* (George Duning) [I]	Decca 29888
				STORIES		
8/25/73	❶²	18	●	1 Brother Louie	Errol Brown/Anthony Wilson...*What Comes After*	Kama Sutra 577
				STORM, Gale		
12/10/55	2³	18	⊙	1 I Hear You Knocking	Dave Bartholomew/Pearl King...*Never Leave Me*	Dot 15412
1/14/56	5	16		2 Memories Are Made Of This	Richard Dehr/Terry Gilkyson/Frank Miller...*Teen Age Prayer*	Dot 15436
1/14/56	6	15		3 Teen Age Prayer	Bernie Lowe/Bix Reichner...*Memories Are Made Of This*	Dot 15436
3/24/56	9	18		4 Why Do Fools Fall In Love	Jimmy Merchant/Herman Santiago...*I Walk Alone*	Dot 15448
5/19/56	6	18		5 Ivory Tower	Jack Fulton/Lois Steele...*I Ain't Gonna Worry*	Dot 15458
6/17/57	4	23		6 Dark Moon	Ned Miller...*A Little Too Late*	Dot 15558
				STRAWBERRY ALARM CLOCK		
11/25/67	❶¹	16	●	1 Incense And Peppermints	John Carter/Tim Gilbert...*The Birdman Of Alkatrash*	Uni 55018
				STRAY CATS		
12/11/82	9	21		1 Rock This Town	Brian Setzer...*You Can't Hurry Love*	EMI America 8132
2/26/83	3³	19		2 Stray Cat Strut	Brian Setzer...*You Don't Believe Me*	EMI America 8122
10/1/83	5	15		3 (She's) Sexy + 17	Brian Setzer...*Lookin' Better Every Beer*	EMI America 8168
				STREISAND, Barbra		
6/27/64	5	19		1 People	Bob Merrill/Jule Styne...*I Am Woman*	Columbia 42965
1/23/71	6	18		2 Stoney End	Laura Nyro...*I'll Be Home*	Columbia 45236
2/2/74	❶³	23	▲	3 The Way We Were	Alan Bergman/Marilyn Bergman/Marvin Hamlisch...*What Are You Doing The Rest Of Your Life?*	Columbia 45944
3/5/77	❶³	25	▲	4 Evergreen (Love Theme From "A Star Is Born")	Barbra Streisand/Paul Williams...*I Believe In Love*	Columbia 10450
7/30/77	4	17		5 My Heart Belongs To Me	Alan Gordon...*Answer Me*	Columbia 10555
12/2/78	❶²	17	▲	6 You Don't Bring Me Flowers BARBRA & NEIL	Alan Bergman/Marilyn Bergman/Neil Diamond	Columbia 10840
8/11/79	3⁴	17	●	7 The Main Event/Fight	Bob Esty/Paul Jabara/Bruce Roberts	Columbia 11008
11/24/79	❶²	15	▲	8 No More Tears (Enough Is Enough) BARBRA STREISAND/DONNA SUMMER	Paul Jabara/Bruce Roberts...*Wet* (Streisand)	Columbia 11125
10/25/80	❶³	24▲		9 Woman In Love	Barry Gibb/Robin Gibb...*Run Wild*	Columbia 11364
1/10/81	3²	22	●	10 Guilty	Barry Gibb/Maurice Gibb/Robin Gibb...*Life Story* (Streisand)	Columbia 11390
3/21/81	10	16		11 What Kind Of Fool BARBRA STREISAND & BARRY GIBB (above 2)	Albhy Galuten/Barry Gibb...*The Love Inside* (Streisand)	Columbia 11430
12/7/96	8	20	●	12 I Finally Found Someone BARBRA STREISAND and BRYAN ADAMS	Bryan Adams/Marvin Hamlisch/Mutt Lange/Barbra Streisand...*Evergreen (Spanish version* - Streisand)	Columbia 78480
				STRING-A-LONGS, The		
3/6/61	3²	16	⊙	1 Wheels	Richard Stephens/Jimmy Torres...*Tell The World* [I]	Warwick 603
				STRONG, Benny, And His Orchestra		
11/6/48	9	14		1 That Certain Party	Walter Donaldson/Gus Kahn...*My Best Girl*	Tower 1271

PEAK DATE	PEAK POS	WKS CHR	GOLD	ARTIST / Song Title ... Songwriter...B-side	Label & Number
				STUDDARD, Ruben	
6/28/03	2²	10	●	1 Flying Without Wings .... Wayne Hector/Steve Mac...*Superstar*	J Records 51786
2/28/04	9	20		2 Sorry 2004 .... Eric Dawkins/Tony Dixon/Ronnie Jackson/Harvey Mason/Damon Thomas	J Records 57204
				STYLES	
12/7/02	3⁴	20		1 Jenny From The Block .... Miro Arbex/Sam Barnes/Andre Deyo/Jennifer Lopez/Michael Oliver/Troy Oliver/J.C. Olivier/Lawrence Parker/	Epic 79825
				JENNIFER LOPEZ Featuring Jadakiss & Styles Jayson Phillips/Scott Sterling/David Styles	
10/9/04	8	27	○	2 Locked Up .... Aliaune Thiam	SRC 002245
				AKON Feat. Styles P.	
				STYLISTICS, The	
1/22/72	9	16	●	1 You Are Everything .... Thom Bell/Linda Creed...*Country Living*	Avco 4581
5/6/72	3¹	16	●	2 Betcha By Golly, Wow .... Thom Bell/Linda Creed...*Ebony Eyes*	Avco 4591
12/9/72	10	13	●	3 I'm Stone In Love With You .... Anthony Bell/Thom Bell/Linda Creed...*Make It Last*	Avco 4603
4/7/73	5	14	●	4 Break Up To Make Up .... Thom Bell/Linda Creed/Kenny Gamble...*You And Me*	Avco 4611
6/15/74	2²	25	●	5 You Make Me Feel Brand New .... Thom Bell/Linda Creed...*Only For The Children*	Avco 4634
				STYX	
3/8/75	6	17		1 Lady .... Dennis DeYoung...*Children Of The Land*	Wooden Nickel 10102
1/28/78	8	22		2 Come Sail Away .... Dennis DeYoung...*Put Me On*	A&M 1977
12/8/79	❶²	19		3 Babe .... Dennis DeYoung...*I'm O.K.*	A&M 2188
3/21/81	3⁴	19		4 The Best Of Times .... Dennis DeYoung...*Lights*	A&M 2300
5/23/81	9	19		5 Too Much Time On My Hands .... Tommy Shaw...*Queen Of Spades*	A&M 2323
4/16/83	3²	18	●	6 Mr. Roboto .... Dennis DeYoung...*Snowblind*	A&M 2525
7/2/83	6	16		7 Don't Let It End .... Dennis DeYoung...*(A.D. 1928) Rockin' The Paradise*	A&M 2543
3/16/91	3¹	23		8 Show Me The Way .... Dennis DeYoung...*Back To Chicago*	A&M 1536
				SUGARLOAF	
10/17/70	3²	17		1 Green-Eyed Lady .... Jerry Corbetta/J.C. Phillips/David Riordan...*West Of Tomorrow*	Liberty 56183
3/29/75	9	21		2 Don't Call Us, We'll Call You .... John Carter/Jerry Corbetta...*Texas Two-Lane*	Claridge 402
				SUGARLOAF/JERRY CORBETTA	
				SUGAR RAY	
10/18/97	❶⁶	59		1 Fly .... Craig Bullock/Stan Frazier/Murphy Karges/William Maragh/Mark McGrath/Alan Shacklock/Rodney Sheppard	Lava/Atlantic
				SUGAR RAY Featuring Super Cat	
4/3/99	3³	31	●	2 Every Morning .... Richard Bean/Craig Bullock/Stan Frazier/David Kahne/Murphy Karges/Mark McGrath/Joe Nichol/Rodney Sheppard/Pablo Tellez/	Lava/Atlantic 84462
				Abel Zarate...*Even Though*	
10/2/99	7	32		3 Someday .... Craig Bullock/Stan Frazier/David Kahne/Murphy Karges/Mark McGrath/Joe Nichol/Rodney Sheppard...*Every Morning (acoustic version)*	Lava/Atlantic 84536
				SUMMER, Donna	
2/7/76	2²	18	●	1 Love To Love You Baby .... Pete Bellotte/Giorgio Moroder/Donna Summer	Oasis 401
11/12/77	6	23	●	2 I Feel Love .... Pete Bellotte/Giorgio Moroder/Donna Summer...*Can't We Just Sit Down (And Talk It Over)*	Casablanca 884
8/12/78	3²	21	●	3 Last Dance .... Paul Jabara...*With Your Love*	Casablanca 926
11/11/78	❶³	20	●	4 MacArthur Park .... Jimmy Webb...*Once Upon A Time*	Casablanca 939
3/17/79	4	19	●	5 Heaven Knows .... Pete Bellotte/Giorgio Moroder/Donna Summer...*Only One Man*	Casablanca 959
				DONNA SUMMER with Brooklyn Dreams	
6/2/79	❶³	21	▲	6 Hot Stuff .... Pete Bellotte/Harold Faltermeyer/Keith Forsey...*Journey To The Centre Of Your Heart*	Casablanca 978
7/14/79	❶⁵	20	▲	7 Bad Girls .... Joe Esposito/Eddie Hokenson/Bruce Sudano/Donna Summer...*On My Honor*	Casablanca 988
11/10/79	2²	21	●	8 Dim All The Lights .... Donna Summer...*There Will Always Be A You*	Casablanca 2201
11/24/79	❶²	15	▲	9 No More Tears (Enough Is Enough) .... Paul Jabara/Bruce Roberts...*Wet* (Streisand)	Columbia 11125
				BARBRA STREISAND/DONNA SUMMER	
3/8/80	5	17	●	10 On The Radio .... Giorgio Moroder/Donna Summer...*There Will Always Be A You*	Casablanca 2236
11/15/80	3³	20	●	11 The Wanderer .... Giorgio Moroder/Donna Summer...*Stop Me*	Geffen 49563
9/25/82	10	18		12 Love Is In Control (Finger On The Trigger) .... Quincy Jones/Merria Ross/Rod Temperton...*Sometimes Like Butterflies*	Geffen 29982
8/6/83	3³	21		13 She Works Hard For The Money .... Michael Omartian/Donna Summer...*I Do Believe (I Fell In Love)*	Mercury 812370
6/24/89	7	17	●	14 This Time I Know It's For Real .... Matt Aitken/Mike Stock/Donna Summer/Pete Waterman...*If It Makes You Feel Good*	Atlantic 88899
				SUPER CAT	
10/18/97	❶⁶	59		1 Fly .... Craig Bullock/Stan Frazier/Murphy Karges/William Maragh/Mark McGrath/Alan Shacklock/Rodney Sheppard	Lava/Atlantic
				SUGAR RAY Featuring Super Cat	
				SUPERTRAMP	
6/16/79	6	21		1 The Logical Song .... Rick Davies/Roger Hodgson...*Just Another Nervous Wreck*	A&M 2128
12/15/79	10	15		2 Take The Long Way Home .... Rick Davies/Roger Hodgson...*Rudy*	A&M 2193
				SUPREMES, The	
8/22/64	❶²	14	☉	1 Where Did Our Love Go .... Lamont Dozier/Brian Holland/Eddie Holland...*He Means The World To Me*	Motown 1060
10/31/64	❶⁴	13	●	2 Baby Love .... Lamont Dozier/Brian Holland/Eddie Holland...*Ask Any Girl*	Motown 1066
12/19/64	❶²	14	☉	3 Come See About Me .... Lamont Dozier/Brian Holland/Eddie Holland...*Always In My Heart*	Motown 1068
3/27/65	❶²	12	●	4 Stop! In The Name Of Love .... Lamont Dozier/Brian Holland/Eddie Holland...*I'm In Love Again*	Motown 1074
6/12/65	❶¹	11		5 Back In My Arms Again .... Lamont Dozier/Brian Holland/Eddie Holland...*Whisper You Love Me Boy*	Motown 1075
11/20/65	❶²	10		6 I Hear A Symphony .... Lamont Dozier/Brian Holland/Eddie Holland...*Who Could Ever Doubt My Love*	Motown 1083
2/19/66	5	11		7 My World Is Empty Without You .... Lamont Dozier/Brian Holland/Eddie Holland...*Everything Is Good About You*	Motown 1089
5/28/66	9	8		8 Love Is Like An Itching In My Heart .... Lamont Dozier/Brian Holland/Eddie Holland...*He's All I Got*	Motown 1094
9/10/66	❶²	13	☉	9 You Can't Hurry Love .... Lamont Dozier/Brian Holland/Eddie Holland...*Put Yourself In My Place*	Motown 1097
11/19/66	❶²	12	☉	10 You Keep Me Hangin' On .... Lamont Dozier/Brian Holland/Eddie Holland...*Remove This Doubt*	Motown 1101
3/11/67	❶¹	11		11 Love Is Here And Now You're Gone .... Lamont Dozier/Brian Holland/Eddie Holland...*There's No Stopping Us Now*	Motown 1103
5/13/67	❶¹	11		12 The Happening .... Frank DeVol/Lamont Dozier/Brian Holland/Eddie Holland...*All I Know About You*	Motown 1107
				DIANA ROSS AND THE SUPREMES:	
9/9/67	2²	11		13 Reflections .... Lamont Dozier/Brian Holland/Eddie Holland...*Going Down For The Third Time*	Motown 1111
12/9/67	9	8		14 In And Out Of Love .... Lamont Dozier/Brian Holland/Eddie Holland...*I Guess I'll Always Love You*	Motown 1116
11/30/68	❶²	16	☉	15 Love Child .... Deke Richards/Pam Sawyer/R. Dean Taylor/Frank Wilson...*Will This Be The Day*	Motown 1135
1/11/69	2²	13	▲	16 I'm Gonna Make You Love Me .... Kenny Gamble/Jerry Ross/Jerry Williams...*A Place In The Sun*	Motown 1137
				DIANA ROSS AND THE SUPREMES & THE TEMPTATIONS	
2/22/69	10	8		17 I'm Livin' In Shame .... Pam Sawyer/R. Dean Taylor...*I'm So Glad I Got Somebody (Like You Around)*	Motown 1139
12/27/69	❶¹	16	▲	18 Someday We'll Be Together .... Jackey Beavers/Johnny Bristol/Harvey Fuqua...*He's My Sunny Boy*	Motown 1156

PEAK DATE	PEAK POS	WKS CHR	GOLD		ARTIST / Song Title	Songwriter...B-side	Label & Number
					THE SUPREMES:		
4/18/70	10	11		19	Up The Ladder To The Roof	Vincent Dimirco...*Bill, When Are You Coming Home*	Motown 1162
12/19/70	7	14		20	Stoned Love	Yennik Samoht/Frank Wilson...*Shine On Me*	Motown 1172
					SURFACE		
9/16/89	5	19	●	1	Shower Me With Your Love	Bernard Jackson	Columbia 68746
1/26/91	❶²	25	●	2	The First Time	Bernard Jackson/Brian Simpson...*Closer Than Friends*	Columbia 73502
					SURFARIS, The		
8/10/63	2¹	16	☉	1	Wipe Out	Bob Berryhill/Pat Connolly/James Fuller/Jim Pash/Ron Wilson...*Surfer Joe* [I]	Dot 16479
					SURVIVOR		
7/24/82	❶⁶	25	▲²	1	Eye Of The Tiger	Jim Peterik/Frankie Sullivan...*Take You On A Saturday*	Scotti Brothers 02912
3/23/85	8	17		2	High On You	Jim Peterik/Frankie Sullivan...*Everlasting*	Scotti Brothers 04685
7/13/85	4	25		3	The Search Is Over	Jim Peterik/Frankie Sullivan...*It's The Singer Not The Song*	Scotti Brothers 04871
2/1/86	2²	22		4	Burning Heart	Jim Peterik/Frankie Sullivan...*Feels Like Love*	Scotti Brothers 05663
1/17/87	9	19		5	Is This Love	Jim Peterik/Frankie Sullivan...*Can't Let You Go*	Scotti Brothers 06381
					SWAN, Billy		
11/23/74	❶²	18	●	1	I Can Help	Billy Swan...*Ways Of A Woman In Love*	Monument 8621
					SWAYZE, Patrick		
2/27/88	3³	21		1	She's Like The Wind	Patrick Swayze/Stacey Widelitz...*Stay* (Maurice Williams & The Zodiacs)	RCA 5363
					PATRICK SWAYZE (featuring Wendy Fraser)		
					SWEAT, Keith		
4/2/88	5	20	●	1	I Want Her	Teddy Riley/Keith Sweat...*(Part 2)*	Vintertainment 69431
2/16/91	7	20		2	I'll Give All My Love To You	Keith Sweat/Bobby Wooten...*I Want Her*	Vintertainment 64915
8/17/96	2¹	38	▲	3	Twisted	LaVonn Battle/Athena Cage/Tabitha Duncan/Eric McCaine/Keith Sweat	Elektra 64282
12/7/96	3²	35	▲	4	Nobody	Fitzgerald Scott/Keith Sweat...*In The Mood*	Elektra 64245
					KEITH SWEAT featuring Athena Cage		
					SWEET		
5/5/73	3³	23	●	1	Little Willy	Mike Chapman/Nicky Chinn...*Man From Mecca*	Bell 45,251
10/18/75	5	25		2	Ballroom Blitz	Mike Chapman/Nicky Chinn...*Restless*	Capitol 4055
1/17/76	5	16	●	3	Fox On The Run	Brian Connolly/Stephen Priest/Andrew Scott/Michael Tucker...*Burn On The Flame*	Capitol 4157
6/24/78	8	25		4	Love Is Like Oxygen	Trevor Griffin/Andrew Scott...*Cover Girl*	Capitol 4549
					SWEET SENSATION		
9/1/90	❶¹	20		1	If Wishes Came True	Deena Charles/Russ DeSalvo/Robert Steele	Atco 98953
					SWIFT, Taylor		
8/30/08	10	3		1	Change	Taylor Swift	Big Machine
11/1/08	9	4	○	2	Fearless	Hillary Lindsey/Liz Rose/Taylor Swift	Big Machine
1/17/09	4	49	△⁴	3	Love Story	Taylor Swift...*That's A Man* (Jack Ingram)	Big Machine 1015
8/29/09	2¹	49	△²	4	You Belong With Me	Liz Rose/Taylor Swift	Big Machine
11/14/09	10	3		5	Jump Then Fall	Taylor Swift	Big Machine
2/6/10	2¹	18	△	6	Today Was A Fairytale	Taylor Swift	Big Machine
8/21/10	3¹	23	△	7	Mine	Taylor Swift	Big Machine
10/23/10	8	3		8	Speak Now	Taylor Swift	Big Machine
10/30/10	6	13↑		9	Back To December	Taylor Swift	Big Machine
					SWING OUT SISTER		
11/14/87	6	23		1	Breakout	Andy Connell/Corinne Drewery/Martin Jackson...*Dirty Money*	Mercury 888016
					SWV (Sisters With Voices)		
5/22/93	6	27	●	1	I'm So Into You	Brian Morgan...*SWV (In The House)*	RCA 62451
7/10/93	❶²	26	▲	2	Weak	Brian Morgan	RCA 62521
10/2/93	2³	22	●	3	Right Here/Human Nature	John Bettis/Brian Morgan/Steve Porcaro...*Downtown*	RCA 62614
6/8/96	5	20	●	4	You're The One	Cheryl Gamble/Allen Gordon/Tamara Johnson/Andrea Martin/Ivan Matias	RCA 64516
					SYLK-E. FYNE		
4/18/98	6	20	●	1	Romeo And Juliet	Gerald Baillergeau/Lamar Johnson/Victor Merritt/Rene Moore/Angela Winbush	RCA 64973
					SYLK-E. FYNE Featuring Chill		
					SYLVERS, The		
5/15/76	❶¹	21	●	1	Boogie Fever	Freddie Perren/Kenny St. Lewis...*Free Style*	Capitol 4179
1/29/77	5	24	●	2	Hot Line	Freddie Perren/Kenny St. Lewis...*That's What Love Is Made Of*	Capitol 4336
					SYLVIA		
6/9/73	3²	21	●	1	Pillow Talk	Michael Burton/Sylvia Robinson...*My Thing*	Vibration 521
					SYNCH		
6/10/89	10	24		1	Where Are You Now?	Richard Congdon/Jimmy Harnen...*Only For The Night*	WTG 68625
					JIMMY HARNEN W/SYNCH		
					SYNDICATE OF SOUND		
7/9/66	8	10		1	Little Girl	Don Baskin/Bob Gonzalez...*You*	Bell 640
					SYSTEM, The		
7/18/87	4	21		1	Don't Disturb This Groove	David Frank/Mic Murphy...*Modern Girl*	Atlantic 89320

T

PEAK DATE	PEAK POS	WKS CHR	GOLD		ARTIST / Song Title	Songwriter...B-side	Label & Number
					TACO		
9/3/83	4	21	●	1	Puttin' On The Ritz	Irving Berlin...*Livin' In My Dream World*	RCA 13574

PEAK DATE	PEAK POS	WKS CHR	GOLD	ARTIST / Song Title	Songwriter...B-side	Label & Number
				TAG TEAM		
7/31/93	2⁷	45	▲⁴	1 Whoomp! (There It Is)	Steve Gibson/Cecil Glenn	Life 79500
				TAKE THAT		
11/11/95	7	30		1 Back For Good	Gary Barlow...*Love Ain't Here Anymore*	Arista 12848
				TALKING HEADS		
10/22/83	9	20		1 Burning Down The House	David Byrne/Chris Frantz/Jerry Harrison/Tina Weymouth...*I Get Wild/Wild Gravity*	Sire 29565
				TAMIA		
4/14/01	10	21		1 Stranger In My House	Anthony Crawford/Shae Jones...*Un'h...To You*	Elektra 67151
9/20/03	4	26		2 Into You FABOLOUS Featuring Ashanti or Tamia	Ken Ifill/John Jackson/Tim Kelly/Ronald LaPread/Lionel Richie/Bob Robinson/Tamia Washington	Desert Storm 67452
				TAMS, The		
2/22/64	9	14		1 What Kind Of Fool (Do You Think I Am)	Ray Whitley...*Laugh It Off*	ABC-Paramount 10502
				TARRIERS, The		
12/22/56	9	19		1 Cindy, Oh Cindy VINCE MARTIN with The Tarriers	Bob Barron/Burt Long...*Only If You Praise The Lord*	Glory 247
2/9/57	4	19	⊙	2 The Banana Boat Song	Alan Arkin/Bob Carey/Erik Darling...*No Hidin' Place*	Glory 249
				TASTE OF HONEY, A		
9/9/78	❶³	23	▲	1 Boogie Oogie Oogie	Janice Johnson/Perry Kibble...*World Spin*	Capitol 4565
6/13/81	3³	24	●	2 Sukiyaki	Buzz Cason/Rohusuke Ei/Tom Leslie/Hachidai Nakamura...*Don't You Lead Me On*	Capitol 4953
				TAVARES		
10/25/75	10	18		1 It Only Takes A Minute	Dennis Lambert/Brian Potter...*I Hope She Chooses Me*	Capitol 4111
				TAYLOR, James		
10/31/70	3³	16		1 Fire And Rain	James Taylor...*Anywhere Like Heaven*	Warner 7423
7/31/71	❶¹	14	●	2 You've Got A Friend	Carole King...*You Can Close Your Eyes*	Warner 7498
3/23/74	5	16	●	3 Mockingbird CARLY SIMON & JAMES TAYLOR	Charlie Foxx/Inez Foxx...*Grownup* (Simon)	Elektra 45880
8/30/75	5	15		4 How Sweet It Is (To Be Loved By You)	Lamont Dozier/Brian Holland/Eddie Holland...*Sarah Maria*	Warner 8109
9/10/77	4	20		5 Handy Man	Otis Blackwell/Jimmy Jones...*Bartender's Blues*	Columbia 10557
				TAYLOR, Johnnie		
12/7/68	5	14	●	1 Who's Making Love	Homer Banks/Bettye Crutcher/Don Davis/Raymond Jackson...*I'm Trying*	Stax 0009
4/3/76	❶⁴	19	▲	2 Disco Lady	Don Davis/Harvey Scales/Al Vance...*You're The Best In The World*	Columbia 10281
				TAYLOR, R. Dean		
11/7/70	5	15		1 Indiana Wants Me	R. Dean Taylor...*Love's Your Name*	Rare Earth 5013
				T-BONES, The		
2/5/66	3¹	13		1 No Matter What Shape (Your Stomach's In)	Sascha Burland...*Feelin' Fine* [I]	Liberty 55836
				TEARS FOR FEARS		
6/8/85	❶²	24		1 Everybody Wants To Rule The World	Chris Hughes/Roland Orzabal/Ian Stanley...*Pharaohs*	Mercury 880659
8/3/85	❶³	19	●	2 Shout	Roland Orzabal/Ian Stanley...*The Big Chair*	Mercury 880294
11/9/85	3¹	20		3 Head Over Heels	Roland Orzabal/Curt Smith...*When In Love With A Blind Man*	Mercury 880899
10/28/89	2¹	15		4 Sowing The Seeds Of Love	Roland Orzabal/Curt Smith...*Tears Roll Down*	Fontana 874710
				TECHNOTRONIC		
1/20/90	2²	24	▲	1 Pump Up The Jam TECHNOTRONIC Featuring FELLY	Thomas DeQuincey/Manuella Kamosi	SBK 07311
4/7/90	7	20	●	2 Get Up! (Before The Night Is Over)	Jo Bogaert/Manuella Kamosi...*Raw*	SBK 07315
9/5/92	6	23		3 Move This	Jo Bogaert/Manuella Kamosi...*Rockin' Over The Beat*	SBK/EMI 50400
				TEDDY BEARS, The		
12/1/58	❶³	23		1 To Know Him, Is To Love Him	Phil Spector...*Don't You Worry My Little Pet*	Dore 503
				TEENAGERS, The — see LYMON, Frankie		
				TEE SET, The		
3/14/70	5	12		1 Ma Belle Amie	Peter Tetteroo/Hans Van Eijck...*Angels Coming In The Holy Night*	Colossus 107
				TEMPO, Nino, & April Stevens		
7/21/51	6	15		1 I'm In Love Again HENRI RENE and his Orchestra featuring April Stevens	Cole Porter...*Roller Coaster*	RCA Victor 4148
8/18/51	10	5		2 Gimme A Little Kiss, Will Ya Huh? APRIL STEVENS with HENRI RENE and his Orchestra	Maceo Pinkard/Jack Smith/Roy Turk...*Dreamy Melody*	RCA Victor 4208
11/16/63	❶¹	15		3 Deep Purple	Peter DeRose/Mitchell Parish...*I've Been Carrying A Torch For You So Long*	Atco 6273
				TEMPTATIONS, The		
3/6/65	❶¹	13	▲	1 My Girl	Smokey Robinson/Ronnie White...*(Talking 'Bout) Nobody But My Baby*	Gordy 7038
10/1/66	3¹	12	●	2 Beauty Is Only Skin Deep	Eddie Holland/Norman Whitfield...*You're Not An Ordinary Girl*	Gordy 7055
12/31/66	8	10	●	3 (I Know) I'm Losing You	Cornelius Grant/Eddie Holland/Norman Whitfield...*I Couldn't Cry If I Wanted To*	Gordy 7057
6/17/67	8	10		4 All I Need	Eddie Holland/R. Dean Taylor/Frank Wilson...*Sorry Is A Sorry Word*	Gordy 7061
9/16/67	6	12	●	5 You're My Everything	Cornelius Grant/Roger Penzabene/Norman Whitfield...*I've Been Good To You*	Gordy 7063
2/17/68	4	14		6 I Wish It Would Rain	Roger Penzabene/Barrett Strong/Norman Whitfield...*I Truly, Truly Believe*	Gordy 7068
1/4/69	6	12	●	7 Cloud Nine	Barrett Strong/Norman Whitfield...*Why Did She Have To Leave Me (Why Did She Have To Go)*	Gordy 7081
1/11/69	2²	13	▲	8 I'm Gonna Make You Love Me DIANA ROSS AND THE SUPREMES & THE TEMPTATIONS	Kenny Gamble/Jerry Ross/Jerry Williams...*A Place In The Sun*	Motown 1137
3/29/69	6	12	●	9 Run Away Child, Running Wild	Barrett Strong/Norman Whitfield...*I Need Your Lovin'*	Gordy 7084
10/18/69	❶²	17	▲	10 I Can't Get Next To You	Barrett Strong/Norman Whitfield...*Running Away (Ain't Gonna Help You)*	Gordy 7093
2/28/70	7	11	●	11 Psychedelic Shack	Barrett Strong/Norman Whitfield...*That's The Way Love Is*	Gordy 7096
6/27/70	3³	15	▲	12 Ball Of Confusion (That's What The World Is Today)	Barrett Strong/Norman Whitfield...*It's Summer*	Gordy 7099
4/3/71	❶²	15	▲	13 Just My Imagination (Running Away With Me)	Barrett Strong/Norman Whitfield...*You Make Your Own Heaven And Hell Right Here On Earth*	Gordy 7105
12/2/72	❶¹	16		14 Papa Was A Rollin' Stone	Barrett Strong/Norman Whitfield	Gordy 7121

PEAK DATE	PEAK POS	WKS CHR	GOLD	ARTIST Song Title	Songwriter...B-side	Label & Number
				TEMPTATIONS, The (cont'd)		
4/28/73	7	14	●	15 Masterpiece	Norman Whitfield	Gordy 7126
9/21/91	10	17		16 The Motown Song	Larry John McNally...*Sweet Soul Music (live)*	Warner 19322
				ROD STEWART (with The Temptations)		
				10cc		
7/26/75	2³	17		1 I'm Not In Love	Graham Gouldman/Eric Stewart...*Channel Swimmer*	Mercury 73678
4/16/77	5	19	●	2 The Things We Do For Love	Graham Gouldman/Eric Stewart...*Hot To Trot*	Mercury 73875
				TERRELL, Tammi		
				MARVIN GAYE & TAMMI TERRELL:		
11/4/67	5	13		1 Your Precious Love	Nick Ashford/Valerie Simpson...*Hold Me Oh My Darling*	Tamla 54156
1/20/68	10	11		2 If I Could Build My Whole World Around You	Johnny Bristol/Vernon Bullock/Harvey Fuqua...*If This World Were Mine*	Tamla 54161
5/25/68	8	13		3 Ain't Nothing Like The Real Thing	Nick Ashford/Valerie Simpson...*Little Ole Boy, Little Ole Girl*	Tamla 54163
9/14/68	7	12		4 You're All I Need To Get By	Nick Ashford/Valerie Simpson...*Two Can Have A Party*	Tamla 54169
				TERROR SQUAD		
8/21/04	❶³	31	○	1 Lean Back	Joe Cartagena/Remy Smith/Scott Storch	SRC 002704
				TESLA		
1/20/90	10	27	●	1 Love Song	Frank Hannon/Jeff Keith...*I Ain't Superstitious*	Geffen 22856
4/6/91	8	22		2 Signs	Les Emmerson...*Down Fo' Boogie* [L]	Geffen 19653
				TETER, Jack, Trio		
2/4/50	6	23		1 Johnson Rag	Guy Hall/Henry Kleinkauf/Jack Lawrence...*Back Of The Yards*	London 30004
				TEX, Joe		
1/30/65	5	11		1 Hold What You've Got	Joe Tex...*Fresh Out Of Tears*	Dial 4001
12/30/67	10	15	●	2 Skinny Legs And All	Joe Tex...*Watch The One (That Brings The Bad News)* [L-N]	Dial 4063
5/6/72	2²	21	●	3 I Gotcha	Joe Tex...*A Mother's Prayer*	Dial 1010
				THIRD EYE BLIND		
8/9/97	4	43	●	1 Semi-Charmed Life	Stephan Jenkins...*Tattoo Of The Sun*	Elektra 64173
2/14/98	9	52		2 How's It Going To Be	Kevin Cadogan/Stephan Jenkins...*Horror Show*	Elektra 64130
1/30/99	5	20		3 Jumper	Stephan Jenkins...*Graduate*	Elektra 64058
				38 SPECIAL		
7/3/82	10	17		1 Caught Up In You	Don Barnes/Jeff Carlisi/Jim Peterik...*Firestarter*	A&M 2412
5/6/89	6	21		2 Second Chance	Max Carl/Jeff Carlisi/Cal Curtis...*Comin' Down Tonight*	A&M 1273
				THOMAS, B.J.		
4/9/66	8	13		1 I'm So Lonesome I Could Cry	Hank Williams...*Candy Baby*	Scepter 12129
				B.J. THOMAS AND THE TRIUMPHS		
1/11/69	5	16	●	2 Hooked On A Feeling	Mark James...*I've Been Down This Road Before*	Scepter 12230
1/3/70	❶⁴	22	●	3 Raindrops Keep Fallin' On My Head	Burt Bacharach/Hal David...*Never Had It So Good*	Scepter 12265
8/22/70	9	13		4 I Just Can't Help Believing	Barry Mann/Cynthia Weil...*Send My Picture To Scranton, PA.*	Scepter 12283
4/26/75	❶¹	18	●	5 (Hey Won't You Play) Another Somebody Done Somebody Wrong Song	Larry Butler/Chips Moman...*City Boys*	ABC 12054
				THOMAS, Carla		
3/27/61	10	14		1 Gee Whiz (Look At His Eyes)	Carla Thomas...*For You*	Atlantic 2086
				THOMAS, Rob		
10/23/99	❶¹²	58	▲	1 Smooth	Itaal Shur/Rob Thomas...*El Farol*	Arista 13718
				SANTANA Feat. Rob Thomas		
5/21/05	6	34	○	2 Lonely No More	Rob Thomas...*This Is How A Heart Breaks*	Melisma 93896
				THOMAS, Rufus		
12/7/63	10	14	●	1 Walking The Dog	Rufus Thomas...*You Said*	Stax 140
				THOMAS, Timmy		
2/10/73	3¹	15		1 Why Can't We Live Together	Timmy Thomas...*Funky Me*	Glades 1703
				THOMPSON, Sue		
10/23/61	5	14		1 Sad Movies (Make Me Cry)	John D. Loudermilk...*Nine Little Teardrops*	Hickory 1153
2/24/62	3¹	16		2 Norman	John D. Loudermilk...*Never Love Again*	Hickory 1159
				THOMPSON TWINS		
5/5/84	3²	21		1 Hold Me Now	Tom Bailey/Alannah Currie/Joe Leeway...*Let Loving Start*	Arista 9164
11/23/85	6	20		2 Lay Your Hands On Me	Tom Bailey/Alannah Currie/Joe Leeway...*The Lewis Carol (Adventures In Wonderland)*	Arista 9396
3/22/86	8	16		3 King For A Day	Tom Bailey/Alannah Currie/Joe Leeway...*Rollunder*	Arista 9450
				THREE DEGREES, The		
4/20/74	❶²	18	●	1 TSOP (The Sound Of Philadelphia)	Kenny Gamble/Leon Huff...*Something For Nothing* [I]	Philadelphia I. 3540
				MFSB featuring The Three Degrees		
12/14/74	2¹	18	▲	2 When Will I See You Again	Kenny Gamble/Leon Huff...*Year Of Decision*	Philadelphia I. 3550
				THREE DOG NIGHT		
6/28/69	5	16	●	1 One	Harry Nilsson...*Chest Fever*	Dunhill/ABC 4191
9/27/69	4	13		2 Easy To Be Hard	Galt MacDermot/James Rado/Gerome Ragni...*Dreaming Isn't Good For You*	Dunhill/ABC 4203
11/29/69	10	14		3 Eli's Coming	Laura Nyro...*Circle For A Landing*	Dunhill/ABC 4215
7/11/70	❶²	15	●	4 Mama Told Me (Not To Come)	Randy Newman...*Rock & Roll Widow*	Dunhill/ABC 4239
4/17/71	❶⁶	17	●	5 Joy To The World	Hoyt Axton...*I Can Hear You Calling*	Dunhill/ABC 4272
8/28/71	7	12		6 Liar	Russ Ballard...*Can't Get Enough Of It*	Dunhill/ABC 4282
12/18/71	4	11	●	7 An Old Fashioned Love Song	Paul Williams...*Jam*	Dunhill/ABC 4294
2/12/72	5	12		8 Never Been To Spain	Hoyt Axton...*Peace Of Mind*	Dunhill/ABC 4299
9/16/72	❶¹	11	●	9 Black & White	David Arkin/Earl Robinson...*Freedom For The Stallion*	Dunhill/ABC 4317
7/28/73	3¹	16	●	10 Shambala	Daniel Moore...*Our "B" Side*	Dunhill/ABC 4352
5/25/74	4	19	●	11 The Show Must Go On	David Courtney/Leo Sayer...*On The Way Back Home*	Dunhill/ABC 4382

PEAK DATE	PEAK POS	WKS CHR	GOLD	ARTIST / Song Title	Songwriter...B-side	Label & Number
				3 DOORS DOWN		
11/11/00	3³	53	△	1 Kryptonite	Brad Arnold/Todd Harrell/Matt Roberts	Republic
4/26/03	4	45	○	2 When I'm Gone	Brad Arnold/Todd Harrell/Chris Henderson/Matt Roberts	Republic 156263
11/8/03	5	51	△	3 Here Without You	Brad Arnold/Todd Harrell/Chris Henderson/Matt Roberts	Republic
				THREE FLAMES, The		
3/1/47	❶¹	8		1 Open The Door, Richard	Dusty Fletcher/Don Howell/John Mason/Jack McVea...*Nicholas (Don't Be So Ridiculous)* [N]	Columbia 37268
				3OH!3		
5/30/09	7	37	△²	1 Don't Trust Me	Sean Foreman/Nathaniel Motte	Photo Finish
1/23/10	7	20	△	2 Blah Blah Blah	Sean Foreman/Neon Hitch/Benjamin Levin/Kesha Sebert	Kemosabe
				Ke$ha Featuring 3OH!3		
5/22/10	9	18	○	3 My First Kiss	Sean Foreman/Lukasz Gottwald/Benjamin Levin/Nathaniel Motte	Photo Finish
				3OH!3 Featuring Ke$ha		
				THREE SUNS, The		
9/23/44	7	18		1 How Many Hearts Have You Broken	Al Kaufman/Marty Symes...*Twilight Time*	Hit 7092
3/24/45	8	7		2 Twilight Time	Artie Dunn/Al Nevins/Morty Nevins/Buck Ram...*How Many Hearts Have You Broken* [I]	Hit 7092
4/28/45	10	1		3 All Of My Life	Irving Berlin...*Shaga, Shuga Shuffle*	Hit 7092
10/26/46	7	13		4 Five Minutes More	Sammy Cahn/Jule Styne...*By The Waters Of Minnetonka*	Majestic 7197
11/9/46	7	6		5 Rumors Are Flying	Bennie Benjamin/George Weiss...*It's All Over Now* [I]	Majestic 7205
8/9/47	❶³	19	◉	6 Peg O' My Heart	Alfred Bryan/Fred Fisher...*Across The Alley From The Alamo* [I]	RCA Victor 2272
4/3/48	10	8		7 I'm Looking Over A Four Leaf Clover	Mort Dixon/Harry Woods...*Eccentric*	RCA Victor 2688
				THUNDER, Johnny		
2/9/63	4	11		1 Loop De Loop	Teddy Vann...*Don't Be Ashamed*	Diamond 129
				T.I.		
2/5/05	9	21	○	1 Bring Em Out	Thom Bell/Shawn Carter/Roland Chambers/Kasseem Dean/Kenny Gamble/Clifford Harris...*You Don't Know Me*	Grand Hustle 93395
2/12/05	3¹	21	○	2 Soldier	Dwayne Carter/Sean Garrett/Clifford Harris/Rich Harrison/Beyonce Knowles/Kelly Rowland/Michelle Williams	Columbia 70702
				DESTINY'S CHILD (feat. T.I. and Lil Wayne)		
4/22/06	3³	20	○	3 What You Know	Gabriel Arillo/Aldrin Davis/Clifford Harris/Donny Hathaway/Leroy Hutson/Curtis Mayfield/Billy Roberts...*Ride Wit Me*	Grand Hustle 94251
8/26/06	10	20		4 Shoulder Lean	Clifford Harris/D'Juan Hart/Cordale Quinn...*Gangsta*	Grand Hustle 94282
				YOUNG DRO Featuring T.I.		
11/11/06	❶³	29	△	5 My Love	Clifford Harris/Nathan Hills/Tim Mosley/Justin Timberlake	Jive 02049
				JUSTIN TIMBERLAKE Featuring T.I.		
7/21/07	9	19		6 Big Things Poppin' (Do It)	Clifford Harris/Byron Thomas	Grand Hustle 223868
9/6/08	❶⁷	31	△³	7 Whatever You Like	Clifford Harris/James Schefer/D. Siegel/K. Washington...*Swing Ya Rag*	Grand Hustle 514202
9/27/08	5	20		8 Swagga Like Us	Maya Arulpragasm/Dwayne Carter/Shawn Carter/Clifford Harris/Nicky Headon/Mick Jones/Wesley Pentz/Paul Simonon/Joe Strummer/Kanye West	Roc-A-Fella 012284
				JAY-Z & T.I. Featuring Kanye West & Lil Wayne		
10/18/08	❶⁶	28	△³	9 Live Your Life	Dan Balan/Clifford Harris/Makeba Riddick/Justin Smith	Grand Hustle 516201
				T.I. (Featuring Rihanna)		
2/28/09	2⁵	29	△²	10 Dead And Gone	Clifford Harris/Justin Timberlake	Grand Hustle 519313
				T.I. (Featuring Justin Timberlake)		
				TIFFANY		
11/7/87	❶²	24		1 I Think We're Alone Now	Ritchie Cordell...*No Rules*	MCA 53167
2/6/88	❶²	20		2 Could've Been	Lois Blaisch...*The Heart Of Love*	MCA 53231
4/23/88	7	14		3 I Saw Him Standing There	John Lennon/Paul McCartney...*Mr. Mambo*	MCA 53285
2/11/89	6	21		4 All This Time	Tim James/Steve McClintock...*Can't Stop A Heartbeat*	MCA 53371
				TILLOTSON, Johnny		
11/14/60	2¹	15	◉	1 Poetry In Motion	Mike Anthony/Paul Kaufman...*Princess, Princess*	Cadence 1384
9/18/61	7	13		2 Without You	Johnny Tillotson...*Cutie Pie*	Cadence 1404
6/16/62	3¹	14		3 It Keeps Right On A-Hurtin'	Johnny Tillotson...*She Gave Sweet Love To Me*	Cadence 1418
1/4/64	7	13		4 Talk Back Trembling Lips	John D. Loudermilk...*Another You*	MGM 13181
				TILTON, Martha		
10/7/44	4	24		1 I'll Walk Alone	Sammy Cahn/Jule Styne...*Texas Polka*	Capitol 157
7/28/45	10	1		2 Stranger In Town	Mel Torme...*I Should Care*	Capitol 184
3/29/47	8	5		3 How Are Things In Glocca Morra	E.Y. Harburg/Burton Lane...*Connecticut*	Capitol 345
6/14/47	10	9		4 That's My Desire	Helmy Kresa/Carroll Loveday...*I Wonder, I Wonder, I Wonder*	Capitol 395
7/19/47	9	2		5 I Wonder, I Wonder, I Wonder	Daryl Hutchins...*That's My Desire*	Capitol 395
				'TIL TUESDAY		
7/13/85	8	21		1 Voices Carry	Michael Hausman/Robert Holmes/Aimee Mann/Joey Pesce...*Are You Serious?*	Epic 04795
				TIMBALAND		
7/8/06	❶⁶	26	△	1 Promiscuous	Tim Clayton/Nelly Furtado/Nathan Hills/Tim Mosley	Mosley 006818
				NELLY FURTADO Featuring Timbaland		
9/9/06	❶⁷	36	△²	2 SexyBack	Nathan Hills/Tim Mosley/Justin Timberlake	Jive 88175
				JUSTIN TIMBERLAKE Featuring Timbaland		
4/21/07	❶²	26		3 Give It To Me	Tim Clayton/Nelly Furtado/Nathan Hills/Timothy Mosley/Justin Timberlake	Mosley 008759
				TIMBALAND Featuring Nelly Furtado and Justin Timberlake		
8/25/07	3⁴	38		4 The Way I Are	Floyd Hills/Keri Hilson/John Maultsby/Garland Mosley/Tim Mosley/Balewa Muhammad/Candice Nelson	Mosley
				TIMBALAND Featuring Keri Hilson		
9/29/07	5	20		5 Ayo Technology	Nathan Hills/Curtis Jackson/Tim Mosley/Justin Timberlake	Shady 009807
				50 CENT Featuring Justin Timberlake & Timbaland		
11/10/07	2⁴	47	△³	6 Apologize	Ryan Tedder	Mosley
				TIMBALAND Featuring OneRepublic		
				TIMBERLAKE, Justin		
2/1/03	3¹	20		1 Cry Me A River	Tim Mosley/Scott Storch/Justin Timberlake...*Like I Love You*	Jive 40073
5/10/03	5	22	○	2 Rock Your Body	Chad Hugo/Justin Timberlake/Pharrell Williams	Jive
8/9/03	8	25	○	3 Where Is The Love?	William Adams/Printz Board/Michael Fratantuno/Jaime Gomez/George Pajon/Allan Pineda	A&M 000714
				BLACK EYED PEAS (Featuring Justin Timberlake)		
9/9/06	❶⁷	36	△²	4 SexyBack	Nathan Hills/Tim Mosley/Justin Timberlake	Jive 88175
				JUSTIN TIMBERLAKE Featuring Timbaland		
11/11/06	❶³	29	△	5 My Love	Clifford Harris/Nathan Hills/Tim Mosley/Justin Timberlake	Jive 02049
				JUSTIN TIMBERLAKE Featuring T.I.		
3/3/07	❶¹	25	△	6 What Goes Around...Comes Around	Nathan Hills/Tim Mosley/Justin Timberlake	Jive

PEAK DATE	PEAK POS	WKS CHR	GOLD	ARTIST Song Title	Songwriter...B-side	Label & Number
				TIMBERLAKE, Justin (cont'd)		
4/21/07	❶²	26		7 Give It To Me	Tim Clayton/Nelly Furtado/Nathan Hills/Timothy Mosley/Justin Timberlake	Mosley 008759
				TIMBALAND Featuring Nelly Furtado and Justin Timberlake		
6/9/07	6	20	△	8 Summer Love	Floyd Hills/Tim Mosley/Justin Timberlake	Jive
9/29/07	5	20		9 Ayo Technology	Nathan Hills/Curtis Jackson/Tim Mosley/Justin Timberlake	Shady 009807
				50 CENT Featuring Justin Timberlake & Timbaland		
4/12/08	3²	20	△²	10 4 Minutes	Nathan Hills/Madonna/Tim Mosley/Justin Timberlake	Warner 463036
				MADONNA Featuring Justin Timberlake		
2/28/09	2⁵	29	△²	11 Dead And Gone	Clifford Harris/Justin Timberlake	Grand Hustle 519313
				T.I. (Featuring Justin Timberlake)		
4/11/09	10	12		12 Love Sex Magic	Michael Elizondo/James Fauntleroy/Robin Tadross/Justin Timberlake	LaFace
				CIARA Featuring Justin Timberlake		
				TIME, The		
8/25/90	9	15	●	1 Jerk-Out	Morris Day/Jimmy Jam Harris/Terry Lewis/Prince...*Mo' Jerk Out*	Paisley Park 19750
				TIMEX SOCIAL CLUB		
8/16/86	8	19		1 Rumors	Alex Hill/Michael Marshall/Marcus Thompson	Jay 7001
				TIMMY -T-		
3/23/91	❶¹	25	▲	1 One More Try	Timmy Torres	Quality 15114
				TLC		
4/25/92	6	22	▲	1 Ain't 2 Proud 2 Beg	Dallas Austin/Lisa Lopes	LaFace 24008
8/15/92	2⁶	33	▲	2 Baby-Baby-Baby	Babyface/Daryl Dimmons/L.A. Reid	LaFace 24028
11/21/92	7	27	●	3 What About Your Friends	Dallas Austin/Lisa Lopes	LaFace 24025
1/28/95	❶⁴	32	▲	4 Creep	Dallas Austin	LaFace 24082
4/15/95	2³	22	●	5 Red Light Special	Babyface	LaFace 24097
7/8/95	❶⁷	34	●	6 Waterfalls	Patrick Brown/Marqueze Etheridge/Lisa Lopes/Ray Murray/Rico Wade	LaFace 24107
12/30/95	5	20	●	7 Diggin' On You	Babyface	LaFace 24119
4/10/99	❶⁴	28	●	8 No Scrubs	Kevin Briggs/Kandi Burruss/Tameka Cottle/Lisa Lopes	LaFace 24385
9/18/99	❶³	32	●	9 Unpretty	Dallas Austin/Tionne Watkins	LaFace 24424
				TODD, Art And Dotty		
5/5/58	6	16		1 Chanson D'Amour (Song Of Love)	Wayne Shanklin...*Along The Trail With You*	Era 1064
				TOKENS, The		
12/18/61	❶³	15	●	1 The Lion Sleeps Tonight	Paul Campbell/Luigi Creatore/Roy Ilene/Hugo Peretti/Albert Stanton/George David Weiss...*Tina*	RCA Victor 7954
				TOMMY TUTONE		
5/22/82	4	27	●	1 867-5309/Jenny	Alex Call/Jim Keller...*Not Say Goodbye*	Columbia 02646
				TONE LOC		
2/18/89	2¹	25	▲²	1 Wild Thing	Matt Dike/Anthony Smith/Marvin Young...*Loc'ed After Dark*	Delicious Vinyl 102
4/29/89	3¹	18	▲	2 Funky Cold Medina	Matt Dike/Michael Ross/Marvin Young	Delicious Vinyl 104
				TONY! TONI! TONE!		
11/24/90	9	25	●	1 Feels Good	Tim Christian/Raphael Saadiq/Dwayne Wiggins	Wing 877436
8/7/93	7	21	●	2 If I Had No Loot	John Bautista/Will Harris/Raphael Saadiq	Wing 859056
10/23/93	10	20	●	3 Anniversary	Raphael Saadiq/Carl Wheeler	Wing 859566
10/2/04	8	28		4 Diary	Kerry Brothers/Alicia Keys...*If I Ain't Got You*	J Records 59965
				ALICIA KEYS Feat. Tony! Toni! Tone!		
				TORME, Mel		
4/30/49	❶¹	18		1 Careless Hands	Bob Hilliard/Carl Sigman...*She's A Home Girl*	Capitol 15379
7/16/49	3¹	18		2 Again	Dorcas Cochran/Lionel Newman...*Blue Moon*	Capitol 15428
7/30/49	10	8		3 The Four Winds And The Seven Seas	Hal David/Don Rodney...*It's Too Late Now*	Capitol 671
1/14/50	9	7		4 The Old Master Painter	Haven Gillespie/Beasley Smith...*Bless You (For The Good That's In You)*	Capitol 791
				PEGGY LEE and MEL TORME		
7/8/50	8	12		5 Bewitched	Lorenz Hart/Richard Rodgers...*The Piccolino*	Capitol 1000
				TORNADOES, The		
12/22/62	❶³	16	⊙	1 Telstar	Joe Meek...*Jungle Fever* [I]	London 9561
				TOTAL		
3/21/98	6	24	●	1 What You Want	Mason Betha/Sean Combs/Nashiem Myrick/Keisha Spivey...*Will They Die 4 You?* (w/ Puff Daddy & Lil' Kim)	Bad Boy 79141
				Ma$e (Featuring Total)		
1/9/99	7	20	●	2 Trippin'	Missy Elliott/Tim Mosley/Darryl Pearson	Bad Boy 79185
				TOTAL (Feat. Missy Elliott)		
				TOTO		
1/13/79	5	21	●	1 Hold The Line	David Paich...*Takin' It Back*	Columbia 10830
7/3/82	2⁵	23	●	2 Rosanna	David Paich...*It's A Feeling*	Columbia 02811
2/5/83	❶¹	21	●	3 Africa	David Paich/Jeff Porcaro...*Good For You*	Columbia 03335
5/7/83	10	17		4 I Won't Hold You Back	Steve Lukather...*Afraid Of Love*	Columbia 03597
				TOWNSHEND, Pete		
8/16/80	9	19		1 Let My Love Open The Door	Pete Townshend...*And I Moved*	Atco 7217
				TOYS, The		
10/30/65	2³	15	●	1 A Lover's Concerto	Sandy Linzer/Denny Randell...*This Night*	DynoVoice 209
				T-PAIN		
11/19/05	8	26		1 I'm Sprung	Faheem Najm	Jive 71697
2/18/06	5	20	○	2 I'm N Luv (Wit A Stripper)	Mike Jones/Faheem Najm...*I'm Sprung 2*	Jive 77102
				T-PAIN Featuring Mike Jones		
5/26/07	❶¹	35	△	3 Buy U A Drank (Shawty Snappin')	Faheem Najm/Jasiel Robinson	Konvict 08718
				T-PAIN Featuring Yung Joc		
9/8/07	9	22	○	4 Shawty	Christopher Gholson/Ferrell Miles/Faheem Najm/Algernod Washington	Slip n Slide 230716
				PLIES (Feat. T-Pain)		
9/22/07	5	22	△	5 Bartender	Faheem Najm/Aliaune Thiam	Konvict 11814
				T-PAIN Featuring Akon		

PEAK DATE	PEAK POS	WKS CHR	GOLD	ARTIST / Song Title	Songwriter...B-side	Label & Number
				T-PAIN (cont'd)		
11/3/07	7	30	△²	6 Cyclone	Ronald Bryant/Faheem Najm/Jonathan Smith	Arista
				BABY BASH Featuring T-Pain		
11/10/07	❶³	26	△²	7 Kiss Kiss	Chris Brown/Faheem Najm	Jive 17392
				CHRIS BROWN Featuring T-Pain		
11/10/07	7	21	△	8 Good Life	Aldrin Davis/Michael Dean/James Ingram/Quincy Jones/Faheem Najm/John Stephens/Kanye West	Roc-A-Fella
				KANYE WEST Featuring T-Pain		
1/5/08	❶¹⁰	40	△⁵	9 Low	Tramar Dillard/Montay Humphrey/Faheem Najm...*Jealous*	Poe Boy 346620
				FLO RIDA Featuring T-Pain		
4/5/08	10	12		10 Shawty Get Loose	Niatia Kirkland/Faheem Najm	Jive 27082
				LIL MAMA Featuring Chris Brown & T-Pain		
9/27/08	10	27	△	11 Got Money	Dwayne Carter/Faheem Najm/Juan Salinas/Oscar Salinas	Cash Money
				LIL WAYNE Featuring T-Pain		
10/11/08	7	24		12 Can't Believe It	Dwayne Carter/Faheem Najm	Konvict 36568
				T-PAIN Featuring Lil Wayne		
5/16/09	2¹	27		13 Blame It	J.T. Brown/Jamie Foxx/Christopher Henderson/Brandon Melancon/Faheem Najm/Nate Walker	J Records 46266
				JAMIE FOXX Featuring T-Pain		
				T'PAU		
8/8/87	4	27		1 Heart And Soul	Carol Decker/Ron Rogers...*On The Wing*	Virgin 99466
				TRACE, Al, and His Orchestra		
3/18/44	7	6		1 Mairzy Doats	Milton Drake/Al Hoffman/Jerry Livingston...*Where Did You Get That Girl* [N]	Hit 8079
				AL TRACE and his SILLY SYMPHONISTS		
8/14/48	❶⁶	24	☉	2 You Call Everybody Darlin'	Sam Martin/Ben Trace/Clem Watts...*Linger Awhile*	Regent 117
				AL TRACE And His New Orchestra		
				TRAIN		
6/23/01	5	53	○	1 Drops Of Jupiter (Tell Me)	Charlie Colin/Rob Hotchkiss/Patrick Monahan/Jimmy Stafford/Scott Underwood...*Meet Virginia*	Columbia 79565
4/10/10	3⁴	54	△⁴	2 Hey, Soul Sister	Amund Bjoerklund/Espen Lind/Pat Monahan	Columbia
				TRASHMEN, The		
1/25/64	4	13	☉	1 Surfin' Bird	Al Frazier/John Earl Harris/Carl White/Turner Wilson...*King Of The Surf*	Garrett 4002
				TRAVIS, Randy		
4/4/09	9	18	○	1 I Told You So	Randy Travis	19 Records
				CARRIE UNDERWOOD Featuring Randy Travis		
				TRAVIS & BOB		
4/27/59	8	13		1 Tell Him No	Travis Pritchett...*We're Too Young*	Sandy 1017
				TRAVOLTA, John		
7/24/76	10	20		1 Let Her In	Gary Benson...*Big Trouble*	Midland Int'l. 10623
6/10/78	❶¹	24	▲	2 You're The One That I Want	John Farrar...*Alone At A Drive-In Movie*	RSO 891
				JOHN TRAVOLTA AND OLIVIA NEWTON-JOHN		
9/30/78	5	16	●	3 Summer Nights	Warren Casey/Jim Jacobs...*Rock 'N' Roll Party Queen* (Louis St. Louis)	RSO 906
				JOHN TRAVOLTA, OLIVIA NEWTON-JOHN & CAST		
				TRESVANT, Ralph		
1/26/91	4	20	●	1 Sensitivity	Jimmy Jam Harris/Terry Lewis	MCA 53932
6/13/92	10	20		2 The Best Things In Life Are Free	Michael Bivins/Ronnie DeVoe/Jimmy Jam Harris/Terry Lewis/Ralph Tresvant	Perspective 0010
				LUTHER VANDROSS and JANET JACKSON with BBD and Ralph Tresvant		
				T. REX		
3/4/72	10	15		1 Bang A Gong (Get It On)	Marc Bolan...*Raw Ramp*	Reprise 1032
				TRICK DADDY		
11/27/04	7	22	○	1 Let's Go	Derrick Baker/Robert Daisley/Maurice Marshall/Carl Mitchell/Ozzy Osbourne/Randy Rhoads/James Scheffer/Jonathan Smith/ Charles Young/Maurice Young...*Down Wit Da South*	Slip n Slide 93348
				TRICK DADDY Featuring Twista and Lil Jon		
				TRINA & TAMARA		
11/29/97	4	26	●	1 My Love Is The Shhh!	James Baker/Rochad Holiday/Tamara Powell/Curtis Wilson/Melvin Lee Wilson/Jeff Young	Warner 17327
				SOMETHIN' FOR THE PEOPLE featuring Trina & Tamara		
				TROGGS, The		
7/30/66	❶²	11	☉	1 Wild Thing	Chip Taylor...*With A Girl Like You*	Atco 6415/Fontana 1548
5/18/68	7	16		2 Love Is All Around	Reg Presley...*When Will The Rain Come*	Fontana 1607
				TROY, Doris		
7/27/63	10	14		1 Just One Look	Greg Carroll/Doris Payne...*Bossa Nova Blues*	Atlantic 2188
				TRUE, Andrea, Connection		
7/17/76	4	25	●	1 More, More, More (Pt. 1)	Gregg Diamond...*Pt. II*	Buddah 515
				TRUTH HURTS		
6/8/02	9	20		1 Addictive	David Blake/Stephen Garrett/William Griffin	Aftermath 497710
				TRUTH HURTS featuring Rakim		
				TUBB, Ernest		
8/26/50	10	10		1 Goodnight Irene	Huddie Ledbetter/John Lomax...*Hillbilly Fever #2*	Decca 46255
				RED FOLEY-ERNEST TUBB		
				TUBES, The		
7/2/83	10	20		1 She's A Beauty	David Foster/Steve Lukather/Fee Waybill...*When You're Ready To Come*	Capitol 5217
				TUCKER, Tommy, Time		
10/25/41	4	10		1 I Don't Want To Set The World On Fire	Bennie Benjamin/Eddie Durham/Sol Marcus/Eddie Seiler...*This Love Of Mine*	Okeh 6320
8/25/45	10	3		2 On The Atchison, Topeka And The Santa Fe	Johnny Mercer/Harry Warren...*Welcome Home*	Columbia 36829
				TUNE WEAVERS, The		
10/28/57	5	19		1 Happy, Happy Birthday Baby	Gilbert Lopez/Margo Sylvia...*Ol Man River*	Checker 872
				TURNER, Ike & Tina		
3/27/71	4	13	●	1 Proud Mary	John Fogerty...*Funkier Than A Mosquita's Tweeter*	Liberty 56216

PEAK DATE	PEAK POS	WKS CHR	GOLD	ARTIST / Song Title	SONGWRITER...B-side	Label & Number
				TURNER, Sammy		
8/24/59	3¹	18		1 Lavender-Blue	Eliot Daniel/Larry Morey...*Wrapped Up In A Dream*	Big Top 3016
				TURNER, Tina		
9/1/84	❶³	28	●	1 What's Love Got To Do With It	Terry Britten/Graham Lyle...*Rock And Roll Widow*	Capitol 5354
11/24/84	5	21		2 Better Be Good To Me	Mike Chapman/Nicky Chinn/Holly Knight...*When I Was Young*	Capitol 5387
3/23/85	7	18		3 Private Dancer	Mark Knopfler...*Nutbush City Limits (live)*	Capitol 5433
9/14/85	2¹	18		4 We Don't Need Another Hero (Thunderdome)	Terry Britten/Graham Lyle	Capitol 5491
10/18/86	2³	16		5 Typical Male	Terry Britten/Graham Lyle...*Don't Turn Around*	Capitol 5615
8/14/93	9	24		6 I Don't Wanna Fight	Steve DuBerry/Bill Lawrie/Lulu...*Tina's Wish*	Virgin 12652
				TURTLES, The		
9/18/65	8	11		1 It Ain't Me Babe	Bob Dylan...*Almost There*	White Whale 222
3/25/67	❶³	15	●	2 Happy Together	Garry Bonner/Alan Gordon...*Like The Seasons*	White Whale 244
6/17/67	3²	11		3 She'd Rather Be With Me	Garry Bonner/Alan Gordon...*The Walking Song*	White Whale 249
11/2/68	6	12		4 Elenore	John Barbata/Howard Kaylan/Al Nichol/Jim Pons/Mark Volman...*Surfer Dan*	White Whale 276
3/1/69	6	12		5 You Showed Me	Gene Clark/Roger McGuinn...*Buzz Saw*	White Whale 292
				TWAIN, Shania		
5/2/98	2⁹	42	▲	1 You're Still The One	Mutt Lange/Shania Twain...*Don't Be Stupid (You Know I Love You)*	Mercury 568452
12/19/98	4	14		2 From This Moment On	Mutt Lange/Shania Twain	Mercury 566450
6/12/99	7	28		3 That Don't Impress Me Much	Mutt Lange/Shania Twain	Mercury 172118
				TWEET		
5/4/02	7	20		1 Oops (Oh My)	Charlene Keys/Tim Mosley	Gold Mind 67280
				TWISTA		
2/21/04	❶¹	22		1 Slow Jamz	Burt Bacharach/Hal David/Carl Mitchell/Kanye West...*Badunkadunk*	Atlantic 88288
				TWISTA Featuring Kanye West & Jamie Foxx		
5/22/04	6	20	○	2 Overnight Celebrity	Miri Ben-Ari/Carl Mitchell/Kanye West/Lenny Williams...*Like A 24*	Atlantic 88359
11/27/04	7	22	○	3 Let's Go	Derrick Baker/Robert Daisley/Maurice Marshall/Carl Mitchell/Ozzy Osbourne/Randy Rhoads/James Scheffer/Jonathan Smith/ Charles Young/Maurice Young...*Down Wit Da South*	Slip n Slide 93348
				TRICK DADDY Featuring Twista and Lil Jon		
				TWITTY, Conway		
11/10/58	❶²	21		1 It's Only Make Believe	Jack Nance/Conway Twitty...*I'll Try*	MGM 12677
12/7/59	10	18		2 Danny Boy	Fred Weatherly...*Halfway To Heaven*	MGM 12826
2/8/60	6	15		3 Lonely Blue Boy	Ben Weisman/Fred Wise...*Star Spangled Heaven*	MGM 12857
				2PAC		
4/29/95	9	20	▲	1 Dear Mama	Tony Pizarro/Tupac Shakur...*Old School*	Interscope 98273
6/22/96	6	24		2 California Love	Joe Cocker/Tupac Shakur/Chris Stainton/Larry Troutman/Roger Troutman/Andre Young...*How Do U Want It*	Death Row 854652
				2 PAC (featuring Dr. Dre and Roger Troutman)		
7/13/96	❶²	24	▲²	3 How Do U Want It	James Jackson/Tupac Shakur...*California Love*	Death Row 854652
				2 PAC (featuring KC and JoJo)		
				TYLER, Bonnie		
6/24/78	3²	21	●	1 It's A Heartache	Ronnie Scott/Steve Wolfe...*It's About Time*	RCA 11249
10/1/83	❶⁴	29	▲	2 Total Eclipse Of The Heart	Jim Steinman...*Straight From The Heart*	Columbia 03906
				TYMES, The		
8/3/63	❶¹	15	⊙	1 So Much In Love	William Jackson/Roy Straigis/George Williams...*Roscoe James McClain*	Parkway 871
9/28/63	7	11		2 Wonderful! Wonderful!	Sherman Edwards/Ben Raleigh...*Come With Me To The Sea*	Parkway 884
				TYRESE		
3/29/03	7	25		1 How You Gonna Act Like That	Eric Dawkins/Tyrese Gibson/Harvey Mason/Damon Thomas	J Records
10/7/06	9	20		2 Pullin' Me Back	Howard Bailey/Jermaine Dupri/Brian Morgan/Jaco Pastorius/Jim Phillips	Slot-A-Lot 69129
				CHINGY Featuring Tyrese		

U

PEAK DATE	PEAK POS	WKS CHR	GOLD	ARTIST / Song Title	SONGWRITER...B-side	Label & Number
				UB40		
10/15/88	❶¹	25	●	1 Red Red Wine [rap version]	Neil Diamond...*Sufferin'*	A&M 1244
12/15/90	6	25	●	2 The Way You Do The Things You Do	Smokey Robinson/Robert Rogers...*Splugen*	Virgin 98978
7/13/91	7	25		3 Here I Am (Come And Take Me)	Al Green/Mabon Hodges...*Gator*	Virgin 99141
7/24/93	❶⁷	29	▲	4 Can't Help Falling In Love	Luigi Creatore/Hugo Peretti/George David Weiss...*Jungle Love*	Virgin 12653
				UGLY KID JOE		
5/2/92	9	20		1 Everything About You	Whitfield Crane/Klaus Eichstadt	Mercury 866632
4/10/93	6	20	●	2 Cats In The Cradle	Harry Chapin/Sandra Chapin...*Panhandlin' Prince*	Stardog 864888
				ULLMAN, Tracey		
4/28/84	8	17		1 They Don't Know	Kirsty MacColl...*You Broke My Heart In 17 Places*	MCA/Stiff 52347
				UNCLE KRACKER		
6/9/01	5	33		1 Follow Me	Michael Bradford/Matthew Shafer...*Yeah, Yeah, Yeah*	Lava/Atlantic 85184
8/2/03	9	35		2 Drift Away	Mentor Williams	Lava
				UNCLE KRACKER Featuring Dobie Gray		
				UNCLE SAM		
2/7/98	6	28	▲	1 I Don't Ever Want To See You Again	Nathan Morris	Stonecreek 78689
				UNDERWOOD, Carrie		
7/2/05	❶¹	12	●	1 Inside Your Heaven	Andreas Carlsson/Savan Kotecha/Pelle Nylen...*Independence Day*	Arista Nashville 70859
5/12/07	6	5		2 I'll Stand By You	Chrissie Hynde/Tom Kelly/Billy Steinberg	Fremantle
6/2/07	8	64	△³	3 Before He Cheats	Josh Kear/Chris Tompkins	Arista Nashville
4/4/09	9	18	○	4 I Told You So	Randy Travis	19 Records
				CARRIE UNDERWOOD Featuring Randy Travis		

PEAK DATE	PEAK POS	WKS CHR	GOLD	ARTIST / Song Title	Songwriter...B-side	Label & Number
				UNDISPUTED TRUTH, The		
9/4/71	3²	18		1 Smiling Faces Sometimes	Barrett Strong/Norman Whitfield...*You Got The Love I Need*	Gordy 7108
				UNK		
2/17/07	10	36	△	1 Walk It Out	Montay Humphrey/Anthony Platt/Korey Roberson/Howard Simmons	Big Oomp
				USA FOR AFRICA		
4/13/85	❶⁴	18	▲⁴	1 We Are The World	Michael Jackson/Lionel Richie...*Grace* (Quincy Jones)	Columbia 04839
				USHER		
10/25/97	2⁷	47	▲	1 You Make Me Wanna...	Jermaine Dupri/Usher Raymond/Manuel Seal	LaFace 24265
2/14/98	❶²	23	▲	2 Nice & Slow	Brian Casey/Jermaine Dupri/Usher Raymond/Manuel Seal	LaFace 24290
8/15/98	2³	24	▲	3 My Way	Jermaine Dupri/Usher Raymond/Manuel Seal	LaFace 24323
7/7/01	❶⁴	24		4 U Remind Me	Edmund Clement/Anita McCloud	Arista 13992
12/15/01	❶⁶	32		5 U Got It Bad	Brian Michael Cox/Jermaine Dupri/Usher Raymond	Arista 15036
5/4/02	3¹	26		6 U Don't Have To Call	Charles Hugo/Pharrell Williams	Arista
5/25/02	2⁴	23		7 I Need A Girl (Part One)	Sean Combs/Chauncey Hawkins/Michael Jones/Jack Knight/Sonny Lester/Eric Matlock/J. Karen Thomas	Bad Boy 79436
				P. DIDDY Featuring Usher & Loon		
2/28/04	❶¹²	45	△	8 Yeah!	Christopher Bridges/Sean Garrett/Jonathan Smith/Patrick Smith	Arista 59149
				USHER Featuring Lil Jon & Ludacris		
5/22/04	❶⁸	30	○	9 Burn	Bryan Michael Cox/Jermaine Dupri/Usher Raymond	Arista 61107
7/24/04	❶²	25	○	10 Confessions Part II	Bryan Michael Cox/Jermaine Dupri/Usher Raymond	LaFace 64779
10/30/04	❶⁶	26	○	11 My Boo	Jermaine Dupri/Alicia Keys/Usher Raymond/Manuel Seal/Adonis Shropshire	LaFace 65246
				USHER & ALICIA KEYS		
1/22/05	3³	22		12 Lovers & Friends	Christopher Bridges/Usher Raymond/Jonathan Smith/M. Sterling	BME/TVT
				LIL JON & THE EAST SIDE BOYZ Featuring Usher & Ludacris		
3/26/05	8	27		13 Caught Up	Jason Boyd/Vidal Davis/Andre Harris/Ryan Toby	LaFace 66434
3/15/08	❶³	25	△	14 Love In This Club	Darnell Dalton/Jay Jenkins/Jamal Jones/Ryon Lovett/Usher Raymond/Lamar Taylor/Keith Thomas	LaFace 30018
				USHER Featuring Young Jeezy		
5/15/10	❶⁴	30		15 OMG	William Adams	LaFace
				USHER Featuring will.i.am		
10/9/10	4	28↑		16 DJ Got Us Fallin' In Love	Savan Kotecha/Armando Christian Perez/Martin Sandberg/Johan Schuster...*OMG (club mix)*	LaFace 76763
				USHER Featuring Pitbull		
				US3		
3/5/94	9	27	●	1 Cantaloop	Herbie Hancock/Rahsaan Kelly/Mel Simpson/Geoff Wilkinson	Blue Note 44945
				U2		
5/16/87	❶³	18		1 With Or Without You	Adam Clayton/Dave Evans/Paul Hewson/Larry Mullen...*Luminous Times (Hold On To Love) / Walk To The Water*	Island 99469
8/8/87	❶²	17		2 I Still Haven't Found What I'm Looking For	Adam Clayton/Dave Evans/Paul Hewson/Larry Mullen...*Spanish Eyes / Deep In The Heart*	Island 99430
11/26/88	3¹	17	●	3 Desire	Adam Clayton/Dave Evans/Paul Hewson/Larry Mullen...*Hallelujah Here She Comes*	Island 99250
1/25/92	9	20		4 Mysterious Ways	Adam Clayton/Dave Evans/Paul Hewson/Larry Mullen	Island 866188
5/16/92	10	20		5 One	Adam Clayton/Dave Evans/Paul Hewson/Larry Mullen...*Lady With The Spinning Head / Satellite Of Love*	Island 866533
2/22/97	10	11	●	6 Discotheque	Adam Clayton/Dave Evans/Paul Hewson/Larry Mullen...*Holy Joe*	Island 854774

V

PEAK DATE	PEAK POS	WKS CHR	GOLD	ARTIST / Song Title	Songwriter...B-side	Label & Number
				VALENS, Ritchie		
2/23/59	2²	23		1 Donna	Ritchie Valens...*La Bamba*	Del-Fi 4110
				VALENTE, Caterina		
5/14/55	8	14		1 The Breeze And I	Ernesto Lecuona/Al Stillman...*Jalousie*	Decca 29467
				VALENTINO, Bobby		
5/21/05	8	22	○	1 Slow Down	Tim Kelley/Bob Robinson/Bobby Wilson	DTP
8/6/05	9	20		2 Pimpin' All Over The World	Christopher Bridges/Jamal Jones/Darnley Scantlebury...*Spur Of The Moment*	DTP 004851
				LUDACRIS featuring Bobby Valentino		
				VALLEE, Rudy		
6/19/43	2¹	10		1 As Time Goes By	Herman Hupfeld...*Two In One Blues*	Victor 1526
				VALLI, Frankie		
7/22/67	2¹	16	●	1 Can't Take My Eyes Off You	Bob Crewe/Bob Gaudio...*The Trouble With Me*	Philips 40446
3/22/75	❶¹	23	●	2 My Eyes Adored You	Bob Crewe/Kenny Nolan...*Watch Where You Walk*	Private Stock 45,003
7/26/75	6	14		3 Swearin' To God	Bob Crewe/Denny Randell...*Why*	Private Stock 45,021
8/26/78	❶²	22	▲	4 Grease	Barry Gibb	RSO 897
				VALLI, June		
10/3/53	4	17		1 Crying In The Chapel	Artie Glenn...*Love Every Moment You Live*	RCA Victor 5368
7/31/54	8	12		2 I Understand	Pat Best...*Love, Tears, And Kisses*	RCA Victor 5740
				VANDROSS, Luther		
4/21/90	6	27	●	1 Here And Now	Dave Elliott/Terry Steele...*Come Back*	Epic 73029
6/29/91	4	18		2 Power Of Love/Love Power	Marcus Miller/Luther Vandross/Teddy Vann	Epic 73778
11/2/91	9	20		3 Don't Want To Be A Fool	Marcus Miller/Luther Vandross	Epic 73879
6/13/92	10	20		4 The Best Things In Life Are Free	Michael Bivins/Ronnie DeVoe/Jimmy Jam Harris/Terry Lewis/Ralph Tresvant	Perspective 0010
				LUTHER VANDROSS and JANET JACKSON with BBD and Ralph Tresvant		
10/1/94	2¹	20	●	5 Endless Love	Lionel Richie	Columbia 77629
				LUTHER VANDROSS & MARIAH CAREY		
				VAN DYKE, Leroy		
12/11/61	5	16		1 Walk On By	Kendall Hayes...*My World Is Caving In*	Mercury 71834
				VANGELIS		
5/8/82	❶¹	28		1 Chariots Of Fire - Titles	Vangelis...*Eric's Theme* [I]	Polydor 2189

PEAK DATE	PEAK POS	WKS CHR	GOLD	ARTIST / Song Title	Songwriter...B-side	Label & Number
				VAN HALEN		
2/25/84	❶⁵	21	●	1 Jump	Michael Anthony/David Lee Roth/Alex Van Halen/Eddie Van Halen...*House Of Pain*	Warner 29384
5/17/86	3¹	16		2 Why Can't This Be Love	Michael Anthony/Sammy Hagar/Alex Van Halen/Eddie Van Halen...*Get Up*	Warner 28740
9/10/88	5	19		3 When It's Love	Michael Anthony/Sammy Hagar/Alex Van Halen/Eddie Van Halen...*Cabo Wabo*	Warner 27827
				VANILLA FUDGE		
8/31/68	6	12		1 You Keep Me Hangin' On	Lamont Dozier/Brian Holland/Eddie Holland...*Come By Day, Come By Night*	Atco 6590
				VANILLA ICE		
11/3/90	❶¹	21	▲	1 Ice Ice Baby	David Bowie/Floyd Brown/John Deacon/Mario Johnson/Brian May/Freddie Mercury/Roger Taylor/Robert Van Winkle...*Play That Funky Music*	SBK 07335
2/9/91	4	17	●	2 Play That Funky Music	Robert Parissi...*Go Ill*	SBK 07339
				VANITY FARE		
6/27/70	5	22	●	1 Hitchin' A Ride	Peter Callander/Mitch Murray...*Man Child*	Page One 21,029
				VANNELLI, Gino		
12/9/78	4	21		1 I Just Wanna Stop	Ross Vannelli...*The Surest Things Can Change*	A&M 2072
5/30/81	6	20		2 Living Inside Myself	Gino Vannelli...*Stay With Me*	Arista 0588
				VANWARMER, Randy		
6/16/79	4	20	●	1 Just When I Needed You Most	Randy Vanwarmer...*Your Light*	Bearsville 0334
				VAUGHAN, Sarah		
7/3/48	9	1		1 Nature Boy	Eden Ahbez...*I'm Glad There Is You*	Musicraft 567
9/16/50	10	7		2 (I Love The Girl) I Love The Guy	Cy Coben...*Thinking Of You*	Columbia 38925
1/8/55	6	15		3 Make Yourself Comfortable	Bob Merrill...*Idle Gossip*	Mercury 70469
5/28/55	6	11		4 Whatever Lola Wants	Richard Adler/Jerry Ross...*Oh Yeah*	Mercury 70595
9/7/59	7	19		5 Broken-Hearted Melody	Hal David/Sherman Edwards...*Misty*	Mercury 71477
				VAUGHN, Billy, and His Orchestra		
3/5/55	2¹	27	⊙	1 Melody Of Love	Hans Engelmann/Tom Glazer...*Joy Ride* [I]	Dot 15247
10/22/55	5	15		2 The Shifting Whispering Sands (Parts 1 & 2)	V.C. Gilbert/Mary Hadler...[S]	Dot 15409
12/23/57	10	22		3 Raunchy	Bill Justis/Sid Manker...*Sail Along Silvery Moon* [I]	Dot 15661
2/3/58	5	26	⊙	4 Sail Along Silvery Moon	Harry Tobias/Percy Wenrich...*Raunchy* [I]	Dot 15661
				VEE, Bobby		
10/17/60	6	19		1 Devil Or Angel	Blanche Carter...*Since I Met You Baby*	Liberty 55270
1/9/61	6	14		2 Rubber Ball	Anne Orlowski/Aaron Schroeder...*Everyday*	Liberty 55287
9/18/61	❶³	15	⊙	3 Take Good Care Of My Baby	Gerry Goffin/Carole King...*Bashful Bob*	Liberty 55354
12/25/61	2¹	15		4 Run To Him	Gerry Goffin/Jack Keller...*Walkin' With My Angel*	Liberty 55388
2/2/63	3²	14		5 The Night Has A Thousand Eyes	Marilynn Garrett/Dottie Wayne/Ben Weisman...*Anonymous Phone Call*	Liberty 55521
9/9/67	3³	16	●	6 Come Back When You Grow Up	Martha Sharp...*Swahili Serenade*	Liberty 55964
				VEGA, Suzanne		
8/22/87	3¹	19		1 Luka	Suzanne Vega...*Night Vision*	A&M 2937
12/22/90	5	21	●	2 Tom's Diner	Suzanne Vega	A&M 1529
				D.N.A. Featuring SUZANNE VEGA		
				VENTURES, The		
8/29/60	2¹	18	⊙	1 Walk -- Don't Run	John Smith...*Home* [I]	Dolton 25
8/22/64	8	11		2 Walk-Don't Run '64	John Smith...*The Cruel Sea* [I]	Dolton 96
5/10/69	4	14		3 Hawaii Five-O	Mort Stevens...*Soul Breeze* [I]	Liberty 56068
				VERA, Billy		
1/24/87	❶²	21	●	1 At This Moment	Billy Vera...*I Can Take Care Of Myself* [L]	Rhino 74403
				VERNE, Larry		
10/10/60	❶¹	13	⊙	1 Mr. Custer	Fred Darian/Al DeLory/Joseph Van Winkle...*Okeefenokee Two Step* [N]	Era 3024
				VERTICAL HORIZON		
7/15/00	❶¹	41		1 Everything You Want	Matt Scannell...*The Man Who Would Be Santa*	RCA 65981
				VERVE PIPE, The		
6/7/97	5	42	●	1 The Freshmen	Brian Vander Ark	RCA 64734
				VILLAGE PEOPLE		
2/3/79	2³	26	▲	1 Y.M.C.A.	Henri Belolo/Jacques Morali/Victor Willis...*The Women*	Casablanca 945
5/19/79	3²	18	●	2 In The Navy	Henri Belolo/Jacques Morali/Victor Willis...*Manhattan Woman*	Casablanca 973
				VILLAGE STOMPERS, The		
11/23/63	2¹	14		1 Washington Square	Bob Goldstein/David Shire...*Turkish Delight* [I]	Epic 9617
				VINCENT, Anne		
9/18/48	6	16		1 You Call Everybody Darlin'	Sam Martin/Ben Trace/Clem Watts...*Blue Bird Polka*	Mercury 5155
				VINCENT, Gene, and His Blue Caps		
7/28/56	7	20		1 Be-Bop-A-Lula	Tex Davis/Gene Vincent...*Woman Love*	Capitol 3450
				VINTON, Bobby		
7/14/62	❶⁴	15	●	1 Roses Are Red (My Love)	Al Byron/Paul Evans...*You And I*	Epic 9509
7/6/63	3¹	13		2 Blue On Blue	Burt Bacharach/Hal David...*Those Little Things*	Epic 9593
9/21/63	❶³	15	⊙	3 Blue Velvet	Lee Morris/Bernie Wayne...*Is There A Place (Where I Can Go)*	Epic 9614
1/4/64	❶⁴	13	⊙	4 There! I've Said It Again	Redd Evans/Dave Mann...*The Girl With The Bow In Her Hair*	Epic 9638
3/28/64	9	9		5 My Heart Belongs To Only You	Dorothy Daniels/Frank Daniels...*Warm And Tender*	Epic 9662
12/12/64	❶¹	15		6 Mr. Lonely	Gene Allan/Bobby Vinton...*It's Better To Have Loved*	Epic 9730
11/18/67	6	13		7 Please Love Me Forever	Ollie Blanchard/Johnny Malone...*Miss America*	Epic 10228
12/14/68	9	14	●	8 I Love How You Love Me	Larry Kolber/Barry Mann...*Little Barefoot Boy*	Epic 10397
11/16/74	3²	17	●	9 My Melody Of Love	Henry Mayer/Bobby Vinton...*I'll Be Loving You*	ABC 12022

PEAK DATE	PEAK POS	WKS CHR	GOLD	ARTIST / Song Title	Songwriter...B-side	Label & Number
				VIRTUES, The		
4/27/59	5	16		1 Guitar Boogie Shuffle	Arthur Smith...*Guitar In Orbit* [I]	Hunt 324
				VOGUES, The		
11/13/65	4	12		1 You're The One	Petula Clark/Tony Hatch...*Some Words*	Co & Ce 229
1/15/66	4	14		2 Five O'Clock World	Allen Reynolds...*Nothing To Offer You*	Co & Ce 232
8/17/68	7	15	●	3 Turn Around, Look At Me	Jerry Capehart...*Then*	Reprise 0686
10/12/68	7	10	●	4 My Special Angel	Jimmy Duncan...*I Keep It Hid*	Reprise 0766
				VOICES OF THEORY		
7/25/98	10	31	●	1 Say It	Raymond Basora/Gerald McKetney/Steve Morales...*Dímelo (Spanish version)*	H.O.L.A. 341032

W

PEAK DATE	PEAK POS	WKS CHR	GOLD	ARTIST / Song Title	Songwriter...B-side	Label & Number
				WADE, Adam		
5/1/61	7	14		1 Take Good Care Of Her	Arthur Kent/Ed Warren...*Sleepy Time Gal*	Coed 546
7/3/61	5	11		2 The Writing On The Wall	Mark Barkan/Sandy Baron/George Paxton...*Point Of No Return*	Coed 550
9/4/61	10	10		3 As If I Didn't Know	Scott David/Larry Kusik...*Playin' Around*	Coed 553
				WADSWORTH MANSION		
2/27/71	7	14		1 Sweet Mary	Steve Jablecki...*What's On Tonight*	Sussex 209
				WAGNER, Jack		
1/12/85	2²	22		1 All I Need	Glen Ballard/Clif Magness/David Pack...*Tell Him (That You Won't Go)*	Qwest 29238
				WAITE, John		
9/22/84	❶¹	24		1 Missing You	Mark Leonard/Charles Sandford/John Waite...*For Your Love*	EMI America 8212
				WAKELY, Jimmy		
11/27/48	10	8		1 One Has My Name (The Other Has My Heart)	Hal Blair/Dearest Dean/Eddie Dean...*You're The Sweetest Rose In Texas*	Capitol 15162
11/19/49	❶³	23	⊙	2 Slipping Around	Floyd Tillman...*Wedding Bells*	Capitol 40224
11/26/49	8	10		3 I'll Never Slip Around Again	Teepee Mitchell/Lew Porter...*Six Times a Week And Twice On Sunday*	Capitol 40246
12/16/50	6	15		4 A Bushel And A Peck	Frank Loesser...*Beyond The Reef*	Capitol 1234
				MARGARET WHITING and JIMMY WAKELY (above 3)		
				WALD, Jerry, and his Orchestra		
5/12/45	8	3		1 Laura	Johnny Mercer/David Raksin...*Candy*	Majestic 7129
				WALKER, Jr., & The All Stars		
4/3/65	4	14		1 Shotgun	Jr. Walker...*Hot Cha*	Soul 35008
8/9/69	4	16		2 What Does It Take (To Win Your Love)	Johnny Bristol/Vernon Bullock/Harvey Fuqua...*Brainwasher (Part 1)*	Soul 35062
				WALL, Paul		
1/21/06	❶²	28	△	1 Grillz	Jermaine Dupri/Cameron Gipp/Cornell Haynes/Ali Jones/James Phillips/Paul Slayton	Derrty 005897
				NELLY F/Paul Wall, Ali & Gipp		
				WALLACE, Jerry		
10/26/59	8	21		1 Primrose Lane	George Callender/Wayne Shaklin...*By Your Side*	Challenge 59047
				JERRY WALLACE with The Jewels		
				WALLFLOWERS, The		
5/10/97	2⁵	70		1 One Headlight	Jakob Dylan	Interscope
				WALTERS, Teddy		
5/11/46	4	12		1 Laughing On The Outside (Crying On The Inside)	Ben Raleigh/Bernie Wayne...*You I Love*	ARA 135
				WANG CHUNG		
12/27/86	2²	21		1 Everybody Have Fun Tonight	Nick Feldman/Jack Hues/Peter Wolf...*Fun Tonight: The Early Years*	Geffen 28562
4/11/87	9	18		2 Let's Go!	Nick Feldman/Jack Hues...*The World In Which We Live*	Geffen 28531
				WAR		
8/22/70	3¹	21	●	1 Spill The Wine	Thomas Allen/Harold Brown/Morris Dickerson/Leroy Jordan/Charles Miller/Lee Oskar/Howard Scott...*Magic Mountain*	MGM 14118
				ERIC BURDON AND WAR		
2/10/73	7	16	●	2 The World Is A Ghetto	Thomas Allen/Harold Brown/Morris Dickerson/Lonnie Jordan/Charles Miller/Lee Oskar/Howard Scott...*Four Cornered Room*	United Artists 50975
4/28/73	2²	15	●	3 The Cisco Kid	Thomas Allen/Harold Brown/Morris Dickerson/Lonnie Jordan/Charles Miller/Lee Oskar/Howard Scott...*Beetles In The Bog*	United Artists 163
9/15/73	8	13		4 Gypsy Man	Thomas Allen/Harold Brown/Morris Dickerson/Lonnie Jordan/Charles Miller/Lee Oskar/Howard Scott...*Deliver The Word*	United Artists 281
8/23/75	6	20	●	5 Why Can't We Be Friends?	Thomas Allen/Harold Brown/Morris Dickerson/Jerry Goldstein/Lonnie Jordan/Charles Miller/Lee Oskar/Howard Scott...*In Mazatlan*	United Artists 629
11/29/75	7	15		6 Low Rider	Thomas Allen/Harold Brown/Morris Dickerson/Jerry Goldstein/Lonnie Jordan/Charles Miller/Lee Oskar/Howard Scott...*So*	United Artists 706
9/25/76	7	16	●	7 Summer	Thomas Allen/Harold Brown/Morris Dickerson/Jerry Goldstein/Lonnie Jordan/Charles Miller/Lee Oskar/Howard Scott...*All Day Music*	United Artists 834
				WARD, Anita		
6/30/79	❶²	21		1 Ring My Bell	Frederick Knight...*If I Could Feel That Old Feeling Again*	Juana 3422
				WARING, Fred, And The Pennsylvanians		
12/6/47	7	7	⊙	1 Whiffenpoof Song	Todd Galloway/Meade Minnigerode/George Pomeroy...*Kentucky Babe*	Decca 23990
				BING CROSBY with FRED WARING and the GLEE CLUB		
				WARNES, Jennifer		
5/7/77	6	22		1 Right Time Of The Night	Peter McCann...*Daddy Don't Go*	Arista 0223
11/6/82	❶³	23	▲	2 Up Where We Belong	Will Jennings/Jack Nitzsche/Buffy Sainte-Marie...*Sweet Li'l Woman (Cocker)*	Island 99996
				JOE COCKER and JENNIFER WARNES		
11/28/87	❶¹	21	●	3 (I've Had) The Time Of My Life	John DeNicola/Donald Markowitz/Franke Previte...*Love Is Strange (Mickey & Sylvia)*	RCA 5224
				BILL MEDLEY AND JENNIFER WARNES		

PEAK DATE	PEAK POS	WKS CHR	GOLD	ARTIST / Song Title	Songwriter...B-side	Label & Number
				WARRANT		
9/23/89	2[2]	19	●	1 Heaven	Jani Lane...*In The Sticks*	Columbia 68985
11/3/90	10	19		2 Cherry Pie	Jani Lane...*Thin Disguise*	Columbia 73510
2/23/91	10	19		3 I Saw Red	Jani Lane	Columbia 73597
				WARREN, Fran		
2/4/50	3[1]	13		1 I Said My Pajamas (And Put on My Pray'rs)	Eddie Pola/George Wyle...*Have I Told You Lately That I Love You*	RCA Victor 3119
				TONY MARTIN and FRAN WARREN		
				WARREN G		
7/2/94	2[3]	20	▲	1 Regulate	Warren Griffin/Nathan Hale	Death Row 98280
				WARREN G. & NATE DOGG		
9/10/94	9	20	●	2 This DJ	Warren Griffin...*Regulate*	Violator/RAL 853236
				WARWICK, Dionne		
2/15/64	8	14		1 Anyone Who Had A Heart	Burt Bacharach/Hal David...*The Love Of A Boy*	Scepter 1262
6/13/64	6	13		2 Walk On By	Burt Bacharach/Hal David...*Any Old Time Of The Day*	Scepter 1274
5/14/66	8	12		3 Message To Michael	Burt Bacharach/Hal David...*Here Where There Is Love*	Scepter 12133
12/9/67	4	13	●	4 I Say A Little Prayer	Burt Bacharach/Hal David...*(Theme From) Valley Of The Dolls*	Scepter 12203
2/24/68	2[4]	13		5 (Theme From) Valley Of The Dolls	Andre Previn/Dory Previn...*I Say A Little Prayer*	Scepter 12203
5/18/68	10	12		6 Do You Know The Way To San Jose	Burt Bacharach/Hal David...*Let Me Be Lonely*	Scepter 12216
3/8/69	7	12		7 This Girl's In Love With You	Burt Bacharach/Hal David...*Dream Sweet Dreamer*	Scepter 12241
2/7/70	6	11		8 I'll Never Fall In Love Again	Burt Bacharach/Hal David...*What The World Needs Now Is Love*	Scepter 12273
10/26/74	❶[1]	19	●	9 Then Came You	Sherman Marshall/Phil Pugh...*Just As Long As We Have Love*	Atlantic 3202
				DIONNE WARWICKE AND SPINNERS		
10/20/79	5	24	●	10 I'll Never Love This Way Again	Will Jennings/Richard Kerr...*In Your Eyes*	Arista 0419
1/15/83	10	22		11 Heartbreaker	Barry Gibb/Maurice Gibb/Robin Gibb...*I Can't See Anything (But You)*	Arista 1015
1/18/86	❶[4]	23	●	12 That's What Friends Are For	Burt Bacharach/Carole Bayer Sager...*Two Ships Passing In The Night* (Warwick)	Arista 9422
				DIONNE & FRIENDS (Elton John, Gladys Knight and Stevie Wonder)		
				WASHINGTON, Dinah		
8/10/59	8	20		1 What A Diff'rence A Day Makes	Stanley Adams/Maria Grever...*Come On Home*	Mercury 71435
3/21/60	5	15	⊙	2 Baby (You've Got What It Takes)	Clyde Otis/Murray Stein...*I Do*	Mercury 71565
6/27/60	7	13		3 A Rockin' Good Way (To Mess Around And Fall In Love)	Brook Benton/Luchi DeJesus...*I Believe*	Mercury 71629
				DINAH WASHINGTON & BROOK BENTON (above 2)		
				WASHINGTON, Grover Jr.		
5/2/81	2[3]	24		1 Just The Two Of Us	Ralph MacDonald/William Salter/Bill Withers...*Make Me A Memory (Sad Samba)* (Washington)	Elektra 47103
				GROVER WASHINGTON, JR. (with Bill Withers)		
				WAS (NOT WAS)		
4/1/89	7	16		1 Walk The Dinosaur	Randy Jacobs/David Was/Don Was...*Wedding Vows In Vegas*	Chrysalis 43331
				WATERFRONT		
6/17/89	10	17		1 Cry	Phil Cilia/Chris Duffy...*Saved*	Polydor 871110
				WATERS, Crystal		
7/6/91	8	16	●	1 Gypsy Woman (She's Homeless)	Neal Conway/Crystal Waters	Mercury 868208
				WATLEY, Jody		
5/2/87	2[4]	19		1 Looking For A New Love	Andre Cymone/Jody Watley	MCA 52956
12/19/87	6	23		2 Don't You Want Me	David Bryant/Franne Golde/Jody Watley	MCA 53162
4/16/88	10	17		3 Some Kind Of Lover	Andre Cymone/Jody Watley	MCA 53235
5/20/89	2[2]	18	●	4 Real Love	Andre Cymone/Jody Watley	MCA 53484
8/26/89	9	18		5 Friends	Eric Barrier/Andre Cymone/William Griffin/Jody Watley...*Private Life* (Watley)	MCA 53660
				JODY WATLEY (with Eric B. & Rakim)		
1/20/90	4	23		6 Everything	Gardner Cole/James Newton Howard	MCA 53714
				WATSON, Paula		
1/15/49	6	16		1 A Little Bird Told Me	Harvey Brooks...*Stick By Me Baby*	Supreme 1507
				WAYNE, Bobby		
3/15/52	6	13		1 Wheel Of Fortune	Bennie Benjamin/George Weiss...*Heart Of A Clown*	Mercury 5779
				WAYNE, Jerry		
9/17/49	6	7		1 Room Full Of Roses	Tim Spencer...*I'll Keep The Lovelight Burning (In My Heart)*	Columbia 38525
				WAYNE, Thomas		
3/23/59	5	19		1 Tragedy	Fred Burch/Gerald Nelson...*Saturday Date*	Fernwood 109
				WEAVERS, The		
7/29/50	2[1]	17	⊙	1 Tzena Tzena Tzena	Gordon Jenkins/Spencer Ross...*Goodnight Irene*	Decca 27077
8/19/50	❶[13]	25	⊙	2 Goodnight Irene	Huddie Ledbetter/John Lomax...*Tzena Tzena Tzena*	Decca 27077
2/3/51	4	14		3 So Long (It's Been Good to Know Yuh)	Woody Guthrie...*Lonesome Traveler*	Decca 27376
				GORDON JENKINS and his Orchestra and THE WEAVERS (above 3)		
4/28/51	2[8]	23	⊙	4 On Top Of Old Smoky	Pete Seeger...*Across The Wide Missouri*	Decca 27515
				THE WEAVERS and TERRY GILKYSON		
				WEBBIE		
3/8/08	9	25		1 Independent	Jeremy Allen/Webster Gradney/Torence Hatch/Claude McKnight...*I Miss You*	Trill 511418
				WEBBIE Feat. Lil' Phat & Lil' Boosie		
				WEBER, Joan		
1/1/55	❶[4]	16	⊙	1 Let Me Go Lover	Jenny Lou Carson/Al Hill...*Marionette*	Columbia 40366
				WEEMS, Ted, And His Orchestra		
3/15/47	❶[13]	20	⊙	1 Heartaches	Al Hoffman/John Klenner...*Oh! Monah* [I]	Decca 25017
7/19/47	5	6		2 Peg O' My Heart	Alfred Bryan/Fred Fisher...*Violets*	Mercury 5052
8/30/47	2[5]	17		3 I Wonder Who's Kissing Her Now	Frank Adams/Will Hough/Joseph Howard/Harold Orlob...*That Old Gang Of Mine*	Decca 25078
				TED WEEMS And His Orchestra; Perry Como, vocal		
11/22/47	3[1]	11		4 Mickey	Charles Daniels/Harry Williams...*The Martins And The Coys*	Mercury 5062

PEAK DATE	PEAK POS	WKS CHR	GOLD		ARTIST / Song Title	Songwriter...B-side	Label & Number
					WEEZER		
10/8/05	10	43	○	1	Beverly Hills	Rivers Cuomo	Geffen
					WE FIVE		
9/25/65	3[1]	15		1	You Were On My Mind	Sylvia Fricker...*Small World*	A&M 770
					WEIR, Frank		
6/12/54	4	19		1	The Happy Wanderer	Friedrich Moeller/Antonia Ridge/Florenz Siegesmund...*From Your Lips*	London 1448
					FRANK WEIR with his Saxophone, Chorus and Orchestra		
					WEISSBERG, Eric, & Steve Mandell		
2/24/73	2[4]	14	●	1	Dueling Banjos	Arthur Smith...*End Of A Dream* [I]	Warner 7659
					WELCH, Bob		
1/7/78	8	18		1	Sentimental Lady	Bob Welch...*Hot Love, Cold World*	Capitol 4479
					WELCH, Lenny		
12/28/63	4	16		1	Since I Fell For You	Buddy Johnson...*Are You Sincere*	Cadence 1439
					WELK, Lawrence, And His Orchestra		
5/6/44	2[1]	20		1	Don't Sweetheart Me	Cliff Friend/Charles Tobias...*Mairzy Doats*	Decca 4434
2/14/53	5	10		2	Oh, Happy Day	Don Howard/Nancy Reed...*Your Mother And Mine*	Coral 60893
					LAWRENCE WELK And His Champagne Music		
2/13/61	❶[2]	17	●	3	Calcutta	Heino Gaze/Lee Pockriss/Paul Vance...*My Grandfather's Clock* [I]	Dot 16161
					WELLS, Mary		
6/9/62	8	17		1	The One Who Really Loves You	Smokey Robinson...*I'm Gonna Stay*	Motown 1024
9/22/62	9	12		2	You Beat Me To The Punch	Smokey Robinson/Ronnie White...*Old Love (Let's Try It Again)*	Motown 1032
1/19/63	7	13		3	Two Lovers	Smokey Robinson...*Operator*	Motown 1035
5/16/64	❶[2]	15	◉	4	My Guy	Smokey Robinson...*Oh Little Boy (What Did You Do To Me)*	Motown 1056
					WEST, Kanye		
2/21/04	❶[1]	22		1	Slow Jamz	Burt Bacharach/Hal David/Carl Mitchell/Kanye West...*Badunkadunk*	Atlantic 88288
					TWISTA Featuring Kanye West & Jamie Foxx		
5/22/04	7	20	○	2	All Falls Down	Lauryn Hill/Kanye West...*Get 'Em*	Roc-A-Fella 002018
					KANYE WEST featuring Syleena Johnson		
9/17/05	❶[10]	39	△[2]	3	Gold Digger	Ray Charles/Renald Richard/Kanye West...*Diamonds From Sierra Leone*	Roc-A-Fella 005118
					KANYE WEST featuring Jamie Foxx		
9/29/07	❶[1]	27	△[3]	4	Stronger	Thomas Bangalter/Edwin Birdsong/Michael Dean/Christo Homem/Kanye West	Roc-A-Fella
11/10/07	7	21	△	5	Good Life	Aldrin Davis/Michael Dean/James Ingram/Quincy Jones/Faheem Najm/John Stephens/Kanye West	Roc-A-Fella
					KANYE WEST Featuring T-Pain		
9/27/08	5	20		6	Swagga Like Us	Maya Arulpragasm/Dwayne Carter/Shawn Carter/Clifford Harris/Nicky Headon/Mick Jones/Wesley Pentz/Paul Simonon/Joe Strummer/Kanye West	Roc-A-Fella 012284
					JAY-Z & T.I. Featuring Kanye West & Lil Wayne		
9/27/08	9	30	△[2]	7	American Boy	William Adams/Keith Harris/Josh Lopez/Caleb Spier/Estelle Swaray	Home School 422972
					ESTELLE Featuring Kanye West		
10/4/08	3[2]	23	△[3]	8	Love Lockdown	Kanye West	Roc-A-Fella 012384
2/21/09	2[1]	30	△[2]	9	Heartless	Malik Jones/Scott Mescudi/Kanye West/Ernest Wilson	Roc-A-Fella
6/20/09	3[3]	31		10	Knock You Down	Marcella Araica/Kevin Cossom/Floyd Nathaniel Hills/Keri Hilson/Shaffer Smith/Kanye West	Mosley
					KERI HILSON Featuring Kanye West & Ne-Yo		
10/3/09	2[1]	23	△[2]	11	Run This Town	Alatas Athanasios/Jeff Bhasker/Shawn Carter/Robyn Fenty/Kanye West/Ernest Wilson...*D.O.A. (Death Of Auto-Tune)*	Roc Nation 521199
					JAY-Z, RIHANNA & KANYE WEST		
10/3/09	8	24		12	Forever	Dwayne Carter/Aubrey Graham/Marshall Mathers/Matthew Samuels/Kanye West	Harvey Mason
					DRAKE Featuring Kanye West, Lil Wayne & Eminem		
					WESTON, Paul, and his Orchestra		
12/15/45	6	11		1	It Might As Well Be Spring	Oscar Hammerstein/Richard Rodgers...*How Deep Is The Ocean*	Capitol 214
					PAUL WESTON and his Orchestra With MARGARET WHITING		
12/7/46	6	13		2	Ole Buttermilk Sky	Jack Brooks/Hoagy Carmichael...*Just Squeeze Me (But Don't Tease Me)*	Capitol 285
4/26/47	8	8		3	Linda	Jack Lawrence...*Roses In The Rain*	Capitol 362
					PAUL WESTON AND HIS ORCHESTRA With MATT DENNIS (above 2)		
7/9/49	10	3		4	Bali Ha'i	Oscar Hammerstein/Richard Rodgers...*Some Enchanted Evening* [I]	Capitol 629
9/3/49	9	11		5	Some Enchanted Evening	Oscar Hammerstein/Richard Rodgers...*Bali Ha'i* [I]	Capitol 629
11/4/50	2[1]	18		6	Nevertheless (I'm In Love With You)	Bert Kalmar/Harry Ruby...*Beloved, Be Faithful*	Columbia 38982
1/19/52	8	6		7	Charmaine	Lew Pollack/Erno Rapee...*At Dawning (I Love You)*	Columbia 39616
					PAUL WESTON & his Orchestra with The Norman Luboff Choir (above 2)		
					WET WILLIE		
8/24/74	10	19		1	Keep On Smilin'	John Anthony/Jack Hall/Jimmy Hall/Rick Hirsch/Lewis Ross...*Soul Jones*	Capricorn 0043
					WHAM! — See MICHAEL, George		
					WHISPERS, The		
8/29/87	7	23		1	Rock Steady	Babyface/Dwayne Ladd/L.A. Reid/Bo Watson...*Are You Going My Way*	Solar 70006
					WHITCOMB, Ian		
7/17/65	8	13		1	You Turn Me On (Turn On Song)	Ian Whitcomb...*Poor But Honest*	Tower 134
					IAN WHITCOMB And Bluesville		
					WHITE, Barry		
6/23/73	3[1]	18	●	1	I'm Gonna Love You Just A Little More Baby	Barry White...*Just A Little More Baby*	20th Century 2018
1/12/74	7	18	●	2	Never, Never Gonna Give Ya Up	Barry White	20th Century 2058
9/21/74	❶[1]	12	●	3	Can't Get Enough Of Your Love, Babe	Barry White	20th Century 2120
1/4/75	2[2]	15	●	4	You're The First, The Last, My Everything	Peter Radcliffe/Tony Sepe/Barry White...*More Than Anything, You're My Everything*	20th Century 2133
4/19/75	8	11		5	What Am I Gonna Do With You	Barry White...*What Am I Gonna Do With You Baby*	20th Century 2177
11/12/77	4	22	●	6	It's Ecstasy When You Lay Down Next To Me	Ekundayo Paris/Nelson Pigford...*I Never Thought I'd Fall In Love With You*	20th Century 2350
					WHITE, Karyn		
2/4/89	7	25	●	1	The Way You Love Me	Babyface/L.A. Reid/Daryl Simmons...*Love On The Line*	Warner 27773
4/15/89	8	18	●	2	Superwoman	Babyface/L.A. Reid/Daryl Simmons...*Language Of Love*	Warner 27783
8/26/89	6	21		3	Secret Rendezvous	Babyface/L.A. Reid/Daryl Simmons...*Tell Me Tomorrow*	Warner 27863
11/2/91	❶[1]	20		4	Romantic	Jimmy Jam Harris/Terry Lewis/Karyn White	Warner 19319

PEAK DATE	PEAK POS	WKS CHR	GOLD	ARTIST / Song Title	Songwriter...B-side	Label & Number
				WHITE, Tony Joe		
8/23/69	8	12		1 Polk Salad Annie	Tony Joe White...*Aspen Colorado*	Monument 1104
				WHITE LION		
5/21/88	8	21		1 Wait	Vito Bratta/Mike Tramp...*Don't Give Up*	Atlantic 89126
2/4/89	3[1]	23		2 When The Children Cry	Vito Bratta/Mike Tramp...*Lady Of The Valley*	Atlantic 89015
				WHITESNAKE		
10/10/87	❶[1]	28		1 Here I Go Again	David Coverdale/Bernie Marsden...*Children Of The Night*	Geffen 28339
12/19/87	2[1]	19		2 Is This Love	David Coverdale/John Sykes...*Bad Boys*	Geffen 28233
				WHITFIELD, David		
10/30/54	10	18	◉	1 Cara Mia	Lee Lange/Tulio Trapani...*How, When Or Where*	London 1486
				DAVID WHITFIELD with Mantovani His Orchestra and Chorus		
				WHITING, Margaret		
12/15/45	6	11		1 It Might As Well Be Spring	Oscar Hammerstein/Richard Rodgers...*How Deep Is The Ocean*	Capitol 214
				PAUL WESTON and his Orchestra With MARGARET WHITING		
2/8/47	7	7		2 Oh, But I Do	Leo Robin/Arthur Schwartz...*Guilty*	Capitol 324
4/19/47	4	17		3 Guilty	Harry Akst/Gus Kahn/Richard Whiting...*Oh, But I Do*	Capitol 324
11/22/47	5	10		4 You Do	Mack Gordon/Josef Myrow...*My Future Just Passed*	Capitol 438
1/3/48	8	1		5 Pass That Peace Pipe	Ralph Blane/Roger Edens/Hugh Martin...*Let's Be Sweethearts Again*	Capitol 15010
4/17/48	2[1]	16		6 Now Is The Hour (Maori Farewell Song)	Maewa Kaihan/Clement Scott/Dorothy Stewart...*But Beautiful*	Capitol 15024
10/9/48	❶[5]	23	◉	7 A Tree In The Meadow	Billy Reid...*I'm Sorry But I'm Glad*	Capitol 15122
1/29/49	2[6]	23	◉	8 Far Away Places	Alex Kramer/Joan Whitney...*My Own True Love*	Capitol 15278
5/21/49	5	17		9 Forever And Ever	Malia Rosa/Franz Winkler...*Dreamer With A Penny*	Capitol 15386
7/9/49	3[1]	19		10 Baby, It's Cold Outside	Frank Loesser...*I Never Heard You Say*	Capitol 567
				MARGARET WHITING AND JOHNNY MERCER		
11/19/49	❶[3]	23	◉	11 Slipping Around	Floyd Tillman...*Wedding Bells*	Capitol 40224
11/26/49	8	10		12 I'll Never Slip Around Again	Teepee Mitchell/Lew Porter...*Six Times a Week And Twice On Sunday*	Capitol 40246
12/16/50	6	15		13 A Bushel And A Peck	Frank Loesser...*Beyond The Reef*	Capitol 1234
				MARGARET WHITING and JIMMY WAKELY (above 3)		
				WHITMAN, Slim		
9/20/52	9	14	◉	1 Indian Love Call	Rudolf Friml/Oscar Hammerstein/Otto Harbach...*China Doll*	Imperial 8156
				WHO, The		
11/25/67	9	11		1 I Can See For Miles	Pete Townshend...*Mary-Anne With The Shaky Hands*	Decca 32206
				WIEDLIN, Jane		
7/30/88	9	19		1 Rush Hour	Peter Rafelson/Jane Wiedlin...*The End Of Love*	EMI/Manhattan 50118
				WILD CHERRY		
9/18/76	❶[3]	25	▲	1 Play That Funky Music	Robert Parissi...*The Lady Wants Your Money*	Epic 50225
				WILDE, Kim		
6/6/87	❶[1]	21		1 You Keep Me Hangin' On	Lamont Dozier/Brian Holland/Eddie Holland...*Loving You*	MCA 53024
				WILDER, Matthew		
1/21/84	5	29		1 Break My Stride	Greg Prestopino/Matthew Wilder	Private I 04113
				will.i.am		
1/13/07	2[1]	27	△[2]	1 Fergalicious	William Adams/Dania Birks/Juana Burns/Stacy Ferguson/Juanita Lee/Kim Nazel/Derrick Rahming/Fatimah Shaheed	will.i.am
				FERGIE Featuring will.i.am		
9/20/08	9	21	△	2 In The Ayer	William Adams/Tony Butler/Tramar Dillard...*Elevator*	Poe Boy 506684
				FLO RIDA Featuring will.i.am		
5/15/10	❶[4]	30		3 OMG	William Adams	LaFace
				USHER Featuring will.i.am		
				WILLIAMS, Andy		
9/29/56	7	22		1 Canadian Sunset	Norman Gimbel/Eddie Heywood...*High Upon A Mountain*	Cadence 1297
3/30/57	❶[3]	20	◉	2 Butterfly	Bernie Lowe/Kal Mann...*It Doesn't Take Very Long*	Cadence 1308
7/15/57	8	20		3 I Like Your Kind Of Love	Melvin Endsley...*Stop Teasin' Me*	Cadence 1323
3/24/58	3[1]	17		4 Are You Sincere	Wayne Walker...*Be Mine Tonight*	Cadence 1340
11/9/59	5	16		5 Lonely Street	Carl Belew/Kenny Sowder/W.S. Stevenson...*Summer Love*	Cadence 1370
1/25/60	7	13		6 The Village Of St. Bernadette	Eula Parker...*I'm So Lonesome I Could Cry*	Cadence 1374
4/13/63	2[4]	15	◉	7 Can't Get Used To Losing You	Doc Pomus/Mort Shuman...*Days Of Wine And Roses*	Columbia 42674
4/3/71	9	13		8 (Where Do I Begin) Love Story	Francis Lai/Carl Sigman...*Something*	Columbia 45317
				WILLIAMS, Billy		
8/5/57	3[4]	23	◉	1 I'm Gonna Sit Right Down And Write Myself A Letter	Fred Ahlert/Joe Young...*Date With The Blues*	Coral 61830
				WILLIAMS, Danny		
5/16/64	9	14		1 White On White	Lor Crane/Bernice Ross...*The Comedy Is Ended*	United Artists 685
				WILLIAMS, Deniece		
6/3/78	❶[1]	18	●	1 Too Much, Too Little, Too Late	Nat Kipner/John Vallins...*Emotion*	Columbia 10693
				JOHNNY MATHIS & DENIECE WILLIAMS		
6/12/82	10	17		2 It's Gonna Take A Miracle	Teddy Randazzo/Lou Stallman/Bob Weinstein...*A Part Of Love*	ARC 02812
5/26/84	❶[2]	19	▲	3 Let's Hear It For The Boy	Dean Pitchford/Tom Snow	Columbia 04417
				WILLIAMS, John [The London Symphony Orchestra]		
9/17/77	10	17		1 Star Wars (Main Title)	John Williams...*Cantina Band* [I]	20th Century 2345
				WILLIAMS, Larry		
8/5/57	5	21	◉	1 Short Fat Fannie	Larry Williams...*High School Dance*	Specialty 608
				WILLIAMS, Mason		
8/3/68	2[2]	14		1 Classical Gas	Mason Williams...*Long Time Blues* [I]	Warner 7190

PEAK DATE	PEAK POS	WKS CHR	GOLD	ARTIST — Song Title	Songwriter...B-side	Label & Number
				WILLIAMS, Maurice, & The Zodiacs		
11/21/60	❶¹	18	☉	1 Stay	Maurice Williams...*Do You Believe*	Herald 552
				WILLIAMS, Roger		
10/29/55	❶⁴	26	☉	1 Autumn Leaves	Joseph Kosma/Johnny Mercer...*Take Care* [I]	Kapp 116
9/29/58	10	17		2 Near You	Francis Craig/Kermit Goell...*The Merry Widow Waltz* [I]	Kapp 233
12/17/66	7	21		3 Born Free	John Barry/Don Black...*Jimmie's Train*	Kapp 767
				WILLIAMS, Tex, And His Western Caravan		
8/9/47	❶⁶	17	☉	1 Smoke! Smoke! Smoke! (That Cigarette)	Merle Travis/Tex Williams...*Roundup Polka* [N]	Capitol Americana 40001
				WILLIAMS, Vanessa		
4/8/89	8	20		1 Dreamin'	Lisa Montegomary/Geneva Paschal...*The Right Stuff (instrumental)*	Wing 871078
3/21/92	❶⁵	27	●	2 Save The Best For Last	Phil Galdston/Jon Lind/Wendy Waldman...*Freedom Dance (Get Free!)*	Wing 865136
5/15/93	3¹	28		3 Love Is VANESSA WILLIAMS and BRIAN McKNIGHT	John Keller/Steve Krikorian	Giant 18630
8/26/95	4	23	●	4 Colors Of The Wind	Alan Menken/Stephen Schwartz...*(Spanish version)*	Hollywood 64001
				WILLIS, Bruce		
3/7/87	5	14		1 Respect Yourself	Luther Ingram/Mack Rice...*Fun Time*	Motown 1876
				WILLIS, Chuck		
6/30/58	9	19	☉	1 What Am I Living For	Art Harris/Fred Jay...*Hang Up My Rock And Roll Shoes*	Atlantic 1179
				WILLS, Johnnie Lee, And His Boys		
2/25/50	9	11		1 Rag Mop	Deacon Anderson/Johnnie Lee Wills...*Near Me*	Bullet 696
				WILL TO POWER		
12/3/88	❶¹	24	●	1 Baby, I Love Your Way/Freebird Medley (Free Baby)	Allen Collins/Peter Frampton/Ronnie Van Zant...*Anti-Social*	Epic 08034
2/2/91	7	18		2 I'm Not In Love	Graham Gouldman/Eric Stewart...*Fly Bird (Reprise)*	Epic 73636
				WILSON, Al		
1/19/74	❶¹	22	●	1 Show And Tell	Jerry Fuller...*Listen To Me*	Rocky Road 30073
				WILSON, Ann		
7/14/84	7	20		1 Almost Paradise...Love Theme From **Footloose** MIKE RENO and ANN WILSON	Eric Carmen/Dean Pitchford...*Strike Zone (Loverboy)*	Columbia 04418
3/11/89	6	19		2 Surrender To Me ANN WILSON AND ROBIN ZANDER	Richard Marx/Ross Vannelli...*Tequila Dreams (Dave Grusin w/Lee Ritenour)*	Capitol 44288
				WILSON, Charlie		
4/26/03	6	20		1 Beautiful SNOOP DOGG featuring Pharrell & Uncle Charlie Wilson	Calvin Broadus/Chad Hugo/Pharrell Williams...*Ballin'*	Doggystyle 77887
				WILSON, J. Frank, and The Cavaliers		
11/7/64	2¹	15	☉	1 Last Kiss	Wayne Cochran...*That's How Much I Love You*	Josie 923
				WILSON, Jackie		
2/9/59	7	21	☉	1 Lonely Teardrops	Tyran Carlo/Berry Gordy...*In The Blue Of Evening*	Brunswick 55105
5/9/60	4	17		2 Night	Johnny Lehman/Herb Miller...*Doggin' Around*	Brunswick 55166
11/28/60	8	15		3 Alone At Last	Johnny Lehman...*Am I The Man*	Brunswick 55170
2/6/61	9	9		4 My Empty Arms	Hank Hunter/Al Kasha...*The Tear Of The Year*	Brunswick 55201
4/13/63	5	12		5 Baby Workout	Alonzo Tucker/Jackie Wilson...*I'm Going Crazy (Gotta Get You Off My Mind)*	Brunswick 55239
10/7/67	6	12		6 (Your Love Keeps Lifting Me) Higher And Higher	Gary Jackson/Carl Smith...*I'm The One To Do It*	Brunswick 55336
				WILSON PHILLIPS		
6/9/90	❶¹	25	●	1 Hold On	Glen Ballard/Chynna Phillips/Carnie Wilson...*Over And Over*	SBK 07322
9/15/90	❶²	22	●	2 Release Me	Chynna Phillips/Carnie Wilson/Wendy Wilson...*Eyes Like Twins*	SBK 07327
12/22/90	4	20		3 Impulsive	Steve Kipner/Clif Magness...*Hold On (live) / Release Me (live) / Morning Tea In Tokyo*	SBK 07337
4/20/91	❶¹	19		4 You're In Love	Glen Ballard/Chynna Phillips/Carnie Wilson/Wendy Wilson	SBK 07343
				WINANS, CeCe		
5/4/96	8	20	●	1 Count On Me WHITNEY HOUSTON & CECE WINANS	Babyface/Michael Houston/Whitney Houston...*One Moment In Time (Houston)*	Arista 12976
				WINANS, Mario		
8/3/02	4	26		1 I Need A Girl (Part Two) P. DIDDY AND GINUWINE Featuring Loon, Mario Winans & Tammy Ruggeri	Sean Combs/Chauncey Hawkins/Michael Jones/Frank Romano/Adonis Shropshire/Mario Winans...*So Complete*	Bad Boy 79441
4/24/04	2⁸	30	○	2 I Don't Wanna Know MARIO WINANS Featuring P. Diddy & Enya	Enya/Chauncey Hawkins/Michael Jones/Nicky Ryan/Roma Ryan/Erick Sermon/Parrish Smith/Mario Winans	Bad Boy
				WINDING, Kai, & Orchestra		
8/24/63	8	15		1 More	Nino Oliviero/Riz Ortolani...*Comin' Home Baby* [I]	Verve 10295
				WINEHOUSE, Amy		
6/30/07	9	20	△	1 Rehab	Amy Winehouse...*You Know I'm No Good*	Universal 008491
				WINGS — see **McCARTNEY, Paul**		
				WINSTONS, The		
7/19/69	7	13	●	1 Color Him Father	Richard Spencer...*Amen, Brother*	Metromedia 117
				WINTER, Edgar, Group		
5/26/73	❶¹	20	●	1 Frankenstein	Edgar Winter...*Undercover Man* [I]	Epic 10967
				WINTERHALTER, Hugo, and his Orchestra		
11/5/49	10	6		1 Jealous Heart	Jenny Lou Carson...*Someday (You'll Want Me To Want You)*	Columbia 38593
1/7/50	9	3		2 Blue Christmas	Billy Hayes/Jay Johnson...*You're All I Want For Christmas* [X]	Columbia 38635
1/28/50	7	14		3 I Can Dream, Can't I? TONI ARDEN with HUGO WINTERHALTER and his ORCHESTRA and Choir	Sammy Fain/Irving Kahal...*A Little Love, A Little Kiss*	Columbia 38612
8/12/50	10	20		4 Count Every Star	Bruno Coquatrix/Sammy Gallop...*The Flying Dutchman*	RCA Victor 3221

PEAK DATE	PEAK POS	WKS CHR	GOLD	ARTIST / Song Title	Songwriter...B-side	Label & Number
				WINTERHALTER, Hugo, and his Orchestra (cont'd)		
10/7/50	9	7		5 Mr. Touchdown, U. S. A. ....William Katz/Gene Piller/Ruth Roberts...*The Red We Want Is The Red We've Got (In the Old Red, White and Blue)*		RCA Victor 3913
2/16/52	10	9		6 A Kiss To Build A Dream On....................Oscar Hammerstein/Bert Kalmar/Harry Ruby...*Love Makes The World Go 'Round*		RCA Victor 4455
4/19/52	6	18		7 Blue Tango....................Leroy Anderson...*The Gypsy Trail* [I]		RCA Victor 4518
7/26/52	9	14		8 Vanessa....................Bernie Wayne...*Somewhere Along The Way* [I]		RCA Victor 4691
11/21/53	8	5		9 The Velvet Glove....................Harold Spina...*Elaine* [I]		RCA Victor 5405
				HENRI RENE and HUGO WINTERHALTER		
7/24/54	9	11		10 The Little Shoemaker....................Geoffrey Parsons/Rudi Revil/John Turner...*The Magic Tango*		RCA Victor 5769
10/13/56	2²	31	⊙	11 Canadian Sunset....................Eddie Heywood...*This Is Real (We're In Love, We're In Love, We're In Love)* [I]		RCA Victor 6537
				HUGO WINTERHALTER with EDDIE HEYWOOD		
				WINWOOD, Steve		
4/18/81	7	18		1 While You See A Chance....................Will Jennings/Steve Winwood...*Vacant Chair*		Island 49656
8/30/86	❶¹	22		2 Higher Love....................Will Jennings/Steve Winwood...*And I Go*		Island 28710
4/18/87	8	23		3 The Finer Things....................Will Jennings/Steve Winwood...*Night Train*		Island 28498
12/19/87	9	20		4 Valerie....................Will Jennings/Steve Winwood...*Talking Back To The Night*		Island 28231
7/30/88	❶⁴	18		5 Roll With It....................Will Jennings/Steve Winwood...*The Morning Side*		Virgin 99326
10/29/88	6	17		6 Don't You Know What The Night Can Do?....................Will Jennings/Steve Winwood		Virgin 99290
				WITHERS, Bill		
9/18/71	3²	16	●	1 Ain't No Sunshine....................Bill Withers...*Harlem*		Sussex 219
7/8/72	❶³	19	●	2 Lean On Me....................Bill Withers...*Better Off Dead*		Sussex 235
10/14/72	2²	12	●	3 Use Me....................Bill Withers...*Let Me In Your Life*		Sussex 241
5/2/81	2³	24		4 Just The Two Of Us....................Ralph MacDonald/William Salter/Bill Withers...*Make Me A Memory (Sad Samba)* (Washington)		Elektra 47103
				GROVER WASHINGTON, JR. (with Bill Withers)		
				WIZ KHALIFA		
2/5/11	3↑	16↑	○	1 Black And Yellow....................Mikkel Storleer Eriksen/Tor Erik Hermansen/Cameron Thomaz		Rostrum
				WOMACK, Bobby		
4/27/74	10	17	●	1 Lookin' For A Love....................James W. Alexander/Zelda Samuels...*Let It Hang Out*		United Artists 375
				WONDER, Stevie		
8/10/63	❶³	15	⊙	1 Fingertips - Pt 2....................Henry Cosby/Clarence Paul...*Pt 1* [L]		Tamla 54080
				LITTLE STEVIE WONDER		
2/12/66	3²	14		2 Uptight (Everything's Alright)....................Henry Cosby/Sylvia Moy/Stevie Wonder...*Purple Rain Drops*		Tamla 54124
9/3/66	9	10		3 Blowin In The Wind....................Bob Dylan...*Ain't That Asking For Trouble*		Tamla 54136
12/24/66	9	11		4 A Place In The Sun....................Ron Miller/Bryan Wells...*Sylvia*		Tamla 54139
7/29/67	2²	15		5 I Was Made To Love Her....................Henry Cosby/Lulu Hardaway/Sylvia Moy/Stevie Wonder...*Hold Me*		Tamla 54151
5/25/68	9	13		6 Shoo-Be-Doo-Be-Doo-Da-Day....................Henry Cosby/Sylvia Moy/Stevie Wonder...*Why Don't You Lead Me To Love*		Tamla 54165
12/28/68	2²	14		7 For Once In My Life....................Ron Miller/Orlando Murden...*Angie Girl*		Tamla 54174
7/26/69	4	14		8 My Cherie Amour....................Henry Cosby/Sylvia Moy/Stevie Wonder...*I Don't Know Why*		Tamla 54180
12/13/69	7	14		9 Yester-Me, Yester-You, Yesterday....................Ron Miller/Bryan Wells...*I'd Be A Fool Right Now*		Tamla 54188
8/8/70	3²	14		10 Signed, Sealed, Delivered I'm Yours....................Lee Garrett/Lulu Hardaway/Stevie Wonder/Syreeta Wright...*I'm More Than Happy (I'm Satisfied)*		Tamla 54196
11/28/70	9	11		11 Heaven Help Us All....................Ron Miller...*I Gotta Have A Song*		Tamla 54200
10/16/71	8	14		12 If You Really Love Me....................Stevie Wonder/Syreeta Wright...*Think Of Me As Your Soldier*		Tamla 54208
1/27/73	❶¹	16		13 Superstition....................Stevie Wonder...*You've Got It Bad Girl*		Tamla 54226
5/19/73	❶¹	17		14 You Are The Sunshine Of My Life....................Stevie Wonder...*Tuesday Heartbreak*		Tamla 54232
10/13/73	4	14		15 Higher Ground....................Stevie Wonder...*Too High*		Tamla 54235
1/12/74	8	17		16 Living For The City....................Stevie Wonder...*Visions*		Tamla 54242
11/2/74	❶¹	19		17 You Haven't Done Nothin....................Stevie Wonder...*Big Brother*		Tamla 54252
2/1/75	3²	17		18 Boogie On Reggae Woman....................Stevie Wonder...*Seems So Long*		Tamla 54254
1/22/77	❶¹	17		19 I Wish....................Stevie Wonder...*You And I*		Tamla 54274
5/21/77	❶³	17		20 Sir Duke....................Stevie Wonder...*He's Misstra Know-It-All*		Tamla 54281
12/22/79	4	18		21 Send One Your Love....................Stevie Wonder		Tamla 54303
12/6/80	5	23		22 Master Blaster (Jammin')....................Stevie Wonder		Tamla 54317
3/20/82	4	18		23 That Girl....................Stevie Wonder...*All I Do*		Tamla 1602
5/15/82	❶⁷	19	●	24 Ebony And Ivory....................Paul McCartney...*Rainclouds* (McCartney)		Columbia 02860
				PAUL McCARTNEY (with Stevie Wonder)		
10/13/84	❶³	26	●	25 I Just Called To Say I Love You....................Stevie Wonder		Motown 1745
11/2/85	❶¹	21		26 Part-Time Lover....................Stevie Wonder		Tamla 1808
2/1/86	10	17		27 Go Home....................Stevie Wonder		Tamla 1817
				WOOD, Brenton		
10/14/67	9	15		1 Gimme Little Sign....................Joseph Hooven/Alfred Smith/Jerry Winn...*I Think You've Got Your Fools Mixed Up*		Double Shot 116
				WOOD, Del		
11/24/51	4	25		1 Down Yonder....................Wolfe Gilbert...*Mine, All Mine* [I]		Tennessee 775
				WOOLEY, Sheb		
6/9/58	❶⁶	14	⊙	1 The Purple People Eater....................Sheb Wooley...*I Can't Believe You're Mine* [N]		MGM 12651
				WRECKX-N-EFFECT		
12/26/92	2³	28	▲²	1 Rump Shaker....................Aqil Davidson/Anton Hollins/Markell Riley/Teddy Riley/David Wynn		MCA 54388
				WRIGHT, Betty		
1/29/72	6	14	●	1 Clean Up Woman....................Willie Clarke/Clarence Reid...*I'll Love You Forever*		Alston 4601
7/8/78	8	28		2 Dance With Me....................Peter Brown/Robert Rans...*For Your Love*		Drive 6269
				PETER BROWN with Betty Wright		
				WRIGHT, Gary		
3/27/76	2³	20	●	1 Dream Weaver....................Gary Wright...*Let It Out*		Warner 8167
7/31/76	2²	27		2 Love Is Alive....................Gary Wright...*Much Higher*		Warner 8143

X

XSCAPE
10/23/93	2[1]	21	▲	1 Just Kickin' It	Jermaine Dupri/Manuel Seal...*W.S.S. Deez Nuts*	So So Def 77119
2/19/94	8	20	●	2 Understanding	Manuel Seal...*With You*	So So Def 77335
11/18/95	8	20	●	3 Who Can I Run To?	Frank Alstin/Rich Roebuck/Charles Simmons...*Feels So Good*	So So Def 78056
6/1/96	10	20	●	4 Keep On, Keepin' On	Jermaine Dupri/Lana Moorer	Flavor Unit 64302
				MC LYTE Featuring Xscape		
5/30/98	7	20	●	5 The Arms Of The One Who Loves You	Diane Warren	So So Def 78788
10/24/98	9	14		6 My Little Secret	Jermaine Dupri/LaTocha Scott/Manuel Seal	So So Def 79036

Y

YANKOVIC, Frankie, & his Yanks
| 6/19/48 | 9 | 14 | | 1 Just Because | Sid Robin/Bob Shelton/Joe Shelton...*A Night In May* | Columbia 12359 |

YANKOVIC, "Weird Al"
| 10/21/06 | 9 | 20 | △ | 1 White & Nerdy | Anthony Henderson/Juan Carlos Salinas/Oscar Salinas/Hakeem Seriki/Al Yankovic [N] | Way Moby |

YARDBIRDS, The
| 7/3/65 | 6 | 12 | | 1 For Your Love | Graham Gouldman...*Got To Hurry* | Epic 9790 |
| 9/25/65 | 9 | 12 | | 2 Heart Full Of Soul | Graham Gouldman...*Steeled Blues* | Epic 9823 |

YES
| 1/21/84 | ❶[2] | 23 | | 1 Owner Of A Lonely Heart | Jon Anderson/Trevor Horn/Trevor Rabin/Chris Squire...*Our Song* | Atco 99817 |

YING YANG TWINS
10/25/03	2[1]	45		1 Get Low	D'Angelo Holmes/Eric Jackson/Sammie Norris/Jonathan Smith...*Throw It Up*	BME/TVT 2377
				LIL JON & THE EAST SIDE BOYZ Featuring Ying Yang Twins		
2/14/04	9	26		2 Salt Shaker	D'Angelo Holmes/Eric Jackson/L. Jefferson/C. Love/Jonathan Smith	TVT 2485
				YING YANG TWINS Feat. Lil Jon & The East Side Boyz		
5/13/06	7	24		3 Ms. New Booty	Michael Crooms/Deongelo Holmes/Eric Jackson/Warren Mathis	New South 50658
				BUBBA SPARXXX Feat. Ying Yang Twins & Mr. ColliPark		

YORGESSON, Yogi
| 12/31/49 | 5 | 5 | ◉ | 1 I Yust Go Nuts At Christmas | Harry Stewart...*Yingle Bells* [X-N] | Capitol 781 |
| 12/31/49 | 7 | 4 | | 2 Yingle Bells | James Pierpont...*I Yust Go Nuts At Christmas* [X-N] | Capitol 781 |

YOUNG, John Paul
| 10/14/78 | 7 | 21 | | 1 Love Is In The Air | Harry Vanda/George Young...*Where The Action Is* | Scotti Brothers 402 |

YOUNG, Kathy, with The Innocents
| 12/12/60 | 3[1] | 17 | ◉ | 1 A Thousand Stars | Eugene Pearson...*Eddie My Darling* | Indigo 108 |

YOUNG, Neil
| 3/18/72 | ❶[1] | 14 | ● | 1 Heart Of Gold | Neil Young...*Sugar Mountain (live)* | Reprise 1065 |

YOUNG, Paul
| 7/27/85 | ❶[1] | 23 | ● | 1 Everytime You Go Away | Daryl Hall...*This Means Anything* | Columbia 04867 |
| 10/6/90 | 8 | 23 | | 2 Oh Girl | Eugene Record...*Leaving Home* | Columbia 73377 |

YOUNG, Victor, And His Singing Strings
9/30/50	7	15		1 Mona Lisa	Ray Evans/Jay Livingston...*The 3rd Man Theme*	Decca 27048
				VICTOR YOUNG And His Orchestra And Chorus And DON CHERRY		
9/4/54	6	14		2 The High And The Mighty	Dimitri Tiomkin/Ned Washington...*Moonlight And Roses (Bring Mem'ries Of You)* [I]	Decca 29203

YOUNGBLOODS, The
| 9/6/69 | 5 | 17 | ● | 1 Get Together | Chet Powers...*Beautiful* | RCA Victor 9752 |

YOUNGBLOODZ
11/1/03	4	32		1 Damn!	Jeffrey Grigsby/Sean Paul Joseph/Cedric Leonard/Jonathan Smith	So So Def 52215
				YOUNGBLOODZ Featuring Lil' Jon		
5/27/06	7	28		2 Snap Yo Fingers	Sean Paul Joseph/Jonathan Smith/Earl Stevens	BME/TVT 2841
				LIL JON Feat. E-40 & Sean Paul of YoungBloodZ		

YOUNG DRO
| 8/26/06 | 10 | 20 | | 1 Shoulder Lean | Clifford Harris/D'Juan Hart/Cordale Quinn...*Gangsta* | Grand Hustle 94282 |
| | | | | YOUNG DRO Featuring T.I. | | |

YOUNG-HOLT UNLIMITED
| 1/18/69 | 3[1] | 13 | ● | 1 Soulful Strut | Eugene Record/William Sanders...*Country Slicker Joe* [I] | Brunswick 55391 |

YOUNG JEEZY
11/12/05	4	24	△	1 Soul Survivor	Jay Jenkins/Aliaune Thiam	Def Jam 005290
				YOUNG JEEZY featuring Akon		
3/15/08	❶[3]	25	△	2 Love In This Club	Darnell Dalton/Jay Jenkins/Jamal Jones/Ryon Lovett/Usher Raymond/Lamar Taylor/Keith Thomas	LaFace 30018
				USHER Featuring Young Jeezy		
1/30/10	8	20	△	3 Hard	Robyn Fenty/Jay Jenkins/Terius Nash/Christopher Stewart	SRP
				RIHANNA Featuring Jeezy		

YOUNG M.C.
| 10/14/89 | 7 | 39 | ▲ | 1 Bust A Move | Matt Dike/Michael Ross/Marvin Young...*Got More Rhymes* | Delicious Vinyl 105 |

YOUNG MONEY
7/4/09	10	20	○	1 Every Girl	Dwayne Carter/Aubrey Graham/Justin Henderson/Carl Lilly/Jarvis Mills/Jermaine Preyan/Chris Whitacre	Young Money
3/13/10	2[1]	25		2 BedRock	Jasper Cameron/Dwayne Carter/Aubrey Graham/Daniel Johnson/Carl Lilly/Onika Maraj/Jarvis Mills/Lloyd Polite/Michael Stevenson	Universal Motown
				YOUNG MONEY Featuring Lloyd		

YOUNG RASCALS, The — see RASCALS, The

PEAK DATE	PEAK POS	WKS CHR	GOLD	ARTIST Song Title	Songwriter...B-side	Label & Number
4/5/08	3¹	26	△	**YUNG BERG** 1 Sexy Can I RAY J & YUNG BERG	Victor Carraway/Noel Fisher/Willie Norwood/Christian Ward	Koch/Epic
6/24/06	3¹	28		**YUNG JOC** 1 It's Goin' Down YUNG JOC Featuring Nitti	Chadron Moore/Jasiel Robinson	Bad Boy 94249
5/26/07	❶¹	35	△	2 Buy U A Drank (Shawty Snappin') T-PAIN Featuring Yung Joc	Faheem Najm/Jasiel Robinson	Konvict 08718
9/11/61	4	12		**YURO, Timi** 1 Hurt	Jimmie Crane/Al Jacobs...*I Apologize*	Liberty 55343

Z

PEAK DATE	PEAK POS	WKS CHR	GOLD	ARTIST Song Title	Songwriter...B-side	Label & Number
3/31/58	6	13		**ZACHERLE, John, "The Cool Ghoul"** 1 Dinner With Drac (Part 1)	Dave Appell/Kal Mann...*Part 2* [N]	Cameo 130
7/12/69	❶⁶	13	●	**ZAGER & EVANS** 1 In The Year 2525	Rick Evans...*Little Kids*	RCA Victor 0174
10/30/93	6	24	●	**ZHANE** 1 Hey Mr. D.J.	Kay Gee/Zane Grey/Renee Neufville/Leon Ware	Flavor Unit 77177
8/21/99	10	17	●	2 Jamboree NAUGHTY BY NATURE (Featuring Zhane)	Vincent Brown/Anthony Criss/Kier Gist/Benny Golson...*On The Run*	Arista 13712
1/3/98	2²	6	▲	**ZOMBIE, Rob** 1 It's All About The Benjamins PUFF DADDY & THE FAMILY Feat. The Notorious B.I.G./Lil' Kim/The Lox/Dave Grohl/Perfect/FuzzBubble/Rob Zombie	Deric Angelettie/Sean Combs/Sean Jacobs/Kim Jones/Jayson Phillips/David Styles/Christopher Wallace ...*Been Around The World* (Puff Daddy)	Bad Boy 79130
12/12/64	2¹	15	⊙	**ZOMBIES, The** 1 She's Not There	Rod Argent...*You Make Me Feel So Good*	Parrot 9695
2/27/65	6	11		2 Tell Her No	Rod Argent...*Leave Me Be*	Parrot 9723
3/29/69	3²	13	●	3 Time Of The Season	Rod Argent...*Friends Of Mine*	Date 1628
7/21/84	8	19		**ZZ TOP** 1 Legs	Frank Beard/Billy Gibbons/Dusty Hill...*Bad Girl*	Warner 29272
12/14/85	8	17		2 Sleeping Bag	Frank Beard/Billy Gibbons/Dusty Hill...*Party On The Patio*	Warner 28884

CHART KINGS & QUEENS of POP'S TOP 10 HITS 1940-2010

1. **Bing Crosby**
T10s: 77 / #1s: 14

2. **Perry Como**
T10s: 50 / #1s: 14

3. **Frank Sinatra**
T10s: 49 / #1s: 6

4. **Glenn Miller Orch.**
T10s: 42 / #1s: 7

5. **Elvis Presley**
T10s: 38 / #1s: 18

6. **Madonna**
T10s: 37 / #1s: 12

7. **Sammy Kaye Orch.**
T10s: 36 / #1s: 5

8. **Tommy Dorsey Orch.**
T10s: 36 / #1s: 3

9. **Jo Stafford**
T10s: 35 / #1s: 4

10. **The Beatles**
T10s: 34 / #1s: 20

11. **Dinah Shore**
T10s: 33 / #1s: 4

12. **Andrews Sisters**
T10s: 30 / #1s: 6

12. **Harry James Orch.**
T10s: 30 / #1s: 6

14. **Janet Jackson**
T10s: 29 / #1s: 10

15. **Guy Lombardo Orch.**
T10s: 29 / #1s: 3

16. **Mariah Carey**
T10s: 28 / #1s: 18

17. **Michael Jackson**
T10s: 28 / #1s: 13

18. **Jimmy Dorsey Orch.**
T10s: 28 / #1s: 7

19. **Stevie Wonder**
T10s: 27 / #1s: 9

20. **Elton John**
T10s: 27 / #1s: 8

21. **Dick Haymes**
T10s: 27 / #1s: 1

22. **Vaughn Monroe**
T10s: 25 / #1s: 5

23. **Eddie Fisher**
T10s: 25 / #1s: 4

24. **Patti Page**
T10s: 24 / #1s: 4

25. **Kay Kyser Orch.**
T10s: 24 / #1s: 3

CHART KINGS & QUEENS of POP'S TOP 10 HITS 1940-2010

26. Whitney Houston
T10s: 23 / #1s: 11

27. The Rolling Stones
T10s: 23 / #1s: 8

28. Paul McCartney
T10s: 22 / #1s: 9

29. George Michael
T10s: 21 / #1s: 10

30. Nat "King" Cole
T10s: 21 / #1s: 4

31. The Supremes
T10s: 20 / #1s: 12

32. Chicago
T10s: 20 / #1s: 3

32. Les Paul & Mary Ford
T10s: 20 / #1s: 3

34. Prince
T10s: 19 / #1s: 5

35. Freddy Martin Orch.
T10s: 19 / #1s: 4

36. Ricky Nelson
T10s: 19 / #1s: 2

37. Pat Boone
T10s: 18 / #1s: 6

38. Marvin Gaye
T10s: 18 / #1s: 3

39. Rihanna
T10s: 17 / #1s: 9

40. Jay-Z
T10s: 17 / #1s: 4

41. Frankie Laine
T10s: 17 / #1s: 3

42. Aretha Franklin
T10s: 17 / #1s: 2

43. Usher
T10s: 16 / #1s: 9

44. Daryl Hall & John Oates
T10s: 16 / #1s: 6

45. Ludacris
T10s: 16 / #1s: 5

45. Puff Daddy
T10s: 16 / #1s: 5

47. Ink Spots
T10s: 16 / #1s: 4

47. Rod Stewart
T10s: 16 / #1s: 4

47. The Temptations
T10s: 16 / #1s: 4

50. Connie Francis
T10s: 16 / #1s: 3